Essays

Essays

HENRY D. THOREAU

A FULLY ANNOTATED EDITION

Edited by Jeffrey S. Cramer

Yale UNIVERSITY PRESS   New Haven and London

Frontispiece: *Four Autumn Leaves*, © Kazuo Honzawa/
orion/amanaimages/Corbis.

Yale University Press books may be purchased in
quantity for educational, business, or promotional use.
For information, please e-mail sales.press@yale.edu
(U.S. office) or sales@yaleup.co.uk (U.K. office).

Designed by Sonia Shannon.
Set in Adobe Garamond type by Tseng Information
Systems, Inc.
Printed in the United States of America.

Library of Congress Cataloging-in-Publication Data
Thoreau, Henry David, 1817–1862.
[Essays. Selections]
Essays : a fully annotated edition / Henry D. Thoreau ;
edited by Jeffrey S. Cramer.
     pages   cm
Includes bibliographical references and index.
ISBN 978-0-300-16498-5 (cloth : alk. paper)
I. Cramer, Jeffrey S., 1955–, editor of compilation.
II. Title.
PS3042.C73 2013
814'.3—dc23
                                        2012038780

A catalogue record for this book is available from the
British Library.

This paper meets the requirements of ANSI/NISO
Z39.48-1992 (Permanence of Paper).

10 9 8 7 6 5 4 3 2 1

publication of this book is enabled by a grant from

Figure Foundation

To Scott Greenberg

My friend is one . . . who takes me for what I am.

—Thoreau in his journal, 23 October 1852

Contents

Acknowledgments

A work like this could not have been made without the help of literally hundreds of people, known and unknown. Many are acknowledged below or in the bibliography, but there are many who, I regret, have become anonymous, and for these omissions of credit I apologize. There are generosity and enthusiasm in the world, for which I am appreciative, and it is rewarding to know that such dedication and passion exist.

Special thanks to the staffs of the College of Staten Island; Staten Island Historical Society at Historic Richmond Town; the New York Public Library; the Boston Public Library; and the Concord Public Library; and to the following individuals for their help with various conundrums: Jeffrey Auerbach, California State University, Northridge; Alastair Cameron; Eric Homberger; Nancy V. Flood, managing editor, *Encyclopedia of New York City;* Kevin Van Anglen; Elizabeth Bouvier, head of archives, Massachusetts Supreme Judicial Court, for looking through the 1846 Middlesex County Court of Common Pleas criminal records; and the late Jan Chadbourne, Fine Arts Department, Boston Public Library, who will be missed as both a colleague and a friend.

As always, particular thanks to Greg Joly for being a constant sounding board for all the ideas that made it into this book and the many that did not.

To my editor at Yale University Press, Jennifer Banks: it's good to have you back!

And to my family—my wife, Julia Berkley, and our daughters, Kazia and Zoë—who once again welcomed this transcendental visitor into our home.

Introduction

THOREAU AND THE PERIODIC PRESS

I may yet accomplish something in the literary way—
— Thoreau to his mother, 29 August 1843

After Thoreau's death Thomas Wentworth Higginson told the story about asking Thoreau's sister Sophia "for leave to publish something from his numerous volumes of journals and natural observations, now so largely in print." Sophia, Higginson recalled, "had refused, and I applied confidently to Judge Hoar. When I got through, the judge said placidly, between puffs of his cigar, 'Whereunto? You have not yet unfolded the preliminary question. Why should any one wish to have a sentence of Henry Thoreau's put in print?'"

From a present-day perspective, which places Thoreau in the pantheon of masters of American prose, Hoar's comments may cause an exasperated snigger, but it took a long while before Thoreau's reputation became as prominent and as far-reaching as it is today. Although he always had his champions, such as Higginson, Ralph Waldo Emerson, Horace Greeley, and Bronson Alcott, he also had his detractors. James Russell Lowell's 1848 *A Fable for Critics,* for instance, satirically dismissed him as little more than an Emerson imitator who had "stolen all his apples from Emerson's orchard." Lowell was not alone in dismissing Thoreau as an Emerson aspirant. Several contemporaries noted that Thoreau not only imitated his friend intellectually but seemed to have adopted some of Emerson's physical attributes. Now, nearing the bicentennial of his birth, he serves as a paradigm, the quintessential writer who examines man's place in nature in conjunction with man's duties and obligations to society. Wendell Berry has called him a figurehead; Gary Snyder has called him an elder.

On the sixth of May, 1843, Henry David Thoreau left his native and much-beloved Concord for New York. Although the purported and mundane reason for his going was to tutor the children of Ralph Waldo Emerson's brother William, an attorney living in Staten Island, the move also placed the aspiring writer in the heart of the American publishing world.

Thoreau began to keep a journal on 22 October 1837 at the instigation of Ralph Waldo Emerson, who asked, "What are you doing now? Do you keep a journal?" "So I make my first entry to-day," was Thoreau's response. From the beginning he used his journal as a storehouse for his thoughts: thoughts that would evolve into lectures, lectures that would be redacted into essays, essays that would become chapters of books. Even in the earliest extant entries, which he culled into a section he titled "Gleanings or What Time has not Reaped of my Journal," there is the presumption of an audience and the self-assuredness, as well as the self-consciousness, of an incipient writer.

The craft or art of writing was always paramount with Thoreau. Less than six months after writing his first entry in his journal he asked: "But what does all this scribbling amount to? What is now scribbled in the heat of the moment one can contemplate with somewhat of satisfaction, but alas! to-morrow—aye, to-night—it is stale, flat, and unprofitable,—in fine, is not, only its shell remains, some red parboiled lobster-shell which, kicked never so often, still stares at you in the path."

In mid-1840 he wrote, "I am startled when I consider how little I am *actually* concerned about the things I write in my journal."

He had not yet come to the understanding that he would realize in 1841, that "nothing goes by luck in composition. It allows of no trick. The best you can write will be the best you are. Every sentence is the result of a long probation. The author's character is read from title-page to end. Of this he never corrects the proofs." The few writings of Thoreau's that failed to find a solid readership—"The Landlord," for example, or "An Excursion to Canada"—fell short because of his own personal distance in the writing. As he wrote his friend H. G. O. Blake, "I do not wonder that you do not like my Canada story. It concerns me but little, and probably is not worth the time it took to tell it."

As he would conclude in his journal on 18 March 1842, "Whatever book or sentence will bear to be read twice, we may be sure was thought twice."

THE *DIAL*

The Dial: A Magazine for Literature, Philosophy, and Religion was published over a four-year period, putting out sixteen issues before it folded. It was an outgrowth of what has been called the Transcendental Club, or the Hedge Club, a group of like-minded individuals who usually met when one of their members, Frederic H. Hedge, was able to get into Boston from Maine. Members included Margaret Fuller, Bronson Alcott, George Ripley, Elizabeth Peabody, Theodore Parker, and Emerson, who described it this way:

> I think there prevailed at that time a general belief in Boston that there was some concert of doctrinaires to establish certain opinions and inaugurate some movement in literature, philosophy and religion, of which design the supposed con-

spirators were quite innocent; for there was no concert, and only here and there two or three men or women who read and wrote, each alone, with unusual vivacity. Perhaps they only agreed in having fallen upon Coleridge and Wordsworth and Goethe, then on Carlyle, with pleasure and sympathy. . . . I suppose all of them were surprised at this rumor of a school or sect, and certainly at the name of Transcendentalism, given nobody knows by whom, or when it was first applied. As these persons became in the common chances of society acquainted with each other, there resulted certainly strong friendships, which of course were exclusive in proportion to their heat: and perhaps those persons who were mutually the best friends were the most private and had no ambition of publishing their letters, diaries or conversation.

From that time meetings were held for conversation, with very little form, from house to house, of people engaged in studies, fond of books, and watchful of all the intellectual light from whatever quarter it flowed. Nothing could be less formal, yet the intelligence and character and varied ability of the company gave it some notoriety and perhaps waked curiosity as to its aims and results.

Nothing more serious came of it than the modest quarterly journal called *The Dial*. . . . All its papers were unpaid contributions, and it was rather a work of friendship among the narrow circle of students than the organ of any party.

Thirty pieces by Thoreau were published in eleven of its sixteen issues, most of which after March 1842, when Emerson took over the editorship from Margaret Fuller. These included essays, poems, translations, and edited selections from "ethical scriptures." Thoreau's time with the *Dial* served as a literary apprenticeship in which he experienced all aspects of authorship: rejection (both the essay "The Service" and two poems—"The Fisher's Son" and the piece published later in "A Walk to Wachusett"—were rejected by Fuller) and editorial emendations to his text ("A Winter Walk" contained extensive revisions and deletions by Emerson), as well as numerous acceptances. He also shared in the role of assistant editor to Emerson.

NATURAL HISTORY OF MASSACHUSETTS
Dial *(July 1842)*

"Natural History of Massachusetts" is a review of four reports published under the auspices of the Commissioners on the Zoological and Botanical Survey of the State. As in any Thoreau work, even in this early period, the purported theme or genre, whether a review, an excursion, or something that approaches autobiography, is minor compared with the holistic and organic reality of the piece. As Nathaniel Hawthorne perceptively noted in his journal, Thoreau had

> written a good article, a rambling disquisition on Natural History, in the last *Dial,* which, he says, was chiefly made up from journals of his own observations. Methinks this article gives a very fair image of his mind and character,— so true, innate, and literal in observation, yet giving the spirit as well as letter of what he sees, even as a lake reflects its wooded banks, showing every leaf, yet giving the wild beauty of the whole scene. Then there are in the article passages of cloudy and dreamy metaphysics, and also passages where his thoughts seem to measure and attune themselves into spontaneous verse, as they rightfully may, since there

is real poetry in them. There is a basis of good sense and of moral truth, too, throughout the article, which also is a reflection of his character; for he is not unwise to think and feel, and I find him a healthy and wholesome man to know.

A WINTER WALK
Dial *(October 1843)*

Most of the material for "A Winter Walk" had been culled from Thoreau's 1841 journal. When Emerson wrote to Thoreau on 21 May 1843 requesting "something good by the 10th of June" for the July issue of the *Dial,* Thoreau replied: "If I can finish an account of a winter's walk in Concord in the midst of a Staten Island summer—not so wise or true I trust—I will send it to you soon." By 8 June, Thoreau was able to send Emerson the completed essay only to find that Emerson had already wrapped up the July issue. Emerson wrote: "I may not have place now for the Winter's Walk in the July Dial which is just making up its last sheets & somehow I must end it to-morrow—when I go to Boston. I shall then keep it for October, subject however to your order if you find a better disposition for it."

Thoreau had no inclination to find another place for his essay unless Emerson ultimately rejected it. After receiving the July issue he wrote: "As for the 'Winter's Walk' I should be glad to have it printed in the D. if you think it good enough, and will criticise it—otherwise send it to me and I will dispose of it." In this same letter Thoreau wrote one of his early and perceptive comments on writing: "It is the height of art that on the first perusal plain common sense should appear—on the second severe truth—and on a third beauty—and having these warrants for its depth and reality, we may then enjoy the beauty forever more."

Emerson did criticize the essay, as Thoreau has asked, but within the privacy of his journal. In an undated entry from this period he wrote:

H.D.T. sends me a paper with the old fault of unlimited contradiction. The trick of his rhetoric is soon learned. It consists in substituting for the obvious word & thought its diametrical antagonist. He praises wild mountains & winter forests for their domestic air; snow & ice for their warmth; villagers & wood choppers for their urbanity and the wilderness for resembling Rome & Paris. With the constant inclination to dispraise cities & civilization, he yet can find no way to honour woods & woodmen except by paralleling them with towns & townsmen.

Although William Ellery Channing declared to Emerson that it was an "excellent" piece, it made Emerson "nervous & wretched to read it, with all its merits." To Thoreau he wrote just prior to publication:

I mean to send the Winter's Walk to the printer to-morrow for the Dial. I had some hesitation about it, notwithstanding its faithful observation and its fine sketches of the pickerel-fisher and of the woodchopper, on account of *mannerism,* an old charge of mine, — as if, by attention, one could get the trick of the rhetoric; for example, to call a cold place sultry, a solitude public, a wilderness *domestic* (a favorite word), and in the woods to insult over cities, whilst the woods, again, are dignified by comparing them to cities, armies, etc. By pretty free omissions, however, I have removed my principal objections. I ought to say that

Ellery Channing admired the piece loudly and long, and only stipulated for the omission of Douglas and one copy of verses on the Smoke.

Following publication Thoreau wrote to Emerson in a manner that could be either humble honesty or the carefully couched feelings of a still grateful young author not wishing to damage the relationship he had with the man who had been mentor, advocate, and friend: "I see that I was very blind to send you my manuscript in such a state, but I have a good second sight (?) at least. I could still shake it in the wind to some advantage, if it would hold together." Thoreau was unable to be more severe than his dismay at typesetting errors: "There are some sad mistakes in the printing."

Despite Emerson's objections to the essay, or perhaps because of his editorial changes, a short excerpt was published in the 27 October 1843 *New-York Daily Tribune.* The *Knickerbocker Magazine,* distinguishing four pieces including Thoreau's, considered this issue of the *Dial* to have "much less of the new style of verbal affectation in the present than in preceding numbers" and reported it to be thus "more readable and attractive." The *Knickerbocker* reviewer called Thoreau an "observant and thoughtful essayist" and mentioned his "delicate appreciation of the little accessories of the season."

A WALK TO WACHUSETT
Boston Miscellany of Literature and Fashion *(January 1843)*

Except for a brief obituary published in the Concord *Yeoman's Gazette* in 1837, "A Walk to Wachusett" was Thoreau's first piece published outside of the *Dial.* As the *Boston Miscellany* suspended publication after the following issue in February, Thoreau's initial publication in the general periodical press beyond the subscription-supported *Dial* brought no payment.

Thoreau tried to get the remuneration owed him, but any attempt he made, or others made on his behalf, failed. Elizabeth Peabody wrote him on 26 February 1843: "I hope you have got your money from Bradbury & Soden. I have done all I could about it." In an 8 June letter to Emerson in which he expressed his want of cash, Thoreau wrote: "Bradbury told me, when I passed through Boston, that he was coming to New York the following Saturday, and would then settle with me, but he has not made his appearance yet." On 7 July, Thoreau wrote his mother that he didn't get his money "in Boston and probably shall not at all." Emerson continued to do his bidding, writing on 20 July:

> I am sorry to say that when I called on Bradbury & Soden nearly a month ago, their partner in their absence informed me that they could not pay you at present any part of their debt on account of the B. Miscellany. After much talking, all the promise he could offer, was, "that within a year it would probably be paid," a probability which certainly looks very slender. The very worst thing he said was the proposition that you should take your payment in the form of B. Miscellanies! I shall not fail to refresh their memory at intervals.

The following month Thoreau resigned himself to not being paid at all, telling Emerson not to "think of Bradbury and Soden any more. . . . I see that they have given up their shop here."

The *New-York Daily Tribune* of 16 December 1842 reviewed this issue of the *Boston Miscellany,* noting that it contained articles "of a good degree of literary merit, of which 'The Walk to Wachusett' is perhaps the best." With this early essay Thoreau had already begun to show his ability to make the local universal, the personal communal, and the objectively descriptive subjectively moral, as if he were prophetically following the advice he would give in 1857 to H. G. O. Blake, who wanted to write about an excursion to Mount Washington:

> Let me suggest a theme for you: to state to yourself precisely and completely what that walk over the mountains amounted to for you,—returning to this essay again and again, until you are satisfied that all that was important in your experience, is in it. Give this good reason to yourself for having gone over the mountains, for mankind is ever going over a mountain. . . . It did not take very long to get over the mountain, you thought; but have you got over it indeed? If you have been to the top of Mount Washington, let me ask, what did you find there? . . . It is after we get home that we really go over the mountain, if ever. What did the mountain say? What did the mountain do?

In the same year "The Landlord" was also published in the *United States Magazine and Democratic Review.* Written while living on Staten Island, it is Thoreau's only essay written specifically to appeal to the general reading public. As Thoreau wrote his mother: "I see that they have printed a short piece which I wrote to sell in the Dem Review."

"PARADISE (TO BE) REGAINED"
United States Magazine and Democratic Review *(November 1843)*

"Paradise (To Be) Regained" is Thoreau's review of the second English edition of John Adolphus Etzler's *The Paradise within the Reach of all Men, without Labor, by Powers of Nature and Machinery. An Address to all Intelligent Men,* published in 1842. Emerson's writing to Thoreau in February 1843 asking if he's "given any shape to the comment on Etzler" indicates that Thoreau was already, in early 1843, thinking of writing a review of Etzler's book and that Emerson was considering it as a piece for the *Dial.* On 15 February 1843 Thoreau wrote Emerson, referring to Etzler's work, "here is the book still, and I will try."

In May of that year Thoreau had moved to New York. Whether for that reason or another remains unknown, but Thoreau's review ultimately went to the *United States Magazine and Democratic Review.* He had met its editor, John L. O'Sullivan, in January, when O'Sullivan visited Concord to call on Nathaniel Hawthorne. During their initial meeting, according to Thoreau, "We had nothing to say, and therefore we said a great deal! He, however, made a point of asking me to write for his Review, which I shall be glad to do."

The review was at first rejected because O'Sullivan, as Thoreau wrote his mother, "could not adopt the sentiments" he expressed, although Thoreau was not the first to disparage Etzler's ideas. Criticism of his books caused Etzler to write in his own defense his 1842 *Dialogue on Etzler's Paradise: Between Messrs. Clear, Flat, Dunce, and Grudge.* Thoreau explained to Emerson in September that "O'Sullivan is printing the manuscript I sent him some time ago, having objected only to my want of sympathy with the Communities," but it soon suffered another delay. Thoreau wrote home that the review was being held back "that I may include in it a notice of another book by the same author, which they have found, and are going to send me." The other book was Etzler's *The New World; or, Mechanical System, to Perform the Labours of Man and Beast by Inanimate Powers, That Cost Nothing, for Producing and Preparing the Substances of Life,* about which Thoreau would write that "we have not been able to ascertain whether it has been published, or only exists as yet in the design of the author."

Thoreau's primary criticism came from the standpoint of the transcendental self-reformer who had little patience for organized reform or Fourierist communities, both of which place the individual in a subservient role to the society of which they are a part. He had no faith in a paradise "without labor" because he valued the labor itself for what it could teach. As he wrote in his journal of 23 March 1842, "I am sure I write the tougher truth for these calluses on my palms."

In "Paradise (To Be) Regained" Thoreau quoted liberally from Etzler's *Paradise within the Reach of all Men*—liberally in the sense both of quoting generously and freely adapting his quotations. There are hundreds of variations from Etzler's text, ranging from minor incidentals to wholesale juxtaposition of nonconsecutive sentences.[1]

By today's print standards of textual accuracy, the atrocious handling—Thoreau called them "liberties"—of his source material has caused consternation among his readers. To many critics it has seemed that Thoreau, in his unfettered changes to Etzler's text, failed to hold himself to the same standard by which he would soon criticize other editors. It is also possible, however, to see the writer who had not yet fully realized the evolving understanding he would develop as a professionally established writer over the next ten or fifteen years.

WENDELL PHILLIPS BEFORE CONCORD LYCEUM
Liberator *(28 March 1845)*

Rather than being a formal essay, "Wendell Phillips Before Concord Lyceum" was a letter to William Lloyd Garrison, editor of the *Liberator*. Wendell Phillips, sometimes called the "Golden Trumpet" of abolitionism, had spoken at the Concord Lyceum on 21 December 1842, at Thoreau's invitation, and again on 18 January 1844. Abolitionism was a contentious topic, and the outspoken Phillips was not a welcome speaker to the more conservative curators of the Lyceum.

When Phillips was again being considered as a speaker in 1845, several curators resigned, being replaced by Samuel Barrett, Emerson, and Thoreau. Phillips was forthwith invited to speak and came on 11 March 1845. Thoreau sent his letter to the *Liberator* on the next day, although portions may have been written following one or the other of Phillips's previous lectures. Thoreau's letter is a paean to free speech, under which "the most revolutionary and heretical opinions, when frankly and adequately, and in some sort cheerfully, expressed" serve to "whet and clarify the intellect of all parties," furnishing each side "an additional argument for that right he asserted."

THOMAS CARLYLE AND HIS WORKS
Graham's Magazine *(March 1847, April 1847)*

In 1842, having recently met Thoreau in Concord, Horace Greeley—political reformer, author, journalist, and founder of the *New-York Tribune*—became the self-appointed agent for Thoreau's work, finding places for his essays in journals, promoting his writings in the pages of the *Tribune*, and even assisting in the collection of fees owed Thoreau. Greeley wrote Thoreau, after reading his essay on Carlyle, "But I know you have written a good thing about Carlyle—too solidly good, I fear, to be profitable to yourself or attractive to publishers." Nonetheless Greeley was able to place the essay, writing to Thoreau the next month:

I learned to-day, through Mr. Griswold, former editor of "Graham's Magazine," that your lecture is accepted, to appear in that magazine. Of course it is to be paid for at the usual rate, as I expressly so stated when I inclosed it to Graham. He has not written me a word on the subject, which induces me to think he may have written to you on the subject. Please write me if you would have me speak further on the subject. The pay, however, is sure, though the amount may not be large, and I think you may wait until the article appears, before making further stipulations on the subject.

Toward the end of October, Greeley wrote again:

I have to-day received a letter from Griswold, in Philadelphia, who says: "The article by Thoreau on Carlyle is in type, and will be paid for liberally." "Liberally" is quoted as an expression of Graham's. I know well the difference between a publisher's and an author's idea of what is "liberally"; but I give you the best I can get as the result of three letters to Philadelphia on this subject.

Success to you, my friend!

This rarely reprinted essay is often dismissed as nothing more than Thoreau's comprehensive review of the writings of the Scottish writer Thomas Carlyle, written for the purpose of bringing Carlyle more prominently before an American audience. In assessing the work of one writer, Thoreau was also reassessing the work of another writer: himself. In the same way that Proust's writings on translating Ruskin's "The Bibles of Amiens" and "Sesames and Lilies" reveal more about Proust than about Ruskin,

Thoreau's review of Carlyle's career was less a revaluation of Carlyle than an evaluation of what a writer, as seen through the lens of Thoreau's first decade of writing, could be.

In the following year, 1848, came the five-part serial publication of "Ktaadn and the Maine Woods" in Sartain's *Union Magazine*.

"RESISTANCE TO CIVIL GOVERNMENT"
Aesthetic Papers *(May 1849)*

On 23 or 24 July 1846 Thoreau was stopped by Concord tax collector and jailor Sam Staples, who asked Thoreau to pay his poll tax. When Thoreau refused, Staples offered to pay the tax himself, which Thoreau would not allow. Thoreau was taken to the Concord jail, where he shared a cell with an Irishman named Hugh Connell, who was accused of burning a barn in the neighboring town of Sudbury. Despite Thoreau's belief that his cellmate's transgression had been accidental—a sympathy that would partly stem from Thoreau's own accidental burning of hundreds of acres of woodland two years before—Connell would soon serve five years in prison. That evening an unidentified person paid Thoreau's tax to Staples's daughter Ellen. Although Thoreau should have been released, Staples had already removed his boots and decided to let his prisoner remain in jail for the night. When released the next day, Thoreau was angry at the intervention of his anonymous taxpayer.

Bronson Alcott had a similar but less notorious experience two and a half years before his friend Thoreau's refusal and arrest. In Alcott's journal of 17 January 1843 the following entry was written by his wife: "A day of some excitement, as Mr. Alcott had refused to pay his town tax and they had gone through the form of taking him to jail. After waiting some time to be committed, he was told it was paid by a friend." Alcott, on 4 May 1846, wrote:

Staples, the town collector, called to assure me that he should next week advertise my land to pay for the tax, unless it was paid before that time. Land for land, man for man. I would, were it possible, know nothing of this economy called "the State," but it will force itself upon the freedom of the freeborn and the wisest bearing is to over-bear it, let it have its own way, the private person never going out of his way to meet it. It shall put its hand into a person's pocket if it will, but I shall not put mine there on its behalf.

Charles Lane wrote an account of Alcott's arrest in the 27 January 1843 issue of the *Liberator:* "State Slavery—Imprisonment of Amos Bronson Alcott (1799–1888)—Dawn of Liberty":

Being convinced that the payment of the town tax involved principles and practices most degrading and injurious to man, he had long determined not to be a party to its continuance. . . . To the county jail, therefore, Mr. Alcott went, or rather was forced by the benignant State and its delicate instrument. . . . This act of non-resistance, you will perceive, does not rest on the plea of poverty. For Mr. Alcott has always supplied some poor neighbor with food and clothing to a much higher amount than his tax. Neither is it wholly based on the iniquitous purposes to which the money when collected is applied. For part of it is devoted to education, and education has not a heartier friend in the world than Bronson Alcott. But it is founded on the moral instinct which forbids every moral being to be a party, either actively or permissively, to the destructive principles of power and might over peace and love.

At first, according to Alcott, Emerson thought Thoreau's going to jail "mean and skulking, and in bad taste," but Emerson soon had qualms with the abolitionists who spoke for freedom and yet were not willing to give up a lifestyle that ultimately supported the institution they decried. Reevaluating the incident in his journals, Emerson concluded that his "friend Mr Thoreau has gone to jail rather than pay his tax. . . . The abolitionists denounce the war & give much time to it, but they pay the tax."

In order to explain his actions and principles, Thoreau gave two lectures, or two variants or parts of the same lecture, in Concord on 26 January ("The Relation of the Individual to the State") and 16 February 1848 ("The Rights and Duties of the Individual in Relation to the State"). When Elizabeth Peabody began to plan the first and, as it turned out, the only issue of *Aesthetic Papers* in 1849, she asked Thoreau to contribute a manuscript based on one or both of these lectures that she had heard about. He wrote Peabody on 5 April 1849 in what must have seemed in many ways a favorable and coveted position for a writer to be in: "I have so much writing to do at present, with the printers in the rear of me,"— for his first book, *A Week on the Concord and Merrimack Rivers*— "that I have almost no time left, but for bodily exercise; however, I will send you the article in question before the end of next week," adding a postscript: "I offer the paper to your *first volume* only."

First published as "Resistance to Civil Government" in *Aesthetic Papers,* it was collected posthumously under its more universally known title "Civil Disobedience" in *A Yankee in Canada, with Anti-Slavery and Reform Papers.* Thoreau also related the incident briefly in *A Week on the Concord and Merrimack Rivers:*

When I have not paid the tax which the State demanded for that protection which I did not want, itself has robbed me;

when I have asserted the liberty it presumed to declare, itself has imprisoned me. Poor creature! if it knows no better I will not blame it. If it cannot live but by these means, I can. I do not wish, it happens, to be associated with Massachusetts, either in holding slaves or in conquering Mexico. . . . If, for instance, a man asserts the value of individual liberty over the merely political commonweal, his neighbor still tolerates him, that is he who is *living near* him, sometimes even sustains him, but never the State. Its officer, as a living man, may have human virtues and a thought in his brain, but as the tool of an institution, a jailer or constable it may be, he is not a whit superior to his prison key or his staff. Herein is the tragedy; that men doing outrage to their proper natures, even those called wise and good, lend themselves to perform the office of inferior and brutal ones. Hence come war and slavery in; and what else may not come in by this opening? But certainly there are modes by which a man may put bread into his mouth which will not prejudice him as a companion and neighbor.

In *Walden* Thoreau wrote:

One afternoon, near the end of the first summer, when I went to the village to get a shoe from the cobbler's, I was seized and put into jail, because, as I have elsewhere related, I did not pay a tax to, or recognize the authority of, the state which buys and sells men, women, and children, like cattle at the door of its senate-house. I had gone down to the woods for other purposes. But, wherever a man goes, men will pursue and paw him with their dirty institutions, and, if they can, constrain him to belong to their desperate odd-fellow society. It is true, I might have resisted forcibly with more or less effect, might have run "amok" against society; but I preferred that society should run "amok" against me, it being the desperate party. However, I was released the next day, obtained my mended shoe, and returned to the woods in season to get my dinner of huckleberries on Fair Haven Hill.

Thoreau's essay is what Wendell Berry called an "essay in the literal sense: a trial." In it we, as readers and as citizens, try our times against Thoreau's days, try ourselves against Thoreau, and try the morals and ethics we espouse against the ideals Thoreau set forth and lived by. The philosopher and theologian Martin Buber encapsulated the essence of this essay and all of Thoreau's writings when he wrote that the author "addressed his reader . . . in such a way that the reader not only discovered why Thoreau acted as he did . . . but also that the reader—assuming him of course to be honest and dispassionate—would have to act in just such a way whenever the proper occasion arose, provided he was seriously engaged in fulfilling his existence as a human person."

In 1852 Sartain's *Union Magazine,* which had published "Ktaadn and the Maine Woods" four years previously, brought out two excerpts from Thoreau's forthcoming book about his life at Walden Pond: "The Iron Horse" in July and "A Poet Buying a Farm" in August. The August issue was the final issue of the magazine, and Thoreau found himself again an unpaid contributor, as he had been with "A Walk to Wachusett" in the *Boston Miscellany of Literature and Fashion.*

The following year "An Excursion to Canada" was published in three consecutive issues of *Putnam's Magazine.* Although it was originally planned for five issues, Thoreau pulled the essay when the editor of *Putnam's,* George William Curtis, editorially removed lines about Catholicism. Greeley tried to make Thoreau understand that when a journal publishes a piece editorially and anonymously, as had been done in *Putnam's,* then the "elimination of very flagrant heresies (like your defiant Pantheism) becomes a necessity." Thoreau responded to Greeley by writing, "I am sorry that my manuscript should be so mangled, insignificant as it is, but I do not know how I could have helped it fairly, since I was born to be a pantheist—if that be the name of me, and I do the deeds of one."

SLAVERY IN MASSACHUSETTS
The Liberator *(21 July 1854)*

On 24 May 1854 Anthony Burns, a fugitive slave, was arrested in Boston. Speeches in Faneuil Hall by Wendell Phillips and Theodore Parker incited a small band, which included Bronson Alcott and was led by the Reverend Thomas Wentworth Higginson, to attempt to batter down the doors of the courthouse to free Burns, but officers armed with cutlasses held the protesters at bay until military troops could be mustered to keep order. The rescue attempt having failed, Burns was placed aboard a U.S. cutter and returned to Virginia. Burns's case infused Thoreau's essay.

Selections from "Slavery in Massachusetts" were first read at the 4 July 1954 antislavery convention in Framingham, Massachusetts, where it was heard by Garrison, who, at the same convention, publicly burned a copy of the Constitution in protest of the protections it afforded the institution of slavery. It is likely that the lecture was prepared hurriedly from the furor caused by the Burns case and was not complete at this time, which would explain the reading of excerpts only and the note in the record of the meeting that the whole would be published later in the *Liberator*. Thoreau's name did not appear in any of the advance notices of the convention that appeared in the *Liberator* the month before the meeting. The complete essay was published in the *Liberator* a few weeks later, and reprinted the next month in Greeley's *New-York Daily Tribune,* and, with a few excisions, in the *National Anti-Slavery Standard.*

The association of slavery with the North as well as the South did not originate with Thoreau. He probably read and was influenced by Greeley's 1845 essay "Slavery at Home: Answer to an Invitation to Attend an Anti-Slavery Meeting":

> *I understand by Slavery, that condition in which one human being exists mainly as a convenience for other human beings—*
> . . . You will readily understand, therefore, that if I regard your enterprise with less absorbing interest than you do, it is not that I deem Slavery a less but a greater evil. If I am less troubled concerning the Slavery in Charlestown or New-Orleans, it is because I see so much Slavery in New York, which appears to claim my first efforts. . . . Still less would I undertake to say that the Slavery of the South is not more hideous in kind and degree than that which prevails at the North.

Many of the ideas found in Thoreau—ideas we now label Thoreauvian—he himself found in those who came before him: not only was his concept of a northern slavery preceded by that of Horace Greeley and his nonpayment of taxes preceded by that of Bronson Alcott, but even his most iconic gesture, his stay in the woods, was preceded by that of his friend Charles Stearns Wheeler. As Emerson wrote, "The originals are not original. There is imitation, model, and suggestion, to the very archangels, if we knew their history. The first book tyrannizes over the second. Read Tasso, and you think of Virgil; read Virgil, and you think of Homer; and Milton forces you to reflect how narrow are the limits of human invention."

Thoreau's use of his sources adds to an understanding of him. Thoreau was a master at absorbing what had come before him and turning it uniquely into his own. In this day and age in which total originality is paramount, no distinction is made between a legalistic view of plagiarism and the artistic and literary notion of homage to and respect for the masters that have come before. That Thoreau could take what he read and heard and saw and adapt them in ways that made them seem nothing other than Thoreauvian to his readers is the key to his strength and individuality. "The borrowing is often honest enough," Emerson wrote, "and comes of magnanimity and stoutness. A great man quotes bravely, and will not draw on his invention when his memory serves him with a word as good. What he quotes, he fills with his own voice and humor, and the whole cyclopaedia of his table-talk is presently believed to be his own."

In 1855 *Putnam's Magazine* began serial publication of Thoreau's *Cape Cod.* As with Thoreau's previous experience with *Putnam's,* his submission was not printed in its entirety. Although this time Thoreau seemed more accommodating to Curtis's editorial requests, *Putnam's* ultimately discontinued publication of Thoreau's Cape Cod essays.

Thoreau's second Maine Woods piece, "Chesuncook," was published in the *Atlantic Monthly* in three monthly installments from June through August 1858. When a sentence about the pine tree—"It is as immortal as I am, and perchance will go to as high a heaven, there to tower above me still"—was deleted, Thoreau complained to James Russell Lowell, the editor, that he had "in this case, no more right to omit a sentiment than to insert one, or put words into my mouth. . . . I am not willing to be associated in any way, unnecessarily, with parties who will confess themselves so bigoted & timid as this implies. I could excuse a man who was afraid of an uplifted fist, but if one manifests fear at the utterance of a sincere thought, I must think that his life is a kind of nightmare continued into broad daylight." Thoreau would not publish anything else in the *Atlantic Monthly* until after Lowell's resignation as editor in early 1861.

TWO JOHN BROWN ESSAYS:

A PLEA FOR CAPTAIN JOHN BROWN
Echoes of Harper's Ferry, *edited by James Redpath (Boston: Thayer and Eldridge, 1860)*

THE LAST DAYS OF JOHN BROWN
The Liberator *(27 July 1860)*

Thoreau spoke publically and wrote formally about John Brown more than he did about any other of his contemporaries, perhaps following his own advice from his journal of 24 March 1857:

> If you are describing any occurrence, or a man, make two
> or more distinct reports at different times. Though you may
> think you have said all, you will to-morrow remember a
> whole new class of facts which perhaps interested most of all
> at the time, but did not present themselves to be reported.
> If we have recently met and talked with a man, and would

report our experience, we commonly make a very partial report at first, failing to seize the most significant, picturesque, and dramatic points; we describe only what we have had time to digest and dispose of in our minds, without being conscious that there were other things really more novel and interesting to us, which will not fail to recur to us and impress us suitably at last. How little that occurs to us in any way are we prepared at once to appreciate! We discriminate at first only a few features, and we need to reconsider our experience from many points of view and in various moods, to preserve the whole fruit of it.

A few days later he reiterated:

I would fain make two reports in my Journal, first the incidents and observations of to-day; and by to-morrow I review the same and record what was omitted before, which will often be the most significant and poetic part. I do not know at first what it is that charms me. The men and things of to-day are wont to lie fairer and truer in to-morrow's memory.

Thoreau's support of John Brown has often proved a difficult period for many of Thoreau's readers. The man who carefully praised Wendell Phillips's abolitionist efforts by emphasizing Phillips's declaration that he was born not to abolish slavery but to do right would later write aggressive endorsements of Brown's efforts: "I do not complain of any tactics that are effective of good, whether one wields the quill or the sword, but I shall not think him mistaken who quickest succeeds to liberate the slave. I will judge of the tactics by the fruit." He acknowledged, "I do not wish to kill or to be killed, but I can foresee circumstances in which both these things would be by me unavoidable."

Although he has become the exemplar of civil disobedience or passive resistance, it is a mistake to take any single statement that Thoreau made to represent who he was, and what he thought, from 1817 to 1862. "Is it not a fact," Herman Melville asked in *The Confidence Man*, "that, in real life, a consistent character is a *rara avis?*" Thoreau's support of John Brown, though, is not far from the military stance he offered in his early essay "The Service," or in "Resistance to Civil Government," in which he wrote: "When a sixth of the population of a nation which has undertaken to be the refuge of liberty are slaves, and a whole country is unjustly overrun and conquered by a foreign army, and subjected to military law, I think that it is not too soon for honest men to rebel and revolutionize."

When Thoreau spoke in 1860 at a public meeting protesting the attempted arrest of Frank Sanborn for his involvement with Brown's secret six—abolitionists who helped fund and support John Brown's war on slavery—it was reported in the *Boston Journal* that the author advocated "resistance even to the law, when it opposed justice." His ideas reflected the concepts on which our nation was founded and in particular the words of Thomas Jefferson, who wrote, "When patience has begotten false estimates of its motives, when wrongs are pressed because it is believed they will be borne, resistance becomes morality," and, referring to life, liberty, and the pursuit of happiness, "Whenever any form of government becomes destructive of these ends, it is the right of the people to alter or abolish it."

In part Thoreau's support of Brown was in reaction to a long series of events. In November 1844, Concord lawyer and former Massachusetts Congressman Samuel Hoar was appointed to negotiate a settlement of an old dispute with South Carolina. Free black sailors were forcibly being taken off Massachusetts's ships in Charleston harbor. Hoar, who had been accompanied by his daughter, Elizabeth, was thrust back onto a ship under the seemingly real threat of being lynched if he remained in Charleston.

In 1850, as part of the Missouri Compromise, Congress adopted the Fugitive Slave Act, which made it legally incumbent on all citizens, including those in free states, to help slave catchers. A one thousand–dollar fine was levied on persons found helping escaped slaves. On 15 February 1851 a federal marshal seized a fugitive slave from Virginia by the name of Shadrach Minkins, who had been working in Boston as a waiter. That afternoon he was seized from the courthouse by two black men, and on the following day he was brought to Concord; from there, with the help of the town blacksmith, Francis Bigelow, Minkins was sent to Canada. Two months later, in April, Thomas Sims, who had escaped from Georgia, was arrested with different results. The courthouse was surrounded by a large police force, and Sims, bound in chains, was returned to slavery. This was followed a few years later by the Burns affair.

While the topic of slavery formed a continuous hum in the background, and the above events increased the pitch, John Brown came to Concord, first in March 1857 and again in May 1859. Thoreau found in Brown a "man of rare common sense and directness of speech, as of action; a transcendentalist above all, a man of ideas and principles,—that was what distinguished him." When Brown was arrested after his failed raid on the federal arsenal at Harpers Ferry, during which more than a dozen people were killed, it did not take long for Thoreau to turn him into a martyr who exhibited a selflessness equivalent to that of Christ.

Notwithstanding a brief disillusionment—"I subscribed a

trifle when he was here three years ago, I had so much confidence in the man,—that he would do right,—but it would seem that he had not confidence enough in me, nor in anybody else that I know, to communicate his plans to us."—Thoreau found himself thinking so much about Brown that he put paper and pencil under his pillow so he could write in the dark when he couldn't sleep. "When I reflect to what a cause this man devoted himself, and how religiously, and then reflect to what cause his judges and all who condemn him so angrily and fluently devote themselves, I see that they are as far apart as the heavens and earth are asunder."

Two weeks after Brown's raid, on 30 October 1859, Thoreau was delivering a talk on "The Character and Actions of Capt. John Brown." He was the first to speak out publicly on Brown's behalf, unabashedly and unstintingly supportive:

> I trust that you will pardon me for being here. I do not wish to force my thoughts upon you, but I feel forced myself. . . . Think of him—of his rare qualities! such a man as it takes ages to make, and ages to understand; no mock hero, nor the representative of any party. A man such as the sun may not rise upon again in this benighted land. . . . I rejoice that I live in this age—that I am his contemporary.

At the time Thoreau delivered his lecture there was nothing in Brown's future but a noose. Thoreau had no misguided optimism about saving John Brown from the gallows. What would be titled in print "A Plea for Captain John Brown" was a plea neither for his release nor for commutation of his sentence. It was a plea for his character. It was a plea for principle. It was a plea for the heroic ideal.

Emerson recalled in his eulogy of Thoreau:

One man, whose personal acquaintance he had formed, he honored with exceptional regard. Before the first friendly word had been spoken for Captain John Brown, he sent notices to most houses in Concord that he would speak in a public hall on the condition and character of John Brown, on Sunday evening, and invited all people to come. The Republican Committee, the Abolitionist Committee, sent him word that it was premature and not advisable. He replied, — "I did not send to you for advice, but to announce that I am to speak." The hall was filled at an early hour by people of all parties, and his earnest eulogy of the hero was heard by all respectfully, by many with a sympathy that surprised themselves.

Emerson's son Edward noted that Thoreau delivered his paper on Brown "as if it burned him." He also recalled that many of "those who had come to scoff remained to pray," perceptively echoing Oliver Goldsmith's "The Deserted Village":

At church, with meek and unaffected grace,
His looks adorn'd the venerable place;
Truth from his lips prevailed with double sway,
And fools, who came to scoff, remain'd to pray.

Thoreau would deliver his paper twice more: in Boston on 1 November as a replacement for Frederick Douglass, who had fled to Canada to avoid arrest for association with Brown, and again on 3 November in Worcester, Massachusetts.

On 4 July 1860 a memorial celebration was held in North Elba, New York, on the Brown farm, where he was buried. Thoreau did not attend. As he had written in his "A Plea for Captain John

Brown": "I do not think it is quite sane for one to spend his whole life in talking or writing about this matter, unless he is continuously inspired, and I have not done so. A man may have other affairs to attend to." Nonetheless he sent along a short manuscript that would be posthumously titled, in *A Yankee in Canada, with Anti-Slavery and Reform Papers,* "The Last Days of John Brown," although the paper had little to say on Brown's final days. Thoreau's paper was read by Richard Josiah Hinton, the antislavery advocate and journalist, who prefaced them by saying:

> In conclusion, Mr. President, I desire to read the manuscript I hold. It was handed to me at Concord, with a note, while on my way here, by one whom all must honor who know him—Henry D. Thoreau. Of a fearless, truthful soul, living near to Nature, with ear attuned to catch her simplest and most subtle thought, and heart willing to interpret them to his eager brain, he often speaks undisguised, in most nervous Saxon, the judgment upon great events which others, either timid or powerless of speech, so long to hear expressed. So it was last fall. Mr. Thoreau's voice was the first which broke the disgraceful silence or hushed senseless babble with which the grandest deed of our time was met. Herein, Mr. Thoreau gives us some recollections of that eventful period:—

In addition to the two John Brown pieces included in this volume, Thoreau also compiled some readings for the "Exercises at the Town Hall, in Concord, on Friday, December 2, 1859, at 2 O'clock, P.M." "After the Death of John Brown," as it was called when collected in the posthumous *Miscellanies,* contains little of substance by Thoreau, mostly comprising readings appropriate to Brown's perceived martyrdom with brief introductions.

AN ADDRESS ON THE SUCCESSION
OF FOREST TREES
New-York Weekly Tribune *(6 October 1860)*

First given as an address at the Middlesex Agricultural Society's annual agricultural fair, the Middlesex Cattle Show and Ploughing Match, on 20 September 1860, Thoreau's essay was meant to answer the question "I have often been asked, as many of you have been, if I could tell how it happened, that when a pine wood was cut down an oak one sprang up, and *vice versa*. To which I have answered, and now answer, that I can tell—that it is no mystery to me."

It was no mystery because Thoreau spent his life in extensive and close study of the natural world around him. His life of observation and interest enabled him to address with confidence and a bit of scorn the popular theory of abiogenesis, the hypothesis that life spontaneously generated from nonorganic materials. Many natural philosophers and scientists, including Louis Agassiz, professor of zoology and geology at Harvard, had supported that idea. Thoreau was not the first person to observe forest succession or to doubt abiogenesis, but he was the first to formulate his theories and present them publically, for what may now be considered peer review, to an audience of farmers.

At the end of November 1860 Thoreau suffered a bad cold. On 3 May 1861 he wrote his friend H. G. O. Blake:

> I am still as much an invalid as when you and Brown were here, if not more of one, and at this rate there is danger that the cold weather may come again, before I get over my bronchitis. The doctor accordingly tells me that I must "clear out" to the West Indies, or elsewhere,—he does not

seem to care much where. But I decide against the West Indies, on account of their muggy heat in the summer, and the South of Europe, on account of the expense of time and money, and have at last concluded that it will be most expedient for me to try the air of Minnesota, say somewhere about St. Paul's. I am only waiting to be well enough to start. Hope to get off within a week or ten days.

The inland air may help me at once, or it may not.

Ultimately the inland air did not help. On his return he wrote Daniel Ricketson that his "ordinary pursuits, both indoors and out, have been for the most part omitted, or seriously interrupted—walking, boating, scribbling, &c. Indeed I have been sick so long that I have almost forgotten what it is to be well, yet I feel that it all respects only my envelope." At this point Thoreau was aware that he was gravely ill, writing Ricketson in somewhat couched but, in hindsight, prescient terms, "If I do not mend very quickly I shall be obliged to go to another climate again very soon." During his final months Thoreau redacted four lectures for posthumous publication in the *Atlantic Monthly*.

WALKING
Atlantic Monthly *(June 1862)*

"Walking" is composed of two lectures Thoreau had given in the 1850s, "Walking" and "The Wild"; these had been the more substantive parts extracted from a longer piece, "Walking or the Wild," which had been too long to read in full to an audience.

"Walking" contains one of his most quoted and most misquoted lines: "In Wildness is the preservation of the world." Often quoted as *Wilderness*, not *Wildness*, as if the two terms were equivalent, wildness is neither wilderness nor nature but is that which wilderness or nature represents, a freedom not subject to the dictates and demands of a "culture merely civil," as he called it in "Walking."

"Whatever has not come under the sway of man is wild. In this sense original and independent men are wild, — not tamed and broken by society," Thoreau wrote in his journal. Wildness is synonymous with deliberation. It is to be infused with spirit, to follow our genius: what Emerson called not only our natural bias but the "spontaneous perception and exhibition of truth" or what Sampson Reed simply called "divine truth."

To follow the essence of wildness in the way in which Thoreau understood it is to live a willful and deliberate life free from the external forces that cause us to live in discord with our true nature.

Thoreau's concept of wildness grew out of his 1853 reading of Richard Trench's *The Study of Words,* in which he found: "'Wild' is the participle past of 'to will'; a 'wild' horse is a 'willed' or self-willed horse, one that has never been tamed or taught to submit its will to the will of another; and so with a man." Based on this reading, Thoreau noted in his journal: "a wild man is a willed man. Well, then, a man of will who does what he wills or wishes, a man of hope and of the future tensed, for not only the obstinate is willed, but far more the constant and persevering. The obstinate man, properly speaking, is one who will not. The perseverance of the saints is positive willedness, not a mere passive willingness. The fates are wild, for they will; and the Almighty is wild above all."

"Walking" was Thoreau's call for a "Nature" with a capital "N": "I wish to speak a word for Nature, for absolute freedom and wildness, as contrasted with a freedom and culture merely civil, — to regard man as an inhabitant, or a part and parcel of Nature, rather than a member of society." The first half of the statement is important for what it tells of what Thoreau had hoped to, and did, discover in the natural world: absolute freedom and wildness. The second, however—particularly the phrase "to regard man as an inhabitant, or a part and parcel of Nature"—serves as a reminder that human life is passing *within* nature. We are not something discrete, something outside of nature, but, as Thoreau said, "part and parcel."

Considered by many to be the father of the American environmental movement, Thoreau found his place comfortably and naturally within Nature, while many environmentalists look at man as something that is not "part and parcel" of the natural world, but something discreet, outside of, or even above it. Unlike the spiritual or religious position in which the Transcendentalists found a divinity in man while acknowledging that this was different from being divine, separation of man and nature was not a Transcendental worldview.

AUTUMNAL TINTS
Atlantic Monthly *(October 1862)*

"Autumnal Tints" was first prepared as a lecture in 1859. It was culled from a botanical study that Thoreau referred to as a "very large imperfect" project. Although at the point at which he was preparing the text for the *Atlantic Monthly* it was clear that he would not live to perfect his imperfect project, he nonetheless requested the manuscript's return in order to help reestablish the larger work's integrity, perhaps with the hope that someone would continue, or at least understand, his work.

When Thoreau gave the lecture, he "always carried," as he explained to William Ticknor and James Fields of the *Atlantic Monthly,* "a very large & handsome" scarlet oak leaf "displayed on a white ground, which did me great service with the audience," suggesting that they "will see the advantage of having a simple outline engraving of this leaf & also of the White Oak leaf on the opposite page, that the readers may the better appreciate my words." Thoreau sent the smallest scarlet oak leaf from his collection in order that it best fit the magazine's pages, expressing his desire "simply for a faithful outline engraving of the leaf bristles & all."

Given Thoreau's redaction of this 1859 lecture as he lay dying, several passages take on a personal significance for the author. He could not have missed, for example, in his musings from 1853 on the fall of the leaf, the foreshadowing of his own approaching death: "It is the emblem of a successful life concluded by a death not premature, which is an ornament to Nature. What if we were to mature as perfectly, root and branch, glowing in the midst of our decay, like the Poke!" Elsewhere he describes how "contentedly" the leaves go to "their graves":

So they troop to their last resting-place, light and frisky. They put on no weeds, but merrily they go scampering over the earth, selecting the spot, choosing a lot, ordering no iron fence, whispering all through the woods about it,—some choosing the spot where the bodies of men are mouldering beneath, and meeting them half-way. How many flutterings before they rest quietly in their graves! They that soared so loftily, how contentedly they return to dust again, and are laid low, resigned to lie and decay at the foot of the tree, and afford nourishment to new generations of their kind, as well as to flutter on high! They teach us how to die.

WILD APPLES
Atlantic Monthly *(November 1862)*

"Wild Apples" was the last of the essays Thoreau sent to the *Atlantic Monthly* from his deathbed. When given as a lecture in Concord on 8 February 1860, according to Annie Russell Marble, it was acknowledged as "the best lecture of the season, and at its close there was long, continued applause." After hearing it, Bronson Alcott wrote in his journal, "It is a piece of exquisite sense, a celebrating of the infinity of Nature, exemplified with much learning and original observation, beginning with the apple in Eden and down to the wildings in our woods. I listened with uninterrupted interest and delight, and it told on the good company present."

Thoreau's essays are often categorized as natural history essays or essays of social reform, but it is limiting to treat any of his writings as belonging to either genre exclusively. The opening sentence of "Wild Apples" — "It is remarkable how closely the history of the apple tree is connected with the history of man" — sets the tone: this natural history essay about apples is also about man and society, and any essay on man and society from Thoreau's pen is an essay of social reform.

Thoreau had absorbed and transformed Emerson's use of language in his first book, *Nature:*

All the facts in natural history, taken by themselves, have no value, but are barren, like a single sex. But marry it to human history, and it is full of life. Whole Floras, all Linnaeus' and Buffon's volumes, are dry catalogues of facts; but the most trivial of these facts, the habit of a plant, the organs, or work, or noise of an insect applied to the illustration of a fact in intellectual philosophy, or, in any way associated to human nature, affects us in the most lively and agreeable manner.

As Thoreau wrote in his journal later in the same month in which he first gave this lecture, "A fact stated barely is dry. It must be the vehicle of some humanity in order to interest us. It is like giving a man a stone when he asks you for bread. Ultimately the moral is all in all . . ."

In spite of the lecture's apparent success, Thoreau concluded just one week after presenting "Wild Apples" to his Concord audience:

> Always you have to contend with the stupidity of men. It is like a stiff soil, a hard-pan. If you go deeper than usual, you are sure to meet with a pan made harder even by the superficial cultivation. The stupid you have always with you. . . . Read to them a lecture on "Education," naming that subject, and they will think that they have heard something important, but call it "Transcendentalism," and they will think it moonshine.

Although he wrote in late 1854 that he would "rather write books than lectures," Thoreau nonetheless never swerved from his authorial principle, written in his journal on 24 March 1842, that authors "are successful who do not *write down* to others, but make their own taste and judgment their audience." Failure can come when men, as he wrote on 18 October 1856,

> exaggerate the theme. Some themes they think are significant and others insignificant. I feel that my life is very homely, my pleasures very cheap. Joy and sorrow, success

and failure, grandeur and meanness, and indeed most words in the English language do not mean for me what they do for my neighbors. I see that my neighbors look with compassion on me, that they think it is a mean and unfortunate destiny which makes me to walk in these fields and woods so much and sail on this river alone. But so long as I find here the only real elysium, I cannot hesitate in my choice. My work is writing, and I do not hesitate, though I know that no subject is too trivial for me, tried by ordinary standards; for, ye fools, the theme is nothing, the life is everything. All that interests the reader is the depth and intensity of the life excited.

LIFE WITHOUT PRINCIPLE
Atlantic Monthly *(October 1863)*

Thoreau redacted "Life Without Principle" from a lecture that he presented more often than any other, delivering it seven times over six years. It was first given as "Getting a Living" in New Bedford, Massachusetts, in late 1854, and was repeated in Nantucket, Worcester, Concord, Boston, and Lowell, Massachusetts, as well as in Perth Amboy, New Jersey, under such varying titles as, "The Connection between Man's Employment and His Higher Life," "Life Misspent," and "What Shall It Profit?" In correspondence with Ticknor and Fields it was referred to as "The Higher Law" before Thoreau either suggested or agreed to its present title. As it turned out, this was the last of Thoreau's four final essays to be published, and as such, accidentally or not, serves as a culmination.

The theme of the essay was presented like the text of a sermon: "Let us consider the way in which we spend our lives." As he wrote in his journal on 13 February 1860, "The more you have thought and written on a given theme, the more you can still write," and in this essay one finds themes, as represented in the several titles, which ran through other essays, *A Week on the Concord and Merrimack River,* and, in particular, *Walden.* As Thoreau wrote on 3 February 1859:

> The writer must to some extent inspire himself. Most of his sentences may at first lie dead in his essay, but when all are arranged, some life and color will be reflected on them from the mature and successful lines; they will appear to pulsate with fresh life, and he will be enabled to eke out their slumbering sense, and make them worthy of their neighborhood. In his first essay on a given theme, he produces scarcely more than a frame and groundwork for his sentiment and poetry. Each clear thought that he attains to draws in its train many divided thoughts or perceptions. The writer has much to do even to create a theme for himself. Most that is first written on any subject is a mere groping after it, mere rubble-stone and foundation. It is only when many observations of different periods have been brought together that he begins to grasp his subject and can make one pertinent and just observation.

Thoreau called his first lectures on his Walden experience, "A History of Myself," something that could aptly be used as a subtitle for any of Thoreau's works. "Is not the poet bound to write his own biography?" he asked himself on 21 October 1857. "We do not wish to know how his imaginary hero, but how he, the actual hero, lived from day to day." He understood that for any piece to be interesting, whether it was popular or polemic, informal or expository, a natural history essay or an essay of social reform, it all had to be filtered through his very personal and individual lens. Ulti-mately there is no difference between the various types of essays under which we tend to categorize his writings. They are all a his-tory of one: Henry David Thoreau. As he acknowledged when he wrote on 18 October 1856: "Man is all in all, Nature nothing, but as she draws him out and reflects him." On 18 March 1861 he wrote in his journal:

> You can't read any genuine history—as that of Herodotus
> or the Venerable Bede—without perceiving that our interest
> depends not on the subject but on the man,—on the
> manner in which he treats the subject and the importance
> he gives it. A feeble writer and without genius must have
> what he thinks a great theme, which we are already inter-
> ested in through the accounts of others, but a genius—a
> Shakespeare, for instance—would make the history of his
> parish more interesting than another's history of the world.

"Wherever men have lived," Thoreau wrote in the same passage, "there is a story to be told, and it depends chiefly on the story-teller or historian whether that is interesting or not." When that storyteller is Thoreau, the history of one man is the history of all men; the history of Concord is the history of the world.

NOTE

1 Thoreau's changes to his source are clearly deliberate, although his reasons for them are less transparent. Therefore no attempt has been made in this volume to emend Thoreau's text to match his source. The parts of Etzler's text from which Thoreau quoted are printed in the appendix.

Abbreviations

The following abbreviations for Thoreau's works are used in notes.

C   *The Correspondence of Henry David Thoreau.* Edited by
     Walter Harding and Carl Bode. New York: New York
     University Press, 1958.

J   *The Journal of Henry Thoreau.* Edited by Bradford Torrey
     and Francis H. Allen. Boston: Houghton Mifflin, 1906.

PJ   *Journal.* Edited by John C. Broderick et al. Princeton:
     Princeton University Press, 1981–.

W   *The Writings of Henry D. Thoreau.* Walden edition. Boston:
     Houghton Mifflin, 1906.

Wa   *Walden: A Fully Annotated Edition.* Edited by Jeffrey S.
     Cramer. New Haven: Yale University Press, 2004.

All biblical quotations in the notes are from the King James
Version.

Essays

Natural History of Massachusetts

Reports—on the Fishes, Reptiles, and Birds; the Herbaceous Plants and Quadrupeds; the Insects Injurious to Vegetation; and the Invertebrate Animals—of Massachusetts.
Published agreeably to an Order of the Legislature, by the Commissioners on the Zoological and Botanical Survey of the State.[1]

PRELIMINARY NOTE

We were thinking how we might best celebrate the good deed which the State of Massachusetts has done, in procuring the Scientific Survey of the Commonwealth, whose result is recorded in these volumes, when we found a near neighbor and friend of ours, dear also to the Muses, a native and an inhabitant of the town of Concord, who readily undertook to give us such comments as he had made on these books, and, better still, notes of his own conversation with nature in the woods and waters of this town. With all thankfulness we begged our friend to lay down the oar and fishing line, which none can handle better, and assume the pen, that Isaak Walton and White of Selborne might not want a successor, nor the fair meadows, to which we also have owed a home and the happiness of many years, their poet.

Editor of the Dial.[2]

CONCORD, MASS.

Books of natural history make the most cheerful winter reading. I read in Audubon[3] with a thrill of delight,

1 The four reports consisted of Chester Dewey, *Report on the Herbaceous Flowering Plants of Massachusetts, and on the Quadrupeds of Massachusetts* (Cambridge, Mass.: Folsom, Wells and Thurston, 1840); Augustus A. Gould, *Report on the Invertebrata of Massachusetts, Comprising the Mollusca, Crustacea, Annelida, and Radiata* (Cambridge, Mass.: Folsom, Wells and Thurston, 1841); Thaddeus William Harris, *A Report on the Insects of Massachusetts, Injurious to Vegetation* (Cambridge, Mass.: Folsom, Wells and Thurston, 1841); and David Humphreys Storer, *Report on the Fishes, Reptiles, and Birds of Massachusetts* (Boston: Dutton and Wentworth, 1839).
2 In 1842 Ralph Waldo Emerson (1803–1882) edited *The Dial: A Magazine for Literature, Philosophy, and Religion* (1840–1844).
3 John James Audubon (1785–1851), French-American naturalist and painter, wrote about the magnolia and the Florida Keys in *Ornithological Biography; or, An Account of the Habits of the Birds of the United States of America.*

4 Bobolink (*Dolichonyx oryzivorus*).
5 Saint-John's-wort (*Hypericum perforatum*).
6 Meadow.
7 British name for the European thrush (*Turdus pilaris*).

when the snow covers the ground, of the magnolia, and the Florida keys, and their warm sea breezes; of the fence-rail, and the cotton-tree, and the migrations of the rice-bird;[4] of the breaking up of winter in Labrador, and the melting of the snow on the forks of the Missouri; and owe an accession of health to these reminiscences of luxuriant nature.

> Within the circuit of this plodding life
> There enter moments of an azure hue,
> Untarnished fair as is the violet
> Or anemone, when the spring strews them
> By some meandering rivulet, which make
> The best philosophy untrue that aims
> But to console man for his grievances.
> I have remembered when the winter came,
> High in my chamber in the frosty nights,
> When in the still light of the cheerful moon,
> On every twig and rail and jutting sprout,
> The icy spears were adding to their length
> Against the arrows of the coming sun,
> How in the shimmering noon of summer past
> Some unrecorded beam slanted across
> The upland pastures where the Johnswort[5] grew;
> Or heard, amid the verdure of my mind,
> The bee's long smothered hum, or the blue flag
> Loitering amidst the mead;[6] or busy rill,
> Which now through all its course stands still and
>   dumb
> Its own memorial,—purling at its play
> Along the slopes, and through the meadows next,
> Until its youthful sound was hushed at last
> In the staid current of the lowland stream;
> Or seen the furrows shine but late upturned,
> And where the fieldfare[7] followed in the rear,
> When all the fields around lay bound and hoar

Beneath a thick integument of snow.
So by God's cheap economy made rich
To go upon my winter's task again.[8]

I am singularly refreshed in winter when I hear of service berries,[9] poke-weed, juniper. Is not heaven made up of these cheap summer glories? There is a singular health in those words Labrador and East Main,[10] which no desponding creed recognises. How much more than federal are these states. If there were no other vicissitudes than the seasons, our interest would never tire. Much more is adoing than Congress wots[11] of. What journal do the persimmon and the buckeye keep, and the sharp-shinned hawk? What is transpiring from summer to winter in the Carolinas, and the Great Pine Forest,[12] and the Valley of the Mohawk?[13] The merely political aspect of the land is never very cheering; men are degraded when considered as the members of a political organization. On this side all lands present only the symptoms of decay. I see but Bunker Hill and Sing-Sing,[14] the District of Columbia and Sullivan's Island,[15] with a few avenues connecting them. But paltry are they all beside one blast of the east or the south wind which blows over them.

In society you will not find health, but in nature. Unless our feet at least stood in the midst of nature, all our faces would be pale and livid. Society is always diseased, and the best is the most so. There is no scent in it so wholesome as that of the pines, nor any fragrance so penetrating and restorative as the life-everlasting[16] in high pastures. I would keep some book of natural history always by me as a sort of elixir, the reading of which should restore the tone of the system. To the sick, indeed, nature is sick, but to the well, a fountain of health. To him who contemplates a trait of natural beauty no harm nor disappointment can come. The doctrines of despair, of spiritual or political tyranny or servitude, were

8 All poetry not otherwise identified is Thoreau's own.
9 Fruit of the service berry, or shadbush.
10 In northern Canada.
11 Knows.
12 In Pennsylvania, also known as the Great Pine Swamp.
13 River in New York.
14 Sing-Sing Prison in Ossining, New York, on the Hudson River.
15 Sullivan's Island: in Charleston harbor, South Carolina, and home of Fort Moultrie, site of a battle between Colonial forces and the British.
16 American cudweed.

17 Canadian provinces.
18 In northern Canada.
19 Eskimo: a general term applied to indigenous peoples inhabiting northern Canada, Alaska,
Greenland, and eastern Siberia.
20 Allusion to William Miller (1782–1849), who
predicted the end of the world in 1843 following
the Second Coming of Jesus Christ.
21 Possible response to Lucius Annaeus Seneca
(4 B.C.E.–65 C.E.), Roman philosopher and
dramatist, who wrote in his *Morals:* "Death is the
condition of life."
22 Clock case.

never taught by such as shared the serenity of nature. Surely good courage will not flag here on the Atlantic border, as long as we are flanked by the Fur Countries.[17] There is enough in that sound to cheer one under any circumstances. The spruce, the hemlock, and the pine will not countenance despair. Methinks some creeds in vestries and churches do forget the hunter wrapped in furs by the Great Slave Lake,[18] and that the Esquimaux[19] sledges are drawn by dogs, and in the twilight of the northern night, the hunter does not give over to follow the seal and walrus on the ice. They are of sick and diseased imaginations who would toll the world's knell so soon.[20] Cannot these sedentary sects do better than prepare the shrouds and write the epitaphs of those other busy living men? The practical faith of all men belies the preacher's consolation. What is any man's discourse to me, if I am not sensible of something in it as steady and cheery as the creak of crickets? In it the woods must be relieved against the sky. Men tire me when I am not constantly greeted and refreshed as by the flux of sparkling streams. Surely joy is the condition of life.[21] Think of the young fry that leap in ponds, the myriads of insects ushered into being on a summer evening, the incessant note of the hyla with which the woods ring in the spring, the nonchalance of the butterfly carrying accident and change painted in a thousand hues upon its wings, or the brook minnow stoutly stemming the current, the lustre of whose scales worn bright by the attrition is reflected upon the bank.

We fancy that this din of religion, literature, and philosophy, which is heard in pulpits, lyceums, and parlors, vibrates through the universe, and is as catholic a sound as the creaking of the earth's axle; but if a man sleep soundly, he will forget it all between sunset and dawn. It is the three-inch swing of a pendulum in a cupboard,[22] which the great pulse of nature vibrates by and through each instant. When we lift our eyelids and open our ears, it disappears with smoke and rattle like the cars on a railroad. When I detect a beauty in any of the recesses of nature, I am reminded, by the serene and retired spirit in which it requires to be contemplated, of the inexpressible privacy of a life,—how silent and unambitious it is. The beauty there is in mosses must be considered from the holiest, quietest nook. What an admirable training is science for the more active warfare of life. Indeed, the unchallenged bravery, which these studies imply, is far more impressive than the trumpeted valor of the warrior. I am pleased to learn that Thales[23] was up and stirring by night not unfrequently, as his astronomical discoveries prove. Linnaeus,[24] setting out for Lapland, surveys his "comb" and "spare shirt," "leathern breeches" and "gauze cap to keep off gnats,"[25] with as much complacency as Bonaparte a park of artillery for the Russian campaign.[26] The quiet bravery of the man is admirable. His eye is to take in fish, flower, and bird, quadruped and biped. Science is always brave, for to know, is to know good; doubt and danger quail before her eye. What the coward overlooks in his hurry, she calmly scrutinizes, breaking ground like a pioneer for the array of arts that follow in her train. But cowardice is unscientific; for there cannot be a science of ignorance. There may be a science of bravery, for that advances; but a retreat is rarely well conducted; if it is, then it is an orderly advance in the face of circumstances.

But to draw a little nearer to our promised topics. Entomology extends the limits of being in a new direction, so that I walk in nature with a sense of greater space and freedom. It suggests besides, that the universe is not rough-hewn, but perfect in its details. Nature will bear the closest inspection; she invites us to lay our eye level with the smallest leaf, and take an insect view of its plain. She has no interstices; every part is full of life. I explore,

23 Thales of Miletus (ca. 624–ca. 546 B.C.E.), Greek philosopher known for his study of astronomy.
24 Carolus Linnaeus (Carl von Linné, 1707–1778), Swedish naturalist who established the classification of organisms in terms of genus and species, utilizing a Latin binomial nomenclature.
25 Thoreau noted these items in his journal of 22 November 1839 from his reading in Linnaeus's *Lachesis Lapponica; or, A tour of Lapland.*
26 Napoleon I (1769–1821), who defeated the Russian army, 1805–1806.

27 Cicada.

28 Thoreau's translation from the "Anacreontea," a collection of poems in the *Carminum Poetarum Nouem* (1554) falsely attributed to Greek poet Anacreon (582–485 B.C.E.).

29 Allusion to Apollo, in Greek mythology, god of music and poetry.

30 Beetle (*Xestobium rufovillosum*), the head of which makes a clicking sound as it burrows into wood. The sound was regarded as a portent of death.

too, with pleasure, the sources of the myriad sounds which crowd the summer noon, and which seem the very grain and stuff of which eternity is made. Who does not remember the shrill roll-call of the harvest fly?[27] There were ears for these sounds in Greece long ago, as Anacreon's ode[28] will show.

"We pronounce thee happy, Cicada,
For on the tops of the trees,
Drinking a little dew,
Like any king thou singest.
For thine are they all,
Whatever thou seest in the fields,
And whatever the woods bear.
Thou art the friend of the husbandmen,
In no respect injuring any one;
And thou art honored among men,
Sweet prophet of summer.
The Muses love thee,
And Phoebus[29] himself loves thee,
And has given thee a shrill song;
Age does not wrack thee,
Thou skilful, earthborn, song-loving,
Unsuffering, bloodless one;
Almost thou art like the gods."

In the autumn days, the creaking of crickets is heard at noon over all the land, and as in summer they are heard chiefly at night-fall, so then by their incessant chirp they usher in the evening of the year. Nor can all the vanities that vex the world alter one whit the measure that night has chosen. Every pulse-beat is in exact time with the cricket's chant and the tickings of the deathwatch[30] in the wall. Alternate with these if you can.

About two hundred and eighty birds either reside permanently in the State, or spend the summer only, or make us a passing visit. Those which spend the winter with us have obtained our warmest sympathy. The nuthatch and chicadee flitting in company through the dells of the wood, the one harshly scolding at the intruder, the other with a faint lisping note enticing him on, the jay screaming in the orchard, the crow cawing in unison with the storm, the partridge, like a russet link extended over from autumn to spring, preserving unbroken the chain of summers, the hawk with warrior-like firmness abiding the blasts of winter, the robin[31] and lark lurking by warm springs in the woods, the familiar snow-bird[32] culling a few seeds in the garden, or a few crumbs in the yard, and occasionally the shrike, with heedless and unfrozen melody bringing back summer again;—

His steady sails he never furls
At any time o' year,
And perching now on Winter's curls,
He whistles in his ear.

As the spring advances and the ice is melting in the river, our earliest and straggling visitors make their appearance. Again does the old Teian poet[33] sing as well for New England as for Greece, in the

RETURN OF SPRING.

"Behold, how spring appearing,
The Graces send forth roses;
Behold, how the wave of the sea
Is made smooth by the calm;
Behold, how the duck dives;
Behold, how the crane travels;
And Titan[34] shines constantly bright.
The shadows of the clouds are moving;
The works of man shine;
The earth puts forth fruits;

[31] Thoreau's note: "A white robin and a white quail have occasionally been seen. It is mentioned in Audubon as remarkable that the nest of a robin should be found on the ground; but this bird seems to be less particular than most in the choice of a building spot. I have seen its nest placed under the thatched roof of a deserted barn, and in one instance, where the adjacent country was nearly destitute of trees, together with two of the phoebe, upon the end of a board in the loft of a sawmill, but a few feet from the saw, which vibrated several inches with the motion of the machinery."

[32] Junco.

[33] Anacreon was born in Teos, an Ionian maritime city.

[34] Helios, in Greek mythology, the sun deity.

The fruit of the olive puts forth.
The cup of Bacchus is crowned,
Along the leaves, along the branches,
The fruit, bending them down, flourishes."[35]

The ducks alight at this season in the still water, in company with the gulls, which do not fail to improve an east wind to visit our meadows, and swim about by twos and threes, pluming themselves, and diving to peck at the root of the lily, and the cranberries which the frost has not loosened. The first flock of geese is seen beating to north, in long harrows[36] and waving lines, the gingle[37] of the song-sparrow salutes us from the shrubs and fences, the plaintive note of the lark comes clear and sweet from the meadow, and the bluebird, like an azure ray, glances past us in our walk. The fish-hawk, too, is occasionally seen at this season sailing majestically over the water, and he who has once observed it will not soon forget the majesty of its flight. It sails the air like a ship of the line, worthy to struggle with the elements, falling back from time to time like a ship on its beam ends, and holding its talons up as if ready for the arrows, in the attitude of the national bird.[38] It is a great presence, as of the master of river and forest. Its eye would not quail before the owner of the soil, but make him feel like an intruder on its domains. And then its retreat, sailing so steadily away, is a kind of advance. I have by me one of a pair of ospreys, which have for some years fished in this vicinity, shot by a neighboring pond, measuring more than two feet in length, and six in the stretch of its wings. Nuttall mentions that "The ancients, particularly Aristotle, pretended that the ospreys taught their young to gaze at the sun, and those who were unable to do so were destroyed. Linnaeus even believed, on ancient authority, that one of the feet of this bird had all the toes divided, while the other was partly webbed, so that it could swim with one

35 Thoreau's translation from the "Anacreontea."
36 Diagonal arrangements formed by migratory fowl in flight.
37 Jingle.
38 On the Great Seal of the United States.

foot, and grasp a fish with the other."[39] But that educated eye is now dim, and those talons are nerveless. Its shrill scream seems yet to linger in its throat, and the roar of the sea in its wings. There is the tyranny of Jove[40] in its claws, and his wrath in the erectile feathers of the head and neck. It reminds me of the Argonautic expedition,[41] and would inspire the dullest to take flight over Parnassus.[42]

The booming of the bittern, described by Goldsmith[43] and Nuttall,[44] is frequently heard in our fens, in the morning and evening, sounding like a pump, or the chopping of wood in a frosty morning in some distant farm-yard. The manner in which this sound is produced I have not seen anywhere described. On one occasion, the bird has been seen by one of my neighbors to thrust its bill into the water, and suck up as much as it could hold, then raising its head, it pumped it out again with four or five heaves of the neck, throwing it two or three feet, and making the sound each time.[45]

At length the summer's eternity is ushered in by the cackle of the flicker among the oaks on the hill-side, and a new dynasty begins with calm security.

In May and June the woodland quire[46] is in full tune, and given the immense spaces of hollow air, and this curious human ear, one does not see how the void could be better filled.

Each summer sound
Is a summer round.

As the season advances, and those birds which make us but a passing visit depart, the woods become silent again, and but few feathers ruffle the drowsy air. But the solitary rambler may still find a response and expression for every mood in the depths of the wood.

39 Quoted from Thomas Nuttall's (1786–1859) *A Manual of the Ornithology of the United States and Canada,* with one minor variant: "with the other" for "in the other."
40 Allusion to Aeschylus's (525–456 B.C.E.) *Prometheus Bound,* translated by Thomas Medwin (London, 1832). Thoreau rendered it as the "tyranny of Zeus" in his translation published in the *Dial* (April 1843).
41 Reference to the Argo, the ship in Greek mythology on which Jason sailed in search of the Golden Fleece.
42 Mountain in central Greece; in Greek mythology, the place where the Muses resided, and as such a source of poetic inspiration.
43 Allusion to Oliver Goldsmith's (1728–1774) *A History of the Earth and Animated Nature:* "There is none so dismally hollow as the booming of the bittern."
44 Allusion to Nuttall's *A Manual of the Ornithology of the United States and of Canada:* "We often hear the loud booming note of this bird from the marshes of Fresh Pond, morning and evening, and sometimes even during the day"; Nuttall follows with Goldsmith's description.
45 George Minott, sometimes Minot (1783–1861), who, Thoreau noted at a later date, "says he has seen them when making the noise" [J 3:66]. Minott a neighbor during Thoreau's first tenure in the Emerson home, which began in April 1841.
46 Choir.

47 Thoreau's note: "This bird, which is so well described by Nuttall, but is apparently unknown by the author of the Report, is one of the most common in the woods in this vicinity, and in Cambridge I have heard the college yard ring with its trill. The boys call it 'yorrick,' from the sound of its querulous and chiding note, as it flits near the traveller through the underwood. The cowbirds's egg is occasionally found in its nest, as mentioned by Audubon."

48 Christian name of Metacomet (ca. 1639–1676), leader of the Wampanoag Indians of Massachusetts and Rhode Island.

49 Wa-hun-sn-a-cawh (ca. 1550–1618) leader of the Algonquin Indians of North America.

50 John Winthrop (1588–1649), Puritan leader and first governor of the Massachusetts Bay Colony.

51 John Smith (ca. 1579–1631), English explorer, soldier, and author, and one of the founders of Jamestown, Virginia.

Sometimes I hear the veery's[47] clarion,
Or brazen trump of the impatient jay,
And in secluded woods the chicadee
Doles out her scanty notes, which sing the praise
Of heroes, and set forth the loveliness
Of virtue evermore.

The phoebe still sings in harmony with the sultry weather by the brink of the pond, nor are the desultory hours of noon in the midst of the village without their minstrel.

Upon the lofty elm tree sprays
The vireo rings the changes sweet,
During the trivial summer days,
Striving to lift our thoughts above the street.

With the autumn begins in some measure a new spring. The plover is heard whistling high in the air over the dry pastures, the finches flit from tree to tree, the bobolinks and flickers fly in flocks, and the goldfinch rides on the earliest blast, like a winged hyla peeping amid the rustle of the leaves. The crows, too, begin now to congregate; you may stand and count them as they fly low and straggling over the landscape, singly or by twos and threes, at intervals of half a mile, until a hundred have passed.

I have seen it suggested somewhere that the crow was brought to this country by the white man; but I shall as soon believe that the white man planted these pines and hemlocks. He is no spaniel to follow our steps; but rather flits about the clearings like the dusky spirit of the Indian, reminding me oftener of Philip[48] and Powhatan,[49] than of Winthrop[50] and Smith.[51] He is a relic of the dark ages. By just so slight, by just so lasting a tenure does superstition hold the world ever; there is the rook in England, and the crow in New England.

Thou dusky spirit of the wood,
Bird of an ancient brood,
Flitting thy lonely way,
A meteor in the summer's day,
From wood to wood, from hill to hill,
Low over forest, field and rill,
What wouldst thou say?
Why shouldst thou haunt the day?
What makes thy melancholy float?
What bravery inspires thy throat,
And bears thee up above the clouds,
Over desponding human crowds,
Which far below
Lay thy haunts low?

The late walker or sailer, in the October evenings, may hear the murmuring of the snipe, circling over the meadows, the most spirit-like sound in nature; and still later in the autumn, when the frosts have tinged the leaves, a solitary loon pays a visit to our retired ponds, where he may lurk undisturbed till the season of moulting is passed,[52] making the woods ring with his wild laughter. This bird, the Great Northern Diver, well deserves its name; for when pursued with a boat, it will dive, and swim like a fish under water, for sixty rods or more, as fast as a boat can be paddled, and its pursuer, if he would discover his game again, must put his ear to the surface to hear where it comes up. When it comes to the surface, it throws the water off with one shake of its wings, and calmly swims about until again disturbed.

These are the sights and sounds which reach our senses oftenest during the year. But sometimes one hears a quite new note, which has for back ground other Carolinas and Mexicos than the books describe, and learns that his ornithology has done him no service.

It appears from the Report that there are about forty

52 Late winter.

53 John Hayward (1781–1869) wrote in *The New England Gazetteer:* "Its Indian title was *Musketaquid.*"
54 Quoted from Lemuel Shattuck's (1793–1859) *A History of the Town of Concord* (1835).

quadrupeds belonging to the State, and among these one is glad to hear of a few bears, wolves, lynxes, and wildcats.

When our river overflows its banks in the spring, the wind from the meadows is laden with a strong scent of musk, and by its freshness advertises me of an unexplored wildness. Those backwoods are not far off then. I am affected by the sight of the cabins of the musk-rat, made of mud and grass, and raised three or four feet along the river, as when I read of the barrows of Asia. The musk-rat is the beaver of the settled States. Their number has even increased within a few years in this vicinity. Among the rivers which empty into the Merrimack, the Concord is known to the boatmen as a dead stream. The Indians are said to have called it Musketaquid, or Prairie river.[53] Its current being much more sluggish, and its water more muddy than the rest, it abounds more in fish and game of every kind. According to the History of the town, "The fur trade here was once very important. As early as 1641, a company was formed in the colony, of which Major Willard of Concord was superintendent, and had the exclusive right to trade with the Indians in furs and other articles; and for this right they were obliged to pay into the public treasury one twentieth of all the furs they obtained."[54] There are trappers in our midst still, as well as on the streams of the far west, who night and morning go the round of their traps, without fear of the Indian. One of these takes from one hundred and fifty to two hundred musk-rats in a year, and even thirty-six have been shot by one man in a day. Their fur, which is not nearly as valuable as formerly, is in good condition in the winter and spring only; and upon the breaking up of the ice, when they are driven out of their holes by the water, the greatest number is shot from boats, either swimming or resting on their stools, or slight supports of grass and reeds, by the side of the stream. Though they exhibit considerable cunning at other times, they are easily taken in a trap, which has only to be placed in their holes, or wherever they frequent, without any bait being used, though it is sometimes rubbed with their musk. In the winter the hunter cuts holes in the ice, and shoots them when they come to the surface. Their burrows are usually in the high banks of the river, with the entrance under water, and rising within to above the level of high water. Sometimes their nests, composed of dried meadow grass and flags, may be discovered where the bank is low and spongy, by the yielding of the ground under the feet. They have from three to seven or eight young in the spring.

Frequently, in the morning or evening, a long ripple is seen in the still water, where a musk-rat is crossing the stream, with only its nose above the surface, and sometimes a green bough in its mouth to build its house with. When it finds itself observed, it will dive and swim five or six rods[55] under water, and at length conceal itself in its hole, or the weeds. It will remain under water for ten minutes at a time, and on one occasion has been seen, when undisturbed, to form an air bubble under the ice, which contracted and expanded as it breathed at leisure. When it suspects danger on shore, it will stand erect like a squirrel, and survey its neighborhood for several minutes, without moving.

In the fall, if a meadow intervene between their burrows and the stream, they erect cabins of mud and grass, three or four feet high, near its edge. These are not their breeding places, though young are sometimes found in them in late freshets, but rather their hunting lodges, to which they resort in the winter with their food, and for shelter. Their food consists chiefly of flags[56] and fresh water muscles, the shells of the latter being left in large quantities around their lodges in the spring.

The Penobscot Indian[57] wears the entire skin of a

55 Eighty to one hundred feet; a rod equals sixteen and a half feet.
56 Calamus or sweet flag, a marsh herb.
57 Of the Penobscot River region of Maine.

58 Pilpai, or Bidpai, supposed author of a collection of Sanskrit fables, the *Hitopadesa*. Thoreau would have known Charles Wilkins's (1750–1836) translation, *The Hĕĕtōpădēs of Vĕĕshnŏŏ-Sărmā, in a Series of Connected Fables, Interspersed with Moral, Prudential. And Political Maxims*, a selection from which was published in the July 1842 issue of the *Dial*.
59 Aesop (ca. 620–560 B.C.E.) told several fables about the fox, including "The Fox and the Grapes," "The Fox and the Crow," and "The Fox without a Tail."

muskrat, with the legs and tail dangling, and the head caught under his girdle, for a pouch, into which he puts his fishing tackle, and essences to scent his traps with.

The bear, wolf, lynx, wildcat, deer, beaver, and marten, have disappeared; the otter is rarely if ever seen at present; and the mink is less common than formerly.

Perhaps of all our untamed quadrupeds, the fox has obtained the widest and most familiar reputation, from the time of Pilpay[58] and Aesop[59] to the present day. His recent tracks still give variety to a winter's walk. I tread in the steps of the fox that has gone before me by some hours, or which perhaps I have started, with such a tiptoe of expectation, as if I were on the trail of the Spirit itself which resides in the wood, and expected soon to catch it in its lair. I am curious to know what has determined its graceful curvatures, and how surely they were coincident with the fluctuations of some mind. I know which way a mind wended, what horizon it faced, by the setting of these tracks, and whether it moved slowly or rapidly, by their greater or less intervals and distinctness; for the swiftest step leaves yet a lasting trace. Sometimes you will see the trails of many together, and where they have gambolled and gone through a hundred evolutions, which testify to a singular listlessness and leisure in nature.

When I see a fox run across the pond on the snow, with the carelessness of freedom, or at intervals trace his course in the sunshine along the ridge of a hill, I give up to him sun and earth as to their true proprietor. He does not go in the sun, but it seems to follow him, and there is a visible sympathy between him and it. Sometimes, when the snow lies light, and but five or six inches deep, you may give chase and come up with one on foot. In such a case he will show a remarkable presence of mind, choosing only the safest direction, though he may lose ground by it. Notwithstanding his fright, he will take no step which is not beautiful. His pace is a sort of leopard canter, as if he were in no wise impeded by the snow, but were husbanding his strength all the while. When the ground is uneven, the course is a series of graceful curves, conforming to the shape of the surface. He runs as though there were not a bone in his back, occasionally dropping his muzzle to the ground for a rod or two, and then tossing his head aloft, when satisfied of his course. When he comes to a declivity, he will put his fore feet together, and slide swiftly down it, shoving the snow before him. He treads so softly that you would hardly hear it from any nearness, and yet with such expression, that it would not be quite inaudible at any distance.[60]

Of fishes, seventy-five genera and one hundred and seven species are described in the Report. The fisherman will be startled to learn that there are but about a dozen kinds in the ponds and streams of any inland town; and almost nothing is known of their habits. Only their names and residence make one love fishes. I would know even the number of their fin rays, and how many scales compose the lateral line. I am the wiser in respect to all knowledges, and the better qualified for all fortunes, for knowing that there is a minnow in the brook. Methinks I have need even of his sympathy and to be his fellow in a degree.

I have experienced such simple delight in the trivial matters of fishing and sporting, formerly, as might have inspired the muse of Homer or Shakespeare; and now when I turn the pages and ponder the plates of the Angler's Souvenir,[61] I am fain to exclaim, —

"Can these things be,
And overcome us like a summer's cloud?"[62]

Next to nature it seems as if man's actions were the most natural, they so gently accord with her. The small

60 In his corrected copy of the *Dial* Thoreau referenced the following 1844 journal passage: "Yesterday I skated after a fox over the ice. Occasionally he sat on his haunches and barked at me like a young wolf. . . . The fox manifested an almost human suspicion of mystery in my actions. While I skated directly after him, he cantered at the top of his speed; but when I stood still, though his fear was not abated, some strange but inflexible law of his nature caused him to stop also, and sit again on his haunches. While I still stood motionless, he would go slowly a rod to one side, then sit and bark, then a rod to the other side, and sit and bark again, but did not retreat, as if spellbound. When, however, I commenced the pursuit again, he found himself released from his durance" [J 1:470].
61 Book by William Andrew Chatto (1799–1864) published under the pseudonym P. Fisher, Esq.
62 Variant, similarly found in Emerson's *Nature*, of William Shakespeare's (1564–1616) *Macbeth* III. iv.111–112: "Can such things be, / And overcome us like a summer's cloud, / Without our special wonder?"

63 Possible allusion to the eponymous hero of Daniel Defoe's (1660–1731) novel *Robinson Crusoe,* who was shipwrecked on an unnamed island and saw footprints in the sand.
64 Large open farm wagon.
65 Thoreau's 10-line poem "The Thaw," as written in his journal of 11 January 1839, began:

> I saw the civil sun drying the earth's tears,
> Her tears of joy, that only faster flowed. [J 1:71]

seines of flax stretched across the shallow and transparent parts of our river, are no more intrusion than the cobweb in the sun. I stay my boat in mid current, and look down in the sunny water to see the civil meshes of his nets, and wonder how the blustering people of the town could have done this elvish work. The twine looks like a new river weed, and is to the river as a beautiful memento of man's presence in nature, discovered as silently and delicately as a foot-print in the sand.[63]

When the ice is covered with snow, I do not suspect the wealth under my feet; that there is as good as a mine under me wherever I go. How many pickerel are poised on easy fin fathoms below the loaded wain.[64] The revolution of the seasons must be a curious phenomenon to them. At length the sun and wind brush aside their curtain, and they see the heavens again.

Early in the spring, after the ice has melted, is the time for spearing fish. Suddenly the wind shifts from north-east and east to west and south, and every icicle, which has tinkled on the meadow grass so long, trickles down its stem, and seeks its level unerringly with a million comrades. The steam curls up from every roof and fence.

> I see the civil sun drying earth's tears,
> Her tears of joy, which only faster flow.[65]

In the brooks is heard the slight grating sound of small cakes of ice, floating with various speed, full of content and promise, and where the water gurgles under a natural bridge, you may hear these hasty rafts hold conversation in an under tone. Every rill is a channel for the juices of the meadow. In the ponds the ice cracks with a merry and inspiriting din, and down the larger streams is whirled grating hoarsely, and crashing its way along, which was so lately a highway for the woodman's team and the fox, sometimes with the tracks of the skaters still fresh upon it, and the holes cut for pickerel. Town committees anxiously inspect the bridges and causeways, as if by mere eye-force to intercede with the ice, and save the treasury.

The river swelleth more and more,[66]
Like some sweet influence stealing o'er
The passive town; and for a while
Each tussuck makes a tiny isle,
Where, on some friendly Ararat,
Resteth the weary water-rat.

No ripple shows Musketaquid,
Her very current e'en is hid,
As deepest souls do calmest rest,
When thoughts are swelling in the breast,
And she that in the summer's drought
Doth make a rippling and a rout,
Sleeps from Nahshawtuck[67] to the Cliff,[68]
Unruffled by a single skiff.
But by a thousand distant hills
The louder roar a thousand rills,
And many a spring which now is dumb,
And many a stream with smothered hum,
Doth swifter well and faster glide,
Though buried deep beneath the tide.

Our village shows a rural Venice,
Its broad lagoons where yonder fen is;
As lovely as the Bay of Naples
Yon placid cove amid the maples;
And in my neighbor's field of corn
I recognise the Golden Horn.[69]

Here Nature taught from year to year,
When only red men came to hear,

66 Lines 15–48 of Thoreau's 48-line poem "The Freshet," as written in his journal of 24 February 1840.
67 Sometimes spelled Nawshawtuct, and also known as Lee's Hill: a hill in Concord, west of where the Sudbury and Assabet Rivers meet.
68 Fair Haven Hill was on the shore of the Sudbury River, about one half mile southwest of Walden, and was also known as the Cliffs.
69 Allusion to an inlet of the Bosporus on which Constantinople (now Istanbul) was situated, so called for its curved shape and great beauty.

71 Sometimes, cucujo or cucuyo: West Indian firefly.

72 In Greek mythology, god of the underworld. Charon was the ferryman who conveyed souls across the river Styx from the land of the living to the land of the dead.

73 Will-o'-the-wisp: a phosphorescent light that hovers or flits over marshy or swampy ground; also something that deludes or misleads by its visionary or evanescent nature.

74 Allusion to Venus, the morning star, also called Lucifer or Phosphorus.

Methinks 't was in this school of art
Venice and Naples learned their part,
But still their mistress, to my mind,
Her young disciples leaves behind.

The fisherman now repairs and launches his boat. The best time for spearing is at this season, before the weeds have begun to grow, and while the fishes lie in the shallow water, for in summer they prefer the cool depths, and in the autumn they are still more or less concealed by the grass. The first requisite is fuel for your crate; and for this purpose the roots of the pitch pine are commonly used, found under decayed stumps, where the trees have been felled eight or ten years.

With a crate, or jack,[70] made of iron hoops, to contain your fire, and attached to the bow of your boat about three feet from the water, a fish-spear with seven tines, and fourteen feet long, a large basket, or barrow, to carry your fuel and bring back your fish, and a thick outer garment, you are equipped for a cruise. It should be a warm and still evening; and then with a fire crackling merrily at the prow, you may launch forth like a cucullo[71] into the night. The dullest soul cannot go upon such an expedition without some of the spirit of adventure; as if he had stolen the boat of Charon and gone down the Styx on a midnight expedition into the realms of Pluto.[72] And much speculation does this wandering star afford to the musing night-walker, leading him on and on, jack-o'lantern-like,[73] over the meadows; or if he is wiser, he amuses himself with imagining what of human life, far in the silent night, is flitting moth-like round its candle. The silent navigator shoves his craft gently over the water, with a smothered pride and sense of benefaction, as if he were the phosphor,[74] or light-bringer, to these dusky realms, or some sister moon, blessing the spaces with her light. The waters, for a rod or two on either hand and several feet in depth, are lit up with more than noon-day distinctness, and he enjoys the opportunity which so many have desired, for the roofs of a city are indeed raised, and he surveys the midnight economy[75] of the fishes. There they lie in every variety of posture, some on their backs, with their white bellies uppermost, some suspended in mid water, some sculling gently along with a dreamy motion of the fins, and others quite active and wide awake,—a scene not unlike what the human city would present. Occasionally he will encounter a turtle selecting the choicest morsels, or a musk-rat resting on a tussuck. He may exercise his dexterity, if he sees fit, on the more distant and active fish, or fork the nearer into his boat, as potatoes out of a pot, or even take the sound sleepers with his hands.[76] But these last accomplishments he will soon learn to dispense with, distinguishing the real object of his pursuit, and find compensation in the beauty and never ending novelty of his position. The pines growing down to the water's edge will show newly as in the glare of a conflagration, and as he floats under the willows with his light, the song-sparrow will often wake on her perch, and sing that strain at midnight, which she had meditated for the morning. And when he has done, he may have to steer his way home through the dark by the north star, and he will feel himself some degrees nearer to it for having lost his way on the earth.

The fishes commonly taken in this way are pickerel, suckers, perch, eels, pouts, breams, and shiners,—from thirty to sixty weight[77] in a night. Some are hard to be recognised in the unnatural light, especially the perch, which his dark bands being exaggerated, acquires a ferocious aspect. The number of these transverse bands, which the Report states to be seven, is, however, very variable, for in some of our ponds they have nine and ten even.

75 From the Greek, meaning management of a household or of household affairs. Thoreau often went to the root meaning of a word, here plumbing beneath the narrow common use of *economy* as a community's method of wealth creation or as frugality.

76 Moncure Daniel Conway (1832–1907) recalled in *Life of Nathaniel Hawthorne* that "Thoreau used to amuse us by gently raising fish out of the water."

77 Fisherman's weight, in pounds, also known as river-weight: the weight of a fish as guessed at, but not determined on a scale.

78 In his corrected copy of the *Dial* Thoreau emended the month to May.

79 Thoreau described a pigeon-bed in his journal of 15 August 1854 as a place "where the pigeons were being baited" [J 6:445].

It appears that we have eight kinds of tortoises, twelve snakes,—but one of which is venomous,—nine frogs and toads, nine salamanders, and one lizard, for our neighbors.

I am particularly attracted by the motions of the serpent tribe. They make our hands and feet, the wings of the bird, and the fins of the fish seem very superfluous, as if nature had only indulged her fancy in making them. The black snake will dart into a bush when pursued, and circle round and round with an easy and graceful motion, amid the thin and bare twigs, five or six feet from the ground, as a bird flits from bough to bough, or hang in festoons between the forks. Elasticity and flexibleness in the simpler forms of animal life are equivalent to a complex system of limbs in the higher; and we have only to be as wise and wily as the serpent, to perform as difficult feats without the vulgar assistance of hands and feet.

In April,[78] the snapping turtle, *Emysaurus serpentina,* is frequently taken on the meadows and in the river. The fisherman, taking sight over the calm surface, discovers its snout projecting above the water, at the distance of many rods, and easily secures his prey through its unwillingness to disturb the water by swimming hastily away, for, gradually drawing its head under, it remains resting on some limb or clump of grass. Its eggs, which are buried at a distance from the water, in some soft place, as a pigeon bed,[79] are frequently devoured by the skunk. It will catch fish by day-light, as a toad catches flies, and is said to emit a transparent fluid from its mouth to attract them.

Nature has taken more care than the fondest parent for the education and refinement of her children. Consider the silent influence which flowers exert, no less upon the ditcher in the meadow than the lady in the bower. When I walk in the woods, I am reminded that a wise purveyor has been there before me; my most delicate experience is typified there. I am struck with the pleasing friendships and unanimities of nature, as when the moss[80] on the trees takes the form of their leaves. In the most stupendous scenes you will see delicate and fragile features, as slight wreaths of vapor, dew-lines, feathery sprays, which suggest a high refinement, a noble blood and breeding, as it were. It is not hard to account for elves and fairies; they represent this light grace, this ethereal gentility. Bring a spray from the wood, or a crystal[81] from the brook, and place it on your mantel, and your household ornaments will seem plebeian beside its nobler fashion and bearing. It will wave superior there, as if used to a more refined and polished circle. It has a salute and a response to all your enthusiasm and heroism.

In the winter, I stop short in the path to admire how the trees grow up without forethought, regardless of the time and circumstances. They do not wait as man does, but now is the golden age of the sapling. Earth, air, sun, and rain, are occasion enough; they were not better in primeval centuries. The "winter of *their* discontent"[82] never comes. Witness the buds of the native poplar standing gaily out to the frost on the sides of its bare switches. They express a naked confidence. With cheerful heart one could be a sojourner[83] in the wilderness, if he were sure to find there the catkins of the willow or the alder. When I read of them in the accounts of northern adventurers, by Baffin's Bay[84] or Mackenzie's river,[85] I see how even there too I could dwell. They are our little vegetable redeemers. Methinks our virtue will hold out till they come again. They are worthy to have had a greater than Minerva[86] or Ceres[87] for their inventor. Who was the benignant goddess that bestowed them on mankind?

Nature is mythical and mystical always, and works with the license and extravagance of genius. She has her luxurious and florid style as well as art. Having a pil-

80 In his corrected copy of the *Dial* Thoreau changed *moss* to *lichens*.
81 Quartz.
82 Allusion to the opening of Shakespeare's *Richard III* I.i.1–2: "Now is the winter of our discontent / Made glorious summer by this son of York." It was an allusion Thoreau liked, as evidenced by his use of it here, in *Walden*, and in his journal, on 13 October 1851 and 31 October 1857 [J 10:150].
83 One whose stay is temporary. Although Thoreau wrote in an early journal entry, "I don't want to feel as if my life were a sojourn any longer" [J 1:299], he looked at various stages of his life as temporary sojourns or experiments.
84 Between Baffin Island and the coast of Greenland.
85 In the Canadian Rocky Mountains.
86 In Roman mythology, the goddess of wisdom; Athena, in Greek mythology.
87 In Roman mythology, the goddess of agriculture.

88 Colloquial or Thoreauvian name for an un-identified plant, but possibly the skunk cabbage, *Symplocarpus foetidus,* which Thoreau described on 23 June 1853: "a skunk-cabbage leaf makes the best vessel to drink out of at a spring, it is so large, already somewhat dishing, oftenest entire, and grows near at hand, and, though its odor when the stem is cut off is offensive, it does not flavor the water and is not perceived in drinking" [J 5:296].

89 Tapered or pointing projection, as in a pitcher.

90 In Greek mythology, sea gods.

91 In his journal of 28 November 1837 Thoreau wrote: "Every tree, fence, and spire of grass that could raise its head above the snow was this morning covered with a dense hoar frost. . . . The branches and taller grasses were covered with a wonderful ice-foliage, answering leaf for leaf to their summer dress" [J 1:14].

92 From the Latin, meaning "begetter," it referred originally to an attendant spirit.

93 Stumps, or parts of stalk, left in a field after harvesting.

grim's cup[88] to make, she gives to the whole, stem, bowl, handle, and nose,[89] some fantastic shape, as if it were to be the car of some fabulous marine deity, a Nereus or Triton.[90]

In the winter, the botanist needs not confine himself to his books and herbarium, and give over his outdoor pursuits, but study a new department of vegetable physiology, what may be called crystalline botany, then. The winter of 1837 was unusually favorable for this.[91] In December of that year the Genius[92] of vegetation seemed to hover by night over its summer haunts with unusual persistency. Such a hoar-frost, as is very uncommon here or anywhere, and whose full effects can never be witnessed after sunrise, occurred several times. As I went forth early on a still frosty morning, the trees looked like airy creatures of darkness caught napping, on this side huddled together with their grey hairs streaming in a secluded valley, which the sun had not penetrated, on that hurrying off in Indian file along some water-course, while the shrubs and grasses, like elves and fairies of the night, sought to hide their diminished heads in the snow. The river, viewed from the high bank, appeared of a yellowish green color, though all the landscape was white. Every tree, shrub, and spire of grass, that could raise its head above the snow, was covered with a dense ice-foliage, answering, as it were, leaf for leaf to its summer dress. Even the fences had put forth leaves in the night. The centre, diverging, and more minute fibres were perfectly distinct, and the edges regularly indented. These leaves were on the side of the twig or stubble[93] opposite to the sun, meeting it for the most part at right angles, and there were others standing out at all possible angles upon these and upon one another, with no twig or stubble supporting them. When the first rays of the sun slanted over the scene, the grasses seemed hung with innumerable jewels, which jingled merrily as they were brushed by the foot of the traveller, and re-flected all the hues of the rainbow as he moved from side to side. It struck me that these ghost leaves and the green ones whose forms they assume, were the creatures of but one law; that in obedience to the same law the vegetable juices swell gradually into the perfect leaf, on the one hand, and the crystalline particles troop to their standard in the same order, on the other. As if the material were indifferent, but the law one and invariable, and every plant in the spring but pushed up into and filled a per-manent and eternal mould, which, summer and winter, forever is waiting to be filled.

This foliate structure is common to the coral and the plumage of birds, and to how large a part of animate and inanimate nature. The same independence of law on matter is observable in many other instances, as in the natural rhymes, when some animal form, color, or odor, has its counterpart in some vegetable. As, indeed, all rhymes imply an eternal melody, independent of any particular sense.

As confirmation of the fact, that vegetation is but a kind of crystallization, every one may observe how, upon the edge of the melting frost on the window, the needle-shaped particles are bundled together so as to resemble fields waving with grain, or shocks rising here and there from the stubble; on one side the vegetation of the torrid zone, high towering palms and wide-spread bannians, such as are seen in pictures of oriental scenery; on the other, arctic pines stiff frozen, with downcast branches.

Vegetation has been made the type of all growth; but as in crystals the law is more obvious, their material being more simple, and for the most part more transient and fleeting, would it not be as philosophical as convenient, to consider all growth, all filling up within the limits of nature, but a crystallization more or less rapid?[94]

On this occasion, in the side of the high bank of the

94 In his corrected copy of the *Dial* Thoreau referenced an undated 1848 journal passage in which he wrote: "What in short is all art at length but a kind of vegetation or crystallization (It is) the production of nature manured & quickened with mind— . . . . The naturalist at last finds it impossible to distinguish animal from vegetable productions When the artist works simply and naturally enough his work will seem to grow under his hands touch like the coral insects The Tahi-tians regarded the first nails they saw as vegetable productions. . . . This was not merely childish but contained in it a germ of truth—" [PJ 3:7–8].

95 Allusion to Lilliput, a land of very small people in Jonathan Swift's (1667–1745) *Gulliver's Travels.*
96 Gothic architecture was characterized by vaulting and pointed arches, slender vertical piers, and counterbalancing buttresses.

river, wherever the water or other cause had formed a cavity, its throat and outer edge, like the entrance to a citadel, bristled with a glistening ice-armor. In one place you might see minute ostrich feathers, which seemed the waving plumes of the warriors filing into the fortress; in another, the glancing, fan-shaped banners of the Lilliputian host;[95] and in another, the needle-shaped particles collected into bundles, resembling the plumes of the pine, might pass for a phalanx of spears. From the under side of the ice in the brooks, where there was a thicker ice below, depended a mass of crystallization, four or five inches deep, in the form of prisms, with their lower ends open, which, when the ice was laid on its smooth side, resembled the roofs and steeples of a Gothic city,[96] or the vessels of a crowded haven under a press of canvas. The very mud in the road, where the ice had melted, was crystallized with deep rectilinear fissures, and the crystalline masses in the sides of the ruts resembled exactly asbestos in the disposition of their needles. Around the roots of the stubble and flower-stalks, the frost was gathered into the form of irregular conical shells, or fairy rings. In some places the ice-crystals were lying upon granite rocks, directly over crystals of quartz, the frost-work of a longer night, crystals of a longer period, but to some eye unprejudiced by the short term of human life, melting as fast as the former.

In the Report on the Invertebrate Animals, this singular fact is recorded, which teaches us to put a new value on time and space. "The distribution of the marine shells is well worthy of notice as a geological fact. Cape Cod, the right arm of the Commonwealth, reaches out into the ocean, some fifty or sixty miles. It is nowhere many miles wide; but this narrow point of land has hitherto proved a barrier to the migrations of many species of Mollusca. Several genera and numerous species, which are separated by the intervention of only a few miles of land, are effectually prevented from mingling by the Cape, and do not pass from one side to the other. * * * * * Of the one hundred and ninety-seven marine species, eighty-three do not pass to the south shore, and fifty are not found on the north shore of the Cape."[97]

That common muscle, the *Unio complanatus,* or more properly *fluviatilis,* left in the spring by the musk-rat upon rocks and stumps, appears to have been an important article of food with the Indians. In one place, where they are said to have feasted, they are found in large quantities, at an elevation of thirty feet above the river, filling the soil to the depth of a foot, and mingled with ashes and Indian remains.

The works we have placed at the head of our chapter, with as much license as the preacher selects his text, are such as imply more labor than enthusiasm. The State wanted complete catalogues of its natural riches, with such additional facts merely as would be directly useful.

The Reports on Fishes, Reptiles, Insects, and Invertebrate Animals, however, indicate labor and research, and have a value independent of the object of the legislature.

Those on Herbaceous Plants and Birds cannot be of much value, as long as Bigelow[98] and Nuttall are accessible. They serve but to indicate, with more or less exactness, what species are found in the State. We detect several errors ourselves, and a more practised eye would no doubt expand the list.

The Quadrupeds deserve a more final and instructive report than they have obtained.

These volumes deal much in measurements and minute descriptions, not interesting to the general reader, with only here and there a colored sentence to allure him, like those plants growing in dark forests, which bear only leaves without blossoms.[99] But the ground was comparatively unbroken, and we will not complain of the pioneer, if he raises no flowers with his first crop.

97 Quoted from Gould's *Report on the Invertebrata of Massachusetts,* with one minor variant: "mingling" for "intermingling"

98 Jacob Bigelow (1786–1879), author of *Florula Bostoniensis: A Collection of the Plants of Boston and Its Vicinity* (Boston: Hillard Gray, Little and Wilkins, 1829).

99 An allusion to Augustin Pyramus de Candolle (1778–1841) and Kurt Polycarp Joachim Sprengel's (1766–1833) *Elements of the Philosophy of Plants:* "It is not uncommon, with the *Rubus fruticosus,* when in dark forests it is deprived of the sun's light, to put forth only leaves instead of blossoms." Thoreau noted in his journal of 16 December 1837: "Those plants growing in dark forests, which 'put forth only leaves instead of blossoms.'" [J 1:18].

100 Quoted from *The Characters of Theophrastus:* "The natural attitude of inspection is prone: we do not often observe accurately any object that rises much above the level of the eye." Theophrastus (ca. 372–ca. 287 B.C.E.) was a Greek philosopher and student of Aristotle.

101 Reference to an attendant spirit or genius in Greek mythology, not to be confused with the malignant Judeo-Christian demon.

102 Allusion to the scientific methods of Francis Bacon (1561–1626), who wrote in his *Aphorisms Concerning the Interpretation of Nature and the Kingdom of Man:* "There are and can be only two ways of searching into and discovering truth. The one flies from the senses and particulars to the most general axioms, and from these principles, the truth of which it takes for settled and immoveable, proceeds to judgment and to the discovery of middle axioms. And this way is now in fashion. The other derives axioms from the senses and particulars, rising by a gradual and unbroken ascent, so that it arrives at the most general axioms last of all. This is the true way, but as yet untried." In *The Great Instauration* he explained: "For man is but the servant and interpreter of nature: what he does and what he knows is only what he has observed of nature's order in fact or in thought; beyond this he knows nothing and can do nothing. . . . And all depends on keeping the eye steadily fixed upon the facts of nature and so receiving their images simply as they are."

103 Thoreau wrote in *The Maine Woods:* "Often, when an Indian says, "I don't know,' . . . he does not mean what a white man would by these words, for his Indian instinct may tell him still as much as the most confident white man knows" [MW 172]. Emerson, in "Self-Reliance," called this transcendent wisdom "the essence of genius, of virtue, and of life, which we call Spontaneity or Instinct. We denote this primary wisdom as Intuition. . . . In that deep force, the last fact behind which analysis cannot go, all things find their common origin."

Let us not underrate the value of a fact; it will one day flower in a truth. It is astonishing how few facts of importance are added in a century to the natural history of any animal. The natural history of man himself is still being gradually written. Men are knowing enough after their fashion. Every countryman and dairymaid knows that the coats of the fourth stomach of the calf will curdle milk, and what particular mushroom is a safe and nutritious diet. You cannot go into any field or wood, but it will seem as if every stone had been turned, and the bark on every tree ripped up. But after all, it is much easier to discover than to see when the cover is off. It has been well said that "the attitude of inspection is prone."[100] Wisdom does not inspect, but behold. We must look a long time before we can see. Slow are the beginnings of philosophy. He has something demoniacal[101] in him, who can discern a law, or couple two facts. We can imagine a time when, — "Water runs down hill," — may have been taught in the schools. The true man of science will know nature better by his finer organization; he will smell, taste, see, hear, feel, better than other men. His will be a deeper and finer experience. We do not learn by inference and deduction, and the application of mathematics to philosophy, but by direct intercourse and sympathy. It is with science as with ethics, we cannot know truth by contrivance and method; the Baconian[102] is as false as any other, and with all the helps of machinery and the arts, the most scientific will still be the healthiest and friendliest man, and possess a more perfect Indian wisdom.[103]

A Winter Walk

1 Venetian blinds made of thin wooden laths attached to strips of cloth.
2 House or shed for storing wood.
3 Earth orbits between the planets Venus and Mars.
4 In Roman mythology, goddess of agriculture, specifically corn and harvests.
5 Emerson wrote to Thoreau that he "had some hesitation about it, notwithstanding its faithful observation and its fine sketches of the pickerel-fisher and of the woodchopper, on account of mannerism, an old charge of mine,—as if, by attention, one could get the trick of the rhetoric; for example, to call a cold place sultry, a solitude public, a wilderness domestic."

The wind has gently murmured through the blinds,[1] or puffed with feathery softness against the windows, and occasionally sighed like a summer zephyr lifting the leaves along the livelong night. The meadow mouse has slept in his snug gallery in the sod, the owl has sat in a hollow tree in the depth of the swamp, the rabbit, the squirrel, and the fox have all been housed. The watch-dog has lain quiet on the hearth, and the cattle have stood silent in their stalls. The earth itself has slept, as it were its first, not its last sleep, save when some street-sign or wood-house[2] door, has faintly creaked upon its hinge, cheering forlorn nature at her midnight work.—The only sound awake twixt Venus and Mars,[3]—advertising us of a remote inward warmth, a divine cheer and fellowship, where gods are met together, but where it is very bleak for men to stand. But while the earth has slumbered, all the air has been alive with feathery flakes, descending, as if some northern Ceres[4] reigned, showering her silvery grain over all the fields.

We sleep and at length awake to the still reality of a winter morning. The snow lies warm[5] as cotton or down upon the window-sill; the broadened sash and frosted panes admit a dim and private light, which enhances the snug cheer within. The stillness of the morning is impressive. The floor creaks under our feet as we move toward the window to look abroad through some clear space over the fields. We see the roofs stand under their snow burden. From the eaves and fences hang stalactites of snow, and in the yard stand stalagmites covering some

6 Related to Tartarus, the lowest section of the underworld in Greek mythology, described in Homer's *Iliad* as being as far below Hades as heaven is above earth.

7 Cattle.

8 Cf. "Natural History of Massachusetts," note 72.

9 In Greek mythology, the main river of Hades, across which the spirits of the dead are ferried.

10 Ecclesiastically, the first of seven canonical hours, but generally, the time of dawn worship, prayer, or song.

concealed core. The trees and shrubs rear white arms to the sky on every side, and where were walls and fences, we see fantastic forms stretching in frolic gambols across the dusky landscape, as if nature had strewn her fresh designs over the fields by night as models for man's art.

Silently we unlatch the door, letting the drift fall in, and step abroad to face the cutting air. Already the stars have lost some of their sparkle, and a dull leaden mist skirts the horizon. A lurid brazen light in the east proclaims the approach of day, while the western landscape is dim and spectral still, and clothed in a sombre Tartarean[6] light, like the shadowy realms. They are Infernal sounds only that you hear,—the crowing of cocks, the barking of dogs, the chopping of wood, the lowing of kine,[7] all seem to come from Pluto's[8] barn-yard and beyond the Styx;[9]—not for any melancholy they suggest, but their twilight bustle is too solemn and mysterious for earth. The recent tracks of the fox or otter, in the yard, remind us that each hour of the night is crowded with events, and the primeval nature is still working and making tracks in the snow. Opening the gate, we tread briskly along the lone country road, crunching the dry and crisp snow under our feet, or aroused by the sharp clear creak of the wood-sled, just starting for the distant market, from the early farmer's door, where it has lain the summer long, dreaming amid the chips and stubble. Far through the drifts and powdered windows we see the farmer's early candle, like a paled star, emitting a lonely beam, as if some severe virtue were at its matins[10] there. And one by one the smokes begin to ascend from the chimneys amidst the trees and snows.

> The sluggish smoke curls up from some deep dell,
> The stiffened air exploring in the dawn,
> And makes slow acquaintance with the day;
> Delaying now upon its heavenward course,

In wreathed loiterings dallying with itself,
With as uncertain purpose and slow deed,
As its half-wakened master by the hearth,
Whose mind still slumbering and sluggish
    thoughts
Have not yet swept into the onward current
Of the new day;—and now it streams afar,
The while the chopper goes with step direct,
And mind intent to swing the early axe.
       First in the dusky dawn he sends abroad
His early scout, his emissary, smoke,
The earliest, latest pilgrim from the roof,
To feel the frosty air, inform the day;
And while he crouches still beside the hearth,
Nor musters courage to unbar the door,
It has gone down the glen with the light wind,
And o'er the plain unfurled its venturous wreath,
Draped the tree tops, loitered upon the hill,
And warmed the pinions of the early bird;
And now, perchance, high in the crispy air,
Has caught sight of the day o'er the earth's edge,
And greets its master's eye at his low door,
As some refulgent cloud in the upper sky.

We hear the sound of wood-chopping at the farmers' doors, far over the frozen earth, the baying of the house dog, and the distant clarion of the cock. The thin and frosty air conveys only the finer particles of sound to our ears, with short and sweet vibrations, as the waves subside soonest on the purest and lightest liquids, in which gross substances sink to the bottom. They come clear and bell-like, and from a greater distance in the horizon, as if there were fewer impediments than in summer to make them faint and ragged. The ground is sonorous, like seasoned wood, and even the ordinary rural sounds are melodious, and the jingling of the ice on the trees is sweet and liquid. There is the least possible moisture in the atmosphere, all being dried up, or congealed, and it is of such extreme tenuity and elasticity, that it becomes a source of delight. The withdrawn and tense sky seems groined like the aisles of a cathedral, and the polished air sparkles as if there were crystals of ice floating in it. Those who have resided in Greenland, tell us, that, when it freezes, "the sea smokes like burning turf land, and a fog or mist arises, called frost smoke," which "cutting smoke frequently raises blisters on the face and hands, and is very pernicious to the health."[11] But this pure stinging cold is an elixir to the lungs, and not so much a frozen mist, as a crystallized mid-summer haze, refined and purified by cold.

The sun at length rises through the distant woods, as if with the faint clashing swinging sound of cymbals, melting the air with his beams, and with such rapid steps the morning travels, that already his rays are gilding the distant western mountains. We step hastily along through the powdery snow, warmed by an inward heat, enjoying an Indian summer[12] still, in the increased glow of thought and feeling. Probably if our lives were more conformed to nature, we should not need to defend ourselves against her heats and colds, but find her our constant nurse and friend, as do plants and quadrupeds. If our bodies were fed with pure and simple elements, and not with a stimulating and heating diet, they would afford no more pasture for cold than a leafless twig, but thrive like the trees, which find even winter genial to their expansion.

The wonderful purity of nature at this season is a most pleasing fact. Every decayed stump and moss-grown stone and rail, and the dead leaves of autumn, are concealed by a clean napkin of snow. In the bare fields and tinkling woods, see what virtue survives. In the coldest and bleakest places, the warmest charities still maintain

11 Quoted from Charles Giesecke's (1761–1833) "Greenland" in the *Edinburgh Encyclopedia*, as found in *Library of Useful Knowledge. Natural Philosophy:* "Sir Charles Giesecké, who lived seven years in Greenland, describes this phenomenon in the following words: 'Previous to that operation of nature, (*viz.* the freezing of the sea,) the sea smokes like burning turf-land, and a fog or mist arises, called *frost smoke.* This cutting smoke frequently raises blisters on the face and hands, and is very pernicious to the health. It appears to consist of small particles of ice, and produces the sensation of needles pricking the skin."

12 During an autumnal period of mild, sunny weather in October 1850, Thoreau called Indian summer "the finest season of the year" [J 2:76].

a foot-hold. A cold and searching wind drives away all contagion, and nothing can withstand it but what has a virtue in it; and accordingly, whatever we meet with in cold and bleak places, as the tops of mountains, we respect for a sort of sturdy innocence, a Puritan toughness. All things beside seem to be called in for shelter, and what stays out must be part of the original frame of the universe, and of such valor as God himself. It is invigorating to breathe the cleansed air. Its greater fineness and purity are visible to the eye, and we would fain[13] stay out long and late, that the gales may sigh through us too, as through the leafless trees, and fit us for the winter:—as if we hoped so to borrow some pure and steadfast virtue, which will stead us in all seasons.

At length we have reached the edge of the woods, and shut out the gadding[14] town. We enter within their covert as we go under the roof of a cottage, and cross its threshold, all ceiled and banked up with snow. They are glad and warm still, and as genial and cheery in winter as in summer. As we stand in the midst of the pines, in the flickering and checkered light which straggles but little way into their maze, we wonder if the towns have ever heard their simple story. It seems to us that no traveller has ever explored them, and notwithstanding the wonders which science is elsewhere revealing every day, who would not like to hear their annals? Our humble villages in the plain, are their contribution. We borrow from the forest the boards which shelter, and the sticks which warm us. How important is their evergreen to the winter, that portion of the summer which does not fade, the permanent year, the unwithered grass. Thus simply, and with little expense of altitude, is the surface of the earth diversified. What would human life be without forests, those natural cities? From the tops of mountains they appear like smooth shaven lawns, yet whither shall we walk but in this taller grass?

13 Happily, willingly.
14 Going about without a specific aim or purpose.

A Winter Walk 31

15 Any large snowstorm, as in Thoreau's 28 March 1856 journal entry: "Uncle Charles buried. He was born in February, 1780, the winter of the Great Snow, and he dies in the winter of another great snow,—a life bounded by great snows" [J 8:230].

16 Sown in the autumn for spring or summer harvest, but called "winter" rye because it survives through the winter.

17 Narrow passages or ways.

There is a slumbering subterranean fire in nature which never goes out, and which no cold can chill. It finally melts the great snow,[15] and in January or July is only buried under a thicker or thinner covering. In the coldest day it flows somewhere, and the snow melts around every tree. This field of winter rye,[16] which sprouted late last fall, and now speedily dissolves the snow, is where the fire is very thinly covered. We feel warmed by it. In the winter, warmth stands for all virtue, and we resort in thought to a trickling rill, with its bare stones shining in the sun, and to warm springs in the woods, with as much eagerness as rabbits and robins. The steam which rises from swamps and pools is as dear and domestic as that of our own kettle. What fire could ever equal the sunshine of a winter's-day, when the meadow mice come out by the wallsides, and the chickadee lisps in the defiles[17] of the wood? The warmth comes directly from the sun, and is not radiated from the earth, as in summer; and when we feel his beams on our backs as we are treading some snowy dell, we are grateful as for a special kindness, and bless the sun which has followed us into that by-place.

This subterranean fire has its altar in each man's breast, for in the coldest day, and on the bleakest hill, the traveller cherishes a warmer fire within the folds of his cloak than is kindled on any hearth. A healthy man, indeed, is the complement of the seasons, and in winter, summer is in his heart. There is the south. Thither have all birds and insects migrated, and around the warm springs in his breast are gathered the robin and the lark.

In this glade covered with bushes of a year's growth see how the silvery dust lies on every seared leaf and twig, deposited in such infinite and luxurious forms as by their very variety atone for the absence of color. Observe the tiny tracks of mice around every stem, and the triangular tracks of the rabbit. A pure elastic heaven hangs over all, as if the impurities of the summer sky refined and shrunk by the chaste winter's cold, had been winnowed from the heavens upon the earth.

Nature confounds her summer distinctions at this season. The heavens seem to be nearer the earth. The elements are less reserved and distinct. Water turns to ice, rain to snow. The day is but a Scandinavian night. The winter is an arctic summer.

How much more living is the life that is in nature, the furred life which still survives the stinging nights, and, from amidst fields and woods covered with frost and snow, sees the sun rise.

> "The foodless wilds
> Pour forth their brown inhabitants."[18]

The grey-squirrel and rabbit are brisk and playful in the remote glens, even on the morning of the cold Friday.[19] Here is our Lapland and Labrador, and for our Esquimaux and Knistenaux, Dog-ribbed Indians, Novazemblaites, and Spitzbergeners,[20] are there not the ice-cutter and wood-chopper, the fox, muskrat, and mink?

Still, in the midst of the arctic day, we may trace the summer to its retreats, and sympathize with some contemporary life. Stretched over the brooks, in the midst of the frost-bound meadows, we may observe the submarine cottages of the caddice worms, the larvae of the Plicipennes.[21] Their small cylindrical cases built around themselves, composed of flags, sticks, grass, and withered leaves, shells and pebbles, in form and color like the wrecks which strew the bottom—now drifting along over the pebbly bottom, now whirling in tiny eddies and dashing down steep falls, or sweeping rapidly along with the current, or else swaying to and fro at the end of some grass blade or root. Anon they will leave their sunken habitations, and crawling up the stems of plants,

18 Quoted from the Scottish poet James Thomson's (1700–1748) *The Seasons*, "Winter, A Poem" (ll. 233–234).
19 On 19 January 1810 New England experienced gale winds and a sudden overnight temperature drop of fifty degrees to subzero temperatures. Thoreau wrote that his mother remembered that the "people in the kitchen . . . drew up close to the fire, but the dishes which the Hardy girl was washing froze as fast as she washed them, close to the fire. They managed to keep warm in the parlor, by the great fire" [J 9:213]. George Minott (cf. "Natural History of Massachusetts," note 45) remembered "seeing them toss up water in a shoemaker's shop, usually a very warm place, and when it struck the floor it was frozen, and rattled like so many shot" [J 9:230].
20 Northern places and peoples: Lapland and Labrador, northernmost parts of Europe and Newfoundland, respectively; Esquimaux (Eskimo or Inuit), Knistenaux (Christenaux or Cree), Dog-ribbed Indians (Dogrib or Tlicho), peoples of North America; Novazemblaites and Spitzbergeners, inhabitants of the Arctic islands of Nova Zembla (Novaya Zemlya) and Spitzbergen, respectively.
21 Caddis fly.

22 Allusion to William Kirby (1759–1850) and William Spence's (1783–1860) *An Introduction to Entomology; or, Elements of the Natural History of Insects:* "Amongst perfect insects, troops of *Trichocera biemalis*, the gnat whose choral dances have been before described, may be constantly seen gamboling in the air in the depth of winter when it is mild and calm."

or floating on the surface like gnats, or perfect insects,[22] henceforth flutter over the surface of the water, or sacrifice their short lives in the flame of our candles at evening. Down yonder little glen the shrubs are drooping under their burden, and the red alder-berries contrast with the white ground. Here are the marks of a myriad feet which have already been abroad. The sun rises as proudly over such a glen, as over the valley of the Seine or the Tiber, and it seems the residence of a pure and self-subsistent valor, such as they never witnessed; which never knew defeat nor fear. Here reign the simplicity and purity of a primitive age, and a health and hope far remote from towns and cities. Standing quite alone, far in the forest, while the wind is shaking down snow from the trees, and leaving the only human tracks behind us, we find our reflections of a richer variety than the life of cities. The chicadee and nut-hatch are more inspiring society than statesmen and philosophers, and we shall return to these last, as to more vulgar companions. In this lonely glen, with its brook draining the slopes, its creased ice and crystals of all hues, where the spruces and hemlocks stand up on either side, and the rush and sere wild oats in the rivulet itself, our lives are more serene and worthy to contemplate.

As the day advances, the heat of the sun is reflected by the hillsides, and we hear a faint but sweet music, where flows the rill released from its fetters, and the icicles are melting on the trees; and the nut-hatch and partridge are heard and seen. The south wind melts the snow at noon, and the bare ground appears with its withered grass and leaves, and we are invigorated by the perfume which exhales from it, as by the scent of strong meats.

Let us go into this deserted woodman's hut, and see how he has passed the long winter nights and the short and stormy days. For here man has lived under this south hill-side, and it seems a civilized and public spot. We have such associations as when the traveller stands by the ruins of Palmyra[23] or Hecatompolis.[24] Singing birds and flowers perchance have begun to appear here, for flowers as well as weeds follow in the footsteps of man. These hemlocks whispered over his head, these hickory logs were his fuel, and these pitch-pine roots kindled his fire; yonder fuming rill in the hollow, whose thin and airy vapor still ascends as busily as ever, though he is far off now, was his well. These hemlock boughs, and the straw upon this raised platform, were his bed, and this broken dish held his drink. But he has not been here this season, for the phoebes built their nest upon this shelf last summer. I find some embers left, as if he had but just gone out, where he baked his pot of beans; and while at evening he smoked his pipe, whose stemless bowl lies in the ashes,[25] chatted with his only companion, if perchance he had any, about the depth of the snow on the morrow, already falling fast and thick without, or disputed whether the last sound was the screech of an owl, or the creak of a bough, or imagination only; and through his broad chimney-throat,[26] in the late winter evening, ere he stretched himself upon the straw, he looked up to learn the progress of the storm, and seeing the bright stars of Cassiopeia's chair[27] shining brightly down upon him, fell contentedly asleep.

See how many trees from which we may learn the chopper's history. From this stump we may guess the sharpness of his axe, and from the slope of the stroke, on which side he stood, and whether he cut down the tree without going round it or changing hands; and from the flexure[28] of the splinters we may know which way it fell. This one chip contains inscribed on it the whole history of the wood-chopper and of the world. On this scrap of paper, which held his sugar or salt, perchance, or was the wadding of his gun, sitting on a log in the forest, with what interest we read the tattle of cities, of those larger

23 Ancient Syrian city, north of Damascus.
24 Thebes, ancient capital of Parthia, was also called Hecatompylos for its many gates.
25 Clay pipes were fragile and the stem would break or shorten over time until reduced to just a bowl.
26 Narrowest portion of the flue.
27 Group of five stars resembling a W (or M) in the constellation Cassiopeia.
28 Bend or curvature.

huts, empty and to let, like this, in High-streets, and Broad-ways. The eaves are dripping on the south side of this simple roof, while the titmouse lisps in the pine, and the genial warmth of the sun around the door is somewhat kind and human.

After two seasons, this rude dwelling does not deform the scene. Already the birds resort to it, to build their nests, and you may track to its door the feet of many quadrupeds. Thus, for a long time, nature overlooks the encroachment and profanity of man. The wood still cheerfully and unsuspiciously echoes the strokes of the axe that fells it, and while they are few and seldom, they enhance its wildness, and all the elements strive to naturalize the sound.

Now our path begins to ascend gradually to the top of this high hill, from whose precipitous south side, we can look over the broad country, of forest, and field, and river, to the distant snowy mountains. See yonder thin column of smoke curling up through the woods from some invisible farm-house; the standard raised over some rural homestead. There must be a warmer and more genial spot there below, as where we detect the vapor from a spring forming a cloud above the trees. What fine relations are established between the traveller who discovers this airy column from some eminence in the forest, and him who sits below. Up goes the smoke as silently and naturally as the vapor exhales from the leaves, and as busy disposing itself in wreathes as the housewife on the hearth below. It is a hieroglyphic of man's life, and suggests more intimate and important things than the boiling of a pot. Where its fine column rises above the forest, like an ensign, some human life has planted itself,—and such is the beginning of Rome, the establishment of the arts, and the foundation of empires, whether on the prairies of America, or the steppes of Asia.

And now we descend again to the brink of this woodland lake,[29] which lies in a hollow of the hills, as if it were their expressed juice, and that of the leaves, which are annually steeped in it. Without outlet or inlet to the eye,[30] it has still its history, in the lapse of its waves, in the rounded pebbles on its shore, and in the pines which grow down to its brink. It has not been idle, though sedentary, but, like Abu Musa,[31] teaches that "sitting still at home is the heavenly way; the going out is the way of the world."[32] Yet in its evaporation it travels as far as any. In summer it is the earth's liquid eye; a mirror in the breast of nature.[33] The sins of the wood are washed out in it. See how the woods form an amphitheatre about it, and it is an arena for all the genialness of nature. All trees direct the traveller to its brink, all paths seek it out, birds fly to it, quadrupeds flee to it, and the very ground inclines toward it. It is nature's saloon,[34] where she has sat down to her toilet.[35] Consider her silent economy and tidiness; how the sun comes with his evaporation to sweep the dust from its surface each morning, and a fresh surface is constantly welling up; and annually, after whatever impurities have accumulated herein, its liquid transparency appears again in the spring. In summer a hushed music seems to sweep across its surface. But now a plain sheet of snow conceals it from our eyes, except where the wind has swept the ice bare, and the sere leaves are gliding from side to side, tacking and veering on their tiny voyages. Here is one just keeled up against a pebble on shore, a dry beech leaf, rocking still, as if it would soon start again. A skilful engineer, methinks, might project its course since it fell from the parent stem. Here are all the elements for such a calculation. Its present position, the direction of the wind, the level of the pond, and how much more is given. In its scarred edges and veins is its log rolled up.

We fancy ourselves in the interior of a larger house.

29 Walden Pond.
30 Walden Pond is a flow-through lake, gaining water from the aquifer, a layer of rock or soil able to hold or transmit water, along its eastern perimeter and losing water to the aquifer along its western perimeter.
31 Abu Musa Alishari (ca. 721–ca. 815), Arab alchemist and mystic.
32 Quoted from Simon Ockley's (1678–1720) *History of the Saracens:* "There came some of the *Hagis,* or Pilgrims . . . and asked *Abu Musa,* what he thought of *going out?* Meaning, to assist *Ali,* to which he gravely answer'd, *My opinion to Day is different from what it was Yesterday. What you despised in Time past, hath drawn upon you what you see now.* The going out, and sitting still at home are two things. Sitting still at Home *is the Heavenly Way.* The going out, *is the Way of the World. Therefore take your Choice.*"
33 In *Walden* Thoreau wrote: "A lake is the landscape's most beautiful and expressive feature. It is earth's eye; looking into which the beholder measures the depth of his own nature" [Wa 180].
34 Spacious or elegant room for receiving company or for displaying works of art.
35 Dressing table.

36 Table made of deal, i.e., pine or fir.
37 Alexander the Great of Macedon (356–323 B.C.E.).
38 A soft murmuring or rustling sound.

The surface of the pond is our deal table[36] or sanded floor, and the woods rise abruptly from its edge, like the walls of a cottage. The lines set to catch pickerel through the ice look like a larger culinary preparation, and the men stand about on the white ground like pieces of forest furniture. The actions of these men, at the distance of half a mile over the ice and snow, impress us as when we read the exploits of Alexander[37] in history. They seem not unworthy of the scenery, and as momentous as the conquest of kingdoms.

Again we have wandered through the arches of the wood, until from its skirts we hear the distant booming of ice from yonder bay of the river, as if it were moved by some other and subtler tide than oceans know. To me it has a strange sound of home, thrilling as the voice of one's distant and noble kindred. A mild summer sun shines over forest and lake, and though there is but one green leaf for many rods, yet nature enjoys a serene health. Every sound is fraught with the same mysterious assurance of health, as well now the creaking of the boughs in January, as the soft sough[38] of the wind in July.

> When Winter fringes every bough
>   With his fantastic wreath,
> And puts the seal of silence now
>   Upon the leaves beneath;
>
> When every stream in its pent-house
>   Goes gurgling on its way,
> And in his gallery the mouse
>   Nibbleth the meadow hay;
>
> Methinks the summer still is nigh,
>   And lurketh underneath,
> As that same meadow mouse doth lie
>   Snug in that last year's heath.

And if perchance the Chickadee
    Lisp a faint note anon,
The snow is summer's canopy,
    Which she herself put on.

Fair blossoms deck the cheerful trees,
    And dazzling fruits depend,
The north wind sighs a summer breeze,
    The nipping frosts to fend,

Bringing glad tidings unto me,
    The while I stand all ear,
Of a serene eternity,
    Which need not winter fear.

Out on the silent pond straightway
    The restless ice doth crack,
And pond sprites merry gambols play
    Amid the deafening rack.

Eager I hasten to the vale,
    As if I heard brave news,
How nature held high festival,
    Which it were hard to lose.

I gambol with my neighbor ice,
    And sympathizing quake,
As each new crack darts in a trice
    Across the gladsome lake.

One with the cricket in the ground,
    And faggot on the hearth,
Resounds the rare domestic sound
    Along the forest path.

Before night we will take a journey on skates along the course of this meandering river, as full of novelty to one who sits by the cottage fire all the winter's day, as if it were over the polar ice, with Captain Parry or Franklin;[39]

39 Sir William Edward Parry (1790–1855) and Sir John Franklin (1786–1847), English Arctic explorers. Thoreau read Parry's *Three Voyages for the Discovery of the Northwest Passage from the Atlantic to the Pacific* and Franklin's *Narrative of a Journey to the Shores of the Polar Seas in the Years 1819, 20, 21 & 22.*

following the winding of the stream, not flowing amid hills, now spreading out into fair meadows, and forming a myriad coves and bays where the pine and hemlock overarch. The river flows in the rear of the towns, and we see all things from a new and wilder side. The fields and gardens come down to it with a frankness, and freedom from pretension, which they do not wear on the highway. It is the outside and edge of the earth. Our eyes are not offended by violent contrasts. The last rail of the farmer's fence is some swaying willow bough, which still preserves its freshness, and here at length all fences stop, and we no longer cross any road. We may go far up within the country now by the most retired and level road, never climbing a hill, but by broad levels ascending to the upland meadows. It is a beautiful illustration of the law of obedience, the flow of a river; the path for a sick man, a highway down which an acorn cup may float secure with its freight. Its slight occasional falls, whose precipices would not diversify the landscape, are celebrated by mist and spray, and attract the traveller from far and near. From the remote interior, its current conducts him by broad and easy steps, or by one gentle inclined plane, to the sea. Thus by an early and constant yielding to the inequalities of the ground, it secures itself the easiest passage.

No domain of nature is quite closed to man at all times, and now we draw near to the empire of the fishes. Our feet glide swiftly over unfathomed depths, where in summer our line tempted the pout and perch, and where the stately pickerel lurked in the long corridors, formed by the bulrushes. The deep, impenetrable marsh, where the heron waded, and bittern squatted, is made pervious to our swift shoes, as if a thousand railroads had been made into it. With one impulse we are carried to the cabin of the muskrat, that earliest settler, and see him dart away under the transparent ice, like a furred fish, to his hole in the bank; and we glide rapidly over meadows where lately "the mower whet his scythe,"[40] through beds of frozen cranberries mixed with meadow grass. We skate near to where the blackbird, the pewee, and the kingbird hung their nests over the water, and the hornets builded from the maple in the swamp. How many gay warblers now following the sun, have radiated from this nest of silver birch and thistle down. On the swamp's outer edge was hung the supermarine village, where no foot penetrated. In this hollow tree the wood-duck reared her brood, and slid away each day to forage in yonder fen.

In winter, nature is a cabinet of curiosities,[41] full of dried specimens, in their natural order and position. The meadows and forests are a *hortus siccus.*[42] The leaves and grasses stand perfectly pressed by the air without screw or gum,[43] and the birds' nests are not hung on an artificial twig, but where they builded them. We go about dry shod to inspect the summer's work in the rank swamp, and see what a growth have got the alders, the willows, and the maples; testifying to how many warm suns, and fertilizing dews and showers. See what strides their boughs took in the luxuriant summer,—and anon these dormant buds will carry them onward and upward another span into the heavens.

Occasionally we wade through fields of snow, under whose depths the river is lost for many rods, to appear again to the right or left, where we least expected; still holding on its way underneath, with a faint, stertorous, rumbling sound, as if, like the bear and marmot, it too had hibernated, and we had followed its faint summer trail to where it earthed itself in snow and ice. At first we should have thought that rivers would be empty and dry in mid winter, or else frozen solid till the spring thawed them; but their volume is not diminished even, for only a superficial cold bridges their surface. The thousand

40 Thoreau's variant of John Milton's (1608–1674) "L'Allegro," l. 66—"the mower whets his scythe"—which Thoreau copied into his journal of 27 April 1843, indicating the change of tense as "whet" [PJ 1:456].

41 Originally a room, and later a piece of furniture, devoted to the display of rare and unique items.

42 Latin: dry garden. A herbarium or collection of specimens of plants, dried and preserved, and arranged systematically.

43 Methods by which naturalists pressed and preserved plant specimens.

44 Native of Finland but here also one from the land of fins.

45 Heavy cloth, often woolen, coat, called "fearnaughts" in *Walden* [Wa 274].

46 Possible allusion to Shakespeare's *1 Henry IV* III.i.154: "And of a dragon, and a finless fish."

47 Pacific Ocean inlet or sound on west coast of Vancouver, British Columbia. Early navigators include Captain James Cook (1728–1779), whose *The Three Voyages of Capt. James Cook Round the World* Thoreau read.

springs which feed the lakes and streams are flowing still. The issues of a few surface springs only are closed, and they go to swell the deep reservoirs. Nature's wells are below the frost. The summer brooks are not filled with snow-water, nor does the mower quench his thirst with that alone. The streams are swollen when the snow melts in the spring, because nature's work has been delayed, the water being turned into ice and snow, whose particles are less smooth and round, and do not find their level so soon.

Far over the ice, between the hemlock woods and snow-clad hills, stands the pickerel fisher, his lines set in some retired cove, like a Finlander,[44] with his arms thrust into the pouches of his dreadnought;[45] with dull, snowy, fishy thoughts, himself a finless fish,[46] separated a few inches from his race; dumb, erect, and made to be enveloped in clouds and snows, like the pines on shore. In these wild scenes, men stand about in the scenery, or move deliberately and heavily, having sacrificed the sprightliness and vivacity of towns to the dumb sobriety of nature. He does not make the scenery less wild, more than the jays and muskrats, but stands there as a part of it, as the natives are represented in the voyages of early navigators, at Nootka sound,[47] and on the Northwest coast, with their furs about them, before they were tempted to loquacity by a scrap of iron. He belongs to the natural family of man, and is planted deeper in nature and has more root than the inhabitants of towns. Go to him, ask what luck, and you will learn that he too is a worshiper of the unseen. Hear with what sincere deference and waving gesture in his tone, he speaks of the lake pickerel, which he has never seen, his primitive and ideal race of pickerel. He is connected with the shore still, as by a fish-line, and yet remembers the season when he took fish through the ice on the pond, while the peas were up in his garden at home.

But now, while we have loitered, the clouds have gathered again, and a few straggling snow-flakes are beginning to descend. Faster and faster they fall, shutting out the distant objects from sight. The snow falls on every wood and field, and no crevice is forgotten; by the river and the pond, on the hill and in the valley. Quadrupeds are confined to their coverts, and the birds sit upon their perches this peaceful hour. There is not so much sound as in fair weather, but silently and gradually every slope, and the grey walls and fences, and the polished ice, and the sere leaves, which were not buried before, are concealed, and the tracks of men and beasts are lost. With so little effort does nature reassert her rule, and blot out the traces of men. Hear how Homer has described the same. "The snow flakes fall thick and fast on a winter's day. The winds are lulled, and the snow falls incessant, covering the tops of the mountains, and the hills, and the plains where the lotus tree grows, and the cultivated fields, and they are falling by the inlets and shores of the foaming sea, but are silently dissolved by the waves."[48] The snow levels all things, and infolds them deeper in the bosom of nature, as, in the slow summer, vegetation creeps up to the entablature of the temple, and the turrets of the castle, and helps her to prevail over art.

The surly night-wind rustles through the wood, and warns us to retrace our steps, while the sun goes down behind the thickening storm, and birds seek their roosts, and cattle their stalls.

> "Drooping the lab'rer ox
> Stands covered o'er with snow, and *now* demands
> The fruit of all his toil."[49]

Though winter is represented in the almanac as an old man, facing the wind and sleet, and drawing his cloak about him, we rather think of him as a merry wood-

48 Quoted from Homer's *Iliad* XII:278–286.
49 Quoted, with minor variants, from Thomson's *The Seasons*, "Winter, A Poem" (ll. 240–242).

50 Northern.

51 Cf. "Natural History of Massachusetts": "I read in Audubon with a thrill of delight, when the snow covers the ground, of the magnolia, and the Florida keys, and their warm sea breezes; of the fence-rail, and the cotton-tree, and the migrations of the rice-bird; of the breaking up of winter in Labrador, and the melting of the snow on the forks of the Missouri."

chopper, and warm-blooded youth, as blithe as summer. The unexplored grandeur of the storm keeps up the spirits of the traveller. It does not trifle with us, but has a sweet earnestness. In winter we lead a more inward life. Our hearts are warm and cheery, like cottages under drifts, whose windows and doors are half concealed, but from whose chimneys the smoke cheerfully ascends. The imprisoning drifts increase the sense of comfort which the house affords, and in the coldest days we are content to sit over the hearth and see the sky through the chimney top, enjoying the quiet and serene life that may be had in a warm corner by the chimney side, or feeling our pulse by listening to the low of cattle in the street, or the sound of the flail in distant barns all the long afternoon. No doubt a skillful physician could determine our health by observing how these simple and natural sounds affected us. We enjoy now, not an oriental, but a boreal[50] leisure, around warm stoves and fire-places, and to watch the shadow of motes in the sunbeams.

Sometimes our fate grows too homely and familiarly serious ever to be cruel. Consider how for three months the human destiny is wrapped in furs. The good Hebrew revelation takes no cognizance of all this cheerful snow. Is there no religion for the temperate and frigid zones? We know of no scripture which records the pure benignity of the gods on a New England winter night. Their praises have never been sung, only their wrath deprecated. The best scripture, after all, records but a meagre faith. Its saints live reserved and austere. Let a brave devout man spend the year in the woods of Maine or Labrador, and see if the Hebrew scriptures speak adequately to his condition and experience, from the setting in of winter to the breaking up of the ice.

Now commences the long winter evening around the farmer's hearth, when the thoughts of the indwellers travel far abroad,[51] and men are by nature and necessity charitable and liberal to all creatures. Now is the happy resistance to cold, when the farmer reaps his reward, and thinks of his preparedness for winter, and through the glittering panes, sees with equanimity "the mansion of the northern bear,"[52] for now the storm is over,

> The full ethereal round,
> Infinite worlds disclosing to the view,
> Shines out intensely keen; and all one cope
> Of starry glitter glows from pole to pole."[53]

[52] Unidentified quotation. The northern bear is a reference to the constellation Ursa Major, the Big Dipper.

[53] Quoted from Thomson's *The Seasons*, "Winter, A Poem" (ll. 738–741).

1 Highest mountain in Greece and, in Greek mythology, the homes of the gods, called "many-peaked" in Homer's *Iliad* V:940. The following sentence was added in *Excursions* (1863): "Thus we spoke our minds to them, standing on the Concord cliffs. —" [*Excursions* 73]
2 Relating to regions of ancient Italy and Greece, respectively.
3 Allusion to Alexander von Humboldt's (1769–1859) *Personal Narrative of Travels to the Equinoctial Regions of America During the Years 1799–1804*.

A Walk to Wachusett

The needles of the pine,
All to the west incline.

Concord, July 19, 1842.

Summer and winter our eyes had rested on the dim outline of the mountains, to which distance and indistinctness lent a grandeur not their own, so that they served equally to interpret all the allusions of poets and travellers; whether with Homer, on a spring morning, we sat down on the many-peaked Olympus,[1] or, with Virgil, and his compeers, roamed the Etrurian and Thessalian[2] hills, or with Humboldt measured the more modern Andes and Teneriffe.[3]

With frontier strength ye stand your ground,
With grand content ye circle round,
Tumultuous silence for all sound,
Ye distant nursery of rills,
Monadnock, and the Peterboro' hills;
Like some vast fleet,
Sailing through rain and sleet,
Through winter's cold and summer's heat;
Still holding on, upon your high emprise,
Until ye find a shore amid the skies;
Not skulking close to land,
With cargo contraband,
For they who sent a venture out by ye
Have set the sun to see

Their honesty.
Ships of the line,[4] each one,
Ye to the westward run,
Always before the gale,
Under a press of sail,
With weight of metal all untold.
I seem to feel ye, in my firm seat here,
Immeasurable depth of hold,
And breadth of beam, and length of running
    gear.

Methinks ye take luxurious pleasure
In your novel western leisure;
So cool your brows, and freshly blue,
As Time had nought for ye to do;
For ye lie at your length,
An unappropriated strength,
Unhewn primeval timber,
For knees[5] so stiff, for masts so limber;
The stock of which new earths are made,
One day to be our western trade,
Fit for the stanchions of a world
Which through the seas of space is hurled.

While we enjoy a lingering ray,
Ye still o'ertop the western day,
Reposing yonder, on God's croft,[6]
Like solid stacks of hay.
Edged with silver, and with gold,
The clouds hang o'er in damask fold,
And with such depth of amber light
The west is dight,[7]
Where still a few rays slant,
That even heaven seems extravagant.
On the earth's edge mountains and trees
Stand as they were on air graven,
Or as the vessels in a haven

4 Warships.
5 In shipbuilding, a piece of timber somewhat in the shape of the bent human knee, having two branches or arms and used to connect the beams of a ship with its sides or timbers.
6 Small enclosed field or pasture.
7 Dressed.

A Walk to Wachusett 47

8 Cf. "A Winter Walk," note 17.

9 Ancient Greek and Roman writers divided the history of the universe into a number of Ages. The Golden Age was a time of perfection. The Greek poet Hesiod (eighth century B.C.E.) wrote in *Works and Days* of an ideal golden age in the past from which period there had been a progressive decline. The Silver Age was the period of achievement secondary to the Golden Age.

10 Thoreau's poem appeared with variants in *A Week on the Concord and Merrimack Rivers*. It had been rejected by Margaret Fuller (1810–1850) when submitted for publication in the *Dial*. Fuller wrote to Thoreau on 18 October 1841:

> I do not find the poem on the mountain improved by mere compression, though it might be by fusion and glow.
>
> Its merits to me are a noble recognition of nature, two or three manly thoughts, and, in one place, a plaintive music. The image of the ships does not please me originally. It illustrates the greater by the less and affects me as when Byron compares the light on Jura to that of the dark eyes of woman. I cannot define my position here, and a large class of readers would differ from me.

11 Allusion to Samuel Johnson's (cf. "Thomas Carlyle and His Works," note 38) *The History of Rasselas, Prince of Abyssinia*. Rasselas lived in a happy valley from which he longed to escape, learning that variety is necessary to be content, or, as his sister Nekayah said: "None are happy but by the anticipation of change: the change itself is nothing: when we have made it, the next wish is to change again. The world is not yet exhausted; let me see something to-morrow which I never saw before."

Await the morning breeze.
I fancy even
Through your defiles[8] windeth the way to heaven;
And yonder still, in spite of history's page,
Linger the golden and the silver age;[9]
Upon the laboring gale
The news of future centuries is brought,
And of new dynasties of thought,
From your remotest vale.

But special I remember thee,
Wachusett, who like me
Standest alone without society.
Thy far blue eye,
A remnant of the sky,
Seen through the clearing or the gorge,
Or from the windows of the forge,
Doth leaven all it passes by.
Nothing is true,
But stands 'tween me and you,
Thou western pioneer,
Who know'st not shame nor fear,
By venturous spirit driven,
Under the eaves of heaven,
And can'st expand thee there,
And breathe enough of air?
Upholding heaven, holding down earth,
Thy pastime from thy birth,
Not steadied by the one, nor leaning on the
    other;
May I approve myself thy worthy brother![10]

At length, like Rasselas,[11] and other inhabitants of happy valleys, we resolved to scale the blue wall which bounds the western horizon, though not without misgivings, that thereafter no visible fairy land would exist for us. But we will not leap at once to our journey's end, though near, but imitate Homer, who conducts his reader over the plain, and along the resounding sea, though it be but to the tent of Achilles.[12] In the spaces of thought are the reaches of land and water, where men go and come. The landscape lies far and fair within, and the deepest thinker is the farthest travelled. Taking advantage of the early hour, on a pleasant morning in July,[13] my companion[14] and I passed rapidly through Acton and Stow, stopping to rest and refresh us on the bank of a small stream, a tributary of the Assabet, in the latter town. As we traversed the cool woods of Acton, with stout staves in our hands,[15] we were cheered by the song of the red-eye,[16] the thrushes, the phoebe, and the cuckoo; and as we passed through the open country, we inhaled the fresh scent of every field, and all nature lay passive, to be viewed and travelled. Every rail, every farm-house, seen dimly in the twilight, every tinkling sound told of peace and purity, and we moved happily along the dank roads, enjoying not such privacy as the day leaves when it withdraws, but such as it has not profaned. It was solitude with light, which is better than darkness. But anon, the sound of the mower's rifle[17] was heard in the fields, and this, too, mingled with the herd of days.[18]

This part of our route lay through the country of hops. Perhaps there is no plant which so well supplies the want of the vine in American scenery, and reminds the traveller so often of Italy, and the South of France, as this, whether he traverses the country when the hop-fields, as now, present solid and regular masses of verdure, hanging in graceful festoons from pole to pole, the cool coverts where fresh gales are born to refresh the way-farer, or in September, when the women and children, and the neighbors from far and near, are gathered to pick the hops into long troughs, or later still, when the

12 In Greek mythology, hero of Homer's *Iliad*, of whom Thoreau wrote similarly in *A Week on the Concord and Merrimack Rivers*: "If his messengers repair but to the tent of Achilles, we do not wonder how they got there, but accompany them step by step" [W 1:96].

13 Thoreau's travelling companion, Richard Frederick Fuller (1824–1869), brother of Margaret Fuller, wrote an account of their excursion, only part of which is extant: "Mr. Thoreau and myself swallowing a good breakfast, and not heeding a threatened storm, with knapsacks filed with a day's provisions and a tent to be alternately carried by each, at about a quarter of five, started." On this date Emerson wrote to Margaret Fuller: "This morning your brother . . . set out with H.T. on the road to Wachusett. I am sorry that you, & the world after you, do not like my brave Henry any better."

14 Fuller had come to Concord in September 1841, where he was tutored by Thoreau. In his *Recollections* Fuller wrote that Thoreau "furnished me with a good deal of companionship. . . . He was thoroughly unselfish, truly refined, sincere, and of a true spirit." As a memento of their excursion and in gratitude for Thoreau's tutoring Fuller sent Thoreau a music box at the end of 1842.

15 While passing through a wood between Concord and Stow, according to Fuller, each man cut himself a cane.

16 Red-eyed vireo (*Vireo olivaceus*).

17 An instrument used after the manner of a whetstone for sharpening scythes.

18 Variant of deys: dairymaids or milkmaids.

19 In Bolton.

poles stand piled in immense pyramids in the yards, or lie in heaps by the roadside.

The culture of the hop, with the processes of picking, drying in the kiln, and packing for the market, as well as the uses to which it is applied, so analogous to the culture and uses of the grape, may afford a theme for future poets.

The mower in the adjacent meadow could not tell us the name of the brook on whose banks we had rested, or whether it had any, but his younger companion, perhaps his brother, knew that it was Great Brook.[19] Though they stood very near together in the field, the things they knew were very far apart; nor did they suspect each other's reserved knowledge, till the stranger came by. In Bolton, while we rested on the rails of a cottage fence, the strains of music which issued from within, perhaps in compliment to us sojourners, reminded us that thus far men were fed by the accustomed pleasures. So soon did we begin to learn that man's life is rounded with the same few facts, the same simple relations everywhere, and it is vain to travel to find it new. The flowers grow more various ways than he. But coming soon to higher land, which afforded a prospect of the mountains, we thought we had not travelled in vain, if it were only to hear a truer and wilder pronunciation of their names, from the lips of a farmer by the road-side; not *Way*-tatic, *Way*-chusett, but *Wor*-tatic, *Wor*-chusett. It made us ashamed of our tame and civil pronunciation, and we looked upon him as born and bred farther west than we. His tongue had a more generous accent than ours, as if breath was cheaper where it wagged. A countryman, who speaks but seldom, talks copiously, as it were, as his wife sets cream and cheese before you without stint. Before noon we had reached the highlands in the western part of Bolton, overlooking the valley of Lancaster, and affording the first fair and open prospect into the west, and here, on the top of a hill, in the shade of some oaks, near to where a spring bubbled out from a leaden pipe, we rested during the heat of the day, reading Virgil, and enjoying the scenery. It was such a place as one feels to be on the outside of the earth, for from it we could, in some measure, see the form and structure of the globe. There lay the object of our journey, lowering upon us with unchanged proportions, though with a less ethereal aspect than had greeted our morning gaze, while further north, in successive order, slumbered the sister mountains[20] along the horizon.

We could get no further into the Aeneid than

—atque altae moenia Romae,
—and the wall of high Rome,[21]

before we were constrained to reflect by what myriad tests a work of genius has to be tried; that Virgil, away in Rome, two thousand years off, should have to unfold his meaning, the inspiration of Italian vales, to the pilgrim on the New England hills. This life so raw and modern, that so civil and ancient, and yet we read Virgil, mainly to be reminded of the identity of human nature in all ages, and by the poet's own account, we are both the children of a late age, and live equally under the reign of Jupiter.[22]

"He shook honey from the leaves, and removed
    fire,
And stayed the wine, everywhere flowing in
    rivers,
That experience, by meditating, might invent
    various arts
By degrees, and seek the blade of corn in furrows,
And strike out hidden fire from the veins of the
    flint."[23]

20 Mount Monadnock and the Peterborough hills.
21 From Virgil's *Aeneid* I:7 with Thoreau's translation.
22 In Roman mythology, the supreme god; Zeus, in Greek mythology.
23 Thoreau's translation of Virgil's *Georgics* I:131–135.

24 King Philip's War (1675–1676), an Indian up-
rising to resist English expansion, led by Philip: cf.
"Natural History of Massachusetts," note 48.
25 Latin: cold valleys. Allusion to Claudian's (fl.
fourth century C.E.) *De Consulatu Stilichonis* I:131.
26 Quoted from William Collins's (1721–1759)
"Hassan; or, The Camel-Driver," 7–8 from his *Persian Eclogues.*
27 Quoted from Collins's "Hassan; or the Camel-
Driver," 13–14.

The old world stands serenely behind the new, as one
mountain yonder towers behind another, more dim and
distant. Rome imposes her story still upon this late generation. The very children in the school we have that
morning passed, had gone through her wars, and recited
her alarms, ere they had heard of the wars of the neighboring Lancaster.[24] The roving eye still rests inevitably
on her hills. She still holds up the skirts of the sky, and
makes the past remote.

The lay of the land hereabouts is well worthy the attention of the traveller. The hill on which we were resting
makes part of an extensive range, running from south-west
to north-east, across the country, and separating the waters
of the Nashua from those of the Concord, whose banks we
had left in the morning, and by bearing in mind this fact,
we could easily determine whither each brook was bound
that crossed our path. Parallel to this, and fifteen miles further west, beyond the deep and broad valley in which lie
Groton, Shirley, Lancaster, and Boylston, runs the Wachusett range, in the same general direction. The descent into
the valley on the Nashua side, is by far the most sudden;
and a couple of miles brought us to the southern branch
of that river, a shallow but rapid stream, flowing between
high and gravelly banks. But we soon learned that there
were no *gelidae valles*[25] into which we had descended, and
missing the coolness of the morning air, feared it had become the sun's turn to try his power upon us.

"The sultry sun had gained the middle sky,
And not a tree, and not an herb was nigh,"[26]

and with melancholy pleasure we echoed the melodious
plaint of our fellow-traveller Hassan, in the desert,

"Sad was the hour, and luckless was the day,
When first from Schiraz' walls I bent my way."[27]

The air lay lifeless between the hills, as in a seething caldron, with no leaf stirring, and instead of the fresh odor of grass and clover, with which we had before been regaled, the dry scent of every herb seemed merely medicinal. Yielding, therefore, to the heat, we strolled into the woods, and along the course of a rivulet, on whose banks we loitered, observing at our leisure the products of these new fields. He who traverses the woodland paths, at this season, will have occasion to remember the small drooping bell-like flowers and slender red stem of the dogs-bane, and the coarser stem and berry of the poke, which are both common in remoter and wilder scenes; and if "the sun casts such a reflecting heat from the sweet fern,"[28] as makes him faint, when he is climbing the bare hills, as they complained who first penetrated into these parts, the cool fragrance of the swamp pink[29] restores him again, when traversing the valleys between.

On we went, and late in the afternoon refreshed ourselves by bathing our feet in every rill that crossed the road, and anon, as we were able to walk in the shadows of the hills, recovered our morning elasticity. Passing through Sterling, we reached the banks of the Stillwater, in the western part of the town, at evening, where is a small village[30] collected. We fancied that there was already a certain western look about this place, a smell of pines and roar of water, recently confined by dams, belying its name, which were exceedingly grateful.[31] When the first inroad has been made, a few acres levelled, and a few houses erected, the forest looks wilder than ever. Left to herself, nature is always more or less civilized, and delights in a certain refinement; but where the axe has encroached upon the edge of the forest, the dead and unsightly limbs of the pine, which she had concealed with green banks of verdure, are exposed to sight. This village had, as yet, no post-office, nor any settled name. As

28 Quoted from Edward Johnson (ca. 1599–1672) *A History of New-England From the English Planting in the Yeere 1628 untill the Yeere 1652,* better known as *The Wonder-working Providence of Sion's Saviour in New England,* as found in Emerson's "Historical Discourse in Concord."
29 Swamp azalea (*Rhododendron viscosum*).
30 Now West Sterling.
31 In the sense of agreeable, pleasing, gratifying.

32 From Thoreau's journal entry of 5 May 1838 while traveling in Maine: "Each one's world is but a clearing in the forest, so much open and inclosed ground. When the mail coach rumbles into one of these, the villagers gaze after you with a compassionate look, as much as to say: 'Where have you been all this time, that you make your début in the world at this late hour? Nevertheless, here we are; come and study us, that you may learn men and manners'" [J 1:47–48].

33 Quoted, with one variant—*Trolhate* for *Trollhatte*—from Richard Sharp's (1759–1835) *Letters and Essays in Prose and Verse*, which Thoreau had copied into his journal of 21 January 1838.

34 Allusion to Genesis 49:26: "The blessings of thy father have prevailed above the blessings of my progenitors unto the utmost bound of the everlasting hills."

we entered upon its street, the villagers gazed after us, with a complacent, almost compassionate look, as if we were just making our debut in the world, at a late hour. "Nevertheless," did they seem to say, "come and study us, and learn men and manners." So is each one's world but a clearing in the forest, so much open and inclosed ground.[32] The landlord had not yet returned from the field with his men, and the cows had yet to be milked. But though we met with no very hospitable reception here at first, we remembered the inscription on the wall of the Swedish inn, and were comforted, "You will find at Trolhate excellent bread, meat, and wine, provided you bring them with you."[33] But I must confess it did somewhat disturb our pleasure, in this withdrawn spot, to have our own village newspaper handed us by our host, as if the greatest charm the country offered to the traveller was the facility of communication with the town. Let it recline on its own everlasting hills,[34] and not be looking out from their summits for some petty Boston or New York in the horizon.

At intervals we heard the murmuring of water, and the slumbrous breathing of crickets throughout the night, and left the inn the next morning in the grey twilight, after it had been hallowed by the night air, and when only the innocent cows were stirring, with a kind of regret. It was only four miles to the base of the mountain, and the scenery was already more picturesque. Our road lay along the course of the Stillwater, which was brawling at the bottom of a deep ravine, filled with pines and rocks, tumbling fresh from the mountains, so soon, alas! to commence its career of usefulness. At first a cloud hung between us and the summit, but it was soon blown away. As we gathered the raspberries, which grew abundantly by the roadside, that action seemed consistent with a lofty prudence, as well as agreeable to the palate, as if the traveller who ascends into a mountainous region should fortify himself by eating of such light ambrosial fruits as grow there, and drinking of the springs which gush out from the mountain sides, as he gradually inhales the subtler and purer atmosphere of those elevated places, thus propitiating the mountain gods, by a sacrifice of their own fruits. The gross products of the plains and valleys are for such as dwell therein; but surely the juices of this berry have relation to the thin air of the mountain tops.

In due time we began to ascend the mountain, passing, first, through a maple wood,[35] then a denser forest, which gradually became dwarfed, till there were no trees whatever. We at length pitched our tent on the summit. It is but nineteen hundred feet above the village of Princeton, and three thousand above the level of the sea;[36] but by this slight elevation, it is infinitely removed from the plain, and when we reached it, we felt a sense of remoteness, as if we had travelled into distant regions, to Arabia Petrea,[37] or the farthest east, so withdrawn and solitary it seems. A robin upon a staff, was the highest object in sight, thus easily triumphing over the height of nature. Swallows were flying about us, and the chewink[38] and cuckoos were heard near at hand. The summit consists of a few acres, destitute of trees, covered with bare rocks, interspersed with blueberry bushes, raspberries, gooseberries, strawberries, moss, and a fine wiry grass. The common yellow lily, and dwarf cornel, grow abundantly in the crevices of the rocks. This clear space, which is gently rounded, is bounded a few feet lower by a thick shrubbery of oaks, with maples, aspens, beeches, cherries, and occasionally a mountain-ash intermingled, among which we found the bright blue berries of the Solomon's Seal,[39] and the fruit of the pyrola.[40] From the foundation of a wooden observatory, which was formerly erected on the highest point, forming a rude hollow structure of stone, a dozen feet in diameter, and five or

35 In *Excursions* the phrase "which bore the marks of the augur" was added, and the misspelled "augur" corrected to "auger" in *The Writings of Henry David Thoreau* (1906).
36 Thoreau read in Edward Hitchcock's (1793–1864) *Report on the Geology, Mineralogy, Botany, and Zoology of Massachusetts*: "This mountain is in Princeton, whose general elevation, above the ocean, is 1100 feet: and the mountain lifts its conical head 1900 feet higher, so as to be 3000 feet above Massachusetts Bay."
37 During the time of the Roman Empire, the eastern of the three zones that made up the whole of Arabia.
38 Rufous-sided towhee (*Pipilo erythrophthlamus*), which Thoreau also called the ground-robin. On 19 September 1858 Thoreau wrote of the "chewink's chewink" [J 9:169].
39 *Polygonatum*: a genus of flowering plants within the family Ruscaceae, formerly classified in the lily family.
40 Wintergreen.

41 Allusion to Felicia Hemans's (1793–1835) ballad "O'er the Far Blue Mountain."

42 In his journal of 9 August 1842 this phrase read: "blue Atlantic island" [PJ 1:436].

43 Quoted from William Wordsworth's (1770–1850) *Peter Bell* I: 224–230.

44 Mountain in the Lake District of England, near which Wordsworth lived.

45 See "Natural History of Massachusetts," note 42.

six in height, we could dimly see Monadnock, rising in simple grandeur, in the north-west, nearly a thousand feet higher, still the "far blue mountain,"[41] though with an altered profile. But the first day the weather was so hazy that it was in vain we endeavored to unravel the obscurity. It was like looking into the sky again, and the patches of forest here and there seemed to flit like clouds over a lower heaven. As to voyagers of an aerial Polynesia, the earth seemed like an island in the ether; on every side, even as low as we, the sky shutting down, like an unfathomable deep, around it. A blue Pacific island,[42] where who knows what islanders inhabit? and as we sail near its shores we see the waving of trees, and hear the lowing of kine.

We read Virgil and Wordsworth in our tent, with new pleasure there, while waiting for a clearer atmosphere, nor did the weather prevent our appreciating the simple truth and beauty of Peter Bell:

"And he had lain beside his asses,
On lofty Cheviot hills."

"And he had trudged through Yorkshire dales,
Among the rocks and winding *scars,*
Where deep and low the hamlets lie
Beneath their little patch of sky,
And little lot of stars."[43]

Who knows but this hill may one day be a Helvellyn,[44] or even a Parnassus,[45] and the Muses haunt here, and other Homers frequent the neighboring plains,

Not unconcerned Wachusett rears his head
Above the field, so late from nature won,
With patient brow reserved, as one who read
New annuals in the history of man.

The blueberries which the mountain afforded, added to the milk we had brought, made our frugal supper,[46] while for entertainment, the even-song[47] of the wood-thrush rung along the ridge. Our eyes rested on no painted ceiling, nor carpeted hall, but on skies of nature's painting, and hills and forests of her embroidery. Before sunset, we rambled along the ridge to the north, while a hawk soared still above us. It was a place where gods might wander, so solemn and solitary, and removed from all contagion with the plain.[48] As the evening came on, the haze was condensed in vapor, and the landscape became more distinctly visible, and numerous sheets of water were brought to light,

Et jam summa procul villarum culmina fumant,
Majoresque cadunt altis de montibus umbrae.

And now the tops of the villas smoke afar off,
And the shadows fall longer from the high
    mountains.[49]

As we stood on the stone tower while the sun was setting, we saw the shades of night creep gradually over the valleys of the east, and the inhabitants withdrew to their houses, and shut their doors, while the moon silently rose up, and took possession of that part. And then the same scene was repeated on the west side, as far as the Connecticut and the Green Mountains, and the sun's rays fell on us two alone, of all New England men.

It was the night but one before the full of the moon, so that we enjoyed uninterrupted light, so bright that we could see to read Wordsworth distinctly, and when in the evening we strolled on the summit, there was a fire blazing on Monadnock, which lighted up the whole western horizon, and by making us aware of a community of mountains, made our position seem less solitary.

46 Thoreau wrote in *Wild Fruits:* "Many years ago, when camping on Wachusett mountain, having carried up milk for drink because there was no water there, I picked blueberries enough through the holes in the buffalo skin on which I lay in my tent to have berries and milk for supper" [*Wild Fruits* 22].

47 Ecclesiastically, the sixth of seven canonical hours, but generally, the time of early evening worship, prayer or song.

48 Allusion to Sodom and Gomorrah and the cities of the plain in Genesis 19.

49 Quoted from Virgil's *Eclogue* I:83–84, followed by Thoreau's translation.

50 Cedar waxwing (*Bombycilla cedrorum*)

But at length the wind drove us to the shelter of our tent, and we closed its door for the night, and fell asleep.

It was a rich treat to hear the wind roar over the rocks, at intervals, when we waked, for it had grown quite cold and windy. The night was, in its elements, simple even to majesty in that bleak place—a bright moonlight and a piercing wind. It was at no time darker than twilight within the tent, and we could easily see the moon through its transparent roof as we lay; for there was the moon still above us, with Jupiter and Saturn on either hand, looking down on Wachusett, and it was a satisfaction to know that they were our fellow-travellers still, as high and out of our reach, as our own destiny. Truly the stars were given for a consolation to man. We should not know but our life were fated to be always grovelling, but it is permitted to behold them, and surely they are deserving of a fair destiny. We see laws which never fail, of whose failure we never conceived; and their lamps burn all the night, too, as well as all day, so rich and lavish is that nature, which can afford this superfluity of light.

The morning twilight began as soon as the moon had set, and we arose and kindled our fire, whose blaze might have been seen for thirty miles around. As the day-light increased, it was remarkable how rapidly the wind went down. There was no dew on the summit, but coldness supplied its place. When the dawn had reached its prime, we enjoyed the view of a distinct horizon line, and could fancy ourselves at sea, and the distant hills the waves in the horizon, as seen from the deck of a vessel. The cherry-birds[50] flitted around us, the nuthatch and flicker were heard among the bushes, the titmouse perched within a few feet, and the song of the woodthrush again rung along the ridge. At length we saw the sun rise up out of the sea, and shine on Massachusetts, and from this moment the atmosphere grew more and more transparent till the time of our departure, and we began to realize the extent of the view, and how the earth, in some degree, answered to the heavens in breadth, the white villages to the constellations in the sky. There was little of the sublimity and grandeur which belong to mountain scenery, but an immense landscape to ponder on a summer's day. We could see how ample and roomy is nature. As far as the eye could reach, there was little life in the landscape; the few birds that flitted past did not crowd. The travellers on the remote highways, which intersect the country on every side, had no fellow-travellers for miles, before or behind. On every side, the eye ranged over successive circles of towns, rising one above another, like the terraces of a vineyard, till they were lost in the horizon. Wachusett is, in fact, the observatory of the state. There lay Massachusetts, spread out before us in its length and breadth, like a map. There was the level horizon, which told of the sea on the east and south, the well-known hills of New Hampshire on the north, and the misty summits of the Hoosac and Green Mountains, first made visible to us the evening before, blue and unsubstantial, like some bank of clouds which the morning wind would dissipate, on the north-west and west. These last distant ranges, on which the eye rests unwearied, commence with an abrupt boulder in the north, beyond the Connecticut, and travel southward, with three or four peaks dimly seen. But Monadnock, rearing its masculine front in the north-west, is the grandest feature. As we beheld it we knew that it was the height of land between the two rivers, on this side the valley of the Merrimack, on that of the Connecticut, fluctuating with their blue seas of air. These rival vales, gradually extending their population and commerce along their respective streams, to what destiny who shall tell?[51] Watatic,[52] and the neighboring hills in this state and in New Hampshire, are a continuation of the same elevated range on which we were standing. But that New Hamp-

51 In *Excursions* this reads: "blue seas of air,— these rival gales, already teeming with Yankee men along their respective streams, born to what destiny who shall tell?" [*Excursions* 91].
52 Mount Watatic, on the border of Massachusetts and New Hampshire.

shire bluff—that promontory of a state—causing day and night on this our state of Massachusetts, will longest haunt our dreams.

We could, at length, realize the place mountains occupy on the land, and how they come into the general scheme of the universe. When first we climb their summits, and observe their lesser irregularities, we do not give credit to the comprehensive intelligence which shaped them; but when afterward we behold their outlines in the horizon, we confess that the hand which moulded their opposite slopes, making one to balance the other, worked round a deep centre, and was privy to the plan of the universe. So is the least part of nature in its bearings referred to all space. These lesser mountain ranges, as well as the Alleghanies, run from north-east to south-west, and parallel with these mountain streams are the more fluent rivers, answering to the general direction of the coast, the bank of the great ocean stream itself. Even the clouds, with their thin bars, fall into the same direction by preference, and such is the course of the prevailing winds, and the migration of men and birds. A mountain chain determines many things for the statesman and philosopher. The improvements of civilization rather creep along its sides than cross its summit. How often is it a barrier to prejudice and fanaticism? In passing over these heights of land, through their thin atmosphere, the follies of the plain are refined and purified. As many species of plants do not scale their summits, so many species of folly do not cross the Alleghanies; it is only the hardy mountain plant that creeps quite over the ridge, and descends into the valley beyond.

It adds not a little grandeur to our conception of the flight of birds, especially of the duck tribe, and such as fly high in the air, to have ascended a mountain. We can now see what landmarks they are to their migrations; how the Catskills and Highlands have hardly sunk to them, when Wachusett and Monadnock open a passage to the north-east—how they are guided, too, in their course by the rivers and valleys, and who knows but by the stars, as well as the mountain ranges, and not by the petty landmarks which we use. The bird whose eye takes in the Green Mountains[53] on the one side, and the ocean on the other, need not be at a loss to find its way.

At noon we descended the mountain, and having returned to the abodes of men, turned our faces to the east again; measuring our progress, from time to time, by the more ethereal hues, which the mountain assumed. Passing swiftly through Stillwater and Sterling, as with a downward impetus, (the reader will excuse the abruptness of the descent,) we found ourselves almost at home again in the green meadows of Lancaster, so like our own Concord, for both are watered by two streams which unite near their centres, and have many other features in common. There is an unexpected refinement about this scenery; level prairies of great extent, interspersed with elms, and hop-fields, and groves of trees, give it almost a classic appearance. This, it will be remembered, was the scene of Mrs. Rowlandson's capture,[54] and of other events in the Indian wars, but from this July afternoon, and under that mild exterior, those times seemed as remote as the irruption of the Goths.[55] They were the dark age of New England. On beholding a picture of a New England village as it then appeared, with a fair open prospect, and a light on trees and river, as if it were broad noon, we find we had not thought the sun shone in those days, or that men lived in broad daylight then. We do not imagine the sun shining on hill and valley during Philip's war, nor on the war-path of Paugus,[56] or Standish,[57] or Church,[58] or Lovell,[59] with serene summer weather, but a dim twilight or night did those events transpire in. They must have fought in the shade of their own dusky deeds.

53 Forested mountain range running north-south from northern Vermont to western Massachusetts.

54 Mary Rowlandson (ca. 1635–ca. 1678) was captured on 10 February 1676 when the Narragansett raided Lancaster during King Philip's War. She was held captive for eighty-two days and later wrote *The sovereignty & goodness of God, together with the faithfulness of his promises displayed, being a narrative of the captivity and restoration of Mrs. Mary Rowlandson.*

55 A Teutonic people which made several incursions into the Roman Empire during the third through fifth centuries.

56 War chief of the Pequawkets, killed in Lovewell's Fight during King Philip's War, and also mentioned in *The Maine Woods.*

57 Miles Standish (1584–1656), English-born professional soldier hired as military adviser to the Pilgrims.

58 Captain Benjamin Church (1639–1718), Indian fighter, who wrote *The History of King Philip's War,* mentioned by Thoreau in his 1840 journal and an 1857 letter.

59 John Lovewell, sometimes Lovell (1691–1725), Indian fighter with whom Thoreau was familiar from "The Ballad of Lovewell's Fight" and the *History of the Old Township of Dunstable.*

At length, as we plodded along the dusty roads, our thoughts became as dusty as they; all thought indeed stopped, thinking broke down, or proceeded only passively in a sort of rhythmical cadence of the confused material of thought, and we found ourselves mechanically repeating some familiar measure which timed with our tread; some verse of the Robin Hood ballads, for instance, which one can recommend to travel by.

> "Sweavens are swift, sayd lyttle John,
>   As the wind blows over the hill;
> For if it be never so loud this night,
>   To-morrow it may be still."

And so it went up hill and down till a stone interrupted the line, when a new verse was chosen.

> "His shoote it was but loosely shot,
>   Yet flewe not the arrowe in vaine,
> For it met one of the sheriffe's men,
>   And William-a-Trent was slaine."[60]

There is, however, this consolation to the most way-worn traveller, upon the dustiest road, that the path his feet describe is so perfectly symbolical of human life—now climbing the hills, now descending into the vales. From the summits he beholds the heavens and the horizon, from the vales he looks up to the heights again. He is treading his old lessons still, and though he may be very weary and travel-worn, it is yet sincere experience.

Leaving the Nashua, we changed our route a little, and arrived at Stillriver village, in the western part of Harvard,[61] just as the sun was setting. From this place, which lies to the northward, upon the western slope of the same range of hills, on which we had spent the noon before, in the adjacent town, the prospect is beautiful,

60 Quoted from "Robin Hood and Guy of Gisborne" from *Robin Hood: A Collection of All the Ancient Poems, Songs, and Ballads*, compiled by Joseph Ritson (1795), several verses of which Thoreau copied into his literary notebook.
61 Town approximately thirteen miles west of Concord.

and the grandeur of the mountain outlines unsurpassed. There was such a repose and quiet here at his hour, as if the very hill-sides were enjoying the scene, and as we passed slowly along, looking back over the country we had traversed, and listening to the evening song of the robin, we could not help contrasting the equanimity of nature with the bustle and impatience of man. His words and actions presume always a crisis near at hand, but she is forever silent and unpretending.

We rested that night at Harvard, and the next morning, while one bent his steps to the nearer village of Groton,[62] the other took his separate and solitary way to the peaceful meadows of Concord; but let him not forget to record the brave[63] hospitality of a farmer and his wife, who generously entertained him at their board, though the poor wayfarer could only congratulate the one on the continuance of hayweather, and silently accept the kindness of the other. Refreshed by this instance of generosity, no less than by the substantial viands set before him, he pushed forward with new vigor, and reached the banks of the Concord before the sun had climbed many degrees into the heavens.

And now that we have returned to the desultory life of the plain, let us endeavor to import a little of that mountain grandeur into it. We will remember within what walls we lie, and understand that this level life too has its summit, and why from the mountain top the deepest valleys have a tinge of blue; that there is elevation in every hour, as no part of the earth is so low that the heavens may not be seen from, and we have only to stand on the summit of our hour to command an uninterrupted horizon.[64]

62 The Fuller family moved to Groton in 1833.
63 Excellent, admirable.
64 The final two paragraphs were reversed in *Excursions*.

A Walk to Wachusett 63

1 John Adolphus Etzler (1791–ca. 1846) emigrated in 1831.

2 J. A. Etzler, *The Paradise within the Reach of all Men, Without Labor, by Powers of Nature and Machinery. An Address to All Intelligent Men* (Pittsburgh: Etzler and Reinhold, 1833).

3 Thoreau's review is based on the first part of the second English edition, printed by James H. Young and published by J. Cleave, 1842.

4 Charles Fourier (1772–1837), French philosopher, who self-sustaining cooperative communities called phalansteries emphasized social cooperation. Brook Farm adopted Fourieristic principles in 1844, three years after its founding.

5 The excerpts from Etzler in this essay have all been silently edited by Thoreau, who often juxtaposes noncontiguous quotations with no mark of ellipses or other indication and in one case gives as one sentence portions of two different sentences. The nonedited texts as they appeared in Thoreau's source can be found in the appendix, pp. 369–382.

Paradise (To Be) Regained

We learn that Mr. Etzler is a native of Germany,[1] and originally published his book in Pennsylvania, ten or twelve years ago;[2] and now a second English edition,[3] from the original American one, is demanded by his readers across the water, owing, we suppose, to the recent spread of Fourier's doctrines.[4] It is one of the signs of the times. We confess that we have risen from reading this book with enlarged ideas, and grander conceptions of our duties in this world. It did expand us a little. It is worth attending to, if only that it entertains large questions. Consider what Mr. Etzler proposes:[5]

"Fellow Men! I promise to show the means of creating a paradise within ten years, where everything desirable for human life may be had by every man in superabundance, without labor, and without pay; where the whole face of nature shall be changed into the most beautiful forms, and man may live in the most magnificent palaces, in all imaginable refinements of luxury, and in the most delightful gardens; where he may accomplish, without labor, in one year, more than hitherto could be done in thousands of years; may level mountains, sink valleys, create lakes, drain lakes and swamps, and intersect the land everywhere with beautiful canals, and roads for transporting heavy loads of many thousand tons, and for travelling one thousand miles in twenty-four hours; may cover the ocean with floating islands movable in any desired direction with immense power and celerity, in perfect security, and with all comforts and luxuries, bearing gardens and palaces, with thousands of families, and provided with rivulets of sweet water; may explore the interior of the globe, and travel from pole to pole in a fortnight; provide himself with means, unheard of yet, for increasing his knowledge of the world, and so his intelligence; lead a life of continual happiness, of enjoyments yet unknown; free himself from almost all the evils that afflict mankind, except death, and even put death far beyond the common period of human life, and finally render it less afflicting. Mankind may thus live in and enjoy a new world, far superior to the present, and raise themselves far higher in the scale of being."

It would seem from this and various indications beside, that there is a transcendentalism in mechanics as well as in ethics. While the whole field of the one reformer lies beyond the boundaries of space, the other is pushing his schemes for the elevation of the race to its utmost limits. While one scours the heavens, the other sweeps the earth. One says he will reform himself, and then nature and circumstances will be right. Let us not obstruct ourselves, for that is the greatest friction. It is of little importance though a cloud obstruct the view of the astronomer compared with his own blindness. The other will reform nature and circumstances, and then man will be right. Talk no more vaguely, says he, of reforming the world—I will reform the globe itself. What matters it whether I remove this humor out of my flesh, or this pestilent humor from the fleshy part of the globe? Nay, is not the latter the more generous course? At present the globe goes with a shattered constitution in its orbit. Has it not asthma, and ague, and fever, and dropsy, and flatu-

6 Ailments or afflictions.

7 In Greek mythology, the goddess of health.

8 Allusion to heaven as expressed as a land or country, as in Hebrews 11:16: "But now they desire a better country, that is, an heavenly."

9 Thoreau referred to "a certain fertility, an Ohio soil," in his journal of 16 March 1852 [J 3:353].

10 Allusion to the Noachian deluge from Genesis 6–7.

11 Self-referencing pun, as in "Life without Principle," in which Thoreau referred to himself as a "thoroughfare."

lence, and pleurisy, and is it not afflicted with vermin? Has it not its healthful laws counteracted, and its vital energy which will yet redeem it? No doubt the simple powers of nature properly directed by man would make it healthy and a paradise; as the laws of man's own constitution but wait to be obeyed, to restore him to health and happiness. Our panaceas cure but few ails,[6] our general hospitals are private and exclusive. We must set up another Hygeia[7] than is now worshipped. Do not the quacks even direct small doses for children, larger for adults, and larger still for oxen and horses? Let us remember that we are to prescribe for the globe itself.

This fair homestead has fallen to us, and how little have we done to improve it, how little have we cleared and hedged and ditched! We are too inclined to go hence to a "better land,"[8] without lifting a finger, as our farmers are moving to the Ohio soil;[9] but would it not be more heroic and faithful to till and redeem this New-England soil of the world? The still youthful energies of the globe have only to be directed in their proper channel. Every gazette brings accounts of the untutored freaks of the wind—shipwrecks and hurricanes which the mariner and planter accept as special or general providences; but they touch our consciences, they remind us of our sins. Another deluge would disgrace mankind.[10] We confess we never had much respect for that antediluvian race. A thorough-bred[11] business man cannot enter heartily upon the business of life without first looking into his accounts. How many things are now at loose ends. Who knows which way the wind will blow to-morrow? Let us not succumb to nature. We will marshal the clouds and restrain the tempests; we will bottle up pestilent exhalations, we will probe for earthquakes, grub them up; and give vent to the dangerous gases; we will disembowel the volcano, and extract its poison, take its seed out. We will wash water, and warm fire, and cool ice, and underprop the earth. We will teach birds to fly, and fishes to swim, and ruminants to chew the cud. It is time we had looked into these things.

And it becomes the moralist, too, to inquire what man might do to improve and beautify the system; what to make the stars shine more brightly, the sun more cheery and joyous, the moon more placid and content. Could he not heighten the tints of flowers and the melody of birds? Does he perform his duty to the inferior races? Should he not be a god to them? What is the part of magnanimity to the whale and the beaver? Should we not fear to exchange places with them for a day, lest by their behavior they should shame us? Might we not treat with magnanimity the shark and the tiger, not descend to meet them on their own level, with spears of sharks' teeth and bucklers of tiger's skin? We slander the hyaena; man is the fiercest and cruelest animal.[12] Ah! he is of little faith;[13] even the erring comets and meteors would thank him, and return his kindness in their kind.

How meanly and grossly do we deal with nature! Could we not have a less gross labor? What else do these fine inventions suggest, — magnetism, the daguerreo-type,[14] electricity? Can we not do more than cut and trim the forest, — can we not assist in its interior economy, in the circulation of the sap? Now we work superficially and violently. We do not suspect how much might be done to improve our relation with animated nature; what kind-ness and refined courtesy there might be.

There are certain pursuits which, if not wholly poetic and true, do at least suggest a nobler and finer relation to nature than we know. The keeping of bees, for in-stance, is a very slight interference. It is like directing the sunbeams. All nations, from the remotest antiquity, have thus fingered nature. There are Hymettus[15] and Hybla,[16] and how many bee-renowned spots beside? There is nothing gross in the idea of these little herds, —

12 In early books of natural history the hyena was referred to as "fierce, cruel, and rapacious" (William Wood [fl. 1629–1635], *Zoology*) or "cer-tainly the fiercest of quadrupeds" (William For-dyce Mavor [1758–1837], *The Elements of Natural History*).
13 Allusion to Jesus' accusation "O ye of little faith," found in Matthew and Luke.
14 Early negativeless form of photograph print on glass plates, invented in the mid-1830s by the French photographic pioneer Louis Jacques Mandé Daguerre (1789–1851).
15 Mountain in Attica.
16 Hybla Major: an ancient town in Sicily.

17 Lucian Junius Moderatus Columella (4–70 C.E.), Roman writer on agriculture.

18 Quoted from a lengthy and unsigned review in the *Quarterly Review* (141:13) on "The Honey-bee, and Bee-books."

19 Allusion to a description in "The Honey-bee, and Bee-books" of the "most pleasing picture . . . of the floating bee-houses of the Nile, mentioned by old and modern writers."

20 Allusion in "The Honey-bee, and Bee-books" to the "old man, who was generally set down as being no wiser than his neighbors" but who was "very observant of the habits of his little friends. . . . The honey-harvest came round, and when he had stored away just double what any of the rest had saved, he called his friends and neighbors together . . . and he pointed to the inclination of his hives—one degree more to the east than was generally adopted."

21 Latin: at full length.

22 Benefit, the word choice furnishing Thoreau with an equine pun.

their hum like the faintest low of kine in the meads. A pleasant reviewer has lately reminded us that in some places they are led out to pasture where the flowers are most abundant. "Columella[17] tells us," says he, "that the inhabitants of Achaia sent their hives into Attica to benefit by the later-blowing flowers."[18] Annually are the hives, in immense pyramids, carried up the Nile in boats, and suffered to float slowly down the stream by night, resting by day, as the flowers put forth along the banks; and they determine the richness of any locality, and so the profitableness of delay, by the sinking of the boat in the water.[19] We are told, by the same reviewer, of a man in Germany, whose bees yielded more honey than those of his neighbors, with no apparent advantage; but at length he informed them that he had turned his hives one degree more to the east, and so his bees, having two hours the start in the morning, got the first sip of honey.[20] True, there is treachery and selfishness behind all this; but these things suggest to the poetic mind what might be done.

Many examples there are of a grosser interference, yet not without their apology. We saw last summer, on the side of a mountain, a dog employed to churn for a farmer's family, travelling upon a horizontal wheel, and though he had sore eyes, an alarming cough, and withal a demure aspect, yet their bread did get buttered for all that. Undoubtedly, in the most brilliant successes, the first rank is always sacrificed. Much useless travelling of horses, *in extenso*,[21] has of late years been improved for man's behoof,[22] only two forces being taken advantage of,—the gravity of the horse, which is the centripetal, and his centrifugal inclination to go a-head. Only these two elements in the calculation. And is not the creature's whole economy better economized thus? Are not all finite beings better pleased with motions relative than absolute?

And what is the great globe itself but such a wheel,—a larger tread-mill,—so that our horse's freest steps over prairies are oftentimes balked and rendered of no avail by the earth's motion on its axis? But here he is the central agent and motive power; and, for variety of scenery, being provided with a window in front, do not the ever-varying activity and fluctuating energy of the creature himself work the effect of the most varied scenery on a country road? It must be confessed that horses at present work too exclusively for men, rarely men for horses; and the brute degenerates in man's society.

It will be seen that we contemplate a time when man's will shall be law to the physical world, and he shall no longer be deterred by such abstractions as time and space, height and depth, weight and hardness, but shall indeed be the lord of creation.[23] "Well," says the faithless reader, "'life is short, but art is long';[24] where is the power that will effect all these changes?" This it is the very object of Mr. Etzler's volume to show. At present, he would merely remind us that there are innumerable and immeasurable powers already existing in nature, unimproved on a large scale, or for generous and universal ends, amply sufficient for these purposes. He would only indicate their existence, as a surveyor makes known the existence of a water-power on any stream; but for their application he refers us to a sequel to this book, called the "Mechanical System."[25] A few of the most obvious and familiar of these powers are, the Wind, the Tide, the Waves, the Sunshine. Let us consider their value.

First, there is the power of the Wind, constantly exerted over the globe. It appears from observation of a sailing-vessel, and from scientific tables, that the average power of the wind is equal to that of one horse for every one hundred square feet. "We know," says our author—

[23] Allusion to Genesis 1:26, in which man is given "dominion over the fish of the sea, and over the fowl of the air, and over the cattle, and over all the earth, and over every creeping thing that creepeth upon the earth."

[24] Translation of *Ars longa, vita brevis,* from the maxim of the Greek physician Hippocrates (ca. 460–ca. 377 B.C.E.), known as the "Father of Medicine": "Life is short, the art long, opportunity fleeting, experiment treacherous, judgment difficult."

[25] *The New World; or, Mechanical System, to Perform the Labours of Man and Beast by Inanimate Powers, That Cost Nothing, for Producing and Preparing the Substances of Life* (Philadelphia: C. F. Stollmeyer, 1841).

"that ships of the first class carry sails two hundred feet high; we may, therefore, equally, on land, oppose to the wind surfaces of the same height. Imagine a line of such surfaces one mile, or about 5,000 feet, long; they would then contain 1,000,000 square feet. Let these surfaces intersect the direction of the wind at right angles, by some contrivance, and receive, consequently, its full power at all times. Its average power being equal to one horse for every 100 square feet, the total power would be equal to 1,000,000 divided by 100, or 10,000 horses' power. Allowing the power of one horse to equal that of ten men, the power of 10,000 horses is equal to 100,000 men. But as men cannot work uninterruptedly, but want about half the time for sleep and repose, the same power would be equal to 200,000 men. . . . We are not limited to the height of 200 feet; we might extend, if required, the application of this power to the height of the clouds, by means of kites."

But we will have one such fence for every square mile of the globe's surface, for, as the wind usually strikes the earth at an angle of more than two degrees, which is evident from observing its effect on the high sea, it admits of even a closer approach. As the surface of the globe contains about 200,000,000 square miles, the whole power of the wind on these surfaces would equal 40,000,000,000,000 men's power, and "would perform 80,000 times as much work as all the men on earth could effect with their nerves."

If it should be objected that this computation includes the surface of the ocean and uninhabitable regions of the earth, where this power could not be applied for our purposes, Mr. Etzler is quick with his reply—

"But, you will recollect," says he, "that I have promised to show the means for rendering the ocean as inhabitable as the most fruitful dry land; and I do not exclude even the polar regions."

The reader will observe that our author uses the fence only as a convenient formula for expressing the power of the wind, and does not consider it a necessary method of its application. We do not attach much value to this statement of the comparative power of the wind and horse, for no common ground is mentioned on which they can be compared. Undoubtedly, each is incomparably excellent in its way, and every general comparison made for such practical purposes as are contemplated, which gives a preference to the one, must be made with some unfairness to the other. The scientific tables are, for the most part, true only in a tabular sense. We suspect that a loaded wagon, with a light sail, ten feet square, would not have been blown so far by the end of the year, under equal circumstances, as a common racer or dray horse[26] would have drawn it. And how many crazy structures on our globe's surface, of the same dimensions, would wait for dry-rot if the traces[27] of one horse were hitched to them, even to their windward side? Plainly, this is not the principle of comparison. But even the steady and constant force of the horse may be rated as equal to his weight at least. Yet we should prefer to let the zephyrs and gales bear, with all their weight, upon our fences, than that Dobbin,[28] with feet braced, should lean ominously against them for a season.

Nevertheless, here is an almost incalculable power at our disposal, yet how trifling the use we make of it. It only serves to turn a few mills, blow a few vessels across the ocean, and a few trivial ends besides. What a poor compliment do we pay to our indefatigable and energetic servant!

26 Draft horse: horse used for drawing a dray, a low cart or carriage on wheels.
27 Straps, chains, or ropes in a harness by which a carriage or sleigh is drawn.
28 Common name for a workhorse.

"If you ask, perhaps, why this power is not used, if the statement be true, I have to ask in return, why is the power of steam so lately come to application? so many millions of men boiled water every day for many thousand years; they must have frequently seen that boiling water, in tightly closed pots or kettles, would lift the cover or burst the vessel with great violence. The power of steam was, therefore, as commonly known down to the least kitchen or wash-woman, as the power of wind; but close observation and reflection were bestowed neither on the one nor the other."

Men having discovered the power of falling water, which after all is comparatively slight, how eagerly do they seek out and improve these *privileges?* Let a difference of but a few feet in level be discovered on some stream near a populous town, some slight occasion for gravity to act, and the whole economy of the neighborhood is changed at once. Men do indeed speculate about and with this power as if it were the only privilege. But meanwhile this aerial stream is falling from far greater heights with more constant flow, never shrunk by drought, offering mill-sites wherever the wind blows; a Niagara in the air, with no Canada side;—only the application is hard.

There are the powers too of the Tide and Waves, constantly ebbing and flowing, lapsing and relapsing, but they serve man in but few ways. They turn a few tide mills, and perform a few other insignificant and accidental services only. We all perceive the effect of the tide; how imperceptibly it creeps up into our harbors and rivers, and raises the heaviest navies as easily as the lightest ship. Everything that floats must yield to it. But man, slow to take nature's constant hint of assistance, makes slight and irregular use of this power, in careening[29] ships and getting them afloat when aground.

The following is Mr. Etzler's calculation on this head: To form a conception of the power which the tide affords, let us imagine a surface of 100 miles square, or 10,000 square miles, where the tide rises and sinks, on an average, 10 feet; how many men would it require to empty a basin of 10,000 square miles area, and 10 feet deep, filled with sea-water, in 6¼ hours and fill it again in the same time? As one man can raise 8 cubic feet of sea-water per minute, and in 6¼ hours 3,000, it would take 1,200,000,000 men, or as they could work only half the time, 2,400,000,000, to raise 3,000,000,000,000 cubic feet, or the whole quantity required in the given time.

This power may be applied in various ways. A large body, of the heaviest materials that will float, may first be raised by it, and being attached to the end of a balance reaching from the land, or from a stationary support, fastened to the bottom, when the tide falls, the whole weight will be brought to bear upon the end of the balance. Also when the tide rises it may be made to exert a nearly equal force in the opposite direction. It can be employed whenever a *point d'appui*[30] can be obtained.

"However, the application of the tide being by establishments fixed on the ground, it is natural to begin with them near the shores in shallow water, and upon sands, which may be extended gradually further into the sea. The shores of the continent, islands, and sands, being generally surrounded by shallow water, not exceeding from 50 to 100 fathoms in depth, for 20, 50, or 100 miles and upward. The coasts of North America, with their extensive sand-banks, islands, and rocks, may easily afford, for this purpose, a ground about 3,000

29 Heaving or bringing a ship to lay on one side, for the purpose of caulking, repairing, cleansing, or paying over with pitch, the other side.
30 French: point of support.

miles long, and, on an average, 100 miles broad, or 300,000 square miles, which, with a power of 240,000 men per square mile, as stated, at 10 feet tide, will be equal to 72,000 millions of men, or for every mile of coast, a power of 24,000,000 men."

"Rafts, of any extent, fastened on the ground of the sea, along the shore, and stretching far into the sea, may be covered with fertile soil, bearing vegetables and trees, of every description, the finest gardens, equal to those the firm land may admit of, and buildings and machineries, which may operate, not only on the sea, where they are, but which also, by means of mechanical connections, may extend their operations for many miles into the continent. (Etzler's Mechanical System, page 24.) Thus this power may cultivate the artificial soil for many miles upon the surface of the sea, near the shores, and, for several miles, the dry land, along the shore, in the most superior manner imaginable; it may build cities along the shore, consisting of the most magnificent palaces, every one surrounded by gardens and the most delightful sceneries; it may level the hills and unevennesses, or raise eminences for enjoying open prospect into the country and upon the sea; it may cover the barren shore with fertile soil, and beautify the same in various ways; it may clear the sea of shallows, and make easy the approach to the land, not merely of vessels, but of large floating islands, which may come from, and go to distant parts of the world, islands that have every commodity and security for their inhabitants which the firm land affords."

"Thus may a power, derived from the gravity of the moon and the ocean, hitherto but the objects of idle curiosity to the studious man, be made eminently subservient for creating the most delightful abodes along the coasts, where men may enjoy at the same time all the advantages of sea and dry land; the coasts may hereafter be continuous paradisiacal skirts between land and sea, everywhere crowded with the densest population. The shores and the sea along them will be no more as raw nature presents them now, but everywhere of easy and charming access, not even molested by the roar of waves, shaped as it may suit the purposes of their inhabitants; the sea will be cleared of every obstruction to free passage every-where, and its productions in fishes, etc., will be gathered in large, appropriate receptacles, to present them to the inhabitants of the shores and of the sea."

Verily, the land would wear a busy aspect at the spring and neap tide,[31] and these island ships—these *terrae infirmae*[32]—which realise the fables of antiquity, affect our imagination. We have often thought that the fittest locality for a human dwelling was on the edge of the land, that there the constant lesson and impression of the sea might sink deep into the life and character of the landsman, and perhaps impart a marine tint to his imagination. It is a noble word, that *mariner*—one who is conversant with the sea.[33] There should be more of what it signifies in each of us. It is a worthy country to belong to—we look to see him not disgrace it. Perhaps we should be equally mariners and terreners,[34] and even our Green Mountains need some of that sea-green to be mixed with them.

The computation of the power of the waves is less satisfactory. While only the average power of the wind, and the average height of the tide, were taken before now, the extreme height of the waves is used, for they are made to

31 Spring tides have the maximum range between high and low tide; neap tides have the minimum range.
32 Latin: unstable ground, as opposed to the more common term *terra firma,* solid ground.
33 Definition of the Greek word *halistrephes* as found in John Pickering's (1777–1846) *A Greek and English Lexicon.*
34 A Thoreauism, after mariner, meaning one who navigates on dry land, or following Thoreau, one who is conversant with the land.

35 Concave mirrors used to concentrate the sun's rays. Allusion to Archimedes (287–212 B.C.E.), Greek mathematician, physicist, engineer, astronomer, and philosopher, who is reported to have used mirrors to burn the Roman fleet during the siege of Syracuse.

rise ten feet above the level of the sea, to which, adding ten more for depression, we have twenty feet, or the extreme height of a wave. Indeed, the power of the waves, which is produced by the wind blowing obliquely and at disadvantage upon the water, is made to be, not only three thousand times greater than that of the tide, but one hundred times greater than that of the wind itself, meeting its object at right angles. Moreover, this power is measured by the area of the vessel, and not by its length mainly, and it seems to be forgotten that the motion of the waves is chiefly undulatory, and exerts a power only within the limits of a vibration, else the very continents, with their extensive coasts, would soon be set adrift.

Finally, there is the power to be derived from Sunshine, by the principle on which Archimedes contrived his burning mirrors,[35] a multiplication of mirrors reflecting the rays of the sun upon the same spot, till the requisite degree of heat is obtained. The principal application of this power will be to the boiling of water and production of steam.

"How to create rivulets of sweet and wholesome water, on floating islands, in the midst of the ocean, will be no riddle now. Sea-water changed into steam, will distil into sweet water, leaving the salt on the bottom. Thus the steam engines on floating islands, for their propulsion and other mechanical purposes, will serve, at the same time, for the distillery of sweet water, which, collected in basins, may be led through channels over the island, while, where required, it may be refrigerated by artificial means, and changed into cool water, surpassing, in salubrity, the best spring water, because nature hardly ever distils water so purely, and without admixture of less wholesome matter."

So much for these few and more obvious powers, already used to a trifling extent. But there are innumerable others in nature, not described nor discovered. These, however, will do for the present. This would be to make the sun and the moon equally our satellites. For, as the moon is the cause of the tides, and the sun the cause of the wind, which, in turn, is the cause of the waves, all the work of this planet would be performed by these far influences.

"But as these powers are very irregular and subject to interruptions; the next object is to show how they may be converted into powers that operate continually and uniformly for ever, until the machinery be worn out, or, in other words, into perpetual motions." . . . "Hitherto the power of the wind has been applied immediately upon the machinery for use, and we have had to wait the chances of the wind's blowing; while the operation was stopped as soon as the wind ceased to blow. But the manner, which I shall state hereafter, of applying this power, is to make it operate only for collecting or storing up power, and then to take out of this store, at any time, as much as may be wanted for final operation upon the machines. The power stored up is to react as required, and may do so long after the original power of the wind has ceased. And though the wind should cease for intervals of many months, we may have by the same power a uniform perpetual motion in a very simple way."

"The weight of a clock being wound up gives us an image of reaction. The sinking of this weight is the reaction of winding it up. It is not necessary to wait till it has run down before we wind up the weight, but it may be wound up at any time,

36 One quarter of an acre.

partly or totally; and if done always before the weight reaches the bottom, the clock will be going perpetually. In a similar, though not in the same way, we may cause a reaction on a larger scale. We may raise, for instance, water by the immediate application of wind or steam to a pond upon some eminence, out of which, through an outlet, it may fall upon some wheel or other contrivance for setting machinery a-going. Thus we may store up water in some eminent pond, and take out of this store, at any time, as much water through the outlet as we want to employ, by which means the original power may react for many days after it has ceased." . . . "Such reservoirs of moderate elevation or size need not be made artificially, but will be found made by nature very frequently, requiring but little aid for their completion. They require no regularity of form. Any valley with lower grounds in its vicinity, would answer the purpose. Small crevices may be filled up. Such places may be eligible for the beginning of enterprises of this kind."

The greater the height, of course the less water required. But suppose a level and dry country; then hill and valley, and "eminent pond," are to be constructed by main force; or if the springs are unusually low, then dirt and stones may be used, and the disadvantage arising from friction will be counterbalanced by their greater gravity. Nor shall a single rood[36] of dry land be sunk in such artificial ponds as may be wasted, but their surfaces "may be covered with rafts decked with fertile earth, and all kinds of vegetables which may grow there as well as anywhere else."

And finally, by the use of thick envelopes retaining the heat, and other contrivances, "the power of steam caused by sunshine may react at will, and thus be rendered perpetual, no matter how often or how long the sunshine may be interrupted. (Etzler's Mechanical System)."

Here is power enough, one would think, to accomplish somewhat. These are the powers below. Oh ye millwrights, ye engineers, ye operatives and speculators of every class, never again complain of a want of power; it is the grossest form of infidelity. The question is not how we shall execute, but what. Let us not use in a niggardly manner what is thus generously offered.

Consider what revolutions are to be effected in agriculture. First, in the new country, a machine is to move along taking out trees and stones to any required depth, and piling them up in convenient heaps; then the same machine, "with a little alteration," is to plane the ground perfectly, till there shall be no hills nor valleys, making the requisite canals, ditches and roads, as it goes along. The same machine, "with some other little alterations," is then to sift the ground thoroughly, supply fertile soil from other places if wanted, and plant it; and finally, the same machine "with a little addition," is to reap and gather in the crop, thresh and grind it, or press it to oil, or prepare it any way for final use. For the description of these machines we are referred to "Etzler's Mechanical System, pages 11 to 27." We should be pleased to see that "Mechanical System," though we have not been able to ascertain whether it has been published, or only exists as yet in the design of the author. We have great faith in it. But we cannot stop for applications now.

"Any wilderness, even the most hideous and sterile, may be converted into the most fertile and delightful gardens. The most dismal swamps may be cleared of all their spontaneous growth, filled up and levelled, and intersected by canals, ditches and aqueducts, for draining them entirely. The soil, if required, may be meliorated, by covering or mixing it with rich soil taken from distant places, and the same be mouldered to fine dust, levelled, sifted from all roots, weeds and stones, and sowed and planted in the most beautiful order and symmetry, with fruit trees and vegetables of every kind that may stand the climate."

New facilities for transportation and locomotion are to be adopted:

"Large and commodious vehicles, for carrying many thousand tons, running over peculiarly adapted level roads, at the rate of forty miles per hour, or one thousand miles per day, may transport men and things, small houses, and whatever may serve for comfort and ease, by land. Floating islands, constructed of logs, or of wooden-stuff prepared in a similar manner, as is to be done with stone, and of live trees, which may be reared so as to interlace one another, and strengthen the whole, may be covered with gardens and palaces, and propelled by powerful engines, so as to run at an equal rate through seas and oceans. Thus, man may move, with the celerity of a bird's flight, in terrestrial paradises, from one climate to another, and see the world in all its variety, exchanging, with distant nations, the surplus of productions. The journey from one pole to another may be performed in a fortnight; the visit to a transmarine country in a week or two; or a journey round the world in one or two months by land and water. And why pass a dreary winter every year while there is yet room enough on the globe where nature is blessed with a perpetual summer, and with a far greater variety and luxuriance of vegetation? More than one-half the surface of the globe has no winter. Men will have it in their power to remove and prevent all bad influences of climate, and to enjoy, perpetually, only that temperature which suits their constitution and feeling best."

Who knows but by accumulating the power until the end of the present century, using meanwhile only the smallest allowance, reserving all that blows, all that shines, all that ebbs and flows, all that dashes, we may have got such a reserved accumulated power as to run the earth off its track into a new orbit, some summer, and so change the tedious vicissitude of the seasons? Or, perchance, coming generations will not abide the dissolution of the globe, but, availing them-selves of future inventions in aerial locomotion, and the navigation of space, the entire race may migrate from the earth, to settle some vacant and more western planet, it may be still healthy, perchance unearthly, not composed of dirt and stones, whose primary strata only are strewn, and where no weeds are sown. It took but little art, a simple application of natural laws, a canoe, a paddle, and a sail of matting,[37] to people the isles of the Pacific, and a little more will people the shining isles of space. Do we not see in the firmament the lights carried along the shore by night, as Columbus did?[38] Let us not despair nor mutiny.

"The dwellings also ought to be very different from what is known, if the full benefit of our means is to be enjoyed. They are to be of a structure for which we have no name yet. They are to be neither palaces, nor temples, nor cities, but a combination of all, superior to whatever is known. Earth may be baked into bricks, or even vitrified stone by heat,—we may bake large masses of any size and form into stone and vitrified substance of the

37 Course fabric, usually hemp or straw.
38 Thoreau may have read in Washington Irving's (1783–1859) *History of the Life and Voyages of Christopher Columbus* or other sources of the light Columbus (1451–1506) saw on the night of 11 October 1492 and which he thought of as a harbinger of inhabited land.

greatest durability, lasting even thousands of years, out of clayey earth, or of stones ground to dust, by the application of burning mirrors. This is to be done in the open air, without other preparation than gathering the substance, grinding and mixing it with water and cement, moulding or casting it, and bringing the focus of the burning mirrors of proper size upon the same. The character of the architecture is to be quite different from what it ever has been hitherto; large solid masses are to be baked or cast in one piece, ready shaped in any form that may be desired. The building may, therefore, consist of columns two hundred feet high and upwards, of proportionate thickness, and of one entire piece of vitrified substance; huge pieces are to be moulded so as to join and hook on to each other firmly, by proper joints and folds, and not to yield in any way without breaking."

"Foundries, of any description, are to be heated by burning mirrors, and will require no labor, except the making of the first moulds and the superintendence for gathering the metal and taking the finished articles away."

Alas, in the present state of science, we must take the finished articles away; but think not that man will always be a victim of circumstances.

The countryman who visited the city and found the streets cluttered with bricks and lumber, reported that it was not yet finished, and one who considers the endless repairs and reforming of our houses, might well wonder when they will be done. But why may not the dwellings of men on this earth be built once for all of some durable material, some Roman or Etruscan masonry which will stand, so that time shall only adorn and beautify them? Why may we not finish the outward world for posterity, and leave them leisure to attend to the inner? Surely, all the gross necessities and economies might be cared for in a few years. All might be built and baked and stored up, during this, the term-time[39] of the world, against the vacant eternity, and the globe go provisioned and furnished like our public vessels, for its voyage through space, as through some Pacific ocean, while we would "tie up the rudder and sleep before the wind,"[40] as those who sail from Lima to Manilla.[41]

But, to go back a few years in imagination, think not that life in these crystal palaces[42] is to bear any analogy to life in our present humble cottages. Far from it. Clothed, once for all, in some "flexible stuff," more durable than George Fox's suit of leather,[43] composed of "fibres of vegetables," "glutinated"[44] together by some "cohesive substances," and made into sheets, like paper, of any size or form, man will put far from him corroding care and the whole host of ills.

> "The twenty-five halls in the inside of the square are to be each two hundred feet square and high; the forty corridors, each one hundred feet long and twenty wide; the eighty galleries, each from 1,000 to 1,250 feet long; about 7,000 private rooms, the whole surrounded and intersected by the grandest and most splendid colonnades imaginable; floors, ceilings, columns with their various beautiful and fanciful intervals all shining, and reflecting to infinity all objects and persons, with splendid lustre of all beautiful colors, and fanciful shapes and pictures. All galleries, outside and within the halls, are to be provided with many thousand commodious and most elegant vehicles, in which persons may move up and down, like birds, in perfect security, and without exertion. Any member may procure himself all the common articles of his daily wants,

39 Gestation period.
40 Quoted from Sir Thomas Browne's (1605–1682) "A Letter to a Friend": "In this virtuous voyage let not disappointment cause despondency nor difficulty despair. Think not that you are sailing from Lima to Manilla wherein thou mayest tie up the rudder and sleep before the wind but expect rough seas flaws and contrary blasts and it is well if by many cross tacks and veerings thou arrivest at thy port."
41 From Lima, Peru, to Manila in the Philippines, thus crossing the Pacific Ocean from east to west carried by the South Equatorial Current.
42 Fantastic palaces such as those described in the *Vishnu Purana:* "Setting off therefore on a visit to the hermitage of Saubhari, he beheld upon his arrival a row of beautiful crystal palaces shining as brilliantly as the rays of the sun, and situated amidst lovely gardens, and reservoirs of pellucid water."
43 George Fox (1624–1691), founder of the Society of Friends, or Quakers, who, as a young man wore leather breeches, doublet, and hat, clothing usually associated with the working class.
44 Glued.

by a short turn of some crank, without leaving his apartment; he may, at any time, bathe himself in cold or warm water, or in steam, or in some artificially prepared liquor for invigorating health. He may, at any time, give to the air in his apartment that temperature that suits his feeling best. He may cause, at any time, an agreeable scent of various kinds. He may, at any time, meliorate his breathing air,—that main vehicle of vital power. Thus, by a proper application of the physical knowledge of our days, man may be kept in a perpetual serenity of mind, and if there is no incurable disease or defect in his organism, in constant vigor of health, and his life be prolonged beyond any parallel which present times afford."

"One or two persons are sufficient to direct the kitchen business. They have nothing else to do but to superintend the cookery, and to watch the time of the victuals being done, and then to remove them, with the table and vessels, into the dining-hall, or to the respective private apartments, by a slight motion of the hand at some crank. Any extraordinary desire of any person may be satisfied by going to the place where the thing is to be had; and anything that requires a particular preparation in cooking or baking, may be done by the person who desires it."

This is one of those instances in which the individual genius is found to consent, as indeed it always does, at last, with the universal. These last sentences have a certain sad and sober truth, which reminds us of the scripture of all nations. All expression of truth does at length take the deep ethical form. Here is hint of a place the most eligible of any in space, and of a servitor, in comparison with whom, all other helps dwindle into insignificance. We hope to hear more of him anon, for even a crystal palace would be deficient without his invaluable services.

And as for the environs of the establishment,

"There will be afforded the most enrapturing views to be fancied, cut of the private apartments, from the galleries, from the roof, from its turrets and cupolas,—gardens as far as the eye can see, full of fruits and flowers, arranged in the most beautiful order, with walks, colonnades, aqueducts, canals, ponds, plains, amphitheatres, terraces, fountains, sculptural works, pavilions, gondolas, places for public amusement, etc., to delight the eye and fancy, the taste and smell." . . . "The walks and roads are to be paved with hard vitrified, large plates, so as to be always clean from all dirt in any weather or season. . . . The channels being of vitrified substance, and the water perfectly clear, and filtrated or distilled if required, may afford the most beautiful scenes imaginable, while a variety of fishes is seen clear down to the bottom playing about, and the canals may afford at the same time, the means of gliding smoothly along between various sceneries of art and nature, in beautiful gondolas, while their surface and borders may be covered with fine land and aquatic birds. The walks may be covered with porticos adorned with magnificent columns, statues and sculptural works; all of vitrified substance, and lasting for ever, while the beauties of nature around heighten the magnificence and deliciousness."

"The night affords no less delight to fancy and feelings. An infinite variety of grand, beautiful and fanciful objects and sceneries, radiating with crystalline brilliancy, by the illumination of gas-light; the human figures themselves, arrayed in the most beautiful pomp fancy may suggest, or the eye desire, shining even with brilliancy of stuffs and diamonds, like stones of various colors, elegantly shaped and arranged around the body; all reflected a thousand-fold in huge mirrors and reflectors of various forms; theatrical scenes of a grandeur and magnificence, and enrapturing illusions, unknown yet, in which any person may be either a spectator or actor; the speech and the songs reverberating with increased sound, rendered more sonorous and harmonious than by nature, by vaultings that are moveable into any shape at any time; the sweetest and most impressive harmony of music, produced by song and instruments partly not known yet, may thrill through the nerves and vary with other amusements and delights."

"At night the roof, and the inside and outside of the whole square, are illuminated by gas-light, which in the mazes of many-colored crystal-like colonnades and vaultings, is reflected with a brilliancy that gives to the whole a lustre of precious stones, as far as the eye can see, — such are the future abodes of men." . . . "Such is the life reserved to true intelligence, but withheld from ignorance, prejudice, and stupid adherence to custom." . . . "Such is the domestic life to be enjoyed by every human individual that will partake of it. Love and affection may there be fostered and enjoyed without any of the obstructions that oppose, diminish, and destroy them in the present state of men." . . . "It would be as ridiculous, then, to dispute and quarrel about the means of life, as it would be now about water to drink along mighty rivers, or about the permission to breathe air in the atmosphere, or about sticks in our extensive woods."

Thus is Paradise to be Regained,[45] and that old and stern decree at length reversed. Man shall no more earn his living by the sweat of his brow. All labor shall be reduced to "a short turn of some crank," and "taking the finished article away." But there is a crank,—oh, how hard to be turned! Could there not be a crank upon a crank,—an infinitely small crank?—we would fain inquire. No,—alas! not. But there is a certain divine energy in every man, but sparingly employed as yet, which may be called the crank within,—the crank after all,—the prime mover in all machinery,—quite indispensable to all work. Would that we might get our hands on its handle! In fact no work can be shirked. It may be postponed indefinitely, but not infinitely. Nor can any really important work be made easier by co-operation or machinery. Not one particle of labor now threatening any man can be routed without being performed. It cannot be hunted out of the vicinity like jackals and hyenas. It will not run. You may begin by sawing the little sticks, or you may saw the great sticks first, but sooner or later you must saw them both.

We will not be imposed upon by this vast application of forces. We believe that most things will have to be accomplished still by the application called Industry. We are rather pleased after all to consider the small private, but both constant and accumulated force, which stands behind every spade in the field. This it is that makes the valleys shine, and the deserts really bloom. Sometimes, we confess, we are so de-generate as to reflect with pleasure on the days when men were yoked like cattle, and drew a crooked stick for a plough. After all, the great interests and methods were the same.

It is a rather serious objection to Mr. Etzler's schemes, that they require time, men, and money, three very superfluous and inconvenient things for an honest and well-disposed man to deal with. "The whole world,"

45 Allusion to Milton's *Paradise Regained*.

46 On common sense as practical sense, Thoreau wrote in *A Week on the Concord and Merrimack Rivers* that "common sense always takes a hasty and superficial view" [W 1:347]. For Thoreau, however, common sense also carried with it the meaning that came out of the Scottish common-sense school of philosophy, in particular, Thomas Reid's (1710–1796) *An Inquiry into the Human Mind, on the Principles of Common Sense,* which emphasized common sense as natural judgment from a set of innate principles of conception and belief implanted in the human mind by God. This is the antecedent of the concept of inspiration, which Emerson called in "Self-Reliance" "the essence of genius, of virtue, and of life, which we call Spontaneity or Instinct. We denote this primary wisdom as Intuition. . . . In that deep force, the last fact behind which analysis cannot go, all things find their common origin."

he tells us, "might therefore be really changed into a paradise, within less than ten years, commencing from the first year of an association for the purpose of constructing and applying the machinery." We are sensible of a startling incongruity when time and money are mentioned in this connection. The ten years which are proposed would be a tedious while to wait, if every man were at his post and did his duty, but quite too short a period, if we are to take time for it. But this fault is by no means peculiar to Mr. Etzler's schemes. There is far too much hurry and bustle, and too little patience and privacy, in all our methods, as if something were to be accomplished in centuries. The true reformer does not want time, nor money, nor co-operation, nor advice. What is time but the stuff delay is made of? And depend upon it, our virtue will not live on the interest of our money. He expects no income, but outgoes; so soon as we begin to count the cost the cost begins. And as for advice, the information floating in the atmosphere of society is as evanescent and unserviceable to him as gossamer for clubs of Hercules. There is absolutely no common sense;[46] it is common nonsense. If we are to risk a cent or a drop of our blood, who then shall advise us? For ourselves, we are too young for experience. Who is old enough? We are older by faith than by experience. In the unbending of the arm to do the deed there is experience worth all the maxims in the world.

> "It will now be plainly seen that the execution of the proposals is not proper for individuals. Whether it be proper for government at this time, before the subject has become popular, is a question to be decided; all that is to be done, is to step forth, after mature reflection, to confess loudly one's conviction, and to constitute societies. Man is powerful but in union with many. Nothing

great, for the improvement of his own condition, or that of his fellow men, can ever be effected by individual enterprise."

Alas! this is the crying sin of the age, this want of faith in the prevalence of a man. Nothing can be effected but by one man. He who wants help wants everything. True, this is the condition of our weakness, but it can never be the means of our recovery. We must first succeed alone, that we may enjoy our success together. We trust that the social movements which we witness indicate an aspiration not to be thus, cheaply satisfied. In this matter of reforming the world, we have little faith in corporations; not thus was it first formed.

But our author is wise enough to say, that the raw materials for the accomplishment of his purposes, are "iron, copper, wood, earth chiefly, and a union of men whose eyes and understanding are not shut up by preconceptions." Aye, this last may be what we want mainly,—a company of "odd fellows" indeed.[47]

"Small shares of twenty dollars will be sufficient,"—in all, from "200,000 to 300,000,"—"to create the first establishment for a whole community of from 3000 to 4000 individuals"—at the end of five years we shall have a principal of 200 millions of dollars, and so paradise will be wholly regained at the end of the tenth year. But, alas, the ten years have already elapsed, and there are no signs of Eden yet, for want of the requisite funds to begin the enterprise in a hopeful manner. Yet it seems a safe investment. Perchance they could be hired at a low rate, the property being mortgaged for security, and, if necessary, it could be given up in any stage of the enterprise, without loss, with the fixtures.

Mr. Etzler considers this "Address as a touchstone, to try whether our nation is in any way accessible to these great truths, for raising the human creature to a superior

47 Allusion to the fraternal organization, the Independent Order of Odd Fellows, to which Thoreau also referred in "Resistance to Civil Government": "The American has dwindled into an Odd Fellow,—one who may be known by the development of his organ of gregariousness, and a manifest lack of intellect and cheerful self-reliance; . . . who, in short, ventures to live only by the aid of the mutual insurance company, which has promised to bury him decently." The purpose of the organization was to give aid to those in need and to pursue projects for the benefit of all.

48 Quoted from Euripides' (ca. 480–406 B.C.E.) *Orestes* 420. When asked by Menelaus whether Loxias helps in his affliction, Orestes replies: "Not yet; and with respect to the future my prospects are no better."

state of existence, in accordance with the knowledge and the spirit of the most cultivated minds of the present time." He has prepared a constitution, short and concise, consisting of twenty-one articles, so that wherever an association may spring up, it may go into operation without delay; and the editor informs us that "Communications on the subject of this book may be addressed to C. F. Stollmeyer, No. 6, Upper Charles street, Northampton square, London."

But we see two main difficulties in the way. First, the successful application of the powers by machinery, (we have not yet seen the "Mechanical System,") and, secondly, which is infinitely harder, the application of man to the work by faith. This it is, we fear, which will prolong the ten years to ten thousand at least. It will take a power more than "80,000 times greater than all the men on earth could effect with their nerves," to persuade men to use that which is already offered them. Even a greater than this physical power must be brought to bear upon that moral power. Faith, indeed, is all the reform that is needed; it is itself a reform. Doubtless, we are as slow to conceive of Paradise as of Heaven, of a perfect natural as of a perfect spiritual world. We see how past ages have loitered and erred; "Is perhaps our generation free from irrationality and error? Have we perhaps reached now the summit of human wisdom, and need no more to look out for mental or physical improvement?" Undoubtedly, we are never so visionary as to be prepared for what the next hour may bring forth.

Μέλλει τὸ θεῖον δ'εστι τοιοῦτον φύσει.[48]

The Divine is about to be, and such is its nature. In our wisest moments we are secreting a matter, which, like the lime of the shell fish, incrusts us quite over, and well for us, if, like it, we cast our shells from time to time, though they be pearl and of fairest tint. Let us consider under what disadvantages science has hitherto labored before we pronounce thus confidently on her progress.

"There was never any system in the productions of human labor; but they came into existence and fashion as chance directed men." "Only a few professional men of learning occupy themselves with teaching natural philosophy, chemistry, and the other branches of the sciences of nature, to a very limited extent, for very limited purposes, with very limited means." "The science of mechanics is but in a state of infancy. It is true, improvements are made upon improvements, instigated by patents of government; but they are made accidentally or at hap-hazard. There is no general system of this science, mathematical as it is, which developes its principles in their full extent, and the outlines of the application to which they lead. There is no idea of comparison between what is explored and what is yet to be explored in this science. The ancient Greeks placed mathematics at the head of their education. But we are glad to have filled our memory with notions, without troubling ourselves much with reasoning about them."

Mr. Etzler is not one of the enlightened practical men, the pioneers of the actual, who move with the slow deliberate tread of science, conserving the world; who execute the dreams of the last century, though they have no dreams of their own; yet he deals in the very raw but still solid material of all inventions. He has more of the practical than usually belongs to so bold a schemer, so resolute a dreamer. Yet his success is in theory, and not in practice, and he feeds our faith rather than contents our understanding. His book wants order, serenity, dignity,

49 Thomas Carlyle (cf. "Thomas Carlyle and His Works") described the Islamic heaven in his *On Heroes, Hero-worship, and the Heroic in History* as a "gross sensual Paradise" but also wrote that "however gross and material," it is "an emblem of an everlasting truth, not always so well remembered elsewhere."

50 Carlyle also wrote in the above work: "On the whole, we will repeat that this Religion of Mahomet's is a kind of Christianity; has a genuine element of what is spiritually highest looking through it, not to be hidden by all its imperfections."

51 Allusion to Royall Tyler's (1757–1826) *The Contrast,* in which the character of Jonathan, in differentiating between a "servant" and a "waiter," is said to have made a "true Yankee distinction, egad, without a difference." Thoreau used the phrase in "Ktaadn," in "Slavery in Massachusetts," and several times in his journal.

everything,—but it does not fail to impart what only man can impart to man of much importance, his own faith. It is true his dreams are not thrilling nor bright enough, and he leaves off to dream where he who dreams just before the dawn begins. His castles in the air fall to the ground, because they are not built lofty enough; they should be secured to heaven's roof. After all, the theories and speculations of men concern us more than their puny execution. It is with a certain coldness and languor that we loiter about the actual and so called practical. How little do the most wonderful inventions of modern times detain us. They insult nature. Every machine, or particular application, seems a slight outrage against universal laws. How many fine inventions are there which do not clutter the ground? We think that those only succeed which minister to our sensible and animal wants, which bake or brew, wash or warm, or the like. But are those of no account which are patented by fancy and imagination, and succeed so admirably in our dreams that they give the tone still to our waking thoughts? Already nature is serving all those uses which science slowly derives on a much higher and grander scale to him that will be served by her. When the sunshine falls on the path of the poet, he enjoys all those pure benefits and pleasures which the arts slowly and partially realize from age to age. The winds which fan his cheek waft him the sum of that profit and happiness which their lagging inventions supply.

The chief fault of this book is, that it aims to secure the greatest degree of gross comfort and pleasure merely. It paints a Mahometan's heaven,[49] and stops short with singular abruptness when we think it is drawing near to the precincts of the Christian's,[50]—and we trust we have not made here a distinction without a difference.[51] Undoubtedly if we were to reform this outward life truly and thoroughly, we should find no duty of the inner omitted.

It would be employment for our whole nature; and what we should do there-after would be as vain a question as to ask the bird what it will do when its nest is built and its brood reared. But a moral reform must take place first, and then the necessity of the other will be superseded, and we shall sail and plough by its force alone. There is a speedier way than the Mechanical System can show to fill up marshes, to drown the roar of the waves, to tame hyenas, secure agreeable environs, diversify the land, and refresh it with "rivulets of sweet water," and that is by the power of rectitude and true behavior. It is only for a little while, only occasionally, methinks, that we want a garden. Surely a good man need not be at the labor to level a hill for the sake of a prospect, or raise fruits and flowers, and construct floating islands, for the sake of a paradise. He enjoys better prospects than lie behind any hill. Where an angel travels it will be paradise all the way, but where Satan travels it will be burning marl and cinders. What says Veeshnoo Sarma?[52] "He whose mind is at ease is possessed of all riches. Is it not the same to one whose foot is enclosed in a shoe, as if the whole surface of the earth were covered with leather?"[53]

He who is conversant with the supernal powers will not worship these inferior deities of the wind, the waves, tide, and sunshine. But we would not disparage the importance of such calculations as we have described. They are truths in physics, because they are true in ethics. The moral powers no one would presume to calculate. Suppose we could compare the moral with the physical, and say how many horse-power the force of love, for instance, blowing on every square foot of a man's soul, would equal. No doubt we are well aware of this force; figures would not increase our respect for it; the sunshine is equal to but one ray of its heat. The light of the sun is but the shadow of love. "The souls of men loving and fearing God," says Raleigh, "receive influence from

[52] Cf. "Natural History of Massachusetts," note 58.
[53] This quotation was included in "Extracts from the Heetopades of Veeshnoo Sarma," published in the July 1842 issue of *The Dial*.

54 Plato (428–347 B.C.E.), Greek philosopher and teacher.

55 Quoted from Sir Walter Raleigh's (1552 or 1554–1618) *The History of the World*. Thoreau lectured on Raleigh on 8 February 1843, incorporating parts of the lecture into *A Week on the Concord and Merrimack Rivers*.

56 Allusion to Archimedes, who is reported to have said, in describing the power of the lever: "Give me a place to stand and I will move the Earth." Thoreau similarly wrote in "Resistance to Civil Government": "They speak of moving society, but have no resting-place without it."

that divine light itself, whereof the sun's clarity, and that of the stars, is by Plato[54] called but a shadow. *Lumen est umbra Dei, Deus est Lumen Luminis.* Light is the shadow of God's brightness, who is the light of light,"[55] and, we may add, the heat of heat. Love is the wind, the tide, the waves, the sunshine. Its power is incalculable; it is many horse power. It never ceases, it never slacks; it can move the globe without a resting-place;[56] it can warm without fire; it can feed without meat; it can clothe without garments; it can shelter without roof; it can make a paradise within which will dispense with a paradise with-out. But though the wisest men in all ages have labored to publish this force, and every human heart is, sooner or later, more or less, made to feel it, yet how little is actually applied to social ends. True, it is the motive power of all successful social machinery; but, as in physics, we have made the elements do only a little drudgery for us, steam to take the place of a few horses, wind of a few oars, water of a few cranks and hand-mills; as the mechanical forces have not yet been generously and largely applied to make the physical world answer to the ideal, so the power of love has been but meanly and sparingly applied, as yet. It has patented only such machines as the almshouse, the hospital, and the Bible Society, while its infinite wind is still blowing, and blowing down these very structures, too, from time to time. Still less are we accumulating its power, and preparing to act with greater energy at a future time. Shall we not contribute our shares to this enterprise, then?

Wendell Phillips Before Concord Lyceum

1 Wendell Phillips (1811–1884), lawyer, politician, and social reformer, was a staunch supporter of the "no union with slaveholders" doctrine. He had spoken at the Concord Lyceum on 21 December 1842, 18 January 1844, and for the third time on 11 March 1845.

2 Allusion to the come-outers, an epithet coined in the 1830s for abolitionists who withdrew from established organizations, such as church or government, to protest a failure to take a strong position opposing slavery. The term comes from 2 Corinthians 6:17: "Wherefore come out from among them, and be ye separate, saith the Lord, and touch not the unclean thing; and I will receive you."

3 Allusion to Milton's *Paradise Lost* VII:31, in which the poet pleads with his muse to "fit audience find, though few."

Concord, Mass. March 12th, 1845.

Mr. Editor:

We have now, for the third winter, had our spirits refreshed, and our faith in the destiny of the Commonwealth strengthened, by the presence and the eloquence of Wendell Phillips;[1] and we wish to tender to him our thanks and our sympathy. The admission of this gentleman into the Lyceum has been strenuously opposed by a respectable portion of our fellow-citizens, who themselves, we trust, whose descendants, at least, we know, will be as faithful conservers of the true order, whenever that shall be the order of the day,—and in each instance, the people have voted that they *would hear him,* by coming themselves and bringing their friends to the lecture room, and being very silent that they *might* hear. We saw some men and women, who had long ago *come out,*[2] *going in* once more through the free and hospitable portals of the Lyceum; and many of our neighbors confessed, that they had had a "sound season" this once.

It was the speaker's aim to show what the State, and above all the Church, had to do, and now, alas! have done, with Texas and Slavery, and how much, on the other hand, the individual should have to do with Church and State. These were fair themes, and not mistimed; and his words were addressed to "fit audience, *and not few.*"[3]

We must give Mr. Phillips the credit of being a clean, erect, and what was once called a consistent man. He

4 Phillips probably made a similar statement to that he made before the American Ant-Slavery Society in New York on 7 May 1844, when he referred to "us, as the official representatives of the American Society."

5 Phrase found at the end of John Hancock's (1737–1793) "Proclamation for a Public Day of Thanksgiving," issued on 5 October 1791.

6 Echo of the phrase "There shall not be left here one stone upon another," found variantly in each of the four Gospels.

7 Frederick Douglass (1818–1895), abolitionist, orator, and writer.

at least is not responsible for slavery, nor for American Independence; for the hypocrisy and superstition of the Church, nor the timidity and selfishness of the State; nor for the indifference and willing ignorance of any. He stands so distinctly, so firmly, and so effectively, alone, and one honest man is so much more than a host, that we cannot but feel that he does himself injustice when he reminds us of "the American Society, which he represents."[4] It is rare that we have the pleasure of listening to so clear and orthodox a speaker, who obviously has so few cracks or flaws in his moral nature—who, having words at his command in a remarkable degree, has much more than words, if these should fail, in his unquestionable earnestness and integrity—and, aside from their admiration at his rhetoric, secures the genuine respect of his audience. He unconsciously tells his biography as he proceeds, and we see him early and earnestly deliberating on these subjects, and wisely and bravely, without counsel or consent of any, occupying a ground at first, from which the varying tides of public opinion cannot drive him.

No one could mistake the genuine modesty and truth with which he affirmed, when speaking of the framers of the Constitution,—"I am wiser than they," who with him has improved these sixty years' experience of its working; or the uncompromising consistency and frankness of the prayer which concluded, not like the Thanksgiving proclamations, with—"God save the Commonwealth of Massachusetts,"[5] but God dash it into a thousand pieces, till there shall not remain a fragment[6] on which a man can stand, and dare not tell his name—referring to the case of Frederick——;[7] to our disgrace we know not what to call him, unless Scotland will lend us the spoils of one of her Douglasses, out of history or fiction, for a season, till we be hospitable and brave enough to hear his proper name,—a fugitive slave in one more sense than we; who has proved himself the possessor of a *fair* intellect, and has won a colorless reputation in these parts; and who, we trust, will be as superior to degradation from the sympathies of Freedom, as from the antipathies of Slavery. When, said Mr. Phillips, he communicated to a New-Bedford audience, the other day,[8] his purpose of writing his life,[9] and telling his name, and the name of his master, and the place he ran from, the murmur ran round the room, and was anxiously whispered by the sons of the Pilgrims, "He had better not!" and it was echoed under the shadow of Concord monument,[10] "He had better not!"

We would fain express our appreciation of the freedom and steady wisdom, so rare in the reformer, with which he declared that he was not born to abolish slavery, but to do right. We have heard a few, a very few, good political speakers, who afforded us the pleasure of great intellectual power and acuteness, of soldier-like steadiness, and of a graceful and natural oratory; but in this man the audience might detect a sort of moral principle and integrity, which was more stable than their firmness, more discriminating than his own intellect, and more graceful than his rhetoric, which was not working for temporary or trivial ends. It is so rare and encouraging to listen to an orator, who is content with another alliance than with the popular party, or even with the sympathizing school of the martyrs, who can afford sometimes to be his own auditor if the mob stay away, and hears himself without reproof, that we feel ourselves in danger of slandering all mankind by affirming, that here is one, who is at the same time an eloquent speaker and a righteous man.

Perhaps, on the whole, the most interesting fact elicited by these addresses, is the readiness of the people at large, of whatever sect or party, to entertain, with good will and hospitality, the most revolutionary and heretical opinions, when frankly and adequately, and in some sort

8 Douglass had lived in New Bedford from 1838 to 1841. It was during this time he adopted the name Frederick Douglass.
9 Douglass's autobiography, *The Narrative of the Life of Frederick Douglass, An American Slave, Written by Himself,* was published in 1845.
10 Monument completed in 1837 to commemorate the site of the battle of 19 April 1775 when five hundred "Minutemen" successfully repelled the British at Concord.

11 Medicine composed of powders, or other in-
gredients, incorporated with some conserve,
honey, or syrup to the desired consistency to be
taken in doses.

12 Pagan.

13 As expressed in 2 Peter 1:5–7, these include
faith, virtue, knowledge, temperance, patience,
godliness, brotherly kindness, and charity.

14 Reference to an enclosed ground or field of
battle being open to allow acceptance of a challenge or engagement in a contest.

15 Allusion to the Redcrosse Knight in Edmund
Spenser's (1552–1599) *The Faerie Queene.*

cheerfully, expressed. Such clear and candid declaration of opinion served like an electuary[11] to whet and clarify the intellect of all parties, and furnished each one with an additional argument for that right he asserted.

We consider Mr. Phillips one of the most conspicuous and efficient champions of a true Church and State now in the field, and would say to him, and such as are like him—"God speed you." If you know of any champion in the ranks of his opponents, who has the valor and courtesy even of Paynim[12] chivalry, if not the Christian graces[13] and refinement of this knight, you will do us a service by directing him to these fields forthwith, where the lists[14] are now open, and he shall be hospitably enter-tained. For as yet the Red-cross knight[15] has shown us only the gallant device upon his shield, and his admi-rable command of his steed, prancing and curvetting in the empty lists; but we wait to see who, in the actual breaking of lances, will come tumbling upon the plain.

Thomas Carlyle and His Works

Thomas Carlyle[1] is a Scotchman, born about fifty years ago, "at Ecclefechan, Annandale," according to one authority.[2] "His parents 'good farmer people,' his father[3] an elder in the Secession church[4] there, and a man of strong native sense, whose words were said to 'nail a subject to the wall.'" We also hear of his "excellent mother,"[5] still alive, and of "her fine old covenanting accents, concerting with his transcendental tones."[6] He seems to have gone to school at Annan, on the shore of the Solway Frith, and there, as he himself writes, "heard of famed professors, of high matters classical, mathematical, a whole Wonderland of Knowledge," from Edward Irving,[7] then a young man "fresh from Edinburgh, with college prizes, &c." — "come to see our schoolmaster, who had also been his."[8] From this place, they say, you can look over into Wordsworth's country.[9] Here first he may have become acquainted with Nature, with woods, such as are there, and rivers and brooks, some of whose names we have heard, and the last lapses of Atlantic billows. He got some of his education, too, more or less liberal, out of the University of Edinburgh, where, according to the same authority, he had to "support himself," partly by "private tuition, translations for the booksellers, &c.," and afterward, as we are glad to hear, "taught an academy in Dysart, at the same time that Irving was teaching in Kirkaldy," the usual middle passage of a literary life. He was destined for the church, but not by the powers that rule man's life; made his literary debut in Fraser's Magazine,[10] long ago; read here and there in English and French, with more or

1 Thomas Carlyle (1795–1881), Scottish historian and essayist.

2 Quoted from George Gilfillan's (1813–1878) *Sketches of Modern Literature, and Eminent Literary Men.*

3 James Carlyle (1757–1832), a stonemason.

4 Founded in 1820, a Scottish Presbyterian denomination formed by a union of churches which had seceded from the Church of Scotland.

5 Margaret Aitken Carlyle (1771–1853) was James Carlyle's second wife.

6 Quoted from Gilfillan's *Sketches of Modern Literature, and Eminent Literary Men.*

7 Edward Irving (1792–1834), Scottish Presbyterian minister, who was convinced that the second coming of Christ was imminent and was accused of heresy by the London Presbytery when he developed his views on the human side of Christ. Carlyle met Jane Welsh, his future wife, through Irving.

8 Quoted from Carlyle's "Death of the Rev. Edward Irving," in his *Critical and Miscellaneous Pieces.*

9 The Lake District in the northwest of England, associated with William Wordsworth, Samuel Taylor Coleridge (1772–1834), and Robert Southey (1774–1843).

10 *Fraser's Magazine for Town and Country,* which began publication in London in 1830 and in which Carlyle published his "Jean Paul Friedrich Richter Again." This piece was not his literary debut and had been preceded by several pieces published in the *Edinburg Review* and the *Foreign Review.*

11 Quoted from Gilfillan's *Sketches of Modern Literature, and Eminent Literary Men.*

12 In 1833, following the death of his first wife, Ellen Tucker Emerson (1811–1831), Emerson went to England, where he met Wordsworth, Coleridge, and Carlyle, among others.

13 *The Correspondence of Thomas Carlyle and Ralph Waldo Emerson, 1834–1872* was collected and published in 1883.

14 Quoted from Carlyle's "Death of the Rev. Edward Irving" in his *Critical and Miscellaneous Pieces.*

15 Gilfillan wrote in *Sketches of Modern Literature, and Eminent Literary Men:* "He entered into a correspondence with Goethe, which lasted, at intervals, till the latter's death."

16 Probably from Emerson.

17 John Sterling (1806–1844), British novelist and poet whose papers were left to Carlyle and Julius Charles Hare (1795–1855).

18 A part of London known as a borough for artists.

19 Quoted from Elizur Wright's (1804–1885) description of Carlyle as published in Robert Turnbull's (1809–1877) *The Genius of Scotland.*

20 Quoted from Wright's description of Carlyle in Turnbull's *The Genius of Scotland.*

less profit, we may suppose, such of us at least as are not particularly informed, and at length found some words which spoke to his condition in the German language, and set himself earnestly to unravel that mystery—with what success many readers know.

After his marriage he "resided partly at Comely Bank, Edinburgh; and for a year or two at Craigenputtock, a wild and solitary farm-house in the upper part of Dumfriesshire,"[11] at which last place, amid barren heather hills, he was visited by our countryman Emerson.[12] With Emerson he still corresponds.[13] He was early intimate with Edward Irving, and continued to be his friend until the latter's death. Concerning this "freest, brotherliest, bravest human soul,"[14] and Carlyle's relation to him, those whom it concerns will do well to consult a notice of his death in Fraser's Magazine for 1835, reprinted in the Miscellanies. He also corresponded with Goethe.[15] Latterly, we hear,[16] the poet Sterling[17] was his only intimate acquaintance in England.

He has spent the last quarter of his life in London, writing books; has the fame, as all readers know, of having made England acquainted with Germany, in late years, and done much else that is novel and remarkable in literature. He especially is the literary man of those parts. You may imagine him living in altogether a retired and simple way, with small family, in a quiet part of London, called Chelsea,[18] a little out of the din of commerce, in "Cheyne Row," there, not far from the "Chelsea Hospital." "A little past this, and an old ivy-clad church, with its buried generations lying around it," writes one traveler, "you come to an antique street running at right angles with the Thames, and, a few steps from the river, you find Carlyle's name on the door."[19]

"A Scotch lass ushers you into the second story front chamber, which is the spacious workshop of the world maker."[20] Here he sits a long time together, with many books and papers about him; many new books, we have been told,[21] on the upper shelves, uncut,[22] with the "author's respects" in them; in late months, with many manuscripts in an old English hand, and innumerable pamphlets, from the public libraries, relating to the Cromwellian period;[23] now, perhaps, looking out into the street on brick and pavement, for a change, and now upon some rod of grass ground in the rear; or, perchance, he steps over to the British Museum, and makes that his studio for the time.[24] This is the fore part of the day; that is the way with literary men commonly; and then in the afternoon, we presume, he takes a short run of a mile or so through the suburbs out into the country; we think he would run that way, though so short a trip might not take him to very sylvan or rustic places. In the meanwhile, people are calling to *see* him, from various quarters, very few worthy of being *seen* by him, "distinguished travelers from America,"[25] not a few, to all and sundry of whom he gives freely of his yet unwritten rich and flashing soliloquy, in exchange for whatever they may have to offer; speaking his English, as they say, with a "broad Scotch accent,"[26] talking, to their astonishment and to ours, very much as he writes, a sort of Carlylese, his discourse "coming to its climaxes, ever and anon, in long, deep, chest-shaking bursts of laughter."[27]

He goes to Scotland sometimes to visit his native heath-clad hills, having some interest still in the earth there; such names as Craigenputtock and Ecclefechan, which we have already quoted, stand for habitable places there to him; or he rides to the seacoast of England in his vacations, upon his horse Yankee, bought by the sale of his books here, as we have been told.[28]

How, after all, he gets his living; what proportion of his daily bread he earns by day-labor or job-work with his pen, what he inherits, what steals—questions whose answers are so significant, and not to be omitted in his

21 Probably by Emerson.
22 Books with the adjacent pages still joined at the fore edge (i.e., unread).
23 Research for his *Oliver Cromwell's Letters and Speeches: With Elucidations* (London: Chapman and Hall, 1845).
24 The collections of the British Museum, which opened in 1759, were open to "all studious and curious Persons."
25 Thoreau's source for this quotation is unknown.
26 Several contemporary portraits of Carlyle refer to his "broad Scotch accent."
27 Quoted from Gilfillan's *Sketches of Modern Literature, and Eminent Literary Men.*
28 By Emerson, who read in Carlyle's letter to him of 25 September 1838: "My Wife says she received your American Bill of so many pounds sterling for the Revolution Book. . . . I will buy something permanent, I think, out of this £50, and call it either *Ebenezer* or *Yankee-doodle-doo.*" Carlyle never purchased the horse because he was given one.

29 Quoted from Gilfillan's *Sketches of Modern Literature, and Eminent Literary Men.*

30 Carlyle was six feet tall.

31 Raiders operating in the bogs on the borders of England and Scotland during the seventeenth century.

32 By Daniel Maclise (1806–1870) and published in the June 1833 issue of *Fraser's Magazine.*

33 By Alfred, Count D'Orsay (1801–1852), described by Emerson in a letter of 15 February 1842 to David H. Barlow as a "lithographed profile taken by Count D'Orsay who is, you know, the Emperor of European Dandies."

34 Emerson wrote in his journal of 19 October 1832: "If Carlyle knew what an interest I have in his persistent goodness, would it not be worth one effort more, one prayer, one meditation?"

35 Daniel Boone (1734–1820) and Davy Crockett (1786–1836), frontiersmen. Thoreau's spellings of their surnames were common in the nineteenth century.

biography—we, alas! are unable to answer here. It may be worth the while to state that he is not a Reformer, in our sense of the term, eats, drinks, and sleeps, thinks and believes, professes and practices, not according to the New England standard, nor to the Old English wholly. Nevertheless, we are told that he is a sort of lion in certain quarters there, "an amicable centre for men of the most opposite opinions," and "listened to as an oracle," "smoking his perpetual pipe."[29]

A rather tall,[30] gaunt figure, with intent face, dark hair and complexion, and the air of a student; not altogether well in body, from sitting too long in his workhouse, he, born in the border country and descended from moss-troopers,[31] it may be. We have seen several pictures of him here; one, a full length portrait, with hat and overall,[32] if it did not tell us much, told the fewest lies; another, we remember, was well said to have "too combed a look";[33] one other also we have seen in which we discern some features of the man we are thinking of; but the only ones worth remembering, after all, are those which he has unconsciously drawn of himself.

When we remember how these volumes came over to us, with their encouragement and provocation from month to month, and what commotion they created in many private breasts,[34] we wonder that the country did not ring, from shore to shore, from the Atlantic to the Pacific, with its greeting; and the Boons and Crockets[35] of the West make haste to hail him, whose wide humanity embraces them too. Of all that the packets have brought over to us, has there been any richer cargo than this? What else has been English news for so long a season? What else, of late years, has been England to us—to us who read books, we mean? Unless we remembered it as the scene where the age of Wordsworth was spending itself, and a few younger muses were trying their wings, and from time to time, as the residence of Landor;[36] Carlyle alone, since the death of Coleridge, has kept the promise of England. It is the best apology for all the bustle and the sin of commerce, that it has made us acquainted with the thoughts of this man. Commerce would not concern us much if it were not for such results as this. New England owes him a debt which she will be slow to recognize. His earlier essays reached us at a time when Coleridge's were the only recent words which had made any notable impression so far,[37] and they found a field unoccupied by him, before yet any words of moment had been uttered in our midst. He had this advantage, too, in a teacher, that he stood near to his pupils; and he has no doubt afforded reasonable encouragement and sympathy to many an independent but solitary thinker. Through him, as usher, we have been latterly, in a great measure, made acquainted with what philosophy and criticism the nineteenth century had to offer—admitted, so to speak, to the privileges of the century; and what he may yet have to say, is still expected here with more interest than any thing else from that quarter.

It is remarkable, but on the whole, perhaps, not to be lamented, that the world is so unkind to a new book. Any distinguished traveler who comes to our shores, is likely to get more dinners and speeches of welcome than he can well dispose of, but the best books, if noticed at all, meet with coldness and suspicion, or, what is worse, gratuitous, off-hand criticism. It is plain that the reviewers, both here and abroad, do not know how to dispose of this man. They approach him too easily, as if he were one of the men of letters about town, who grace Mr. Somebody's administration, merely; but he already belongs to literature, and depends neither on the favor of reviewers, nor the honesty of booksellers, nor the pleasure of readers for his success. He has more to impart than to receive from his generation. He is another such

36 William Savage Landor (1775–1864), best known for his *Imaginary Conversations,* whom Emerson met in 1833.
37 Coleridge, who died in 1834, was a major influence to the Transcendentalists through such philosophical works as *The Friend* (1810) and *Aids to Reflection* (1825).

38 Samuel Johnson (1709–1784), British author of *The History of Rasselas, Prince of Abyssinia* (cf. "A Walk to Wachusett," note 11) and *A Dictionary of the English Language.*

39 Many early reviews refer to what they considered defects in Carlyle's style. John Stuart Mill (1806–1873) wrote that the peculiarities of his style included "mannerisms, arising from some casual association of ideas, or some habit accidentally picked up; and what is worse, many sterling thoughts are so disguised in phraseology borrowed from the spiritualist school of German poets and metaphysicians, as not only to obscure the meaning, but to raise, in the minds of most English readers, a not unnatural nor inexcusable presumption of there being no meaning at all." William Makepeace Thackeray (1811–1863) wrote that never did "a man's style so mar his subject and dim his genius. It is stiff, short, and rugged, it abounds with Germanisms and Latinisms, strange epithets, and choking double words."

40 William Blackstone (1723–1780), British jurist and educator whose historical and analytic four-volume treatise *Commentaries on the Laws of England* was the most comprehensive work on English law.

41 The longest river in the Peloponnesus, which, according to Greek mythology, passes under the sea and emerges at Syracuse (Italy) in the fountain of Arethusa.

a strong and finished workman in his craft as Samuel Johnson[38] was, and like him, makes the literary class respectable. As few are yet out of their apprenticeship, or even if they learn to be able writers, are at the same time able and valuable thinkers. The aged and critical eye, especially, is incapacitated to appreciate the works of this author. To such their meaning is impalpable and evanescent, and they seem to abound only in obstinate mannerisms, Germanisms, and whimsical ravings of all kinds, with now and then an unaccountably true and sensible remark.[39] On the strength of this last, Carlyle is admitted to have what is called genius. We hardly know an old man to whom these volumes are not hopelessly sealed. The language, they say, is foolishness and a stumbling-block to them; but to many a clear-headed boy, they are plainest English, and despatched with such hasty relish as his bread and milk. The fathers wonder how it is that the children take to this diet so readily, and digest it with so little difficulty. They shake their heads with mistrust at their free and easy delight, and remark that "Mr. Carlyle is a very learned man"; for they, too, not to be out of fashion, have got grammar and dictionary, if the truth were known, and with the best faith cudgelled their brains to get a little way into the jungle, and they could not but confess, as often as they found the clue, that it was as intricate as Blackstone[40] to follow, if you read it honestly. But merely reading, even with the best intentions, is not enough, you must almost have written these books yourself. Only he who has had the good fortune to read them in the nick of time, in the most perceptive and recipient season of life, can give any adequate account of them.

Many have tasted of this well with an odd suspicion, as if it were some fountain Arethuse[41] which had flowed under the sea from Germany, as if the materials of his books had lain in some garret there, in danger of being appropriated for waste paper. Over what German ocean, from what Hercynian forest,[42] he has been imported, piece-meal, into England, or whether he has now all arrived, we are not informed. This article is not invoiced in Hamburg, nor in London. Perhaps it was contraband. However, we suspect that this sort of goods cannot be imported in this way. No matter how skillful the stevedore, all things being got into sailing trim, wait for a Sunday, and aft wind, and then weigh anchor, and run up the main-sheet—straightway what of transcendent and permanent value is there resists the aft wind, and will doggedly stay behind that Sunday—it does not travel Sundays; while biscuit and pork make headway, and sailors cry heave-yo! it must part company, if it open a seam. It is not quite safe to send out a venture in this kind, unless yourself go supercargo.[43] Where a man goes, there he is; but the slightest virtue is immovable—it is real estate, not personal; who would keep it, must consent to be bought and sold with it.

However, we need not dwell on this charge of a German extraction, it being generally admitted, by this time, that Carlyle is English, and an inhabitant of London. He has the English for his mother tongue, though with a Scotch accent, or never so many accents, and thoughts also, which are the legitimate growth of native soil, to utter therewith. His style is eminently colloquial—and no wonder it is strange to meet with in a book. It is not literary or classical; it has not the music of poetry, nor the pomp of philosophy, but the rhythms and cadences of conversation endlessly repeated. It resounds with emphatic, natural, lively, stirring tones, muttering, rattling, exploding, like shells and shot, and with like execution. So far as it is a merit in composition, that the written answer to the spoken word, and the spoken word to a fresh and pertinent thought in the mind, as well as to the half thoughts, the tumultuary misgivings and ex-

42 Hercynian Forest, an ancient forest of central Germany, extending at one time from the Rhine to the Carpathian Mountains, and described by Julius Caesar as having "gigantic oaks, uninjured by the lapse of ages, and contemporary with the creation of the world, by their near approach to immortality surpass all other marvels known. Not to speak of other matters that would surpass all belief, it is a well-known fact that their roots, as they meet together, upheave vast hills; or, if the earth happens not to accumulate with them, rise aloft to the very branches even, and, as they contend for the mastery, form arcades, like so many portals thrown open, and large enough to admit of the passage of a squadron of horse."

43 Person or officer placed in charge of specific cargo not by the owner of the vessel on which it is shipped but by the owner of the cargo.

44 From Samuel Butler's (1612–1680) "Hudibras" and quoted by Carlyle in "Goethe" in his *Critical and Miscellaneous Pieces:* "These funereal choristers, in Germany a loud, haggard, tumultuous, as well as tearful class, were named the *Kraftmänner,* or Power-men, but have all long since, like sick children, cried themselves to rest. Byron was our English Sentimentalist and Power-man; the strongest of his kind in Europe; the wildest, the gloomiest, and it may be hoped the last. For what good is it to 'whine, put finger i' the eye, and sob,' in such a case?"

45 Thoreau's source for this quotation is unknown.

46 Isaac Newton (1642–1727), British physicist who formulated laws of gravitation and motion; Sir Richard Arkwright (1732–1792), British inventor who established cotton mills utilizing machinery on a large scale; Humphrey Davy (1778–1829), British chemist and pioneer in electrochemistry.

47 Carlyle's 1837 prose work *The French Revolution: A History.* Thoreau used *poem* in the sense of which he wrote in *A Week on the Concord and Merrimack Rivers:* "A poem is one undivided, unimpeded expression fallen ripe into literature" [W 1:350]. Emerson wrote in "The Poet" that "it is not metres, but a metre-making argument, that makes a poem."

pectancies, this author is, perhaps, not to be matched in literature. In the streets men laugh and cry, but in books, never; they "whine, put finger i' the eye, and sob"[44] only. One would think that all books of late, had adopted the falling inflexion. "A mother, if she wishes to sing her child to sleep," say the musical men, "will always adopt the falling inflexion."[45] Would they but choose the rising inflexion, and wake the child up for once.

He is no mystic either, more than Newton or Arkwright, or Davy[46] — and tolerates none. Not one obscure line, or half line, did he ever write. His meaning lies plain as the daylight, and he who runs may read; indeed, only he who runs *can* read, and keep up with the meaning. It has the distinctness of picture to his mind, and he tells us only what he sees printed in largest English type upon the face of things. He utters substantial English thoughts in plainest English dialects; for it must be confessed, he speaks more than one of these. All the shires of England, and all the shires of Europe, are laid under contribution to his genius; for to be English does not mean to be exclusive and narrow, and adapt one's self to the apprehension of his nearest neighbor only. And yet no writer is more thoroughly Saxon. In the translation of those fragments of Saxon poetry, we have met with the same rhythm that occurs so often in his poem on the French Revolution.[47] And if you would know where many of those obnoxious Carlyleisms and Germanisms came from, read the best of Milton's prose, read those speeches of Cromwell which he has brought to light, or go and listen once more to your mother's tongue. So much for his German extraction.

Indeed, for fluency and skill in the use of the English tongue, he is a master unrivaled. His felicity and power of expression surpass even any of his special merits as a historian and critic. Therein his experience has not failed him, but furnished him with such a store of winged, aye, and legged words, as only a London life, perchance, could give account of; we had not understood the wealth of the language before. Nature is ransacked, and all the resorts and purlieus of humanity are taxed, to furnish the fittest symbol for his thought. He does not go to the dictionary, the word-book, but to the word-manufactory itself, and has made endless work for the lexicographers—yes, he has that same English for his mother-tongue, that you have, but with him it is no dumb, muttering, mumbling faculty, concealing the thoughts, but a keen, unwearied, resistless weapon. He has such command of it as neither you nor I have; and it would be well for any who have a lost horse to advertise, or a town-meeting warrant, or a sermon, or a letter to write, to study this universal letter-writer, for he knows more than the grammar or the dictionary.

The style is worth attending to, as one of the most important features of the man which we at this distance can discern. It is for once quite equal to the matter. It can carry all its load, and never breaks down nor staggers. His books are solid and workmanlike, as all that England does; and they are graceful and readable also. They tell of huge labor done, well done, and all the rubbish swept away, like the bright cutlery which glitters in shop-windows, while the coke and ashes, the turnings, filings, dust, and borings, lie far away at Birmingham,[48] unheard of. He is a masterly clerk, scribe, reporter, and writer. He can reduce to writing most things—gestures, winks, nods, significant looks, patois, brogue, accent, panto-mime, and how much that had passed for silence before, does he represent by written words. The countryman who puzzled the city lawyer, requiring him to write, among other things, his call to his horses,[49] would hardly have puzzled him; he would have found a word for it, all right and classical, that would have started his team for him. Consider the ceaseless tide of speech forever

48 In England, considered the first manufacturing town.

49 Thoreau's source for this anecdote is unknown.

50 Quoted from Carlyle's *The French Revolution: A History.*
51 Delivery of goods or letters.
52 Quoted from Carlyle's *The French Revolution: A History.*

flowing in countless cellars, garrets, *parlors;* that of the French, says Carlyle, "only ebbs toward the short hours of night,"[50] and what a drop in the bucket is the printed word. Feeling, thought, speech, writing, and we might add, poetry, inspiration—for so the circle is completed; how they gradually dwindle at length, passing through successive colanders, into your history and classics, from the roar of the ocean, the murmur of the forest, to the squeak of a mouse; so much only parsed and spelt out, and punctuated, at last. The few who can talk like a book, they only get reported commonly. But this writer reports a new "Lieferung."[51]

One wonders how so much, after all, was expressed in the old way, so much here depends upon the emphasis, tone, pronunciation, style, and spirit of the reading. No writer uses so profusely all the aids to intelligibility which the printer's art affords. You wonder how others had contrived to write so many pages without emphatic or italicised words, they are so expressive, so natural, so indispensable here, as if none had ever used the demonstrative pronouns demonstratively before. In another's sentences the thought, though it may be immortal, is, as it were, embalmed, and does not *strike* you, but here it is so freshly living, even the body of it, not having passed through the ordeal of death, that it stirs in the very extremities, and the smallest particles and pronouns are all alive with it. It is not simple dictionary *it,* yours or mine, but IT. The words did not come at the command of grammar, but of a tyrannous, inexorable meaning; not like standing soldiers, by vote of parliament, but any able-bodied countryman pressed into the service, for "sire, it is not a revolt, it is a revolution."[52]

We have never heard him speak, but we should say that Carlyle was a rare talker. He has broken the ice, and streams freely forth like a spring torrent. He does not trace back the stream of his thought, silently adventurous, up to its fountain-head, but is borne away with it, as it rushes through his brain like a torrent to overwhelm and fertilize. He holds a talk with you. His audience is such a tumultuous mob of thirty thousand, as assembled at the University of Paris, before printing was invented. Philosophy, on the other hand, does not talk, but write, or, when it comes personally before an audience, lecture or read; and therefore it must be read to-morrow, or a thousand years hence. But the talker must naturally be attended to at once; he does not talk on without an audience; the winds do not long bear the sound of his voice. Think of Carlyle reading his French Revolution to any audience. One might say it was never written, but spoken; and thereafter reported and printed, that those not within sound of his voice might know something about it. Some men read to you something which they have written, in a dead *language,* of course, but it may be in a living *letter,* in a Syriac, or Roman, or Runic character. Men must *speak* English who can *write* Sanscrit; and they must speak a modern language who write, perchance, an ancient and universal one. We do not live in those days when the learned used a learned language. There is no writing of Latin with Carlyle, but as Chaucer, with all reverence to Homer, and Virgil, and Messieurs the Normans, sung his poetry in the homely Saxon tongue; and Locke[53] has at least the merit of having done philosophy into English—so Carlyle has done a different philosophy still further into English, and thrown open the doors of literature and criticism to the populace.

Such a style—so diversified and variegated! It is like the face of a country; it is like a New England landscape, with farm-houses and villages, and cultivated spots, and belts of forests and blueberry-swamps round about it, with the fragrance of shad-blossoms and violets on certain winds. And as for the reading of it, it is novel enough

53 John Locke (1632–1704), British philosopher who wrote that knowledge is determined experientially through sensual perception.

54 Public stagecoach.

55 In New York, a system of passenger, freight, and mail coaches between Albany and Buffalo.

56 Roads were constructed in the beginning of the nineteenth century through the Simplon Pass between the Pennine and Lepontine Alps in Switzerland.

57 Winged horse of Greek mythology, a favorite of the muses and so associated with poetic inspiration.

58 Road or causeway constructed of logs laid together.

59 Long piece of timber, especially a principal horizontal beam.

60 Six-horse hitch.

61 Cracker at the end of a whip used to direct the lead horse.

62 Professor Gottfried Sauerteig, one of Carlyle's fictional mouthpieces, found in *Frederick the Great* and several essays. *Sauerteig* means "sourdough."

63 Wrestling moves possibly learned of his maternal uncle, Charles Dunbar (1780–1856), of whom he wrote: "People are talking about my Uncle Charles. Minott tells how he heard Tilly Brown once asking him to show him a peculiar (inside?) lock in wrestling. 'Now, don't hurt me, don't throw me hard.' He struck his antagonist inside his knees with his feet, and so deprived him of his legs" [J 8:245]. George Minott: cf. "Natural History of Massachusetts," note 45.

to the reader who has used only the diligence,[54] and old-line mail-coach.[55] It is like travelling, sometimes on foot, sometimes in a gig tandem; sometimes in a full coach, over highways, mended and unmended, for which you will prosecute the town; on level roads, through French departments, by Simplon roads over the Alps,[56] and now and then he hauls up for a relay, and yokes in an unbroken colt of a Pegasus[57] for a leader, driving off by cart-paths, and across lots, by corduroy roads[58] and gridiron bridges; and where the bridges are gone, not even a string-piece[59] left, and the reader has to set his breast and swim. You have got an expert driver this time, who has driven ten thousand miles, and was never known to upset; can drive six in hand[60] on the edge of a precipice, and touch the leaders anywhere with his snapper.[61]

With wonderful art he grinds into paint for his picture all his moods and experiences, so that all his forces may be brought to the encounter. Apparently writing without a particular design or responsibility, setting down his soliloquies from time to time, taking advantage of all his humors, when at length the hour comes to declare himself, he puts down in plain English, without quotation marks, what he, Thomas Carlyle, is ready to defend in the face of the world, and fathers the rest, often quite as defensible, only more modest, or plain spoken, or insinuating, upon "Sauerteig,"[62] or some other gentleman long employed on the subject. Rolling his subject how many ways in his mind, he meets it now face to face, wrestling with it at arm's length, and striving to get it down, or throws it over his head; and if that will not do, or whether it will do or not, tries the back-stitch and side-hug[63] with it, and downs it again—scalps it, draws and quarters it, hangs it in chains, and leaves it to the winds and dogs. With his brows knit, his mind made up, his will resolved and resistless, he advances, crashing his way through the host of weak, half-formed, *dilet-*

tante opinions, honest and dishonest ways of thinking, with their standards raised, sentimentalities and conjectures, and tramples them all into dust. See how he prevails; you don't even hear the groans of the wounded and dying. Certainly it is not so well worth the while to look through any man's eyes at history, for the time, as through his; and his way of looking at things is fastest getting adopted by his generation.

It is not in man to determine what his style shall be. He might as well determine what his thoughts shall be. We would not have had him write always as in the chapter on Burns,[64] and the Life of Schiller,[65] and elsewhere. No; his thoughts were ever irregular and impetuous. Perhaps as he grows older and writes more he acquires a truer expression; it is in some respects manlier, freer, struggling up to a level with its fountain-head. We think it is the richest prose style we know of.

Who cares what a man's style is, so it is intelligible— as intelligible as his thought. Literally and really, the style is no more than the *stylus,* the pen he writes with—and it is not worth scraping and polishing, and gilding, unless it will write his thoughts the better for it. It is something for use, and not to look at. The question for us is not whether Pope[66] had a fine style, wrote with a peacock's feather, but whether he uttered useful thoughts. Translate a book a dozen times from one language to another, and what becomes of its style? Most books would be worn out and disappear in this ordeal. The pen which wrote it is soon destroyed, but the poem survives. We believe that Carlyle has, after all, more readers, and is better known today for this very originality of style, and that posterity will have reason to thank him for emancipating the language, in some measure, from the fetters which a merely conservative, aimless, and pedantic literary class had imposed upon it, and setting an example of greater freedom and naturalness. No man's thoughts

64 "The Hero as Man of Letters. Johnson, Rousseau, Burns," in *On Heroes, Hero-Worship, and the Heroic in History.* Robert Burns (1759–1796) was a Scottish poet.

65 Carlyle's *The Life of Friedrich Schiller Comprehending an Examination of His Works* was published in 1825. Johann Christoph Friedrich von Schiller (1759–1805) was a German poet, philosopher, and playwright.

66 Alexander Pope (1688–1774), British poet known for his mock-epic poems "The Rape of the Lock" and "The Dunciad," as well as his translation of Homer. Thoreau had *The Iliad of Homer,* the 1812 two-volume edition of Pope's translation, with him at Walden.

67 Related to the Titans, the primordial giant gods of Greek mythology who ruled the earth before Zeus and were symbolic of great power and force.
68 Quoted from Carlyle's "Jean Paul Friedrich Richter Again," in *Critical and Miscellaneous Pieces*. Jean Paul Richter (1763–1825), German writer, two of whose works Carlyle published as "Army Chaplain Schmelzle's Journey to Flaetz" and "Life of Quintus Fixlein Down to Our Own Times Extracted From Fifteen Letter-Boxes by Jean-Paul."
69 The Augustan Age, in Rome, after Augustus Caesar (63 B.C.E.–14 C.E.) was a period of cultural advancement.

are new, but the style of their expression is the never failing novelty which cheers and refreshes men. If we were to answer the question, whether the mass of men, as we know them, talk as the standard authors and reviewers write, or rather as this man writes, we should say that he alone begins to write their language at all, and that the former is, for the most part, the mere effigies of a language, not the best method of concealing one's thoughts even, but frequently a method of doing without thoughts at all.

In his graphic description of Richter's style, Carlyle describes his own pretty nearly; and no doubt he first got his own tongue loosened at that fountain, and was inspired by it to equal freedom and originality. "The language," as he says of Richter, "groans with indescribable metaphors and allusions to all things, human and divine, flowing onward, not like a river, but like an inundation; circling in complex eddies, chafing and gurgling, now this way, now that"; but in Carlyle, "the proper current" never "sinks out of sight amid the boundless uproar." Again: "His very language is Titanian[67]—deep, strong, tumultuous, shining with a thousand hues, fused from a thousand elements, and winding in labyrinthic mazes."[68]

In short, if it is desirable that a man be eloquent, that he talk much, and address himself to his own age mainly, then this is not a bad style of doing it. But if it is desired rather that he pioneer into unexplored regions of thought, and speak to silent centuries to come, then, indeed, we could wish that he had cultivated the style of Goethe more, that of Richter less; not that Goethe's is the kind of utterance most to be prized by mankind, but it will serve commencing for a model of the best that can be successfully cultivated.

But for style, and fine writing, and Augustan ages[69]—that is but a poor style, and vulgar writing, and a degenerate age, which allows us to remember these things. This man has something to communicate. Carlyle's are not, in the common sense, works of art in their origin and aim; and yet, perhaps, no living English writer evinces an equal literary talent. They are such works of art only as the plough, and corn-mill, and steam-engine—not as pictures and statues. Others speak with greater emphasis to scholars, as such, but none so earnestly and effectually to all who can read. Others give their advice, he gives his sympathy also. It is no small praise that he does not take upon himself the airs, has none of the whims, none of the pride, the nice vulgarities, the starched, impoverished isolation, and cold glitter of the spoiled children of genius. He does not need to husband his pearl, but excels by a greater humanity and sincerity.

He is singularly serious and untrivial. We are every where impressed by the rugged, unwearied, and rich sincerity of the man. We are sure that he never sacrificed one jot of his honest thought to art or whim, but to utter himself in the most direct and effectual way, that is the endeavor. These are merits which will wear well. When time has worn deeper into the substance of these books, this grain will appear. No such sermons have come to us here out of England, in late years, as those of this preacher; sermons to kings, and sermons to peasants, and sermons to all intermediate classes. It is in vain that John Bull,[70] or any of his cousins, turns a deaf ear, and pretends not to hear them, nature will not soon be weary of repeating them. There are words less obviously true, more for the ages to hear, perhaps, but none so impossible for this age not to hear. What a cutting cimiter[71] was that "Past and Present," going through heaps of silken stuffs, and glibly through the necks of men, too, without their knowing it, leaving no trace. He has the earnestness of a prophet. In an age of pedantry and dilettantism, he has no grain of these in his com-

70 Common nineteenth-century name for the English.
71 Scimitar, a sword with a thin curved blade, known for its sharpness.

72 Muhammad (570–632), founder of Islam, and considered a prophet by Muslims.
73 Martin Luther (1483–1546), German theologian who taught that salvation came through faith, His opposition to sacerdotalism—salvation through the intervention of the priesthood—initiated the Protestant Reformation.
74 Latin: all works, i.e., collected works.
75 In his journal of 18 March 1842 Thoreau wrote: "He is essentially a humorist. But humors will not feed a man; they are the least satisfactory morsel to a healthy appetite" [J 1:336].
76 A place consecrated to religion, as a temple or church.

position. There is no where else, surely, in recent readable English, or other books, such direct and effectual teaching, reproving, encouraging, stimulating, earnestly, vehemently, almost like Mahomet,[72] like Luther;[73] not looking behind him to see how his *Opera Omnia*[74] will look, but forward to other work to be done. His writings are a gospel to the young of this generation; they will hear his manly, brotherly speech with responsive joy, and press forward to older or newer gospels.

We should omit a main attraction in these books, if we said nothing of their humor. Of this indispensable pledge of sanity, without some leaven, of which the abstruse thinker may justly be suspected of mysticism, fanaticism, or insanity, there is a super-abundance in Carlyle.[75] Especially the transcendental philosophy needs the leaven of humor to render it light and digestible. In his later and longer works it is an unfailing accompaniment, reverberating through pages and chapters, long sustained without effort. The very punctuation, the italics, the quotation marks, the blank spaces and dashes, and the capitals, each and all are pressed into its service.

Every man, of course, has his fane,[76] from which even the most innocent conscious humor is excluded; but in proportion as the writer's position is high above his fellows, the range of his humor is extended. To the thinker, all the institutions of men, as all imperfection, viewed from the point of equanimity, are legitimate subjects of humor. Whatever is not necessary, no matter how sad or personal, or universal a grievance, is, indeed, a jest more or less sublime.

Carlyle's humor is vigorous and Titanic, and has more sense in it than the sober philosophy of many another. It is not to be disposed of by laughter and smiles merely; it gets to be too serious for that—only they may laugh who are not hit by it. For those who love a merry jest, this is a strange kind of fun—rather too practical joking, if they understand it. The pleasant humor which the public loves, is but the innocent pranks of the ball-room, harmless flow of animal spirits, the light plushy pressure of dandy pumps, in comparison. But when an elephant takes to treading on your corns, why then you are lucky if you sit high, or wear cowhide. His humor is always subordinate to a serious purpose, though often the real charm for the reader, is not so much in the essential progress and final upshot of the chapter, as in this indirect side-light illustration of every hue. He sketches first with strong, practical English pencil, the essential features in outline, black on white, more faithfully than Dryasdust[77] would have done, telling us wisely whom and what to mark, to save time, and then with brush of camel's hair,[78] or sometimes with more expeditious swab, he lays on the bright and fast colors of his humor everywhere. One piece of solid work, be it known, we have determined to do, about which let there be no jesting, but all things else under the heavens, to the right and left of that, are for the time fair game. To us this humor is not wearisome, as almost every other is. Rabelais,[79] for instance, is intolerable; one chapter is better than a volume—it may be sport to him, but it is death to us. A mere humorist, indeed, is a most unhappy man; and his readers are most unhappy also.

Humor is not so distinct a quality as for the purposes of criticism, it is commonly regarded, but allied to every, even the divinest faculty. The familiar and cheerful conversation about every hearth-side, if it be analyzed, will be found to be sweetened by this principle. There is not only a never-failing, pleasant, and earnest humor kept up there, embracing the domestic affairs, the dinner, and the scolding, but there is also a constant run upon the neighbors, and upon church and state, and to cherish and maintain this, in a great measure, the fire is kept

77 The Reverend Doctor Jonathan Dryasdust, a fictitious antiquarian to whom Sir Walter Scott (1771–1832) dedicated some of his novels, and who Carlyle resurrected in several of his own works.
78 Small brush used by painters for fine work.
79 François Rabelais (ca. 1490–1553), French author, priest, and doctor. Emerson referred to "Rabelais's gigantic humors which astonish in order to force attention" in a 5 January 1872 letter to Carlyle.

80 In his "Jean Paul Friedrich Richter," in *Critical and Miscellaneous Pieces,* Carlyle wrote that humor is "the ruling quality with Richter; as it were the central fire that pervades and vivifies his whole being. He is a humorist from his inmost soul; he thinks as a humorist, he feels, imagines, acts as a humorist: Sport is the element in which his nature lives and works. A tumultuous element for such a nature, and wild work he makes in it! A Titan in his sport as in his earnestness, he oversteps all bound, and riots without law or measure."

burning, and the dinner provided. There will be neighbors, parties to a very genuine, even romantic friendship, whose whole audible salutation and intercourse, abstaining from the usual cordial expressions, grasping of hands, or affectionate farewells, consists in the mutual play and interchange of a genial and healthy humor, which excepts nothing, not even themselves, in its lawless range. The child plays continually, if you will let it, and all its life is a sort of practical humor of a very pure kind, often of so fine and ethereal a nature, that its parents, its uncles and cousins, can in no wise participate in it, but must stand aloof in silent admiration and reverence even. The more quiet the more profound it is. Even nature is observed to have her playful moods or aspects, of which man seems sometimes to be the sport.

But, after all, we could sometimes dispense with the humor, though unquestionably incorporated in the blood, if it were replaced by this author's gravity. We should not apply to himself, without qualification, his remarks on the humor of Richter.[80] With more repose in his inmost being, his humor would become more thoroughly genial and placid. Humor is apt to imply but a half satisfaction at best. In his pleasantest and most genial hour, man smiles but as the globe smiles, and the works of nature. The fruits *dry* ripe, and much as we relish some of them in their green and pulpy state, we lay up for our winter store, not out of these, but the rustling autumnal harvests. Though we never weary of this vivacious wit, while we are perusing its work, yet when we remember it from afar, we sometimes feel balked and disappointed, missing the security, the simplicity, and frankness, even the occasional magnanimity of acknowledged dullness and bungling. This never-failing success and brilliant talent become a reproach. To the most practical reader the humor is certainly too obvious and constant a quality. When we are to have dealings with a man, we prize the good faith and valor of soberness and gravity. There is always a more impressive statement than consists with these victorious comparisons. Besides, humor does not wear well. It is commonly enough said, that a joke will not bear repeating. The deepest humor will not keep. Humors do not circulate but stagnate, or circulate partially. In the oldest literature, in the Hebrew, the Hindoo, the Persian, the Chinese, it is rarely humor, even the most divine, which still survives, but the most sober and private, painful or joyous thoughts, maxims of duty, to which the life of all men may be referred. After time has sifted the literature of a people, there is left only their SCRIPTURE, for that is WRITING, *par excellence.* This is as true of the poets, as of the philosophers and moralists by profession; for what subsides in any of these is the moral only, to reappear as dry land at some remote epoch.

We confess that Carlyle's humor is rich, deep, and variegated, in direct communication with the back bone and risible[81] muscles of the globe—and there is nothing like it; but much as we relish this jovial, this rapid and detergous[82] way of conveying one's views and impressions, when we would not converse but meditate, we pray for a man's diamond edition[83] of his thought, without the colored illuminations in the margin—the fishes and dragons, and unicorns, the red or the blue ink, but its initial letter in distinct skeleton type,[84] and the whole so clipped and condensed down to the very essence of it, that time will have little to do. We know not but we shall immigrate soon, and would fain take with us all the treasures of the east, and all kinds of *dry,* portable soups, in small tin canisters, which contain whole herds of English beeves,[85] boiled down, will be acceptable.

The difference between this flashing, fitful writing and pure philosophy, is the difference between flame and light. The flame, indeed, yields light, but when we are

81 Having the faculty or power for, or inclination toward, laughter.
82 Cleansing.
83 An edition of a work printed in diamond, or in some other very small, type.
84 Any type in which the outline only of the letter or character is printed.
85 Plural of beef.

86 Allusion to Prometheus, who, in Greek mythology, stole fire from the gods and gave it to humankind.

so near as to observe the flame, we are apt to be incommoded by the heat and smoke. But the sun, that old Platonist, is set so far off in the heavens, that only a genial summer-heat and ineffable day-light can reach us. But many a time, we confess, in wintery weather, we have been glad to forsake the sun-light, and warm us by these Promethean flames.[86]

Carlyle must undoubtedly plead guilty to the charge of mannerism. He not only has his vein, but his peculiar manner of working it. He has a style which can be imitated, and sometimes is an imitator of himself. Every man, though born and bred in the metropolis of the world, will still have some provincialism adhering to him; but in proportion as his aim is simple and earnest, he approaches at once the most ancient and the most modern men. There is no mannerism in the Scriptures. The style of proverbs, and indeed of all *maxims,* whether measured by sentences or by chapters, if they may be said to have any style, is one, and as the expression of one voice, merely an account of the matter by the latest witness. It is one advantage enjoyed by men of science, that they use only formulas which are universal. The common language and the common sense of mankind, it is most uncommon to meet with in the individual. Yet liberty of thought and speech is only liberty to think the universal thought, and speak the universal language of men, instead of being enslaved to a particular mode. Of this universal speech there is very little. It is equable and sure; from a depth within man which is beyond education and prejudice.

Certainly, no critic has anywhere said what is more to the purpose, than this which Carlyle's own writings furnish, which we quote, as well for its intrinsic merit as for its pertinence here. "It is true," says he, thinking of Richter, "the beaten paths of literature lead the safeliest to the goal; and the talent pleases us most, which submits to shine with new gracefulness through old forms. Nor is the noblest and most peculiar mind too noble or peculiar for working by prescribed laws; Sophocles, Shakspeare, Cervantes,[87] and in Richter's own age, Goethe, how little did they innovate on the given forms of composition, how much in the spirit they breathed into them! All this is true; and Richter must lose of our esteem in proportion."[88] And again, in the chapter on Goethe, "We read Goethe for years before we come to see wherein the distinguishing peculiarity of his understanding, of his disposition, even of his way of writing, consists! It seems quite a simple style—that of his; remarkable chiefly for its calmness, its perspicuity, in short, its commonness; and yet it is the most uncommon of all styles."[89] And this, too, translated for us by the same pen from Schiller, which we will apply not merely to the outward form of his works, but to their inner form and substance. He is speaking of the artist. "Let some beneficent divinity snatch him, when a suckling, from the breast of his mother, and nurse him with the milk of a better time, that he may ripen to his full stature beneath a distant Grecian sky. And having grown to manhood, let him return, a foreign shape, into his century; not, however, to delight it by his presence, but, dreadful, like the son of Agamemnon,[90] to purify it. The matter of his works he will take from the present, but their form he will derive from a nobler time; nay, from beyond all time, from the absolute unchanging unity of his own nature."[91]

But enough of this. Our complaint is already out of all proportion to our discontent.

Carlyle's works, it is true, have not the stereotyped success which we call classic. They are a rich but inexpensive entertainment, at which we are not concerned lest the host has strained or impoverished himself to feed his guests. It is not the most lasting word, nor the loftiest wisdom, but rather the word which comes last.

87 Miguel de Cervantes (1547–1616), Spanish author of *Don Quixote*.
88 Quoted from Carlyle's "Jean Paul Friedrich Richter," in *Critical and Miscellaneous Pieces*.
89 Quoted from "Goethe." in *Critical and Miscellaneous Pieces*.
90 Orestes, in Greek mythology, was the son of Agamemnon and Clytemnestra. With his sister, Electra, he avenged the murder of his father by killing his mother and her lover Aegisthus.
91 Quoted from "State of German Literature," in *Critical and Miscellaneous Pieces*.

92 Cf. "Natural History of Massachusetts," note 74.

For his genius it was reserved to give expression to the thoughts which were throbbing in a million breasts. He has plucked the ripest fruit in the public garden; but this fruit already least concerned the tree that bore it, which was rather perfecting the bud at the foot of the leaf stalk. His works are not to be studied, but read with a swift satisfaction. Their flavor and gust is like what poets tell of the froth of wine, which can only be tasted once and hastily. On a review we can never find the pages we had read. The first impression is the truest and the deepest, and there is no reprint, no *double entendre,* so to speak, for the alert reader. Yet they are in some degree true natural products in this respect. All things are but once, and never repeated. The first faint blushes of the morning, gilding the mountain tops, the pale phosphor[92] and saffron-colored clouds do verily transport us to the morning of creation; but what avails it to travel eastward, or look again there an hour hence? We should be as far in the day ourselves, mounting toward our meridian. These works were designed for such complete success that they serve but for a single occasion. It is the luxury of art, when its own instrument is manufactured for each particular and present use. The knife which slices the bread of Jove ceases to be a knife when this service is rendered.

But he is wilfully and pertinaciously unjust, even scurrilous, impolite, ungentlemanly; calls us "Imbeciles," "Dilettants," "Philistines," implying sometimes what would not sound well expressed. If he would adopt the newspaper style, and take back these hard names—but where is the reader who does not derive some benefit from these epithets, applying them to himself? Think not that with each repetition of them there is a fresh overflowing of bile; oh no! Perhaps none at all after the first time, only a faithfulness, the right name being found, to apply it—"They are the same ones we meant before"—and ofttimes with a genuine sympathy and encouragement expressed. Indeed, there appears in all his writings a hearty and manly sympathy with all misfortune and wretchedness, and not a weak and sniveling one. They who suspect a Mephistophiles,[93] or sneering, satirical devil, under all, have not learned the secret of true humor, which sympathizes with the gods themselves, in view of their grotesque, half-finished creatures.

He is, in fact, the best tempered, and not the least impartial of reviewers. He goes out of his way to do justice to profligates and quacks. There is somewhat even Christian, in the rarest and most peculiar sense,[94] in his universal brotherliness, his simple, child-like endurance, and earnest, honest endeavor, with sympathy for the like. And this fact is not insignificant, that he is almost the only writer of biography, of the lives of men, in modern times. So kind and generous a tribute to the genius of Burns cannot be expected again, and is not needed. We honor him for his noble reverence for Luther,[95] and his patient, almost reverent study of Goethe's genius,[96] anxious that no shadow of his author's meaning escape him for want of trustful attention. There is nowhere else, surely, such determined and generous love of whatever is manly in history. His just appreciation of any, even inferior talent, especially of all sincerity, under whatever guise, and all true men of endeavor, must have impressed every reader. Witness the chapters on Werner, Heyne, even Cagliostro, and others.[97] He is not likely to underrate his man. We are surprised to meet with such a discriminator of kingly qualities in these republican and democratic days, such genuine loyalty all thrown away upon the world.

Carlyle, to adopt his own classification, is himself the hero, as literary man. There is no more notable working-man in England, in Manchester or Birmingham, or the mines round about. We know not how many hours a-day

93 In the Faust legend, the devil, or evil spirit, to whom Faust sold his soul.

94 Acting in the manner, or having the spiritual character, proper to a follower of Christ and not of the church, as Thoreau specifies elsewhere: "The Christians, now and always, are they who obey the higher law" [J 6:362], or "I expect the Christian not to be superstitious but to be distinguished by the clearness of his knowledge, the strength of his faith, the breadth of his humanity" [J 3:21].

95 Carlyle wrote about Luther in "Luther's Psalm" in *Critical and Miscellaneous Essays* and in "The Hero as Priest. Luther; Reformation: Knox; Puritanism," in *On Heroes, Hero-Worship, and the Heroic in History.*

96 In Carlyle's essays "Goethe's Helena," "Goethe," "Goethe's Portrait," "Death of Goethe," and "Goethe's Works" and his translations "Novelle" and "The Tale," all collected in *Critical and Miscellaneous Pieces.*

97 Carlyle's "Life and Writings of Werner," "The Life of Heyne," "Count Cagliostro: *Flight First,*" and "Count Cagliostro: *Flight Last,*" all collected in *Critical and Miscellaneous Pieces.*

98 Allusion to Genesis 3:19: "In the sweat of thy face shalt thou eat bread, till thou return unto the ground."

he toils, nor for what wages, exactly, we only know the results for us. We hear through the London fog and smoke the steady systole, diastole, and vibratory hum, from "Somebody's Works" there; the "Print Works," say some; the "Chemicals," say others; where something, at any rate, is manufactured which we remember to have seen in the market. This is the place, then. Literature has come to mean, to the ears of laboring men, something idle, something cunning and pretty merely, because the nine hundred and ninety-nine really write for fame or for amusement. But as the laborer works, and soberly by the sweat of his brow earns bread for his body,[98] so this man *works* anxiously and *sadly,* to get bread of life, and dispense it. We cannot do better than quote his own estimate of labor from Sartor Resartus.

"Two men I honor, and no third. First; the toil-worn craftsman that with earth-made implement laboriously conquers the earth, and makes her man's. Venerable to me is the hard hand; crooked, coarse, wherein, notwithstanding, lies a cunning virtue, indefeasibly royal, as of the sceptre of this planet. Venerable, too, is the rugged face, all weather-tanned, besoiled, with its rude intelligence; for it is the face of a man living manlike. Oh, but the more venerable for thy rudeness, and even because we must pity as well as love thee. Hardly-entreated brother! For us was thy back so bent, for us were thy straight limbs and fingers so deformed; thou wert our conscript, on whom the lot fell, and fighting our battles wert so marked. For in thee, too, lay a god-created form, but it was not to be unfolded; encrusted must it stand with the thick adhesions and defacements of labor; and thy body, like thy soul, was not to know freedom. Yet toil on, toil on; *thou* art in thy duty, be out of it who may; thou toilest for the altogether indispensable, for daily bread."

"A second man I honor, and still more highly; him who is seen toiling for the spiritually indispensable; not daily bread, but the bread of life. Is not he, too, in his duty, endeavoring toward inward harmony, revealing this, by act or by word, through all his out-ward endeavors, be they high or low? Highest of all, when his outward and his inward endeavor are one; when we can name him Artist; not earthly craftsman only, but inspired thinker, that with heaven-made implement conquers heaven for us. If the poor and humble toil that we have food, must not the high and glorious toil for him in return, that he have light, have guidance, freedom, immortality? These two in all their degrees, I honor; all else is chaff and dust, which let the wind blow whither it listeth."

"Unspeakably touching is it, however, when I find both dignities united; and he that must toil outwardly for the lowest of man's wants, is also toiling inwardly for the highest. Sublimer in this world know I nothing than a peasant saint, could such now anywhere be met with. Such a one will take thee back to Nazareth itself; thou wilt see the splendor of heaven spring forth from the humblest depths of earth, like a light shining in great darkness."[99]

Notwithstanding the very genuine, admirable, and loyal tributes to Burns, Schiller, Goethe, and others, Carlyle is not a critic of poetry. In the book of heroes, Shakspeare, the hero, as poet, comes off rather slimly. His sympathy, as we said, is with the men of endeavor; not using the life got, but still bravely getting their life. "In fact," as he says of Cromwell, "every where we have

[99] Quoted, with minor variants, from Carlyle's *Sartor Resartus.*

100 Quoted from "The Hero as King. Cromwell. Napoleon. Modern Revolutionism," in *On Heroes, Hero-Worship, and the Heroic in History*.

101 Allusion to Antaeus, in Greek mythology, a giant who, whenever he touched the earth, his mother, became stronger. He was defeated by Hercules, who, raising him so that he no longer made contact with the earth, squeezed him to death.

102 A pastoral elegy and a masque, respectively, by Milton.

103 Originally called the *Edinburgh Monthly Magazine* when William Blackwood (1776–1834) published the first number appeared in 1817, it was renamed *Blackwood's Magazine* with the seventh number.

104 Phrase coined by Carlyle in *Chartism* to emphasize the conditions of the working class in England.

105 No facts are known of Homer's life, but a tradition exists that he lived as a beggar, stemming from an ancient couplet found in the *Greek Anthology* and translated by Thomas Seward (1708–1790): "Seven wealthy towns contend for Homer dead / Through which the living Homer begged his bread."

106 Historical region of India.

107 Carlyle wrote about poetry in "The Hero as Poet. Dante. Shakespeare" and about the Norse Edda in "The Hero as Divinity. Odin. Paganism: Scandinavian Mythology," in *On Heroes, Hero-Worship, and the Heroic in History*.

to notice the decisive, practical *eye* of this man; how he drives toward the practical and practicable; has a genuine insight into what *is* fact."[100] You must have very stout legs to get noticed at all by him. He is thoroughly English in his love of practical men, and dislike for cant, and ardent enthusiastic heads that are not supported by any legs. He would kindly knock them down that they may regain some vigor by touching their mother earth.[101] We have often wondered how he ever found out Burns, and must still refer a good share of his delight in him to neighborhood and early association. The Lycidas and Comus[102] appearing in Blackwood's Magazine,[103] would probably go unread by him, nor lead him to expect a Paradise Lost. The condition of England question[104] is a practical one. The condition of England demands a hero, not a poet. Other things demand a poet; the poet answers other demands. Carlyle in London, with this question pressing on him so urgently, sees no occasion for minstrels and rhapsodists there. Kings may have their bards when there are any kings. Homer would *certainly* go a begging there.[105] He lives in Chelsea, not on the plains of Hindostan,[106] nor on the prairies of the West, where settlers are scarce, and a man must at least go *whistling* to himself.

What he says of poetry is rapidly uttered, and suggestive of a thought, rather than the deliberate development of any. He answers your question, What is poetry? by writing a special poem, as that Norse one,[107] for instance, in the Book of Heroes, altogether wild and original;—answers your question, What is light? by kindling a blaze which dazzles you, and pales sun and moon, and not as a peasant might, by opening a shutter. And, certainly, you would say that this question never could be answered but by the grandest of poems; yet he has not dull breath and stupidity enough, perhaps, to give the most deliberate and universal answer, such as the fates wring from illiterate and unthinking men. He answers like Thor,[108] with a stroke of his hammer, whose dint makes a valley in the earth's surface.

Carlyle is not a *seer*,[109] but a brave looker-on and *reviewer;* not the most free and catholic observer of men and events, for they are likely to find him pre-occupied, but unexpectedly free and catholic when they fall within the focus of his lens. He does not live in the present hour, and read men and books as they occur for his theme, but having chosen this, he directs his studies to this end.

But if he supplies us with arguments and illustrations against himself, we will remember that we may perhaps be convicted of error from the same source — stalking on these lofty reviewer's stilts so far from the green pasturage around. If we look again at his page, we are apt to retract somewhat that we have said. Often a genuine poetic feeling dawns through it, like the texture of the earth seen through the dead grass and leaves in the spring. There is indeed more poetry in this author than criticism on poetry. He often reminds us of the ancient Scald,[110] inspired by the grimmer features of life, dwelling longer on Dante than on Shakspeare. We have not recently met with a more solid and unquestionable piece of poetic work than that episode of "The Ancient Monk," in Past and Present,[111] at once idyllic, narrative, heroic; a beautiful restoration of a past age. There is nothing like it elsewhere that we know of. The History of the French Revolution is a poem, at length got translated into prose; an Iliad, indeed, as he himself has it — "The destructive wrath of Sansculottism:[112] this is what we speak, having unhappily no voice for singing."[113]

One improvement we could suggest in this last, as indeed in most epics, that he should let in the sun oftener upon his picture. It does not often enough appear, but it is all revolution, the old way of human life turned simply bottom upward, so that when at length we are inadver-

108 In Norse mythology, god of thunder.
109 Literally one who sees, and by extension a prophet, but also a poet, as Thoreau wrote in *A Week on the Concord and Merrimack Rivers:* "The bard has in a great measure lost the dignity and sacredness of his office. Formerly he was called a seer, but now it is thought that one man sees as much as another" [W I:392]. Emerson in his "Divinity School Address" wrote: "Always the seer is a sayer. Somehow his dream is told; somehow he publishes it with solemn joy: sometimes with pencil on canvas, sometimes with chisel on stone, sometimes in towers and aisles of granite, his soul's worship is builded; sometimes in anthems of indefinite music; but clearest and most permanent, in words."
110 Ancient Scandinavian poet.
111 "The Ancient Monk," in Carlyle's *Past and Present,* was about Jocelin of Brakelond (d. 1211), French monk, known only through his chronicle of *Chronica Jocelini de Brakelond de Rebus Gestis Samsonis Abbatis Monasterii Sancti Edmundi.*
112 Holding extreme republican principles, from the sans-culottes, meaning "without breeches," and used as a name of reproach.
113 Quoted from *The French Revolution: A History.*

114 Shipping between Brest, France, and the French Caribbean sugar colony Saint-Domingue.
115 Revolutions followed the emancipation of slaves in 1791.
116 Knotted to increase damage or pain inflicted during a whipping.
117 Archibald Alison's (1792–1867) multivolume *History of Europe from the Commencement of the French Revolution in 1789 to the Restoration of the Bourbons in 1814.*
118 In Norse mythology, a race of giants.

tently reminded of the "Brest Shipping," a St. Domingo colony,[114] and that anybody thinks of owning plantations, and simply turning up the soil there, and that now at length, after some years of this revolution, there is a falling off in the importation of sugar, we feel a queer surprise.[115] Had they not sweetened their water with Revolution then? It would be well if there were several chapters headed "Work for the Month"—Revolution-work inclusive, of course—"Altitude of the Sun," "State of the Crops and Markets," "Meteorological Observations," "Attractive Industry," "Day Labor," &c., just to remind the reader that the French peasantry did something beside go without breeches, burn châteaus, get ready knotted cords,[116] and embrace and throttle one another by turns. These things are sometimes hinted at, but they deserve a notice more in proportion to their importance. We want not only a background to the picture, but a ground under the feet also. We remark, too, occasionally, an unphilosophical habit, common enough elsewhere, in Alison's History of Modern Europe,[117] for instance, of saying, undoubtedly with effect, that if a straw had not fallen this way or that, why then—but, of course, it is as easy in philosophy to make kingdoms rise and fall as straws. The old adage is as true for our purpose, which says that a miss is as good as a mile. Who shall say how near the man came to being killed who was not killed? If an apple had not fallen then we had never heard of Newton and the law of gravitation; as if they could not have contrived to let fall a pear as well.

The poet is blithe and cheery ever, and as well as nature. Carlyle has not the simple Homeric health of Wordsworth, nor the deliberate philosophic turn of Coleridge, nor the scholastic taste of Landor, but, though sick and under restraint, the constitutional vigor of one of his old Norse heroes, struggling in a lurid light, with Jötuns[118] still, striving to throw the old woman,

and "she was Time"—striving to lift the big cat—
and that was "The Great World-Serpent which, tail in
mouth, girds and keeps up the whole created world."[119]
The smith, though so brawny and tough, I should not
call the healthiest man. There is too much shop-work,
too great extremes of heat and cold, and incessant ten-
pound-ten[120] and thrashing of the anvil, in his life. But
the haymaker's is a true sunny perspiration, produced
by the extreme of summer heat only, and conversant
with the blast of the zephyr, not of the forge-bellows.
We know very well the nature of this man's sadness, but
we do not know the nature of his gladness. There sits
Bull in the court all the year round, with his hoarse bark
and discontented growl—not a cross dog, only a canine
habit, verging to madness some think—now separated
from the shuddering travelers only by the paling, now
heard afar in the horizon, even melodious there; baying
the moon o' nights, *baying the sun by day,* with his mastiff
mouth. He never goes after the cows, nor stretches in the
sun, nor plays with the children. Pray give him a longer
rope, ye gods, or let him go at large, and never taste raw
meat more.

The poet will maintain serenity in spite of all disap-
pointments. He is expected to preserve an unconcerned
and healthy outlook over the world while he lives. *Philosophia practica est eruditionis meta,*[121] philosophy practiced is the goal of learning; and for that other, *Ora-
toris est celare artem,*[122] we might read, *Herois est celare
pugnam,* the hero will conceal his struggles. Poetry is the
only life got, the only work done, the only pure product
and free labor of man, performed only when he has put
all the world under his feet, and conquered the last of his
foes.

Carlyle speaks of Nature with a certain unconscious
pathos for the most part. She is to him a receded but ever
memorable splendor, casting still a reflected light over all

119 Quoted from "The Hero as Divinity. Odin.
Paganism: Scandinavian Mythology," in *On
Heroes, Hero-Worship, and the Heroic in History.*
120 Ten-pound hammer and anvil.
121 Listed under "Ethicas" under "Theses Philosophicaus" from "The Theses of the First Class of
Graduates from Harvard College, in 1642."
122 Listed under "Rhetoricas" under "Theses
Philosophicaus" from "The Theses of the First
Class of Graduates from Harvard College, in
1642."

123 Chief god of Norse mythology.

his scenery. As we read his books here in New England, where there are potatoes enough, and every man can get his living peacefully and sportively as the birds and bees, and need think no more of that, it seems to us as if by the world he often meant London, at the head of the tide upon the Thames, the sorest place on the face of the earth, the very citadel of conservatism. Possibly a South African village might have furnished a more hopeful, and more exacting audience, or in the silence of the wilderness and the desert, he might have addressed himself more entirely to his true audience posterity.

In his writings, we should say that he, as conspicuously as any, though with little enough expressed or even conscious sympathy, represents the Reformer class, and all the better for not being the acknowledged leader of any. In him the universal plaint is most settled, unappeasable and serious. Until a thousand named and nameless grievances are righted, there will be no repose for him in the lap of nature, or the seclusion of science and literature. By foreseeing it he hastens the crisis in the affairs of England, and is as good as many years added to her history.

As we said, we have no adequate word from him concerning poets—Homer, Shakspeare; nor more, we might add, of Saints—Jesus; nor philosophers—Socrates, Plato; nor mystics—Swedenborg. He has no articulate sympathy at least with such as these as yet. Odin,[123] Mahomet, Cromwell, will have justice at his hands, and we would leave him to write the eulogies of all the giants of the will, but the kings of men, whose kingdoms are wholly in the hearts of their subjects, strictly transcendent and moral greatness, what is highest and worthiest in character, he is not inclined to dwell upon or point to. To do himself justice, and set some of his readers right, he should give us some transcendent hero at length, to rule his demigods and Titans; develop, perhaps, his re-

served and dumb reverence for Christ, not speaking to
a London or Church of England audience merely. Let
not "sacred silence meditate that sacred matter"[124] forever, but let us have sacred speech and sacred scripture
thereon. True reverence is not necessarily dumb, but ofttimes prattling and hilarious as children in the spring.

Every man will include in his list of worthies those
whom he himself best represents. Carlyle, and our
countryman Emerson, whose place and influence
must ere long obtain a more distinct recognition, are,
to a certain extent, the complement of each other. The
age could not do with one of them, it cannot do with
both. To make a broad and rude distinction, to suit
our present purpose, the former, as critic, deals with
the men of action—Mahomet, Luther, Cromwell; the
latter with the thinkers—Plato, Shakspeare, Goethe,
for though both have written upon Goethe, they do
not meet in him. The one has more sympathy with the
heroes, or practical reformers, the other with the observers, or philosophers. Put these worthies together,
and you will have a pretty fair representation of mankind; yet with one or more memorable exceptions. To
say nothing of Christ, who yet awaits a just appreciation from literature, the peacefully practical hero, whom
Columbus may represent, is obviously slighted; but
above and after all, the Man of the Age, come to be
called working-man, it is obvious that none yet speaks
to his condition, for the speaker is not yet in his condition. There is poetry and prophecy to cheer him, and
advice of the head and heart to the hands; but no very
memorable coöperation, it must be confessed, since the
Christian era, or rather since Prometheus tried it. It is
even a note-worthy fact, that a man addresses effectually in another only himself still, and what he himself
does and is, alone can he prompt the other to do and
to become. Like speaks to like only; labor to labor, phi-

124 Quoted from "The Hero as Divinity. Odin.
Paganism: Scandinavian Mythology," in *On
Heroes, Hero-Worship, and the Heroic in History:* "The greatest of all Heroes is One whom
we do not name here! The greatest of all Heroes
is One whom we do not name here! Let sacred
silence meditate that sacred matter; you will find
it the ultimate perfection of a principle extant
throughout man's whole history on earth."

125 Traps, snares.
126 Roof formed like an inclined plane, the slope being all on one side.

losophy to philosophy, criticism to criticism, poetry to poetry, &c. Literature speaks how much still to the past, how little to the future, how much to the east, how little to the west—

In the East fames are won,
In the West deeds are done.

One more merit in Carlyle, let the subject be what it may, is the freedom of prospect he allows, the entire absence of cant and dogma. He removes many cart-loads of rubbish, and leaves open a broad highway. His writings are all unfenced on the side of the future and the possible. He does not place himself across the passage out of his books, so that none may go freely out, but rather by the entrance, inviting all to come in and go through. No gins,[125] no net-work, no pickets here, to restrain the free thinking reader. In many books called philosophical, we find ourselves running hither and thither, under and through, and sometimes quite unconsciously straddling some imaginary fence-work, which in our clairvoyance we had not noticed, but fortunately, not with such fatal consequences as happen to those birds which fly against a white-washed wall, mistaking it for fluid air. As we proceed the wreck of this dogmatic tissue collects about the organs of our perception, like cobwebs about the muzzles of hunting dogs in dewy mornings. If we look up with such eyes as these authors furnish, we see no heavens, but a low pent-roof[126] of straw or tiles, as if we stood under a shed, with no sky-light through which to glimpse the blue.

Carlyle, though he does but inadvertently direct our eyes to the open heavens, nevertheless, lets us wander broadly underneath, and shows them to us reflected in innumerable pools and lakes. We have from him, occasionally, some hints of a possible science of astronomy even, and revelation of heavenly arcana,[127] but nothing definite hitherto.

These volumes contain not the highest, but a very practicable wisdom, which startles and provokes, rather than informs us. Carlyle does not oblige us to think; we have thought enough for him already, but he compels us to act. We accompany him rapidly through an endless gallery of pictures, and glorious reminiscences of experiences unimproved. "Have you not had Moses and the prophets? Neither will ye be persuaded if one should rise from the dead."[128] There is no calm philosophy of life here, such as you might put at the end of the Almanac, to hang over the farmer's hearth, how men shall live in these winter, in these summer days. No philosophy, properly speaking, of love, or friendship, or religion, or politics, or education, or nature, or spirit; perhaps a nearer approach to a philosophy of kingship, and of the place of the literary man, than of any thing else. A rare preacher, with prayer, and psalm, and sermon, and benediction, but no contemplation of man's life from serene oriental ground, nor yet from the stirring occidental. No thanksgiving sermon for the holydays, or the Easter vacations, when all men submit to float on the full currents of life. When we see with what spirits, though with little heroism enough, wood-choppers, drovers, and apprentices, take and spend life, playing all day long, sunning themselves, shading themselves, eating, drinking, sleeping, we think that the philosophy of their life written would be such a level natural history as the Gardener's Calendar,[129] and the works of the early botanists, inconceivably slow to come to practical conclusions; its premises away off before the first morning light, ere the heather was introduced into the British isles, and no inferences to be drawn during this noon of the day, not till after the remote evening shadows have begun to fall around.

127 Secrets; mysteries.
128 Allusion to Luke 16:31: "And he said unto him, If they hear not Moses and the prophets, neither will they be persuaded, though one rose from the dead."
129 Possible reference to Bernard M'Mahon's (or McMahon) (ca. 1775–1816) *American Gardeners Calendar* published in 1802 or similar works.

130 Attributed to, among others, Socrates (469–399 B.C.E.) although its origin is unknown. It is found chiseled over the portals of the ancient Greek temple of Apollo at Delphi. *Demosthenes* 3 in Plutarch's *Parallel Lives*, which Thoreau is known to have read, contains the line: "If the 'Know thyself' of the oracle were an easy thing for every man, it would not be held to be a divine injunction." Emerson, in "The American Scholar," wrote, "And, in fine, the ancient precept, 'Know thyself,' and the modern precept, 'Study nature,' become at last one maxim."

131 Carlyle wrote in *Past and Present*: "'Know thyself': long enough has that poor 'self' of thine tormented thee; thou wilt never get to 'know' it, I believe! . . . Thou art an unknowable individual: know what thou canst work at, and work at like, like a Hercules! That will be a better plan."

132 Sophia Hawthorne (1809–1871)—wife of Nathaniel Hawthorne (1804–1864)—described Thoreau as "an experienced skater" who figured "dithyrambic dances and Bacchic leaps on the ice."

133 Quagmire related to Lake Serbonis in Egypt, which Milton described in *Paradise Lost* II:592–594 as a "gulf profound . . . / Betwixt *Damiata* and Mount *Casius* old, / Where Armies whole have sunk."

134 All three quotations, from *Sartor Resartus,* are based on lines from Goethe's *Wilhelm Meister*. Thoreau quoted the last in his journal of 8 August 1856: "When I came forth, thinking to empty my boat and go a-meditating along the river . . . I learned to my chagrin that Father's pig was gone. He had leaped out of the pen some time since his breakfast, but his dinner was untouched. . . . I felt chagrined, it is true, but I could not ignore the fact nor shirk the duty that lay so near to me. Do the duty that lies nearest to thee" [J 8:451].

There is no philosophy here for philosophers, only as every man is said to have his philosophy. No system but such as is the man himself; and, indeed, he stands compactly enough. No progress beyond the first assertion and challenge, as it were, with trumpet blast. One thing is certain, that we had best be doing something in good earnest, henceforth forever; that's an indispensable philosophy. The before impossible precept, *"know thyself,"*[130] he translates into the partially possible one, *"know what thou canst work at."*[131] Sartor Resartus is, perhaps, the sunniest and most philosophical, as it is the most autobiographical of his works, in which he drew most largely on the experience of his youth. But we miss everywhere a calm depth, like a lake, even stagnant, and must submit to rapidity and whirl, as on skates, with all kinds of skillful and antic motions, sculling, sliding, cutting punch-bowls and rings, forward and backward.[132] The talent is very nearly equal to the genius. Sometimes it would be preferable to wade slowly through a Serbonian bog,[133] and feel the juices of the meadow. We should say that he had not speculated far, but faithfully, living up to it. He lays all the stress still on the most elementary and initiatory maxims, introductory to philosophy. It is the experience of the religionist. He pauses at such a quotation as, "It is only with renunciation that life, properly speaking, can be said to begin"; or, "Doubt of any sort cannot be removed except by action"; or, "Do the duty which lies nearest thee."[134] The chapters entitled, "The Everlasting No," and "The Everlasting Yea," contain what you might call the religious experience of his hero. In the latter, he assigns to him these words, brief, but as significant as any we remember in this author—"One BIBLE I know, of whose plenary inspiration doubt is not so much as possible; nay, with my own eyes I saw the God's-hand writing it: thereof all other Bibles are but leaves." This belongs to "The Everlasting Yea"; yet he lingers unaccountably in "The Everlasting No," under the negative pole. "Truth!" he still cries with Teufelsdröckh, "though the heavens crush me for following her: no falsehood! though a whole celestial Lubberland[135] were the price of apostacy."[136] Again, "Living without God in the world, of God's light I was not utterly bereft; if my as yet sealed eyes, with their unspeakable longing, could nowhere see Him, nevertheless, in my heart He was present, and His heaven-written law still stood legible and sacred there."[137] Again, "Ever from that time, [*the era of his Protest,*] the temper of my misery was changed: not fear or whining sorrow was it, but indignation and grim, fire-eyed defiance." And in the "Centre of Indifference," as editor, he observes, that "it was no longer a quite hopeless unrest," and then proceeds, not in his best style, "For the fire-baptized soul, long so scathed and thunder-riven, here feels its own freedom, which feeling is its Baphometic Baptism:[138] the citadel of its whole kingdom it has thus gained by assault, and will keep inexpugnable;[139] outward from which the remaining dominions, not, indeed, without hard battling, will doubtless by degrees be conquered and pacificated."

Beside some philosophers of larger vision, Carlyle stands like an honest, half-despairing boy, grasping at some details only of their world systems. Philosophy, certainly, is some account of truths, the fragments and very insignificant parts of which man will practice in this work-shop; truths infinite and in harmony with infinity; in respect to which the very objects and ends of the so-called practical philosopher, will be mere propositions, like the rest. It would be no reproach to a philosopher, that he knew the future better than the past, or even than the present. It is better worth knowing. He will prophesy, tell what is to be, or in other words, what alone is, under appearances, laying little stress on the boiling of the pot, or the Condition of England question. He has

135 Land of Cockaigne, an imaginary land of luxury and idleness.
136 Quoted from *Sartor Resartus*. Carlyle's book purports to be the life and opinions of a German philosopher named Diogenes Teufelsdröckh Teufelsdröckh ("devil's dung").
137 Quoted from *Sartor Resartus*, as are the following quotations.
138 A baptism of fire. Baphomet was a symbolical figure, a corruption of Mahomet, which the Templars were said to have used in their rites.
139 Not to be subdued by force; impregnable.

140 Allusion to Robert Burns's 1795 song by the same name.

141 Allusion to Hamlet I.v.168–169: "There are more things in heaven and earth, Horatio, / Than are dreamt of in our philosophy."

no more to do with the condition of England than with her national debt, which a vigorous generation would not inherit. The philosopher's conception of things will, above all, be truer than other men's, and his philosophy will subordinate all the circumstances of life. To live like a philosopher, is to live, not foolishly, like other men, but wisely, and according to universal laws. In this, which was the ancient sense, we think there has been no philosopher in modern times. The wisest and most practical men of recent history, to whom this epithet has been hastily applied, have lived comparatively meagre lives, of conformity and tradition, such as their fathers transmitted to them. But a man may live in what style he can. Between earth and heaven, there is room for all kinds. If he take counsel of fear and prudence, he has already failed. One who believed, by his very constitution, some truth which a few words express, would make a revolution never to be forgotten in this world; for it needs but a fraction of truth to found houses and empires on.

However, such distinctions as poet and philosopher, do not much assist our final estimate of a man; we do not lay much stress on them. "A man's a man for a' that."[140] If Carlyle does not take two steps in philosophy, are there any who take three? Philosophy having crept clinging to the rocks, so far, puts out its feelers many ways in vain. It would be hard to surprise him by the relation of any important human experience, but in some nook or corner of his works, you will find that this, too, was sometimes dreamed of in his philosophy.[141]

To sum up our most serious objections, in a few words, we should say that Carlyle indicates a depth,—and we mean not impliedly, but distinctly,—which he neglects to fathom. We want to know more about that which he wants to know as well. If any luminous star, or undissolvable nebula, is visible from his station, which is not visible from ours, the interests of science require that the fact be communicated to us. The universe expects every man to do his duty in his parallel of latitude. We want to hear more of his inmost life; his hymn and prayer, more; his elegy and eulogy, less; that he should speak more from his character, and less from his talent;[142] communicate centrally with his readers, and not by a side; that he should say what he believes, without suspecting that men disbelieve it, out of his never-misunderstood nature. Homer and Shakspeare speak directly and confidently to us. The confidence implied in the unsuspicious tone of the world's worthies, is a great and encouraging fact. Dig up some of the earth you stand on, and show that. If he gave us religiously the meagre results of his experience, his style would be less picturesque and diversified, but more attractive and impressive. His genius can cover all the land with gorgeous palaces, but the reader does not abide in them, but pitches his tent rather in the desert and on the mountain peak.

When we look about for something to quote, as the fairest specimen of the man, we confess that we labor under an unusual difficulty; for his philosophy is so little of the proverbial or sentential kind, and opens so gradually, rising insensibly from the reviewer's level, and developing its thought completely and in detail, that we look in vain for the brilliant passages, for point and antithesis, and must end by quoting his works entire. What in a writer of less breadth would have been the proposition which would have bounded his discourse, his column of victory, his Pillar of Hercules,[143] and *ne plus ultra*,[144] is in Carlyle frequently the same thought unfolded; no Pillar of Hercules, but a considerable prospect, north and south, along the Atlantic coast. There are other pillars of Hercules, like beacons and light-houses, still further in the horizon toward Atlantis,[145] set up by a few ancient and modern travelers; but, so far as this traveler goes, he clears and colonizes, and all the surplus

142 Thoreau wrote: "Talent only indicates a depth of character in some direction" [J 1:215].
143 Two promontories on the Strait of Gibraltar which, in Greek mythology, mark the westernmost extent traveled by Hercules.
144 Latin: the greatest extent, literally "no more beyond."
145 Fabled island which, according to legend, lay at the bottom of the Atlantic Ocean off the Strait of Gibraltar. According to Plato, who described it in the *Timaeus* and *Critias* as beautiful and prosperous, Atlantis ruled part of Europe and Africa, but the Athenians defeated its kings when it attempted to conquer the rest, and the sea overwhelmed it.

146 Peisistratos (sixth century B.C.E.): Athenian tyrant who reduced the privileges of the aristocracy, helped the poor, funded artistic and religious programs including the Panathenaea, and attempted to produce a definitive version of Homer's epic poems.

147 In ancient Greece, a public place for instruction.

148 Gerald of Wales (d. 1223) claimed to be present at the exhumation of King Arthur at Glastonbury Abbey ca. 1190, and in 1278 a second exhumation was ordered by Edward I to have the bones transferred to a marble tomb.

population of London is bound thither at once. What we would quote is, in fact, his vivacity, and not any particular wisdom or sense, which last is ever synonymous with sentence, [*sententia,*] as in his cotemporaries, Coleridge, Landor and Wordsworth.

We have not attempted to discriminate between his works, but have rather regarded them all as one work as is the man himself. We have not examined so much as remembered them. To do otherwise, would have required a more indifferent, and perhaps even less just review, than the present. The several chapters were thankfully received, as they came out, and now we find it impossible to say which was best, perhaps each was best in its turn. They do not require to be remembered by chapters—that is a merit—but are rather remembered as a well-known strain, reviving from time to time, when it had nearly died away, and always inspiring us to worthier and more persistent endeavors.

In his last work, "The Letters and Speeches of Oliver Cromwell," Carlyle has added a chapter to the history of England; has actually written a chapter of her history, and, in comparison with this, there seems to be no other,—this, and the thirty thousand or three hundred thousand pamphlets in the British Museum, and that is all. This book is a practical comment on Universal History. What if there were a British Museum in Athens and Babylon, and nameless cities! It throws light on the history of the Iliad and the labors of Pisistratus.[146] History is, then, an account of memorable events that have sometime transpired, and not an incredible and confused fable, quarters for scholars merely, or a gymnasium[147] for poets and orators. We may say that he has dug up a hero, who was buried alive in his battle-field, hauled him out of his cairn, on which every passer had cast a pamphlet. We had heard of their digging up Arthurs[148] before to be sure they were there; and, to be sure they were there, their bones, seven feet of them; but they had to bury them again. Others have helped to make known Shakspeare, Milton, Herbert,[149] to give a name to such treasures as we all possessed; but, in this instance, not only a lost character has been restored to our imaginations, but palpably a living body, as it were, to our senses, to wear and sustain the former. His Cromwell's restoration, if England will read it faithfully, and addressed to New England too. Every reader will make his own application.

To speak deliberately, we think that in this instance, vague rumor and a vague history have for the first time been subjected to a rigid scrutiny, and the wheat, with at least novel fidelity, sifted from the chaff; so that there remain for result,—First, Letters and Speeches of Oliver Cromwell, now for the first time read or readable, and well nigh as complete as the fates will permit; secondly, Deeds, making an imperfect and fragmentary life, which may, with probability, be fathered upon him; thirdly, this wreck of an ancient picture, the present editor has, to the best of his ability, restored, sedulously scraping away the daubings of successive bunglers, and endeavoring to catch the spirit of the artist himself. Not the worst, nor a barely possible, but for once the most favorable construction has been put upon this evidence of the life of a man, and the result is a picture of the ideal Cromwell, the perfection of the painter's art. Possibly this was the actual man. At any rate, this only can contain the actual hero. We confess that when we read these Letters and Speeches, unquestionably Cromwell's, with open and confident mind, we get glimpses occasionally of a grandeur and heroism, which even this editor has not proclaimed. His "Speeches" make us forget modern orators, and might go right into the next edition of the Old Testament, without alteration. Cromwell *was* another sort of man than *we* had taken him to be. These Letters and Speeches have supplied the lost key to his character.

149 George Herbert (1593–1633), English poet.

Thomas Carlyle and His Works 137

150 Allusion to Cromwell's praise on 4 July 1653 of "that famous Psalm, sixty-eighth Psalm; which is indeed a glorious prophecy. . . . And the triumph of that Psalm is exceeding high and great; and God is accomplishing it."

151 Book recording the arms of the nobility and gentry.

152 Allusion to Cromwell's statement following the Battle of Worcester, at which the Parliamentarians defeated the Royalist forces: "The dimensions of this mercy are above my thoughts. It is, for aught I know, a crowning mercy."

153 The dispensation of the Hebraic law to Moses in Exodus.

154 Allusion to Joshua 6:20.

155 Allusion to the "theia mania" described by Plato in *Phaedrus* as a "divine gift."

156 In *Oliver Cromwell's Letters and Speeches: With Elucidations* Carlyle wrote: "Sansculottism, as we said above, has to lie submerged for almost two centuries yet. . . . It ceases dibbling beans on St. George's Hill near Cobham; ceases galloping in mutiny across the Isis to Burford;—takes into Quakerisms, and kingdoms which are not of this world." "Dibbling beans" referred to the Diggers, a Protestant group believing in equality through an agrarian community, and who began by planting vegetables on common land on Saint George's Hill.

157 Quoted from *Oliver Cromwell's Letters and Speeches: With Elucidations*. John Maidston, steward of Cromwell's household.

158 Quoted from Milton's sonnet "To the Lord General Cromwell" 1–4:

> Cromwell, our chief of men, who through a cloud
> Not of war only, but detractions rude,
> Guided by faith and matchless fortitude,
> To peace and truth thy glorious way hast plough'd.

159 Carlyle himself.

Verily another soldier than Bonaparte; rejoicing in the triumph of a psalm;[150] to whom psalms were for Magna Charta and Heralds' Book,[151] and whose victories were "crowning mercies."[152] For stern, antique, and practical religion, a man unparalleled, since the Jewish dispensation,[153] in the line of kings. An old Hebrew warrior, indeed, and last right-hand man of the Lord of Hosts, that has blown his ram's horn about Jericho.[154] Yet, with a remarkable common sense and unexpected liberality, there was joined in him, too, such a divine madness,[155] though with large and sublime features, as that of those dibblers of beans on St. George's Hill, whom Carlyle tells of.[156] He still listened to ancient and decaying oracles. If his actions were not always what Christianity or the truest philosophy teaches, still they never fail to impress us as noble, and however violent, will always be pardoned to the great purpose and sincerity of the man. His unquestionable hardness, not to say willfulness, not prevailing by absolute truth and greatness of character, but honestly striving to bend things to his will, is yet grateful to consider in this or any age. As John Maidston said, "He was a strong man in the dark perils of war; in the high places of the field, hope shone in him like a pillar of fire, when it had gone out in the others."[157] And as Milton sang, whose least testimony cannot be spared—

> "Our chief of men,
> Guided by faith and matchless fortitude."[158]

None ever spake to Cromwell before, sending a word of cheer across the centuries—not the "hear!" "hear!" of modern parliaments, but the congratulation and sympathy of a brother soul. The Letters and Speeches owe not a little to the "Intercalations" and "Annotations" of the "latest of the Commentators."[159] The reader will not soon forget how like a happy merchant in the crowd, listening to his favorite speaker, he is all on the alert, and sympathetic, nudging his neighbors from time to time, and throwing in his responsive or interrogatory word. All is good, both that which he didn't hear, and that which he did. He not only makes him speak audibly, but he makes all parties listen to him, all England sitting round, and give in their comments, "groans," or "blushes," or "assent"; indulging sometimes in triumphant malicious applications to the present day, when there is a palpable hit;[160] supplying the look and attitude of the speaker, and the tone of his voice, and even rescuing his unutterable, wrecked and submerged thought,—for this orator begins speaking anywhere within sight of the beginning, and leaves off when the conclusion is visible. Our merchant listens, restless, meanwhile, encouraging his fellow-auditors, when the speech grows dim and involved, and pleasantly congratulating them, when it runs smoothly; or, in touching soliloquy, he exclaims, "Poor Oliver, noble Oliver"—"Courage, my brave one!"[161]

And all along, between the Letters and Speeches, as readers well remember, he has ready such a fresh top-of-the-morning salutation as conjures up the spirits of those days, and men go marching over English sward, not wired skeletons,[162] but with firm, elastic muscles, and clang of armor on their thighs, if they wore swords, or the twang of psalms and canticles on their lips. His blunt, "Who are you?" put to the shadowy ghosts of history, they vanish into deeper obscurity than ever. Vivid phantasmagorian pictures of what is transpiring in England in the meanwhile, there are, not a few, better than if you had been there to see.

All of Carlyle's works might well enough be embraced under the title of one of them, a good specimen brick, "On Heroes, Hero-worship, and the Heroic in History." Of this department, he is the Chief Professor in the World's University, and even leaves Plutarch[163] be-

160 Allusion to *Hamlet* V.ii.281: "A hit, a very palpable hit."
161 Carlyle's "elucidations" to Speech V and Speech XVI respectively, as found in *Oliver Cromwell's Letters and Speeches.*
162 Used as specimens in medical schools.
163 Plutarch (ca. 45–125 C.E.), Greek essayist and author of *Parallel Lives,* a series of Greek and Roman biographies the object of which was not simply to write the histories but to examine the character of famous men.

164 Pen name of François-Marie Arouet (1694–1778), French writer and philosopher.
165 Honoré-Gabriel Victor Riqueti, Comte de Mirabeau (1749–1791), French revolutionary statesman of whom Thoreau wrote in *Walden:* "It is said that Mirabeau took to highway robbery 'to ascertain what degree of resolution was necessary in order to place one's self in formal opposition to the most sacred laws of society.' . . . It is not for a man to put himself in such an attitude to society, but to maintain himself in whatever attitude he find himself through obedience to the laws of his being, which will never be one of opposition to a just government, if he should chance to meet with such" [Wa 312–313].

hind. Such intimate and living, such loyal and generous sympathy with the heroes of history, not one in one age only, but forty in forty ages, such an unparalleled reviewing and greeting of all past worth, with exceptions, to be sure,—but exceptions were the rule, before,—it was, indeed, to make this the age of review writing, as if now one period of the human story were completing itself, and getting its accounts settled. This soldier has told the stories with new emphasis, and will be a memorable hander-down of fame to posterity. And with what wise discrimination he has selected his men, with reference both to his own genius and to theirs: Mahomet,—Dante,—Cromwell,—Voltaire,[164]—Johnson,—Burns,—Goethe,—Richter,—Schiller,—Mirabeau;[165] could any of these have been spared? These we wanted to hear about. We have not as commonly the cold and refined judgment of the scholar and critic merely, but something more human and affecting. These eulogies have the glow and warmth of friendship. There is sympathy not with mere fames, and formless, incredible things, but with kindred men,—not transiently, but lifelong he has walked with them.

The attitude of some, in relation to Carlyle's love of heroes, and men of the sword, reminds us of the procedure at the anti-slavery meetings, when some member, being warmed, begins to speak with more latitude than usual of the Bible or the Church, for a few prudent and devout ones to spring a prayer upon him, as the saying is; that is, propose suddenly to unite in prayer, and so solemnize the minds of the audience, or dismiss them at once; which may oftener be to interrupt a true prayer by most gratuitous profanity. But the spring of this trap, we are glad to learn, has grown somewhat rusty, and is not so sure of late.

No doubt, some of Carlyle's worthies, should they ever return to earth, would find themselves unpleasantly

put upon their good behavior, to sustain their characters; but if he can return a man's life more perfect to
our hands, than it was left at his death, following out
the design of its author, we shall have no great cause to
complain. We do not want a Daguerreotype[166] likeness.
All biography is the life of Adam,—a much-experienced
man,—and time withdraws something partial from the
story of every individual, that the historian may supply
something general. If these virtues were not in this man,
perhaps they are in his biographer,—no fatal mistake.
Really, in any other sense, we never do, nor desire to,
come at the historical man,—unless we rob his grave,
that is the nearest approach. Why did he die, then? *He* is
with his bones, surely.

No doubt, Carlyle has a propensity to *exaggerate* the
heroic in history, that is, he creates you an ideal hero
rather than another thing, he has most of that material.
This we allow in all its senses, and in one narrower sense
it is not so convenient. Yet what were history if he did
not exaggerate it? How comes it that history never has to
wait for facts, but for a man to write it? The ages may go
on forgetting the facts never so long, he can remember
two for every one forgotten. The musty records of history, like the catacombs, contain the perishable remains,
but only in the breast of genius are embalmed the souls
of heroes. There is very little of what is called criticism
here; it is love and reverence, rather, which deal with
qualities not relatively, but absolutely great; for whatever
is admirable in a man is something infinite, to which we
cannot set bounds. These sentiments allow the mortal to
die, the immortal and divine to survive. There is something antique, even in his style of treating his subject,
reminding us that Heroes and Demi-gods, Fates and
Furies, still exist, the common man is nothing to him,
but after death the hero is apotheosized and has a place
in heaven, as in the religion of the Greeks.

166 Cf. "Paradise (To Be) Regained," note 14.

Thomas Carlyle and His Works 141

Exaggeration! was ever any virtue attributed to a man without exaggeration? was ever any vice, without infinite exaggeration? Do we not exaggerate ourselves to ourselves, or do we recognize ourselves for the actual men we are? Are we not all great men? Yet what are we actually to speak of? We live by exaggeration, what else is it to anticipate more than we enjoy? The lightning is an exaggeration of the light. Exaggerated history is poetry, and truth referred to a new standard. To a small man every greater is an exaggeration. He who cannot exaggerate is not qualified to utter truth. No truth we think was ever expressed but with this sort of emphasis, so that for the time there seemed to be no other. Moreover, you must speak loud to those who are hard of hearing, and so you acquire a habit of shouting to those who are not. By an immense exaggeration we appreciate our Greek poetry and philosophy, and Egyptian ruins; our Shakspeares and Miltons, our Liberty and Christianity. We give importance to this hour over all other hours. We do not live by justice, but by grace. As the sort of justice which concerns us in our daily intercourse is not that administered by the judge, so the historical justice which we prize is not arrived at by nicely balancing the evidence. In order to appreciate any, even the humblest man, you must first, by some good fortune, have acquired a sentiment of admiration, even of reverence, for him, and there never were such exaggerators as these. Simple admiration for a hero renders a juster verdict than the wisest criticism, which necessarily degrades what is high to its own level. There is no danger in short of saying too much in praise of one man, provided you can say more in praise of a better man. If by exaggeration a man can create for us a hero, where there was nothing but dry bones before, we will thank him, and let Dryasdust administer historical justice. This is where a true history properly begins, when some genius arises, who can turn the dry and musty records into poetry. As we say, looking to the future, that what is best is truest, so, in one sense, we may say looking into the past, for the only past that we are to look at, must also be future to us. The great danger is not of excessive partiality or sympathy with one, but of a shallow justice to many, in which, after all, none gets his deserts. Who has not experienced that praise is truer than naked justice? As if man were to be the judge of his fellows, and should repress his rising sympathy with the prisoner at the bar, considering the many honest men abroad, whom he had never countenanced.

To try him by the German rule of referring an author to his own standard,[167] we will quote the following from Carlyle's remarks on history, and leave the reader to consider how far his practice has been consistent with his theory. "Truly, if History is Philosophy teaching by experience, the writer fitted to compose history, is hitherto an unknown man. The experience itself would require all knowledge to record it, were the All-wisdom needful for such Philosophy as would interpret it, to be had for asking. Better were it that mere earthly historians should lower such pretensions, more suitable for omniscience than for human science; and aiming only at some picture of the things acted, which picture itself, will at best be a poor approximation, leave the inscrutable purport of them an acknowledged secret; or, at most, in reverent Faith, far different from that teaching of Philosophy, pause over the mysterious vestiges of Him, whose path is in the great deep of Time, whom history indeed reveals, but only all History and in Eternity, will clearly reveal."[168]

Who lives in London to tell this generation who have been the great men of our race? We have read that on some exposed place in the city of Geneva, they have fixed a brazen indicator for the use of travelers, with the names

167 George Henry Lewes (1817–1878) wrote in "State of Criticism in France" (*British and Foreign Review*, January 1844) that the "radical virtue of German criticism is precisely this desired flexibility, which, so far from reducing all works to one standard, endeavors to appreciate them from their own central point. . . . —with what power did they not only see into the nature of art but also throw off their own national predilections, to view each artist from his own central point!"
168 Quoted from Carlyle's "On History," in *Critical and Miscellaneous Essays.*

169 Quoted from George Barrell Cheever's (1807–1890) *Wanderings of a Pilgrim in the Shadow of Mount Blanc.*

of the mountain summits in the horizon marked upon it, "so that by taking sight across the index you can distinguish them at once. You will not mistake Mont Blanc, if you see him, but until you get accustomed to the panorama, you may easily mistake one of his court for the king."[169] It stands there a piece of mute brass, that seems nevertheless to know in what vicinity it is: and there perchance it will stand, when the nation that placed it there has passed away, still in sympathy with the mountains, forever discriminating in the desert.

So, we may say, stands this man, pointing as long as he lives, in obedience to some spiritual magnetism, to the summits in the historical horizon, for the guidance of his fellows.

Truly, our greatest blessings are very cheap. To have our sunlight without paying for it, without any duty levied,—to have our poet there in England, to furnish us entertainment, and what is better provocation, from year to year, all our lives long, to make the world seem richer for us, the age more respectable, and life better worth the living,—all without expense of acknowledgment even, but silently accepted out of the east, like morning light as a matter of course.

Resistance to Civil Government

1 Allusion to the motto found on the title page of the *United States Magazine, and Democratic Review:* "The best government is that which governs least," taken from John O'Sullivan's (1813–1895) introductory article "The Democratic Review: An Introductory Statement on the Democratic Principle." Emerson similarly wrote in "Politics": "The less government we have the better."

2 Not a quotation but Thoreau's amplification of the motto.

3 On maintaining a permanent army during peace and war, Elbridge Gerry (1744–1814) said at the 1787 Constitutional Convention: "Standing armies in time of peace are inconsistent with the principles of republican Governments, dangerous to the liberties of a free people, and generally converted into destructive engines for establishing despotism."

4 The United States declared war on Mexico on 13 May 1846 over the territory of Texas. Although a "present" war when Thoreau's composition was presented as a lecture, it was no longer so when this essay was published in 1849.

5 At the time of Thoreau's jailing, the American Revolution was a mere seventy years in the past, and the formation of the American government, with the adoption of the Constitution in 1787, more recent.

6 Wooden guns were used in training.

I heartily accept the motto,—"That government is best which governs least";[1] and I should like to see it acted up to more rapidly and systematically. Carried out, it finally amounts to this, which also I believe,—"That government is best which governs not at all";[2] and when men are prepared for it, that will be the kind of government which they will have. Government is at best but an expedient; but most governments are usually, and all governments are sometimes, inexpedient. The objections which have been brought against a standing army,[3] and they are many and weighty, and deserve to prevail, may also at last be brought against a standing government. The standing army is only an arm of the standing government. The government itself, which is only the mode which the people have chosen to execute their will, is equally liable to be abused and perverted before the people can act through it. Witness the present Mexican war,[4] the work of comparatively a few individuals using the standing government as their tool; for, in the outset, the people would not have consented to this measure.

This American government,—what is it but a tradition, though a recent one,[5] endeavoring to transmit itself unimpaired to posterity, but each instant losing some of its integrity? It has not the vitality and force of a single living man; for a single man can bend it to his will. It is a sort of wooden gun to the people themselves; and, if ever they should use it in earnest as a real one against each other, it will surely split.[6] But it is not the less necessary for this; for the people must have some complicated machinery or other, and hear its din, to satisfy that idea of

7 Those who held to a higher law than the political, such as William Lloyd Garrison (1805–1879), who wrote in his 1838 "Declaration of Sentiments Adopted by the Peace Convention": "We recognize but one King and Lawgiver. We are bound by the laws of a kingdom which is not of this world." In the same declaration he advocated complete nonparticipation with government: "If *we* cannot occupy a seat in the legislature, or on the bench, neither can we elect *others* to act as our substitutes in any such capacity."

government which they have. Governments show thus how successfully men can be imposed on, even impose on themselves, for their own advantage. It is excellent, we must all allow; yet this government never of itself furthered any enterprise, but by the alacrity with which it got out of its way. *It* does not keep the country free. *It* does not settle the West. *It* does not educate. The character inherent in the American people has done all that has been accomplished; and it would have done somewhat more, if the government had not sometimes got in its way. For government is an expedient by which men would fain succeed in letting one another alone; and, as has been said, when it is most expedient, the governed are most let alone by it. Trade and commerce, if they were not made of India rubber, would never manage to bounce over the obstacles which legislators are continually putting in their way; and, if one were to judge these men wholly by the effects of their actions, and not partly by their intentions, they would deserve to be classed and punished with those mischievous persons who put obstructions on the railroads.

But, to speak practically and as a citizen, unlike those who call themselves no-government men,[7] I ask for, not at once no government, but *at once* a better government. Let every man make known what kind of government would command his respect, and that will be one step toward obtaining it.

After all, the practical reason why, when the power is once in the hands of the people, a majority are permitted, and for a long period continue, to rule, is not because they are most likely to be in the right, nor because this seems fairest to the minority, but because they are physically the strongest. But a government in which the majority rule in all cases cannot be based on justice, even as far as men understand it. Can there not be a government in which the majorities do not virtually decide right and wrong, but conscience?—in which majorities decide only those questions to which the rule of expediency is applicable?[8] Must the citizen ever for a moment, or in the least degree, resign his conscience to the legislator? Why has every man a conscience, then? I think that we should be men first, and subjects[9] afterward. It is not desirable to cultivate a respect for the law, so much as for the right. The only obligation which I have a right to assume, is to do at any time what I think right. It is truly enough said, that a corporation has no conscience;[10] but a corporation of conscientious men is a corporation *with* a conscience. Law never made men a whit more just; and, by means of their respect for it, even the well-disposed are daily made the agents on injustice. A common and natural result of an undue respect for law is, that you may see a file of soldiers, colonel, captain, corporal, privates, powder-monkeys[11] and all, marching in admirable order over hill and dale to the wars, against their wills, aye, against their common sense and consciences, which makes it very steep marching indeed, and produces a palpitation of the heart. They have no doubt that it is a damnable business in which they are concerned; they are all peaceably inclined. Now, what are they? Men at all? or small moveable forts and magazines, at the service of some unscrupulous man in power? Visit the Navy Yard,[12] and behold a marine, such a man as an American government can make, or such as it can make a man with its black arts, a mere shadow and reminiscence of humanity, a man laid out alive and standing, and already, as one may say, buried under arms with funeral accompaniments, though it may be

"Not a drum was heard, nor a funeral note,
    As his corse to the ramparts we hurried;
Not a soldier discharged his farewell shot
    O'er the grave where our hero was buried."[13]

8 Allusion to Paley's *The Principles of Moral and Political Philosophy,* first published in 1785: "The danger of error and abuse, is no objection to the rule of expediency, because every other rule is liable to the fame or greater; and every rule that can be propounded upon the subject (like all rules which appeal to, or bind, the conscience) must in the application depend upon private judgment. It may be observed, however, that it ought equally to be accounted the exercise of a man's private judgment, whether he be determined by reasonings and conclusions of his own, or submit to be directed by the advice of others, provided he be free to choose his guide."

9 Persons who owe allegiance to a government.

10 Incorrectly attributed to the English jurist Sir Edward Coke (1552–1634) by Jeremy Bentham (1748–1832), who wrote: "A corporation, according to Lord Coke (who was not ill acquainted with them,) has no conscience." Coke wrote that the "corporate aggregate . . . cannot commit treason, nor be outlawed, nor excommunicated, for they have no souls."

11 One who carries gunpowder or other explosives from a storehouse.

12 In Boston, the United States Navy Yard.

13 Quoted, with minor variants, from Charles Wolfe's (1791–1823) "The Burial of Sir John Moore." Thoreau's variants—"nor a funeral" for "not a funeral" and "ramparts" for "rampart"— were found in many printed sources of his day. John Moore (1761–1809) was a British general killed near La Coruña, Spain, in the campaign against Napoleon I.

14 Thoreau wrote in *Walden:* "He has not time to be any thing but a machine" [Wa 5].

15 Latin: power of the county. A group of citizens called together by a sheriff to assist in the maintaining of peace and the pursuing of felons.

16 Cf. "Paradise (To Be) Regained" note 46.

17 Quoted from Shakespeare's *Hamlet* V.i.236–237: "Imperial Caesar, dead and turn'd to clay, / Might stop a hole to keep the wind away."

18 Quoted from Shakespeare's *King John* V.ii.79–82.

The mass of men serve the State thus, not as men mainly, but as machines, with their bodies.[14] They are the standing army, and the militia, jailers, constables, *posse comitatus,*[15] &c. In most cases there is no free exercise whatever of the judgment or of the moral sense;[16] but they put themselves on a level with wood and earth and stones; and wooden men can perhaps be manufactured that will serve the purpose as well. Such command no more respect than men of straw, or a lump of dirt. They have the same sort of worth only as horses and dogs. Yet such as these even are commonly esteemed good citizens. Others, as most legislators, politicians, lawyers, ministers, and office-holders, serve the State chiefly with their heads; and, as they rarely make any moral distinctions, they are as likely to serve the devil, without intending it, as God. A very few, as heroes, patriots, martyrs, reformers in the great sense, and *men,* serve the State with their consciences also, and so necessarily resist it for the most part; and they are commonly treated by it as enemies. A wise man will only be useful as a man, and will not submit to be "clay," and "stop a hole to keep the wind away,"[17] but leave that office to his dust at least:—

"I am too high-born to be propertied,
To be a secondary at control,
Or useful serving-man and instrument
To any sovereign state throughout the world."[18]

He who gives himself entirely to his fellow-men appears to them useless and selfish; but he who gives himself partially to them is pronounced a benefactor and philanthropist.

How does it become a man to behave toward the American government to-day? I answer that he cannot without disgrace be associated with it. I cannot for an instant recognize that political organization as *my* government which is the *slave's* government also.

All men recognize the right of revolution; that is, the right to refuse allegiance to and to resist the government, when its tyranny or its inefficiency are great and unendurable. But almost all say that such is not the case now. But such was the case, they think, in the Revolution of '75.[19] If one were to tell me that this was a bad government because it taxed certain foreign commodities brought to its ports, it is most probable that I should not make an ado about it, for I can do without them: all machines have their friction; and possibly this does enough good to counterbalance the evil. At any rate, it is a great evil to make a stir about it. But when the friction comes to have its machine, and oppression and robbery are organized, I say, let us not have such a machine any longer. In other words, when a sixth of the population of a nation which has undertaken to be the refuge of liberty are slaves, and a whole country is unjustly overrun and conquered by a foreign army, and subjected to military law, I think that it is not too soon for honest men to rebel and revolutionize. What makes this duty the more urgent is that fact, that the country so overrun is not our own, but ours is the invading army.

Paley,[20] a common authority with many on moral questions, in his chapter on the "Duty of Submission to Civil Government," resolves all civil obligation into expediency; and he proceeds to say, "that so long as the interest of the whole society requires it, that is, so long as the established government cannot be resisted or changed without public inconveniency, it is the will of God that the established government be obeyed, and no longer." — "This principle being admitted, the justice of every particular case of resistance is reduced to a computation of the quantity of the danger and grievance on the one side, and of the probability and expense of re-

19 The beginning of the American Revolution, on 19 April 1775, the first battles of which were fought in Concord and Lexington, Massachusetts.
20 William Paley (1743–1805), British philosopher and theologian, whose *The Principles of Moral and Political Philosophy* was one of Thoreau's textbooks at Harvard.

21 Quoted from "The Duty of Submission to Civil Government Explained" in Paley's *The Principles of Moral and Political Philosophy*.

22 Allusion to the question found in Marcus Tullius Cicero's (ca. 106–43 B.C.E.) *De Officiis* III.xxiii: "If a fool should snatch a plank from a wreck, shall a wise man wrest it from him if he is able?"

23 Allusion to Paley's *The Principles of Moral and Political Philosophy*: "It is by virtue of a compact, that the subject owes obedience to civil government, it will follow, that he ought to abide by the form of government which he finds established, be it ever so absurd, or inconvenient. He is bound by his bargain. It is not permitted to any man to retreat from his engagement, merely because he finds the performance disadvantageous."

24 Allusion to Luke 9:24 (or the variant at Matthew 10:39): "For whosoever will save his life shall lose it: but whosoever will lose his life for my sake, the same shall save it."

25 A woman who is negligent of cleanliness and whose dress and home are dirty or in disarray.

26 Quoted from Cyril Tourneur's (ca. 1575–1626)—now attributed to Thomas Middleton (1580–1627)—*The Revenger's Tragedy* IV.iv.72–73, which Thoreau copied in his literary notebooks from *Specimens of English Dramatic Poets, Who Lived about the Time of Shakespeare*, edited by Charles Lamb.

27 The Cotton Whigs of Massachusetts were dependent on the cotton mills and therefore on the cotton produced through slavery.

28 Allusion to 1 Corinthians 5:6: "Know ye not that a little leaven leaveneth the whole lump?"

dressing it on the other."[21] Of this, he says, every man shall judge for himself. But Paley appears never to have contemplated those cases to which the rule of expediency does not apply, in which a people, as well as an individual, must do justice, cost what it may. If I have unjustly wrested a plank from a drowning man, I must restore it to him though I drown myself.[22] This, according to Paley, would be inconvenient.[23] But he that would save his life, in such a case, shall lose it.[24] This people must cease to hold slaves, and to make war on Mexico, though it cost them their existence as a people.

In their practice, nations agree with Paley; but does any one think that Massachusetts does exactly what is right at the present crisis?

> "A drab of state, a cloth-o'-silver slut,[25]
> To have her train borne up, and her soul trail in
> the dirt."[26]

Practically speaking, the opponents to a reform in Massachusetts are not a hundred thousand politicians at the South, but a hundred thousand merchants[27] and farmers here, who are more interested in commerce and agriculture than they are in humanity, and are not prepared to do justice to the slave and to Mexico, *cost what it may.* I quarrel not with far-off foes, but with those who, near at home, co-operate with, and do the bidding of those far away, and without whom the latter would be harmless. We are accustomed to say, that the mass of men are unprepared; but improvement is slow, because the few are not materially wiser or better than the many. It is not so important that many should be good as you, as that there be some absolute goodness somewhere; for that will leaven the whole lump.[28] There are thousands who are *in opinion* opposed to slavery and to the war, who yet in effect do nothing to put an end to them;

who, esteeming themselves children of Washington and Franklin, sit down with their hands in their pockets, and say that they know not what to do, and do nothing; who even postpone the question of freedom to the question of free-trade, and quietly read the prices-current[29] along with the latest advices from Mexico, after dinner, and, it may be, fall asleep over them both. What is the price-current of an honest man and patriot to-day? They hesitate, and they regret, and sometimes they petition; but they do nothing in earnest and with effect. They will wait, well-disposed, for others to remedy the evil, that they may no longer have it to regret. At most, they give only a cheap vote, and a feeble countenance and God-speed, to the right, as it goes by them. There are nine hundred and ninety-nine patrons of virtue to one virtuous man; but it is easier to deal with the real possessor of a thing than with the temporary guardian of it.

All voting is a sort of gaming, like chequers or back-gammon, with a slight moral tinge to it, a playing with right and wrong, with moral questions; and betting naturally accompanies it. The character of the voters is not staked. I cast my vote, perchance, as I think right;[30] but I am not vitally concerned that that right should prevail. I am willing to leave it to the majority. Its obligation, therefore, never exceeds that of expediency. Even voting *for the right* is *doing* nothing for it. It is only expressing to men feebly your desire that it should prevail. A wise man will not leave the right to the mercy of chance, nor wish it to prevail through the power of the majority. There is but little virtue in the action of masses of men. When the majority shall at length vote for the abolition of slavery, it will be because they are indifferent to slavery, or because there is but little slavery left to be abolished by their vote. *They* will then be the only slaves. Only *his* vote can hasten the abolition of slavery who asserts his own freedom by his vote.

29 Published lists of current prices for goods recently sold.
30 Thoreau wrote figuratively here, as he is not known ever to have voted.

31 The 1848 Democratic Convention, at which Lewis Cass (1782–1866) was nominated.
32 Thoreau similarly wrote in his journal of 17 January 1852: "Those old Northmen were not like so many men in these days, whom you can pass your hand through because they have not any backbone" [J 3:203].
33 Cf. "Paradise (To Be) Regained," note 47.
34 Allusion to phrenology, a popular pseudo-science in Thoreau's day, in which the shape of the skull reflected the development of the underlying parts, or organs, of the brain in which the various mental processes were assumed to take place. The organ of gregariousness, or adhesiveness, controlled sociability.
35 *Toga virilis*, the adult clothing which a Roman boy was allowed to wear after the age of fourteen.

I hear of a convention to be held at Baltimore, or elsewhere, for the selection of a candidate for the Presidency,[31] made up chiefly of editors, and men who are politicians by profession; but I think, what is it to any independent, intelligent, and respectable man what decision they may come to, shall we not have the advantage of his wisdom and honesty, nevertheless? Can we not count upon some independent votes? Are there not many individuals in the country who do not attend conventions? But no: I find that the respectable man, so called, has immediately drifted from his position, and despairs of his country, when his country has more reasons to despair of him. He forthwith adopts one of the candidates thus selected as the only *available* one, thus proving that he is himself *available* for any purposes of the demagogue. His vote is of no more worth than that of any unprincipled foreigner or hireling native, who may have been bought. Oh for a man who is a *man,* and, as my neighbor says, has a bone in his back which you cannot pass your hand through![32] Our statistics are at fault: the population has been returned too large. How many *men* are there to a square thousand miles in this country? Hardly one. Does not America offer any inducement for men to settle here? The American has dwindled into an Odd Fellow,[33] — one who may be known by the development of his organ of gregariousness,[34] and a manifest lack of intellect and cheerful self-reliance; whose first and chief concern, on coming into the world, is to see that the alms-houses are in good repair; and, before yet he has lawfully donned the virile garb,[35] to collect a fund for the support of the widows and orphans that may be; who, in short, ventures to live only by the aid of the mutual insurance company, which has promised to bury him decently.

It is not a man's duty, as a matter of course, to devote himself to the eradication of any, even the most enormous wrong; he may still properly have other concerns to engage him; but it is his duty, at least, to wash his hands of it, and, if he gives it no thought longer, not to give it practically his support. If I devote myself to other pursuits and contemplations, I must first see, at least, that I do not pursue them sitting upon another man's shoulders. I must get off him first, that he may pursue his contemplations too. See what gross inconsistency is tolerated. I have heard some of my townsmen say, "I should like to have them order me out to help put down an insurrection of the slaves, or to march to Mexico,—see if I would go"; and yet these very men have each, directly by their allegiance, and so indirectly, at least, by their money, furnished a substitute. The soldier is applauded who refuses to serve in an unjust war by those who do not refuse to sustain the unjust government which makes the war; is applauded by those whose own act and authority he disregards and sets at nought; as if the State were penitent to that degree that it hired one to scourge it while it sinned, but not to that degree that it left off sinning for a moment. Thus, under the name of order and civil government, we are all made at last to pay homage to and support our own meanness. After the first blush of sin, comes its indifference; and from immoral it becomes, as it were, *un*moral, and not quite unnecessary to that life which we have made.

The broadest and most prevalent error requires the most disinterested virtue to sustain it. The slight reproach to which the virtue of patriotism is commonly liable, the noble are most likely to incur. Those who, while they disapprove of the character and measures of a government, yield to it their allegiance and support, are undoubtedly its most conscientious supporters, and so frequently the most serious obstacles to reform. Some are petitioning the State to dissolve the Union,[36] to disregard the requisitions of the President.[37] Why do they not dissolve

36 On 24 January 1842 former president John Quincy Adams (1767–1848) presented a petition to the House of Representatives signed by forty-six citizens of Haverhill, Massachusetts, "peaceably to dissolve the union of these States: First, because no union can be agreeable or permanent, which does not present prospects of reciprocal benefit; second, because a vast proportion of the resources of one section of the union is annually drained to sustain the views and course of another section without any adequate return; third, because (judging from history of past nations) this union, if persisted in, in the present course of things, will certainly overwhelm the whole nation in utter destruction."

37 Requisition from President James K. Polk (1795–1849; president 1845–1849) to various state governors, including Henry J. Gardner (1818–1892) of Massachusetts, to call volunteer regiments into active service.

38 Nicolaus Copernicus (1473–1543), Polish astronomer whose *De Revolutionibus Orbium Coelestium* (1543) stated that the planets revolve around the sun. The Catholic Church banned his work although he died before he could be excommunicated.

39 Martin Luther: cf. "Thomas Carlyle and His Works," note 73. Pope Leo X (1483–1546) excommunicated Luther for refusing to recant his beliefs.

it themselves,—the union between themselves and the State,—and refuse to pay their quota into its treasury? Do not they stand in same relation to the State, that the State does to the Union? And have not the same reasons prevented the State from resisting the Union, which have prevented them from resisting the State?

How can a man be satisfied to entertain an opinion merely, and enjoy *it?* Is there any enjoyment in it, if his opinion is that he is aggrieved? If you are cheated out of a single dollar by your neighbor, you do not rest satisfied with knowing you are cheated, or with saying that you are cheated, or even with petitioning him to pay you your due; but you take effectual steps at once to obtain the full amount, and see that you are never cheated again. Action from principle,—the perception and the performance of right,—changes things and relations; it is essentially revolutionary, and does not consist wholly with any thing which was. It not only divides states and churches, it divides families; aye, it divides the *individual,* separating the diabolical in him from the divine.

Unjust laws exist: shall we be content to obey them, or shall we endeavor to amend them, and obey them until we have succeeded, or shall we transgress them at once? Men generally, under such a government as this, think that they ought to wait until they have persuaded the majority to alter them. They think that, if they should resist, the remedy would be worse than the evil. But it is the fault of the government itself that the remedy *is* worse than the evil. *It* makes it worse. Why is it not more apt to anticipate and provide for reform? Why does it not cherish its wise minority? Why does it cry and resist before it is hurt? Why does it not encourage its citizens to put out its faults, and *do* better than it would have them? Why does it always crucify Christ, and excommunicate Copernicus[38] and Luther,[39] and pronounce Washington and Franklin rebels?

One would think, that a deliberate and practical denial of its authority was the only offense never contemplated by government; else, why has it not assigned its definite, its suitable and proportionate penalty? If a man who has no property refuses but once to earn nine shillings[40] for the State, he is put in prison for a period unlimited by any law that I know, and determined only by the discretion of those who placed him there; but if he should steal ninety times nine shillings from the State, he is soon permitted to go at large again.

If the injustice is part of the necessary friction of the machine of government, let it go, let it go: perchance it will wear smooth,—certainly the machine will wear out. If the injustice has a spring, or a pulley, or a rope, or a crank, exclusively for itself, then perhaps you may consider whether the remedy will not be worse than the evil; but if it is of such a nature that it requires you to be the agent of injustice to another, then, I say, break the law. Let your life be a counter friction to stop the machine.[41] What I have to do is to see, at any rate, that I do not lend myself to the wrong which I condemn.

As for adopting the ways which the State has provided for remedying the evil, I know not of such ways. They take too much time, and a man's life will be gone. I have other affairs to attend to.[42] I came into this world, not chiefly to make this a good place to live in, but to live in it, be it good or bad. A man has not every thing to do, but something; and because he cannot do *every thing*, it is not necessary that he should do *something* wrong. It is not my business to be petitioning the governor or the legislature any more than it is theirs to petition me; and, if they should not hear my petition, what should I do then? But in this case the State has provided no way: its very Constitution is the evil.[43] This may seem to be harsh and stubborn and unconciliatory; but it is to treat with the utmost kindness and consideration the only spirit

40 The amount of the poll tax was $1.50. A shilling was equal to one-sixth of a dollar, thus nine shillings was equal to $1.50. It was not uncommon in Thoreau's day to make accounts in shillings.
41 Friction applied to stop a moving part, as in a wagon brake.
42 Thoreau wrote in "A Plea for Captain John Brown": "I do not think it is quite sane for one to spend his whole life in talking or writing about this matter, unless he is continuously inspired, and I have not done so. A man may have other affairs to attend to."
43 In his resolution adopted by the Anti-Slavery Society in 1843, Garrison called the Constitution "a covenant with death and an agreement with hell."

44 Allusion to the concept traced back to John Knox (ca. 1514–1572), founder of Scottish Presbyterianism, that "One man with God is always in the majority."

45 Sam Staples (d. 1895), Concord tax collector and jailer, with whom Thoreau remained on good terms and who was sometimes employed by Thoreau to assist in his surveying work. Thoreau reported in his journal of 8 December 1857 that Staples said there was "one thing he liked," and when asked by Thoreau what it was, replied, "An honest man" [J 10:222].

that can appreciate or deserves it. So is all change for the better, like birth and death which convulse the body.

I do not hesitate to say, that those who call themselves abolitionists should at once effectually withdraw their support, both in person and property, from the government of Massachusetts, and not wait till they constitute a majority of one, before they suffer the right to prevail through them. I think that it is enough if they have God on their side,[44] without waiting for that other one. Moreover, any man more right than his neighbors, constitutes a majority of one already.

I meet this American government, or its representative the State government, directly, and face to face, once a year, no more, in the person of its tax-gatherer; this is the only mode in which a man situated as I am necessarily meets it; and it then says distinctly, Recognize me; and the simplest, the most effectual, and, in the present posture of affairs, the indispensablest mode of treating with it on this head, of expressing your little satisfaction with and love for it, is to deny it then. My civil neighbor, the tax-gatherer,[45] is the very man I have to deal with,—for it is, after all, with men and not with parchment that I quarrel,—and he has voluntarily chosen to be an agent of the government. How shall he ever know well what he is and does as an officer of the government, or as a man, until he is obliged to consider whether he shall treat me, his neighbor, for whom he has respect, as a neighbor and well-disposed man, or as a maniac and disturber of the peace, and see if he can get over this obstruction to his neighborliness without a ruder and more impetuous thought or speech corresponding with his action? I know this well, that if one thousand, if one hundred, if ten men whom I could name,—if ten *honest* men only,—aye, if *one* HONEST man, in this State of Massachusetts, *ceasing to hold slaves,* were actually to withdraw from this co-partnership, and be locked up in the county jail therefor, it would be the abolition of slavery in America.[46] For it matters not how small the beginning may seem to be: what is once well done is done for ever. But we love better to talk about it: that we say is our mission. Reform keeps many scores of newspapers in its service, but not one man. If my esteemed neighbor, the State's ambassador, who will devote his days to the settlement of the question of human rights in the Council Chamber, instead of being threatened with the prisons of Carolina,[47] were to sit down the prisoner of Massachusetts, that State which is so anxious to foist the sin of slavery upon her sister,—though at present she can discover only an act of inhospitality to be the ground of a quarrel with her,—the Legislature would not wholly waive the subject the following winter.

Under a government which imprisons unjustly, the true place for a just man is also a prison. The proper place to-day, the only place which Massachusetts has provided for her freer and less desponding spirits, is in her prisons, to be put out and locked out of the State by her own act, as they have already put themselves out by their principles. It is there that the fugitive slave, and the Mexican prisoner on parole, and the Indian come to plead the wrongs of his race,[48] should find them; on that separate, but more free and honorable ground, where the State places those who are not *with* her but *against* her,[49]—the only house in a slave-state in which a free man can abide with honor. If any think that their influence would be lost there, and their voices no longer afflict the ear of the State, that they would not be as an enemy within its walls, they do not know by how much truth is stronger than error, nor how much more eloquently and effectively he can combat injustice who has experienced a little in his own person. Cast your whole vote, not a strip of paper merely, but your whole influence. A minority is powerless while it conforms to the majority; it is not

46 Echo of the Greek philosopher Diogenes' (412–323 B.C.E.) search for an honest man and of Abraham's request in Genesis 18:22–33 that God spare Sodom if fifty righteous people could be found among the wicked, reducing the number needed after each agreement to forty-five, then forty, and finally to ten.

47 In November 1844 the Concord lawyer and former Massachusetts Congressman Samuel Hoar (1778–1856) was appointed to negotiate a settlement of an old dispute with South Carolina. Free black sailors were being forcibly removed from Massachusetts ships in Charleston harbor. Hoar was thrust back onto a ship under the seemingly real threat of violence if he remained in Charleston. Nathaniel Rogers editorialized in *Herald of Freedom* (22 May 1846):

> Slavery may perpetrate any thing—and New England can't see it. It can *horse-whip* the old Commonwealth of Massachusetts and spit in her governmental face, and she will not recognize it as an offence. She sent her Hon. Sam. Hoar to Charleston, on a state embassy. Slavery caught him and sent him most ignominiously home. The solemn great man came back in a hurry. He returned on a most undignified trot. . . . Her grave old Senator, who no more thought of ever having to break his stately walk, than he had of being flogged at school for stealing apples, came back from Carolina upon the full run—out of breath, as well as out of dignity. Well, what's the result? Why, nothing.

48 In *The Maine Woods* Thoreau wrote: "I observed a short shabby washerwoman-looking Indian; they commonly have the woe-begone look of the girl that cried for spilt milk—just from 'up river,'—land on the Oldtown side near a grocery, and drawing up his canoe, take out a bundle of skins in one hand, and an empty keg or half-barrel in the other, and scramble up the bank with them. This picture will do to put before the

49 Allusion to Matthew 12:30: "Whoever is not
with me is against me, and whoever does not
gather with me scatters."

50 Thoreau may have recalled the phrase "Aye, we
must die an everlasting death," from Christopher
Marlowe's (1564–1593) *Doctor Faustus.*

51 According to the statutes of Massachusetts,
for any person who did not pay his tax, the tax
collector would, with certain exceptions, "levy the
same by distress and sale of his goods," and if unable to "find sufficient goods, upon which it may
be levied, he may take the body of such person
and commit him to prison."

even a minority then; but it is irresistible when it clogs
by its whole weight. If the alternative is to keep all just
men in prison, or give up war and slavery, the State will
not hesitate which to choose. If a thousand men were
not to pay their tax-bills this year, that would not be a
violent and bloody measure, as it would be to pay them,
and enable the State to commit violence and shed innocent blood. This is, in fact, the definition of a peaceable
revolution, if any such is possible. If the tax-gatherer, or
any other public officer, asks me, as one has done, "But
what shall I do?" my answer is, "If you really wish to do
any thing, resign your office." When the subject has refused allegiance, and the officer has resigned from office,
then the revolution is accomplished. But even suppose
blood should flow. Is there not a sort of blood shed when
the conscience is wounded? Through this wound a man's
real manhood and immortality flow out, and he bleeds
to an everlasting death.[50] I see this blood flowing now.

I have contemplated the imprisonment of the of-
fender, rather than the seizure of his goods,[51]—though
both will serve the same purpose,—because they who
assert the purest right, and consequently are most dangerous to a corrupt State, commonly have not spent
much time in accumulating property. To such the State
renders comparatively small service, and a slight tax is
wont to appear exorbitant, particularly if they are obliged
to earn it by special labor with their hands. If there were
one who lived wholly without the use of money, the
State itself would hesitate to demand it of him. But the
rich man—not to make any invidious comparison—is
always sold to the institution which makes him rich.
Absolutely speaking, the more money, the less virtue; for
money comes between a man and his objects, and ob-
tains them for him; and it was certainly no great virtue to
obtain it. It puts to rest many questions which he would
otherwise be taxed to answer; while the only new ques-

tion which it puts is the hard but superfluous one, how to spend it. Thus his moral ground is taken from under his feet. The opportunities of living are diminished in proportion as what are called the "means" are increased. The best thing a man can do for his culture when he is rich is to endeavour to carry out those schemes which he entertained when he was poor. Christ answered the Herodians [52] according to their condition. "Show me the tribute-money," said he;—and one took a penny out of his pocket;—If you use money which has the image of Caesar on it, and which he has made current and valuable, that is, *if you are men of the State,* and gladly enjoy the advantages of Caesar's government, then pay him back some of his own when he demands it; "Render therefore to Caesar that which is Caesar's, and to God those things which are God's," [53]—leaving them no wiser than before as to which was which; for they did not wish to know.

When I converse with the freest of my neighbors, I perceive that, whatever they may say about the magnitude and seriousness of the question, and their regard for the public tranquillity, the long and the short of the matter is, that they cannot spare the protection of the existing government, and they dread the consequences of disobedience to it to their property and families. For my own part, I should not like to think that I ever rely on the protection of the State. But, if I deny the authority of the State when it presents its tax-bill, it will soon take and waste all my property, and so harass me and my children without end. This is hard. This makes it impossible for a man to live honestly and at the same time comfortably in outward respects. It will not be worth the while to accumulate property; that would be sure to go again. You must hire or squat somewhere, and raise but a small crop, and eat that soon.[54] You must live within yourself, and depend upon yourself, always tucked up and ready for a

52 Followers of King Herod (Herod Antipas) (ca. 20 B.C.E.–CA. 39 C.E.).
53 Allusion to Matthew 22:17–21: "Tell us therefore, What thinkest thou? Is it lawful to give tribute unto Caesar, or not? But Jesus perceived their wickedness, and said, Why tempt ye me, ye hypocrites? Shew me the tribute money. And they brought unto him a penny. And he saith unto them, Whose is this image and superscription? They say unto him, Caesar's. Then saith he unto them, Render therefore unto Caesar the things which are Caesar's; and unto God the things that are God's."
54 Thoreau's arrest took place while he was living on Emerson's land. Although he had permission to live on Emerson's land, Thoreau liked to refer to himself as a squatter.

55 Possible allusion to Bias (ca. sixth century B.C.E.), one of the Seven Wise Men of Greece, referred to in *Walden,* and in Thoreau's journal of 12 July 1840: "In the sack of Priene, when the inhabitants with much hurry and bustle were carrying their effects to a place of safety, some one asked Bias, who remained tranquil amid the confusion, why he was not thinking how he should save something, as the others were. 'I do so,' said Bias, 'for I carry all my effects with me.'" [J 1:169–170]. Thoreau probably read of Bias in François de Salignac de La Mothe Fénelon's (1651–1715) *The Lives and Most Remarkable Maxims of the Antient Philosophers.*

56 The Turkish Empire had been in a steady decline since the sixteenth century and was referred to in Thoreau's time as the "sick man" of Europe.

57 Kung Fu-tze (ca. 551–478 B.C.E.), Chinese philosopher of ethical precepts for good management of family and society.

58 Thoreau's translation of *Analects* 8:13 from Jean-Pierre-Guillaume Pauthier's (1801–1873) French translation of Confucius as found in his *Confucius et Mencius: Les Quatre Livres de Philosophie Moral et Politique de la Chine* (Paris: Charpentier, 1841).

59 Although Massachusetts, in 1834, disestablished churches—that is, abrogated any official connection between church and state—unless a person officially "signed off" from his parish church, he was still considered a member.

60 Church tax bill of 1840, which Thoreau did not pay, was in support of Barzillai Frost (1804–1858), the minister of the First Parish Church of Concord from 1837 to 1857.

61 The Middlesex County Jail, a three-story granite building near the town center.

62 It is unknown who may have paid Thoreau's church tax bill of 1840. Because he signed off in 1841, this would have been the last tax year for which he would have been responsible.

63 Thoreau and his brother John (1815–1842) ran the Concord Academy from 1838 to 1841, charging a subscription of six dollars per quarter.

start,[55] and not have many affairs. A man may grow rich in Turkey even, if he will be in all respects a good subject of the Turkish government.[56] Confucius[57] said,—"If a State is governed by the principles of reason, poverty and misery are subjects of shame; if a State is not governed by the principles of reason, riches and honors are subjects of shame."[58] No: until I want the protection of Massachusetts to be extended to me in some distant southern port, where my liberty is endangered, or until I am bent solely on building up an estate at home by peaceful enterprise, I can afford to refuse allegiance to Massachusetts, and her right to my property and life. It costs me less in every sense to incur the penalty of disobedience to the State, than it would to obey. I should feel as if I were worth less in that case.

Some years ago, the State met me in behalf of the church,[59] and commanded me to pay a certain sum toward the support of a clergyman[60] whose preaching my father attended, but never I myself. "Pay it," it said, "or be locked up in the jail."[61] I declined to pay. But, unfortunately, another man saw fit to pay it.[62] I did not see why the schoolmaster should be taxed to support the priest, and not the priest the schoolmaster; for I was not the State's schoolmaster, but I supported myself by voluntary subscription.[63] I did not see why the lyceum[64] should not present its tax-bill, and have the State to back its demand, as well as the church. However, at the request of the selectmen, I condescended to make some such statement as this in writing:—"Know all men by these presents, that I, Henry Thoreau, do not wish to be regarded as a member of any incorporated society which I have not joined."[65] This I gave to the town-clerk;[66] and he has it. The State, having thus learned that I did not wish to be regarded as a member of that church, has never made a like demand on me since; though it said that it must adhere to its original presumption that time.

If I had known how to name them, I should then have signed off in detail from all the societies which I never signed on to; but I did not know where to find such a complete list.

I have paid no poll-tax[67] for six years.[68] I was put into a jail once on this account, for one night; and, as I stood considering the walls of solid stone, two or three feet thick, the door of wood and iron, a foot thick, and the iron grating which strained the light, I could not help being struck with the foolishness of that institution which treated me as if I were mere flesh and blood and bones, to be locked up. I wondered that it should have concluded at length that this was the best use it could put me to, and had never thought to avail itself of my services in some way. I saw that, if there was a wall of stone between me and my townsmen, there was a still more difficult one to climb or break through, before they could get to be as free as I was. I did not for a moment feel confined, and the walls seemed a great waste of stone and mortar. I felt as if I alone of all my townsmen had paid my tax. They plainly did not know how to treat me, but behaved like persons who are underbred. In every threat and in every compliment there was a blunder; for they thought that my chief desire was to stand the other side of that stone wall. I could not but smile to see how industriously they locked the door on my meditations, which followed them out again without let or hinderance, and *they* were really all that was dangerous. As they could not reach me, they had resolved to punish my body; just as boys, if they cannot come at some person against whom they have a spite, will abuse his dog. I saw that the State was half-witted, that it was timid as a lone woman with her silver spoons, and that it did not know its friends from its foes, and I lost all my remaining respect for it, and pitied it.

Thus the State never intentionally confronts a man's

64 The lyceum was a local association for the discussion of topics of current interest. The Concord Lyceum began in 1829. Thoreau was elected secretary of the Lyceum in October 1839 and curator in November 1839. In 1840 he was again elected curator and secretary, but declined, retiring from the position in December 1840 only to be again elected curator several more times. Thoreau gave nineteen lectures at the Lyceum, the first of which, "Society," was delivered on 11 April 1838, and the last of which, "Wild Apples," was given on 8 February 1860.

65 Thoreau's statement, written on 6 January 1841, was actually more specific: "I do not wish to be considered a member of the First Parish in this town. Henry D. Thoreau."

66 Cyrus Stow (1787–1876).

67 Tax levied on individual adult males, not on goods or property, which must be paid in order to vote.

68 Thoreau probably stopped paying his poll tax in 1843. Although the implication of this essay is that his refusal to pay the levy was a protest against the war with Mexico, he had stopped paying the tax before war was declared.

69 Moral or religious principles, or laws of con-science, that take precedence over the constitu-tions or statutes of society. The term was popu-larized by the New York senator William Henry Seward (1801–1872) in his argument against the Fugitive Slave Bill on 11 March 1850: "The Con-stitution devotes the national domain to union, to justice, to defence, to welfare and to liberty. But there is a higher law than the Constitution." Echoing Seward, Thoreau wrote in "Slavery in Massachusetts": "What is wanted is men, not of policy, but of probity—who recognize a higher law than the Constitution, or the decision of the majority."

The concept of higher law can be found in the Judeo-Christian belief in moral law, as well as in the idea of a natural law formulated by Plato and by Cicero, who wrote in his "On the Re-public": "There is in fact a true law—namely, right reason—which is in accordance with nature, ap-plies to all men, and is unchangeable and eternal. By its commands it summons men to the perfor-mance of their duties; by its prohibitions it re-strains them from doing wrong. To invalidate this law by human legislation is never morally right, nor is it permissible ever to restrict its operation; and to annul it wholly is impossible." Emerson wrote in *Nature:* "The moral law lies at the center of nature and radiates to the circumference." In nineteenth-century New England, as debates about the legality and morality of slavery raged, the call to a higher law became paramount.
70 These were narrow cells eighteen feet in length.
71 Hugh Connell (sometimes O'Connell), born in Ireland ca. 1820.

sense, intellectual or moral, but only his body, his senses. It is not armed with superior wit or honesty, but with superior physical strength. I was not born to be forced. I will breathe after my own fashion. Let us see who is the strongest. What force has a multitude? They only can force me who obey a higher law[69] than I. They force me to become like themselves. I do not hear of *men* being *forced* to live this way or that by masses of men. What sort of life were that to live? When I meet a government which says to me, "Your money or your life," why should I be in haste to give it my money? It may be in a great strait, and not know what to do: I cannot help that. It must help itself; do as I do. It is not worth the while to snivel about it. I am not responsible for the successful working of the machinery of society. I am not the son of the engineer. I perceive that, when an acorn and a chestnut fall side by side, the one does not remain inert to make way for the other, but both obey their own laws, and spring and grow and flourish as best they can, till one, perchance, overshadows and destroys the other. If a plant cannot live according to its nature, it dies; and so a man.

The night in prison was novel and interesting enough. The prisoners in their shirt-sleeves were enjoying a chat and the evening air in the door-way, when I entered. But the jailer said, "Come, boys, it is time to lock up"; and so they dispersed, and I heard the sound of their steps returning into the hollow apartments.[70] My room-mate was introduced to me by the jailer, as "a first-rate fellow and a clever man."[71] When the door was locked, he showed me where to hang my hat, and how he man-aged matters there. The rooms were whitewashed once a month; and this one, at least, was the whitest, most simply furnished, and probably neatest apartment in the town. He naturally wanted to know where I came from, and what brought me there; and, when I had told him, I asked him in my turn how he came there, presuming him to be an honest man, of course; and, as the world goes, I believe he was. "Why," said he, "they accuse me of burning a barn; but I never did it."[72] As near as I could discover, he had probably gone to bed in a barn when drunk, and smoked his pipe there; and so a barn was burnt. He had the reputation of being a clever man, had been there some three months waiting for his trial to come on, and would have to wait as much longer; but he was quite domesticated and contented, since he got his board for nothing, and thought that he was well treated.

He occupied one window, and I the other; and I saw, that, if one stayed there long, his principal business would be to look out the window. I had soon read all the tracts that were left there, and examined where former prisoners had broken out, and where a grate had been sawed off, and heard the history of the various occupants of that room; for I found that even here there was a history and a gossip which never circulated beyond the walls of the jail. Probably this is the only house in the town where verses are composed, which are afterward printed in a circular form, but not published. I was shown quite a long list of verses which were composed by some young men who had been detected in an attempt to escape, who avenged themselves by singing them.

I pumped my fellow-prisoner as dry as I could, for fear I should never see him again; but at length he showed me which was my bed, and left me to blow out the lamp.

It was like travelling into a far country, such as I had never expected to behold, to lie there for one night. It seemed to me that I never had heard the town-clock strike before, nor the evening sounds of the village; for we slept with the windows open, which were inside the grating. It was to see my native village in the light of the middle ages, and our Concord was turned into a Rhine

72 Connell, who had been arraigned in the Middlesex County Court of Common Pleas, pleaded not guilty to the March 1846 burning of Israel Hunt's (1783–1865) barn in Sudbury. He was found guilty in October when the court sat for criminal cases. He appealed and was again found guilty when the court sat in Lowell in December. He was remanded to the Charlestown State Prison for five years, being discharged on 8 December 1851.

73 The Middlesex Hotel, a four-story wooden hotel, the back of which stood near the jail.

74 A seat of county government.

75 It is unknown who may have paid Thoreau's poll tax. It may have been his Aunt Maria Thoreau (1794–1881). Edward Emerson (1844–1930) wrote that Staples "told me that he never knew who paid it, but, if I recollect rightly, said that he supposed that it was Miss Elizabeth Hoar, or her father." Staples may have been misremembering Samuel Hoar paying Amos Bronson Alcott's tax a few years before.

76 Allusion to George Herbert's (1593–1633) "The Answer": "Like summer friends, / Flies of estate and sunshine."

stream, and visions of knights and castles passed before me. They were the voices of old burghers that I heard in the streets. I was an involuntary spectator and auditor of whatever was done and said in the kitchen of the adjacent village-inn,[73]—a wholly new and rare experience to me. It was a closer view of my native town. I was fairly inside of it. I never had seen its institutions before. This is one of its peculiar institutions; for it is a shire town.[74] I began to comprehend what its inhabitants were about.

In the morning, our breakfasts were put through the hole in the door, in small oblong-square tin pans, made to fit, and holding a pint of chocolate, with brown bread, and an iron spoon. When they called for the vessels again, I was green enough to return what bread I had left; but my comrade seized it, and said that I should lay that up for lunch or dinner. Soon after, he was let out to work at haying in a neighboring field, whither he went every day, and would not be back till noon; so he bade me good-day, saying that he doubted if he should see me again.

When I came out of prison,—for some one interfered, and paid that tax,[75]—I did not perceive that great changes had taken place on the common, such as he observed who went in a youth, and emerged a tottering and gray-headed man; and yet a change had to my eyes come over the scene,—the town, and State, and country,— greater than any that mere time could effect. I saw yet more distinctly the State in which I lived. I saw to what extent the people among whom I lived could be trusted as good neighbors and friends; that their friendship was for summer weather only;[76] that they did not greatly propose to do right; that they were a distinct race from me by their prejudices and superstitions, as the Chinamen and Malays are; that, in their sacrifices to humanity, they ran no risks, not even to their property; that, after all, they were not so noble but they treated the thief as he had treated them,[77] and hoped, by a certain outward observance and a few prayers, and by walking in a particular straight though useless path[78] from time to time, to save their souls. This may be to judge my neighbors harshly; for I believe that most of them are not aware that they have such an institution as the jail in their village.

It was formerly the custom in our village, when a poor debtor came out of jail, for his acquaintances to salute him, looking through their fingers, which were crossed to represent the grating of the jail window, "How do ye do?" My neighbors did not thus salute me, but first looked at me, and then at one another, as if I had returned from a long journey. I was put into jail as I was going to the shoemaker's[79] to get a shoe which was mended. When I was let out the next morning, I proceeded to finish my errand, and, having put on my mended shoe, joined a huckleberry party,[80] who were impatient to put themselves under my conduct; and in half an hour,—for the horse was soon tackled,[81]—was in the midst of a huckleberry field, on one of our highest hills, two miles off;[82] and then the State was nowhere to be seen.

This is the whole history[83] of "My Prisons."[84]

I have never declined paying the highway tax, because I am as desirous of being a good neighbor as I am of being a bad subject; and, as for supporting schools, I am doing my part to educate my fellow-countrymen now. It is for no particular item in the tax-bill that I refuse to pay it. I simply wish to refuse allegiance to the State, to withdraw and stand aloof from it effectually. I do not care to trace the course of my dollar, if I could, till it buys a man, or a musket to shoot one with,—the dollar is innocent,—but I am concerned to trace the effects of my allegiance. In fact, I quietly declare war with the State,

77 Inversion of the Golden Rule found in the New Testament—Matthew 5:44, 7:12 and Luke 6:31: "And as ye would that men should do to you, do ye also to them likewise"—as well as the Talmud, the Koran, the Analects of Confucius, and other religious and philosophical writings.

78 Allusion to Matthew 7:14: "Because strait *is the* gate, and narrow *is* the way, which leadeth unto life, and few there be that find it."

79 There were several shoemakers in Concord. Emerson wrote in "The Fortunes of the Republic": "In Massachusetts, every twelfth man is a shoemaker."

80 Emerson was disappointed in what he saw as a lack of ambition, and wrote in his eulogy of Thoreau: "Wanting this, instead of engineering for all America, he was captain of a huckleberry party."

81 Harnessed to a wagon.

82 As he wrote in *Walden*, Thoreau "returned to the woods in season to get my dinner of huckleberries on Fair Haven Hill" [Wa 166].

83 One incident which Thoreau left out of his "whole history" was recounted by Edward Emerson: "He was kept awake by a man in the cell below ejaculating, 'What is life?' and, 'So this is life!' with a painful monotony. As last, willing to get whatever treasure of truth this sonorous earthen vessel might hold, Thoreau put his head to the iron window-bars and asked suddenly, 'Well, What *is* life, then?' but got no other reward than the sleep of the just, which his fellow-martyr did not further molest."

84 Allusion to *My Prisons: Memoirs of Silvio Pellico of Saluzzo*, the 1836 English translation of Silvio Pellico's (1789–1854) *Le Mie Prigioni*.

after my fashion, though I will still make what use and get what advantage of her I can, as is usual in such cases.

If others pay the tax which is demanded of me, from a sympathy with the State, they do but what they have already done in their own case, or rather they abet injustice to a greater extent than the State requires. If they pay the tax from a mistaken interest in the individual taxed, to save his property or prevent his going to jail, it is because they have not considered wisely how far they let their private feelings interfere with the public good.

This, then, is my position at present. But one cannot be too much on his guard in such a case, lest his action be biassed by obstinacy, or an undue regard for the opinions of men. Let him see that he does only what belongs to himself and to the hour.

I think sometimes, Why, this people mean well; they are only ignorant; they would do better if they knew how: why give your neighbors this pain to treat you as they are not inclined to? But I think, again, this is no reason why I should do as they do, or permit others to suffer much greater pain of a different kind. Again, I sometimes say to myself, When many millions of men, without heat, without ill-will, without personal feeling of any kind, demand of you a few shillings only, without the possibility, such is their constitution, of retracting or altering their present demand, and without the possibility, on your side, of appeal to any other millions, why expose yourself to this overwhelming brute force? You do not resist cold and hunger, the winds and the waves, thus obstinately; you quietly submit to a thousand similar necessities. You do not put your head into the fire. But just in proportion as I regard this as not wholly a brute force, but partly a human force, and consider that I have relations to those millions as to so many millions of men, and not of mere brute or inanimate things, I see that appeal is possible, first and instantaneously, from them to the Maker of them, and, secondly, from them to themselves. But, if I put my head deliberately into the fire, there is no appeal to fire or to the Maker of fire, and I have only myself to blame. If I could convince myself that I have any right to be satisfied with men as they are, and to treat them accordingly, and not according, in some respects, to my requisitions and expectations of what they and I ought to be, then, like a good Mussulman[85] and fatalist, I should endeavor to be satisfied with things as they are, and say it is the will of God. And, above all, there is this difference between resisting this and a purely brute or natural force, that I can resist this with some effect; but I cannot expect, like Orpheus, to change the nature of the rocks and trees and beasts.[86]

I do not wish to quarrel with any man or nation. I do not wish to split hairs, to make fine distinctions, or set myself up as better than my neighbors. I seek rather, I may say, even an excuse for conforming to the laws of the land. I am but too ready to conform to them. Indeed I have reason to suspect myself on this head; and each year, as the tax-gatherer comes round, I find myself disposed to review the acts and position of the general and state governments, and the spirit of the people, to discover a pretext for conformity.[87] I believe that the State will soon be able to take all my work of this sort out of my hands, and then I shall be no better patriot than my fellow-countrymen. Seen from a lower point of view, the Constitution, with all its faults, is very good; the law and the courts are very respectable; even this State and this American government are, in many respects, very admirable and rare things, to be thankful for, such as a great many have described them; but seen from a point of view a little higher, they are what I have described them; seen from a higher still, and the highest, who shall say what they are, or that they are worth looking at or thinking of at all?

85 Muslim.

86 In Greek mythology, Orpheus's music had supernatural powers, and his singing could charm animals and inanimate objects.

87 In "Civil Disobedience," the posthumously published version of this essay in *A Yankee in Canada, with Anti-Slavery and Reform Papers,* this line is followed by a quotation from George Peele's (1556–1596) *The Battle of Alcazar* II.ii.425–430:

> "We must affect our country as our parents;
> And if at any time we alienate
> Our love or industry from doing it honor,
> We must respect effects and teach the soul
> Matter of conscience and religion,
> And not desire of rule or benefit."

88 Cf. "Paradise (To Be) Regained," note 56.
89 Daniel Webster (1782–1852), senator from Massachusetts, who would soon alienate abolitionists by his support of the Compromise of 1850 reaffirming fugitive slave laws: cf. "Slavery in Massachusetts," note 30.

However, the government does not concern me much, and I shall bestow the fewest possible thoughts on it. It is not many moments that I live under a government, even in this world. If a man is thought-free, fancy-free, imagination-free, that which *is not* never for a long time appearing *to be* to him, unwise rulers or reformers cannot fatally interrupt him.

I know that most men think differently from myself; but those whose lives are by profession devoted to the study of these or kindred subjects, content me as little as any. Statesmen and legislators, standing so completely within the institution, never distinctly and nakedly behold it. They speak of moving society, but have no resting-place without it.[88] They may be men of a certain experience and discrimination, and have no doubt invented ingenious and even useful systems, for which we sincerely thank them; but all their wit and usefulness lie within certain not very wide limits. They are wont to forget that the world is not governed by policy and expediency. Webster[89] never goes behind government, and so cannot speak with authority about it. His words are wisdom to those legislators who contemplate no essential reform in the existing government; but for thinkers, and those who legislate for all time, he never once glances at the subject. I know of those whose serene and wise speculations on this theme would soon reveal the limits of his mind's range and hospitality. Yet, compared with the cheap professions of most reformers, and the still cheaper wisdom and eloquence of politicians in general, his are almost the only sensible and valuable words, and we thank Heaven for him. Comparatively, he is always strong, original, and, above all, practical. Still his quality is not wisdom, but prudence. The lawyer's truth is not Truth, but consistency, or a consistent expediency. Truth is always in harmony with herself, and is not concerned chiefly to reveal the justice that may consist with wrong-doing. He well deserves to be called, as he has been called, the Defender of the Constitution.[90] There are really no blows to be given by him but defensive ones. He is not a leader, but a follower. His leaders are the men of '87.[91] "I have never made an effort," he says, "and never propose to make an effort; I have never countenanced an effort, and never mean to countenance an effort, to disturb the arrangement as originally made, by which various States came into the Union."[92] Still thinking of the sanction which the Constitution gives to slavery, he says, "Because it was a part of the original compact,—let it stand."[93] Notwithstanding his special acuteness and ability, he is unable to take a fact out of its merely political relations, and behold it as it lies absolutely to be disposed of by the intellect,—what, for instance, it behoves a man to do here in America to-day with regard to slavery, but ventures, or is driven, to make some such desperate answer as the following, while professing to speak absolutely, and as a private man,—from which what new and singular code of social duties might be inferred?—"The manner," says he, "in which the governments of those States where slavery exists are to regulate it, is for their own consideration, under their responsibility to their constituents, to the general laws of propriety, humanity, and justice, and to God. Associations formed elsewhere, springing from a feeling of humanity, or any other cause, have nothing whatever to do with it. They have never received any encouragement from me, and they never will."[94]

They who know of no purer sources of truth, who have traced up its stream no higher, stand, and wisely stand, by the Bible and the Constitution, and drink at it there with reverence and humanity; but they who behold where it comes trickling into this lake or that pool, gird up their loins[95] once more, and continue their pilgrimage toward its fountain-head.

90 An epithet given Webster in 1830 in recognition of his defense of the Union and the Constitution—"liberty and Union, now and forever, one and inseparable"—over states' rights.

91 The men who first drafted the Constitution in 1787 when the Constitutional Convention was held in Philadelphia.

92 Quoted from Webster's speech of 22 December 1845 on "The Admission of Texas," as quoted in his "Speech in the U.S. Senate, March 23, 1848, Upon the War with Mexico."

93 Quoted from Webster's "Speech in the U.S. Senate, March 23, 1848, Upon the War with Mexico."

94 Quoted, with one minor variant—deletion of paragraph break after "and to God"—from Webster's 12 August 1848 speech "On the Oregon Bill" as published in O. C. Gardiner's *The Great Issue; or, The Three Presidential Candidates* (New York: W. C. Bryant, 1848). This quotation was followed by Thoreau's note: "These extracts have been inserted since the Lecture was read."

95 Allusion to Ephesians 6:14: "Stand therefore, having your loins girt about with truth, and having on the breastplate of righteousness."

96 In "Civil Disobedience," the posthumously published version of this essay in *A Yankee in Canada, with Anti-Slavery and Reform Papers*, the following sentence about Confucius was added: "Even the Chinese philosopher was wise enough to regard the individual as the basis of the empire."

No man with a genius for legislation has appeared in America. They are rare in the history of the world. There are orators, politicians, and eloquent men, by the thousand; but the speaker has not yet opened his mouth to speak, who is capable of settling the much-vexed questions of the day. We love eloquence for its own sake, and not for any truth which it may utter, or any heroism it may inspire. Our legislators have not yet learned the comparative value of free-trade and of freedom, of union, and of rectitude, to a nation. They have no genius or talent for comparatively humble questions of taxation and finance, commerce and manufactures and agriculture. If we were left solely to the wordy wit of legislators in Congress for our guidance, uncorrected by the seasonable experience and the effectual complaints of the people, America would not long retain her rank among the nations. For eighteen hundred years, though perchance I have no right to say it, the New Testament has been written; yet where is the legislator who has wisdom and practical talent enough to avail himself of the light which it sheds on the science of legislation.

The authority of government, even such as I am willing to submit to,—for I will cheerfully obey those who know and can do better than I, and in many things even those who neither know nor can do so well,—is still an impure one: to be strictly just, it must have the sanction and consent of the governed. It can have no pure right over my person and property but what I concede to it. The progress from an absolute to a limited monarchy, from a limited monarchy to a democracy, is a progress toward a true respect for the individual.[96] Is a democracy, such as we know it, the last improvement possible in government? Is it not possible to take a step further towards recognizing and organizing the rights of man? There will never be a really free and enlightened State, until the State comes to recognize the individual as a higher and independent power, from which all its own power and authority are derived, and treats him accordingly. I please myself with imagining a State at last which can afford to be just to all men, and to treat the individual with respect as a neighbor; which even would not think it inconsistent with its own repose, if a few were to live aloof from it, not meddling with it, nor embraced by it, who fulfilled all the duties of neighbors and fellowmen. A State which bore this kind of fruit, and suffered it to drop off as fast as it ripened, would prepare the way for a still more perfect and glorious State, which I have also imagined, but not yet anywhere seen.

1 Held on 22 June 1854 to denounce the Kansas-Nebraska Act and work toward the repealing of the Fugitive Slave Law.

2 The Kansas-Nebraska Act, which would be passed by the U.S. Congress in May 1854 following much debate, left the question of slavery open for the settlers in the territories of Kansas and Nebraska to decide for themselves. This act virtually repealed the Missouri Compromise of 1820, which prohibited slavery north of latitude 36°30'.

3 Twelve men were arrested on various charges for their involvement in the attempted rescue of Anthony Burns (see note 18 below), during which federal marshal James Batchelder (1830–1854) was killed. Among those held was Thoreau's friend Thomas Wentworth Higginson (1823–1911), who called the endeavor "one of the very best plots that ever—failed."

4 Allusion to the battle at the North Bridge in Concord on 19 April 1775 signaling the start of the American Revolution.

5 Concord citizens who participated in the battle at the North Bridge.

6 Site of the first battle of the Revolutionary War on 19 April 1775.

7 According to the 1850 census Massachusetts had a population nearing one million citizens.

8 The Fugitive Slave Act of 1850, passed as part of the Compromise of 1850, required the return of runaway slaves to their owners and provided severe penalties for helping fugitive slaves escape.

Slavery in Massachusetts

I lately attended a meeting of the citizens of Concord,[1] expecting, as one among many, to speak on the subject of slavery in Massachusetts; but I was surprised and disappointed to find that what had called my townsmen together was the destiny of Nebraska,[2] and not of Massachusetts, and that what I had to say would be entirely out of order. I had thought that the house was on fire, and not the prairie; but though several of the citizens of Massachusetts are now in prison for attempting to rescue a slave from her own clutches,[3] not one of the speakers at that meeting expressed regret for it, not one even referred to it. It was only the disposition of some wild lands a thousand miles off, which appeared to concern them. The inhabitants of Concord are not prepared to stand by one of their own bridges,[4] but talk only of taking up a position on the highlands beyond the Yellowstone river. Our Buttricks, and Davises, and Hosmers[5] are retreating thither, and I fear that they will have no Lexington Common[6] between them and the enemy. There is not one slave in Nebraska; there are perhaps a million slaves in Massachusetts.[7]

They who have been bred in the school of politics fail now and always to face the facts. Their measures are half measures and make-shifts, merely. They put off the day of settlement indefinitely, and meanwhile, the debt accumulates. Though the Fugitive Slave Law[8] had not been the subject of discussion on that occasion, it was at length faintly resolved by my townsmen, at an adjourned meeting, as I learn, that the compromise compact of 1820[9] having been repudiated by one of the parties, "Therefore, . . . the Fugitive Slave Law must be repealed." But this is not the reason why an iniquitous law should be repealed. The fact which the politician faces is merely, that there is less honor among thieves than was supposed, and not the fact that they are thieves.

As I had no opportunity to express my thoughts at that meeting, will you allow me to do so here?

Again it happens that the Boston Court House is full of armed men,[10] holding prisoner and trying a MAN, to find out if he is not really a SLAVE. Does any one think that Justice or God awaits Mr. Loring's[11] decision? For him to sit there deciding still, when this question is already decided from eternity to eternity, and the unlettered slave himself, and the multitude around, have long since heard and assented to the decision, is simply to make himself ridiculous. We may be tempted to ask from whom he received his commission, and who he is that received it; what novel statutes he obeys, and what precedents are to him of authority. Such an arbiter's very existence is an impertinence. We do not ask him to make up his mind, but to make up his pack.

I listen to hear the voice of a Governor, Commander-in-Chief of the forces of Massachusetts. I hear only the creaking of crickets and the hum of insects which now fill the summer air. The Governor's exploit is to review the troops on muster days. I have seen him on horseback, with his hat off, listening to a chaplain's prayer. It chances that is all I have ever seen of a Governor. I think that I could manage to get along without one. If *he* is not of the least use to prevent my being kidnapped, pray of what important use is he likely to be to me? When freedom is most endangered, he dwells in the deepest obscurity. A distinguished clergyman told me that he chose the profession of a clergyman, because it afforded the

9 Missouri Compromise.
10 The Boston Court House was secured by federal and state troops to prevent the rescue of Anthony Burns. During the Sims affair it was protected by regular, as well as additional specially recruited, policemen.
11 Edward Greely Loring (1802–1890), Boston judge and United States commissioner of the circuit court in Massachusetts, who issued the orders for the capture of both Simms (see next note) and Burns.

12 Thomas Sims, sometimes Simms (b. ca. 1834), a fugitive slave from Georgia who fled in late February 1851 and was arrested in Boston on 4 April 1851.

13 George S. Boutwell (1818–1905), of whom Thoreau wrote in his journal that he was "so named, perchance, because he goes about well to suit the prevailing wind" [J 2:174].

14 Emory Washburn (1800–1877), who served only one term (1854–1855) as governor of Massachusetts.

15 The Latimer Law of March 1843, named after the capturing of fugitive slave George Latimer (1820–1896), made it illegal for the state of Massachusetts to aid in the capture, or the remanding of, a fugitive slave.

16 A prejudgment process ordering the seizure or attachment of property, alleged to be illegally taken or wrongfully withheld.

17 A writ of replevin was served upon the U.S. Marshal Watson Freeman, who refused to comply on the ground that he held Burns by legal process. Freeman had a strong civil and military force backing him. Boston coroner Charles Emery Stevens (1815–1893) expressed his readiness to serve the writ and release the prisoner provided a sufficient force could be enlisted to overcome the Freeman's forces.

most leisure for literary pursuits. I would recommend to him the profession of a Governor.

Three years ago, also, when the Simms tragedy[12] was acted, I said to myself, there is such an officer, if not such a man, as the Governor of Massachusetts,—what has he been about the last fortnight?[13] Has he had as much as he could do to keep on the fence during this moral earthquake? It seemed to me that no keener satire could have been aimed at, no more cutting insult have been offered to that man, than just what happened—the absence of all inquiry after him in that crisis. The worst and the most I chance to know of him is, that he did not improve that opportunity to make himself known, and worthily known. He could at least have *resigned* himself into fame. It appeared to be forgotten that there was such a man, or such an office. Yet no doubt he was endeavoring to fill the gubernatorial chair all the while. He was no Governor of mine. He did not govern me.

But at last, in the present case, the Governor was heard from.[14] After he and the United States Government had perfectly succeeded in robbing a poor innocent black man of his liberty for life, and, as far as they could, of his Creator's likeness in his breast, he made a speech to his accomplices, at a congratulatory supper!

I have read a recent law of this State, making it penal for "any officer of the Commonwealth" to "detain, or aid in the . . . detention," any where within its limits, "of any person, for the reason that he is claimed as a fugitive slave."[15] Also, it was a matter of notoriety that a writ of replevin[16] to take the fugitive out of the custody of the United States Marshal could not be served, for want of sufficient force to aid the officer.[17]

I had thought that the Governor was in some sense the executive officer of the State; that it was his business, as a Governor, to see that the laws of the State were executed; while, as a man, he took care that he did not, by so doing, break the laws of humanity; but when there is any special important use for him, he is useless, or worse than useless, and permits the laws of the State to go unexecuted. Perhaps I do not know what are the duties of a Governor; but if to be a Governor requires to subject one's self to so much ignominy without remedy, if it is to put a restraint upon my manhood, I shall take care never to be Governor of Massachusetts. I have not read far in the statutes of this Commonwealth. It is not profitable reading. They do not always say what is true; and they do not always mean what they say. What I am concerned to know is, that that man's influence and authority were on the side of the slaveholder, and not of the slave—of the guilty, and not of the innocent—of injustice, and not of justice. I never saw him of whom I speak; indeed, I did not know that he was Governor until this event occurred. I heard of him and Anthony Burns[18] at the same time, and thus, undoubtedly, most will hear of him. So far am I from being governed by him. I do not mean that it was any thing to his discredit that I had not heard of him, only that I heard what I did. The worst I shall say of him is, that he proved no better than the majority of his constituents would be likely to prove. In my opinion, he was not equal to the occasion.

The whole military force of the State[19] is at the service of a Mr. Suttle,[20] a slaveholder from Virginia, to enable him to catch a man whom he calls his property; but not a soldier is offered to save a citizen of Massachusetts from being kidnapped! Is this what all these soldiers, all this *training* has been for these seventy-nine years past? Have they been trained merely to rob Mexico,[21] and carry back fugitive slaves to their masters?

These very nights, I heard the sound of a drum in our streets. There were men *training* still; and for what? I could with an effort pardon the cockerels[22] of Concord for crowing still, for they, perchance, had not been

18 Anthony Burns (ca. 1834–1862) was a fugitive slave who was arrested on 24 May 1854. Within days handbills were posted announcing: "A MAN KIDNAPPED! A PUBLIC MEETING AT FANEUIL HALL! WILL BE HELD THIS FRIDAY EVEN'G, May 26th, at 7 o'clock, To secure justice for A MAN CLAIMED AS A SLAVE by a VIRGINIA KIDNAPPER! And NOW IMPRISONED IN BOSTON COURT HOUSE, in defiance of the Laws of Massachusetts, Shall be plunged into the Hell of Virginia Slavery by a Massachusetts Judge of Probate! BOSTON, May 26, 1854."

19 A form of martial law was declared when the Mayor of Boston issued a proclamation on 2 June 1854 stating: "To secure order throughout the city this day, Major-General Edmands and the Chief of Police will make such disposition of the respective forces under their commands as will best promote that important object; and they are clothed with full discretionary power to sustain the laws of the land. All well-disposed citizens and other persons are urgently requested to leave those streets which it may be found necessary to clear temporarily, and under no circumstances to obstruct or molest any officer, civil or military, in the lawful discharge of his duty."

20 Charles F. Suttle of Alexandria, Virginia, who came to Boston to have Burns arrested and remanded.

21 The annexation of Texas in 1845 was considered by many to be the robbing of Mexico of its rightful territory.

22 Young rooster, under one year old.

23 Members of a "train band" training for service in the militia.

24 A rescue having failed, Burns was convicted on 2 June of being a fugitive slave and was brought to the waterfront, shackled, under the escort of 1,500 Massachusetts militiamen, the entire Boston police force, 145 federal troops with cannon, and 100 special deputies, to be placed on ship to return him to slavery in Virginia. An estimated crowd of fifty thousand lined the streets of Boston to witness this. The later fate of Burns—the purchase of his freedom within the year, his attending Oberlin College, his service as a Baptist minister—received no mention in Thoreau's writings.

25 Allusion to the pied clothing of a court fool or jester, with a possible allusion to Walter Scott's *Ivanhoe*, in which a character is described as a "fond fool . . . decked in a painted coat, and jangling as pert and as proud as any popinjay."

26 Anthony Burns.

27 On this date, Sims was sent back into slavery.

beaten that morning; but I could not excuse this rub-a-dub of the "trainers."[23] The slave was carried back by exactly such as these,[24] i.e., by the soldier, of whom the best you can say in this connection is that he is a fool made conspicuous by a painted coat.[25]

Three years ago, also, just a week after the authorities of Boston assembled to carry back a perfectly innocent man, and one whom they knew to be innocent, into slavery,[26] the inhabitants of Concord caused the bells to be rung and the cannons to be fired, to celebrate their liberty—and the courage and love of liberty of their ancestors who fought at the bridge. As if *those* three millions had fought for the right to be free themselves, but to hold in slavery three million others. Now-a-days men wear a fool's cap, and call it a liberty cap. I do not know but there are some, who, if they were tied to a whipping-post, and could get but one hand free, would use it to ring the bells and fire the cannons, to celebrate *their* liberty. So some of my townsmen took the liberty to ring and fire; that was the extent of their freedom; and when the sound of the bells died away, their liberty died away also; when the powder was all expended, their liberty went off with the smoke.

The joke could be no broader, if the inmates of the prisons were to subscribe for all the powder to be used in such salutes, and hire the jailers to do the firing and ringing for them, while they enjoyed it through the grating.

This is what I thought about my neighbors.

Every humane and intelligent inhabitant of Concord, when he or she heard those bells and those cannons, thought not with pride of the events of the 19th of April, 1775, but with shame of the events of the 12th of April, 1851.[27] But now we have half buried that old shame under a new one.

Massachusetts sat waiting Mr. Loring's decision, as if

it could in any way affect her own criminality. Her crime, the most conspicuous and fatal crime of all, was permitting him to be the umpire in such a case. It was really the trial of Massachusetts. Every moment that she hesitated to set this man free—every moment that she now hesitates to atone for her crime, she is convicted. The Commissioner on her case is God; not Edward G. God,[28] but simple God.

I wish my countrymen to consider, that whatever the human law may be, neither an individual nor a nation can ever commit the least act of injustice against the obscurest individual, without having to pay the penalty for it. A government which deliberately enacts injustice, and persists in it, will at length ever become the laughing-stock of the world.

Much has been said about American slavery, but I think that we do not even yet realize what slavery is. If I were seriously to propose to Congress to make mankind into sausages,[29] I have no doubt that most of the members would smile at my proposition, and if any believed me to be in earnest, they would think that I proposed something much worse than Congress had ever done. But if any of them will tell me that to make a man into a sausage would be much worse,—would be any worse, than to make him into a slave,—than it was to enact the Fugitive Slave Law, I will accuse him of foolishness, of intellectual incapacity, of making a distinction without a difference. The one is just as sensible a proposition as the other.

I hear a good deal said about trampling this law under foot. Why, one need not go out of his way to do that. This law rises not to the level of the head or the reason; its natural habitat is in the dirt. It was born and bred, and has its life only in the dust and mire, on a level with the feet, and he who walks with freedom, and does not with Hindoo mercy avoid treading on every venomous

28 Reference to Edward G. Loring.
29 Echo of Jonathan Swift's "A Modest Proposal," in which he proposed the eating of Irish children "for preventing the children of poor people in Ireland from being a burden to their parents or country, and for making them beneficial to the public."

30 Associated with Daniel Webster (cf. "Resistance to Civil Government," note 89), although it was James M. Mason, (1798–1871) Senator from Virginia, who wrote the bill. So strong was the sentiment against Webster in Massachusetts that Emerson wrote several diatribes in his journal, including "Pho! Let Mr Webster for decency's sake shut his lips once & forever on this word. The word *liberty* in the mouth of Mr Webster sounds like the word *love* in the mouth of a courtesan," and "Tell him that he who was their pride in the woods & mountains of New England is now their mortification; that they never name him; they have taken his picture from the wall & torn it—dropped the pieces in the gutter[;] they have taken his book of speeches from the shelf & put it in the stove."
31 The dung beetle, *Phanaus vindex*, buries its eggs in a ball of dung.

reptile, will inevitably tread on it, and so trample it under foot,—and Webster, its maker,[30] with it, like the dirt-bug and its ball.[31]

Recent events will be valuable as a criticism on the administration of justice in our midst, or, rather, as showing what are the true resources of justice in any community. It has come to this, that the friends of liberty, the friends of the slave, have shuddered when they have understood that his fate was left to the legal tribunals of the country to be decided. Free men have no faith that justice will be awarded in such a case; the judge may decide this way or that; it is a kind of accident, at best. It is evident that he is not a competent authority in so important a case. It is no time, then, to be judging according to his precedents, but to establish a precedent for the future. I would much rather trust to the sentiment of the people. In their vote, you would get something of some value, at least, however small; but, in the other case, only the trammelled judgment of an individual, of no significance, be it which way it might.

It is to some extent fatal to the courts, when the people are compelled to go behind them. I do not wish to believe that the courts were made for fair weather, and for very civil cases merely,—but think of leaving it to any court in the land to decide whether more than three millions of people, in this case, a sixth part of a nation, have a right to be freemen or not! But it has been left to the courts of *justice,* so-called—to the Supreme Court of the land—and, as you all know, recognizing no authority but the Constitution, it has decided that the three millions are, and shall continue to be, slaves. Such judges as these are merely the inspectors of a picklock and murderer's tools, to tell him whether they are in working order or not, and there they think that their responsibility ends. There was a prior case on the docket, which they, as judges appointed by God, had no right to skip; which having been justly settled, they would have been saved from this humiliation. It was the case of the murderer himself.

The law will never make men free; it is men who have got to make the law free. They are the lovers of law and order, who observe the law when the government breaks it.

Among human beings, the judge whose words seal the fate of a man furthest into eternity, is not he who merely pronounces the verdict of the law, but he, whoever he may be, who, from a love of truth, and unprejudiced by any custom or enactment of men, utters a true opinion or *sentence* concerning him. He it is that *sentences* him. Whoever has discerned truth, has received his commission from a higher source than the chiefest justice in the world, who can discern only law. He finds himself constituted judge of the judge. — Strange that it should be necessary to state such simple truths.

I am more and more convinced that, with reference to any public question, it is more important to know what the country thinks of it, than what the city thinks. The city does not *think* much. On any moral question, I would rather have the opinion of Boxboro[32] than of Boston and New York put together. When the former speaks, I feel as if somebody *had* spoken, as if *humanity* was yet, and a reasonable being had asserted its rights, — as if some unprejudiced men among the country's hills had at length turned their attention to the subject, and by a few sensible words redeemed the reputation of the race. When, in some obscure country town, the farmers come together to a special town meeting, to express their opinion on some subject which is vexing the land, that, I think, is the true Congress, and the most respectable one that is ever assembled in the United States.

It is evident that there are, in this Commonwealth, at least, two parties, becoming more and more distinct —

32 A small farming town Northwest of Concord where, Thoreau wrote on 15 January 1853, "they go to church as of old" [J 4:467].

the party of the city, and the party of the country. I know that the country is mean enough, but I am glad to believe that there is a slight difference in her favor. But as yet, she has few, if any organs, through which to express herself. The editorials which she reads, like the news, come from the sea-board. Let us, the inhabitants of the country, cultivate self-respect. Let us not send to the city for aught more essential than our broadcloths and groceries, or, if we read the opinions of the city, let us entertain opinions of our own.

Among measures to be adopted, I would suggest to make as earnest and vigorous an assault on the Press as has already been made, and with effect, on the Church. The Church has much improved within a few years; but the Press is almost, without exception, corrupt. I believe that, in this country, the press exerts a greater and a more pernicious influence than the Church did in its worst period. We are not a religious people, but we are a nation of politicians. We do not care for the Bible, but we do care for the newspaper. At any meeting of politicians,—like that at Concord the other evening, for instance,—how impertinent it would be to quote from the Bible! how pertinent to quote from a newspaper or from the Constitution! The newspaper is a Bible which we read every morning and every afternoon, standing and sitting, riding and walking. It is a Bible which every man carries in his pocket, which lies on every table and counter, and which the mail, and thousands of missionaries, are continually dispensing. It is, in short, the only book which America has printed, and which America reads. So wide is its influence. The editor is a preacher whom you voluntarily support. Your tax is commonly one cent daily, and it costs nothing for pew hire. But how many of these preachers preach the truth? I repeat the testimony of many an intelligent foreigner as well as my own convictions, when I say, that probably no country was ever ruled by so mean a class of tyrants as, with a few noble exceptions, are the editors of the periodical press in *this* country. And as they live and rule only by their servility, and appealing to the worst, and not the better nature of man, the people who read them are in the condition of the dog that returns to his vomit.

The *Liberator* and the *Commonwealth*[33] were the only papers in Boston, as far as I know, which made themselves heard in condemnation of the cowardice and meanness of the authorities of that city, as exhibited in '51. The other journals, almost without exception, by their manner of referring to and speaking of the Fugitive Slave Law, and the carrying back of the slave Simms, insulted the common sense of the country, at least. And, for the most part, they did this, one would say, because they thought so to secure the approbation of their patrons, not being aware that a sounder sentiment prevailed to any extent in the heart of the Commonwealth. I am told that some of them have improved of late; but they are still eminently time-serving.[34] Such is the character they have won.

But, thank fortune, this preacher can be even more easily reached by the weapons of the reformer than could the recreant priest. The free men of New England have only to refrain from purchasing and reading these sheets, have only to withhold their cents, to kill a score of them at once. One whom I respect told me that he purchased Mitchell's *Citizen*[35] in the cars, and then threw it out the window. But would not his contempt have been more fatally expressed, if he had not bought it?

Are they Americans? are they New Englanders? are they inhabitants of Lexington, and Concord, and Framingham, who read and support the Boston *Post, Mail, Journal, Advertiser, Courier,* and *Times?*[36] Are these the Flags of our Union?[37] I am not a newspaper reader,[38] and may omit to name the worst.

33 William Lloyd Garrison's abolitionist newspaper the *Liberator* and the Free-Soil paper the *Commonwealth.*
34 Obsequiously complying with the humors of men in power, often implying a surrender of independence and integrity.
35 John Mitchell's (1815–1875) pro-slavery paper the *Citizen.*
36 Contemporary Boston newspapers.
37 Allusion to the popular newspaper *Flag of Our Union,* published in Boston beginning in 1846 and, according to its masthead, "independent of party or sect."
38 Despite his dismissive attitude in "Life Without Principle" and in his journal, where he wrote, "Do not read the newspapers" [J 2:45], Thoreau was an avid reader of newspapers. In *A Week on the Concord and Merrimack Rivers* he wrote: "With a bending sail we glided rapidly by Tyngsborough and Chelmsford, each holding in one hand half of a tart country apple pie which we had purchased to celebrate our return, and in the other a fragment of the newspaper in which it was wrapped, devouring these with divided relish, and learning the news which had transpired since we sailed" [W 1:384]. Franklin Benjamin Sanborn (1831–1917) made the substantiating claim that few Concordians "read the newspapers (particularly the *New-York Tribune*) more eagerly than Thoreau."

39 Founded in 1846 to be, according to its first editor, William O. Eaton (1823–1880), "independent in politics and religion; liberal, industrious, enterprising, critically concerned with literacy and dramatic matters, and diligent in its mission to report and analyze the news, local and global."

40 Tavern or drinking place, usually considered of a low or disreputable class.

41 Allusion to the Unitarian minister Orville Dewey's (1794–1882) pronouncement: "I would *consent* that my own brother, my own son, should go—*ten times rather* would I go myself into slavery—than that this Union should be sacrificed for me or for us."

Could slavery suggest a more complete servility than some of these journals exhibit? Is there any dust which their conduct does not lick, and make fouler still with its slime? I do not know whether the Boston *Herald* [39] is still in existence, but I remember to have seen it about the streets when Simms was carried off. Did it not act its part well—serve its master faithfully? How could it have gone lower on its belly? How can a man stoop lower than he is low? do more than put his extremities in the place of the head he has? than make his head his lower extremity? When I have taken up this paper with my cuffs turned up, I have heard the gurgling of the sewer through every column. I have felt that I was handling a paper picked out of the public gutters, a leaf from the gospel of the gambling-house, the groggery [40] and the brothel, harmonizing with the gospel of the Merchants' Exchange.

The majority of the men of the North, and of the South, and East, and West, are not men of principle. If they vote, they do not send men to Congress on errands of humanity, but while their brothers and sisters are being scourged and hung for loving liberty, while—I might here insert all that slavery implies and is,—it is the mismanagement of wood and iron and stone and gold which concerns them. Do what you will, O Government! with my wife and children, my mother and brother, my father and sister, [41] I will obey your commands to the letter. It will indeed grieve me if you hurt them, if you deliver them to overseers to be hunted by hounds or to be whipped to death; but nevertheless, I will peaceably pursue my chosen calling on this fair earth, until perchance, one day, when I have put on mourning for them dead, I shall have persuaded you to relent. Such is the attitude, such are the words of Massachusetts.

Rather than do thus, I need not say what match I would touch, what system endeavor to blow up,—but as I love my life, I would side with the light, and let the dark earth roll from under me, calling my mother and my brother to follow.

I would remind my countrymen, that they are to be men first, and Americans only at a late and convenient hour. No matter how valuable law may be to protect your property, even to keep soul and body together, if it do not keep you and humanity together.

I am sorry to say, that I doubt if there is a judge in Massachusetts who is prepared to resign his office, and get his living innocently, whenever it is required of him to pass sentence under a law which is merely contrary to the law of God. I am compelled to see that they put themselves, or rather, are by character, in this respect, exactly on a level with the marine who discharges his musket in any direction he is ordered to. They are just as much tools and as little men. Certainly, they are not the more to be respected, because their master enslaves their understandings and consciences, instead of their bodies.

The judges and lawyers,—simply as such, I mean,—and all men of expediency,[42] try this case by a very low and incompetent standard. They consider, not whether the Fugitive Slave Law is right, but whether it is what they call *constitutional*. Is virtue constitutional, or vice? Is equity constitutional, or iniquity? In important moral and vital questions like this, it is just as impertinent to ask whether a law is constitutional or not, as to ask whether it is profitable or not. They persist in being the servants of the worst of men, and not the servants of humanity. The question is not whether you or your grandfather, seventy years ago, did not enter into an agreement to serve the devil, and that service is not accordingly now due; but whether you will not now, for once and at last, serve God,—in spite of your own past recreancy,[43] or that of your ancestor,—by obeying that eternal and only just CONSTITUTION, which He, and not any Jefferson or Adams, has written in your being.

42 Allusion to Paley: cf. "Resistance to Civil Government," note 8.
43 A cowardly yielding; mean-spiritedness.

44 The phrase—*and obey the successful candidate,*—found in his journal of 17 June 1854 under the section, "June 9th, continued." was added in *A Yankee in Canada, with Anti-Slavery and Reform Papers.*

45 Avarice, riches and worldly gain personified as a false god in Luke 16:13: "No servant can serve two masters. . . . You cannot serve God and mammon."

46 The Sabbath. In the "Sunday" chapter of *A Week on the Concord and Merrimack Rivers,* being observed with brother John traveling on Sunday, Thoreau called themselves "the truest observers of this sunny day. According to Hesiod,—'The seventh is a holy day, / For then Latona brought forth golden-rayed Apollo,' and by our reckoning this was the seventh day of the week, not the first" [W 1:64].

47 Confused noise or uproar.

48 Cf. "Resistance to Civil Government," note 69.

The amount of it is, if the majority vote the devil to be God, the minority will live and behave accordingly, and obey the successful candidate,[44] trusting that some time or other, by some Speaker's casting vote, perhaps, they may reinstate God. This is the highest principle I can get out of or invent for my neighbors. These men act as if they believed that they could safely slide down hill a little way—or a good way—and would surely come to a place, by and by, where they could begin to slide up again. This is expediency, or choosing that course which offers the slightest obstacles to the feet, that is, a downhill one. But there is no such thing as accomplishing a righteous reform by the use of "expediency." There is no such thing as sliding up hill. In morals, the only sliders are backsliders.

Thus we steadily worship Mammon,[45] both School, and State, and Church, and the Seventh Day[46] curse God with a tintamar[47] from one end of the Union to the other.

Will mankind never learn that policy is not morality—that it never secures any moral right, but considers merely what is expedient? chooses the available candidate, who is invariably the devil,—and what right have his constituents to be surprised, because the devil does not behave like an angel of light? What is wanted is men, not of policy, but of probity—who recognize a higher law[48] than the Constitution, or the decision of the majority. The fate of the country does not depend on how you vote at the polls—the worst man is as strong as the best at that game; it does not depend on what kind of paper you drop into the ballot-box once a year, but on what kind of man you drop from your chamber into the street every morning.

What should concern Massachusetts is not the Nebraska Bill, nor the Fugitive Slave Bill, but her own slave-holding and servility. Let the State dissolve her union with the slaveholder. She may wriggle and hesitate, and ask leave to read the Constitution once more; but she can find no respectable law or precedent which sanctions the continuance of such a Union for an instant.

Let each inhabitant of the State dissolve his union with her, as long as she delays to do her duty.

The events of the past month teach me to distrust Fame. I see that she does not finely discriminate, but coarsely hurrahs. She considers not the simple heroism of an action, but only as it is connected with its apparent consequences. She praises till she is hoarse the easy exploit of the Boston tea party, but will be comparatively silent about the braver and more disinterestedly heroic attack on the Boston Court-House, simply because it was unsuccessful!

Covered with disgrace, the State has sat down coolly to try for their lives and liberties the men who attempted to do its duty for it. And this is called *justice!* They who have shown that they can behave particularly well may perchance be put under bonds for *their good behavior.* They whom truth requires at present to plead guilty, are of all the inhabitants of the State, pre-eminently innocent. While the Governor, and the Mayor,[49] and countless officers of the Commonwealth, are at large, the champions of liberty are imprisoned.

Only they are guiltless, who commit the crime of contempt of such a Court. It behooves every man to see that his influence is on the side of justice, and let the courts make their own characters. My sympathies in this case are wholly with the accused, and wholly against the accusers and their judges. Justice is sweet and musical; but injustice is harsh and discordant. The judge still sits grinding at his organ,[50] but it yields no music, and we hear only the sound of the handle. He believes that all the music resides in the handle, and the crowd toss him their coppers the same as before.

49 Jerome Van Croninsfield Smith (1800–1879), "Know-Nothing" mayor of Boston from 1854 to 1856. The American, or Know-Nothing, Party was founded in 1841 by a state convention in Louisiana, asserting principles that promoted the exclusion of foreign-born citizens from all offices of trust and emolument in the government, whether federal, state, or municipal.
50 Barrel organ that is played by the action of turning or grinding a revolving cylinder fitted with pegs or pins that open pipe valves supplied by a bellows.

Do you suppose that that Massachusetts which is now doing these things,—which hesitates to crown these men, some of whose lawyers, and even judges, perchance, may be driven to take refuge in some poor quibble, that they may not wholly outrage their instinctive sense of justice,—do you suppose that she is any thing but base and servile? that she is the champion of liberty?

Show me a free State, and a court truly of justice, and I will fight for them, if need be; but show me Massachusetts, and I refuse her my allegiance, and express contempt for her courts.

The effect of a good government is to make life more valuable,—of a bad one, to make it less valuable. We can afford that railroad, and all other merely material stock, should lose some of its value, for that only compels us to live more simply and economically; but suppose that the value of life itself should be diminished! How can we make a less demand on man and nature, how live more economically in respect to virtue and all noble qualities, than we do? I have lived for the last month,—and I think that every man in Massachusetts capable of the sentiment of patriotism must have had a similar experience,—with the sense of having suffered a vast and indefinite loss. I did not know at first what ailed me. At last it occurred to me that what I had lost was a country. I had never respected the Government near to which I had lived, but I had foolishly thought that I might manage to live here, minding my private affairs, and forget it. For my part, my old and worthiest pursuits have lost I cannot say how much of their attraction, and I feel that my investment in life here is worth many per cent. less since Massachusetts last deliberately sent back an innocent man, Anthony Burns, to slavery. I dwelt before, perhaps, in the illusion that my life passed somewhere only *between* heaven and hell, but now I cannot persuade myself that I do not dwell *wholly within* hell. The site of that political organization called Massachusetts is to me morally covered with volcanic scoriae[51] and cinders, such as Milton describes in the infernal regions.[52] If there is any hell more unprincipled than our rulers, and we, the ruled, I feel curious to see it. Life itself being worth less, all things with it, which minister to it, are worth less. Suppose you have a small library, with pictures to adorn the walls—a garden laid out around—and contemplate scientific and literary pursuits, &c., and discover all at once that your villa,[53] with all its contents, is located in hell, and that the justice of the peace has a cloven foot and a forked tail—do not these things suddenly lose their value in your eyes?

I feel that, to some extent, the State has fatally interfered with my lawful business. It has not only interrupted me in my passage through Court street[54] on errands of trade, but it has interrupted me and every man on his onward and upward path, on which he had trusted soon to leave Court street far behind. What right had it to remind me of Court street? I have found that hollow which even I had relied on for solid.

I am surprised to see men going about their business as if nothing had happened. I say to myself—Unfortunates! they have not heard the news. I am surprised that the man whom I just met on horseback should be so earnest to overtake his newly bought cows running away—since all property is insecure—and if they do not run away again, they may be taken away from him when he gets them. Fool! does he not know that his seed-corn is worth less this year—that all beneficent harvests fail as you approach the empire of hell? No prudent man will build a stone house under these circumstances, or engage in any peaceful enterprise which requires a long time to accomplish. Art is as long as ever,[55] but life is more interrupted and less available for a man's proper pursuits. It is not an era of repose. We have used up all our inherited

51 Loose, cinderlike lava.
52 Allusion to Milton's *Paradise Lost* 10:570: "With soot and cinders fill'd . . ."
53 Probable allusion to Andrew Jackson Downing's (1815–1852) definition in *The Architecture of Country Houses* (1850) that "this word *villa*—the same in Latin, Italian, Spanish, and English, signifies only 'a country house or abode'; or, according to others, 'a rural or country seat'—as *village* means a small collection of houses in the country."
54 Location of the Municipal Courthouse, in which Burns was imprisoned.
55 Cf. "Paradise (To Be) Regained," note 24.

56 Possible allusion to Matthew 16:25: "For who-soever will save his life shall lose it."

57 Two weeks after Burns was sent back Thoreau wrote on 16 June 1854: "Again I scent the white water-lily & a season I had waited for is arrived" [PJ 8:195].

58 An invented nomenclature alluding to Senator Stephen A. Douglas (1813–1861) of Illinois, who was instrumental in the passing of the Compromise of 1850.

freedom. If we would save our lives, we must fight for them.[56]

I walk toward one of our ponds, but what signifies the beauty of nature when men are base? We walk to lakes to see our serenity reflected in them; when we are not serene, we go not to them. Who can be serene in a country where both the rulers and the ruled are without principle? The remembrance of my country spoils my walk. My thoughts are murder to the State, and involuntarily go plotting against her.

But it chanced the other day that I scented a white water-lily,[57] and a season I had waited for had arrived. It is the emblem of purity. It bursts up so pure and fair to the eye, and so sweet to the scent, as if to show us what purity and sweetness reside in, and can be extracted from, the slime and muck of earth. I think I have plucked the first one that has opened for a mile. What confirmation of our hopes is in the fragrance of this flower! I shall not so soon despair of the world for it, notwithstanding slavery, and the cowardice and want of principle of Northern men. It suggests what kind of laws have prevailed longest and widest, and still prevail and that the time may come when man's deeds will smell as sweet. Such is the odor which the plant omits. If Nature can compound this fragrance still annually, I shall believe her still young and full of vigor, her integrity and genius unimpaired, and that there is virtue even in man, too who is fitted to perceive and love it. It reminds me that Nature has been partner to no Missouri Compromise. I scent no compromise in the fragrance of the water-lily. It is not a *Nymphoea Douglassii*.[58] In it, the sweet, and pure, and innocent, are wholly sundered from the obscene and baleful. I do not scent in this time the time-serving irresolution of a Massachusetts Governor, nor of a Boston Mayor. So behave that the odor of your actions may enhance the general sweetness of the atmosphere, that when we behold or scent a flower, we may not be reminded how inconsistent your deeds are with it; for all odor is but one form of advertisement of a moral quality, and if fair actions had not been performed, the lily would not smell sweet. The foul slime stands for the sloth and vice of man, the decay of humanity; the fragrant flower that springs from it, for the purity and courage which are immortal.

Slavery and servility have produced no sweet-scented flower annually, to charm the senses of men, for they have no real life: they are merely a decaying and a death, offensive to all healthy nostrils. We do not complain that they *live,* but that they do not *get buried.* Let the living bury them;[59] even they are good for manure.

59 Allusion to Luke 9:60: "Jesus said unto him, Let the dead bury their dead: but go thou and preach the kingdom of God."

1 Thoreau read his lecture on "The Character and Actions of Capt. John Brown" in the vestry of the First Parish Meetinghouse in Concord. Edward Emerson said that Thoreau read his plea "as if it burned him" and that "many of those who came to scoff remained to pray."

2 Thoreau repeated his lecture in Boston at the Tremont Temple as a replacement for Frederick Douglass, who was scheduled to speak but fled to Canada due to allegations of his connections with Brown, and again on 3 November in the Mechanic's Hall Building in Worcester.

3 John Brown (1726–1776), Brown's paternal grandfather, joined the Continental Army but died from dysentery shortly after enlistment.

4 On 9 May 1800 in West Torrington, Connecticut.

5 The Brown family moved to Hudson, Ohio, in 1805.

6 Thoreau met Brown when he was in Concord in March 1857 and again in May 1859. Brown spoke publicly on 12 March 1857 in the Concord Town Hall. Thoreau later complained in his journal: "I subscribed a trifle when he was here there years ago, I had so much confidence in the man . . . but it would seem that he had not confidence enough in me, nor in anybody else that I know, to communicate his plans to us" [J 12:437].

A Plea for Captain John Brown

Read to the citizens of Concord, Mass., Sunday Evening, October 30, 1859;[1] also as the Fifth Lecture of the Fraternity Course, in Boston, November 1.[2]

I trust that you will pardon me for being here. I do not wish to force my thoughts upon you, but I feel forced myself. Little as I know of Captain Brown, I would fain do my part to correct the tone and the statements of the newspapers, and of my countrymen generally, respecting his character and actions. It costs us nothing to be just. We can at least express our sympathy with, and admiration of, him and his companions, and that is what I now propose to do.

First, as to his history. I will endeavor to omit, as much as possible, what you have already read. I need not describe his person to you, for probably most of you have seen and will not soon forget him. I am told that his grandfather, John Brown, was an officer in the Revolution;[3] that he himself was born in Connecticut about the beginning of this century,[4] but early went with his father to Ohio.[5] I heard him say[6] that his father was a contractor who furnished beef to the army there, in the war of 1812; that he accompanied him to the camp, and assisted him in that employment, seeing a good deal of military life, more, perhaps, than if he had been a soldier, for he was often present at the councils of the officers. Especially, he learned by experience how armies are supplied and maintained in the field—a work which, he observed, requires at least as much experience and skill as to lead them in battle. He said that few persons had any conception of the cost, even the pecuniary cost, of firing a single bullet in war.[7] He saw enough, at any rate, to disgust him with a military life; indeed, to excite in him a great abhorrence of it; so much so, that though he was tempted by the offer of some petty office in the army, when he was about eighteen, he not only declined that, but he also refused to train when warned, and was fined for it. He then resolved that he would never have any thing to do with any war, unless it were a war for liberty.

When the troubles in Kansas began,[8] he sent several of his sons thither to strengthen the party of the Free State men,[9] fitting them out with such weapons as he had; telling them that if the troubles should increase, and there should be need of him, he would follow to assist them with his hand and counsel. This, as you all know, he soon after did; and it was through his agency, far more than any other's, that Kansas was made free.[10]

For a part of his life he was a surveyor, and at one time he was engaged in wool-growing, and he went to Europe as an agent about that business. There, as every where, he had his eyes about him, and made many original observations. He said, for instance, that he saw why the soil of England was so rich, and that of Germany[11] (I think it was) so poor, and he thought of writing to some of the crowned heads about it. It was because in England the peasantry live on the soil which they cultivate, but in Germany they are gathered into villages, at night. It is a pity that he did not make a book of his observations.

I should say that he was an old-fashioned man in his respect for the Constitution, and his faith in the permanence of this Union. Slavery he deemed to be wholly opposed to these, and he was its determined foe.

He was by descent and birth a New England farmer, a man of great common sense,[12] deliberate and practical as

7 Many of Brown's undocumented remarks and personal accounts were said during his visits to Concord and were either heard firsthand by Thoreau or passed to him in conversation with Sanborn, Emerson, or others.
8 Fighting over the question of whether slavery would be allowed in the territory.
9 Members of the Kansas Free State Party, formed in 1855.
10 As of October 1857 the Free State Party had gained control of Kansas, but slavery was not constitutionally prohibited until January 1861.
11 Brown visited Hamburg, Germany, in 1849 as part of his European travels, during which he hoped to sell wool in England.
12 Cf. "Paradise (To Be) Regained," note 46.

13 Revolutionary War battle sites.

14 Two heroes of the American Revolution. Ethan Allen (1738–1789) organized the Green Mountain Boys, a volunteer militia, which helped capture Fort Ticonderoga from the British in 1775. John Stark (1728–1822), major general in the Continental Army, countermanding his orders, led his troops to meet the Hessians at the Battle of Bennington in Walloomsac, New York.

15 Quoted from the *New-York Daily Tribune,* 24 October 1859, reprinted from the *Chicago Press and Tribune,* 20 October 1859: "His rural exterior has enabled him to pass through scores of perils, where his life would have paid the forfeit of his discovery."

16 Harvard was Thoreau's alma mater (Latin: fostering mother), from which he graduated in 1837.

17 Not of the Puritan era but one who held to the Puritan ideals represented by strict moral and religious principles.

18 Oliver Cromwell (1599–1658), who ruled England from 1653 to 1658 following the Puritan Reformation.

19 Approximately twenty-one thousand Puritans immigrated into New England between 1620 and 1641.

20 The tradition of Forefathers' Day, begun in 1820 by the newly formed Pilgrim Society to commemorate the landing of the Pilgrims, included placing five kernels of parched corn on each dinner plate, alluding to the time in 1623 when, because corn was so scarce, that was the portion allowed to each individual.

that class is, and tenfold more so. He was like the best of those who stood at Concord Bridge once, on Lexington Common, and on Bunker Hill,[13] only he was firmer and higher principled than any that I have chanced to hear of as there. It was no abolition lecturer that converted him. Ethan Allen and Stark,[14] with whom he may in some respects be compared, were rangers in a lower and less important field. They could bravely face their country's foes, but he had the courage to face his country herself, when she was in the wrong. A Western writer says, to account for his escape from so many perils, that he was concealed under a "rural exterior";[15] as if, in that prairie land, a hero should, by good rights, wear a citizen's dress only.

He did not go to the college called Harvard, good old Alma Mater[16] as she is. He was not fed on the pap that is there furnished. As he phrased it, "I know no more of grammar than one of your calves." But he went to the great university of the West, where he sedulously pursued the study of Liberty, for which he had early betrayed a fondness, and having taken many degrees, he finally commenced the public practice of Humanity in Kansas, as you all know. Such were *his humanities,* and not any study of grammar. He would have left a Greek accent slanting the wrong way, and righted up a falling man.

He was one of that class of whom we hear a great deal, but, for the most part, see nothing at all—the Puritans.[17] It would be in vain to kill him. He died lately in the time of Cromwell,[18] but he reappeared here. Why should he not? Some of the Puritan stock are said to have come over and settled in New England.[19] They were a class that did something else than celebrate their forefathers' day, and eat parched corn in remembrance of that time.[20] They were neither Democrats nor Republicans, but men of simple habits, straightforward, prayerful; not thinking much of rulers who did not fear God, not making many compromises, nor seeking after available candidates.

"In his camp," as one has recently written, and as I have myself heard him state, "he permitted no profanity; no man of loose morals was suffered to remain there, unless, indeed, as a prisoner of war. 'I would rather,' said he, 'have the small-pox, yellow fever, and cholera, all together in my camp, than a man without principle. * * * It is a mistake, sir, that our people make, when they think that bullies are the best fighters, or that they are the fit men to oppose these Southerners. Give me men of good principles,—God-fearing men,—men who respect themselves, and with a dozen of them I will oppose any hundred such men as these Buford ruffians.'"[21] He said that if one offered himself to be a soldier under him, who was forward to tell what he could or would do, if he could only get sight of the enemy, he had but little confidence in him.

He was never able to find more than a score or so of recruits whom he would accept, and only about a dozen, among them his sons, in whom he had perfect faith. When he was here, some years ago, he showed to a few a little manuscript book,—his "orderly book"[22] I think he called it,—containing the names of his company in Kansas, and the rules by which they bound themselves; and he stated that several of them had already sealed the contract with their blood. When some one remarked that, with the addition of a chaplain, it would have been a perfect Cromwellian troop,[23] he observed that he would have been glad to add a chaplain to the list, if he could have found one who could fill that office worthily. It is easy enough to find one for the United States army. I believe that he had prayers in his camp morning and evening, nevertheless.

He was a man of Spartan habits,[24] and at sixty was scrupulous about his diet at your table, excusing himself

21 James Redpath's (1833–1891) meeting with John Brown in 1856 was recorded in the Boston *Atlas and Daily Bee* the Monday before Thoreau's speech. The Buford Ruffians were a band of approximately four hundred southerners led by Jefferson Buford (1807–1862) for the purpose of fighting the Free State settlers of the Kansas Territory. Thoreau's ellipsis represents an interjection by Redpath. None of Brown's words were deleted.
22 Book kept for a military troop or regiment listing general or regimental orders.
23 Allusion to Cromwell's remark during the Protestant Revolution: "We can only resist the superior training of the King's soldiers, by enlisting godly men."
24 Rigorously self-disciplined, resolute, courageous, and austere.

25 According to Frank Sanborn, based on Brown's notes, during his Concord speech Brown said: "I, together with four of my sons, was called out to help defend Lawrence in the fall of 1855, and travelled most of the way on foot, and during a dark night, a distance of thirty-five miles. . . . On or about the 30th May last two of my sons, with several others, were imprisoned without other crime than opposition to bogus enactments, and most barbarously treated for a time,—one being held about one month, the other about four months. Both had their families in Kansas, and destitute of homes, being burned out after they were imprisoned. In this burning all the eight were sufferers, as we all had our effects at the two houses. One of my sons had his oxen taken from him at this time, and never recovered them. Here is the chain with which one of them was confined, after the cruelty, sufferings, and anxiety he underwent had rendered him a maniac. . . . I, with five sick and wounded sons and son-in-law, was obliged for some time to lie on the ground, without shelter, our boots and clothes worn out, destitute of money, and at times almost in a state of starvation, and dependent on the charities of the Christian Indian and his wife whom I before named."

26 Pro-slavery militants from Missouri who fought along the Kansas-Missouri border.

27 This is not in the extant copy of Brown's speech and may have been given in answer to a specific question.

28 Insincere speech-making for the gratification of the constituents, or to gain public applause, from Felix Walker (1753–1828), congressman from Buncombe County in North Carolina. During the 16th Congress, after long and tedious speeches were made regarding the Missouri question, Walker secured the floor and, when asked to sit down, said that he was making a speech for Buncombe.

by saying that he must eat sparingly and fare hard, as became a soldier or one who was fitting himself for difficult enterprises, a life of exposure.

A man of rare common sense and directness of speech, as of action; a transcendentalist above all, a man of ideas and principles,—that was what distinguished him. Not yielding to a whim or transient impulse, but carrying out the purpose of a life. I noticed that he did not overstate any thing, but spoke within bounds. I remember, particularly, how, in his speech here, he referred to what his family had suffered in Kansas,[25] without ever giving the least vent to his pent-up fire. It was a volcano with an ordinary chimney-flue. Also referring to the deeds of certain Border Ruffians,[26] he said, rapidly paring away his speech, like an experienced soldier, keeping a reserve of force and meaning, "They had a perfect right to be hung."[27] He was not in the least a rhetorician, was not talking to Buncombe[28] or his constituents any where, had no need to invent any thing, but to tell the simple truth, and communicate his own resolution; therefore he appeared incomparably strong, and eloquence in Congress and elsewhere seemed to me at a discount. It was like the speeches of Cromwell compared with those of an ordinary king.

As for his tact and prudence, I will merely say, that at a time when scarcely a man from the Free States was able to reach Kansas by any direct route, at least without having his arms taken from him, he, carrying what imperfect guns and other weapons he could collect, openly and slowly drove an ox-cart through Missouri, apparently in the capacity of a surveyor, with his surveying compass exposed in it, and so passed unsuspected, and had ample opportunity to learn the designs of the enemy. For some time after his arrival he still followed the same profession. When, for instance, he saw a knot of the ruffians on the prairie, discussing, of course, the single topic which then occupied their minds, he would, perhaps, take his compass and one of his sons, and proceed to run an imaginary line right through the very spot on which that conclave had assembled,[29] and when he came up to them, he would naturally pause and have some talk with them, learning their news, and, at last, all their plans perfectly; and having thus completed his real survey, he would resume his imaginary one, and run on his line till he was out of sight.

When I expressed surprise that he could live in Kansas at all, with a price set upon his head,[30] and so large a number, including the authorities, exasperated against him, he accounted for it by saying, "It is perfectly well understood that I will not be taken." Much of the time for some years he has had to skulk in swamps, suffering from poverty and from sickness, which was the consequence of exposure, befriended only by Indians and a few whites. But though it might be known that he was lurking in a particular swamp, his foes commonly did not care to go in after him. He could even come out into a town where there were more Border Ruffians than Free State men, and transact some business, without delaying long, and yet not be molested; for said he, "No little handful of men were willing to undertake it, and a large body could not be got together in season."

As for his recent failure, we do not know the facts about it. It was evidently far from being a wild and desperate attempt. His enemy, Mr. Vallandigham, is compelled to say, that "it was among the best planned and executed conspiracies that ever failed."[31]

Not to mention his other successes, was it a failure, or did it show a want of good management, to deliver from bondage a dozen human beings, and walk off with them by broad daylight, for weeks if not months, at a leisurely pace, through one State after another, for half the length of the North,[32] conspicuous to all parties, with a price set

29 According to John Brown, Jr. (1821–1895): "Early in the spring of 1856 Colonel Buford of Alabama arrived with a regiment of armed men mostly from South Carolina and Georgia. They came with the openly declared purpose to make Kansas a slave State at all hazards. A company of these men was reported to us as being encamped near the Marais des Cygnes . . . distant from our place about two miles. Father took his surveyor's compass and with him four of my brothers,— Owen, Frederick, Salmon, and Oliver,—as chain-carriers, ax-man, and marker, and found a section line which, on following, led through the camp of these men. The Georgians indulged in the utmost freedom of expression."

30 President James Buchanan (1791–1868) offered a $250 reward for Brown's capture, and the state of Missouri offered $3,000, following Brown's December 1858 raid into Missouri.

31 Clement L. Vallandigham (1820–1871), representative from Ohio, participated in the interrogation of Brown after his capture. On 22 October 1859 he wrote to the Cincinnati *Enquirer*: "The conspiracy was, unquestionably, far more extended than yet appears, numbering among the conspirators many more than the handful of followers who assailed Harper's Ferry, and having in the North and West, if not also the South, as its counsellors and abettors, men of intelligence, position and wealth. Certainly it was one among the best-planned and executed conspiracies that ever failed."

32 On 20 December 1858 Brown, with twenty men, liberated eleven slaves from two Missouri farms, leading them on an eighty-two-day trek eastward to Detroit, from where they were sent to Canada.

upon his head, going into a court room on his way and telling what he had done, thus convincing Missouri that it was not profitable to try to hold slaves in his neighborhood?—and this, not because the government menials were lenient, but because they were afraid of him.

Yet he did not attribute his success, foolishly, to "his star," or to any magic. He said, truly, that the reason why such greatly superior numbers quailed before him, was, as one of his prisoners confessed, because they *lacked a cause*—a kind of armor which he and his party never lacked. When the time came, few men were found willing to lay down their lives in defence of what they knew to be wrong; they did not like that this should be their last act in this world.

But to make haste to *his* last act, and its effects.

The newspapers seem to ignore, or perhaps are really ignorant of the fact, that there are at least as many as two or three individuals to a town throughout the North, who think much as the present speaker does about him and his enterprise. I do not hesitate to say that they are an important and growing party. We aspire to be something more than stupid and timid chattels, pretending to read history and our Bibles, but desecrating every house and every day we breathe in. Perhaps anxious politicians may prove that only seventeen white men and five negroes were concerned in the late enterprise; but their very anxiety to prove this might suggest to themselves that all is not told. Why do they still dodge the truth? They are so anxious because of a dim consciousness of the fact, which they do not distinctly face, that at least a million of the free inhabitants of the United States would have rejoiced if it had succeeded. They at most only criticise the tactics. Though we wear no crape, the thought of that man's position and probable fate is spoiling many a man's day here at the North for other thinking. If any one who has seen him here can pursue successfully any other train of thought, I do not know what he is made of. If there is any such who gets his usual allowance of sleep, I will warrant him to fatten easily under any circumstances which do not touch his body or purse. I put a piece of paper and a pencil under my pillow, and when I could not sleep, I wrote in the dark.

On the whole, my respect for my fellow-men, except as one may outweigh a million, is not being increased these days. I have noticed the cold-blooded way in which newspaper writers and men generally speak of this event, as if an ordinary malefactor, though one of unusual "pluck,"—as the Governor of Virginia is reported to have said, using the language of the cock-pit,[33] "the gamest man he ever saw,"[34]—had been caught, and were about to be hung. He was not dreaming of his foes when the governor thought he looked so brave. It turns what sweetness I have to gall, to hear, or hear of, the remarks of some of my neighbors. When we heard at first that he was dead, one of my townsmen observed that "he died as the fool dieth";[35] which, pardon me, for an instant suggested a likeness in him dying to my neighbor living. Others, craven-hearted, said disparagingly, that "he threw his life away," because he resisted the government. Which way have they thrown *their* lives, pray?— Such as would praise a man for attacking singly an ordinary band of thieves or murderers. I hear another ask, Yankee-like, "What will he gain by it?" as if he expected to fill his pockets by this enterprise. Such a one has no idea of gain but in this worldly sense. If it does not lead to a "surprise" party,[36] if he does not get a new pair of boots, or a vote of thanks, it must be a failure. "But he won't gain any thing by it." Well, no, I don't suppose he could get four-and-sixpence[37] a day for being hung, take the year round; but then he stands a chance to save a considerable part of his soul—and *such* a soul!—when *you* do not. No doubt you can get more in your market

33 In ships of war, a room near the after hatchway, under the lower gun deck, in which wounded men are dressed; the fore cockpit is a place leading to the magazine passage and the storeroom of the boatswain, gunner, and carpenter.
34 Henry A. Wise (1806–1876), Governor of Virginia, whose remark "He is the gamest man I ever saw" was printed in the *Richmond Whig* (October 1859) and reprinted widely, including in the *New-York Daily Tribune* of 22 October 1859, Thoreau's probable source.
35 Thoreau wrote in his journal of 19 October 1959 that one comment he "heard of by the postmaster"—Charles B. Davis—"of this village on the news of Brown's death: 'He died as the fool dieth'" [J 12:400–401]. There had been erroneous reports that Brown was killed, not captured.
36 An uninvited group of people bringing food and gifts to a person's house as an act of support and charity.
37 Common figure used to indicate a trifling sum.

38 Now Balaklava, where, during the Crimean War (1853–1856), the British suffered a monumental defeat, losing more than five hundred soldiers.
39 Alfred, Lord Tennyson (1809–1892), in "The Charge of the Light Brigade."
40 In his journal Thoreau noted that the "remarks of my neighbors upon Brown's death and supposed fate, with very few exceptions, are, 'He is undoubtedly insane,' 'Died as the fool dieth,' 'Served him right'" [J 12:403].
41 Cf. "Thomas Carlyle and His Works," note 163.
42 Israel Putnam (1718–1790), Revolutionary War general who, in the winter of 1742–1743, killed a wolf in Pomfret, Connecticut, that had been preying on local sheep.
43 The New England Tract Society, later the American Tract Society, founded to publish and disseminate Christian literature.
44 From the fable by Aesop.
45 Established in 1810 by the New England Congregationalists as the first American foreign missionary society.

for a quart of milk than for a quart of blood, but that is not the market that heroes carry their blood to.

Such do not know that like the seed is the fruit, and that, in the moral world, when good seed is planted, good fruit is inevitable, and does not depend on our watering and cultivating; that when you plant, or bury, a hero in his field, a crop of heroes is sure to spring up. This is a seed of such force and vitality, that it does not ask our leave to germinate.

The momentary charge at Balaclava,[38] in obedience to a blundering command, proving what a perfect machine the soldier is, has, properly enough, been celebrated by a poet laureate;[39] but the steady, and for the most part successful charge of this man, for some years, against the legions of Slavery, in obedience to an infinitely higher command, is as much more memorable than that, as an intelligent and conscientious man is superior to a machine. Do you think that that will go unsung?

"Served him right" — "A dangerous man" — "He is undoubtedly insane."[40] So they proceed to live their sane, and wise, and altogether admirable lives, reading their Plutarch[41] a little, but chiefly pausing at that feat of Putnam, who was let down into a wolf's den;[42] and in this wise they nourish themselves for brave and patriotic deeds some time or other. The Tract Society[43] could afford to print that story of Putnam. You might open the district schools with the reading of it, for there is nothing about Slavery or the Church in it; unless it occurs to the reader that some pastors are *wolves* in sheep's clothing.[44] "The American Board of Commissioners for Foreign Missions"[45] even, might dare to protest against *that* wolf. I have heard of boards, and of American boards, but it chances that I never heard of this particular lumber till lately. And yet I hear of Northern men, women, and children, by families, buying a "life membership" in such societies as these;—a life-membership in the grave! You can get buried cheaper than that.

Our foes are in our midst and all about us. There is hardly a house but is divided against itself,[46] for our foe is the all but universal woodenness of both head and heart, the want of vitality in man, which is the effect of our vice; and hence are begotten fear, superstition, bigotry, persecution, and slavery of all kinds. We are mere figure-heads upon a hulk, with livers in the place of hearts. The curse is the worship of idols, which at length changes the worshipper into a stone image himself; and the New Englander is just as much an idolater as the Hindoo. This man was an exception, for he did not set up even a political graven image between him and his God.

A church that can never have done with excommunicating Christ while it exists! Away with your broad and flat churches, and your narrow and tall churches! Take a step forward, and invent a new style of out-houses. Invent a salt that will save you, and defend our nostrils.[47]

The modern Christian is a man who has consented to say all the prayers in the liturgy, provided you will let him go straight to bed and sleep quietly afterward. All his prayers begin with "Now I lay me down to sleep,"[48] and he is forever looking forward to the time when he shall go to his "*long* rest."[49] He has consented to perform certain old established charities, too, after a fashion, but he does not wish to hear of any new-fangled ones; he doesn't wish to have any supplementary articles added to the contract, to fit it to the present time. He shows the whites of his eyes on the Sabbath, and the blacks all the rest of the week. The evil is not merely a stagnation of blood, but a stagnation of spirit. Many, no doubt, are well disposed, but sluggish by constitution and by habit, and they cannot conceive of a man who is actuated by higher motives than they are. Accordingly they pro-

46 Allusion to Matthew 12:25: "And Jesus knew their thoughts, and said unto them, Every kingdom divided against itself is brought to desolation; and every city or house divided against itself shall not stand," with a possible allusion to Abraham Lincoln's use of it in his June 1858 speech accepting the Republican nomination: "'A house divided against itself cannot stand.' I believe this government cannot endure, permanently half *slave* and half *free*. I do not expect the Union to be *dissolved*—I do not expect the house to *fall*—but I *do* expect it will cease to be divided. It will become *all* one thing or *all* the other."
47 Smelling salts (carbonate of ammonia), used for provoking consciousness.
48 Beginning of children's prayer printed in the *New England Primer:*

> Now I lay me down to sleep,
> I pray the Lord my soul to keep,
> If I shall die before I wake,
> I pray the Lord my soul to take.

49 Allusion to Tennyson's "The Lotus Eaters," ll. 96–98: "All things have rest, and ripen toward the grave / In silence—ripen, fall, and cease: / Give us long rest or death, dark death, or dreamful ease."

50 A Russian measure of length of approximately two-thirds of a mile.

51 In *Walden* Thoreau wrote: "A man thinking or working is always alone, let him be where he will" [Wa 131].

52 Henry Wilson (1812–1875), Republican senator from Massachusetts, who, although he had met Brown and was a Free-Soiler, did not support Brown's actions.

53 Of these columns Thoreau wrote in "Life Without Principle": "The newspapers, I perceive, devote some of their columns specially to politics or government without charge; and this, one would say, is all that saves it; but, as I love literature, and, to some extent, the truth also, I never read those columns at any rate."

nounce this man insane, for they know that *they* could never act as he does, as long as they are themselves.

We dream of foreign countries, of other times and races of men, placing them at a distance in history or space; but let some significant event like the present occur in our midst, and we discover, often, this distance and this strangeness between us and our nearest neighbors. *They* are our Austrias, and Chinas, and South Sea Islands. Our crowded society becomes well spaced all at once, clean and handsome to the eye, a city of magnificent distances. We discover why it was that we never got beyond compliments and surfaces with them before; we become aware of as many versts[50] between us and them as there are between a wandering Tartar and a Chinese town. The thoughtful man becomes a hermit in the thoroughfares of the market-place.[51] Impassable seas suddenly find their level between us, or dumb steppes stretch themselves out there. It is the difference of constitution, of intelligence, and faith, and not streams and mountains, that make the true and impassable boundaries between individuals and between states. None but the like-minded can come plenipotentiary to our court.

I read all the newspapers I could get within a week after this event, and I do not remember in them a single expression of sympathy for these men. I have since seen one noble statement, in a Boston paper, not editorial. Some voluminous sheets decided not to print the full report of Brown's words to the exclusion of other matter. It was as if a publisher should reject the manuscript of the New Testament, and print Wilson's last speech.[52] The same journal which contained this pregnant news, was chiefly filled, in parallel columns, with the reports of the political conventions that were being held.[53] But the descent to them was too steep. They should have been spared this contrast, been printed in an extra at least. To turn from the voices and deeds of earnest men to the *cackling* of political conventions! Office-seekers and speech-makers, who do not so much as lay an honest egg, but wear their breasts bare upon an egg of chalk![54] Their great game is the game of straws, or rather that universal aboriginal game of the platter, at which the Indians cried *hub, bub!*[55] Exclude the reports of religious and political conventions, and publish the words of a living man.

But I object not so much to what they have omitted, as to what they have inserted. Even the *Liberator* called it "a misguided, wild, and apparently insane—effort."[56] As for the herd of newspapers and magazines, I do not chance to know an editor in the country who will deliberately print any thing which he knows will ultimately and permanently reduce the number of his subscribers. They do not believe that it would be expedient. How then can they print truth? If we do not say pleasant things, they argue, nobody will attend to us. And so they do like some travelling auctioneers, who sing an obscene song in order to draw a crowd around them. Republican editors, obliged to get their sentences ready for the morning edition, and accustomed to look at every thing by the twilight of politics, express no admiration, nor true sorrow even, but call these men "deluded fanatics"—"mistaken men"—"insane," or "crazed." It suggests what a *sane* set of editors we are blessed with, *not* "mistaken men"; who know very well on which side their bread is buttered, at least.

A man does a brave and humane deed, and at once, on all sides, we hear people and parties declaring, "I didn't do it, nor countenance *him* to do it, in any conceivable way. It can't be fairly inferred from my past career." I, for one, am not interested to hear you define your position. I don't know that I ever was, or ever shall be. I think it is mere egotism, or impertinent at this time. Ye needn't take so much pains to wash your skirts of him. No intelligent man will ever be convinced that he was any creature

54 Used to induce a hen to lay.

55 Thoreau read in John Ogilby's (1600–1676) *America, Being the Latest and Most Accurate Description of the New World:* "Hubbub is five small Bones in a small Tray; the Bones be like a Die, but something flatter, black on the one side and white on the other, which they place on the Ground, against which violently thumping the Platter, the Bones mount, changing Colour with the windy whisking of their Hands to and fro; which action in that sport they much use, smiting themselves on the Breasts and Thighs, crying out Hub Hub Hub."

56 William Lloyd Garrison wrote in the 21 October 1859 issue: "The particulars of a misguided, wild, and apparently insane, though disinterested and well-intended effort by insurrection to emancipate the slaves in Virginia . . . may be found on our third page. Our views of war and bloodshed, even in the best of causes, are too well known to need repeating here; but let no one who glories in the revolutionary struggle of 1776, deny the right of the slaves to imitate the example of our fathers."

57 From Brown's interrogation on 18 October 1859 as reported in the *New York Herald* (21 October 1859) in answer to the question: "Did you go out to Kansas under the auspices of the Emigrant Aid Society?"

58 Allusion to the proverb, at least as old as the seventeenth century, "Spare at the spile, or spigot, and let run out at the bung-hole." A pile is a wooden faucet; a bung is the hole in a cask through which it is filled.

59 Quoted from the unattributed "Who Is Brown, The Leader?" in the *New York Herald*, 19 October 1859, as reprinted in the *Boston Journal*, 21 October 1859.

60 Horace Greeley (1811–1872), political reformer, author, journalist, and founder of the *New-York Tribune*, wrote in that paper (19 October 1859): "Believing that the way to universal emancipation lies not through insurrection, civil war, and bloodshed, but through peace, discussion and quiet diffusion of sentiments of humanity and justice, we deeply regret this outbreak; but, remembering that, if their fault was grievous, grievously have they answered it, we will not, by one reproachful word, disturb the bloody shrouds wherein John Brown and his compatriots are sleeping. They dared and died for what they felt to be the right, though in a manner which seems to us fatally wrong."

of yours. He went and came, as he himself informs us, "under the auspices of John Brown and nobody else."[57] The Republican party does not perceive how many his *failure* will make to vote more correctly than they would have them. They have counted the votes of Pennsylvania &. Co., but they have not correctly counted Captain Brown's vote. He has taken the wind out of their sails, the little wind they had, and they may as well lie to and repair.

What though he did not belong to your clique! Though you may not approve of his method or his principles, recognize his magnanimity. Would you not like to claim kindredship with him in that, though in no other thing he is like, or likely, to you? Do you think that you would lose your reputation so? What you lost at the spile, you would gain at the bung.[58]

If they do not mean all this, then they do not speak the truth, and say what they mean. They are simply at their old tricks still.

"It was always conceded to him," *says one who calls him crazy*, "that he was a conscientious man, very modest in his demeanor, apparently inoffensive, until the subject of Slavery was introduced, when he would exhibit a feeling of indignation unparalleled."[59]

The slave-ship is on her way, crowded with its dying victims; new cargoes are being added in mid ocean; a small crew of slaveholders, countenanced by a large body of passengers, is smothering four millions under the hatches, and yet the politician asserts that the only proper way by which deliverance is to be obtained, is by "the quiet diffusion of the sentiments of humanity," without any "outbreak."[60] As if the sentiments of humanity were ever found unaccompanied by its deeds, and you could disperse them, all finished to order, the pure article, as easily as water with a watering-pot, and so lay the dust. What is that that I hear cast overboard? The bodies of the dead that have found deliverance. That is the way we are "diffusing" humanity, and its sentiments with it.

Prominent and influential editors, accustomed to deal with politicians, men of an infinitely lower grade, say, in their ignorance, that he acted "on the principle of revenge."[61] They do not know the man. They must enlarge themselves to conceive of him. I have no doubt that the time will come when they will begin to see him as he was. They have got to conceive of a man of faith and of religious principle, and not a politician nor an Indian; of a man who did not wait till he was personally interfered with or thwarted in some harmless business before he gave his life to the cause of the oppressed.

If Walker[62] may be considered the representative of the South, I wish I could say that Brown was the representative of the North. He was a superior man. He did not value his bodily life in comparison with ideal things. He did not recognize unjust human laws, but resisted them as he was bid. For once we are lifted out of the trivialness and dust of politics into the region of truth and manhood. No man in America has ever stood up so persistently and effectively for the dignity of human nature, knowing himself for a man, and the equal of any and all governments. In that sense he was the most American of us all. He needed no babbling lawyer, making false issues, to defend him. He was more than a match for all the judges that American voters, or office-holders of whatever grade, can create. He could not have been tried by a jury of his peers, because his peers did not exist. When a man stands up serenely against the condemnation and vengeance of mankind, rising above them literally *by a whole body,*—even though he were of late the vilest murderer, who has settled that matter with himself,—the spectacle is a sublime one,—didn't ye know it, ye Liberators, ye Tribunes, ye Republicans?[63]—and

61 During his interrogation Brown said: "I pity the poor in bondage that have none to help them; that is why I am here; not to gratify any personal animosity, revenge or vindictive spirit. It is my sympathy with the oppressed and the wronged that are as good as you and as precious in the sight of God." According to Richard Davis Webb's (1805–1872) *The Life and Letters of Captain John Brown,* a gentleman reported: "There is one thing he charged me to do when I last saw him. It is this:—'Do not allow any one to say I acted from revenge. I claim no man has a right to revenge himself.'"
62 Probably Robert J. Walker (1801–1869), proslavery governor of the Kansas Territory from 1857 to 1858.
63 Whig and, later, Republican newspapers.

we become criminal in comparison. Do yourselves the honor to recognize him. He needs none of your respect.

As for the Democratic journals,[64] they are not human enough to affect me at all. I do not feel indignation at any thing they may say.

I am aware that I anticipate a little, that he was still, at the last accounts, alive in the hands of his foes; but that being the case, I have all along found myself thinking and speaking of him as physically dead.

I do not believe in erecting statues to those who still live in our hearts, whose bones have not yet crumbled in the earth around us,[65] but I would rather see the statue of Captain Brown in the Massachusetts State-House yard, than that of any other man whom I know. I rejoice that I live in this age—that I am his contemporary.

What a contrast, when we turn to that political party which is so anxiously shuffling him and his plot out of its way, and looking around for some available slaveholder, perhaps, to be its candidate, at least for one who will execute the Fugitive Slave Law, and all those other unjust laws which he took up arms to annul!

Insane! A father and six sons, and one son-in-law, and several more men besides,—as many at least as twelve disciples,—all struck with insanity at once; while the sane tyrant holds with a firmer gripe[66] than ever his four millions of slaves, and a thousand sane editors, his abettors, are saving their country and their bacon! Just as insane were his efforts in Kansas. Ask the tyrant who is his most dangerous foe, the sane man or the insane. Do the thousands who know him best, who have rejoiced at his deeds in Kansas, and have afforded him material aid there, think him insane? Such a use of this word is a mere trope with most who persist in using it, and I have no doubt that many of the rest have already in silence retracted their words.

Read his admirable answers to Mason and others.[67]

---

64 The Democratic journals included the *New York Times* and the *New York World*.

65 On 18 September 1859 Thoreau wrote in his journal: "Dr. Bartlett handed me a paper to-day, desiring me to subscribe for a statue to Horace Mann. I declined, and said that I thought a man ought not any more to take up room in the world after he was dead. We shall lose one advantage of a man's dying if we are to have a statue of him forthwith. . . . It is very offensive to my imagination to see the dying stiffen into statues at this rate. We should wait till their bones begin to crumble—and then avoid too near a likeness to the living" [ITM 401–402].

66 Archaic spelling of *grip*.

67 After his capture on 18 October, the wounded Brown was questioned by James M. Mason in the presence of Governor Wise, Colonel Robert E. Lee (1808–1870), and others.

How they are dwarfed and defeated by the contrast! On the one side, half brutish, half timid questioning; on the other, truth, clear as lightning, crashing into their obscene temples. They are made to stand with Pilate,[68] and Gesler,[69] and the Inquisition.[70] How ineffectual their speech and action! and what a void their silence! They are but helpless tools in this great work. It was no human power that gathered them about this preacher.

What have Massachusetts and the North sent a few *sane* representatives to Congress for, of late years?—to declare with effect what kind of sentiments? All their speeches put together and boiled down,—and probably they themselves will confess it,—do not match for manly directness and force, and for simple truth, the few casual remarks of crazy John Brown, on the floor of the Harper's Ferry engine house;—that man whom you are about to hang, to send to the other world, though not to represent *you* there. No, he was not our representative in any sense. He was too fair a specimen of a man to represent the like of us. Who, then, *were* his constituents? If you read his words understandingly you will find out. In his case there is no idle eloquence, no made, nor maiden speech, no compliments to the oppressor. Truth is his inspirer, and earnestness the polisher of his sentences. He could afford to lose his Sharps' rifles,[71] while he retained his faculty of speech, a Sharps' rifle of infinitely surer and longer range.

And the *New York Herald* reports the conversation "*verbatim*"![72] It does not know of what undying words it is made the vehicle.

I have no respect for the penetration of any man who can read the report of that conversation, and still call the principal in it insane. It has the ring of a saner sanity than an ordinary discipline and habits of life, than an ordinary organization, secure. Take any sentence of it— "Any questions that I can honorably answer, I will; not

68 Pontius Pilate, Roman prefect who interrogated Jesus and ordered his crucifixion.
69 Allusion to the fourteenth-century Austrian despot Albrecht (sometimes Hermann) Gessler (sometimes Gesler), who, according to legend, ordered the Swiss folk hero William Tell on 18 November 1307 to shoot an apple from his son's head using a bow and arrow.
70 Inquisition of the Roman Catholic Church begun in the twelfth century, which allowed the use of torture against heretics.
71 A long-range cartridge rifle designed by Christian Sharps (1811–1874).
72 The *New York Herald* (21 October 1859) called Brown's interrogation a "conversation."

73 Brown refused to answer questions about anyone other than himself.

74 From Brown's interrogation on 18 October 1859.

75 Lewis W. Washington (1812–1871), great-grandnephew of George Washington and one of the hostages taken by Brown during the raid.

76 Oliver Brown (1839–1859) was wounded on 17 October 1859 and died the following day; Watson Brown (1835–1859) also was wounded on 17 October when sent outside by his father with a white flag and died following his capture.

77 Aaron Dwight Stevens (1831–1860) and Edwin Coppoc (1835–1859).

78 Quoted, with variants, from the *Richmond Whig* (October 1859) and reprinted widely, including in the *New-York Daily Tribune* of 22 October 1859, Thoreau's probable source.

79 On 22 October 1859 Vallandigham wrote to the Cincinnati *Enquirer:* "And now allow me to add that it is vain to underrate either the man or his conspiracy. Captain John Brown is as brave and resolute a man as ever headed an insurrection, and, in a good cause, and with a sufficient force, would have been a consummate partisan commander. He has coolness, daring, persistency, the stoic faith and patience, and a firmness of will and purpose unconquerable. . . . Though engaged in a wicked, mad and fanatical enterprise, he is the farthest possible remove from the ordinary ruffian, fanatic or madman."

80 Allusion to such statements as "Peace and quiet are restored at Harper's Ferry" in the *New York Herald*, 20 October 1859.

otherwise. So far as I am myself concerned,[73] I have told every thing truthfully. I value my word, sir."[74] The few who talk about his vindictive spirit, while they really admire his heroism, have no test by which to detect a noble man, no amalgam to combine with his pure gold. They mix their own dross with it.

It is a relief to turn from these slanders to the testimony of his more truthful, but frightened, jailers and hangmen. Governor Wise speaks far more justly and appreciatingly of him than any Northern editor, or politician, or public personage, that I chance to have heard from. I know that you can afford to hear him again on this subject. He says: "They are themselves mistaken who take him to be a madman. . . . He is cool, collected, and indomitable, and it is but just to him to say, that he was humane to his prisoners. . . . And he inspired me with great trust in his integrity as a man of truth. He is a fanatic, vain and garrulous," (I leave that part to Mr. Wise,) "but firm, truthful, and intelligent. His men, too, who survive, are like him. . . . Colonel Washington[75] says that he was the coolest and firmest man he ever saw in defying danger and death. With one son dead by his side, and another shot through,[76] he felt the pulse of his dying son with one hand, and held his rifle with the other, and commanded his men with the utmost composure, encouraging them to be firm, and to sell their lives as dear as they could. Of the three white prisoners, Brown, Stevens, and Coppoc,[77] it was hard to say which was most firm."[78]

Almost the first Northern men whom the slaveholder has learned to respect!

The testimony of Mr. Vallandigham, though less valuable, is of the same purport, that "it is vain to underrate either the man or his conspiracy. . . . He is the farthest possible remove from the ordinary ruffian, fanatic, or madman."[79]

"All is quiet at Harper's Ferry," say the journals.[80]

What is the character of that calm which follows when the law and the slaveholder prevail? I regard this event as a touchstone designed to bring out, with glaring distinctness, the character of this government. We needed to be thus assisted to see it by the light of history. It needed to see itself. When a government puts forth its strength on the side of injustice, as ours to maintain Slavery and kill the liberators of the slave, it reveals itself a merely brute force, or worse, a demoniacal force. It is the head of the Plug Uglies.[81] It is more manifest than ever that tyranny rules. I see this government to be effectually allied with France and Austria[82] in oppressing mankind. There sits a tyrant holding fettered four millions of slaves; here comes their heroic liberator. This most hypocritical and diabolical government looks up from its seat on the gasping four millions, and inquires with an assumption of innocence, "What do you assault me for? Am I not an honest man? Cease agitation on this subject, or I will make a slave of you, too, or else hang you."

We talk about a *representative* government; but what a monster of a government is that where the noblest faculties of the mind, and the *whole* heart, are not *represented*. A semi-human tiger or ox, stalking over the earth, with its heart taken out and the top of its brain shot away. Heroes have fought well on their stumps when their legs were shot off, but I never heard of any good done by such a government as that.

The only government that I recognize, — and it matters not how few are at the head of it, or how small its army, — is that power that establishes justice in the land, never that which establishes injustice. What shall we think of a government to which all the truly brave and just men in the land are enemies, standing between it and those whom it oppresses? A government that pretends to be Christian and crucifies a million Christs every day!

81 Ruffians who practiced political intimidation, but specifically a gang operating in Baltimore between 1854 and 1860, which was sometimes referred to as a "political club." William Lloyd Garrison referred to the Plug Uglies as a "lawless horde."

82 Autocratically ruled nations: France was under the rule of Napoleon III (1808–1873) and Austria under Emperor Franz Joseph (1830–1916).

83 Brown was charged in Virginia with murder, conspiring to start a slave revolt, and treason, although the last charge is legally incorrect, as Brown was not a citizen of that state.

84 Cannons in which the barrels are cast with spiral grooves, and the balls embossed to fit those grooves, giving them greater accuracy and longer range.

85 One who casts the metal, in a foundry, for cannons.

86 Group chained together in a line.

87 A company of United States Marines arrived at Harpers Ferry on 18 October under the command of Robert E. Lee.

88 Allusion to the Boston Vigilance Committee, founded in 1841 to protect fugitive slaves from capture.

89 A Muslim judge or magistrate.

Treason![83] Where does such treason take its rise? I cannot help thinking of you as you deserve, ye governments. Can you dry up the fountains of thought? High treason, when it is resistance to tyranny here below, has its origin in, and is first committed by the power that makes and forever recreates man. When you have caught and hung all these human rebels, you have accomplished nothing but your own guilt, for you have not struck at the fountain head. You presume to contend with a foe against whom West Point cadets and rifled cannon[84] *point* not. Can all the art of the cannon-founder[85] tempt matter to turn against its maker? Is the form in which the founder thinks he casts it more essential than the constitution of it and of himself?

The United States have a coffle[86] of four millions of slaves. They are determined to keep them in this condition; and Massachusetts is one of the confederated overseers to prevent their escape. Such are not all the inhabitants of Massachusetts, but such are they who rule and are obeyed here. It was Massachusetts, as well as Virginia, that put down this insurrection at Harper's Ferry. She sent the marines there,[87] and she will have to pay the penalty of her sin.

Suppose that there is a society in this State that out of its own purse and magnanimity saves all the fugitive slaves that run to us, and protects our colored fellow-citizens, and leaves the other work to the Government, so-called. Is not that government fast losing its occupation, and becoming contemptible to mankind? If private men are obliged to perform the offices of government, to protect the weak and dispense justice, then the government becomes only a hired man, or clerk, to perform menial or indifferent services. Of course, that is but the shadow of a government whose existence necessitates a Vigilant Committee.[88] What should we think of the oriental Cadi[89] even, behind whom worked in secret a Vigilant Committee? But such is the character of our Northern States generally; each has its Vigilant Committee. And, to a certain extent, these crazy governments recognize and accept this relation. They say, virtually, "We'll be glad to work for you on these terms, only don't make a noise about it." And thus the government, its salary being insured, withdraws into the back shop, taking the constitution with it, and bestows most of its labor on repairing that. When I hear it at work sometimes, as I go by, it reminds me, at best, of those farmers who in winter contrive to turn a penny by following the coopering business.[90] And what kind of spirit is their barrel made to hold? They speculate in stocks, and bore holes in mountains, but they are not competent to lay out even a decent highway. The only *free* road, the Underground Railroad, is owned and managed by the Vigilant Committee. *They* have tunnelled under the whole breadth of the land. Such a government is losing its power and respectability as surely as water runs out of a leaky vessel, and is held by one that can contain it.

I hear many condemn these men because they were so few. When were the good and the brave ever in a majority? Would you have had him wait till that time came?—till you and I came over to him? The very fact that he had no rabble or troop of hirelings about him, would alone distinguish him from ordinary heroes. His company was small indeed, because few could be found worthy to pass muster. Each one who there laid down his life for the poor and oppressed was a picked man, culled out of many thousands, if not millions; apparently a man of principle, of rare courage and devoted humanity; ready to sacrifice his life at any moment for the benefit of his fellow-man. It may be doubted if there were as many more their equals in these respects in all the country—I speak of his followers only—for their leader, no doubt, scoured the land far and wide, seeking to swell his troop.

90 The making of barrels, tubs, and casks of various kinds.

These alone were ready to step between the oppressor and the oppressed. Surely they were the very best men you could select to be hung. That was the greatest compliment which this country could pay them. They were ripe for her gallows. She has tried a long time, she has hung a good many, but never found the right one before.

When I think of him, and his six sons, and his son-in-law,—not to enumerate the others,—enlisted for this fight; proceeding coolly, reverently, humanely to work, for months if not years, sleeping and waking upon it, summering and wintering the thought, without expecting any reward but a good conscience, while almost all America stood ranked on the other side, I say again, that it affects me as a sublime spectacle. If he had had any journal advocating "*his cause,*" any organ, as the phrase is, monotonously and wearisomely playing the same old tune, and then passing round the hat, it would have been fatal to his efficiency. If he had acted in any way so as to be let alone by the government, he might have been suspected. It was the fact that the tyrant must give place to him, or he to the tyrant, that distinguished him from all the reformers of the day that I know.

It was his peculiar doctrine that a man has a perfect right to interfere by force with the slaveholder, in order to rescue the slave. I agree with him. They who are continually shocked by slavery have some right to be shocked by the violent death of the slaveholder, but no others. Such will be more shocked by his life than by his death. I shall not be forward to think him mistaken in his method who quickest succeeds to liberate the slave. I speak for the slave when I say, that I prefer the philanthropy of Captain Brown to that philanthropy which neither shoots me nor liberates me. At any rate, I do not think it is quite sane for one to spend his whole life in talking or writing about this matter, unless he is continuously inspired, and I have not done so. A man may have other affairs to attend to.[91] I do not wish to kill nor to be killed, but I can foresee circumstances in which both these things would be by me unavoidable. We preserve the so-called peace of our community by deeds of petty violence every day. Look at the policeman's billy and handcuffs! Look at the jail! Look at the gallows! Look at the chaplain of the regiment! We are hoping only to live safely on the outskirts of *this* provisional army. So we defend ourselves and our hen-roosts, and maintain slavery. I know that the mass of my countrymen think that the only righteous use that can be made of Sharps' rifles and revolvers is to fight duels with them, when we are insulted by other nations, or to hunt Indians, or shoot fugitive slaves with them, or the like. I think that for once the Sharps' rifles and the revolvers were employed in a righteous cause. The tools were in the hands of one who could use them.

The same indignation that is said to have cleared the temple once[92] will clear it again. The question is not about the weapon, but the spirit in which you use it. No man has appeared in America, as yet, who loved his fellow-man so well, and treated him so tenderly. He lived for him. He took up his life and he laid it down for him. What sort of violence is that which is encouraged, not by soldiers but by peaceable citizens, not so much by laymen as by ministers of the gospel, not so much by the fighting sects as by the Quakers, and not so much by Quaker men as by Quaker women?[93]

This event advertises me that there is such a fact as death—the possibility of a man's dying. It seems as if no man had ever died in America before, for in order to die you must first have lived. I don't believe in the hearses, and palls, and funerals that they have had. There was no death in the case, because there had been no life; they merely rotted or sloughed off, pretty much as they had rotted or sloughed along. No temple's vail was rent,[94] only

91 Thoreau wrote in "Resistance to Civil Government": "As for adopting the ways of the State has provided for remedying the evil, I know not of such ways. They take too much time, and a man's life will be gone. I have other affairs to attend to."
92 Allusion to Jesus' clearing or cleansing of the Temple, related in all four Gospels, as in Mark 11:15–18: "Jesus went into the temple, and began to cast out them that sold and bought in the temple, and overthrew the tables of the money-changers, and the seats of them that sold doves; And would not suffer that any man should carry any vessel through the temple. And he taught, saying unto them, Is it not written, My house shall be called of all nations the house of prayer? but ye have made it a den of thieves. And the scribes and chief priests heard it, and sought how they might destroy him: for they feared him, because all the people was astonished at his doctrine."
93 Allusion to the support of Brown by many Quakers, as evidenced by this "Letter from a Quaker Lady to John Brown" of 27 October 1859: "You can never know how very many dear Friends love thee with all their hearts, for thy brave efforts in behalf of the poor oppressed; and though we, who are non-resistants, and religiously believe it better to reform by moral, and not by carnal weapons, could not approve of bloodshed, yet we know thee was animated by the most generous and philanthropic motives. Very many thousands openly approve thy intentions, though most Friends would not think it right to take up arms. . . . If Moses let out thousands of Jewish slaves from their bondage, and God destroyed the Egyptians in the sea because they went after the Israelites to bring them back to Slavery, then surely, by the same reasoning, we may judge thee a deliverer who wished to release millions from a more cruel oppression."
94 During the Crucifixion, when Jesus died, as told in Matthew 27:51 (and variantly in Mark and Luke): "And, behold, the veil of the temple was rent in twain from the top to the bottom; and the earth did quake, and the rocks rent."

A Plea for Captain John Brown 211

95 Cf. "Slavery in Massachusetts," note 60.

96 Latin: remember you will die.

97 Quoted from the *New-York Daily Tribune*, 24 October 1859, reprinted from the *Chicago Press and Tribune*, 20 October 1859: "He seems to have been laboring under a religious hallucination. . . . His evident hallucination caused all clear-headed men in Kansas to avoid him. . . . The same feeling made him dreaded by the Missourians, as a supernatural being."

a hole dug somewhere. Let the dead bury their dead.[95] The best of them fairly ran down like a clock. Franklin—Washington—they were let off without dying; they were merely missing one day. I hear a good many pretend that they are going to die; or that they have died, for aught that I know. Nonsense! I'll defy them to do it. They haven't got life enough in them. They'll deliquesce like fungi, and keep a hundred eulogists mopping the spot where they left off. Only half a dozen or so have died since the world began. Do you think that you are going to die, sir? No! there's no hope of you. You haven't got your lesson yet. You've got to stay after school. We make a needless ado about capital punishment—taking lives, when there is no life to take. *Memento mori!*[96] We don't understand that sublime sentence which some worthy got sculptured on his gravestone once. We've interpreted it in a grovelling and snivelling sense; we've wholly forgotten how to die.

But be sure you do die, nevertheless. Do your work, and finish it. If you know how to begin, you will know when to end.

These men, in teaching us how to die, have at the same time taught us how to live. If this man's acts and words do not create a revival, it will be the severest possible satire on the acts and words that do. It is the best news that America has ever heard. It has already quickened the feeble pulse of the North, and infused more and more generous blood into her veins and heart, than any number of years of what is called commercial and political prosperity could. How many a man who was lately contemplating suicide has now something to live for!

One writer says that Brown's peculiar monomania made him to be "dreaded by the Missourians as a supernatural being."[97] Sure enough, a hero in the midst of us cowards is always so dreaded. He is just that thing. He shows himself superior to nature. He has a spark of divinity in him.[98]

> "Unless above himself he can
> Erect himself, how poor a thing is man!"[99]

Newspaper editors argue also that it is a proof of his *insanity* that he thought he was appointed to do this work which he did—that he did not suspect himself for a moment! They talk as if it were impossible that a man could be "divinely appointed" in these days to do any work whatever;[100] as if vows and religion were out of date as connected with any man's daily work,—as if the agent to abolish Slavery could only be somebody appointed by the President, or by some political party. They talk as if a man's death were a failure, and his continued life, be it of whatever character, were a success.

When I reflect to what a cause this man devoted himself, and how religiously, and then reflect to what cause his judges and all who condemn him so angrily and fluently devote themselves, I see that they are as far apart as the heavens and earth are asunder.

The amount of it is, our "*leading men*" are a harmless kind of folk, and they know *well enough* that *they* were not divinely appointed, but elected by the votes of their party.

Who is it whose safety requires that Captain Brown be hung? Is it indispensable to any Northern man? Is there no resource but to cast these men also to the Minotaur?[101] If you do not wish it, say so distinctly. While these things are being done, beauty stands veiled and music is a screeching lie. Think of him—of his rare qualities! such a man as it takes ages to make, and ages to understand; no mock hero, nor the representative of any

[98] Allusion to Joseph Addison's (1672–1719) *Cato* V.i:

> 'T is the Divinity that stirs within us;
> 'T is Heaven itself that points out an hereafter,
> And intimates eternity to man.

The idea of a divinity within allowed for a personal innate relationship with God and separated the Transcendentalists from the Unitarians, who were grounded in historical Christianity. In his *Nature* Emerson wrote simply: "I am part or particle of God." William Ellery Channing (1780–1842) wrote in his sermon "Likeness to God": "Men, as by a natural inspiration, have agreed to speak of conscience as the voice of God, as the Divinity within us. This principle, reverently obeyed, makes us more and more partakers of the moral perfection of the Supreme Being, of that very excellence, which constitutes the rightfulness of his sceptre, and enthrones him over the universe. Without this inward law, we should be as incapable of receiving a law from Heaven, as the brute. Without this, the thunders of Sinai might startle the outward ear, but would have no meaning, no authority to the mind. I have expressed here a great truth. Nothing teaches so encouragingly our relation and resemblance to God."

[99] Quoted from Samuel Daniel's (ca. 1562–1619) "Epistle to the Lady Margaret, Countess of Cumberland," 95–96.

[100] Thoreau wrote in his journal: "If Christ should appear on earth he could on all hands be denounced as a mistaken, misguided man, insane and crazed" [J 12:407].

[101] In Greek mythology, a monster with a bull's head and a man's body housed within the labyrinth created by Daedalus.

party. A man such as the sun may not rise upon again in this benighted land. To whose making went the costliest material, the finest adamant;[102] sent to be the redeemer of those in captivity; and the only use to which you can put him is to hang him at the end of a rope! You who pretend to care for Christ crucified, consider what you are about to do to him who offered himself to be the savior of four millions of men.

Any man knows when he is justified, and all the wits in the world cannot enlighten him on that point. The murderer always knows that he is justly punished; but when a government takes the life of a man without the consent of his conscience, it is an audacious government, and is taking a step towards its own dissolution. Is it not possible that an individual may be right and a government wrong? Are laws to be enforced simply because they were made? or declared by any number of men to be good, if they are *not* good? Is there any necessity for a man's being a tool to perform a deed of which his better nature disapproves? Is it the intention of law-makers that *good* men shall be hung ever? Are judges to interpret the law according to the letter, and not the spirit?[103] What right have *you* to enter into a compact with yourself that you *will* do thus or so, against the light within you? Is it for *you* to *make up* your mind—to form any resolution whatever—and not accept the convictions that are forced upon you, and which ever pass your understanding? I do not believe in lawyers, in that mode of attacking or defending a man, because you descend to meet the judge on his own ground, and, in cases of the highest importance, it is of no consequence whether a man breaks a human law or not. Let lawyers decide trivial cases. Business men may arrange that among themselves. If they were the interpreters of the everlasting laws which rightfully bind man,[104] that would be another thing. A counterfeiting law-factory, standing half in a slave land

---

102 Name applied with more or less indefiniteness to various metals or minerals, real or imaginary, characterized by extreme hardness, thus any substance of impenetrable or surpassing hardness which is impregnable to any force.
103 Allusion to 2 Corinthians 3:6, also used in "Last Days of John Brown": "The letter killeth, but the spirit giveth life."
104 Higher law: cf. "Resistance to Civil Government," note 69.

and half in a free! What kind of laws for free men can you expect from that?

I am here to plead his cause with you. I plead not for his life, but for his character—his immortal life; and so it becomes your cause wholly, and is not his in the least. Some eighteen hundred years ago Christ was crucified; this morning, perchance, Captain Brown was hung. These are the two ends of a chain which is not without its links. He is not Old Brown any longer; he is an angel of light.[105]

I see now that it was necessary that the bravest and humanest man in all the country should be hung. Perhaps he saw it himself. I *almost fear* that I may yet hear of his deliverance, doubting if a prolonged life, if *any* life, can do as much good as his death.

"Misguided"! "Garrulous"! "Insane"! "Vindictive"! So ye write in your easy chairs, and thus he wounded responds from the floor of the Armory, clear as a cloudless sky, true as the voice of nature is: "No man sent me here; it was my own prompting and that of my Maker. I acknowledge no master in human form."[106]

And in what a sweet and noble strain he proceeds, addressing his captors, who stand over him: "I think, my friend, you are guilty of a great wrong against God and humanity,[107] and it would be perfectly right for any one to interfere with you so far as to free those you wilfully and wickedly hold in bondage."[108]

And referring to his movement: "It is, in my opinion, the greatest service a man can render to God."[109]

"I pity the poor in bondage that have none to help them; that is why I am here; not to gratify any personal animosity, revenge, or vindictive spirit. It is my sympathy with the oppressed and the wronged, that are as good as you, and as precious in the sight of God."[110]

You don't know your testament when you see it.

"I want you to understand that I respect the rights of

105 Allusion to 2 Corinthians 11:12–15 in which Paul defends himself as a disciple of Christ: "But what I do, that I will do, that I may cut off occasion from them which desire occasion; that wherein they glory, they may be found even as we. For such *are* false apostles, deceitful workers, transforming themselves into the apostles of Christ. And no marvel; for Satan himself is transformed into an angel of light. Therefore *it is* no great thing if his ministers also be transformed as the ministers of righteousness; whose end shall be according to their works."
106 This was in answer to the question, "Mr. Brown, who sent you here?" Brown's full reply was: "No man sent me here; it was my own prompting and that of my Maker, or that of the Devil,—whichever you please to ascribe it to. I acknowledge no master in human form."
107 Thoreau here deleted the phrase "I say it without wishing to be offensive."
108 Brown's answer to the question: "How do you justify your acts?"
109 In answer to the question: "Do you consider this a religious movement?"
110 Allusion to Psalms 116:15: "Precious in the sight of the Lord is the death of his saints." This was in answer to the question: "Upon what principle do you justify your acts?" Brown prefaced his answer with: "Upon the Golden Rule."

the poorest and weakest of colored people, oppressed by the slave power, just as much as I do those of the most wealthy and powerful."

"I wish to say, furthermore, that you had better, all you people at the South, prepare yourselves for a settlement of that question, that must come up for settlement sooner than you are prepared for it. The sooner you are prepared the better. You may dispose of me very easily. I am nearly disposed of now; but this question is still to be settled—this negro question, I mean; the end of that is not yet."[111]

I foresee the time when the painter will paint that scene, no longer going to Rome for a subject; the poet will sing it; the historian record it; and, with the Landing of the Pilgrims and the Declaration of Independence,[112] it will be the ornament of some future national gallery, when at least the present form of Slavery shall be no more here. We shall then be at liberty to weep for Captain Brown. Then, and not till then, we will take our revenge.[113]

111 Asked whether he had anything further to say, Brown began by saying: "I have nothing to say, only that I claim to be here in carrying out a measure I believe perfectly justifiable, and not to act the part of an incendiary or ruffian, but to aid those suffering great wrong."

112 Allusion to paintings by Henry Sargent (1770–1845) and John Trumbull (1756–1843), respectively.

113 This is at variance with both Thoreau's position in "Sir Walter Raleigh" ("Revenge is most unheroic" [EE&M 185]) and Brown's principles: cf. note 61 above.

The Last Days of John Brown

John Brown's career for the last six weeks[1] of his life was meteor-like, flashing through the darkness in which we live. I know of nothing so miraculous in our history.

If any person, in a lecture or conversation at that time, cited any ancient example of heroism, such as Cato[2] or Tell[3] or Winkelried,[4] passing over the recent deeds and words of Brown, it was felt by any intelligent audience of Northern men to be tame and inexcusably far-fetched.

For my own part, I commonly attend more to nature than to man, but any affecting human event may blind our eyes to natural objects. I was so absorbed in him as to be surprised whenever I detected the routine of the natural world surviving still, or met persons going about their affairs indifferent. It appeared strange to me that the "little dipper"[5] should be still diving quietly in the river, as of yore; and it suggested that this bird might continue to dive here when Concord should be no more.

I felt that he, a prisoner in the midst of his enemies, and under sentence of death, if consulted as to his next step or resource, could answer more wisely than all his countrymen beside. He best understood his position; he contemplated it most calmly. Comparatively, all other men, North and South, were beside themselves. Our thoughts could not revert to any greater or wiser or better man with whom to contrast him, for he, then and there, was above them all. The man this country was about to hang appeared the greatest and best in it.

Years were not required for a revolution of public opinion; days, nay, hours, produced marked changes in

1 Period from Brown's 16 October raid on Harpers Ferry to his execution on 2 December 1859.
2 Marcus Porcius Cato (95–46 B.C.E.), also called Cato the Younger, Roman politician who opposed Julius Caesar (100–44 B.C.E.). Refusing to acknowledge Caesar's power, he committed suicide.
3 Swiss folk hero William Tell, who was compelled by the local bailiff on November 18, 1307, to shoot an apple from the head of his son with a crossbow.
4 Arnold Winkelried (d. 1386), legendary Swiss hero who allegedly saved the victory of the Swiss Confederacy during the Battle of Sempach against an invading Austrian army. According to the legend, when the Swiss were unable to break the close ranks of the enemy soldiers, Winkelried rushed forward, gathering a number of his comrades' spears together against his breast, thus breaching the enemy line.
5 Colloquial name for various small diving birds, often the pied-billed or horned grebe.

6 On 30 October 1859, at which "A Plea for Captain John Brown" was read.

7 Cf. "A Plea for Captain John Brown," note 1.

8 James Montgomery's (1771–1854) hymn "Go to the grave in all thy glorious prime" was sung at the "Exercises at the Town Hall, in Concord, on Friday, December 2, 1859, at 2 O'clock, P.M."

9 Unidentified further.

10 Sunday school teacher, unidentified further.

11 Cf. "Resistance to Civil Government," note 77, and "A Plea for Captain John Brown," note 109. When sentenced, Brown addressed the court: "I see a book kissed which I suppose to be the Bible, or at least the New Testament, which teaches me that all things whatsoever I would that men should do to me, I should do to them."

12 Allusion to followers of Robert Browne (d. 1663), founder of Congregationalism, who taught that every church is complete and independent in itself when organized.

13 Cf. "A Plea for Captain John Brown," note 102.

this case. Fifty who were ready to say on going into our meeting in honor of him in Concord,[6] that he ought to be hung, would not say it when they came out.[7] They heard his words read; they saw the earnest faces of the congregation; and perhaps they joined at last in singing the hymn in his praise.[8]

The order of instructors was reversed. I heard that one preacher, who at first was shocked and stood aloof, felt obliged at last, after he was hung, to make him the subject of a sermon, in which, to some extent, he eulogized the man, but said that his act was a failure.[9] An influential class-teacher[10] thought it necessary, after the services, to tell his grown-up pupils, that at first he thought as the preacher did then, but now he thought that John Brown was right. But it was understood that his pupils were as much ahead of the teacher, as he was ahead of the priest; and I know for a certainty, that very little boys at home had already asked their parents, in a tone of surprise, why God did not interfere to save him. In each case, the constituted teachers were only half conscious that they were not *leading,* but being *dragged,* with some loss of time and power.

The more conscientious preachers, the Bible men, they who talk about principle, and *doing* to others as you would that they should do unto you,[11]—how could they fail to recognize him, by far the greatest preacher of them all, with the Bible in his life and in his acts, the embodiment of principle, who actually carried out the golden rule? All whose moral sense had been aroused, who had a calling from on high to preach, sided with him. What confessions he extracted from the cold and conservative! It is remarkable, but on the whole it is well, that it did not prove the occasion for a new sect of *Brownites*[12] being formed in our midst.

They, whether within the Church or out of it, who adhere to the spirit and let go the letter,[13] and are ac-

cordingly called infidel, were as usual foremost to recognize him. Men have been hung in the South before
for attempting to rescue slaves, and the North was not
much stirred by it. Whence, then, this wonderful difference? We were not so sure of *their* devotion to principle. We made a subtle distinction, forgot human laws,
and did homage to an idea. The North, I mean the *living*
North, was suddenly all transcendental. It went behind
the human law, it went behind the apparent failure, and
recognized eternal justice and glory. Commonly, men
live according to a formula, and are satisfied if the order
of law is observed, but in this instance they, to some
extent, returned to original perceptions, and there was
a slight revival of old religion. They saw that what was
called order was confusion, what was called justice, injustice, and that the best was deemed the worst. This attitude suggested a more intelligent and generous spirit
than that which actuated our forefathers, and the possibility, in the course of ages, of a revolution in behalf of
another and an oppressed people.

Most Northern men, and a few Southern ones, were
wonderfully stirred by Brown's behavior and words. They
saw and felt that they were heroic and noble, and that
there had been nothing quite equal to them in their kind
in this country, or in the recent history of the world. But
the minority were unmoved by them. They were only
surprised and provoked by the attitude of their neighbors. They saw that Brown was brave, and that he believed that he had done right, but they did not detect
any further peculiarity in him. Not being accustomed
to make fine distinctions, or to appreciate magnanimity,
they read his letters and speeches as if they read them
not. They were not aware when they approached a heroic
statement—they did not know when they *burned*. They
did not feel that he spoke with authority, and hence
they only remembered that the *law* must be executed.

14 Democrats accused the Republican Party of encouraging and supporting slave revolts, to which Abraham Lincoln responded in his 27 February 1860 Cooper Union Address: "You charge that we stir up insurrections among your slaves. We deny it; and what is your proof? Harper's Ferry! John Brown!! John Brown was no Republican; and you have failed to implicate a single Republican in his Harper's Ferry enterprise."

15 Thick-skinned.

16 Literally one who follows the doctrines of Christ.

17 Term used for a religious conversion, as in John 3:3: "Jesus answered and said unto him, 'Verily, verily, I say unto thee, except a man be born again, he cannot see the kingdom of God.'"

They remembered the old formula, but did not hear the new revelation. The man who does not recognize in Brown's words a wisdom and nobleness, and therefore an authority, superior to our laws, is a modern Democrat.[14] This is the test by which to discover him. He is not wilfully but constitutionally blind on this side, and he is consistent with himself. Such has been his past life; no doubt of it. In like manner he has read history and his Bible, and he accepts, or seems to accept, the last only as an established formula, and not because he has been convicted by it. You will not find kindred sentiments in his common-place book, if he has one.

When a noble deed is done, who is likely to appreciate it? They who are noble themselves. I was not surprised that certain of my neighbors spoke of John Brown as an ordinary felon, for who are they? They have either much flesh, or much office, or much coarseness of some kind. They are not etherial natures in any sense. The dark qualities predominate in them. Several of them are decidedly pachydermatous.[15] I say it in sorrow, not in anger. How can a man behold the light, who has no answering inward light? They are true to their *right,* but when they look this way they *see* nothing, they are blind. For the children of the light to contend with them is as if there should be a contest between eagles and owls. Show me a man who feels bitterly toward John Brown, and let me hear what noble verse he can repeat. He'll be as dumb as if his lips were stone.

It is not every man who can be a Christian,[16] even in a very moderate sense, whatever education you give him. It is a matter of constitution and temperament, after all. He may have to be born again[17] many times. I have known many a man who pretended to be a Christian, in whom it was ridiculous, for he had no genius for it. It is not every man who can be a free-man, even.

Editors persevered for a good while in saying that

Brown was crazy: but at last they said only that it was "a crazy scheme," and the only evidence brought to prove it was that it cost him his life. I have no doubt that if he had gone with five thousand men, liberated a thousand slaves, killed a hundred or two slaveholders, and had as many more killed on his own side, but not lost his own life, these same editors would have called it by a more respectable name. Yet he has been far more successful than that. He has liberated many thousands of slaves, both North and South. They seem to have known nothing about living or dying for a principle. They all called him crazy then; who calls him crazy now?

All through the excitement occasioned by his remarkable attempt and subsequent behavior, the Massachusetts Legislature, not taking any steps for the defence of her citizens who were likely to be carried to Virginia as witnesses[18] and exposed to the violence of a slaveholding mob, was wholly absorbed in a liquor-agency question,[19] and indulging in poor jokes on the word "extension."[20] Bad spirits occupied their thoughts. I am sure that no statesman up to the occasion could have attended to that question at all at that time,—a very vulgar question to attend to at any time.

When I looked into a liturgy of the Church of England,[21] printed near the end of the last century, in order to find a service applicable to the case of Brown, I found that the only martyr recognized and provided for by it was King Charles the First,[22] an eminent scamp. Of all the inhabitants of England and of the world, he was the only one, according to this authority, whom that church had made a martyr and saint of; and for more than a century it had celebrated his martyrdom, so called, by an annual service. What a satire on the Church is that!

Look not to legislatures and churches for your guidance, nor to any soulless *incorporated* bodies, but to *inspirited* or inspired ones.

18 Henry A. Wise (1806–1876) was trying to have Frank Sanborn, among others, arrested and extradited, for his possible involvement with Brown.
19 Hearings were being held before the Legislative Committee in 1859 to investigate the conduct of the State Liquor Agency.
20 Permission for sale of alcoholic beverages later than the proscribed legal closing time.
21 There were several editions of *The Book of Common Prayer and Administration of the Sacraments and Other Rites and Ceremonies of the Church of England* published at the end of the eighteenth century.
22 Charles I (1600–1649), king of England from 1625 until 1649, when he was beheaded for treason. An entry for "K. Charles Martyr" is found at 30 January in the Kalendar in all editions of the Book of Common Prayer published between 1662 and 1859.

23 Allusion to *The History of the World*, written while Raleigh was imprisoned by James I of England (also James VI of Scotland, 1566–1625) for treason.
24 Reference to the several letters of Brown written from prison and published in newspapers.
25 On 16 November 1859 Brown wrote: "The music of the broom, wash-tub, needle, spindle, loom, axe, scythe, hoe, flail, etc., should be first learned at all events, and that of the piano, etc. afterwards."
26 Benjamin Franklin's (1706–1790) *Poor Richard's Almanack*, published annually from 1732 to 1757.
27 The American author Washington Irving died on 28 November 1859.
28 Cf. "A Plea for Captain John Brown," note 7.
29 Demosthenes (384–322 B.C.E.), whom is said to have overcome his stammer by practicing oratory with pebbles in his mouth.

What avail all your scholarly accomplishments and learning, compared with wisdom and manhood? To omit his other behavior, see what a work this comparatively unread and unlettered man wrote within six weeks. Where is our professor of *belles lettres* or of logic and rhetoric, who can write so well? He wrote in prison, not a history of the world, like Raleigh,[23] but an American book which I think will live longer than that.[24] I do not know of such words, uttered under such circumstances, and so copiously withal, in Roman or English or any history. What a variety of themes he touched on in that short space! There are words in that letter to his wife, respecting the education of his daughters,[25] which deserve to be framed and hung over every mantlepiece in the land. Compare this earnest wisdom with that of Poor Richard.[26]

The death of Irving,[27] which at any other time would have attracted universal attention, having occurred while these things were transpiring, went almost unobserved. I shall have to read of it in the biography of authors.

Literary gentlemen, editors and critics, think that they know how to write, because they have studied grammar and rhetoric; but they are egregiously mistaken. The *art* of composition is as simple as the discharge of a bullet from a rifle, and its master-pieces imply an infinitely greater force behind them. This unlettered man's speaking and writing are standard English. Some words and phrases deemed vulgarisms and Americanisms before, he has made standard American; such as "*It will pay.*"[28] It suggests that the one great rule of composition—and if I were a professor of rhetoric, I should insist on this—is to *speak the truth*. This first, this second, this third; pebbles in your mouth[29] or not. This demands earnestness and manhood chiefly.

We seem to have forgotten that the expression, a *liberal* education, originally meant among the Romans one worthy of *free* men;[30] while the learning of trades and professions by which to get your livelihood merely, was considered worthy of *slaves* only. But taking a hint from the word, I would go a step further and say, that it is not the man of wealth and leisure simply, though devoted to art, or science, or literature, who, in a true sense, is *liberally* educated, but only the earnest and *free* man. In a slaveholding country like this, there can be no such thing as a *liberal* education tolerated by the State; and those scholars of Austria and France who, however learned they may be, are contented under their tyrannies, have received only a *servile* education.

Nothing could his enemies do, but it redounded to his infinite advantage—that is, to the advantage of his cause. They did not hang him at once, but reserved him to preach to them. And then there was another great blunder. They did not hang his four followers with him; that scene was still postponed; and so his victory was prolonged and completed. No theatrical manager could have arranged things so wisely to give effect to his behavior and words. And who, think you, was the manager? Who placed the slave woman and her child, whom he stooped to kiss for a symbol, between his prison and the gallows?[31]

We soon saw, as he saw, that he was not to be pardoned or rescued by men. That would have been to disarm him, to restore to him a material weapon, a Sharps' rifle, when he had taken up the sword of the spirit—the sword with which he has really won his greatest and most memorable victories. Now he has not laid aside the sword of the spirit, for he is pure spirit himself, and his sword is pure spirit also.

"He nothing common did or mean
Upon that memorable scene,

. . . .

30 *Liberal*, from the Latin *liberalis*, meaning suitable for or befitting a free man.

31 Brown was led to the gallows with his hands tied, surrounded by armed soldiers. The apocryphal story of Brown kissing a slave child on the way to his execution, which Thoreau would have read, originated with an account by an unnamed "correspondent" in the *New-York Tribune* on 5 December 1859: "As he stepped out of door a black woman, with her little child in her arms, stood near his way. The twain were of the despised race, for whose emancipation and elevation to the dignity of children of God, he was about to lay down his life. His thoughts at that moment none can know except as his acts interpret them. He stopped for a moment in his course, stooped over, and, with the tenderness of one whose love is as broad as the brotherhood of man, kissed it affectionately."

32 Quoted from Andrew Marvell's (1621–1678) "An Horatian Ode upon Cromwell's Return from Ireland," ll. 57–64, from which Thoreau also quoted in "Wild Apples." Two lines are dropped after the second line of the quotation: "But with his keener eye / The axe's edge did try."

33 In astronomy, the passage of a heavenly body across the meridian, or the passage of a celestial body across the sun.

34 From mortal to immortal.

35 In New York, where Brown moved with his family in 1849 and the site of his grave.

36 During his interrogation on 18 October 1859 as reported in the *New York Herald* (21 October 1859), in answer to the question why he worked secretly, Brown said: "Because I thought that necessary to success; no other reason."

Nor called the gods with vulgar spite,
To vindicate his helpless right;
But bowed his comely head
Down as upon a bed."[32]

What a transit[33] was that of his horizontal body alone, but just cut down from the gallows-tree! We read, that at such a time it passed through Philadelphia, and by Saturday night had reached New York. Thus, like a meteor it shot through the Union from the southern regions toward the north! No such freight had the cars borne since they carried him southward alive.

On the day of his translation,[34] I heard, to be sure, that he was *hung,* but I did not know what that meant; I felt no sorrow on that account; but not for a day or two did I even *hear* that he was *dead,* and not after any number of days shall I believe it. Of all the men who were said to be my contemporaries, it seemed to me that John Brown was the only one who *had not died.* I never hear of a man named Brown now,—and I hear of them pretty often,—I never hear of any particularly brave and earnest man, but my first thought is of John Brown, and what relation he may be to him. I meet him at every turn. He is more alive than ever he was. He has earned immortality. He is not confined to North Elba[35] nor to Kansas. He is no longer working in secret.[36] He works in public, and in the clearest light that shines on this land.

An Address on the Succession
of Forest Trees

1 The Middlesex Agricultural Society's annual agricultural fair, the Middlesex Cattle Show and Ploughing Match, later the Annual Exhibition of the Middlesex Agricultural Society, was held in Concord each September or October. Middlesex is the county of which Concord is part.
2 Thoreau wrote in his journal of 29 September 1857: "All sorts of men come to Cattle-Show. I see one with a blue hat" [J 10:51].
3 Cabinet of curiosities: cf. "A Winter Walk," note 41.

Every man is entitled to come to Cattle-shows,[1] even a transcendentalist; and for my part I am more interested in the men than in the cattle.[2] I wish to see once more those old familiar faces, whose names I do not know, which for me represent the Middlesex country, and come as near being indigenous to the soil as a white man can; the men who are not above their business, whose coats are not too black, whose shoes do not shine very much, who never wear gloves to conceal their hands. It is true, there are some queer specimens of humanity attracted to our festival, but all are welcome. I am pretty sure to meet once more that weak-minded and whimsical fellow, generally weak-bodied too, who prefers a crooked stick for a cane; perfectly useless, you would say, only bizarre, fit for a cabinet,[3] like a petrified snake. A ram's horn would be as convenient, and is yet more curiously twisted. He brings that much indulged bit of the country with him, from some town's end or other, and introduces it to Concord groves, as if he had promised it so much sometime.

So some, it seems to me, elect their rulers for their crookedness. But I think that a straight stick makes the best cane, and an upright man the best ruler. Or why choose a man to do plain work who is distinguished for his "oddity"? However, I do not know but you will think that they have committed this mistake who invited me to speak to you to-day.

In my capacity of surveyor, I have often talked with

some of you, my employers, at your dinner-tables, after having gone round and round and behind your farming, and ascertained exactly what its limits were. Moreover, taking a surveyor's and a naturalist's liberty, I have been in the habit of going across your lots much oftener than is usual, as many of you, perhaps to your sorrow, are aware. Yet many of you, to my relief, have seemed not to be aware of it; and, when I came across you in some out-of-the-way nook of your farms, have inquired, with an air of surprise, if I were not lost, since you had never seen me in that part of the town or county before; when, if the truth were known, and it had not been for betraying my secret, I might with more propriety have inquired if *you* were not lost, since I had never seen *you* there before. I have several times shown the proprietor the shortest way out of his wood-lot.

Therefore, it would seem that I have some title to speak to you to-day; and, considering what that title is, and the occasion that has called us together, I need offer no apology if I invite your attention for the few moments that are allotted me, to a purely scientific subject.

At those dinner-tables referred to, I have often been asked, as many of you have been, if I could tell how it happened, that when a pine wood was cut down an oak one sprang up, and *vice versa*. To which I have answered, and now answer, that I can tell—that it is no mystery to me. As I am not aware that this has been clearly shown by any one, I shall lay the more stress on this point. Let me lead you back into your wood-lots again.

When a single tree or a forest springs up naturally where none of its kind grew before, I do not hesitate to say, though in some quarters still it may sound paradoxical, that it came from a seed. Of the various ways by which trees are *known* to be propagated—by transplanting, cuttings, and the like—this is the only supposable one under these circumstances. No such tree has ever been known to spring from any thing else. If any one asserts that it sprang from something else, or from nothing, the burden of proof lies with him.

It remains then only to show how the seed is transported from where it grows, to where it is planted. This is done chiefly by the agency of the wind, water and animals. The lighter seeds, as those of pines and maples, are transported chiefly by wind and water; the heavier, as acorns and nuts, by animals.

In all the pines, a very thin membrane, in appearance much like an insect's wing, grows over and around the seed, and independent of it, while the latter is being developed within its base. Indeed, this is often perfectly developed, though the seed is abortive, nature being, you would say, more sure to provide the means of transporting the seed, than to provide the seed to be transported. In other words, a beautiful thin sack is woven around the seed, with a handle to it such as the wind can take hold of, and it is then committed to the wind, expressly that it may transport the seed and extend the range of the species; and this it does as effectually as when seeds are sent by mail in a different kind of sack from the patent office.[4] There is a patent office at the seat of government of the universe, whose managers are as much interested in the dispersion of seeds as any body at Washington can be, and their operations are infinitely more extensive and regular.

There is then no necessity for supposing that the pines have sprung up from nothing, and I am aware that I am not at all peculiar in asserting that they come from seeds, though the mode of their propagation *by nature* has been but little attended to. They are very extensively raised from the seed in Europe, and are beginning to be here.

When you cut down an oak wood, a pine wood will not *at once* spring up there unless there are, or have been,

4 From 1836 to 1862 the U.S. Patent Office distributed seeds through the mail.

5 Abiogenesis: the hypothesis that life can spontaneously come into being from nonliving materials, an idea that originated with Aristotle and was supported by many natural philosophers and scientists, including Louis Agassiz (1807–1873), the Swiss-born naturalist who came to the United States in 1846 and in 1848 became a professor of zoology and geology at Harvard.
6 The wall of a ripened fruit or seed.

quite recently, seed-bearing pines near enough for the seeds to be blown from them. But, adjacent to a forest of pines, if you prevent other crops from growing there, you will surely have an extension of your pine forest, provided the soil is suitable.

As for the heavy seeds and nuts which are not furnished with wings, the notion is still a very common one that, when the trees which bear these spring up where none of their kind were noticed before, they have come from seeds or other principles spontaneously generated there in an unusual manner,[5] or which have lain dormant in the soil for centuries, or perhaps been called into activity by the heat of a burning. I do not believe these assertions, and I will state some of the ways in which, according to my observation, such forests are planted and raised.

Every one of these seeds, too, will be found to be winged or legged in another fashion. Surely it is not wonderful that cherry-trees of all kinds are widely dispersed, since their fruit is well known to be the favorite food of various birds. Many kinds are called bird-cherries, and they appropriate many more kinds, which are not so called. Eating cherries is a bird-like employment, and unless we disperse the seeds occasionally as they do I shall think that the birds have the best right to them. See how artfully the seed of a cherry is placed in order that a bird may be compelled to transport it—in the very midst of a tempting pericarp,[6] so that the creature that would devour this must commonly take the stone also into its mouth or bill. If you ever ate a cherry, and did not make two bites of it, you must have perceived it—right in the centre of the luscious morsel, a large earthy residuum left on the tongue. We thus take into our mouths cherry stones as big as peas, a dozen at once, for Nature can persuade us to do almost anything when she would compass her ends. Some wild men and children instinctively swallow these like the birds when in a hurry as the shortest way to get rid of them. Thus, though these seeds are not provided with vegetable wings, Nature has impelled the thrush tribe to take them into their bills and fly away with them, and they are winged in another sense, and more effectually than the seeds of pines, for these are carried even against the wind. The consequence is, that cherry trees grow not only here but there. The same is true of a great many other seeds.

But to come to the observation which suggested these remarks. As I have said, I suspect that I can throw some light on the fact, that when hereabouts a dense pine wood is cut down, oaks and other hard woods may at once take its place. I have got only to show that the acorns and nuts, provided they are grown in the neighborhood, are regularly planted in such woods; for I assert that if an oak tree has not grown within ten miles, and man has not carried acorns thither, then an oak wood will not spring up at once when a pine wood is cut down.

Apparently, there were only pines there before. They are cut off, and after a year or two you see oaks and other hard woods springing up there, with scarcely a pine amid them, and the wonder commonly is how the seed could have been lying in the ground so long without decaying. But the truth is, that it has not lain in the ground so long, but is regularly planted each year by various quadrupeds and birds.

In this neighborhood, where oak and pines are about equally dispersed, if you look through the thickest pine wood, even the seemingly exclusive pitch-pine ones, you will commonly detect many little oaks, birches, and other hard woods, sprung from seeds carried into the thicket by squirrels and other animals, and also blown thither, but which are overshadowed and choked by the pines. The denser the evergreen wood, the more likely it is to be well planted with these seeds, because the planters

7 Thoreau wrote: "All that I have met with of importance on the subject of the succession of forest trees is contained in a few numbers of the *Memoirs of the Philadelphia Society for Promoting Agriculture,* which appeared about 1808, and in an article by John William Dawson of Picton in the *Edinburgh New Philosophical Journal* for April 1847" [*Faith in a Seed* 207]. None of those works account for the squirrel as an instrument of succession.

incline to resort with their forage to the closest covert. They also carry it into birch and other woods. This planting is carried on annually, and the plants annually die; but when the pines are cleared off, the oaks, having got just the start they want, and now secured favorable conditions, immediately spring up to trees.

Apparently, the shade of a dense pine wood is more unfavorable to the springing up of pines than of oaks within it, though the former may come up abundantly when the pines are cut, if there chance to be sound seed in the ground.

But when you cut off a lot of hard wood, very often the little pines mixed with it, have a similar start, for the squirrels have carried off the nuts to the pines, and not to the more open wood, and they commonly make pretty clean work of it — to say nothing about the soil being, in a measure, exhausted for the same kind of crop.

If a pine wood is surrounded by a white oak one chiefly, white oaks may be expected to succeed when the pines are cut. If it is surrounded instead by an edging of shrub-oaks, then you will probably have a dense shrub-oak thicket.

I have no time to go into details, but will say, in a word, that while the wind is conveying the seeds of pines into hard woods and open lands, the squirrels and other animals are conveying the seeds of oaks and walnuts into the pine woods, and thus a rotation of crops is kept up.

I affirmed this confidently many years ago, and an occasional examination of dense pine woods confirmed me in my opinion. It has long been known to observers that squirrels bury nuts in the ground, but I am not aware that any one has thus accounted for the regular succession of forests.[7]

On the 24th of September, in '57, as I was paddling down the Assabet, in this town, I saw a red squirrel run along the bank under some herbage, with something large in its mouth. It stopped near the foot of a hemlock, within a couple of rods of me, and, hastily pawing a hole with its fore feet, dropped its booty into it and covered it up, and retreated part way up the trunk of the tree. As I approached the shore to examine the deposit, the squirrel, descending part way, betrayed no little anxiety about its treasure, and made two or three motions to re-cover it before it finally retreated. Digging there, I found two green pig nuts[8] joined together, with the thick husks on, buried about an inch and a half under the reddish soil of decayed hemlock leaves—just the right depth to plant it. In short, this squirrel was then engaged in accomplishing two objects, to wit, laying up a store of Winter food for itself, and planting a hickory wood for all creation. If the squirrel was killed, or neglected its deposit, a hickory would spring up. The nearest hickory tree was twenty rods distant. These nuts were there still just fourteen days later, but were gone when I looked again, Nov. 21, or six weeks later still.

I have since examined more carefully several dense woods, which are said to be, and are apparently exclusively pine, and always with the same result. For instance, I walked the same day to a small, but very dense and handsome white-pine grove, about fifteen rods square, in the east part of this town. The trees are large for Concord, being from ten to twenty inches in diameter, and as exclusively pine as any wood that I know. Indeed, I selected this wood because I thought it the least likely to contain anything else. It stands on an open plain or pasture, except that it adjoins another small pine wood, which has a few little oaks in it, on the south-east side. On every other side, it was at least thirty rods from the nearest woods. Standing on the edge of this grove and looking through it, for it is quite level and free from underwood, for the most part bare, red-carpeted ground, you would have said that there was not a hard wood tree

8 Seeds of the broom hickory, *Carya glabra.*

in it, young or old. But on looking carefully along over its floor I discovered, though it was not till my eye had got used to the search, that, alternating with thin ferns, and small blueberry bushes, there was, not merely here and there, but as often as every five feet, and with a degree of regularity, a little oak, from three to twelve inches high, and in one place I found a green acorn dropped by the base of a pine.

I confess I was surprised to find my theory so perfectly proved in this case. One of the principal agents in this planting, the red squirrels, were all the while curiously inspecting me, while I was inspecting their plantation. Some of the little oaks had been browsed by cows, which resorted to this wood for shade.

After some years, the hard woods, as I have said, evidently find such a locality unfavorable to their growth, the pines being allowed to stand. As an evidence of this, I observed a red maple twenty-five feet long, which had been recently prostrated, as if by the wind, though it was still covered with green leaves, the only maple in any position in the wood.

But although these oaks almost invariably die if the pines are not cut down, it is probable that they do better for a few years under their shelter than they would anywhere else.

The very extensive and thorough experiments of the English have at length led them to adopt a method of raising oaks almost precisely like this, which somewhat earlier had been adopted by nature and her squirrels here; they have simply re-discovered the value of pines as nurses for oaks. The English experimenters seem early and generally to have found out the importance of using trees of some kind as nurse plants for the young oaks. I quote from Loudon what he describes as "the ultimatum on the subject of planting and sheltering oaks,"—an "abstract of the practice adopted by the Government officers in the national forests"[9] of England, prepared by Alexander Milne.[10]

At first some oaks had been planted by themselves, and others mixed with Scotch pines; "but in all cases," says Mr. Milne, "where oaks were planted actually among the pines, and surrounded by them, [though the soil might be inferior,] the oaks were found to be much the best." "For several years past, the plan pursued has been to plant the enclosures with Scotch pines only, [a tree very similar to our pitch pine,] . . . and when the pines have got to the height of five or six feet,[11] then to put in good strong oak plants of about four or five years' growth among the pines—not cutting away any pines at first, unless they happen to be so strong and thick as to overshadow the oaks. In about two years, it becomes necessary to shred the branches of the pines, to give light and air to the oaks, and in about two or three more years to begin gradually to remove the pines altogether, taking out a certain number each year, so that, at the end of twenty or twenty-five years, not a single Scotch pine shall be left; although, for the first ten or twelve years, the plantation may have appeared to contain nothing else but pines. The advantage of this mode of planting has been found to be that the pines dry and ameliorate the soil, destroying the coarse grass and brambles which frequently choke and injure oaks; and that no mending over is necessary, as scarcely an oak so planted is found to fail."[12]

Thus much the English planters have discovered by patient experiment, and, for aught I know, they have taken out a patent for it; but they appear not to have discovered that it was discovered before, and that they are merely adopting the method of Nature, which she long ago made patent to all. She is all the while planting the oaks amid the pines without our knowledge, and at last, instead of Government officers, we send a party of

[9] Quoted from John Claudius Loudon (1783–1843)'s *Arboretum et Fruticetum Britannicum*.
[10] Alexander Milne (fl. 1818–1850), British commissioner of woods and forests.
[11] Thoreau deleted the phrase "which they will do in as many years," which followed.
[12] Quoted, with minor variants, from Loudon's *Arboretum et Fruticetum Britannicum*.

13 From his journal of 20 August 1854.

14 Common nineteenth-century name for the red squirrel (*Tamiasciurus hudsonicus*), from the sound it makes. In *A Week on the Concord and Merrimack Rivers* Thoreau described the chickaree's "warning of our approach by that peculiar alarum of his, like the winding up of some strong clock, in the top of a pine-tree, and dodged behind its stem, or leaped from tree to tree with such caution and adroitness, as if much depended on the fidelity of his scout, running along the white-pine boughs sometimes twenty rods by our side, with such speed, and by such unerring routes, as if it were some well-worn familiar path to him; and presently, when we have passed, he returns to his work of cutting off the pine-cones, and letting them fall to the ground" [W 1:206].

15 Throwing a club into the tree to knock the chestnut burrs down.

16 The Concord trapper George Melvin (b. 1813).

17 Reported in Thoreau's journal of 16 October 1857.

18 Thoreau noted in his copy of *Walden* that this was *Mus leucopus*, which is the common house mouse, although Thoreau used the term mistakenly to mean *Peromyscus leucopus*, the white-bellied or deer mouse, as shown in a May 1855 journal passage. [J 7:345]

wood-choppers to cut down the pines, and so rescue an oak forest, at which we wonder as if it had dropped from the skies.

As I walk amid hickories, even in August,[13] I hear the sound of green pig-nuts falling from time to time, cut off by the chickaree[14] over my head. In the Fall, I notice on the ground, either within or in the neighborhood of oak woods, on all sides of the town, stout oak twigs three or four inches long, bearing half-a-dozen empty acorn-cups, which have been gnawed off by squirrels, on both sides of the nuts, in order to make them more portable.

The jays scream and the red squirrels scold while you are clubbing[15] and shaking the chestnut trees, for they are there on the same errand, and two of a trade never agree. I frequently see a red or gray squirrel cast down a green chestnut bur, as I am going through the woods, and I used to think, sometimes, that they were cast at me. In fact, they are so busy about it, in the midst of the chestnut season, that you cannot stand long in the woods without hearing one fall.

A sportsman[16] told me that he had, the day before—that was in the middle of October[17]—seen a green chestnut bur dropt on our great river meadow, fifty rods from the nearest wood, and much further from the nearest chestnut tree, and he could not tell how it came there.

Occasionally, when chestnutting in midwinter, I find thirty or forty nuts in a pile, left in its gallery, just under the leaves, by the common wood-mouse (*mus leucopus*).[18]

But especially in the Winter the extent to which this transportation and planting of nuts is carried on is made apparent by the snow. In almost every wood, you will see where the red or gray squirrels have pawed down through the snow in a hundred places, sometimes two feet deep, and almost always directly to a nut or a pine-cone, as directly as if they had started from it and bored upward—which you and I could not have done. It would be difficult for us to find one before the snow falls. Commonly, no doubt, they had deposited them there in the Fall. You wonder if they remember the localities, or discover them by the scent. The red squirrel commonly has its Winter abode in the earth under a thicket of evergreens, frequently under a small clump of evergreens in the midst of a deciduous wood. If there are any nut-trees, which still retain their nuts, standing at a distance without the wood, their paths often lead directly to and from them. We, therefore, need not suppose an oak standing here and there *in* the wood in order to seed it, but if a few stand within twenty or thirty rods of it, it is sufficient.

I think that I may venture to say that every white-pine cone that falls to the earth naturally in this town, before opening and losing its seeds, and almost every pitch-pine one that falls at all, is cut off by a squirrel, and they begin to pluck them long before they are ripe, so that when the crop of white-pine cones is a small one, as it commonly is, they cut off thus almost every one of these before it fairly ripens. I think, moreover, that their design, if I may so speak, in cutting them off green, is partly to prevent their opening and losing their seeds, for these are the ones for which they dig through the snow, and the only white-pine cones which contain anything then. I have counted in one heap, within a diameter of four feet, the cores of 239 pitch-pine cones which had been cut off and stripped by the red squirrel the previous Winter.

The nuts thus left on the surface, or buried just beneath it, are placed in the most favorable circumstances for germinating. I have sometimes wondered how those which merely fell on the surface of the earth got planted; but, by the end of December, I find the chestnuts of the same year partially mixed with the mold, as it were, under the decaying and moldy leaves, where there is all the moisture and manure they want, for the nuts fall fast.

19 Compost pile.

20 Quoted from Loudon's *Arboretum et Fruti-cetum Britannicum.*

21 Stealing attention due to another, from the British dramatist John Dennis (1657–1734), who invented a new method for imitating thunder in his play *Appius and Virginia* at Drury Lane Theatre. When the play failed, the management used his method (stole his thunder) for a performance of *Macbeth.*

22 Allusion to Elisha Kent Kane's (1820–1857) *The U.S. Grinnell Expedition in Search of Sir John Franklin: A Personal Narrative.*

In a plentiful year, a large proportion of the nuts are thus covered loosely an inch deep, and are, of course, somewhat concealed from squirrels. One Winter, when the crop had been abundant, I got, with the aid of a rake, many quarts of these nuts as late as the 10th of January, and though some bought at the store the same day were more than half of them moldy, I did not find a single moldy one among these which I picked from under the wet and moldy leaves, where they had been snowed on once or twice. Nature knows how to pack them best. They were still plump and tender. Apparently, they do not heat there, though wet. In the Spring, they were all sprouting.

Loudon says that "when the nut [of the common walnut of Europe] is to be preserved through the Winter for the purpose of planting in the following spring, it should be laid in a rot heap,[19] as soon as gathered, with the husk on; and the heap should be turned over frequently in the course of the Winter."[20]

Here, again, he is stealing Nature's "thunder."[21] How can a poor mortal do otherwise? for it is she that finds fingers to steal with, and the treasure to be stolen. In the planting of the seeds of most trees, the best gardeners do no more than follow nature, though they may not know it. Generally, both large and small ones are most sure to germinate, and succeed best, when only beaten into the earth with the back of a spade, and then covered with leaves or straw. These results to which planters have arrived, remind us of the experience of Kane and his companions at the North, who, when learning to live in that climate, were surprised to find themselves steadily adopting the customs of the natives, simply becoming Esquimaux.[22] So, when we experiment in planting forests, we find ourselves at last doing as Nature does. Would it not be well to consult with Nature in the outset? for she is the most extensive and experienced planter of us all, not excepting the Dukes of Athol.[23]

In short, they who have not attended particularly to this subject, are but little aware to what an extent quadrupeds and birds are employed, especially in the Fall, in collecting, and so disseminating and planting the seeds of trees. It is the almost constant employment of the squirrels at that season, and you rarely meet with one that has not a nut in its mouth, or is not just going to get one. One squirrel-hunter of this town told me that he knew of a walnut tree which bore particularly good nuts, but that on going to gather them one Fall, he found that he had been anticipated by a family of a dozen red squirrels. He took out of the tree, which was hollow, one bushel and three pecks by measurement without the husks, and they supplied him and his family for the Winter. It would be easy to multiply instances of this kind. How commonly in the Fall you see the cheek-pouches of the striped squirrel distended by a quantity of nuts! This species gets its scientific name *Tamias*,[24] or the steward, from its habit of storing up nuts and other seeds. Look under a nut-tree a month after the nuts have fallen, and see what proportion of sound nuts to the abortive ones and shells you will find ordinarily. They have been already eaten, or dispersed far and wide. The ground looks like a platform before a grocery, where the gossips of the village sit and crack nuts and less savory jokes. You have come, you would say, after the feast was over, and are presented with the shells only.

Occasionally, when threading the woods in the Fall, you will hear a sound as if some one had broken a twig, and, looking up, see a jay pecking at an acorn, or you will see a flock of them at once about it, in the top of an oak, and hear them break them off. They then fly to a suitable limb and, placing the acorn under one foot,

23 James Murray, 2nd Duke of Atholl (1690–1764), planted thousands of larch trees in Scotland, and his son John Murray, 3rd Duke of Atholl (1729–1774), planted fourteen million more. Thoreau may have read this in George B. Emerson's (1797–1881) *A Report on the Trees and Shrubs Growing Naturally in the Forests of Massachusetts*, John S. Springer's (1811–1852) *Forest Life and Forest Trees*, or Loudon's *Arboretum et Fruticetum Britannicum*.

24 From the Greek word meaning one who stores things.

25 Nut-producing or nut-bearing. Thoreau's source mistakenly printed *ruciferous*. There is no indication whether Thoreau consciously or unconsciously corrected the word.

26 William Bartram (1739–1823), American naturalist and author of *Travels Through North and South Carolina*. Alexander Wilson (1766–1813), American ornithologist and author of *American Ornithology*. The quotation is from *Wilson's American Ornithology* (New York: H. S. Samuels, 1852).

27 Fruit and nuts of forest trees, in this case specifically the beech, used as animal food.

28 Quoted from Loudon's *Arboretum et Fruticetum Britannicum*.

hammer away at it busily, making a sound like a wood pecker's tapping, looking round from time to time to see if any foe is approaching, and soon reach the meat, and nibble at it, holding up their heads to swallow, while they hold the remainder very firmly with their claws. Nevertheless, it often drops to the ground before the bird has done with it. I can confirm what Wm. Bartram wrote to Wilson, the Ornithologist, that "The jay is one of the most useful agents in the economy of nature, for disseminating forest trees and other nuciferous[25] and hard-seeded vegetables on which they feed. Their chief employment during the Autumnal season is foraging to supply their Winter stores. In performing this necessary duty they drop abundance of seed in their flight over fields, hedges, and by fences where they alight to deposit them in the post-holes, &c. It is remarkable what numbers of young trees rise up in fields and pastures after a wet Winter and Spring. These birds alone are capable, in a few years' time, to replant all the cleared lands."[26]

I have noticed that squirrels also frequently drop their nuts in open land, which will still further account for the oaks and walnuts which spring up in pastures, for, depend on it, every new tree comes from a seed. When I examine the little oaks, one or two years old, in such places, I invariably find the empty acorn from which they sprung.

So far from the seed having lain dormant in the soil since oaks grew there before, as many believe, it is well known that it is difficult to preserve the vitality of acorns long enough to transport them to Europe; and it is recommended in Loudon's Arboretum, as the safest course, to sprout them in pots on the voyage. The same authority states that "very few acorns of any species will germinate after having been kept a year," that beech mast[27] "only retains its vital properties one year," and the black walnut "seldom more than six months after it has ripened."[28] I have frequently found that in November almost every acorn left on the ground had sprouted or decayed. What with frost, drouth, moisture, and worms, the greater part are soon destroyed. Yet it is stated by one botanical writer that "Acorns that have lain for centuries, on being plowed up, have soon vegetated."[29]

Mr. George B. Emerson, in his valuable Report on the Trees and Shrubs of this State, says of the pines: "The tenacity of life of the seeds is remarkable. They will remain for many years unchanged in the ground, protected by the coolness and deep shade of the forest above them. But when the forest is removed, and the warmth of the sun admitted, they immediately vegetate."[30] Since he does not tell us on what observation his remark is founded, I must doubt its truth. Besides, the experience of nurserymen makes it the more questionable.

The stories of wheat raised from seed buried with an ancient Egyptian,[31] and of raspberries raised from seed found in the stomach of a man in England,[32] who is supposed to have died sixteen or seventeen hundred years ago, are generally discredited, simply because the evidence is not conclusive.

Several men of science, Dr. Carpenter among them, have used the statement that beach-plums sprang up in sand which was dug up forty miles inland in Maine, to prove that the seed had lain there a very long time,[33] and some have inferred that the coast has receded so far.[34] But it seems to me necessary to their argument to show, first, that beach-plums grow only on a beach. They are not uncommon here, which is about half that distance from the shore, and I remember a dense patch a few miles north of us, twenty-five miles inland, from which the fruit was annually carried to market. How much further inland they grow, I know not. Dr. Chas. T. Jackson speaks of finding beach-plums (perhaps they were this kind) more than 100 miles inland in Maine.[35]

29 Quoted from Loring Dudley Chapin's (1798–1846) *The Vegetable Kingdom; or, Hand-book of Plants and Fruits.*

30 Quoted from George B. Emerson's *A Report on the Trees and Shrubs Growing Naturally in the Forests of Massachusetts.*

31 Stories had circulated in Thoreau's day of wheat found among the Egyptian mummies and sown in British soil. In the 1840s reports appeared in papers—The *Concord Freeman* carried one such report on 12 November 1841—about "mummy wheat" discovered in tombs up to 6,000 years old. The London *Times* carried a report on 14 August 1844 of a Mr. Reid's garden in which "we saw a quantity of Egyptian wheat in full ear, and giving promise of an abundant harvest, the seed of which was found in the folds of a mummy unrolled in 1840." Thoreau referred to the mummy wheat in *Walden.*

32 Alphonso Wood (1810–1881) wrote in *A Class-Book of Botany:* "No instance of the longevity of seeds is more remarkable than that related by Dr. Lindley. 'I have before me,' says he, 'three plants of raspberries, raised from seeds which were taken from the stomach of a man whose skeleton was found 30 feet below the surface of the earth. He had been buried with some coins of the emperor Hadrian, and it is therefore probable that the seeds were 1600 or 1700 years old.'" Wood quoted from John Lindley's (1799–1865) *An Introduction to Botany.*

33 William Benjamin Carpenter (1813–1885) wrote in *Vegetable Physiology and Systematic Botany:* "These trees must, therefore, have sprung up from seeds, which had existed in the stratum of sea-sand pierced by the well-diggers; and, until this was dispersed, in such a manner as to expose them to the air, they remained inactive."

34 Inference found in "Where Do Seeds Come From?" (*Transactions of the New Hampshire Agricultural Society, for the Year 1856*): "And whether they had been cast up by some over-flowing of the sea at that place during some convulsion of the elements, or whether the sea had receded from its

former shore by some upheaving of the land, it is equally impossible to say."

35 Charles Thomas Jackson (1805–1880), brother of Lidian Emerson (1802–1892) — wife of Ralph Waldo Emerson (1803–1882) — and of Lucy Jackson Brown (1798–1868), who boarded in the Thoreau family home. No mention of beach plums growing inland appear in any of his official publications as Maine state geologist, but Thoreau may have heard Jackson speak of this on one of his several visits to Concord or at his lecture on geology at the Concord Lyceum on 1 February 1843, when Thoreau was curator. Jackson published a brief obituary in the 1862–1863 *Proceedings of the Boston Society of Natural History* in which he wrote that Thoreau's writings were "full of knowledge of the secrets of nature, and are enlivened by much quaint humor, and warmed with kindness towards all living beings."

36 John Winthrop built this house on land granted to him in 1638, and it was "Adam Winthrop, a *grandson* of the *Governor* who sold the farm to Hunt in 1701" [J 4:487].

37 Stinging nettle, a European plant: see journal of 22 September 1857.

38 Also called feather geranium, a species of goosefoot or pigweed, a garden plant imported from Europe.

39 Common nightshade, imported from Europe.

It chances that similar objections lie against all the more notorious instances of the kind on record.

Yet I am prepared to believe that some seeds, especially small ones, may retain their vitality for centuries under favorable circumstances. In the Spring of 1859, the old Hunt House, so called, in this town, whose chimney bore the date 1703, was taken down. This stood on land which belonged to John Winthrop, the first Governor of Massachusetts, and a part of the house was evidently much older than the above date, and belonged to the Winthrop family.[36] For many years, I have ransacked this neighborhood for plants, and I consider myself familiar with its productions. Thinking of the seeds which are said to be sometimes dug up at an unusual depth in the earth, and thus to reproduce long extinct plants, it occurred to me last Fall that some new or rare plants might have sprung up in the cellar of this house, which had been covered from the light so long. Searching there on the 22d of September, I found, among other rank weeds, a species of nettle (Urtica urens)[37] which I had not found before; dill, which I had not seen growing spontaneously; the Jerusalem oak (Chenopodium botrys)[38] which I had seen wild in but one place; black nightshade (Solanum nigrum,)[39] which is quite rare hereabouts, and common tobacco, which, though it was often cultivated here in the last century, has for fifty years been an unknown plant in this town, and a few months before this not even I had heard that one man in the north part of the town was cultivating a few plants for his own use. I have no doubt that some or all of these plants sprang from seeds which had long been buried under or about that house, and that that tobacco is an additional evidence that the plant was formerly cultivated here. The cellar has been filled up this year, and four of those plants, including the tobacco, are now again extinct in that locality.

It is true, I have shown that the animals consume a great part of the seeds of trees, and so, at least, effectually prevent their becoming trees; but in all these cases, as I have said, the consumer is compelled to be at the same time the disperser and planter, and this is the tax which he pays to nature. I think it is Linnaeus who says that while the swine is rooting for acorns he is planting acorns.[40]

Though I do not believe that a plant will spring up where no seed has been, I have great faith in a seed—a, to me, equally mysterious origin for it. Convince me that you have a seed there, and I am prepared to expect wonders. I shall even believe that the millennium is at hand, and that the reign of justice is about to commence,[41] when the Patent Office, or Government, begins to distribute, and the people to plant the seeds of these things.

In the Spring of '57, I planted six seeds sent to me from the Patent Office, and labeled, I think, "*Poitrine jaune grosse*," large yellow squash. Two came up, and one bore a squash which weighed 123½ pounds, the other bore four, weighing together 186¼ pounds. Who would have believed that there was 310 pounds of *poitrine jaune grosse* in that corner of my garden? These seeds were the bait I used to catch it, my ferrets which I sent into its burrow,[42] my brace of terriers which unearthed it. A little mysterious hoeing and manuring was all the *abra cadabra presto-change* that I used, and lo! true to the label, they found for me 310 pounds of *poitrine jaune grosse* there, where it was never known to be, nor was before. These talismans had perchance sprung from America at first, and returned to it with unabated force. The big squash took a premium at your fair that Fall, and I understood that the man who bought it intended to sell the seeds for 10 cents a piece—were they not cheap at that? But I have more hounds of the same breed. I learn that one which I

40 Allusion to Linnaeus's (cf. "Natural History of Massachusetts," note 24) *Amoenitates Academicae*, translated in *Select Dissertations from the Amoenitates Academicae* as: "the swine, in their search after roots, breaks the ground as much as if it were plowed, covers the scattered seeds with earth, and while they fatten upon acorns, plant oaks."

41 Allusion to the thousand-year period of peace and justice in Revelation 20.

42 Ferrets were sent into burrows in order to cause rabbits or other small game to bolt and be killed or captured by the hunter.

43 Stage name of the celebrated magician Antoni van Zandt (1810–1877).

44 Allusion to John 3:19: "And this is the condemnation, that light is come into the world, and men love darkness rather than the light, because their deeds were evil." Thoreau used the phrase several times in his journal: 15 September 1850, 12 March 1853, 26 January 1856, and 16 October 1859.

despatched to a distant town, true to its instincts, points the large yellow squash there too, where no hound ever found it before, as its ancestors did here and in France.

Other seeds I have which will find other things in that corner of my garden, in like fashion, almost any fruit you wish, every year for ages, until the crop more than fills the whole garden. You have but little more to do than throw up your cap for entertainment these American days. Perfect alchemists I keep, who can transmute substances without end; and thus the corner of my garden is an inexhaustible treasure chest. Here you can dig, not gold, but the value which gold merely represents; and there is no Signor Blitz[43] about it. Yet farmers' sons will stare by the hour to see a juggler draw ribbons from his throat, though he tells them it is all deception. Surely, men love darkness rather than light.[44]

Walking

I wish to speak a word for Nature, for absolute freedom and wildness, as contrasted with a freedom and culture merely civil,—to regard man as an inhabitant, or a part and parcel of Nature, rather than a member of society. I wish to make an extreme statement, if so I may make an emphatic one, for there are enough champions of civilization: the minister, and the school-committee, and every one of you will take care of that.

I have met with but one or two persons in the course of my life who understood the art of Walking, that is, of taking walks,[1]—who had a genius, so to speak, for *sauntering:* which word is beautifully derived "from idle people who roved about the country, in the Middle Ages, and asked charity, under pretence of going *à la Sainte Terre,*"[2] to the Holy Land, till the children exclaimed, "There goes a *Sainte-Terrer,*" a Saunterer,—a Holy-Lander.[3] They who never go to the Holy Land in their walks, as they pretend, are indeed mere idlers and vagabonds; but they who do go there are saunterers in the good sense, such as I mean. Some, however, would derive the word from *sans terre,* without land or a home,[4] which, therefore, in the good sense, will mean, having no particular home, but equally at home everywhere. For this is the secret of successful sauntering. He who sits still in a house all the time may be the greatest vagrant of all; but the saunterer, in the good sense, is no more vagrant than the meandering river, which is all the while sedulously seeking the shortest course to the sea. But I

1 In his journal Thoreau wrote: "I know of but one or two persons with whom I can afford to walk. With most the walk degenerates into a mere vigorous use of your legs, ludicrously purposeless, while you are discussing some mighty argument, each one having his say, spoiling each other's day, worrying one another with conversation, hustling one another with our conversation. I know of no use in the walking part in this case, except that we may seem to be getting on together toward some goal; but of course we keep our original distance all the way" [J 11:296–297].
2 Derived from Samuel Johnson's *A Dictionary of the English Language:* "aller à la sainte terre, from idle people who roved about the country, and asked charity under pretence of going *à la sainte terre,* to the holy land."
3 This is an elaboration by Thoreau, made clear by his inserting the word "perchance" in his journal [J 2:141].
4 From Johnson's *Dictionary:* "or *sans terre,* as having no settled home."

prefer the first, which, indeed, is the most probable derivation. For every walk is a sort of crusade, preached by some Peter the Hermit[5] in us, to go forth and reconquer this Holy Land from the hands of the Infidels.

It is true, we are but faint-hearted crusaders, even the walkers, nowadays, who undertake no persevering, never-ending enterprises. Our expeditions are but tours, and come round again at evening to the old hearth-side from which we set out. Half the walk is but retracing our steps. We should go forth on the shortest walk, perchance, in the spirit of undying adventure, never to return,—prepared to send back our embalmed hearts[6] only as relics to our desolate kingdoms. If you are ready to leave father and mother, and brother and sister, and wife and child and friends, and never see them again,[7]— if you have paid your debts, and made your will, and settled all your affairs, and are a free man, then you are ready for a walk.

To come down to my own experience, my companion and I, for I sometimes have a companion, take pleasure in fancying ourselves knights of a new, or rather an old, order,—not Equestrians or Chevaliers, not Ritters or Riders,[8] but Walkers, a still more ancient and honorable class, I trust. The chivalric and heroic spirit which once belonged to the Rider seems now to reside in, or perchance to have subsided into, the Walker,—not the Knight, but Walker Errant. He is a sort of fourth estate, outside of Church and State and People.

We have felt that we almost alone hereabouts practised this noble art; though, to tell the truth, at least, if their own assertions are to be received, most of my townsmen would fain walk sometimes, as I do, but they cannot. No wealth can buy the requisite leisure, freedom, and independence, which are the capital in this profession. It comes only by the grace of God. It requires a direct dispensation from Heaven to become a walker.[9] You

5 Peter the Hermit, also known as Peter of Amiens (1050–1115), French monk and preacher on the First Crusade.

6 Sometimes during the Crusades the heart of a noble who fell in battle was removed, embalmed, and returned home when returning the body was not possible.

7 Echo of Matthew 19:29: "And every one that hath forsaken houses, or brethren, or sisters, or father, or mother, or wife, or children, or lands, for my name's sake . . ."

8 Not knightly orders but simply terms indicating a rider of horses.

9 In April 1857 Thoreau encountered the Concord farmer Abel Brooks, who, "observed in a loud voice which all could hear, 'Let me see, your society is pretty large, ain't it?' 'Oh, yes, large enough,' said I, not knowing what he meant. . . . 'You mean the walkers; don't you?' 'Ye-es, I call you the Society'" [J 9:331].

must be born into the family of the Walkers. *Ambulator nascitur, non fit.*[10] Some of my townsmen, it is true, can remember and have described to me some walks which they took ten years ago, in which they were so blessed as to lose themselves for half an hour in the woods; but I know very well that they have confined themselves to the highway ever since, whatever pretensions they may make to belong to this select class. No doubt they were elevated for a moment as by the reminiscence of a previous state of existence, when even they were foresters[11] and outlaws.

> "When he came to grene wode,
>   In a mery mornynge,
> There he herde the notes small,
>   Of byrdes mery syngynge.
>
> "It is ferre gone, sayd Robyn,
>   That I was last here;
> Me lyste a lytell for to shote
>   At the donne dere."[12]

I think that I cannot preserve my health and spirits, unless I spend four hours a day at least—and it is commonly more than that—sauntering through the woods and over the hills and fields, absolutely free from all worldly engagements. You may safely say, A penny for your thoughts,[13] or a thousand pounds. When sometimes I am reminded that the mechanics and shopkeepers stay in their shops not only all the forenoon, but all the afternoon too, sitting with crossed legs, so many of them,—as if the legs were made to sit upon, and not to stand or walk upon,—I think that they deserve some credit for not having all committed suicide long ago.

I, who cannot stay in my chamber for a single day without acquiring some rust, and when sometimes I have stolen forth for a walk at the eleventh hour[14] of four

10 Latin: A walker is born, not made. Thoreau's variant of the Latin *Poeta nascitur, non fit* (A poet is born, not made).
11 Officers appointed to maintain or guard the forest, but here one who inhabits a forest or wild country.
12 Quoted from "A Lytell Geste of Robyn Hode," from *Robin Hood: A Collection of All the Ancient Poems, Songs, and Ballads,* several verses of which Thoreau copied into his literary notebook.
13 The earliest known use of this phrase in print is in John Heywood's (ca. 1497–ca. 1580) *Proverbs* (1546): "Freend (quoth the good man) a peny for your thought."
14 Allusion to Matthew 20:6: "And about the eleventh hour he went out, and found others standing idle, and saith unto them, Why stand ye here all the day idle?"

15 Thoreau wrote in an early journal entry: "Sin, I am sure, is not in overt acts or, indeed, in acts of any kind, but is in proportion to the time which has come behind us and displaced eternity,—that degree to which our elements are mixed with the elements of the world" [J 1:300].

16 Reference to Napoleon I, as quoted by Emerson in his 1838 journal from Count Emmanuel Augustin Dieudonné de Las Cases's *Mémorial de Sainte Hélène. Journal of the Private Life and Conversation of the Emperor Napoleon at St. Helena* (Boston, 1823): "As to moral courage, I have rarely met with the *two o'clock in the morning kind*. I mean unprepared courage that which is necessary on an unexpected occasion & which in spite of the most unforeseen events leaves full freedom of judgment & decision." Thoreau reworked this image several times, first in an undated journal passage before it was revised for a deleted paragraph in the first draft of *A Week on the Concord and Merrimack River,* and then in the "Sounds" chapter of *Walden.*

o'clock in the afternoon, too late to redeem the day, when the shades of night were already beginning to be mingled with the daylight, have felt as if I had committed some sin[15] to be atoned for,—I confess that I am astonished at the power of endurance, to say nothing of the moral insensibility, of my neighbors who confine themselves to shops and offices the whole day for weeks and months, ay, and years almost together. I know not what manner of stuff they are of,—sitting there now at three o'clock in the afternoon, as if it were three o'clock in the morning. Bonaparte may talk of the three-o'clock-in-the-morning courage,[16] but it is nothing to the courage which can sit down cheerfully at this hour in the afternoon over against one's self whom you have known all the morning, to starve out a garrison to whom you are bound by such strong ties of sympathy. I wonder that about this time, or say between four and five o'clock in the afternoon, too late for the morning papers and too early for the evening ones, there is not a general explosion heard up and down the street, scattering a legion of antiquated and house-bred notions and whims to the four winds for an airing,—and so the evil cure itself.

How womankind, who are confined to the house still more than men, stand it I do not know; but I have ground to suspect that most of them do not *stand* it at all. When, early in a summer afternoon, we have been shaking the dust of the village from the skirts of our garments, making haste past those houses with purely Doric or Gothic fronts, which have such an air of repose about them, my companion whispers that probably about these times their occupants are all gone to bed. Then it is that I appreciate the beauty and the glory of architecture, which itself never turns in, but forever stands out and erect, keeping watch over the slumberers.

No doubt temperament, and, above all, age, have a good deal to do with it. As a man grows older, his ability to sit still and follow in-door occupations increases. He grows vespertinal[17] in his habits as the evening of life approaches, till at last he comes forth only just before sundown, and gets all the walk that he requires in half an hour.

But the walking of which I speak has nothing in it akin to taking exercise, as it is called, as the sick take medicine at stated hours,—as the swinging of dumb-bells or chairs;[18] but is itself the enterprise and adventure of the day. If you would get exercise, go in search of the springs of life. Think of a man's swinging dumb-bells for his health, when those springs are bubbling up in far-off pastures unsought by him!

Moreover, you must walk like a camel, which is said to be the only beast which ruminates when walking.[19] When a traveller asked Wordsworth's servant to show him her master's study, she answered, "Here is his library, but his study is out of doors."[20]

Living much out of doors, in the sun and wind, will no doubt produce a certain roughness of character,—will cause a thicker cuticle to grow over some of the finer qualities of our nature, as on the face and hands, or as severe manual labor robs the hands of some of their delicacy of touch. So staying in the house, on the other hand, may produce a softness and smoothness, not to say thinness of skin, accompanied by an increased sensibility to certain impressions. Perhaps we should be more susceptible to some influences important to our intellectual and moral growth, if the sun had shone and the wind blown on us a little less; and no doubt it is a nice matter to proportion rightly the thick and thin skin. But methinks that is a scurf[21] that will fall off fast enough,—that the natural remedy is to be found in the proportion which the night bears to the day, the winter to the summer, thought to experience. There will be so much the more air and sunshine in our thoughts. The callous

17 Flowering or active in the evening.

18 On this form of exercise Thoreau wrote: "I see dumb-bells in the minister's study, and some of their dumbness gets into his sermons. Some travellers carry them round the world in their carpetbags. . . . I cannot be interested in these extremely artificial amusements" [J 14:111].

19 Allusion to William Holt Yates's (1802–1874) *The Modern History and Condition of Egypt:* "When crossing the desert, the camel . . . is the only animal that *ruminates* his drink as he walks."

20 Wordsworth told the story in the preface to his 1817 *Complete Poetical Works:* "Nine-tenth of my verses have been murmured out in the open air: and here let me repeat what I believe has already appeared in print. One day a stranger having walked round the garden and grounds of Rydal Mount asked one of the female servants, who happened to be at the door, permission to see her master's study. 'This,' said she, leading him forward, 'is my master's library where he keeps his books, but his study is out of doors.'"

21 Thin flake of dead epidermis shed from the surface of the skin.

22 Public walk.

23 Quoted and paraphrased from John Evelyn's (1620–1706) *Sylva, or a Discourse of Forest-Trees:* "Where-ever they built their sumptuous and magnificent colleges for the exercise of youth in gymnastics, as riding, shooting, wrestling, running, &c. (like to our French academies) and where the graver philosophers also met to converse together and improve their studies, betwixt the xista and *subdiales ambulationes* (which were portico's open to the air) they planted groves and walks of platans, to refresh and shade the Palaestritae." The platan, or platane, is the plane tree; in America, specifically, the sycamore.

24 Country on the west coast of Africa, ruled from 1818 to 1858 by King Gezo.

palms of the laborer are conversant with finer tissues of self-respect and heroism, whose touch thrills the heart, than the languid fingers of idleness. That is mere sentimentality that lies abed by day and thinks itself white, far from the tan and callus of experience.

When we walk, we naturally go to the fields and woods: what would become of us, if we walked only in a garden or a mall?[22] Even some sects of philosophers have felt the necessity of importing the woods to themselves, since they did not go to the woods. "They planted groves and walks of Platanes," where they took *subdiales ambulationes* in porticos open to the air.[23] Of course it is of no use to direct our steps to the woods, if they do not carry us thither. I am alarmed when it happens that I have walked a mile into the woods bodily, without getting there in spirit. In my afternoon walk I would fain forget all my morning occupations and my obligations to society. But it sometimes happens that I cannot easily shake off the village. The thought of some work will run in my head, and I am not where my body is,—I am out of my senses. In my walks I would fain return to my senses. What business have I in the woods, if I am thinking of something out of the woods? I suspect myself, and cannot help a shudder, when I find myself so implicated even in what are called good works,—for this may sometimes happen.

My vicinity affords many good walks; and though for so many years I have walked almost every day, and sometimes for several days together, I have not yet exhausted them. An absolutely new prospect is a great happiness, and I can still get this any afternoon. Two or three hours' walking will carry me to as strange a country as I expect ever to see. A single farm-house which I had not seen before is sometimes as good as the dominions of the King of Dahomey.[24] There is in fact a sort of harmony discoverable between the capabilities of the landscape within a circle of ten miles' radius, or the limits of an afternoon walk, and the threescore years and ten of human life. It will never become quite familiar to you.

Nowadays almost all man's improvements, so called, as the building of houses, and the cutting down of the forest and of all large trees, simply deform the landscape, and make it more and more tame and cheap. A people who would begin by burning the fences and let the forest stand! I saw the fences half consumed, their ends lost in the middle of the prairie, and some worldly miser with a surveyor looking after his bounds, while heaven had taken place around him, and he did not see the angels going to and fro, but was looking for an old post-hole in the midst of paradise. I looked again, and saw him standing in the middle of a boggy, stygian[25] fen, surrounded by devils, and he had found his bounds without a doubt, three little stones, where a stake had been driven, and looking nearer, I saw that the Prince of Darkness[26] was his surveyor.

I can easily walk ten, fifteen, twenty, any number of miles, commencing at my own door, without going by any house, without crossing a road except where the fox and the mink do: first along by the river, and then the brook, and then the meadow and the wood-side. There are square miles in my vicinity which have no inhabitant. From many a hill I can see civilization and the abodes of man afar. The farmers and their works are scarcely more obvious than woodchucks and their burrows. Man and his affairs, church and state and school, trade and commerce, and manufactures and agriculture, even politics, the most alarming of them all,—I am pleased to see how little space they occupy in the landscape. Politics is but a narrow field, and that still narrower highway yonder leads to it. I sometimes direct the traveller thither. If you would go to the political world, follow the great road,—follow that market-man, keep his dust in your

25 Pertaining to the river Styx; cf. "Natural History of Massachusetts," note 72, and "A Winter Walk," note 9.
26 Satan.

27 A common occurrence during his tenure at Walden Pond.
28 A meeting of three or four roads, respectively.
29 Latin: farm or country house.
30 Marcus Terentius Varro (116–27 B.C.E.), Roman scholar and writer of more than seventy works. In *Rerum rusticarum* I.ii.14, his only extant work in complete form, he wrote: "The *vilicus* is appointed for the purpose of tilling the ground, and the name is derived from *villa,* the place into which the crops are hauled (*vehunter*), and out of which they are hauled by him when they are sold. For this reason the peasants even now call a road *veha,* because of the hauling; and the place to which and from which they haul *vella* and not *villa.* In the same way, those who make a living by hauling are said *facere velaturam.*"
31 Latin: of little value, worthless, common, vile.
32 Related to villein or vilayn, lowest class of un-free persons in the feudal system, a serf.
33 It was part of Thoreau's enjoyment of the natural world not to be controlled by fences and property lines. When visiting Canada in 1850 he went "across lots in spite of numerous signs threatening the severest penalties to trespassers" [W 5:98]. On this preferred method of travel Thoreau wrote: "It is true we as yet take liberties and go across lots, and steal, or 'hook,' a good many things, but we naturally take fewer and fewer liberties every year, as we meet with more resistance. In old countries, as England, going across lots is out of the question. You must walk in some beaten path or other, though it may [be] a narrow one. We are tending to the same state of things here, when practically a few will have grounds of their own, but most will have none to walk over but what the few allow them" [J 14:305–306].
34 Horse used on the road, for travel or pleasure, as opposed to a draft horse.
35 Manu, or Menu, was the legendary author of the Hindu code of religious law, *Manusmitri,* compiled in Sanskrit in the first century B.C.E. Manu is also the Hindu archetypal first man, survivor of

eyes, and it will lead you straight to it; for it, too, has its place merely, and does not occupy all space. I pass from it as from a beanfield into the forest,[27] and it is forgotten. In one half-hour I can walk off to some portion of the earth's surface where a man does not stand from one year's end to another, and there, consequently, politics are not, for they are but as the cigar-smoke of a man.

The village is the place to which the roads tend, a sort of expansion of the highway, as a lake of a river. It is the body of which roads are the arms and legs,—a trivial or quadrivial[28] place, the thoroughfare and ordinary of travellers. The word is from the Latin *villa,*[29] which, together with *via,* a way, or more anciently *ved* and *vella,* Varro derives from *veho,* to carry, because the villa is the place to and from which things are carried. They who got their living by teaming were said *vellaturam facere.*[30] Hence, too, apparently, the Latin word *vilis*[31] and our vile; also *villain.*[32] This suggests what kind of degeneracy villagers are liable to. They are wayworn by the travel that goes by and over them, without travelling themselves.

Some do not walk at all; others walk in the highways; a few walk across lots.[33] Roads are made for horses and men of business. I do not travel in them much, comparatively, because I am not in a hurry to get to any tavern or grocery or livery-stable or depot to which they lead. I am a good horse to travel, but not from choice a roadster.[34] The landscape-painter uses the figures of men to mark a road. He would not make that use of my figure. I walk out into a Nature such as the old prophets and poets, Menu,[35] Moses, Homer, Chaucer, walked in. You may name it America, but it is not America: neither Americus Vespucius,[36] nor Columbus, nor the rest were the discoverers of it. There is a truer account of it in mythology than in any history of America, so called, that I have seen.[37]

However, there are a few old roads that may be trodden with profit, as if they led somewhere now that they are nearly discontinued. There is the Old Marlborough Road, which does not go to Marlborough now,[38] methinks, unless that is Marlborough where it carries me. I am the bolder to speak of it here, because I presume that there are one or two such roads in every town.

THE OLD MARLBOROUGH ROAD.

Where they once dug for money,
But never found any;
Where sometimes Martial Miles[39]
Singly files,
And Elijah Wood,[40]
I fear for no good:
No other man,
Save Elisha Dugan, — [41]
O man of wild habits,
Partridges and rabbits,
Who hast no cares
Only to set snares,
Who liv'st all alone,
Close to the bone,
And where life is sweetest[42]
Constantly eatest.
When the spring stirs my blood
    With the instinct to travel,
    I can get enough gravel
On the Old Marlborough Road.
    Nobody repairs it,
    For nobody wears it;
    It is a living way,[43]
    As the Christians say,
Not many there be
    Who enter therein,
Only the guests of the
    Irishman Quin.[44]
What is it, what is it,

the flood and father of the human race. Thoreau compiled a selection, "The Laws of Menu," for the January 1843 issue of the *Dial* from Sir William Jones's (1746–1794) translation of the *Institutes of Hindu Law*.

36 Amerigo Vespucci (1454–1512), Florentine explorer and cartographer for whom the Americas are named.

37 Thoreau wrote in his journal: "I do not know where to find in any literature, whether ancient or modern, any adequate account of that Nature with which I am acquainted. Mythology comes nearest to it of any" [J 2:152].

38 Road which goes southwest from Concord toward Marlborough but which ended in Sudbury.

39 Martial Miles (1820–1890), Concord farmer. Horace Hosmer (1830–1894) described Miles as "full of new kinks and projects."

40 Elijah Wood, Sr. (1776–1861), described by Hosmer as "a strong energetic man; a farmer during the summer and a School teacher in the Winter."

41 Elisha Dugan (b. 1807), son of an emancipated slave, who resorted to living in the woods after losing his father's land. Hosmer described Dugan in 1891 as "a Mulatto. . . . He was unmarried, and lived alone for many years. At present time he is in the Almshouse, Concord."

42 Allusion to the proverb dating back at least as early as Percy's *Ballads* (1559): "The nearer the bone, the sweeter the flesh." Thoreau used a similar phrase in *Walden:* "It is life near the bone where it is sweetest" [Wa 320].

43 Allusion to Hebrews 10:20, in which the way to the "holiest" is by "a new and living way, which he hath consecrated for us, through the veil, that is to say, his flesh."

44 Unidentified.

45 Stone guideposts.
46 Concord families.
47 Engrave.

But a direction out there,
And the bare possibility
    Of going somewhere?
        Great guide-boards of stone,[45]
        But travellers none.
        Cenotaphs of the towns
        Named on their crowns.
        It is worth going to see
        What you *might* be.
        What king
        Did the thing,
        I am still wondering;
        Set up how or when,
        By what selectmen,
        Gourgas or Lee,
        Clark or Darby?[46]
        They're a great endeavor
        To be something forever;
        Blank tablets of stone,
        Where a traveller might groan,
        And in one sentence
        Grave[47] all that is known;
        Which another might read,
        In his extreme need.
        I know one or two
        Lines that would do,
        Literature that might stand
        All over the land,
        Which a man could remember
        Till next December,
        And read again in the spring,
        After the thawing.
If with fancy unfurled
    You leave your abode,
You may go round the world
    By the old Marlborough Road.

At present, in this vicinity, the best part of the land is not private property; the landscape is not owned, and the walker enjoys comparative freedom. But possibly the day will come when it will be partitioned off into so-called pleasure-grounds, in which a few will take a narrow and exclusive pleasure only,—when fences shall be multiplied, and man-traps[48] and other engines invented to confine men to the *public* road, and walking over the surface of God's earth shall be construed to mean trespassing on some gentleman's grounds. To enjoy a thing exclusively is commonly to exclude yourself from the true enjoyment of it. Let us improve our opportunities, then, before the evil days come.

What is it that makes it so hard sometimes to determine whither we will walk? I believe that there is a subtile magnetism in Nature, which, if we unconsciously yield to it, will direct us aright. It is not indifferent to us which way we walk. There is a right way; but we are very liable from heedlessness and stupidity to take the wrong one. We would fain take that walk, never yet taken by us through this actual world, which is perfectly symbolical of the path which we love to travel in the interior and ideal world; and sometimes, no doubt, we find it difficult to choose our direction, because it does not yet exist distinctly in our idea.

When I go out of the house for a walk, uncertain as yet whither I will bend my steps, and submit myself to my instinct to decide for me, I find, strange and whimsical as it may seem, that I finally and inevitably settle southwest, toward some particular wood or meadow or deserted pasture or hill in that direction. My needle is slow to settle,—varies a few degrees, and does not always point due southwest, it is true, and it has good authority for this variation, but it always settles between west and south-southwest. The future lies that way to me, and the

48 A trap to catch trespassers, poachers, or marauders.

49 Australia was first settled in 1788 with the British penal colony at Port Jackson.

50 Alternate spelling of Tatar: a member of a group of Turkic peoples primarily inhabiting Tartary, a vast region of eastern Europe and northern Asia controlled by the Mongols in the thirteenth and fourteenth centuries.

51 Quoted from Évariste Régis Huc's (1813–1860) *Recollections of a Journey Through Tartary, Thibet, and China, During the Years 1844, 1845, and 1846.*

earth seems more unexhausted and richer on that side. The outline which would bound my walks would be, not a circle, but a parabola, or rather like one of those cometary orbits which have been thought to be non-returning curves, in this case opening westward, in which my house occupies the place of the sun. I turn round and round irresolute sometimes for a quarter of an hour, until I decide, for the thousandth time, that I will walk into the southwest or west. Eastward I go only by force; but westward I go free. Thither no business leads me. It is hard for me to believe that I shall find fair landscapes or sufficient wildness and freedom behind the eastern horizon. I am not excited by the prospect of a walk thither; but I believe that the forest which I see in the western horizon stretches uninterruptedly towards the setting sun, and that there are no towns nor cities in it of enough consequence to disturb me. Let me live where I will, on this side is the city, on that the wilderness, and ever I am leaving the city more and more, and withdrawing into the wilderness. I should not lay so much stress on this fact, if I did not believe that something like this is the prevailing tendency of my countrymen. I must walk toward Oregon, and not toward Europe. And that way the nation is moving, and I may say that mankind progress from east to west. Within a few years we have witnessed the phenomenon of a southeastward migration, in the settlement of Australia;[49] but this affects us as a retrograde movement, and, judging from the moral and physical character of the first generation of Australians, has not yet proved a successful experiment. The eastern Tartars[50] think that there is nothing west beyond Thibet. "The World ends there," say they; "beyond there is nothing but a shoreless sea."[51] It is unmitigated East where they live.

We go eastward to realize history and study the works of art and literature, retracing the steps of the race; we go westward as into the future, with a spirit of enterprise and adventure. The Atlantic is a Lethean stream,[52] in our passage over which we have had an opportunity to forget the Old World and its institutions. If we do not succeed this time, there is perhaps one more chance for the race left before it arrives on the banks of the Styx; and that is in the Lethe of the Pacific, which is three times as wide.

I know not how significant it is, or how far it is an evidence of singularity, that an individual should thus consent in his pettiest walk with the general movement of the race; but I know that something akin to the migratory instinct in birds and quadrupeds,—which, in some instances, is known to have affected the squirrel tribe, impelling them to a general and mysterious movement, in which they were seen, say some, crossing the broadest rivers, each on its particular chip, with its tail raised for a sail,[53] and bridging narrower streams with their dead,[54]—that something like the *furor* which affects the domestic cattle in the spring, and which is referred to a worm in their tails,[55]—affects both nations and individuals, either perennially or from time to time. Not a flock of wild geese cackles over our town, but it to some extent unsettles the value of real estate here, and, if I were a broker, I should probably take that disturbance into account.

"Than longen folk to gon on pilgrimages,
And palmeres for to seken strange strondes."[56]

Every sunset which I witness inspires me with the desire to go to a West as distant and as fair as that into which the sun goes down. He appears to migrate westward daily, and tempt us to follow him. He is the Great Western Pioneer[57] whom the nations follow. We dream all night of those mountain-ridges in the horizon, though they may be of vapor only, which were last gilded by his

52 Allusion to Lethe, in Greek mythology, a river in Hades which induces forgetfulness.

53 Allusion to William Wood's (1774–1857) *Zoography*: "If the credit of Linnaeus did not give sanction to what we are going to relate respecting the extraordinary manner in which they cross the broadest rivers, it would hardly be believed.— When they arrive at the edge of the water, and perceive its breadth, they return in a body to the nearest wood in search of bark, which serves them instead of boats, and upon which they boldly commit themselves to the mercy of the waves, every squirrel sitting on its own vessel, and fanning the air with its tail." Thoreau may have also read about this in Wood's probable source, Oliver Goldsmith's (1730–1774) *A History of the Earth and Animated Nature.*

54 Thoreau's source for this statement is unknown.

55 A bovine ailment mistakenly attributed to a worm in the tail.

56 Quoted, with minor variants, from Chaucer's *Canterbury Tales*, prologue, 12–13.

57 Thoreau used a similar epithet of the "western pioneer" to describe Mount Wachusett in "A Walk to Wachusett."

58 Cf. "Thomas Carlyle and His Works," note 145.

59 In Greek mythology, paradisiacal islands of the blessed located in the far west.

60 Two Spanish kingdoms united in 1230. Isabella I (d. 1504) and Ferdinand V (1479–1516) sponsored Columbus's expedition.

61 Quoted from John Milton's "Lycidas," 190–193. Emphasis added by Thoreau.

62 Quoted from François André Michaux's (1770–1855), *The North American Sylva; or, a Description of the Forest Trees of the United States, Canada and Nova Scotia.* Thoreau excerpted several passages from Michaux in his 1851 journal.

63 Allusion to Humboldt's *Personal Narrative of Travels to the Equinoctial Regions of America During the Years 1799–1804.*

rays. The island of Atlantis,[58] and the islands and gardens of the Hesperides,[59] a sort of terrestrial paradise, appear to have been the Great West of the ancients, enveloped in mystery and poetry. Who has not seen in imagination, when looking into the sunset sky, the gardens of the Hesperides, and the foundation of all those fables?

Columbus felt the westward tendency more strongly than any before. He obeyed it, and found a New World for Castile and Leon.[60] The herd of men in those days scented fresh pastures from afar.

"And now the sun had stretched out all the hills,
And now was dropt into the western bay;
At last *he* rose, and twitched his mantle blue;
To-morrow to fresh woods and pastures new."[61]

Where on the globe can there be found an area of equal extent with that occupied by the bulk of our States, so fertile and so rich and varied in its productions, and at the same time so habitable by the European, as this is? Michaux, who knew but part of them, says that "the species of large trees are much more numerous in North America than in Europe; in the United States there are more than one hundred and forty species that exceed thirty feet in height; in France there are but thirty that attain this size."[62] Later botanists more than confirm his observations. Humboldt came to America to realize his youthful dreams of a tropical vegetation, and he beheld it in its greatest perfection in the primitive forests of the Amazon, the most gigantic wilderness on the earth, which he has so eloquently described.[63] The geographer Guyot, himself a European, goes farther,—farther than I am ready to follow him; yet not when he says,—"As the plant is made for the animal, as the vegetable world is made for the animal world, America is made for the man of the Old World. . . . . The man of the Old World sets out upon his way. Leaving the highlands of Asia, he descends from station to station towards Europe. Each of his steps is marked by a new civilization superior to the preceding, by a greater power of development. Arrived at the Atlantic, he pauses on the shore of this unknown ocean, the bounds of which he knows not, and turns upon his footprints for an instant." When he has exhausted the rich soil of Europe, and reinvigorated himself, "then recommences his adventurous career westward as in the earliest ages."[64] So far Guyot.

From this western impulse coming in contact with the barrier of the Atlantic sprang the commerce and enterprise of modern times. The younger Michaux, in his "Travels West of the Alleghanies in 1802," says that the common inquiry in the newly settled West was, "'From what part of the world have you come?' As if these vast and fertile regions would naturally be the place of meeting and common country of all the inhabitants of the globe."[65]

To use an obsolete Latin word, I might say *Ex Oriente lux; ex Occidente FRUX.* From the East light; from the West fruit.

Sir Francis Head,[66] an English traveller and a Governor-General of Canada, tells us that "in both the northern and southern hemispheres of the New World, Nature has not only outlined her works on a larger scale, but has painted the whole picture with brighter and more costly colors than she used in delineating and in beautifying the Old World. . . . . The heavens of America appear infinitely higher, the sky is bluer, the air is fresher, the cold is intenser, the moon looks larger, the stars are brighter, the thunder is louder, the lightning is vivider, the wind is stronger, the rain is heavier, the mountains are higher, the rivers larger, the forests bigger, the plains

64 Quoted from Arnold Henry Guyot's (1807–1884) *The Earth and Man: Lectures on Comparative Physical Geography, in Its Relation to the History of Mankind.*

65 Thoreau's translation of Michaux's *Voyage à l'Ouest des Monts Alléghanys* (Paris: Dentu, 1808). The French text included a translation of the common inquiry—"From what part of the world are you coming?"—which Thoreau did not adopt. François André Michaux is called the "younger Michaux" to differentiate himself from his father, also a naturalist, André Michaux (1746–1802).

66 Sir Francis Bond Head (1793–1875). The extracts are quoted, with minor variants of capitalization and punctuation, from his *The Emigrant.*

67 The French naturalist Georges-Louis Leclerc, Comte de Buffon (1707–1788), who, in his forty-four volume *Natural History* disparaged the New World as being inferior to the Old.

68 Thoreau's translation of Linnaeus, quoted, with variants, from his *Philosophia Botanica* (section VI, Characteres).

69 Thoreau wrote in his journal of 4 February 1854: "Varro says *Africanae bestiae* for savage or ferocious beats" [J 6:93].

broader." This statement will do at least to set against Buffon's account of this part of the world and its productions.[67]

Linnaeus said long ago, "Nescio quae facies *laeta, glabra* plantis Americanis: I know not what there is of joyous and smooth in the aspect of American plants";[68] and I think that in this country there are no, or at most very few, *Africanae bestiae,* African beasts, as the Romans called them,[69] and that in this respect also it is peculiarly fitted for the habitation of man. We are told that within three miles of the center of the East-Indian city of Singapore, some of the inhabitants are annually carried off by tigers; but the traveller can lie down in the woods at night almost anywhere in North America without fear of wild beasts.

These are encouraging testimonies. If the moon looks larger here than in Europe, probably the sun looks larger also. If the heavens of America appear infinitely higher, and the stars brighter, I trust that these facts are symbolical of the height to which the philosophy and poetry and religion of her inhabitants may one day soar. At length, perchance, the immaterial heaven will appear as much higher to the American mind, and the intimations that star it as much brighter. For I believe that climate does thus react on man, — as there is something in the mountain-air that feeds the spirit and inspires. Will not man grow to greater perfection intellectually as well as physically under these influences? Or is it unimportant how many foggy days there are in his life? I trust that we shall be more imaginative, that our thoughts will be clearer, fresher, and more ethereal, as our sky, — our understanding more comprehensive and broader, like our plains, — our intellect generally on a grander scale, like our thunder and lightning, our rivers and mountains and forests, — and our hearts shall even correspond in breadth and depth and grandeur to our inland seas. Perchance there will appear to the traveller something, he knows not what, of *laeta* and *glabra,* of joyous and serene, in our very faces. Else to what end does the world go on, and why was America discovered?

To Americans I hardly need to say,—

"Westward the star of empire takes its way."[70]

As a true patriot, I should be ashamed to think that Adam in paradise was more favorably situated on the whole than the backwoodsman in this country.[71]

Our sympathies in Massachusetts are not confined to New England; though we may be estranged from the South, we sympathize with the West. There is the home of the younger sons, as among the Scandinavians they took to the sea for their inheritance.[72] It is too late to be studying Hebrew; it is more important to understand even the slang of to-day.

Some months ago I went to see a panorama of the Rhine.[73] It was like a dream of the Middle Ages. I floated down its historic stream in something more than imagination, under bridges built by the Romans, and repaired by later heroes, past cities and castles whose very names were music to my ears, and each of which was the subject of a legend. There were Ehrenbreitstein and Rolandseck and Coblentz,[74] which I knew only in history. They were ruins that interested me chiefly. There seemed to come up from its waters and its vine-clad hills and valleys a hushed music as of Crusaders departing for the Holy Land. I floated along under the spell of enchantment, as if I had been transported to a heroic age, and breathed an atmosphere of chivalry.

Soon after, I went to see a panorama of the Mississippi,[75] and as I worked my way up the stream in the light of to-day, and saw the steamboats wooding up,[76]

70 Quoted from George Berkeley's (1685–1753) "On the Prospect of Planting Arts and Learning in America." Berkeley's poem has the word *course* for *star.* As Thoreau's common practice was to emphasize any deliberate change made in a quotation, it is likely that Thoreau's source was either George Bancroft's (1800–1891) *History of the United States of America* or John Quincy Adams's "Oration at Plymouth," which both used the word *star.*

71 This statement was followed in his journal with: "You all know how miserably the former turned out,—or was turned out,—but there is some consolation at least in the fact that it yet remains to be seen how the western Adam in the wilderness will turn out" [J 2:153].

72 Under systems of primogeniture in which the eldest son inherits all, younger sons were forced to travel to seek their fortune.

73 Probably Benjamin Champney's (1817–1907) "The Rhine and Its Banks," which was exhibited in Boston from 11 December 1848 through 9 June 1849.

74 German cities.

75 Probably the John Banvard's (1815–1891) panoramic painting of the Mississippi River which, to be viewed, was stretched between two rollers which were slowly turned to give the appearance of viewing the river from the deck of a steamboat. The Banvard panorama was touring the country ca. 1850, and the "panorama of the Mississippi" was mentioned shortly thereafter in Thoreau's journal of 1851 [J 2:146–47]. This may also be a reference to an earlier panorama, Samuel B. Stockwell's (1813–1854) "Colossal Moving Panorama of the Upper and Lower Mississippi Rivers," which was exhibited in Boston from late August to mid-September 1849.

76 Laying in a supply of wood.

77 In Illinois, on the Mississippi River. In 1846 Nauvoo had been abandoned when ten thousand Mormons were driven west. The Mormons, after being driven out of Missouri, had settled Nauvoo in the early 1840s, making it the largest city in Illinois.

78 River which flows into the Rhine at Koblenz.

79 The French-Canadian explorer Julien Dubuque (1762–1810). According to George Caitlin's (1796–1872) *Letters and Notes on the Manners, Customs, and Conditions of North American Indians:* "Dubuque's Grave is a place of great notoriety on this river. . . . After his death, his body was placed within the tomb [he erected], at his request, lying in state (and uncovered except for his winding sheet), upon a large flat stone, where it was exposed to view, as his bones now are to the gaze of every traveller who takes pains to ascend this beautiful, grassy and lily-covered mount to its top, and peep through the gratings of two little windows, which have admitted the eyes, but stopped the sacrilegious hands of thousands who have taken a walk to it."

80 Sometime called Maiden Rock, in Winona, Mississippi, at the mouth of the Niangua. According to a Native American legend, Okema, Chief of the Osages, fell in love with Winona, a Delaware. Winona had already pledged herself to Minetus and so rejected Okema, who pursued her to this spot, where, to escape capture, she leapt from the cliff and perished. Thoreau's source was probably Frederika Bremer's (1801–1865) "Letter XXVI" from her *The Homes of the New World; Impressions of America:* "Last night we passed through Lake Pepin in the moonlight. It is an extension of the Mississippi, large enough to constitute a lake, surrounded by magnificent hills, which seem to inclose it with their almost perpendicular cliffs, one among which is particularly prominent, and is called Wenona's Cliff, from a young Indian girl who here sang her death-song and then threw herself into the waters below, preferring death to marriage with a young man whom she did not love."

counted the rising cities, gazed on the fresh ruins of Nauvoo,[77] beheld the Indians moving west across the stream, and, as before I had looked up the Moselle,[78] now looked up the Ohio and the Missouri, and heard the legends of Dubuque[79] and of Wenona's Cliff,[80]—still thinking more of the future than of the past or present,—I saw that this was a Rhine stream of a different kind; that the foundations of castles were yet to be laid, and the famous bridges were yet to be thrown over the stream; and I felt that *this was the heroic age itself,* though we know it not, for the hero is commonly the simplest and obscurest of men.

The West of which I speak is but another name for the Wild;[81] and what I have been preparing to say is, that in Wildness is the preservation of the world. Every tree sends its fibres forth in search of the Wild. The cities import it at any price. Men plough and sail for it. From the forest and wilderness come the tonics and barks which brace mankind. Our ancestors were savages. The story of Romulus and Remus being suckled by a wolf is not a meaningless fable.[82] The founders of every State which has risen to eminence have drawn their nourishment and vigor from a similar wild source. It is because the children of the Empire were not suckled by the wolf that they were conquered and displaced by the children of the Northern forests who were.

I believe in the forest, and in the meadow, and in the night in which the corn grows.[83] We require an infusion of hemlock-spruce[84] or arbor-vitae[85] in our tea. There is a difference between eating and drinking for strength and from mere gluttony. The Hottentots[86] eagerly devour the marrow of the koodoo and other antelopes raw, as a matter of course.[87] Some of our northern Indians eat raw the marrow of the Arctic reindeer, as well as various other parts, including the summits of the antlers, as long as they are soft.[88] And herein, perchance, they have stolen a march[89] on the cooks of Paris. They get what usually goes to feed the fire. This is probably better than stall-fed beef and slaughter-house pork to make a man of. Give me a wildness whose glance no civilization can endure,—as if we lived on the marrow of koodoos devoured raw.

There are some intervals[90] which border the strain of the wood-thrush, to which I would migrate,—wild lands where no settler has squatted; to which, methinks, I am already acclimated.

The African hunter Cumming tells us that the skin of the eland, as well as that of most other antelopes just killed, emits the most delicious perfume of trees and grass.[91] I would have every man so much a wild antelope, so much a part and parcel of Nature, that his very person should thus sweetly advertise our senses of his presence, and remind us of those parts of Nature which he most haunts. I feel no disposition to be satirical, when the trapper's coat emits the odor of musquash even; it is a sweeter scent to me than that which commonly exhales from the merchant's or the scholar's garments. When I go into their wardrobes and handle their vestments, I am reminded of no grassy plains and flowery meads which they have frequented, but of dusty merchants' exchanges and libraries rather.

A tanned skin is something more than respectable, and perhaps olive is a fitter color than white for a man,— a denizen of the woods. "The pale white man!"[92] I do not wonder that the African pitied him. Darwin the naturalist says "A white man bathing by the side of a Tahitian was like a plant bleached by the gardener's art, compared with a fine, dark green one, growing vigorously in the open fields."[93]

Ben Jonson exclaims,—

81 Thoreau wrote in his journal of 27 January 1853, citing Richard Chevenix Trench's (1807–1896)*On the Study of Words:* "Trench says a wild man is a *willed* man. Well, then, a man of will who does what he wills or wishes, a man of hope and of the future tensed, for not only the obstinate is willed, but far more the constant and persevering. The obstinate man, properly speaking, is one who will not. The perseverance of the saints is positive willedness, not a mere passive willingness. The fates are wild, for they *will;* and the Almighty is wild above all" [J 4:482].

82 Allusion to the legendary founders of Rome, Romulus and Remus, who were raised by a she-wolf when abandoned as infants, but for a wider context, see Thoreau's February 1851 journal entry: "America is the she wolf to-day, and the children of exhausted Europe exposed on her uninhabited and savage shores are the Romulus and Remus who, having derived new life and vigor from her breast, have founded a new Rome in the West" [J 2:151].

83 Structural echo of the catechism: "I believe in God the Father, the Son, and the Holy Ghost."

84 The needles of the hemlock spruce (*Tsuga Canadensis*).

85 Latin: tree of life; a member of the Cyprus family.

86 The Khoikhoi, a nomadic African people from the southern extremity of Africa.

87 On 30 December 1850 Thoreau noted in his journal, from his reading in Roualeyn George Gordon-Cumming's (1820–1866) *Five Years of a Hunter's Life in the Far Interior of South Africa:* "The Hottentots devoured the marrow of a koodoo raw as a matter of course" [J 2:131]. Gordon-Cumming wrote: "Springing from their horses, they triumphantly seized the skeleton; and, each selecting for himself a couple of stones, they sat down on the ground, cracked the marrow-bones, and greedily devoured the raw contents."

88 Allusion to Sir John Richardson's (1787–1865) *Fauna Boreali-Americana; or, The zoology of the Northern Parts of British America:* "The kidneys,

and part of the intestines, particularly the thin folds of the third stomach or many-plies, are likewise occasionally eaten when raw, and the summits of the antlers, as long as they are soft, are also delicacies in a raw state."

89 Anticipated or gained an advantage.

90 Variant of intervale: a chiefly New England term meaning a tract of low-lying land between hills.

91 Allusion to Gordon-Cumming's *Five Years of a Hunter's Life:* "The skin of the eland I had just shot emitted, like most other antelopes, the most delicious perfume of trees and grasses." Thoreau excerpted several passages from Gordon-Cumming in his journal of December 1850.

92 Not a quotation. In Thoreau's journal entry this was emphasized but not placed in quotation marks: "Olive or red seems the fittest color for a man, a denizen of the woods. The *pale white man!* I do not wonder that the African pitied him" [J 2:32–33].

93 Quoted, with minor variants of punctuation, from Charles Darwin's (1809–1882) *Journal of Researches into the Natural History and Geology of the Countries Visited During the Voyage of H.M.S. Beagle Round the World.*

94 Quoted from Ben Jonson's (1572–1637) masque *Love Freed from Ignorance and Folly* l. 296.

95 Ornamental flower gardens where the paths and beds are arranged in a pattern.

"How near to good is what is fair!"[94]

So I would say,—

How near to good is what is *wild!*

Life consists with Wildness. The most alive is the wildest. Not yet subdued to man, its presence refreshes him. One who pressed forward incessantly and never rested from his labors, who grew fast and made infinite demands on life, would always find himself in a new country or wilderness, and surrounded by the raw material of life. He would be climbing over the prostrate stems of primitive forest-trees.

Hope and the future for me are not in lawns and cultivated fields, not in towns and cities, but in the impervious and quaking swamps. When, formerly, I have analysed my partiality for some farm which I had contemplated purchasing, I have frequently found that I was attracted solely by a few square rods of impermeable and unfathomable bog,—a natural sink in one corner of it. That was the jewel which dazzled me. I derive more of my subsistence from the swamps which surround my native town than from the cultivated gardens in the village. There are no richer parterres[95] to my eyes than the dense beds of dwarf andromeda (*Cassandra calyculata*) which cover these tender places on the earth's surface. Botany cannot go further than tell me the names of the shrubs which grow there,—the high-blueberry, panicled andromeda, lamb-kill, azalea, and rhodora,—all standing in the quaking sphagnum. I often think that I would like to have my house front on this mass of dull red bushes, omitting other flower plots and borders, transplanted spruce and trim box, even gravelled walks,—to have this fertile spot under my windows, not a few imported barrow-fulls of soil only to cover the sand which was thrown out in digging the cellar. Why not put my house, my parlor, behind this plot, instead of behind that meagre assemblage of curiosities, that poor apology for a Nature and Art, which I call my front-yard? It is an effort to clear up and make a decent appearance when the carpenter and mason have departed, though done as much for the passer-by as the dweller within. The most tasteful front-yard fence was never an agreeable object of study to me; the most elaborate ornaments, acorn-tops,[96] or what not, soon wearied and disgusted me. Bring your sills up to the very edge of the swamp, then, (though it may not be the best place for a dry cellar,) so that there be no access on that side to citizens. Front-yards are not made to walk in, but, at most, through, and you could go in the back way.

Yes, though you may think me perverse, if it were proposed to me to dwell in the neighborhood of the most beautiful garden that ever human art contrived, or else of a dismal swamp,[97] I should certainly decide for the swamp. How vain, then, have been all your labors, citizens, for me!

My spirits infallibly rise in proportion to the outward dreariness. Give me the ocean, the desert, or the wilderness! In the desert, pure air and solitude compensate for want of moisture and fertility. The traveller Burton says of it, — "Your *morale* improves; you become frank and cordial, hospitable and single-minded. . . . In the desert spirituous liquors excite only disgust. There is a keen enjoyment in a mere animal existence."[98] They who have been travelling long on the steppes of Tartary say, — "On reëntering cultivated lands, the agitation, perplexity, and turmoil of civilization oppressed and suffocated us; the air seemed to fail us, and we felt every moment as if about to die of asphyxia."[99] When I would recreate myself, I seek the darkest wood, the thickest and most interminable, and, to the citizen, most dismal swamp.

96 Decorative element.

97 Although Thoreau may not have had a specific swamp in mind here—he did not capitalize the name as he did in *Walden*—there is a Dismal Swamp in southeastern Virginia and northeastern North Carolina. It appeared in William Byrd's (1674–1744) *History of the Dividing Line Betwixt Virginia and North Carolina,* Henry Wadsworth Longfellow's (1807–1882) "The Slave in the Dismal Swamp," Thomas Moore's "The Lake of the Dismal Swamp," and Harriet Beecher Stowe's (1811–1896) *Dred.*

98 Quoted from Richard Francis Burton's (1821–1890) *Personal Narrative to Al-Madinah and Meccah.*

99 Quoted from Huc's *Recollections of a Journey Through Tartary, Thibet, and China, During the Years 1844, 1845, and 1846.*

100 Latin: holy of holies; the innermost shrine of a tabernacle or temple, and thus an inviolably private place.

101 Food of John the Baptist in the desert, from Matthew 3:4: "Now John himself had his raiment of camel's hair, and a leathern girdle about his loins; and his food was locusts and wild honey."

102 Thoreau read about this in the ledger of Ephraim Jones (1705–1756). His journal contains four separate entries recording details from and comments on Jones's account books: 27 January, 31 January, 5 February (which entry appeared in the "Winter Animals" chapter of *Walden*), and 5 February (P.M.) 1854. The bark was a source of tannic acid used in tanning.

I enter a swamp as a sacred place,—a *sanctum sanctorum*.[100] There is the strength, the marrow of Nature. The wild-wood covers the virgin mould,—and the same soil is good for men and for trees. A man's health requires as many acres of meadow to his prospect as his farm does loads of muck. There are the strong meats on which he feeds. A town is saved, not more by the righteous men in it than by the woods and swamps that surround it. A township where one primitive forest waves above, while another primitive forest rots below,—such a town is fitted to raise not only corn and potatoes, but poets and philosophers for the coming ages. In such a soil grew Homer and Confucius and the rest, and out of such a wilderness comes the Reformer eating locusts and wild honey.[101]

To preserve wild animals implies generally the creation of a forest for them to dwell in or resort to. So is it with man. A hundred years ago they sold bark[102] in our streets peeled from our own woods. In the very aspect of those primitive and rugged trees, there was, methinks, a tanning principle which hardened and consolidated the fibres of men's thoughts. Ah! already I shudder for these comparatively degenerate days of my native village, when you cannot collect a load of bark of good thickness,—and we no longer produce tar and turpentine.

The civilized nations—Greece, Rome, England—are sustained by the primitive forests which anciently rotted where they stand. They survive as long as the soil is not exhausted. Alas for human culture! little is to be expected of a nation, when the vegetable mould is exhausted, and it is compelled to make manure of the bones of its fathers. There the poet sustains himself merely by his own superfluous fat, and the philosopher comes down on his marrow-bones.

It is said to be the task of the American "to work the virgin soil," and that "agriculture here already assumes proportions unknown everywhere else."[103] I think that the farmer displaces the Indian even because he redeems the meadow, and so makes himself stronger and in some respects more natural. I was surveying for a man the other day a single straight line one hundred and thirty-two rods long, through a swamp, at whose entrance might have been written the words which Dante read over the entrance to the Infernal regions, — "Leave all hope, ye that enter,"[104] — that is, of ever getting out again; where at one time I saw my employer actually up to his neck and swimming for his life in his property, though it was still winter. He had another similar swamp which I could not survey at all, because it was completely under water, and nevertheless, with regard to a third swamp, which I did *survey* from a distance, he remarked to me, true to his instincts, that he would not part with it for any consideration, on account of the mud which it contained. And that man intends to put a girdling ditch round the whole in the course of forty months, and so redeem it by the magic of his spade.[105] I refer to him only as the type of a class.

The weapons with which we have gained our most important victories, which should be handed down as heirlooms from father to son, are not the sword and the lance, but the bush-whack, the turf-cutter, the spade, and the bog-hoe, rusted with the blood of many a meadow, and begrimed with the dust of many a hard-fought field. The very winds blew the Indian's cornfield into the meadow, and pointed out the way which he had not the skill to follow. He had no better implement with which to intrench himself in the land than a clam-shell.[106] But the farmer is armed with plough and spade.

In Literature it is only the wild that attracts us. Dulness is but another name for tameness. It is the uncivilized free and wild thinking in "Hamlet" and the "Iliad," in all the Scriptures and Mythologies, not learned in the

103 Quoted from Guyot's *The Earth and Man*: "For the American, this task is to work the virgin soil, and the wealth of the land Providence has granted to him, for his own benefit and that of the whole world. For this is the first work to be done, that on which the future of America depends. . . . Agriculture here already assumes proportions unknown every where else."

104 Quoted from John A. Carlyle's (1801–1879) "literal prose translation" of Dante Alighieri's (1265–1321) *Divine Comedy: The Inferno*. The translator was Thomas Carlyle's brother.

105 John B. Moore (1817–1887), for whom Thoreau surveyed several times, the first being in 1850. Moore reported to the Concord Farmers' Club in 1854 that on "almost every farm there is more or less low-land, covered with brush, or wet meadows and swamps, which are unproductive in their present condition, but may easily be made the best and most productive grass land on our farms, and after being reclaimed, will produce much more grass with the same manure and labor than dry soils."

106 Thoreau may have forgotten about his 1855 discovery: "Found what I take to be an Indian hoe at Hubbard Bathing-Place, sort of slate stone four or five eighths of an inch thick, semicircular, eight inches one way by four or more the other, chipped down on the edges" [J 5:299].

schools, that delights us. As the wild duck is more swift and beautiful than the tame, so is the wild — the mallard[107] — thought, which, 'mid falling dews[108] wings its way above the fens. A truly good book is something as natural, and as unexpectedly and unaccountably fair and perfect, as a wild flower discovered on the prairies of the West or in the jungles of the East. Genius is a light which makes the darkness visible, like the lightning's flash, which perchance shatters the temple of knowledge itself, — and not a taper lighted at the hearth-stone of the race, which pales before the light of common day.

English literature, from the days of the minstrels to the Lake Poets,[109] — Chaucer and Spenser and Milton, and even Shakspeare, included, — breathes no quite fresh and in this sense wild strain. It is an essentially tame and civilized literature, reflecting Greece and Rome. Her wilderness is a green-wood, — her wild man a Robin Hood. There is plenty of genial love of Nature, but not so much of Nature herself. Her chronicles inform us when her wild animals, but not when the wild man in her, became extinct.

The science of Humboldt is one thing, poetry is another thing.[110] The poet to-day, notwithstanding all the discoveries of science, and the accumulated learning of mankind, enjoys no advantage over Homer.

Where is the literature which gives expression to Nature? He would be a poet who could impress the winds and streams into his service, to speak for him; who nailed words to their primitive senses, as farmers drive down stakes in the spring, which the frost has heaved; who derived his words as often as he used them, — transplanted them to his page with earth adhering to their roots; whose words were so true and fresh and natural that they would appear to expand like the buds at the approach of spring, though they lay half-smothered between two musty leaves in a library, — ay, to bloom and

---

107 From the Middle English, *malarde,* and Old French, *malart,* meaning wild duck.

108 Allusion to the opening of William Cullen Bryant's (1794–1878) "To a Waterfowl":

> Whither, midst falling dew,
> While glow the heavens with the last steps of
> day,
> Far, through their rosy depths, dost though
> pursue
> Thy solitary way?

109 Cf. "Thomas Carlyle and His Works," note 9.

110 In his journal of 1853 Thoreau noted: "It is stated in the Life of Humboldt that he proved 'that the expression, "the ocean reflects the sky," was a purely poetical, but not a scientifically correct one, as the sea is often blue when the sky is almost totally covered with light white clouds.'" [J 5:120–121].

bear fruit there, after their kind, annually, for the faithful reader, in sympathy with surrounding Nature.

I do not know of any poetry to quote which adequately expresses this yearning for the Wild. Approached from this side, the best poetry is tame. I do not know where to find in any literature, ancient or modern, any account which contents me of that Nature with which even I am acquainted. You will perceive that I demand something which no Augustan nor Elizabethan age,[111] which no *culture,* in short, can give. Mythology comes nearer to it than anything. How much more fertile a nature, at least, has Grecian mythology its root in than English literature! Mythology is the crop which the Old World bore before its soil was exhausted, before the fancy and imagination were affected with blight; and which it still bears, wherever its pristine vigor is unabated. All other literatures endure only as the elms which overshadow our houses; but this is like the great dragon-tree of the Western Isles,[112] as old as mankind, and, whether that does or not, will endure as long; for the decay of other literatures makes the soil in which it thrives.

The West is preparing to add its fables to those of the East. The valleys of the Ganges, the Nile, and the Rhine, having yielded their crop,[113] it remains to be seen what the valleys of the Amazon, the Plate, the Orinoco, the St. Lawrence, and the Mississippi will produce. Perchance, when, in the course of ages, American liberty has become a fiction of the past,—as it is to some extent a fiction of the present,—the poets of the world will be inspired by American mythology.

The wildest dreams of wild men, even, are not the less true, though they may not recommend themselves to the sense which is most common among Englishmen and Americans to-day. It is not every truth that recommends itself to the common sense.[114] Nature has a place for the wild clematis as well as for the cabbage. Some ex-

111 Periods of cultural advancement: the Augustan (cf. "Thomas Carlyle and His Works," note 69) and Elizabethan, in England, after Elizabeth I (1533–1603).
112 *Dracaena draco,* found in the Canary Islands, and which Thoreau read about in the section on "The Colossal Dragon-tree of Orotava" in Humboldt's *Views of Nature.*
113 Related to the Hindu, Egyptian, and Roman civilizations, respectively.
114 Cf. "Paradise (To Be) Regained," note 46.

115 Quoted from Robert Hunt's (1807–1887) *The Poetry of Science, or Studies of the Physical Phenomena of Nature.*

116 Thoreau read in Hunt's *The Poetry of Science* of "the Buddaical superstition that the world is supported on a vast elephant, which stands on the back of a tortoise, which again rests on a serpent."

117 Thoreau noted in his journal, from reading Hunt's *The Poetry of Science*: "The fossil tortoise has been found in Asia large enough to support an elephant" [J 2:169]. According to Hunt: "Although the idea of an elephant standing on the back of a tortoise was often laughed at as an absurdity, Captain Cautley and Dr. Falconer at length discovered in the hills of Asia the remains of a tortoise in a fossil state of such a size that an elephant could easily have performed the feat."

118 A Wolof proverb, from Jean Dard's 1826 *Grammaire Wolofe*, which Thoreau read about in an unidentified newspaper clipping in which is found a collection of twenty-eight "Negro Proverbs" prefaced by: "We found yesterday a fragment of an apparently old newspaper, title and date lost, which contained the following proverbs of the Yoloffs, or Woloffs, a nation of negroes on the west coast of Africa, in the vicinity of the river Senegal, extracted from a grammar of the Woloff language, 'published lately,' the fragment says, 'at Paris, by M. Dard, who resided a long time, and still resides among those people.' The Yoloffs, or Woloffs, live under a despotic government, in rude log huts, filled with straw. They can neither read nor write, and their minds are entirely cultivated."

119 In his 1850 journal Thoreau noted: "To-day, May 31st, a red and white cow, being uneasy, broke out of the steam-mill pasture and crossed the bridge and broke into Elijah Wood's grounds. When he endeavored to drive her out by the bars, she boldly took to the water, wading first through the meadows full of ditches, and swam across the river, about forty rods wide at this time, and landed in her own pasture again. She was a buffalo crossing her Mississippi. This exploit con-

pressions of truth are reminiscent,—others merely *sensible,* as the phrase is,—others prophetic. Some forms of disease, even, may prophesy forms of health. The geologist has discovered that the figures of serpents, griffins, flying dragons, and other fanciful embellishments of heraldry, have their prototypes in the forms of fossil species which were extinct before man was created, and hence "indicate a faint and shadowy knowledge of a previous state of organic existence."[115] The Hindoos dreamed that the earth rested on an elephant, and the elephant on a tortoise, and the tortoise on a serpent;[116] and though it may be an unimportant coincidence, it will not be out of place here to state, that a fossil tortoise has lately been discovered in Asia large enough to support an elephant.[117] I confess that I am partial to these wild fancies, which transcend the order of time and development. They are the sublimest recreation of the intellect. The partridge loves peas, but not those that go with her into the pot.[118]

In short, all good things are wild and free. There is something in a strain of music, whether produced by an instrument or by the human voice,—take the sound of a bugle in a summer night, for instance,—which by its wildness, to speak without satire, reminds me of the cries emitted by wild beasts in their native forests. It is so much of their wildness as I can understand. Give me for my friends and neighbors wild men, not tame ones. The wildness of the savage is but a faint symbol of the awful ferity with which good men and lovers meet.

I love even to see the domestic animals reassert their native rights,—any evidence that they have not wholly lost their original wild habits and vigor; as when my neighbor's cow breaks out of her pasture early in the spring and boldly swims the river, a cold, gray tide, twenty-five or thirty rods wide,[119] swollen by the melted snow. It is the buffalo crossing the Mississippi. This exploit confers some dignity on the herd in my eyes, — already dignified. The seeds of instinct are preserved under the thick hides of cattle and horses, like seeds in the bowels of the earth, an indefinite period.

Any sportiveness in cattle is unexpected. I saw one day a herd of a dozen bullocks and cows running about and frisking in unwieldy sport, like huge rats, even like kittens. They shook their heads, raised their tails, and rushed up and down a hill, and I perceived by their horns, as well as by their activity, their relation to the deer tribe. But, alas! a sudden loud *who!* would have damped their ardor at once, reduced them from venison to beef, and stiffened their sides and sinews like the locomotive. Who but the Evil One has cried, "Who!" to mankind? Indeed, the life of cattle, like that of many men, is but a sort of locomotiveness; they move a side at a time, and man, by his machinery, is meeting the horse and ox half-way. Whatever part the whip has touched is thenceforth palsied. Who would ever think of a *side* of any of the supple cat tribe, as we speak of a *side* of beef?

I rejoice that horses and steers have to be broken before they can be made the slaves of men, and that men themselves have some wild oats still left to sow before they become submissive members of society. Undoubtedly, all men are not equally fit subjects for civilization; and because the majority, like dogs and sheep, are tame by inherited disposition, is no reason why the others should have their natures broken that they may be reduced to the same level. Men are in the main alike, but they were made several in order that they might be various. If a low use is to be served, one man will do nearly or quite as well as another; if a high one, individual excellence is to be regarded. Any man can stop a hole to keep the wind away,[120] but no other man could serve so rare a use as the author of this illustration did. Confucius[121] says, — "The skins of the tiger and the leopard, when they are tanned,

ferred some dignity on the herd in my eyes, already dignified, and reflectedly on the river, which I looked on as a kind of Bosporus" [J 2:18–19].
120 Cf. "Resistance to Civil Government," note 17.
121 Cf. "Resistance to Civil Government," note 58.

122 Thoreau's translation of Analects 12:8 from Jean-Pierre-Guillaume Pauthier's (1801–1873) French translation of Confucius: *Confucius et Mencius: Les Quatre Livres de Philosophie Moral et Politique de la Chine.*

123 Probable allusion to Prince Alexander Menshikov (1787–1869), commander in chief of the Russian forces during the Crimean War, 1853–1856. In Thoreau's 1851 journal this passage read: "Looking into a book on dentistry the other day, I observed a list of authors who had written on this subject. There were Ran & Tan and Yungerman, and I was impressed by the fact that there was nothing in a name" [J 2:208].

124 Variant of a common counting rhyme, "Eerie, irey, ickery, Ann," or "One-ery, two-ery, ickery, Ann."

125 Ellery Channing (William Ellery Channing the Younger, 1817–1901) owned a Newfoundland dog named Bose that would often accompany Thoreau and him on their walks together.

126 Thoreau's former pupil Henry Kendall (b. 1829), of whom he wrote on 1 November 1853 that he "climbed daringly to the top of a tall walnut to shake. He had got the nickname Buster for similar exploits, so that some thought he was christened so" [J 5:471].

are as the skins of the dog and the sheep tanned."[122] But it is not the part of a true culture to tame tigers, any more than it is to make sheep ferocious; and tanning their skins for shoes is not the best use to which they can be put.

When looking over a list of men's names in a foreign language, as of military officers, or of authors who have written on a particular subject, I am reminded once more that there is nothing in a name. The name Menschikoff,[123] for instance, has nothing in it to my ears more human than a whisker, and it may belong to a rat. As the names of the Poles and Russians are to us, so are ours to them. It is as if they had been named by the child's rigmarole, — *Iery wiery ichery van, tittle-tol-tan.*[124] I see in my mind a herd of wild creatures swarming over the earth, and to each the herdsman has affixed some barbarous sound in his own dialect. The names of men are of course as cheap and meaningless as *Bose*[125] and *Tray,* the names of dogs.

Methinks it would be some advantage to philosophy, if men were named merely in the gross, as they are known. It would be necessary only to know the genus, and perhaps the race or variety, to know the individual. We are not prepared to believe that every private soldier in a Roman army had a name of his own, — because we have not supposed that he had a character of his own. At present our only true names are nicknames. I knew a boy who, from his peculiar energy, was called "Buster" by his playmates, and this rightly supplanted his Christian name.[126] Some travellers tell us that an Indian had no name given him at first, but earned it, and his name was his fame; and among some tribes he acquired a new name with every new exploit. It is pitiful when a man bears a name for convenience merely, who has earned neither name nor fame.

I will not allow mere names to make distinctions for me, but still see men in herds for all them. A familiar name cannot make a man less strange to me. It may be given to a savage who retains in secret his own wild title earned in the woods. We have a wild savage in us, and a savage name is perchance somewhere recorded as ours. I see that my neighbor, who bears the familiar epithet William, or Edwin, takes it off with his jacket. It does not adhere to him when asleep or in anger, or aroused by any passion or inspiration. I seem to hear pronounced by some of his kin at such a time his original wild name in some jaw-breaking or else melodious tongue.

Here is this vast, savage, howling Mother of ours, Nature, lying all around, with such beauty, and such affection for her children, as the leopard; and yet we are so early weaned from her breast to society, to that culture which is exclusively an interaction of man on man,— a sort of breeding in and in, which produces at most a merely English nobility, a civilization destined to have a speedy limit.

In society, in the best institutions of men, it is easy to detect a certain precocity. When we should still be growing children, we are already little men. Give me a culture which imports much muck from the meadows, and deepens the soil,—not that which trusts to heating manures, and improved implements and modes of culture only.

Many a poor sore-eyed student that I have heard of would grow faster, both intellectually and physically, if, instead of sitting up so very late, he honestly slumbered a fool's allowance.[127]

There may be an excess even of informing light.[128] Niépce,[129] a Frenchman, discovered "actinism," that power in the sun's rays which produces a chemical effect,—that granite rocks, and stone structures, and

127 Allusion to the adage attributed to King George IV (1762–1830) in which he allowed six hours of sleep for a man, seven for a woman, and eight for a fool.
128 In *Walden* Thoreau wrote: "The light which puts out our eyes is darkness to us" [Wa 325].
129 Joseph-Nicéphore Niépce (1765–1833), French inventor of the first permanent photographic image. Thoreau's quotations in this paragraph are from Hunt's *Poetry of Science*.

130 In Greek mythology the letters of the alphabet were brought from Phoenicia to Greece by Cadmus.

131 Allusion to Henry Richard, Lord Holland's (1773–1840) *Foreign Reminiscences:* "What the Spaniard's call strangely enough *Gramatica Parda,* tawny grammar, knowledge and tact without reading. I have heard it applied to Mina; and I translate it *mother wit.*"

132 Founded in 1828 in London to disseminate information to working and middle-class people through a series of publications, including *The Penny Magazine.* Similarly the Boston Society for the Diffusion of Useful Knowledge was founded in 1828, with Daniel Webster as its first president.

133 Axiom commonly attributed to Francis Bacon.

statues of metal, "are all alike destructively acted upon during the hours of sunshine, and, but for provisions of nature no less wonderful, would soon perish under the delicate touch of the most subtile of the agencies of the universe." But he observed that "those bodies which underwent this change during daylight possessed the power of restoring themselves to their original conditions during the hours of night, when this excitement was no longer influencing them." Hence it has been inferred that "the hours of darkness are as necessary to the inorganic creation as we know night and sleep are to the organic kingdom." Not even does the moon shine every night, but gives place to darkness.

I would not have every man nor every part of a man cultivated, any more than I would have very acre of earth cultivated: part will be tillage, but the greater part will be meadow and forest, not only serving an immediate use, but preparing a mould against a distant future, by the annual decay of the vegetation which it supports.

There are other letters for the child to learn than those which Cadmus invented.[130] The Spaniards have a good term to express this wild and dusky knowledge,— *Gramática parda,*[131] tawny grammar,—a kind of mother-wit derived from that same leopard to which I have referred.

We have heard of a Society for the Diffusion of Useful Knowledge.[132] It is said that Knowledge is power;[133] and the like. Methinks there is equal need of a Society for the Diffusion of Useful Ignorance, what we will call Beautiful Knowledge, a knowledge useful in a higher sense: for what is most of our boasted so-called knowledge but a conceit that we know something, which robs us of the advantage of our actual ignorance? What we call knowledge is often our positive ignorance; ignorance our negative knowledge. By long years of patient industry and reading of the newspapers—for what are the libraries of science but files of newspapers?—a man accumulates a myriad facts, lays them up in his memory, and then when in some spring of his life he saunters abroad into the Great Fields of thought, he, as it were, goes to grass like a horse, and leaves all his harness behind in the stable. I would say to the Society for the Diffusion of Useful Knowledge, sometimes,—Go to grass. You have eaten hay long enough. The spring has come with its green crop. The very cows are driven to their country pastures before the end of May; though I have heard of one unnatural farmer who kept his cow in the barn and fed her on hay all the year round. So, frequently, the Society for the Diffusion of Useful Knowledge treats its cattle.

A man's ignorance sometimes is not only useful, but beautiful,—while his knowledge, so called, is oftentimes worse than useless, beside being ugly. Which is the best man to deal with,—he who knows nothing about a subject, and, what is extremely rare, knows that he knows nothing, or he who really knows something about it, but thinks that he knows all?

My desire for knowledge is intermittent; but my desire to bathe my head in atmospheres unknown to my feet is perennial and constant. The highest that we can attain to is not Knowledge, but Sympathy with Intelligence. I do not know that this higher knowledge amounts to anything more definite than a novel and grand surprise on a sudden revelation of the insufficiency of all that we called Knowledge before,—a discovery that there are more things in heaven and earth than are dreamed of in our philosophy.[134] It is the lighting up of the mist by the sun. Man cannot know in any higher sense than this, any more than he can look serenely and with impunity in the face of the sun: Ὡς τὶ νοῶν, οὐ κεῖνον νοήσεις,—"You

134 Cf. "Thomas Carlyle and His Works," note 141.

135 Thoreau copied the original Greek phrase (Fragment 137) into his commonplace book from Isaac Preston Cory's (1802–1842) *Ancient Fragments of the Phoenician, Chaldaean, Egyptian, Tyrian, Carthaginian, Indian, Persian, and Other Writers: with an Introductory Dissertation and an Inquiry into the Philosophy and Trinity of the Ancients*, retranslating slightly Cory's translation: "You will not understand it, as when understanding a particular thing."

136 Allusion to the Scottish clan MacGregor, or Children of the Mist, in Sir Walter Scott's *A Legend of Montrose*, in which he wrote: "Quit not the ancient manners of the Children of the Mist. . . . Live free—requite kindness—avenge the injuries of thy race!" Thoreau wrote of Scott in *A Week on the Concord and Merrimack Rivers:* "No wonder that the Mythology, and Arabian Nights, and Shakespeare, and Scott's novels entertain us" [W 281].

137 The Puranas refer to any of a class of Sanskrit sacred writings on Hindu mythology, folklore, etc., of varying date and origin. They are regarded as divinely inspired texts, each glorifying a particular god, but are also encyclopedias of secular as well as religious knowledge. The Vishnu Purana is the best known of the eighteen main Puranas. Quoted from *Vishnupurāna. The Vishnu Purāña: A System of Hindu Mythology and Tradition.*

138 John Bunyan (1628–1688), author of *Pilgrim's Progress*.

139 Cf. "Thomas Carlyle and His Works," note 50. Thoreau had read Washington Irving's *Mahomet and His Successors* and Carlyle's "The Hero as Prophet. Mahomet: Islam" in *On Heroes, Hero-Worship, and the Heroic in History*.

will not perceive that, as perceiving a particular thing," say the Chaldean Oracles.[135]

There is something servile in the habit of seeking after a law which we may obey. We may study the laws of matter at and for our convenience, but a successful life knows no law. It is an unfortunate discovery certainly, that of a law which binds us where we did not know before that we were bound. Live free, Child of the Mist,—and with respect to knowledge we are all children of the mist.[136] The man who takes the liberty to live is superior to all the laws both of heaven and earth, by virtue of his relation to the law-maker. "That is active duty," says the Vishnu Purana, "which is not for our bondage; that is knowledge which is for our liberation; all other duty is good only unto weariness; all other knowledge is only the cleverness of an artist."[137]

It is remarkable how few events or crises there are in our histories; how little exercised we have been in our minds; how few experiences we have had. I would fain be assured that I am growing apace and rankly, though my very growth disturb this dull equanimity,—though it be with struggle through long, dark, muggy nights or seasons of gloom. It would be well if all our lives were a divine tragedy even, instead of this trivial comedy or farce. Christ, Dante, Bunyan,[138] and others, appear to have been exercised in their minds more than we: they were subjected to a kind of culture such as our district schools and colleges do not contemplate. Even Mahomet,[139] though Christians may scream at his name, had a good deal more to live for, ay, and to die for, than they have commonly.

When, at rare intervals, some thought visits one, as perchance he is walking on a railroad, then indeed the cars go by without his hearing them. But soon, by some inexorable law, our life goes by and the cars return.

"Gentle breeze that wanderest unseen,
And bendest the thistles round Loira[140] of
    storms,
Traveller of the windy glens,
Why hast thou left my ear so soon?"[141]

While almost all men feel an attraction drawing them to society, few are attracted strongly to Nature. In their relation to Nature men appear to me for the most part, notwithstanding their arts, lower than the animals. It is not often a beautiful relation, as in the case of the animals. How little appreciation of the beauty of the landscape there is among us! We have to be told that the Greeks called the world Κόσμος, Beauty, or Order, but we do not see clearly why they did so, and we esteem it at best only a curious philological fact.

For my part, I feel that with regard to Nature I live a sort of border life, on the confines of a world into which I make occasional and transient forays only, and my patriotism and allegiance to the State into whose territories I seem to retreat are those of a moss-trooper.[142] Unto a life which I call natural I would gladly follow even a will-o'-the-wisp[143] through bogs and sloughs unimaginable, but no moon nor fire-fly has shown me the causeway to it. Nature is a personality so vast and universal that we have never seen one of her features. The walker in the familiar fields which stretch around my native town sometimes finds himself in another land than is described in their owners' deeds, as it were in some far-away field on the confines of the actual Concord, where her jurisdiction ceases, and the idea which the word Concord suggests ceases to be suggested.[144] These farms which I have myself surveyed, these bounds which I have set up appear dimly still as through a mist; but they have no chemistry to fix them; they fade from the surface of the glass; and the picture which the painter painted stands out dimly

140 Unidentified river or cataract in Scotland.
141 Quoted from "Ca-Lodin: A Poem" I:2–5, in James MacPherson's (1736–1796) *The Genuine Remains of Ossian, Literally Translated*. MacPherson claimed that the poems were translated from the work of a third-century Gaelic bard, but they are almost universally thought to have been MacPherson's own compositions.
142 Cf. "Thomas Carlyle and His Works," note 31.
143 Cf. "Natural History of Massachusetts," note 73.
144 On 7 January 1857 Thoreau wrote: "I wish to get the Concord, the Massachusetts, the America, out of my head and be sane a part of every day" [J 9:208].

145 Spaulding's farm was located in the village of Carlisle, north of Concord.

146 Thoreau may have misremembered the phrase "knobs and excrescences" which he used in his journal of 16 November 1860 and which he read in William Gilpin's (1724–1804) *Remarks on Forest Scenery and Other Woodland Views, Relative Chiefly to Picturesque Beauty:* "The maple is an uncommon tree. . . . Pliny speaks as highly of the knobs, and excrescences of this tree . . . as Dr. Plot does of those of the ash."

147 Enclosed or protected as by a bay.

from beneath. The world with which we are commonly acquainted leaves no trace, and it will have no anniversary.

I took a walk on Spaulding's Farm[145] the other afternoon. I saw the setting sun lighting up the opposite side of a stately pine-wood. Its golden rays straggled into the aisles of the wood as into some noble hall. I was impressed as if some ancient and altogether admirable and shining family had seated there in that part of the land called Concord, unknown to me,—to whom the sun was servant,—who had not gone into society in the village,—who had not been called on. I saw their park, their pleasure-ground, beyond through the wood, in Spaulding's cranberry-meadow. The pines furnished them with gables as they grew. Their house was not obvious to vision; the trees grew through it. I do not know whether I heard the sounds of a suppressed hilarity or not. They seemed to recline on the sunbeams. They have sons and daughters. They are quite well. The farmer's cart-path, which leads directly through their hall, does not in the least put them out,—as the muddy bottom of a pool is sometimes seen through the reflected skies. They never heard of Spaulding, and do not know that he is their neighbor,—notwithstanding that I heard him whistle as he drove his team through the house. Nothing can equal the serenity of their lives. Their coat of arms is simply a lichen. I saw it painted on the pines and oaks. Their attics were in the tops of the trees. They are of no politics. There was no noise of labor. I did not perceive that they were weaving or spinning. Yet I did detect, when the wind lulled and hearing was done away, the finest imaginable sweet musical hum,—as of a distant hive in May, which perchance was the sound of their thinking. They had no idle thoughts, and no one without could see their work, for their industry was not as in knots and excrescences[146] embayed.[147]

But I find it difficult to remember them. They fade irrevocably out of my mind even now that I speak and endeavor to recall them, and recollect myself. It is only after a long and serious effort to recollect my best thoughts that I become again aware of their cohabitancy. If it were not for such families as this, I think I should move out of Concord.

We are accustomed to say in New England that few and fewer pigeons visit us every year.[148] Our forests furnish no mast[149] for them. So, it would seem, few and fewer thoughts visit each growing man from year to year, for the grove in our minds is laid waste, — sold to feed unnecessary fires of ambition, or sent to mill, and there is scarcely a twig left for them to perch on. They no longer build nor breed with us. In some more genial season, perchance, a faint shadow flits across the landscape of the mind, cast by the wings of some thought in its vernal or autumnal migration, but, looking up, we are unable to detect the substance of the thought itself. Our winged thoughts[150] are turned to poultry. They no longer soar, and they attain only to a Shanghai and Cochin-China[151] grandeur. Those *gra-a-ate* thoughts — those *gra-a-ate*[152] men — you hear of!

We hug the earth, — how rarely we mount! Methinks we might elevate ourselves a little more. We might climb a tree, at least. I found my account in climbing a tree once. It was a tall white pine, on the top of a hill; and though I got well pitched, I was well paid[153] for it, for I discovered new mountains in the horizon which I had never seen before, — so much more of the earth and the heavens. I might have walked about the foot of the tree for threescore years and ten, and yet I certainly should never have seen them. But, above all, I discovered around me, — it was near the end of June, — on the ends of the

148 Thoreau wrote in his journal of 9 May 1852: "Saw pigeons in the woods, with their inquisitive necks and long tails, but few representatives of the great flocks that once broke down our forests" [J 4:44].
149 Cf. "Succession of Forest Trees," note 27.
150 Allusion to Shakespeare's *Henry V* V.ii.8: "Heave him away upon your winged thoughts."
151 Poultry breeds, imported from China.
152 In his journal of 12 September 1854 Thoreau referred to the sound of the pigeon as being "like a dull grating or creaking of bough on bough" [J 7:35].
153 Payed out or smeared with pitch, tar or grease, to protect from water or weather.

154 Cf. "Slavery in Massachusetts," note 8.

topmost branches only, a few minute and delicate red cone-like blossoms, the fertile flower of the white pine looking heavenward. I carried straightway to the village the topmost spire, and showed it to stranger jurymen who walked the streets,—for it was court-week,—and to farmers and lumber-dealers and wood-choppers and hunters, and not one had ever seen the like before, but they wondered as at a star dropped down! Tell of ancient architects finishing their works on the tops of columns as perfectly as on the lower and more visible parts! Nature has from the first expanded the minute blossoms of the forest only toward the heavens, above men's heads and unobserved by them. We see only the flowers that are under our feet in the meadows. The pines have developed their delicate blossoms on the highest twigs of the wood every summer for ages, as well over the heads of Nature's red children as of her white ones; yet scarcely a farmer or hunter in the land has ever seen them.

Above all, we cannot afford not to live in the present. He is blessed over all mortals who loses no moment of the passing life in remembering the past. Unless our philosophy hears the cock crow in every barn-yard within our horizon, it is belated. That sound commonly reminds us that we are growing rusty and antique in our employments and habits of thought. His philosophy comes down to a more recent time than ours. There is something suggested by it not in Plato nor the New Testament. It is a newer testament,—the gospel according to this moment. He has not fallen astern; he has got up early, and kept up early, and to be where he is is to be in season, in the foremost rank of time. It is an expression of the health and soundness of Nature, a brag for all the world,—healthiness as of a spring burst forth, a new fountain of the Muses, to celebrate this last instant of time. Where he lives no fugitive slave laws are passed.[154]

Who has not betrayed his master many times since last he heard that note?[155]

The merit of this bird's strain is in its freedom from all plaintiveness. The singer can easily move us to tears or to laughter, but where is he who can excite in us a pure morning joy? When, in doleful dumps, breaking the awful stillness of our wooden sidewalk on a Sunday, or, perchance, a watcher in the house of mourning, I hear a cockerel crow far or near, I think to myself, "There is one of us well, at any rate,"—and with a sudden gush return to my senses.

We had a remarkable sunset one day last November. I was walking in a meadow, the source of a small brook, when the sun at last, just before setting, after a cold gray day, reached a clear stratum in the horizon, and the softest, brightest morning sunlight fell on the dry grass and on the stems of the trees in the opposite horizon, and on the leaves of the shrub-oaks on the hill-side, while our shadows stretched long over the meadow eastward, as if we were the only motes in its beams. It was such a light as we could not have imagined a moment before, and the air also was so warm and serene that nothing was wanting to make a paradise of that meadow. When we reflected that this was not a solitary phenomenon, never to happen again, but that it would happen forever and ever an infinite number of evenings, and cheer and reassure the latest child that walked there, it was more glorious still.

The sun sets on some retired meadow, where no house is visible, with all the glory and splendor that it lavishes on cities, and, perchance, as it has never set before,—where there is but a solitary marsh-hawk to have his wings gilded by it, or only a musquash looks out from his cabin, and there is some little black-veined brook in the midst of the marsh, just beginning to meander,

155 Allusion to Jesus' words to Peter in Matthew 26:34, 75: "Before the cock crow, thou shalt deny me thrice."

156 In Greek mythology, paradise, located at the westernmost edge of the world.

winding slowly round a decaying stump. We walked in so pure and bright a light, gilding the withered grass and leaves, so softly and serenely bright, I thought I had never bathed in such a golden flood, without a ripple or a murmur to it. The west side of every wood and rising ground gleamed like the boundary of Elysium,[156] and the sun on our backs seemed like a gentle herdsman driving us home at evening.

So we saunter toward the Holy Land, till one day the sun shall shine more brightly than ever he has done, shall perchance shine into our minds and hearts, and light up our whole lives with a great awakening light, so warm and serene and golden as on a bank-side in Autumn.

Autumnal Tints

1 Possible reference to Thomas Cholmondeley's (1823–1863) 1854 visit to Concord, during the autumn of which he spent time with the Thoreaus.
2 Quoted from Thomson's (cf. "A Winter Walk," note 18) *The Seasons*, "Autumn," 948–952 and 1051, respectively.
3 From his journal of 27 October 1858, but no further identification of the person.

Europeans coming to America are surprised by the brilliancy of our autumnal foliage.[1] There is no account of such a phenomenon in English poetry, because the trees acquire but few bright colors there. The most that Thomson says on this subject in his "Autumn" is contained in the lines,—

> "But see the fading many-colored woods,
> Shade deepening over shade, the country round
> Imbrown; a crowded umbrage, dusk and dun,
> Of every hue, from wan declining green
> To sooty dark":—

and in the line in which he speaks of

> "Autumn beaming o'er the yellow woods."[2]

The autumnal change of our woods has not made a deep impression on our own literature yet. October has hardly tinged our poetry.

A great many, who have spent their lives in cities, and have never chanced to come into the country at this season, have never seen this, the flower, or rather the ripe fruit, of the year. I remember riding with one such citizen, who, though a fortnight too late for the most brilliant tints, was taken by surprise, and would not believe that there had been any brighter. He had never heard of this phenomenon before.[3] Not only many in our towns have never witnessed it, but it is scarcely remembered by the majority from year to year.

Most appear to confound changed leaves with withered ones, as if they were to confound ripe apples with rotten ones. I think that the change to some higher color in a leaf is an evidence that it has arrived at a late and perfect maturity, answering to the maturity of fruits. It is generally the lowest and oldest leaves which change first. But as the perfect winged and usually bright-colored insect is short-lived, so the leaves ripen but to fall.[4]

Generally, every fruit, on ripening, and just before it falls, when it commences a more independent and individual existence, requiring less nourishment from any source, and that not so much from the earth through its stem as from the sun and air, acquires a bright tint. So do leaves. The physiologist says it is "due to an increased absorption of oxygen."[5] That is the scientific account of the matter, — only a reassertion of the fact. But I am more interested in the rosy cheek than I am to know what particular diet the maiden fed on. The very forest and herbage, the pellicle[6] of the earth, must acquire a bright color, an evidence of its ripeness, — as if the globe itself were a fruit on its stem, with ever a cheek toward the sun.

Flowers are but colored leaves, fruits but ripe ones. The edible part of most fruits is, as the physiologist says, "the parenchyma or fleshy tissue of the leaf"[7] of which they are formed.

Our appetites have commonly confined our views of ripeness and its phenomena, color, mellowness, and perfectness, to the fruits which we eat, and we are wont to forget that an immense harvest which we do not eat, hardly use at all, is annually ripened by Nature. At our annual Cattle Shows and Horticultural Exhibitions,[8] we make, as we think, a great show of fair fruits, destined, however, to a rather ignoble end, fruits not valued for their beauty chiefly. But round about and within our towns there is annually another show of fruits, on an in-

4 On 3 November 1858 Thoreau wrote: "By fall I mean literally the falling of the leaves, though some mean by it the changing or the acquisition of a brighter color. This I call the autumnal tint, the ripening to the fall" [J 11:280].

5 Quoted from Carpenter's (cf. "An Address on the Succession of Forest Trees," note 33) *Vegetable Physiology and Systematic Botany*.

6 Skin.

7 Quoted from Carpenter's *Vegetable Physiology and Systematic Botany*.

8 Cf. "The Succession of Forest Trees," note 1.

finitely grander scale, fruits which address our taste for beauty alone.

October is the month of painted leaves.[9] Their rich glow now flashes round the world. As fruits and leaves and the day itself acquire a bright tint just before they fall, so the year near its setting. October is its sunset sky; November the later twilight.

I formerly thought[10] that it would be worth the while to get a specimen leaf from each changing tree, shrub, and herbaceous plant, when it had acquired its brightest characteristic color, in its transition from the green to the brown state, outline it, and copy its color exactly, with paint, in a book, which should be entitled, *"October, or Autumnal Tints"*:[11]—beginning with the earliest reddening,—Woodbine and the lake of radical leaves, and coming down through the Maples, Hickories and Sumachs, and many beautifully freckled leaves less generally known, to the latest Oaks and Aspens. What a memento such a book would be! You would need only to turn over its leaves to take a ramble through the autumn woods whenever you pleased. Or if I could preserve the leaves themselves, unfaded, it would be better still. I have made but little progress toward such a book, but I have endeavored, instead, to describe all these bright tints in the order in which they present themselves. The following are some extracts from my notes.

THE PURPLE GRASSES

By the twentieth of August,[12] everywhere in woods and swamps, we are reminded of the fall, both by the richly spotted Sarsaparilla-leaves and Brakes, and the withering and blackened Skunk-Cabbage and Hellebore, and, by the river-side, the already blackening Pontederia.

The Purple Grass (*Eragrostis pectinacea*) is now in the height of its beauty. I remember still when I first noticed

9 Autumnal epithet found in the works of many poets, such as William Cullen Bryant's "Autumn Woods": "the painted leaves are strown / Along the winding way" and Henry Wadsworth Longfellow's "The Song of Hiawatha": "Like the painted leaves of Autumn."
10 Noted in his journal of 22 November 1853.
11 In his journal of 22 November 1853 he suggested the title, "October Hues or Autumnal Tints."
12 Noted in his journal of 23 August 1858.

13 Noted in his journal of 26 August 1854.

14 Land reminiscent of the woven edging of cloth to prevent fraying, as in *Walden,* in which Thoreau described where "Nature has woven a natural selvage, and the eye rises by just gradations from the low shrubs of the shore to the highest trees" [Wa 180].

15 Timothy grass (Phleum pratense).

this grass particularly. Standing on a hill-side near our river, I saw, thirty or forty rods off, a stripe of purple half a dozen rods long, under the edge of a wood, where the ground sloped toward a meadow. It was as high-colored and interesting, though not quite so bright, as the patches of Rhexia, being a darker purple, like a berry's stain laid on close and thick. On going to and examining it, I found it to be a kind of grass in bloom, hardly a foot high, with but few green blades, and a fine spreading panicle of purple flowers, a shallow, purplish mist trembling around me. Close at hand it appeared but a dull purple, and made little impression on the eye; it was even difficult to detect; and if you plucked a single plant, you were surprised to find how thin it was, and how little color it had. But viewed at a distance in a favorable light, it was of a fine lively purple, flower-like, enriching the earth. Such puny causes combine to produce these decided effects. I was the more surprised and charmed because grass is commonly of a sober and humble color.

With its beautiful purple blush it reminds me, and supplies the place, of the Rhexia, which is now leaving off, and it is one of the most interesting phenomena of August.[13] The finest patches of it grow on waste strips or selvages[14] of land at the base of dry hills, just above the edge of the meadows, where the greedy mower does not deign to swing his scythe; for this is a thin and poor grass, beneath his notice. Or, it may be, because it is so beautiful he does not know that it exists; for the same eye does not see this and Timothy.[15] He carefully gets the meadow hay and the more nutritious grasses which grow next to that, but he leaves this fine purple mist for the walker's harvest, — fodder for his fancy stock. Higher up the hill, perchance, grow also Blackberries, John's-Wort, and neglected, withered, and wiry June-Grass. How fortunate that it grows in such places, and not in the midst of the rank grasses which are annually cut! Nature thus keeps use and beauty distinct. I know many such localities, where it does not fail to present itself annually, and paint the earth with its blush. It grows on the gentle slopes, either in a continuous patch or in scattered and rounded tufts a foot in diameter, and it lasts till it is killed by the first smart frosts.

In most plants the corolla or calyx[16] is the part which attains the highest color, and is the most attractive; in many it is the seed-vessel or fruit; in others, as the Red Maple, the leaves; and in others still it is the very culm[17] itself which is the principal flower or blooming part.

The last is especially the case with the Poke or Garget (*Phytolacca decandra*). Some which stand under our cliffs[18] quite dazzle me with their purple stems now and early in September. They are as interesting to me as most flowers, and one of the most important fruits of our autumn. Every part is flower, (or fruit,) such is its superfluity of color,—stem, branch, peduncle, pedicel, petiole, and even the at length yellowish purple-veined leaves. Its cylindrical racemes of berries of various hues, from green to dark purple, six or seven inches long, are gracefully drooping on all sides, offering repasts to the birds; and even the sepals from which the birds have picked the berries are a brilliant lake-red, with crimson flame-like reflections, equal to anything of the kind,— all on fire with ripeness. Hence the *lacca,* from *lac,* lake.[19] There are at the same time flower-buds, flowers, green berries, dark purple or ripe ones, and these flower-like sepals, all on the same plant.

We love to see any redness in the vegetation of the temperate zone. It is the color of colors. This plant speaks to our blood. It asks a bright sun on it to make it show to best advantage, and it must be seen at this season of the year. On warm hill-sides its stems are ripe by the twenty-third of August. At that date I walked through a beautiful grove of them, six or seven feet high, on the side

16 Inner and outer covering of a flower, respectively.

17 Stem of a grass or similar plant.

18 On the shore of the Sudbury River, about a half-mile southwest of Walden, Fair Haven Hill was also known as the Cliffs. This was one of Thoreau's favorite spots, of which he wrote on 12 May 1850: "In all my rambles I have seen no landscape which can make me forget Fair Haven. I still sit on its Cliff in a new spring day, and look over the awakening woods and the river, and hear the new birds sing, with the same delight as ever. It is as sweet a mystery to me as ever, what this world is" [J 2:9].

19 Lake is a pigment made from vegetable matter. The pokeberry is one of the sources of red lake.

20 A measure of wine equivalent to approximately one hundred gallons: see "Life Without Principle," note 26.
21 Thoreau may have read this in Wood's (cf. "An Address on the Succession of Forest Trees," note 32) *A Class-book of Botany:* "In Spain, it is said they are used to color wine."

of one of our cliffs, where they ripen early. Quite to the ground they were a deep brilliant purple with a bloom, contrasting with the still clear green leaves. It appears a rare triumph of Nature to have produced and perfected such a plant, as if this were enough for a summer. What a perfect maturity it arrives at! It is the emblem of a successful life concluded by a death not premature, which is an ornament to Nature. What if we were to mature as perfectly, root and branch, glowing in the midst of our decay, like the Poke! I confess that it excites me to behold them. I cut one for a cane, for I would fain handle and lean on it. I love to press the berries between my fingers, and see their juice staining my hand. To walk amid these upright, branching casks of purple wine, which retain and diffuse a sunset glow, tasting each one with your eye, instead of counting the pipes[20] on a London dock, what a privilege! For Nature's vintage is not confined to the vine. Our poets have sung of wine, the product of a foreign plant which commonly they never saw, as if our own plants had no juice in them more than the singers. Indeed, this has been called by some the American Grape, and, though a native of America, its juices are used in some foreign countries to improve the color of the wine; so that the poetaster may be celebrating the virtues of the Poke[21] without knowing it. Here are berries enough to paint afresh the western sky, and play the bacchanal with, if you will. And what flutes its ensanguined stems would make, to be used in such a dance! It is truly a royal plant. I could spend the evening of the year musing amid the Poke-stems. And perchance amid these groves might arise at last a new school of philosophy or poetry. It lasts all through September.

At the same time with this, or near the end of August, a to me very interesting genus of grasses, Andropogons, or Beard-Grasses, is in its prime. *Andropogon furcatus,* Forked Beard-Grass, or call it Purple-Fingered

Grass; *Andropogon scoparius,* Purple Wood-Grass; and *Andropogon* (now called *Sorghum*) *nutans,* Indian-Grass. The first is a very tall and slender-culmed grass, three to seven feet high, with four or five purple finger-like spikes raying upward from the top. The second is also quite slender, growing in tufts two feet high by one wide, with culms often somewhat curving, which, as the spikes go out of bloom, have a whitish fuzzy look. These two are prevailing grasses at this season on dry and sandy fields and hill-sides. The culms of both, not to mention their pretty flowers, reflect a purple tinge, and help to declare the ripeness of the year. Perhaps I have the more sympathy with them because they are despised by the farmer, and occupy sterile and neglected soil. They are high-colored, like ripe grapes, and express a maturity which the spring did not suggest. Only the August sun could have thus burnished these culms and leaves. The farmer has long since done his upland haying,[22] and he will not condescend to bring his scythe to where these slender wild grasses have at length flowered thinly; you often see spaces of bare sand amid them. But I walk encouraged between the tufts of Purple Wood-Grass, over the sandy fields, and along the edge of the Shrub-Oaks, glad to recognize these simple contemporaries. With thoughts cutting a broad swathe I "get"[23] them, with horse-raking[24] thoughts I gather them into windrows.[25] The fine-eared poet may hear the whetting of my scythe.[26] These two were almost the first grasses that I learned to distinguish, for I had not known by how many friends I was surrounded,—I had seen them simply as grasses standing. The purple of their culms also excites me like that of the Poke-Weed stems.

Think what refuge there is for one, before August is over, from college commencements[27] and society that isolates![28] I can skulk amid the tufts of Purple Wood-Grass on the borders of the "Great Fields."[29] Wherever

22 Haying or harvesting of cultivated grains, chewed or matted grasses, thistles, shrubs, and mowings covered with imported grasses.
23 When scything, the extra stretch or reach to cut the outer grass.
24 Large rake drawn by a horse.
25 Long rows of cut hay or grain left to dry in a field before bundling.
26 Allusion to Milton's "L'Allegro" 66: "And the mower whets his scythe."
27 College commencements were held in July and August. Thoreau's Harvard commencement was held on 30 August 1837.
28 In *Walden* Thoreau wrote: "I never found the companion that was so companionable as solitude. We are for the most part more lonely when we go abroad among men than when we stay in our chambers" [Wa 131].
29 The Concord historian Lemuel Shattuck described these as "extending from the Great Meadows on the north to the Boston south road, and down the river considerably into the present limits of Bedford, and up the river beyond Deacon Hubbard's, and the extensive tract between the two rivers, contained large quantities of open land, which bore some resemblance to the prairies of the western country."

30 A board, as on a guide-post, having directions or information of the way.

31 Thoreau wrote in *Cape Cod:* "To-day it was the Purple Sea, an epithet which I should not before have accepted" [W 4:119].

I walk these afternoons, the Purple-Fingered Grass also stands like a guide-board,[30] and points my thoughts to more poetic paths than they have lately travelled.

A man shall perhaps rush by and trample down plants as high as his head, and cannot be said to know that they exist, though he may have cut many tons of them, littered his stables with them, and fed them to his cattle for years. Yet, if he ever favorably attends to them, he may be overcome by their beauty. Each humblest plant, or weed, as we call it, stands there to express some thought or mood of ours; and yet how long it stands in vain! I had walked over those Great Fields so many Augusts, and never yet distinctly recognized these purple companions that I had there. I had brushed against them and trodden on them, forsooth; and now, at last, they, as it were, rose up and blessed me. Beauty and true wealth are always thus cheap and despised. Heaven might be defined as the place which men avoid. Who can doubt that these grasses, which the farmer says are of no account to him, find some compensation in your appreciation of them? I may say that I never saw them before,—though, when I came to look them face to face, there did come down to me a purple gleam from previous years; and now, wherever I go, I see hardly anything else. It is the reign and presidency of the Andropogons.

Almost the very sands confess the ripening influence of the August sun, and methinks, together with the slender grasses waving over them, reflect a purple tinge. The impurpled sands! Such is the consequence of all this sunshine absorbed into the pores of plants and of the earth. All sap or blood is now wine-colored. At last we have not only the purple sea,[31] but the purple land.

The Chestnut Beard-Grass, Indian-Grass, or Wood-Grass, growing here and there in waste places, but more rare than the former, (from two to four or five feet high,) is still handsomer and of more vivid colors than its congeners,[32] and might well have caught the Indian's eye. It has a long, narrow, one-sided, and slightly nodding panicle of bright purple and yellow flowers, like a banner raised above its reedy leaves. These bright standards are now advanced on the distant hill-sides, not in large armies, but in scattered troops or single file, like the red men.[33] They stand thus fair and bright, representative of the race which they are named after, but for the most part unobserved as they. The expression of this grass haunted me for a week, after I first passed and noticed it, like the glance of an eye. It stands like an Indian chief taking a last look at his favorite hunting-grounds.

THE RED MAPLE

By the twenty-fifth of September,[34] the Red Maples generally are beginning to be ripe. Some large ones have been conspicuously changing for a week, and some single trees are now very brilliant. I notice a small one, half a mile off across a meadow, against the green wood-side there, a far brighter red than the blossoms of any tree in summer, and more conspicuous. I have observed this tree for several autumns invariably changing earlier than its fellows, just as one tree ripens its fruit earlier than another. It might serve to mark the season, perhaps. I should be sorry, if it were cut down. I know of two or three such trees in different parts of our town, which might, perhaps, be propagated from, as early ripeners or September trees, and their seed be advertised in the market, as well as that of radishes, if we cared as much about them.

At present, these burning bushes[35] stand chiefly along the edge of the meadows, or I distinguish them afar on the hill-sides here and there. Sometimes you will see many small ones in a swamp turned quite crimson when all other trees around are still perfectly green, and the former appear so much the brighter for it. They take

32 Belonging to the same genus.
33 In his journal of 4 September 1851 Thoreau referred to the Indian walking "in single file, more solitary, — not side by side, chatting as he went" [J 2:457].
34 Noted in his 1851 journal.
35 Allusion to Exodus 3:2, in which Moses beheld the bush that "burned with fire, and the bush was not consumed."

you by surprise, as you are going by on one side, across the fields, thus early in the season, as if it were some gay encampment of the red men, or other foresters, of whose arrival you had not heard.

Some single trees, wholly bright scarlet, seen against others of their kind still freshly green, or against evergreens, are more memorable than whole groves will be by-and-by. How beautiful, when a whole tree is like one great scarlet fruit full of ripe juices, every leaf, from lowest limb to topmost spire, all aglow, especially if you look toward the sun! What more remarkable object can there be in the landscape? Visible for miles, too fair to be believed. If such a phenomenon occurred but once, it would be handed down by tradition to posterity, and get into the mythology at last.

The whole tree thus ripening in advance of its fellows attains a singular preëminence, and sometimes maintains it for a week or two. I am thrilled at the sight of it, bearing aloft its scarlet standard for the regiment of green-clad foresters around, and I go half a mile out of my way to examine it. A single tree becomes thus the crowning beauty of some meadowy vale, and the expression of the whole surrounding forest is at once more spirited for it.

A small Red Maple has grown, perchance, far away at the head of some retired valley, a mile from any road, unobserved. It has faithfully discharged the duties of a Maple there, all winter and summer, neglected none of its economies, but added to its stature in the virtue which belongs to a Maple, by a steady growth for so many months, never having gone gadding abroad, and is nearer heaven than it was in the spring. It has faithfully husbanded its sap, and afforded a shelter to the wandering bird, has long since ripened its seeds and committed them to the winds, and has the satisfaction of knowing, perhaps, that a thousand little well-behaved

Maples are already settled in life somewhere. It deserves well of Mapledom. Its leaves have been asking it from time to time, in a whisper, "When shall we redden?" And now, in this month of September, this month of travelling, when men are hastening to the sea-side, or the mountains, or the lakes, this modest Maple, still without budging an inch, travels in its reputation,— runs up its scarlet flag on that hill-side, which shows that it has finished its summer's work before all other trees, and withdraws from the contest. At the eleventh hour of the year, the tree which no scrutiny could have detected here when it was most industrious is thus, by the tint of its maturity, by its very blushes, revealed at last to the careless and distant traveller, and leads his thoughts away from the dusty road into those brave solitudes which it inhabits. It flashes out conspicuous with all the virtue and beauty of a Maple,—*Acer rubrum*. We may now read its title, or *rubric*,[36] clear. Its *virtues*, not its sins, are as scarlet.[37]

Notwithstanding the Red Maple is the most intense scarlet of any of our trees, the Sugar-Maple has been the most celebrated, and Michaux in his "Sylva" does not speak of the autumnal color of the former.[38] About the second of October, these trees, both large and small, are most brilliant, though many are still green. In "sprout-lands" they seem to vie with one another, and ever some particular one in the midst of the crowd will be of a peculiarly pure scarlet, and by its more intense color attract our eye even at a distance, and carry off the palm. A large Red-Maple swamp, when at the height of its change, is the most obviously brilliant of all tangible things, where I dwell, so abundant is this tree with us. It varies much both in form and color. A great many are merely yellow, more scarlet, others scarlet deepening into crimson, more red than common. Look at yonder swamp of Maples mixed with Pines, at the base of a Pine-clad hill,

36 *Rubric*, a name or title, so-called because the titles of laws were once written in red, and *rubrum*, the species name of the maple indicating its red color, have the same Latin root: *ruber* (red).
37 Allusion to Isaiah 1:18: "Come now, and let us reason together, saith the Lord: though your sins be as scarlet, they shall be as white as snow; though they be red like crimson, they shall be as wool."
38 Allusion to Michaux's *North American Sylva;* cf. "Walking," note 62.

39 On 7 October 1857 Thoreau was crossing to Bear Garden Hill-side from Bartonia Meadow.
40 Parish officers in early New England whose duty it was to oversee the general morals.

a quarter of a mile off, so that you get the full effect of the bright colors, without detecting the imperfections of the leaves, and see their yellow, scarlet and crimson fires, of all tints, mingled and contrasted with the green. Some Maples are yet green, only yellow or crimson-tipped on the edges of their flakes, as the edges of a Hazel-Nut burr; some are wholly brilliant scarlet, raying out regularly and finely every way, bilaterally, like the veins of a leaf; others, of more irregular form, when I turn my head slightly, emptying out some of its earthiness and concealing the trunk of the tree, seem to rest heavily flake on flake, like yellow and scarlet clouds, wreath upon wreath, or like snow-drifts driving through the air, stratified by the wind. It adds greatly to the beauty of such a swamp at this season, that, even though there may be no other trees interspersed, it is not seen as a simple mass of color, but, different trees being of different colors and hues, the outline of each crescent tree-top is distinct, and where one laps on to another. Yet a painter would hardly venture to make them thus distinct a quarter of a mile off.

As I go across a meadow directly toward a low rising ground this bright afternoon,[39] I see, some fifty rods off toward the sun, the top of a Maple swamp just appearing over the sheeny russet edge of the hill, a stripe apparently twenty rods long by ten feet deep, of the most intensely brilliant scarlet, orange, and yellow, equal to any flowers or fruits, or any tints ever painted. As I advance, lowering the edge of the hill which makes the firm foreground or lower frame of the picture, the depth of the brilliant grove revealed steadily increases, suggesting that the whole of the inclosed valley is filled with such color. One wonders that the tithing-men[40] and fathers of the town are not out to see what the trees mean by their high colors and exuberance of spirits, fearing that some mischief is brewing. I do not see what the Puritans did at this season, when the Maples blaze out in scarlet. They certainly could not have worshipped in groves then. Perhaps that is what they built meeting-houses and fenced them round with horse-sheds for.

THE ELM

Now, too, the first of October, or later, the Elms are at the height of their autumnal beauty, great brownish-yellow masses, warm from their September oven, hanging over the highway. Their leaves are perfectly ripe. I wonder if there is any answering ripeness in the lives of the men who live beneath them. As I look down our street, which is lined with them, they remind me both by their form and color of yellowing sheaves of grain, as if the harvest had indeed come to the village itself, and we might expect to find some maturity and *flavor* in the thoughts of the villagers at last. Under those bright rustling yellow piles just ready to fall on the heads of the walkers, how can any crudity or greenness of thought or act prevail? When I stand where half a dozen large Elms droop over a house, it is as if I stood within a ripe pumpkin-rind, and I feel as mellow as if I were the pulp, though I may be somewhat stringy and seedy withal. What is the late greenness of the English Elm, like a cucumber out of season, which does not know when to have done, compared with the early and golden maturity of the American tree? The street is the scene of a great harvest-home.[41] It would be worth the while to set out these trees, if only for their autumnal value. Think of these great yellow canopies or parasols held over our heads and houses by the mile together, — making the village all one and compact, — an *ulmarium*,[42] which is at the same time a nursery of men! And then how gently and unobserved they drop their burden and let in the sun when it is wanted, their leaves not heard when they fall on our roofs and in our streets;

[41] Festival held to celebrate the completion of a harvest.
[42] A nursery, or plantation, of elm trees.

43 In his journal Thoreau wrote: "Is there, then, indeed, no thought under this ample husk of conversation and manners? There is the sermon husk, the lecture husk, and the book husk, and are they all only good to make mats of and tread under foot?" [J 10:79].

44 Dried or otherwise blighted.

45 Pig-corn is corn grown for animal consumption feed; cob-meal is ground corncobs.

46 Common axiom based on Galatians 6: "Whatsoever a man soweth, that shall he also reap."

47 A military command to lay arms on the ground using a series of prescribed movements.

and thus the village parasol is shut up and put away! I see the market-man driving into the village, and disappearing under its canopy of Elm-tops, with *his* crop, as into a great granary or barn-yard. I am tempted to go thither as to a husking of thoughts,[43] now dry and ripe, and ready to be separated from their integuments; but alas! I foresee that it will be chiefly husks and little thought, blasted[44] pig-corn, fit only for cob-meal,[45]— for as you sow, so shall you reap.[46]

FALLEN LEAVES

By the sixth of October the leaves generally begin to fall, in successive showers, after frost or rain; but the principal leaf-harvest, the acme of the *Fall,* is commonly about the sixteenth. Some morning at that date there is perhaps a harder frost than we have seen, and ice formed under the pump, and now, when the morning wind rises, the leaves come down in denser showers than ever. They suddenly form thick beds or carpets on the ground, in this gentle air, or even without wind, just the size and form of the tree above. Some trees, as small Hickories, appear to have dropped their leaves instantaneously, as a soldier grounds arms[47] at a signal; and those of the Hickory, being bright yellow still, though withered, reflect a blaze of light from the ground where they lie. Down they have come on all sides, at the first earnest touch of autumn's wand, making a sound like rain.

Or else it is after moist and rainy weather that we notice how great a fall of leaves there has been in the night, though it may not yet be the touch that loosens the Rock-Maple leaf. The streets are thickly strewn with the trophies, and fallen Elm-leaves make a dark brown pavement under our feet. After some remarkably warm Indian-summer day or days, I perceive that it is the unusual heat which, more than anything, causes the leaves to fall, there having been, perhaps, no frost nor rain for some time. The intense heat suddenly ripens and wilts them, just as it softens and ripens peaches and other fruits, and causes them to drop.

The leaves of late Red Maples, still bright, strew the earth, often crimson-spotted on a yellow ground, like some wild apples,[48]—though they preserve these bright colors on the ground but a day or two, especially if it rains. On causeways I go by trees here and there all bare and smoke-like,[49] having lost their brilliant clothing; but there it lies, nearly as bright as ever, on the ground on one side, and making nearly as regular a figure as lately on the tree. I would rather say that I first observe the trees thus flat on the ground like a permanent colored shadow, and they suggest to look for the boughs that bore them. A queen might be proud to walk where these gallant trees have spread their bright cloaks in the mud.[50] I see wagons roll over them as a shadow or a reflection, and the drivers heed them just as little as they did their shadows before.

Birds'-nests, in the Huckleberry and other shrubs, and in trees, are already being filled with the withered leaves. So many have fallen in the woods, that a squirrel cannot run after a falling nut without being heard. Boys are raking them in the streets, if only for the pleasure of dealing with such clean crisp substances. Some sweep the paths scrupulously neat, and then stand to see the next breath strew them with new trophies. The swamp-floor is thickly covered, and the *Lycopodium lucidulum*[51] looks suddenly greener amid them. In dense woods they half-cover pools that are three or four rods long. The other day I could hardly find a well-known spring,[52] and even suspected that it had dried up, for it was completely concealed by freshly fallen leaves; and when I swept them aside and revealed it, it was like striking the earth, with Aaron's rod,[53] for a new spring. Wet grounds about the

48 Cf. "Wild Apples," in which Thoreau described apples "freckled or peppered all over on the stem side with fine crimson spots on a white ground."
49 In his 1855 journal Thoreau wrote: "The maple swamps, bare of leaves, here and there about the meadow, look like smoke blown along the edge of the woods" [J 7:493].
50 Thoreau read Thomas Fuller's (1608–1661) account of Raleigh and Elizabeth I in *The works of Sir Walter Ralegh, Kt.*: "Her majesty meeting . . . with a plashy place, made some scruple to go on; when Ralegh (dressed in the gay and genteel habit of those times) presently cast off and spread his new plush cloak on the ground, whereon the queen trod gently over."
51 Species of club moss.
52 On 19 October 1853 Thoreau wrote: "On Sunday last, I could hardly find the Corner Spring" [J 5:441].
53 It was through Aaron's rod that many of the miracles in Exodus were performed. Here specifically Thoreau's allusion is to Numbers 20:11: "And Moses lifted up his hand, and with his rod he smote the rock twice: and the water came out abundantly, and the congregation drank, and their beasts also."

54 Beck Stow's Swamp.

55 Noted in his journal of 18 October 1853.

56 In his journal Thoreau described them as "on the Assabet, just round the Island under Naw-shawtuct Hill" [J 5:64].

57 River north of Concord that joins with the Sudbury River to form the Concord River.

edges of swamps look dry with them. At one swamp,[54] where I was surveying, thinking to step on a leafy shore from a rail, I got into the water more than a foot deep.

When I go to the river the day after the principal fall of leaves, the sixteenth,[55] I find my boat all covered, bottom and seats, with the leaves of the Golden Willow under which it is moored, and I set sail with a cargo of them rustling under my feet. If I empty it, it will be full again to-morrow. I do not regard them as litter, to be swept out, but accept them as suitable straw or matting for the bottom of my carriage. When I turn up into the mouth of the Assabet, which is wooded, large fleets of leaves are floating on its surface, as it were getting out to sea, with room to tack; but next the shore, a little farther up, they are thicker than foam, quite concealing the water for a rod in width, under and amid the Alders, Button-Bushes, and Maples, still perfectly light and dry, with fibre unrelaxed; and at a rocky bend where they are met and stopped by the morning wind, they sometimes form a broad and dense crescent quite across the river. When I turn my prow that way, and the wave which it makes strikes them, list what a pleasant rustling from these dry substances grating on one another! Often it is their undulation only which reveals the water beneath them. Also every motion of the wood-turtle on the shore is betrayed by their rustling there. Or even in mid-channel, when the wind rises, I hear them blown with a rustling sound. Higher up they are slowly moving round and round in some great eddy which the river makes, as that at the "Leaning Hemlocks,"[56] where the water is deep, and the current is wearing into the bank.

Perchance, in the afternoon of such a day, when the water is perfectly calm and full of reflections, I paddle gently down the main stream, and, turning up the Assabet,[57] reach a quiet cove, where I unexpectedly find myself surrounded by myriads of leaves, like fellow-voyagers, which seem to have the same purpose, or want of purpose, with myself. See this great fleet of scattered leaf-boats which we paddle amid, in this smooth river-bay, each one curled up on every side by the sun's skill, each nerve a stiff spruce-knee,[58]—like boats of hide, and of all patterns, Charon's boat[59] probably among the rest, and some with lofty prows and poops, like the stately vessels of the ancients, scarcely moving in the sluggish current,—like the great fleets, the dense Chinese cities of boats, with which you mingle on entering some great mart, some New York or Canton, which we are all steadily approaching together. How gently each has been deposited on the water! No violence has been used towards them yet, though, perchance, palpitating hearts were present at the launching. And painted ducks, too, the splendid wood-duck among the rest, often come to sail and float amid the painted leaves,—barks of a nobler model still!

What wholesome herb-drinks are to be had in the swamps now! What strong medicinal, but rich, scents from the decaying leaves! The rain falling on the freshly dried herbs and leaves, and filling the pools and ditches into which they have dropped thus clean and rigid, will soon convert them into tea,—green, black, brown and yellow teas, of all degrees of strength, enough to set all Nature a-gossiping. Whether we drink them or not, as yet, before their strength is drawn, these leaves, dried on great Nature's coppers,[60] are of such various pure and delicate tints as might make the fame of Oriental teas.

How they are mixed up, of all species, Oak, and Maple and Chestnut and Birch! But Nature is not cluttered with them; she is a perfect husbandman; she stores them all. Consider what a vast crop is thus annually shed on the earth! This, more than any mere grain or seed, is the great harvest of the year. The trees are now repaying the earth with interest what they have taken from it. They are

58 Piece of timber with an angular bend, used in shipbuilding to secure the beams of a ship to its sides.

59 Common name of the boat-shaped leaf *Cymbifolius;* cf. "Natural History of Massachusetts," note 72.

60 Large kettles or boilers, originally made of copper.

61 To count or to pay back again.

62 Mass of dung in a moist state or putrefied vegetable matter.

63 Haggle or negotiate over price; also, talk socially without exchanging much information.

64 Used as a method of branding.

65 Allusion to Philip Massinger's (1583–1640) *The Duke of Milan:* "Be wise, Soar not too high to fall, but stoop to rise."

66 Mourning clothes worn by widows.

discounting.[61] They are about to add a leaf's thickness to the depth of the soil. This is the beautiful way in which Nature gets her muck,[62] while I chaffer[63] with this man and that, who talks to me about sulphur and the cost of carting. We are all the richer for their decay. I am more interested in this crop than in the English grass alone or in the corn. It prepares the virgin mould for future cornfields and forests, on which the earth fattens. It keeps our homestead in good heart.

For beautiful variety no crop can be compared with this. Here is not merely the plain yellow of the grains, but nearly all the colors that we know, the brightest blue not excepted: the early blushing Maple, the Poison-Sumach blazing its sins as scarlet, the mulberry Ash, the rich chrome-yellow of the Poplars, the brilliant red Huckleberry, with which the hills' backs are painted, like those of sheep.[64] The frost touches them, and, with the slightest breath of returning day or jarring of earth's axle, see in what showers they come floating down! The ground is all party-colored with them. But they still live in the soil, whose fertility and bulk they increase, and in the forests that spring from it. They stoop to rise,[65] to mount higher in coming years, by subtle chemistry, climbing by the sap in the trees, and the sapling's first fruits thus shed, transmuted at last, may adorn its crown, when, in after-years, it has become the monarch of the forest.

It is pleasant to walk over the beds of these fresh, crisp, and rustling leaves. How beautifully they go to their graves! how gently lay themselves down and turn to mould!—painted of a thousand hues, and fit to make the beds of us living. So they troop to their last resting-place, light and frisky. They put on no weeds,[66] but merrily they go scampering over the earth, selecting the spot, choosing a lot, ordering no iron fence, whispering all through the woods about it,—some choosing the spot where the bodies of men are mouldering beneath, and meeting them half-way. How many flutterings before they rest quietly in their graves! They that soared so loftily, how contentedly they return to dust again, and are laid low, resigned to lie and decay at the foot of the tree, and afford nourishment to new generations of their kind, as well as to flutter on high! They teach us how to die. One wonders if the time will ever come when men, with their boasted faith in immortality, will lie down as gracefully and as ripe,—with such an Indian-summer serenity will shed their bodies, as they do their hair and nails.

When the leaves fall, the whole earth is a cemetery pleasant to walk in. I love to wander and muse over them in their graves. Here are no lying nor vain epitaphs. What though you own no lot at Mount Auburn?[67] Your lot is surely cast somewhere in this vast cemetery, which has been consecrated from of old. You need attend no auction to secure a place. There is room enough here. The Loosestrife shall bloom and the Huckleberry-bird[68] sing over your bones. The woodman and hunter shall be your sextons, and the children shall tread upon the borders as much as they will. Let us walk in the cemetery of the leaves,—this is your true Greenwood Cemetery.[69]

THE SUGAR-MAPLE

But think not that the splendor of the year is over; for as one leaf does not make a summer, neither does one fallen leaf make an autumn. The smallest Sugar-Maples in our streets make a great show as early as the fifth of October, more than any other trees there. As I look up the Main Street,[70] they appear like painted screens standing before the houses; yet many are green. But now, or generally by the seventeenth of October, when almost all Red Maples, and some White Maples, are bare, the large

67 Established in 1831 in Cambridge, Massachusetts, the first major landscaped cemetery, and part of the rural cemetery movement which, besides providing resting places for the dead, provided places of beauty and contemplation for the living.
68 *Spizella pusilla*, the field or rush sparrow.
69 The Green-Wood Cemetery, established in 1838 in Brooklyn, New York.
70 Thoreau was living at 255 Main Street, Concord, when this was written.

Sugar-Maples also are in their glory, glowing with yellow and red, and show unexpectedly bright and delicate tints. They are remarkable for the contrast they often afford of deep blushing red on one half and green on the other. They become at length dense masses of rich yellow with a deep scarlet blush, or more than blush, on the exposed surfaces. They are the brightest trees now in the street.

The large ones on our Common are particularly beautiful. A delicate, but warmer than golden yellow is now the prevailing color, with scarlet cheeks. Yet, standing on the east side of the Common just before sundown, when the western light is transmitted through them, I see that their yellow even, compared with the pale lemon yellow of an Elm close by, amounts to a scarlet, without noticing the bright scarlet portions. Generally, they are great regular oval masses of yellow and scarlet. All the sunny warmth of the season, the Indian summer, seems to be absorbed in their leaves. The lowest and inmost leaves next the bole are, as usual, of the most delicate yellow and green, like the complexion of young men brought up in the house. There is an auction on the Common to-day,[71] but its red flag is hard to be discerned amid this blaze of color.

Little did the fathers of the town anticipate this brilliant success, when they caused to be imported from farther in the country some straight poles with their tops cut off, which they called Sugar-Maples; and, as I remember, after they were set out, a neighboring merchant's clerk, by way of jest, planted beans about them. Those which were then jestingly called bean-poles are to-day far the most beautiful objects noticeable in our streets. They are worth all and more than they have cost,—though one of the selectmen, while setting them out, took the cold which occasioned his death,—if only because they have filled the open eyes of children with their rich color unstintedly so many Octobers. We will not ask them to yield us sugar in the spring, while they afford us so fair a prospect in the autumn. Wealth indoors may be the inheritance of few, but it is equally distributed on the Common. All children alike can revel in this golden harvest.

Surely trees should be set in our streets with a view to their October splendor; though I doubt whether this is ever considered by the "Tree Society."[72] Do you not think it will make some odds[73] to these children that they were brought up under the Maples? Hundreds of eyes are steadily drinking in this color, and by these teachers even the truants are caught and educated the moment they step abroad. Indeed, neither the truant nor the studious is at present taught color in the schools. These are instead of the bright colors in apothecaries' shops and city windows. It is a pity that we have no more *Red* Maples, and some Hickories, in our streets as well. Our paint-box is very imperfectly filled. Instead of, or beside, supplying such paint-boxes as we do, we might supply these natural colors to the young. Where else will they study color under greater advantages? What School of Design[74] can vie with this? Think how much the eyes of painters of all kinds, and of manufacturers of cloth and paper, and paper-stainers,[75] and countless others, are to be educated by these autumnal colors. The stationer's envelopes may be of very various tints, yet not so various as those of the leaves of a single tree. If you want a different shade or tint of a particular color, you have only to look farther within or without the tree or the wood. These leaves are not many dipped in one dye, as at the dye-house, but they are dyed in light of infinitely various degrees of strength, and left to set and dry there.

Shall the names of so many of our colors continue to be derived from those of obscure foreign localities, as Naples yellow,[76] Prussian blue,[77] raw Sienna,[78] burnt Umber,[79] Gamboge?[80] — (surely the Tyrian purple[81]

72 The Concord Ornamental Tree Society, founded in 1834.
73 Make a difference.
74 Philadelphia School of Design for Women, founded in 1848.
75 Makers of wallpapers.
76 Light yellow based on antimonite lead.
77 Royal blue based on ferro-cyanide of lead.
78 Yellow-brown ocherous earth from Italy.
79 Red-brown ocherous earth from Umbria, Italy.
80 Transparent yellow from plant resin.
81 Crimson from juices derived from various shellfish, so-named from its purported origin in Tyre, a city in ancient Phoenicia, and known for intensifying rather than fading over time.

82 A pigment derived from lapis lazuli, its name means "beyond the sea."

83 Keeper of cabinets of curiosities: cf. "A Winter Walk," note 41.

84 A man skilled or with strong interest in the fine arts or antiquities.

85 A woman of good birth having membership in a royal household as an attendant on a princess or queen.

86 In India, nabobs were provincial governors under the Mogul Empire; begums were ladies of rank, or princesses; and chobdars were members of a superior class of footmen.

87 Concord celebrated two gala days: the anniversary of the Concord fight of 1775 on 19 April and Independence Day on 4 July.

88 Gunpowder for the firing of ceremonial guns.

must have faded by this time)—or from comparatively trivial articles of commerce,—chocolate, lemon, coffee, cinnamon, claret?—(shall we compare our Hickory to a lemon, or a lemon to a Hickory?)—or from ores and oxides which few ever see? Shall we so often, when describing to our neighbors the color of something we have seen, refer them, not to some natural object in our neighborhood, but perchance to a bit of earth fetched from the other side of the planet, which possibly they may find at the apothecary's, but which probably neither they nor we ever saw? Have we not an *earth* under our feet,—ay, and a sky over our heads? Or is the last *all* ultramarine?[82] What do we know of sapphire, amethyst, emerald, ruby, amber, and the like,—most of us who take these names in vain? Leave these precious words to cabinet-keepers,[83] virtuosos,[84] and maids-of-honor,[85]— to the Nabobs, Begums, and Chobdars[86] of Hindostan, or wherever else. I do not see why, since America and her autumn woods have been discovered, our leaves should not compete with the precious stones in giving names to colors; and, indeed, I believe that in course of time the names of some of our trees and shrubs, as well as flowers, will get into our popular chromatic nomenclature.

But of much more importance than a knowledge of the names and distinctions of color is the joy and exhilaration which these colored leaves excite. Already these brilliant trees throughout the street, without any more variety, are at least equal to an annual festival and holiday, or a week of such. These are cheap and innocent gala-days,[87] celebrated by one and all without the aid of committees or marshals, such a show as may safely be licensed, not attracting gamblers nor rum-sellers, nor requiring any special police to keep the peace. And poor indeed must be that New-England village's October which has not the Maple in its streets. This October festival costs no powder,[88] nor ringing of bells, but every tree is a living liberty-pole[89] on which a thousand bright flags are waving.

No wonder that we must have our annual Cattle-Show, and Fall Training,[90] and perhaps Cornwallis,[91] our September Courts,[92] and the like. Nature herself holds her annual fair in October, not only in the streets, but in every hollow and on every hill-side. When lately we looked into that Red-Maple swamp all a-blaze, where the trees were clothed in their vestures of most dazzling tints, did it not suggest a thousand gypsies beneath,—a race capable of wild delight,—or even the fabled fawns, satyrs, and wood-nymphs come back to earth? Or was it only a congregation of wearied wood-choppers, or of proprietors come to inspect their lots, that we thought of? Or, earlier still, when we paddled on the river through that fine-grained September air, did there not appear to be something new going on under the sparkling surface of the stream, a shaking of props,[93] at least, so that we made haste in order to be up in time? Did not the rows of yellowing Willows and Button-Bushes on each side seem like rows of booths, under which, perhaps, some fluviatile egg-pop[94] equally yellow was effervescing? Did not all these suggest that man's spirits should rise as high as Nature's,—should hang out their flag, and the routine of his life be interrupted by an analogous expression of joy and hilarity?

No annual training or muster of soldiery, no celebration with its scarfs and banners, could import into the town a hundredth part of the annual splendor of our October. We have only to set the trees, or let them stand, and Nature will find the colored drapery,—flags of all her nations, some of whose private signals hardly the botanist can read,—while we walk under the triumphal arches[95] of the Elms. Leave it to Nature to appoint the days, whether the same as in neighboring States or not, and let the clergy read her proclamations, if they

89 A tall flagpole to the top of which a liberty cap or the flag of a new republic is attached. Liberty poles were erected in town squares, including that of Concord, in the years before and during the American Revolutionary War.

90 Thoreau described a May training on 27 May 1857: "Some thirty young men are marching in the streets in two straight sections, with each a very heavy and warm cap for the season on his head and a bright red stripe down the legs of his pantaloons, and at their head march two with white stripes down their pants, one beating a drum, the other blowing a fife. I see them all standing in a row by the side of the street in front of their captain's residence, with a dozen or more ragged boys looking on. . . . Thus they march and strut the better part of the clay, going into the tavern two or three times, to abandon themselves to unconstrained positions out of sight, and at night they may be seen going home singly with swelling breasts" [J 9:381–382].

91 Military muster commemorating the end of the American Revolution by the surrender of Charles Cornwallis (1738–1805) at Yorktown on 19 October 1781.

92 The Concord resident Edward Jarvis (1803–1884) wrote that the Court of Common Pleas, which sat during the second week of September, was "a great fair, an occasion for the assemblage of the gay, the fun-loving, the rowdies, and the people who for the time were willing to play the rowdy."

93 Gambling game popular in the 1850s in Boston involving the shaking and tossing of small white seashells which were partially ground down and filled with red wax. Four of these dicelike shells were thrown, the stake being won dependent on the number of red sides were showing.

94 A kind of eggnog.

95 First introduced by ancient Romans, arches in commemoration of a military victory.

96 Allusion to Milton's "Lycidas" 1–2: "Yet once more, O ye Laurels, and once more / Ye Myrtles brown, and Ivy never-sear."

97 Concord, as Thoreau wrote in his journal of 18 October 1858. In the *Atlantic Monthly,* and elsewhere, references to persons or places were often reduced to an initial.

can understand them. Behold what a brilliant drapery is her Woodbine flag! What public-spirited merchant, think you, has contributed this part of the show? There is no handsomer shingling and paint than this vine, at present covering a whole side of some houses. I do not believe that the Ivy *never sear*[96] is comparable to it. No wonder it has been extensively introduced into London. Let us have a good many Maples and Hickories and Scarlet Oaks, then, I say. Blaze away! Shall that dirty roll of bunting in the gun-house be all the colors a village can display? A village is not complete, unless it have these trees to mark the season in it. They are important, like the town-clock. A village that has them not will not be found to work well. It has a screw loose, an essential part is wanting. Let us have Willows for spring, Elms for summer, Maples and Walnuts and Tupeloes for autumn, Evergreens for winter, and Oaks for all seasons. What is a gallery in a house to a gallery in the streets, which every market-man rides through, whether he will or not? Of course, there is not a picture-gallery in the country which would be worth so much to us as is the western view at sunset under the Elms of our main street. They are the frame to a picture which almost daily is painted behind them. An avenue of Elms as large as our largest and three miles long would seem to lead to some admirable place, though only C———[97] were at the end of it.

A village needs these innocent stimulants of bright and cheering prospects to keep off melancholy and superstition. Show me two villages, one embowered in trees and blazing with all the glories of October, the other a merely trivial and treeless waste, or with only a single tree or two for suicides, and I shall be sure that in the latter will be found the most starved and bigoted religionists and the most desperate drinkers. Every wash-tub and milk-can and gravestone will be exposed. The inhabitants will disappear abruptly behind their barns and houses, like desert Arabs amid their rocks, and I shall look to see spears in their hands. They will be ready to accept the most barren and forlorn doctrine,—as that the world is speedily coming to an end, or has already got to it, or that they themselves are turned wrong side outward. They will perchance crack their dry joints at one another and call it a spiritual communication.[98]

But to confine ourselves to the Maples. What if we were to take half as much pains in protecting them as we do in setting them out,—not stupidly tie our horses to our dahlia-stems?

What meant the fathers by establishing this *perfectly living*[99] institution before the church,—this institution which needs no repairing nor repainting, which is continually enlarged and repaired[100] by its growth? Surely they

"Wrought in a sad sincerity;
Themselves from God they could not free;
They *planted* better than they knew;—
The conscious *trees* to beauty grew."[101]

Verily these Maples are cheap preachers, permanently settled,[102] which preach their half-century, and century, aye and century-and-a-half sermons, with constantly increasing unction and influence, ministering to many generations of men; and the least we can do is to supply them with suitable colleagues as they grow infirm.

THE SCARLET OAK

Belonging to a genus which is remarkable for the beautiful form of its leaves, I suspect that some Scarlet-Oak leaves surpass those of all other Oaks in the rich and wild beauty of their outlines. I judge from an acquaintance

98 Considered as signs of a spiritual presence. Thoreau wrote to his sister Sophia on 13 July 1852 about "idiots inspired by the cracking of a restless board, humbly asking, 'Please, Spirit, if you cannot answer by knocks, answer by tips of the table'!!!!!!" [C 284].

99 Living in the way of God, as in Matthew 5:48: "Be perfect, therefore, as your heavenly Father is perfect."

100 In his journal of 18 October 1858 Thoreau placed this phrase, often used in town or church documents, in quotation marks.

101 Quoted, with variants, from Emerson's "The Problem" 21–25, in which "the hand that rounded Peter's dome"

Wrought in a sad sincerity;
Himself from God he could not free;
He builded better than he knew;—
The conscious stone to beauty grew.

102 Established or fixed, and called by the congregation to be their minister, as opposed to occasional or interim.

103 Asa Gray's (1810–1888) *Manual of Botany of the Northern United States* (Boston: Monroe, 1848), which Thoreau owned, lists eighteen species. From his journal references he was most acquainted with the following oaks: black, chestnut, dwarf chinquapin, mossy-cup or bur, pin, red, scarlet, shingle, scrub, swamp white, white, and willow.

104 Latin: solid ground.

105 Allusion to Milton's "L'Allegro": "Come and trip it as ye go, / On the light fantastick toe."

106 Thoreau's note, referring to the illustration which originally appeared on page 398 of the *Atlantic Monthly*, October 1862: "The original of the leaf copied on the next page was picked from such a pile."

with twelve species,[103] and from drawings which I have seen of many others.

Stand under this tree and see how finely its leaves are cut against the sky,—as it were, only a few sharp points extending from a midrib. They look like double, treble, or quadruple crosses. They are far more ethereal than the less deeply scolloped Oak-leaves. They have so little leafy *terra firma*[104] that they appear melting away in the light, and scarcely obstruct our view. The leaves of very young plants are, like those of full-grown Oaks of other species, more entire, simple, and lumpish in their outlines, but these, raised high on old trees, have solved the leafy problem. Lifted higher and higher, and sublimated more and more, putting off some earthiness and cultivating more intimacy with the light each year, they have at length the least possible amount of earthy matter, and the greatest spread and grasp of skyey influences. There they dance, arm in arm with the light,—tripping it on fantastic points,[105] fit partners in those aërial halls. So intimately mingled are they with it, that, what with their slenderness and their glossy surfaces, you can hardly tell at last what in the dance is leaf and what is light. And when no zephyr stirs, they are at most but a rich tracery to the forest-windows.

I am again struck with their beauty, when, a month later they thickly strew the ground in the woods, piled one upon another under my feet. They are then brown above, but purple beneath. With their narrow lobes and their bold deep scollops reaching almost to the middle, they suggest that the material must be cheap, or else there has been a lavish expense in their creation, as if so much had been cut out. Or else they seem to us the remnants of the stuff out of which leaves have been cut with a die. Indeed, when they lie thus one upon another, they remind me of a pile of scrap-tin.[106]

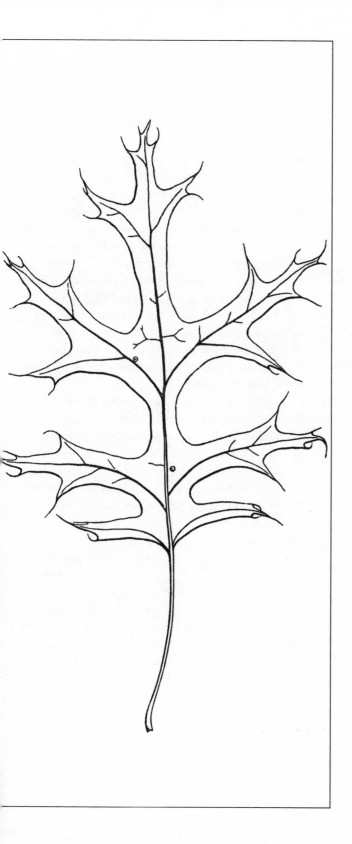

107 A type is the model or form of a letter in metal used in printing; a font is a complete assortment of printing types of one size and style. Oxford University has been associated with printing since the late fifteenth century.

108 Language of the Basques of southern France and northern Spain.

109 Cuneiform script of ancient Sumeria, Assyria, and Persia, called "arrow-headed" from each letter being formed by marks or elements resembling an arrow-head or a wedge.

110 A tablet containing Greek, Egyptian hieroglyphics, and demotic script, which provided the necessary key to deciphering the hieroglyphics.

111 Openings, hollows, or recesses.

112 Cf. "Walking," note 147.

113 Firths: long narrow inlets.

114 Dionysius Periegetes (fourth century C.E.), author of *Oikumenes Periegesis,* and Pliny the Elder, Gaius Plinius Secundus (23–79), Roman historian and naturalist and author of *Naturalis Historia.*

The following comparison is an allusion to Loudon's *Arboretum et Fruticetum Britannicum* (cf. "An Address on the Succession of Forest Trees," note 9): "Dionysius the geographer compares the form of the Morea in the Levant, the ancient Peloponnesus, to the leaf of this tree; and Pliny makes the same remark in allusion to its numerous bays."

115 Southern Grecian peninsula.

116 *Platanus orientalis,* related to the American sycamore or buttonwood, *Platanus occidentalis.*

117 In the nineteenth century, adventurers who organized and led armed expeditions into a foreign country, especially in search of plunder.

Or bring one home, and study it closely at your leisure, by the fireside. It is a type, not from any Oxford font,[107] not in the Basque[108] nor the arrow-headed character,[109] not found on the Rosetta Stone,[110] but destined to be copied in sculpture one day, if they ever get to whittling stone here. What a wild and pleasing outline, a combination of graceful curves and angles! The eye rests with equal delight on what is not leaf and on what is leaf,—on the broad, free, open sinuses,[111] and on the long, sharp, bristle-pointed lobes. A simple oval outline would include it all, if you connected the points of the leaf; but how much richer is it than that, with its half-dozen deep scollops, in which the eye and thought of the beholder are embayed![112] If I were a drawing-master, I would set my pupils to copying these leaves, that they might learn to draw firmly and gracefully.

Regarded as water, it is like a pond with half a dozen broad rounded promontories extending nearly to its middle, half from each side, while its watery bays extend far inland, like sharp friths,[113] at each of whose heads several fine streams empty in,—almost a leafy archipelago.

But it oftener suggests land, and, as Dionysius and Pliny[114] compared the form of the Morea[115] to that of the leaf of the Oriental Plane-tree,[116] so this leaf reminds me of some fair wild island in the ocean, whose extensive coast, alternate rounded bays with smooth strands, and sharp-pointed rocky capes, mark it as fitted for the habitation of man, and destined to become a centre of civilization at last. To the sailor's eye, it is a much-indented shore. Is it not, in fact, a shore to the aërial ocean, on which the windy surf beats? At sight of this leaf we are all mariners,—if not vikings, buccaneers, and filibusters.[117] Both our love of repose and our spirit of adventure are addressed. In our most casual glance, perchance, we think, that, if we succeed in doubling those sharp capes, we shall find deep, smooth, and secure havens in the ample bays. How different from the White-Oak leaf, with its rounded headlands, on which no light-house need be placed! That is an England, with its long civil history, that may be read. This is some still unsettled New-found Island[118] or Celebes.[119] Shall we go and be rajahs there?

By the twenty-sixth of October the large Scarlet Oaks are in their prime, when other Oaks are usually withered. They have been kindling their fires for a week past, and now generally burst into a blaze. This alone of *our* indigenous deciduous trees (excepting the Dogwood, of which I do not know half a dozen, and they are but large bushes) is now in its glory. The two Aspens[120] and the Sugar-Maple come nearest to it in date, but they have lost the greater part of their leaves. Of evergreens, only the Pitch-Pine is still commonly bright.

But it requires a particular alertness, if not devotion to these phenomena, to appreciate the wide-spread, but late and unexpected glory of the Scarlet Oaks. I do not speak here of the small trees and shrubs, which are commonly observed, and which are now withered, but of the large trees. Most go in and shut their doors, thinking that bleak and colorless November has already come, when some of the most brilliant and memorable colors are not yet lit.

This very perfect and vigorous one, about forty feet high, standing in an open pasture, which was quite glossy green on the twelfth, is now, the twenty-sixth, completely changed to bright dark scarlet,—every leaf, between you and the sun, as if it had been dipped into a scarlet dye. The whole tree is much like a heart in form, as well as color. Was not this worth waiting for? Little did you think, ten days ago, that that cold green tree would assume such color as this. Its leaves are still firmly attached, while those of other trees are falling around it. It

118 Possible reference to Newfoundland, Canada, but more likely used as a generic name for any land newly found.

119 Island off central Indonesia.

120 There is no previous mention of the "two Aspens." This is one of the errors which Thoreau did not have time to correct when he redacted his lecture for publication; see "Wild Apples," note 58. In his journal of 1 November 1858 he wrote that the trees "now cannot easily be mistaken for any other, because they are the only conspicuously yellow trees now left in the woods, except a very few aspens of both kinds," and follows it on 5 November with "Judging from the two aspens, this tree, and the willows, one would say that the earliest trees to leaf were, perhaps, the last to lose their leaves" [J 11:271, 288].

seems to say,—"I am the last to blush, but I blush deeper than any of ye. I bring up the rear in my red coat. We Scarlet ones, alone of Oaks, have not given up the fight."

The sap is now, and even far into November, frequently flowing fast in these trees, as in Maples in the spring; and apparently their bright tints, now that most other Oaks are withered, are connected with this phenomenon. They are full of life. It has a pleasantly astringent, acorn-like taste, this strong Oak-wine, as I find on tapping them with my knife.

Looking across this woodland valley, a quarter of a mile wide, how rich those Scarlet Oaks, embosomed in Pines, their bright red branches intimately intermingled with them! They have their full effect there. The Pine-boughs are the green calyx to their red petals. Or, as we go along a road in the woods, the sun striking endwise through it, and lighting up the red tents of the Oaks, which on each side are mingled with the liquid green of the Pines, makes a very gorgeous scene. Indeed, without the evergreens for contrast, the autumnal tints would lose much of their effect.

The Scarlet Oak asks a clear sky and the brightness of late October days. These bring out its colors. If the sun goes into a cloud, they become comparatively indistinct. As I sit on a cliff [121] in the southwest part of our town, the sun is now getting low, and the woods in Lincoln, south and east of me, are lit up by its more level rays; and in the Scarlet Oaks, scattered so equally over the forest, there is brought out a more brilliant redness than I had believed was in them. Every tree of this species which is visible in those directions, even to the horizon, now stands out distinctly red. Some great ones lift their red backs high above the woods, in the next town, like huge roses with a myriad of fine petals; and some more slender ones, in a small grove of White Pines on Pine Hill [122] in the east, on the very verge of the horizon, alternating

121 Lee's Cliff, one and a half miles southwest of Walden Pond.
122 Pine Hill in Lincoln, Massachusetts.

with the Pines on the edge of the grove, and shouldering them with their red coats, look like soldiers in red amid hunters in green. This time it is Lincoln green, too.[123] Till the sun got low, I did not believe that there were so many redcoats in the forest army. Theirs is an intense burning red, which would lose some of its strength, me-thinks, with every step you might take toward them; for the shade that lurks amid their foliage does not report itself at this distance, and they are unanimously red. The focus of their reflected color is in the atmosphere far on this side. Every such tree becomes a nucleus of red, as it were, where, with the declining sun, that color grows and glows. It is partly borrowed fire, gathering strength from the sun on its way to your eye. It has only some comparatively dull red leaves for a rallying-point, or kindling-stuff, to start it, and it becomes an intense scarlet or red mist, or fire, which finds fuel for itself in the very atmosphere. So vivacious is redness. The very rails reflect a rosy light at this hour and season. You see a redder tree than exists.

If you wish to count the Scarlet Oaks, do it now. In a clear day stand thus on a hill-top in the woods, when the sun is an hour high, and every one within range of your vision, excepting in the west, will be revealed. You might live to the age of Methuselah[124] and never find a tithe[125] of them, otherwise. Yet sometimes even in a dark day I have thought them as bright as I ever saw them. Looking westward, their colors are lost in a blaze of light; but in other directions the whole forest is a flower-garden, in which these late roses burn, alternating with green, while the so-called "gardeners," walking here and there, per-chance, beneath, with spade and water-pot, see only a few little asters amid withered leaves.

These are *my* China-asters,[126] *my* late garden-flowers. It costs me nothing for a gardener. The falling leaves, all over the forest, are protecting the roots of my plants.

123 Allusion to the location of Pine Hill but also to the color of cloth made in Lincoln, England, and worn by those who frequented the woods, such as hunters and outlaws, the most famous of whom was Robin Hood.
124 According to Genesis 5:27: "All the days of Methuselah were 969 years and he died."
125 One tenth.
126 *Callistephus chinensis.*

127 Island in the Saint Lawrence River, near Quebec.

128 In *A Yankee in Canada, with Anti-Slavery and Reform Papers,* Thoreau wrote: "They were exceedingly fair and glossy . . . but they were as hard almost as a stone, as if the season was too short to mellow them. . . . I declined eating one, much as I admired it, observing that it would be good *dans le printemps,* in the spring" [W 5:61].

129 Paint came as a block that was ground to a powder and mixed with oil.

130 Lowered or impaired in quality.

Only look at what is to be seen, and you will have garden enough, without deepening the soil in your yard. We have only to elevate our view a little, to see the whole forest as a garden. The blossoming of the Scarlet Oak,— the forest-flower, surpassing all in splendor (at least since the Maple)! I do not know but they interest me more than the Maples, they are so widely and equally dispersed throughout the forest; they are so hardy, a nobler tree on the whole;—our chief November flower, abiding the approach of winter with us, imparting warmth to early November prospects. It is remarkable that the latest bright color that is general should be this deep, dark scarlet and red, the intensest of colors. The ripest fruit of the year; like the cheek of a hard, glossy, red apple from the cold Isle of Orleans,[127] which will not be mellow for eating till next spring![128] When I rise to a hill-top, a thousand of these great Oak roses, distributed on every side, as far as the horizon! I admire them four or five miles off! This my unfailing prospect for a fortnight past! This late forest-flower surpasses all that spring or summer could do. Their colors were but rare and dainty specks comparatively, (created for the near-sighted, who walk amid the humblest herbs and under-woods,) and made no impression on a distant eye. Now it is an extended forest or a mountain-side, through or along which we journey from day to day, that bursts into bloom. Comparatively, our gardening is on a petty scale,—the gardener still nursing a few asters amid dead weeds, ignorant of the gigantic asters and roses, which, as it were, overshadow him, and ask for none of his care. It is like a little red paint ground on a saucer,[129] and held up against the sunset sky. Why not take more elevated and broader views, walk in the great garden, not skulk in a little "debauched"[130] nook of it? consider the beauty of the forest, and not merely of a few impounded herbs?

Let your walks now be a little more adventurous; as-cend the hills. If, about the last of October, you ascend any hill in the outskirts of our town, and probably of yours, and look over the forest, you may see——well, what I have endeavored to describe. All this you surely *will* see, and much more, if you are prepared to see it,—if you *look* for it. Otherwise, regular and universal as this phenomenon is, whether you stand on the hill-top or in the hollow, you will think for threescore years and ten[131] that all the wood is, at this season, sear and brown. Ob-jects are concealed from our view, not so much because they are out of the course of our visual ray as because we do not bring our minds and eyes to bear on them; for there is no power to see in the eye itself, any more than in any other jelly. We do not realize how far and widely, or how near and narrowly, we are to look. The greater part of the phenomena of Nature are for this reason con-cealed from us all our lives. The gardener sees only the gardener's garden. Here, too, as in political economy, the supply answers to the demand.[132] Nature does not cast pearls before swine.[133] There is just as much beauty visible to us in the landscape as we are prepared to ap-preciate,—not a grain more. The actual objects which one man will see from a particular hill-top are just as different from those which another will see as the be-holders are different.[134] The Scarlet Oak must, in a sense, be in your eye when you go forth. We cannot see any-thing until we are possessed with the idea of it, take it into our heads,—and then we can hardly see anything else. In my botanical rambles, I find, that, first, the idea, or image, of a plant occupies my thoughts, though it may seem very foreign to this locality,—no nearer than Hudson's Bay,[135]—and for some weeks or months I go thinking of it, and expecting it, unconsciously, and at length I surely see it. This is the history of my finding a

131 Allusion to Psalms 90:10: "The days of our years are three-score and ten."

132 Thoreau contrasts the economic theory de-veloped as Say's Law, or Say's Law of Economics, from a principle attributed to French businessman and economist Jean-Baptiste Say (1767–1832) stating that supply creates demand. Thoreau wrote in his journal: "The beauty of the earth answers exactly to your demand and appreciation" [J 11:278].

133 Allusion to Matthew 7:6: "Give not that which is holy unto the dogs, neither cast ye your pearls before swine, lest they trample them under their feet, and turn and rend you."

134 As Thoreau wrote in 1858: "It was a new light when my guide gave me Indian names for things for which I had only scientific ones before. In pro-portion as I understood the language, I saw them from a new point of view" [J 10:295].

135 Large bay in northeastern Canada, connected to the Atlantic Ocean.

136 Family name of rushes and grasses, respectively.

137 Elected governing official of a town.

138 From the German, *Brockengespenst,* a mountain specter, so-named from being first observed in 1780 on the Brocken in the Harz Mountains, but actually an optical phenomenon which can occur at high altitudes when the shape of an observer placed between the sun and a cloud is cast as a magnified shadow.

139 Emanuel Swedenborg (1688–1722), Swedish scientist, theologian, and mystic, about whom Emerson wrote in *Representative Men.*

140 Now Fiji.

score or more of rare plants, which I could name. A man sees only what concerns him. A botanist absorbed in the study of grasses does not distinguish the grandest Pasture Oaks. He, as it were, tramples down Oaks unwittingly in his walk, or at most sees only their shadows. I have found that it required a different intention of the eye, in the same locality, to see different plants, even when they were closely allied, as *Juncaceae* and *Gramineae:*[136] when I was looking for the former, I did not see the latter in the midst of them. How much more, then, it requires different intentions of the eye and of the mind to attend to different departments of knowledge! How differently the poet and the naturalist look at objects!

Take a New-England selectman,[137] and set him on the highest of our hills, and tell him to look,—sharpening his sight to the utmost, and putting on the glasses that suit him best, (ay, using a spy-glass, if he likes,)—and make a full report. What, probably, will he *spy?*—what will he *select* to look at? Of course, he will see a Brocken spectre of himself.[138] He will see several meeting-houses, at least, and, perhaps, that somebody ought to be assessed higher than he is, since he has so handsome a wood-lot. Now take Julius Caesar, or Emanuel Swedenborg,[139] or a Fegee-Islander,[140] and set him up there. Or suppose all together, and let them compare notes afterward. Will it appear that they have enjoyed the same prospect? What they will see will be as different as Rome was from Heaven or Hell, or the last from the Fegee Islands. For aught we know, as strange a man as any of these is always at our elbow.

Why, it takes a sharp-shooter to bring down even such trivial game as snipes and woodcocks; he must take very particular aim, and know what he is aiming at. He would stand a very small chance, if he fired at random into the sky, being told that snipes were flying there. And so is it with him that shoots at beauty; though he wait till the sky falls, he will not bag any, if he does not already know its seasons and haunts, and the color of its wing, — if he has not dreamed of it, so that he can *anticipate* it; then, indeed, he flushes it at every step, shoots double and on the wing, with both barrels, even in cornfields. The sportsman trains himself, dresses and watches unweariedly, and loads and primes for his particular game. He prays for it, and offers sacrifices, and so he gets it. After due and long preparation, schooling his eye and hand, dreaming awake and asleep, with gun and paddle and boat he goes out after meadow-hens,[141] which most of his townsmen never saw nor dreamed of, and paddles for miles against a head-wind, and wades in water up to his knees, being out all day without his dinner, and *therefore* he gets them. He had them half-way into his bag when he started, and has only to shove them down. The true sportsman can shoot you almost any of his game from his windows: what else has he windows or eyes for? It comes and perches at last on the barrel of his gun; but the rest of the world never see it *with the feathers on*. The geese fly exactly under his zenith, and honk when they get there, and he will keep himself supplied by firing up his chimney; twenty musquash have the refusal of each one of his traps before it is empty. If he lives, and his game-spirit increases, heaven and earth shall fail him sooner than game; and when he dies, he will go to more extensive, and, perchance, happier hunting-grounds. The fisherman, too, dreams of fish, sees a bobbing cork in his dreams, till he can almost catch them in his sink-spout. I knew a girl who, being sent to pick huckle-berries, picked wild gooseberries by the quart, where no one else knew that there were any, because she was accustomed to pick them up country where she came from.[142] The astronomer knows where to go star-gathering, and

141 Thoreau identified the meadow-hen as the Virginia rail (*Rallus Virginianus*) [J 5:259], now *Rallus limicola*.
142 Unidentified.

sees one clearly in his mind before any have seen it with a glass. The hen scratches and finds her food right under where she stands; but such is not the way with the hawk.

These bright leaves which I have mentioned are not the exception, but the rule; for I believe that all leaves, even grasses and mosses, acquire brighter colors just before their fall. When you come to observe faithfully the changes of each humblest plant, you find that each has, sooner or later, its peculiar autumnal tint; and if you undertake to make a complete list of the bright tints, it will be nearly as long as a catalogue of the plants in your vicinity.

Wild Apples

THE HISTORY OF THE APPLE-TREE

It is remarkable how closely the history of the Apple-tree is connected with that of man. The geologist tells us that the order of the *Rosaceae*,[1] which includes the Apple, also the true Grasses, and the *Labiatae*, or Mints, were introduced only a short time previous to the appearance of man on the globe.[2]

It appears that apples made a part of the food of that unknown primitive people whose traces have lately been found at the bottom of the Swiss lakes, supposed to be older than the foundation of Rome, so old that they had no metallic implements. An entire black and shrivelled Crab-Apple has been recovered from their stores.[3]

Tacitus says of the ancient Germans, that they satisfied their hunger with wild apples (*agrestia poma*) among other things.[4]

Niebuhr observes that "the words for a house, a field, a plough, ploughing, wine, oil, milk, sheep, apples, and others relating to agriculture and the gentler ways of life, agree in Latin and Greek, while the Latin words for all objects pertaining to war or the chase are utterly alien from the Greek."[5] Thus the apple-tree may be considered a symbol of peace no less than the olive.

The apple was early so important, and generally distributed, that its name traced to its root in many languages signifies fruit in general. $M\hat{\eta}\lambda o\nu$, in Greek, means an apple, also the fruit of other trees, also a sheep and any cattle, and finally riches in general.

1 Rose family.
2 Allusion to Louis Agassiz (cf. "An Address on the Succession of Forest Trees," note 5), from Hugh Miller's (1802–1856) *The Testimony of the Rocks; or, Geology in Its Bearing on Two Theologies, Natural and Revealed:* "Agassiz, whose statements must be received with respect by every student of the science, finds reason to conclude that the order of Rosaceae . . . was introduced only a short time previous to the appearance of man."
3 Thoreau's source about the lacustrine habitations near Zurich, Switzerland, is unknown.
4 Allusion to Cornelius Tacitus's (ca. 55–ca. 120 c.e.) *Germania* 23. Thoreau's source was the three-volume *Cornelii Taciti Opera ex Recensione Io.*
5 Quoted from Barthold Georg Niebuhr's (1776–1831) *The History of Rome*, with variants: "It cannot be mere chance, that the words for *a house, a field, a plough, ploughing, wine, oil, milk, kine, swine, sheep, apples,* and others relating to agriculture and gentler ways of life, should agree in Latin and Greek; while the Latin words for all objects pertaining to war or the chase are utterly alien from the Greek."

6 In Genesis 3:3 the "fruit of the tree which is in the midst of the garden" with which Eve was tempted is, in the popular tradition, called an apple.

7 A golden apple inscribed "to the fairest," in Greek mythology, was tossed by Eris, the goddess of Discord, to the guests the wedding of Peleus and Thetis, causing rivalry between Athena, Aphrodite, and Hera and which precipitated the Trojan War.

8 In Greek mythology, Hercules, in order to be released from his servitude to Eurystheus, had to complete twelve seemingly impossible labors, one of which was to bring Eurystheus a golden apple from the Garden of the Hesperides, guarded by a never-sleeping hundred-headed dragon.

9 Quoted from Song of Solomon 2:3.

10 Quoted from Song of Solomon 2:5.

11 Quoted from Psalms 17:8.

12 Greek historian (fifth century B.C.E.).

13 In Greek mythology, king of Phaeacia and father of Nausicaä, who, in Homer's *Odyssey*, aided Odysseus in his return home to Ithaca.

14 Thoreau's translation from Book XI of Homer's *Odyssey*.

15 In the *Odyssey* 7:112–121 Tantalus was condemned to hang from a tree in the underworld as a punishment for deceiving the gods. Thirsty and hungry, when he stretched to reach the pool of water beneath the tree, the pool dried up; when he reached for the fruit which hung above him, the wind lifted the branches just beyond reach.

16 Allusion to Theophrastus, author of *De Causis Plantarum*, of whom Thoreau wrote: "I find that the signs of the weather in Theophrastus are repeated by many more recent writers without being referred to him or through him; *e.g.*, by an authority quoted by Brand in his 'Popular Antiquities,' who evidently does not know that they are in Theophrastus" [J 13:240].

17 The Prose Edda (ca. eleventh to twelfth century), the younger of the two Eddas, collections of old Norse myths and legends, collected from

The apple-tree has been celebrated by the Hebrews, Greeks, Romans, and Scandinavians. Some have thought that the first human pair were tempted by its fruit.[6] Goddesses are fabled to have contended for it,[7] dragons were set to watch it, and heroes employed to pluck it.[8]

The tree is mentioned in at least three places in the Old Testament, and its fruit in two or three more. Solomon sings,—"As the apple-tree among the trees of the wood, so is my beloved among the sons."[9] And again,—"Stay me with flagons, comfort me with apples."[10] The noblest part of man's noblest feature is named from this fruit, the "apple of the eye."[11]

The apple-tree is also mentioned by Homer and Herodotus.[12] Ulysses saw in the glorious garden of Alcinoüs[13] "pears and pomegranates, and apple-trees bearing beautiful fruit" καὶ μηλέαι ἀγλαόκαρποι.[14] And according to Homer, apples were among the fruits which Tantalus could not pluck, the wind ever blowing their boughs away from him.[15] Theophrastus knew and described the apple-tree as a botanist.[16]

According to the Prose Edda,[17] "Iduna keeps in a box the apples which the gods, when they feel old age approaching, have only to taste of to become young again. It is in this manner that they will be kept in renovated youth until Ragnarök"[18] (or the destruction of the gods).

I learn from Loudon that "the ancient Welsh bards were rewarded for excelling in song by the token of the apple-spray";[19] and "in the Highlands of Scotland the apple-tree is the badge of the clan Lamont."[20]

The apple-tree (*Pyrus malus*) belongs chiefly to the northern temperate zone. Loudon says, that it "grows spontaneously in every part of Europe except the frigid zone, and throughout Western Asia, China, and Japan."[21] We have also two or three varieties of the apple indigenous in North America.[22] The cultivated apple-tree was first introduced into this country by the earliest settlers,[23] and it is thought to do as well or better here than anywhere else. Probably some of the varieties which are now cultivated were first introduced into Britain by the Romans.

Pliny, adopting the distinction of Theophrastus, says, — "Of trees there are some which are altogether wild (*sylvestres*), some more civilized (*urbaniores*)."[24] Theophrastus includes the apple among the last; and, indeed, it is in this sense the most civilized of all trees. It is as harmless as a dove, as beautiful as a rose, and as valuable as flocks and herds. It has been longer cultivated than any other, and so is more humanized; and who knows but, like the dog, it will at length be no longer traceable to its wild original? It migrates with man, like the dog and horse and cow: first, perchance, from Greece to Italy, thence to England, thence to America; and our Western emigrant is still marching steadily toward the setting sun with the seeds of the apple in his pocket, or perhaps a few young trees strapped to his load. At least a million apple-trees are thus set farther westward this year than any cultivated ones grew last year. Consider how the Blossom-Week,[25] like the Sabbath, is thus annually spreading over the prairies; for when man migrates, he carries with him not only his birds, quadrupeds, insects, vegetables, and his very sward, but his orchard also.

The leaves and tender twigs are an agreeable food to many domestic animals, as the cow, horse, sheep, and goat; and the fruit is sought after by the first, as well as by the hog. Thus there appears to have existed a natural alliance between these animals and this tree from the first. "The fruit of the Crab in the forests of France" is said to be "a great resource for the wild-boar."[26]

Not only the Indian, but many indigenous insects, birds, and quadrupeds, welcomed the apple-tree to these shores. The tent-caterpillar saddled her eggs on the very first twig that was formed, and it has since shared her af-

oral tradition by Snorri Sturluson in the twelfth century.

18 Quoted from the Prose Edda: Gylfaginning XXVI. Iduna, "The Rejuvenating One," was the goddess of spring who tended the Apples of Immortality in her garden. Ragnarök: Old Norse for "twilight of the gods."

19 Quoted from Loudon's *Arboretum et Fruticetum Britannicum* (cf. "An Address on the Succession of Forest Trees," note 9).

20 Quoted from Loudon's *Arboretum et Fruticetum Britannicum*.

21 Quoted from Loudon's *Arboretum et Fruticetum Britannicum*: "The apple grows spontaneously in every part of Europe, except the torrid zone. It is found throughout Western Asia, China, and Japan." Thoreau corrected Loudon's error of "torrid" zone in reference to Europe which is almost entirely in the temperate zone.

22 Thoreau's correction of Loudon, the next line of the above quotation being: "but not in North America, unless we consider *P. coronaria* as a variety of *P. Málus*."

23 The Pilgrims, as well as Jesuit and Franciscan missionaries, brought seeds and small trees.

24 Allusion to *The Natural History of Pliny* XXXII:19: "There are some trees that are altogether of a wild nature, while there are others, again, that are more civilized, such being the names by which man has thought fit to distinguish the trees." A reference from the word "names" gives the Latin: "'Silvestres,' and 'urbaniores.'" Theophrastus, in his *De Causis Plantarum*, has a chapter on the difference between wild and cultivated trees.

25 Not a specific week but the week in which a particular plant blossoms, such as Thoreau's reference on 25 May 1852: "It is blossom week with the apples" [J 4:71].

26 Quoted from Loudon's *Arboretum et Fruticetum Britannicum*.

27 Cf. "A Walk to Wachusett," note 50.

28 Fly-catcher (*Tyrannus tyrannus*).

29 Thoreau wrote in his journal of 11 October 1860: "Pears, it is truly said, are less poetic than apples. They have neither the beauty nor the fragrance of apples, but their excellence is in their flavor, which speaks to a grosser sense" [J 14:114]. Emerson was very proud of his pears, about which Thoreau wrote: "R.W.E.'s garden is strewn with them. . . . They are a more aristocratic fruit. How much more attention they get from the proprietor! The hired man gathers the apples and barrels them. The proprietor plucks the pears at odd hours for a pastime, and his daughter wraps them each in its paper" [J 14:113].

30 To gently cook in hot, but not boiling, water.

fections with the wild cherry; and the canker-worm also in a measure abandoned the elm to feed on it. As it grew apace, the blue-bird, robin, cherry-bird,[27] king-bird,[28] and many more, came with haste and built their nests and warbled in its boughs, and so became orchard-birds, and multiplied more than ever. It was an era in the history of their race. The downy woodpecker found such a savory morsel under its bark, that he perforated it in a ring quite round the tree, before he left it, — a thing which he had never done before, to my knowledge. It did not take the partridge long to find out how sweet its buds were, and every winter eve she flew, and still flies, from the wood, to pluck them, much to the farmer's sorrow. The rabbit, too, was not slow to learn the taste of its twigs and bark; and when the fruit was ripe, the squirrel half-rolled, half-carried it to his hole; and even the musquash crept up the bank from the brook at evening, and greedily devoured it, until he had worn a path in the grass there; and when it was frozen and thawed, the crow and the jay were glad to taste it occasionally. The owl crept into the first apple-tree that became hollow, and fairly hooted with delight, finding it just the place for him; so, settling down into it, he has remained there ever since.

My theme being the Wild Apple, I will merely glance at some of the seasons in the annual growth of the cultivated apple, and pass on to my special province.

The flowers of the apple are perhaps the most beautiful of any tree's, so copious and delicious to both sight and scent. The walker is frequently tempted to turn and linger near some more than usually handsome one, whose blossoms are two-thirds expanded. How superior it is in these respects to the pear, whose blossoms are neither colored nor fragrant![29]

By the middle of July, green apples are so large as to remind us of coddling,[30] and of the autumn. The sward is commonly strewed with little ones which fall still-born, as it were, — Nature thus thinning them for us. The Roman writer Palladius[31] said, — "If apples are inclined to fall before their time, a stone placed in a split root will retain them."[32] Some such notion, still surviving, may account for some of the stones which we see placed to be overgrown in the forks of trees. They have a saying in Suffolk, England, —

"At Michaelmas[33] time, or a little before,
Half an apple goes to the core."[34]

Early apples begin to be ripe about the first of August; but I think that none of them are so good to eat as some to smell. One is worth more to scent your handkerchief with than any perfume which they sell in the shops. The fragrance of some fruits is not to be forgotten, along with that of flowers. Some gnarly apple which I pick up in the road reminds me by its fragrance of all the wealth of Pomona,[35] — carrying me forward to those days when they will be collected in golden and ruddy heaps in the orchards and about the cider-mills.

A week or two later, as you are going by orchards or gardens, especially in the evenings, you pass through a little region possessed by the fragrance of ripe apples, and thus enjoy them without price, and without robbing anybody.

There is thus about all natural products a certain volatile and ethereal quality which represents their highest value, and which cannot be vulgarized, or bought and sold. No mortal has ever enjoyed the perfect flavor of any fruit, and only the god-like among men begin to taste its ambrosial qualities. For nectar and ambrosia are only those fine flavors of every earthly fruit which our coarse palates fail to perceive, — just as we occupy the heaven of the gods without knowing it. When I see a particularly mean man carrying a load of fair and fragrant early

31 Rutilius Taurus Aemilianus Palladius (fourth or fifth century C.E.), author of *De re rustica*, which Thoreau was familiar with from *Libri de re rustica*, a collection of four Roman agricultural writers from the second century B.C.E. to the fourth century C.E. and often referred to as the *Scriptores rei rusticae*.

32 Thoreau's condensed translation from Book II of Palladius's *De re rustica* follows Thomas Owen's (1749–1812) translation in *The Fourteen Books of Palladius Rutilius Taurus Æmilianus, On Agriculture*: "If the fruit is apt to fall off, a stone fixt in the root will cause the tree to retain it."

33 Feast of Saint Michael, 29 September.

34 Traditional English proverb from John Brand's (1744–1806) *Observations on Popular Antiquities: Chiefly Illustrating the Origin of Our Vulgar Customs, Ceremonies, and Superstitions*, which Thoreau read in the spring of 1860:

At Michaelmas time, or a little before,
Half an apple goes to the core;
At Christmas time, or a little after,
A crab in the hedge, and thanks to the rafter.

35 In Roman mythology, goddess of fruit trees.

36 Allusion to *The Natural History of Pliny* XXIV:1: "It is a common belief, too, that when their load consists of fruit, beasts of burden are immediately sensible of it, and will instantly begin to sweat, however trifling it may be, unless the fruit is duly shown to them before starting."

37 The substance of apples crushed by grinding.

38 According to Thoreau's source, Paul Henri Mallet's (1730–1807) *Northern Antiquities:* "Loki told Iduna that, in a forest at a short distance from the celestial residence, he had found apples growing which he thought were of a much better quality than her own, and that at all events it was worth while making a comparison between them. Iduna, deceived by his words, took her apples, and went with him into the forest, but they had no sooner entered it than Thjassi, clad in his eagle-plumage, flew rapidly towards them, and catching up Iduna, carried her and her treasure off with him to Jötunheim. The gods being thus deprived of their renovating apples, soon became wrinkled and grey."

39 On 24 October 1852 Thoreau and Ellery Channing walked to Stow, where they saw these trees.

apples to market, I seem to see a contest going on between him and his horse, on the one side, and the apples on the other, and, to my mind, the apples always gain it. Pliny says that apples are the heaviest of all things, and that the oxen begin to sweat at the mere sight of a load of them.[36] Our driver begins to lose his load the moment he tries to transport them to where they do not belong, that is, to any but the most beautiful. Though he gets out from time to time, and feels of them, and thinks they are all there, I see the stream of their evanescent and celestial qualities going to heaven from his cart, while the pulp and skin and core only are going to market. They are not apples, but pomace.[37] Are not these still Iduna's apples, the taste of which keeps the gods forever young? and think you that they will let Loki or Thjassi carry them off to Jötunheim, while they grow wrinkled and gray?[38] No, for Ragnarök, or the destruction of the gods, is not yet.

There is another thinning of the fruit, commonly near the end of August or in September, when the ground is strewn with windfalls; and this happens especially when high winds occur after rain. In some orchards you may see fully three-quarters of the whole crop on the ground, lying in a circular form beneath the trees, yet hard and green, — or, if it is a hill-side, rolled far down the hill. However, it is an ill wind that blows nobody any good. All the country over, people are busy picking up the windfalls, and this will make them cheap for early apple-pies.

In October, the leaves falling, the apples are more distinct on the trees. I saw one year in a neighboring town some trees fuller of fruit than I remembered to have ever seen before, small yellow apples hanging over the road.[39] The branches were gracefully drooping with their weight, like a barberry-bush, so that the whole tree acquired a new character. Even the topmost branches, instead of standing erect, spread and drooped in all directions; and there were so many poles supporting the lower ones, that they looked like pictures of banian-trees. As an old English manuscript says, "The mo appelen the tree bereth, the more sche boweth to the folk."[40]

Surely the apple is the noblest of fruits. Let the most beautiful or the swiftest have it. That should be the "going" price of apples.

Between the fifth and twentieth of October I see the barrels lie under the trees. And perhaps I talk with one who is selecting some choice barrels to fulfill an order. He turns a specked one over many times before he leaves it out.[41] If I were to tell what is passing in my mind, I should say that every one was specked which he had handled; for he rubs off all the bloom, and those fugacious[42] ethereal qualities leave it. Cool evenings prompt the farmers to make haste, and at length I see only the ladders here and there left leaning against the trees.

It would be well, if we accepted these gifts with more joy and gratitude, and did not think it enough simply to put a fresh load of compost about the tree. Some old English customs are suggestive at least. I find them described chiefly in Brand's "Popular Antiquities." It appears that "on Christmas eve the farmers and their men in Devonshire take a large bowl of cider, with a toast in it,[43] and carrying it in state[44] to the orchard, they salute the apple-trees with much ceremony, in order to make them bear well the next season."[45] This salutation consists in "throwing some of the cider about the roots of the tree, placing bits of the toast on the branches,"[46] and then, "encircling one of the best bearing trees in the orchard, they drink the following toast three several times: —

    'Here's to thee, old apple-tree,
Whence thou mayst bud, and whence thou mayst
    blow,
And whence thou mayst bear apples enow!

40 From the manuscript, "The Romance of the Monk," held in Scion College, London, as used under the heading, "Appelen, Appelyn," in Thomas Wright's (1810–1877) *Dictionary of Obsolete and Provincial English*.

41 In his journal of 16 October 1856 Thoreau wrote that "Wright, too, is collecting some choice barrels of golden russets. Many times he turns it over before he leaves out a specked one" [J 9:115].

42 Fleeting, volatile.

43 Bread, browned by fire, put in wine or other drink.

44 Publicly, with ceremony.

45 Quoted from Loudon's *Arboretum et Fruticetum*, which in turn quoted from *Mrs. Bray's Borders of the Tamer and the Tovey*.

46 Quoted from Loudon's *Arboretum et Fruticetum*, which in turn quoted from *Mrs. Bray's Borders of the Tamer and the Tovey*.

47 Quoted from Brand's *Observations on Popular Antiquities,* as found in Robert Southey's *Southey's Commonplace Book. Fourth Series.* Brand quoted from a 1791 issue of *Gentleman's Magazine.*

48 Quoted from Brand's *Observations on Popular Antiquities,* as found in *Southey's Commonplace Book. Fourth Series.*

49 Quoted from the *Sussex Archaeological Collections,* as found in *Southey's Commonplace Book. Fourth Series,* with one minor variant: "a cow's horn" for "the cow's horn."

50 Quoted from Brand's *Observations on Popular Antiquities.*

51 Quoted from Robert Herrick's (1591–1674) "Ceremonies for Christmasse" in his *Hesperides.*

52 Hard, or fermented, cider was more common in America than wine at this time.

53 John Phillips, sometimes Philips (1676–1709), author of *Cyder,* a 1,465-line poem, parts of which Thoreau read in Henry Phillips's (1775–1838) *History of Cultivated Vegetables* and in Loudon's *Arboretum et Fruticetum Britannicum.*

54 Native, or natural, seed-grown apple-trees, as opposed to the cultivated varieties which are grown from graft.

Hats-full! caps-full!
Bushel, bushel, sacks-full!
And my pockets full, too! Huzza!'"[47]

Also what was called "apple-howling" used to be practised in various counties of England on New-Year's eve. A troop of boys visited the different orchards, and, encircling the apple-trees, repeated the following words:—

"Stand fast, root! bear well, top!
Pray God send us a good howling crop:
    Every twig, apples big;
    Every bough, apples enow!"[48]

"They then shout in chorus, one of the boys accompanying them on a cow's horn. During this ceremony they rap the trees with their sticks."[49] This is called "wassailing" the trees, and is thought by some to be "a relic of the heathen sacrifice to Pomona."[50]

Herrick sings,—

"Wassaile the trees that they may beare
You many a plum and many a peare;
For more or less fruits they will bring
As you do give them wassailing."[51]

Our poets have as yet a better right to sing of cider than of wine;[52] but it behooves them to sing better than English Phillips[53] did, else they will do no credit to their Muse.

THE WILD APPLE

So much for the more civilized apple-trees (*urbaniores,* as Pliny calls them). I love better to go through the old orchards of ungrafted apple-trees,[54] at whatever season of the year, — so irregularly planted: sometimes two trees standing close together; and the rows so devious that you would think that they not only had grown while the owner was sleeping, but had been set out by him in a somnambulic state. The rows of grafted fruit will never tempt me to wander amid them like these. But I now, alas, speak rather from memory than from any recent experience, such ravages have been made!

Some soils, like a rocky tract called the Easterbrooks Country[55] in my neighborhood, are so suited to the apple, that it will grow faster in them without any care, or if only the ground is broken up once a year, than it will in many places with any amount of care. The owners of this tract allow that the soil is excellent for fruit, but they say that it is so rocky that they have not patience to plough it,[56] and that, together with the distance, is the reason why it is not cultivated. There are, or were recently, extensive orchards there standing without order. Nay, they spring up wild and bear well there in the midst of pines, birches, maples, and oaks. I am often surprised to see rising amid these trees the rounded tops of apple-trees glowing with red or yellow fruit, in harmony with the autumnal tints of the forest.

Going up the side of a cliff about the first of November,[57] I saw a vigorous young apple-tree, which, planted by birds or cows, had shot up amid the rocks and open woods there, and had now much fruit on it, uninjured by the frosts, when all cultivated apples were gathered. It was a rank wild growth, with many green leaves on it still, and made an impression of thorniness. The fruit was hard and green, but looked as if it would be palatable in the winter. Some was dangling on the twigs, but more half-buried in the wet leaves under the tree, or rolled far down the hill amid the rocks. The owner knows nothing of it. The day was not observed when it first blossomed, nor when it first bore fruit, unless by the

55 Estabrook Woods: a large tract in the north of Concord about which Thoreau wrote on 10 June 1853: "What shall this great wild tract over which we strolled be called? Many farmers have pastures there, and wood-lots, and orchards. . . . These orchards are very extensive, and yet many of these apple trees, growing as forest trees, bear good crops of apples. It is a paradise for walkers in the fall. There are also boundless huckleberry pastures as well as many blueberry swamps. Shall we call it the Easterbrooks Country? It would make a princely estate in Europe, yet it is owned by farmers, who live by the labor of their hands and do not esteem it much" [J 5:239–240].

56 According to his journal of 20 October 1857, "Warren Brown, who owns the Easterbrooks place, [on] the west side [of] the road, is picking barberries. Allows that the soil thereabouts is excellent for fruit, but it is so rocky that he has not patience to plow it. That is the reason this tract is not cultivated" [J 10:111].

57 On 28 October 1857.

58 There is no previous mention of the wildness of the crab apple. This is one of the errors which Thoreau did not have time to correct when he redacted his lecture for publication; cf. "Autumnal Tints," note 120.

chickadee. There was no dancing on the green beneath it in its honor, and now there is no hand to pluck its fruit,—which is only gnawed by squirrels, as I perceive. It has done double duty,—not only borne this crop, but each twig has grown a foot into the air. And this is *such* fruit! bigger than many berries, we must admit, and carried home will be sound and palatable next spring. What care I for Iduna's apples so long as I can get these?

When I go by this shrub thus late and hardy, and see its dangling fruit, I respect the tree, and I am grateful for Nature's bounty, even though I cannot eat it. Here on this rugged and woody hill-side has grown an apple-tree, not planted by man, no relic of a former orchard, but a natural growth, like the pines and oaks. Most fruits which we prize and use depend entirely on our care. Corn and grain, potatoes, peaches, melons, etc., depend altogether on our planting; but the apple emulates man's independence and enterprise. It is not simply carried, as I have said, but, like him, to some extent, it has migrated to this New World, and is even, here and there, making its way amid the aboriginal trees; just as the ox and dog and horse sometimes run wild and maintain themselves.

Even the sourest and crabbedest apple, growing in the most unfavorable position, suggests such thoughts as these, it is so noble a fruit.

THE CRAB

Nevertheless, *our* wild apple is wild only like myself, perchance, who belong not to the aboriginal race here, but have strayed into the woods from the cultivated stock. Wilder still, as I have said,[58] there grows elsewhere in this country a native and aboriginal Crab-Apple, *Malus coronaria,* "whose nature has not yet been modified by cultivation." It is found from Western New-York to Minnesota, and southward. Michaux says that its ordinary height "is fifteen or eighteen feet, but it is sometimes found twenty-five or thirty feet high," and that the large ones "exactly resemble the common apple-tree." "The flowers are white mingled with rose-color, and are collected in corymbs."[59] They are remarkable for their delicious odor. The fruit, according to him, is about an inch and a half in diameter, and is intensely acid. Yet they make fine sweet-meats,[60] and also cider of them. He concludes, that, if, on being cultivated, it does not yield new and palatable varieties, it will at least be celebrated for "the beauty of its flowers, and for the sweetness of its perfume."

I never saw the Crab-Apple till May, 1861. I had heard of it through Michaux, but more modern botanists, as far as I know, have not treated it as of any peculiar importance. Thus it was a half-fabulous tree to me. I contemplated a pilgrimage to the "Glades,"[61] a portion of Pennsylvania where it was said to grow to perfection. I thought of sending to a nursery for it, but doubted if they had it, or would distinguish it from European varieties. At last I had occasion to go to Minnesota,[62] and on entering Michigan I began to notice from the cars a tree with handsome rose-colored flowers. At first I thought it some variety of thorn; but it was not long before the truth flashed on me, that this was my long-sought Crab-Apple. It was the prevailing flowering shrub or tree to be seen from the cars at that season of the year,—about the middle of May.[63] But the cars never stopped before one, and so I was launched on the bosom of the Mississippi without having touched one, experiencing the fate of Tantalus. On arriving at St. Anthony's Falls,[64] I was sorry to be told that I was too far north for the Crab-Apple.[65] Nevertheless I succeeded in finding it about eight miles west of the Falls; touched it and smelled it, and secured a lingering corymb of flowers for my herbarium.[66] This must have been near its northern limit.

59 All quotations in this paragraph are quoted from Michaux's *North American Sylva;* cf. "Walking," note 62. Corymbs are flat-topped or convex clusters of flowers in which the outer flowers open first.
60 Fruits preserved with sugar. Michaux wrote in *North American Sylva* that crab apples "make very fine sweet meats."
61 Elevated valleys of the Alleghany Mountains which Michaux described in *North American Sylva* as "the name given to a tract 15 or 18 miles wide, on the summit of the Alleghanies, along the road from Philadelphia to Pittsburg."
62 On 3 May 1861 Thoreau wrote to H. G. O. Blake: "I am still as much an invalid as when you & Brown were here, if not more of one, and at this rate there is danger that the cold weather may come again, before I get over my bronchitis. The Doctor accordingly tells me that I must 'clear out' to the West Indies, or elsewhere, he does not seem to care much where. But I . . . have at last concluded that it will be most expedient for me to try the air of Minnesota" [C 615]. Thoreau left Concord on 13 May 1861, accompanied by Horace Mann, Jr. (1844–1868).
63 On 23 May, Thoreau saw from the railroad car window what he believed to be a crab apple tree (*Pyrus coronaria*).
64 In Minneapolis.
65 Thoreau's source for this information is not identified in his notes from this excursion.
66 On 11 June 1861, when he was staying at the boardinghouse of a Mrs. Elizabeth Hamilton. Despite the implication that Thoreau had searched for and found the elusive crab apple, he was led to it by Jonathan T. Grimes, a local nurseryman. Grimes had set out several trees in the spring which had died, but together the men were able to locate a withered blossom on one of Grimes's transplanted trees.

67 Inhabitants of the forests of frontier settlements, especially in the west.

68 Ten miles southwest of Concord, on the Framingham-Sudbury line.

69 The journal version of this poem contained two additional lines of an incomplete quatrain:

Its heart did bleed all day,
And when the birds were hushed, —[J 10:139]

70 Allusion to the final line in Emerson's "The Rhodora: On Being Asked, Whence is the Flower?": "The self-same Power that brought me there brought you."

HOW THE WILD APPLE GROWS

But though these are indigenous, like the Indians, I doubt whether they are any hardier than those backwoodsmen[67] among the apple-trees, which, though descended from cultivated stocks, plant themselves in distant fields and forests, where the soil is favorable to them. I know of no trees which have more difficulties to contend with, and which more sturdily resist their foes. These are the ones whose story we have to tell. It oftentimes reads thus:—

Near the beginning of May, we notice little thickets of apple-trees just springing up in the pastures where cattle have been,—as the rocky ones of our Easterbrooks Country, or the top of Nobscot Hill, in Sudbury.[68] One or two of these perhaps survive the drought and other accidents,—their very birthplace defending them against the encroaching grass and some other dangers, at first.

In two years' time 't had thus
　　Reached the level of the rocks,
Admired the stretching world,
　　Nor feared the wandering flocks.

But at this tender age
　　Its sufferings began:
There came a browsing ox
　　And cut it down a span.[69]

This time, perhaps, the ox does not notice it amid the grass; but the next year, when it has grown more stout, he recognizes it for a fellow-emigrant from the old country, the flavor of whose leaves and twigs he well knows; and though at first he pauses to welcome it, and express his surprise, and gets for answer, "The same cause that brought you here brought me,"[70] he nevertheless browses it again, reflecting, it may be, that he has some title to it.

Thus cut down annually, it does not despair; but, putting forth two short twigs for every one cut off, it spreads out low along the ground in the hollows or between the rocks, growing more stout and scrubby, until it forms, not a tree as yet, but a little pyramidal, stiff, twiggy mass, almost as solid and impenetrable as a rock. Some of the densest and most impenetrable clumps of bushes that I have ever seen, as well on account of the closeness and stubbornness of their branches as of their thorns, have been these wild-apple scrubs. They are more like the scrubby fir and black spruce on which you stand, and sometimes walk, on the tops of mountains,[71] where cold is the demon they contend with, than anything else. No wonder they are prompted to grow thorns at last, to defend themselves against such foes. In their thorniness, however, there is no malice, only some malic acid.

The rocky pastures of the tract I have referred to— for they maintain their ground best in a rocky field—are thickly sprinkled with these little tufts, reminding you often of some rigid gray mosses or lichens, and you see thousands of little trees just springing up between them, with the seed still attached to them.

Being regularly clipped all around each year by the cows, as a hedge with shears, they are often of a perfect conical or pyramidal form, from one to four feet high, and more or less sharp, as if trimmed by the gardener's art. In the pastures on Nobscot Hill and its spurs,[72] they make fine dark shadows when the sun is low. They are also an excellent covert from hawks for many small birds that roost and build in them. Whole flocks perch in them at night, and I have seen three robins' nests in one which was six feet in diameter.

No doubt many of these are already old trees, if you

71 Thoreau described this experience in *The Maine Woods*: "I began to work my way, scarcely less arduous than Satan's anciently through Chaos, up the nearest, though not the highest peak. At first scrambling on all fours over the tops of ancient black spruce-trees (*Abies nigra*), old as the flood, from two to ten or twelve feet in height, their tops flat and spreading, and their foliage blue and nipt with cold, as if for centuries they had ceased growing upward against the bleak sky, the solid cold. I walked some good rods erect upon the tops of these trees, which were overgrown with moss and mountain-cranberries" [MW 54].

72 Mountains or hills that extend to some distance in a lateral direction from any other mountain or hill.

73 The cow's hide rubs off the outer layer of bark, revealing the reddish sublayer.

reckon from the day they were planted, but infants still when you consider their development and the long life before them. I counted the annual rings of some which were just one foot high, and as wide as high, and found that they were about twelve years old, and quite sound and thrifty! They were so low that they were unnoticed by the walker, while many of their contemporaries from the nurseries were already bearing considerable crops. But what you gain in time is perhaps in this case, too, lost in power, — that is, in the vigor of the tree. This is their pyramidal state.

The cows continue to browse them thus for twenty years or more, keeping them down and compelling them to spread, until at last they are so broad that they become their own fence, when some interior shoot, which their foes cannot reach, darts upward with joy: for it has not forgotten its high calling, and bears its own peculiar fruit in triumph.

Such are the tactics by which it finally defeats its bovine foes. Now, if you have watched the progress of a particular shrub, you will see that it is no longer a simple pyramid or cone, but that out of its apex there rises a sprig or two, growing more lustily perchance than an orchard-tree, since the plant now devotes the whole of its repressed energy to these upright parts. In a short time these become a small tree, an inverted pyramid resting on the apex of the other, so that the whole has now the form of a vast hour-glass. The spreading bottom, having served its purpose, finally disappears, and the generous tree permits the now harmless cows to come in and stand in its shade, and rub against and redden its trunk,[73] which has grown in spite of them, and even to taste of part of its fruit, and so disperse the seed.

Thus the cows create their own shade and food; and the tree, its hour-glass being inverted, lives a second life, as it were.

It is an important question with some nowadays, whether you should trim young apple-trees as high as your nose or as high as your eyes. The ox trims them up as high as he can reach, and that is about the right height, I think.

In spite of wandering kine, and other adverse circumstances, that despised shrub, valued only by small birds as a covert and shelter from hawks, has its blossom-week at last, and in course of time its harvest, sincere, though small.[74]

By the end of some October, when its leaves have fallen, I frequently see such a central sprig, whose progress I have watched, when I thought it had forgotten its destiny, as I had, bearing its first crop of small green or yellow or rosy fruit, which the cows cannot get at over the bushy and thorny hedge which surrounds it, and I make haste to taste the new and undescribed variety. We have all heard of the numerous varieties of fruit invented by Van Mons and Knight.[75] This is the system of Van Cow, and she has invented far more and more memorable varieties than both of them.

Through what hardships it may attain to bear a sweet fruit! Though somewhat small, it may prove equal, if not superior, in flavor to that which has grown in a garden,—will perchance be all the sweeter and more palatable for the very difficulties it has had to contend with. Who knows but this chance wild fruit, planted by a cow or a bird on some remote and rocky hill-side, where it is as yet unobserved by man, may be the choicest of all its kind, and foreign potentates shall hear of it, and royal societies seek to propagate it, though the virtues of the perhaps truly crabbed owner of the soil may never be heard of,—at least, beyond the limits of his village? It was thus the Porter and the Baldwin[76] grew.

Every wild-apple shrub excites our expectation thus, somewhat as every wild child. It is, perhaps, a prince in

74 In Thoreau's journal of 28 October 1857 this is followed by the verse:

> 'T was thirty years ago,
> In a rocky pasture field
> Sprang an infant apple grove
> Unplanted and concealed.
> I sing the wild apple, theme enough for me.
> I love the racy fruit and I reverence the tree.
>   [J 10:138]

75 Jean-Baptiste Van Mons (1765–1842), Belgian horticulturist, cultivated fruit trees to increase their fruit-bearing capacity, and Thomas Andrew Knight (1759–1838), English horticulturist, increased fruit yield through cross-breeding.
76 Varieties of apple.

77 Thoreau's translation and quotation are from Columella's *De Re Rustica* X.16, as found in *Scriptores Rei Rusticae*.

78 Softening, as in Evelyn's *Sylva* (cf. "Walking," note 62), in which he refers to the "pleasanter or plumper or larger Apple being the effect of some Intenaration, which inclines to a kind of Rebatement of the natural Strength of the Tree."

79 Quoted from Marvell's "An Horatian ode upon Cromwell's Return from Ireland," ll. 31–32, from which Thoreau also quoted in "The Last Days of John Brown." The bergamot was prized in Emerson's youth and failed to grow in his garden.

disguise. What a lesson to man! So are human beings, referred to the highest standard, the celestial fruit which they suggest and aspire to bear, browsed on by fate; and only the most persistent and strongest genius defends itself and prevails, sends a tender scion upward at last, and drops its perfect fruit on the ungrateful earth. Poets and philosophers and statesmen thus spring up in the country pastures, and outlast the hosts of unoriginal men.

Such is always the pursuit of knowledge. The celestial fruits, the golden apples of the Hesperides, are ever guarded by a hundred-headed dragon which never sleeps, so that it is an Herculean labor to pluck them.

This is one, and the most remarkable way, in which the wild apple is propagated; but commonly it springs up at wide intervals in woods and swamps, and by the sides of roads, as the soil may suit it, and grows with comparative rapidity. Those which grow in dense woods are very tall and slender. I frequently pluck from these trees a perfectly mild and tamed fruit. As Columella says, "*Et injussu consternitur ubere mali*": And the ground is strewn with the fruit of an unbidden apple-tree.[77]

It is an old notion, that, if these wild trees do not bear a valuable fruit of their own, they are the best stocks by which to transmit to posterity the most highly prized qualities of others. However, I am not in search of stocks, but the wild fruit itself, whose fierce gust has suffered no "inteneration."[78] It is not my

> "highest plot
> To plant the bergamot."[79]

THE FRUIT, AND ITS FLAVOR

The time for wild apples is the last of October and the first of November. They then get to be palatable, for they ripen late, and they are still perhaps as beautiful as ever. I make a great account of these fruits, which the farmers do not think it worth the while to gather,—wild flavors of the Muse, vivacious and inspiriting. The farmer thinks that he has better in his barrels, but he is mistaken, unless he has a walker's appetite and imagination, neither of which can he have.

Such as grow quite wild, and are left out till the first of November, I presume that the owner does not mean to gather. They belong to children as wild as themselves,—to certain active boys that I know,—to the wild-eyed woman of the fields, to whom nothing comes amiss, who gleans after all the world,—and, moreover, to us walkers. We have met with them, and they are ours.[80] These rights, long enough insisted upon, have come to be an institution in some old countries, where they have learned how to live. I hear that "the custom of grippling, which may be called apple-gleaning, is, or was formerly, practised in Herefordshire. It consists in leaving a few apples, which are called the gripples, on every tree, after the general gathering, for the boys, who go with climbing-poles and bags to collect them."[81]

As for those I speak of, I pluck them as a wild fruit, native to this quarter of the earth,—fruit of old trees that have been dying ever since I was a boy and are not yet dead, frequented only by the woodpecker and the squirrel, deserted now by the owner, who has not faith enough to look under their boughs. From the appearance of the tree-top, at a little distance, you would expect nothing but lichens to drop from it, but your faith is rewarded by finding the ground strewn with spirited fruit,—some of it, perhaps, collected at squirrel-holes, with the marks of their teeth by which they carried them,—some containing a cricket or two silently feeding within, and some, especially in damp days, a shelless snail.[82] The very sticks and stones lodged in the tree-top

80 Allusion to Oliver Hazard Perry's (1795–1819) message from the battle of Lake Erie during the War of 1812: "We have met the enemy and they are ours."

81 Quoted from Loudon's *Arboretum et Fruticetum Britannicum*.

82 Slug, described in Thoreau's 1855 journal as "That apparently shell-less snail or slug which is so common this damp day under apple trees, eating the apples, is evidently one of the naked *Mollusca*, the Division *Gasteropoda*, a *Limax*, perhaps the *Limax tunicata* of Gould" [J 7:507–508].

83 Andrew Jackson Downing's *The Fruits and Fruit-Trees of America*.

84 Possibly George Minott (cf. "Natural History of Massachusetts," note 45): "Minott is, perhaps, the most poetical farmer—who most realizes to me the poetry of the farmer's life—that I know. . . . Though he never reads a book,—since he has finished the 'Naval Monument,'—he speaks the best of English" [ITM 104–105]. Thoreau used the term "bow-arrow tang" in his journal of 5 March 1858 and in "The Allegash and East Branch," where the phrase was attributed to "my neighbor."

85 Downing listed William's Favorite, Monk's Favorite, the Hubardston Nonesuch, and the Seek-No-Further in his descriptive catalogue of apple varieties in *The Fruits and Fruit-Trees of America*.

86 Green juice: a liquor expressed from crab apples or unripe grapes, used in sauces, ragouts, etc.

87 Apple family.

might have convinced you of the savoriness of the fruit which has been so eagerly sought after in past years.

I have seen no account of these among the "Fruits and Fruit-Trees of America,"[83] though they are more memorable to my taste than the grafted kinds; more racy and wild American flavors do they possess, when October and November, when December and January, and perhaps February and March even, have assuaged them somewhat. An old farmer in my neighborhood, who always selects the right word,[84] says that "they have a kind of bow-arrow tang."

Apples for grafting appear to have been selected commonly, not so much for their spirited flavor, as for their mildness, their size, and bearing qualities,—not so much for their beauty, as for their fairness and soundness. Indeed, I have no faith in the selected lists of pomological gentlemen. Their "Favorites" and "None-suches" and "Seek-no-furthers,"[85] when I have fruited them, commonly turn out very tame and forgetable. They are eaten with comparatively little zest, and have no real *tang* nor *smack* to them.

What if some of these wildings are acrid and puckery, genuine *verjuice*,[86] do they not still belong to the *Pomaceae*,[87] which are uniformly innocent and kind to our race? I still begrudge them to the cider-mill. Perhaps they are not fairly ripe yet.

No wonder that these small and high-colored apples are thought to make the best cider. Loudon quotes from the "Herefordshire Report" that "apples of a small size are always, if equal in quality, to be preferred to those of a larger size, in order that the rind and kernel may bear the greatest proportion to the pulp, which affords the weakest and most watery juice." And he says, that, "to prove this, Dr. Symonds, of Hereford, about the year 1800, made one hogshead of cider entirely from the rinds and cores of apples, and another from the pulp only, when the first was found of extraordinary strength and flavor, while the latter was sweet and insipid."[88]

Evelyn says that the "Red-strake" was the favorite cider-apple in his day; and he quotes one Dr. Newburg as saying, "In Jersey 't is a general observation, as I hear, that the more of red any apple has in its rind, the more proper it is for this use. Pale-faced apples they exclude as much as may be from their cider-vat."[89] This opinion still prevails.

All apples are good in November. Those which the farmer leaves out as unsalable, and unpalatable to those who frequent the markets, are choicest fruit to the walker. But it is remarkable that the wild apple, which I praise as so spirited and racy when eaten in the fields or woods, being brought into the house, has frequently a harsh and crabbed taste. The Saunterer's Apple not even the saunterer can eat in the house. The palate rejects it there, as it does haws[90] and acorns, and demands a tamed one; for there you miss the November air, which is the sauce it is to be eaten with. Accordingly, when Tityrus, seeing the lengthening shadows, invites Meliboeus to go home and pass the night with him, he promises him *mild* apples and soft chestnuts, —*mitia poma, castaneae molles.*[91] I frequently pluck wild apples of so rich and spicy a flavor that I wonder all orchardists do not get a scion from that tree, and I fail not to bring home my pockets full. But perchance, when I take one out of my desk and taste it in my chamber, I find it unexpectedly crude, —sour enough to set a squirrel's teeth on edge and make a jay scream.

These apples have hung in the wind and frost and rain till they have absorbed the qualities of the weather or season, and thus are highly *seasoned,* and they *pierce* and *sting* and *permeate* us with their spirit. They must be eaten in *season,* accordingly, —that is, out-of-doors.

To appreciate the wild and sharp flavors of these October fruits, it is necessary that you be breathing the

88 Quoted from Loudon's *Encyclopedia of Gardening.* The "Herefordshire Report" was John Duncumb's (1765–1839) *General View of the Agriculture of the County of Hereford.*
89 Quoted from Evelyn's *Sylva,* in which John Newburgh's "Observations Concerning the Making and Preserving of Cider" was reprinted. Newburgh was neither a medical nor a theological doctor.
90 Hawthorn.
91 Quoted from Virgil's *Eclogue* I:80–81. Tityrus and Meliboeus are two shepherds—the first lives on his own land, the second has been dispossessed—and their dialogue forms Virgil's first eclogue.

92 The Reverend Peter Whitney (1744–1816), second town minister of Northborough, located approximately twenty miles southwest of Concord.
93 The American Academy of Arts and Sciences was founded in 1780 in Boston to "cultivate every art and science which may tend to advance the interest, honour, dignity, and happiness of a free, independent, and virtuous people."
94 Quoted, with variants, from Whitney's *The History of the County of Worcester, . . . Massachusetts,* in the first volume, 1785, of the *Memoirs of the American Academy of Arts and Sciences:* "The apples are fair, and, when fully ripe, of a yellow colour, but, evidently, of different tastes—sour and sweet. . . . Two apples growing side by side, on the same limb, will be often of these different tastes, the one all sour, and the other all sweet. And, which is more remarkable, the same apple will frequently be sour on one side, end or part, and the other sweet, and that not in any order or uniformity nor is there any difference in the appearance of the one part from the other."
95 Sometimes called Lee's Hill, located west of the confluence of the Assabet and Sudbury Rivers.
96 In his journal of 29 October 1855, Thoreau wrote "As you cut it . . ." [J 7:526].
97 The *Anasa tristis,* which primarily attacks squash and pumpkins, gives off a foul odor when crushed or disturbed.
98 Quoted from Loudon's *Arboretum et Fruticetum Britannicum.*

sharp October or November air. The out-door air and exercise which the walker gets give a different tone to his palate, and he craves a fruit which the sedentary would call harsh and crabbed. They must be eaten in the fields, when your system is all aglow with exercise, when the frosty weather nips your fingers, the wind rattles the bare boughs or rustles the few remaining leaves, and the jay is heard screaming around. What is sour in the house a bracing walk makes sweet. Some of these apples might be labelled, "To be eaten in the wind."

Of course no flavors are thrown away; they are intended for the taste that is up to them. Some apples have two distinct flavors, and perhaps one-half of them must be eaten in the house, the other out-doors. One Peter Whitney wrote from Northborough[92] in 1782, for the Proceedings of the Boston Academy,[93] describing an apple-tree in that town "producing fruit of opposite qualities, part of the same apple being frequently sour and the other sweet"; also some all sour, and others all sweet, and this diversity on all parts of the tree.[94]

There is a wild apple on Nawshawtuct Hill[95] in our town which has to me a peculiarly pleasant bitter tang, not perceived till it is three-quarters tasted. It remains on the tongue. As you eat it,[96] it smells exactly like a squash-bug.[97] It is a sort of triumph to eat and relish it.

I hear that the fruit of a kind of plum-tree in Provence is "called *Prunes sibarelles,* because it is impossible to whistle after having eaten them, from their sourness."[98] But perhaps they were only eaten in the house and in summer, and if tried out-of-doors in a stinging atmosphere, who knows but you could whistle an octave higher and clearer?

In the fields only are the sours and bitters of Nature appreciated; just as the wood-chopper eats his meal in a sunny glade, in the middle of a winter day, with content, basks in a sunny ray there and dreams of summer in a degree of cold which, experienced in a chamber, would make a student miserable. They who are at work abroad are not cold, but rather it is they who sit shivering in houses. As with temperatures, so with flavors; as with cold and heat, so with sour and sweet. This natural raciness, the sours and bitters which the diseased palate refuses, are the true condiments.

Let your condiments be in the condition of your senses. To appreciate the flavor of these wild apples requires vigorous and healthy senses, *papillae*[99] firm and erect on the tongue and palate, not easily flattened and tamed.

From my experience with wild apples, I can understand that there may be reason for a savage's preferring many kinds of food which the civilized man rejects. The former has the palate of an out-door man. It takes a savage or wild taste to appreciate a wild fruit.

What a healthy out-of-door appetite it takes to relish the apple of life, the apple of the world, then!

"Nor is it every apple I desire,
     Nor that which pleases every palate best;
'Tis not the lasting Deuzan[100] I require,
     Not yet the red-cheeked Queening[101] I
request,
Nor that which first beshrewed[102] the name of
     wife,
Nor that whose beauty caused the golden
     strife:[103]
No, no! bring me an apple from the tree of
     life!"[104]

So there is one *thought* for the field, another for the house. I would have my thoughts, like wild apples, to be food for walkers, and will not warrant them to be palatable, if tasted in the house.

99 Taste buds.
100 Variety of apple.
101 Variety of apple.
102 Cursed; the allusion is to Eve's temptation of Adam.
103 Allusion to the strife, in Greek mythology, over the golden apple: see note 7 above.
104 Quoted from Francis Quarles's (1592–1644) *Emblemes* V.ii.3.

105 Running from north to south on a globe; here, from top to bottom.

THEIR BEAUTY

Almost all wild apples are handsome. They cannot be too gnarly and crabbed and rusty to look at. The gnarliest will have some redeeming traits even to the eye. You will discover some evening redness dashed or sprinkled on some protuberance or in some cavity. It is rare that the summer lets an apple go without streaking or spotting it on some part of its sphere. It will have some red stains, commemorating the mornings and evenings it has witnessed; some dark and rusty blotches, in memory of the clouds and foggy, mildewy days that have passed over it; and a spacious field of green reflecting the general face of Nature, — green even as the fields; or a yellow ground, which implies a milder flavor, — yellow as the harvest, or russet as the hills.

Apples, these I mean, unspeakably fair, — apples not of Discord, but of Concord! Yet not so rare but that the homeliest may have a share. Painted by the frosts, some a uniform clear bright yellow, or red, or crimson, as if their spheres had regularly revolved, and enjoyed the influence of the sun on all sides alike, — some with the faintest pink blush imaginable, — some brindled with deep red streaks like a cow, or with hundreds of fine blood-red rays running regularly from the stem-dimple to the blossom-end, like meridional lines,[105] on a straw-colored ground, — some touched with a greenish rust, like a fine lichen, here and there, with crimson blotches or eyes more or less confluent and fiery when wet, — and others gnarly, and freckled or peppered all over on the stem side with fine crimson spots on a white ground, as if accidentally sprinkled from the brush of Him who paints the autumn leaves. Others, again, are sometimes red inside, perfused with a beautiful blush, fairy food, too beautiful to eat, — apple of the Hesperides, apple of the evening sky! But like shells and pebbles on the sea-shore, they must be seen as they sparkle amid the withering leaves in some dell in the woods, in the autumnal air, or as they lie in the wet grass, and not when they have wilted and faded in the house.

THE NAMING OF THEM

It would be a pleasant pastime to find suitable names for the hundred varieties which go to a single heap at the cider-mill. Would it not tax a man's invention,—no one to be named after a man, and all in the *lingua vernacula?*[106] Who shall stand godfather at the christening of the wild apples? It would exhaust the Latin and Greek languages, if they were used, and make the *lingua vernacula* flag. We should have to call in the sunrise and the sunset, the rainbow and the autumn woods and the wild flowers, and the woodpecker and the purple finch and the squirrel and the jay and the butterfly, the November traveller and the truant boy, to our aid.

In 1836 there were in the garden of the London Horticultural Society more than fourteen hundred distinct sorts.[107] But here are species which they have not in their catalogue, not to mention the varieties which our Crab might yield to cultivation.

Let us enumerate a few of these. I find myself compelled, after all, to give the Latin names of some for the benefit of those who live where English is not spoken,—for they are likely to have a world-wide reputation.[108]

There is, first of all, the Wood-Apple (*Malus sylvatica*); the Blue-Jay Apple; the Apple which grows in Dells in the Woods, (*sylvestrivallis,*) also in Hollows in Pastures (*campestrivallis*); the Apple that grows in an old Cellar-Hole (*Malus cellaris*); the Meadow-Apple; the Partridge-Apple; the Truant's Apple, (*Cessatoris,*) which no boy will ever go by without knocking off some, however *late* it may be; the Saunterer's Apple,—you must lose yourself

106 Latin: native language.
107 Thoreau read of this in George Barrell Emerson's (1797–1881) *A Report on the Trees and Shrubs Growing Naturally in the Forests of Massachusetts.* In his journal of 23 May 1851 Thoreau wrote: "Emerson says, referring to Loudon, 'In 1836, the catalogue of the gardens of the London Horticultural Society contained upwards of 1400 distinct sorts, and new ones are every year added'" [J 2:211].
108 Names invented by Thoreau, followed in some instances by a Latinized version. On 20 November 1850 Thoreau wrote: "It is often the unscientific man who discovers the new species. It would be strange if it were not so. But we are accustomed properly to call that only a scientific discovery which knows the relative value of the thing discovered, uncovers a fact to mankind" [J 2:106].

109 Thoreau similarly wrote in *Walden:* "Not till we are lost, in other words, not till we have lost the world, do we begin to find ourselves, and realize where we are and the infinite extent of our relations" [Wa 166].

110 Allusion to Musketaquid, the Native American name for the Concord River.

111 Cf. "An Address on the Succession of Forest Trees," note 14.

112 Latin: cholera morbus and dysentery, highly esteemed by young boys.

113 In Greek mythology, the virgin huntress Atalanta promised to wed the man who could win a footrace with her. She lost the race to Hippomones, who distracted her with three golden apples.

114 Latin: Walker's solace. Thoreau named it the "Pedestrium solatium in apricis locis" (Latin: Walker's solace in sunny places) in his journal of 31 May 1851 [J 2:223].

115 On 8 August 1851 Thoreau saw "three scythes hanging on an apple tree" [J 2:381–382].

116 Thoreau made two lists in his journal of 23 and 29 May 1851.

117 Thoreau's poem is a translation of a poem by Johannes Bodaeus van Stapel's (1602–1636), which is in turn an adaption of Virgil's *Georgics* II:42–44. Thoreau replaced Bodaeus's final word, *pomoroum,* meaning fruits, with wild apples.

before you can find the way to that;[109] the Beauty of the Air (*Decus Aëris*); December-Eating; the Frozen-Thawed, (*gelato-soluta,*) good only in that state; the Concord Apple, possibly the same with the *Musketaquidensis;*[110] the Assabet Apple; the Brindled Apple; Wine of New England; the Chickaree[111] Apple; the Green Apple (*Malus viridis*);—this has many synonymes; in an imperfect state, it is the *Cholera morbifera aut dysenterifera, puerulis dilectissima;*[112]—the Apple which Atalanta stopped to pick up;[113] the Hedge-Apple (*Malus Sepium*); the Slug-Apple (*limacea*); the Railroad-Apple, which perhaps came from a core thrown out of the cars; the Apple whose Fruit we tasted in our Youth; our Particular Apple, not to be found in any catalogue,—*Pedestrium Solatium;*[114] also the Apple where hangs the Forgotten Scythe;[115] Iduna's Apples, and the Apples which Loki found in the Wood; and a great many more I have on my list,[116] too numerous to mention,—all of them good. As Bodaeus exclaims, referring to the cultivated kinds, and adapting Virgil to his case, so I, adapting Bodaeus,—

> "Not if I had a hundred tongues, a hundred
> mouths,
> An iron voice, could I describe all the forms
> And reckon up all the names of these *wild
> apples.*"[117]

THE LAST GLEANING

By the middle of November the wild apples have lost some of their brilliancy, and have chiefly fallen. A great part are decayed on the ground, and the sound ones are more palatable than before. The note of the chickadee sounds now more distinct, as you wander amid the old trees, and the autumnal dandelion is half-closed and tearful. But still, if you are a skilful gleaner, you may get many a pocket-full even of grafted fruit, long after apples are supposed to be gone out-of-doors. I know a Blue-Pearmain[118] tree, growing within the edge of a swamp, almost as good as wild.[119] You would not suppose that there was any fruit left there, on the first survey, but you must look according to system. Those which lie exposed are quite brown and rotten now, or perchance a few still show one blooming cheek here and there amid the wet leaves. Nevertheless, with experienced eyes, I explore amid the bare alders and the huckleberry-bushes and the withered sedge, and in the crevices of the rocks, which are full of leaves, and pry under the fallen and decaying ferns, which, with apple and alder leaves, thickly strew the ground. For I know that they lie concealed, fallen into hollows long since and covered up by the leaves of the tree itself,—a proper kind of packing. From these lurking-places, anywhere within the circumference of the tree, I draw forth the fruit, all wet and glossy, maybe nibbled by rabbits and hollowed out by crickets and perhaps with a leaf or two cemented to it, (as Curzon an old manuscript from a monastery's mouldy cellar,)[120] but still with a rich bloom on it, and at least as ripe and well kept, if not better than those in barrels, more crisp and lively than they. If these resources fail to yield anything, I have learned to look between the bases of the suckers which spring thickly from some horizontal limb, for now and then one lodges there, or in the very midst of an alder-clump, where they are covered by leaves, safe from cows which may have smelled them out. If I am sharp-set, for I do not refuse the Blue-Pearmain, I fill my pockets on each side; and as I retrace my steps in the frosty eve, being perhaps four or five miles from home, I eat one first from this side, and then from that, to keep my balance.

I learn from Topsell's Gesner,[121] whose authority appears to be Albertus,[122] that the following is the way

118 Variety of apple.

119 While at Bateman's Pond on 2 November 1857 Thoreau found "some good blue pearmains under their tree in a swamp, amid the huckleberry bushes, etc., all fallen. They lie with a rich bloom on them still, though half of them are gnawed by squirrels or rabbits; low in the sedge, with decayed leaves adhering to them" [J 10:155].

120 Allusion to Robert Curzon's (1810–1873) *Visits to Monasteries in the Levant,* in which he wrote of his March 1837 visit to the library of the Souriani monastery. In the oil cellar he discovered "a small closet vaulted with stone which was filled to the depth of two feet or more with the loose leaves of the Syriac manuscripts which now form one of the chief treasures of the British Museum."

121 Allusion to Edward Topsell's (1572–1625) *The Historie of Foure-Footed Beasts and Serpents,* a translation of Konrad Gesner's (1516–1565) *Historiae Animalium.* Thoreau read Topsell in February 1860.

122 Albertus Magnus (1193–1280), German Dominican friar, bishop, and scholar who advocated the harmony between religion and science.

123 Quoted from Topsell's *The Historie of Foure-Footed Beasts and Serpents.*

in which the hedge-hog collects and carries home his apples. He says,—"His meat is apples, worms, or grapes: when he findeth apples or grapes on the earth, he rolleth himself upon them, until he have filled all his prickles, and then carrieth them home to his den, never bearing above one in his mouth; and if it fortune that one of them fall off by the way, he likewise shaketh off all the residue, and walloweth upon them afresh, until they be all settled upon his back again. So, forth he goeth, making a noise like a cart-wheel; and if he have any young ones in his nest, they pull off his load wherewithal he is loaded, eating thereof what they please, and laying up the residue for the time to come."123

THE "FROZEN-THAWED" APPLE

Toward the end of November, though some of the sound ones are yet more mellow and perhaps more edible, they have generally, like the leaves, lost their beauty, and are beginning to freeze. It is finger-cold, and prudent farmers get in their barrelled apples, and bring you the apples and cider which they have engaged; for it is time to put them into the cellar. Perhaps a few on the ground show their red cheeks above the early snow, and occasionally some even preserve their color and soundness under the snow throughout the winter. But generally at the beginning of the winter they freeze hard, and soon, though undecayed, acquire the color of a baked apple.

Before the end of December, generally, they experience their first thawing. Those which a month ago were sour, crabbed, and quite unpalatable to the civilized taste, such at least as were frozen while sound, let a warmer sun come to thaw them, for they are extremely sensitive to its rays, are found to be filled with a rich sweet cider, better than any bottled cider that I know of, and with which I am better acquainted than with wine.

All apples are good in this state, and your jaws are the cider-press. Others, which have more substance, are a sweet and luscious food,—in my opinion of more worth than the pine-apples which are imported from the West Indies. Those which lately even I tasted only to repent of it,—for I am semi-civilized,—which the farmer willingly left on the tree, I am now glad to find have the property of hanging on like the leaves of the young oaks. It is a way to keep cider sweet without boiling. Let the frost come to freeze them first, solid as stones,[124] and then the rain or a warm winter day to thaw them, and they will seem to have borrowed a flavor from heaven through the medium of the air in which they hang. Or perchance you find, when you get home, that those which rattled in your pocket have thawed, and the ice is turned to cider. But after the third or fourth freezing and thawing they will not be found so good.

What are the imported half-ripe fruits of the torrid South, to this fruit matured by the cold of the frigid North? These are those crabbed apples with which I cheated my companion, and kept a smooth face that I might tempt him to eat.[125] Now we both greedily fill our pockets with them,—bending to drink the cup and save our lappets[126] from the overflowing juice,—and grow more social with their wine. Was there one that hung so high and sheltered by the tangled branches that our sticks could not dislodge it?

It is a fruit never carried to market, that I am aware of,—quite distinct from the apple of the markets, as from dried apple and cider,—and it is not every winter that produces it in perfection.

The era of the Wild Apple will soon be past. It is a fruit which will probably become extinct in New England. You may still wander through old orchards of native fruit of great extent, which for the most part went

124 On 11 November 1853 Thoreau noted that apples "are frozen on the trees and rattle like stones in my pocket" [J 5:494].
125 Thoreau's journal of 22 December 1850 does not identify his companion, although it is likely to have been Ellery Channing: cf. "Walking," note 125.
126 Flaps or loose-hanging parts of a garment.

127 In his journal of 13 November 1857 Thoreau wrote that he was "told of an orchard in the town of Russell, on the side of a hill, where the apples rolled down and lay four feet deep (?) against a wall on the lower side, and this the owner cut down" [J 10:177]. Russell is located one hundred miles southwest of Concord.

128 Against fermented cider, as well as the planting of apple trees as the source of fermented cider.

129 Discarded pulp after making cider.

130 A plot or patch of land laid off for or devoted to some particular purpose.

131 Any hairy caterpillar which appears in great numbers, devouring herbage, and wandering about like a palmer, a pilgrim or crusader returning from the Holy Land, but the name is applied also to other voracious insects such as the wingless, or migratory, locust.

to the cider-mill, now all gone to decay. I have heard of an orchard in a distant town, on the side of a hill, where the apples rolled down and lay four feet deep against a wall on the lower side, and this the owner cut down for fear they should be made into cider.[127] Since the temperance reform[128] and the general introduction of grafted fruit, no native apple-trees, such as I see everywhere in deserted pastures, and where the woods have grown up around them, are set out. I fear that he who walks over these fields a century hence will not know the pleasure of knocking off wild apples. Ah, poor man, there are many pleasures which he will not know! Notwithstanding the prevalence of the Baldwin and the Porter, I doubt if so extensive orchards are set out to-day in my town as there were a century ago, when those vast straggling cider orchards were planted, when men both ate and drank apples, when the pomace-heap[129] was the only nursery, and trees cost nothing but the trouble of setting them out. Men could afford then to stick a tree by every wall-side and let it take its chance. I see nobody planting trees to-day in such out-of-the-way places, along the lonely roads and lanes, and at the bottom of dells in the wood. Now that they have grafted trees, and pay a price for them, they collect them into a plat[130] by their houses, and fence them in,—and the end of it all will be that we shall be compelled to look for our apples in a barrel.

This is "The word of the Lord that came to Joel the son of Pethuel.

"Hear this, ye old men, and give ear, all ye inhabitants of the land! Hath this been in your days, or even in the days of your fathers? . . .

"That which the palmer-worm[131] hath left hath the locust eaten; and that which the locust hath left hath the canker-worm eaten; and that which the canker-worm hath left hath the caterpillar eaten.

"Awake, ye drunkards, and weep! and howl, all ye

drinkers of wine, because of the new wine! for it is cut off from your mouth.

"For a nation is come up upon my land, strong, and without number, whose teeth are the teeth of a lion, and he hath the cheek-teeth of a great lion.

"He hath laid my vine waste, and barked my fig-tree; he hath made it clean bare, and cast it away; the branches thereof are made white. . . .

"Be ye ashamed, O ye husbandmen! howl, O ye vine-dressers! . . .

"The vine is dried up, and the fig-tree languisheth; the pomegranate-tree, the palm-tree also, and the apple-tree, even all the trees of the field, are withered: because joy is withered away from the sons of men."[132]

132 Quoted from Joel 1:1–12.

1 Allusion to Emerson's lecture "France," given at the Concord Lyceum on 5 April 1854. In *Walden* Thoreau wrote: "I, on my side, require of every writer, first or last, a simple and sincere account of his own life, and not merely what he has heard of other men's lives; some such account as he would send to his kindred from a distant land; for if he has lived sincerely, it must have been in a distant land to me" [Wa 2].

2 Thoreau sent his paper "The Higher Law" to James Fields of the *Atlantic Monthly* in 1862. On 4 March he wrote: "As for another title for the Higher Law article, I can think of nothing better than, Life without Principle" [C 639].

3 Outer surfaces.

4 Possible reference to Emerson's aunt, Mary Moody Emerson (1774–1863): "She is singular, among women at least, in being really and perseveringly interested to know what thinkers think" [J 3:114].

5 In 1840 Thoreau purchased a combination leveling instrument and circumferentor, a surveying instrument for taking angles. His intention was to introduce surveying in the school he and his brother John ran, in order to give the study of mathematics a more practical and concrete application. This led to a lifelong source of income as a surveyor, as he made more than 150 surveys in the Concord area. The earliest extant record of a Thoreau survey is from December 1845.

6 Thoreau is known to have delivered more than seventy-five lectures.

Life Without Principle

At a lyceum, not long since, I felt that the lecturer had chosen a theme too foreign to himself,[1] and so failed to interest me as much as he might have done.[2] He described things not in or near to his heart, but toward his extremities and superficies.[3] There was, in this sense, no truly central or centralizing thought in the lecture. I would have had him deal with his privatest experience, as the poet does. The greatest compliment that was ever paid me was when one asked me what *I thought,* and attended to my answer.[4] I am surprised, as well as delighted, when this happens, it is such a rare use he would make of me, as if he were acquainted with the tool. Commonly, if men want anything of me, it is only to know how many acres I make of their land, — since I am a surveyor,[5] — or, at most, what trivial news I have burdened myself with. They never will go to law for my meat; they prefer the shell. A man once came a considerable distance to ask me to lecture on Slavery; but on conversing with him, I found that he and his clique expected seven-eighths of the lecture to be theirs, and only one-eighth mine; so I declined. I take it for granted, when I am invited to lecture anywhere, — for I have had a little experience in that business,[6] — that there is a desire to hear what *I think* on some subject, though I may be the greatest fool in the country, — and not that I should say pleasant things merely, or such as the audience will assent to; and I resolve, accordingly, that I will give them a strong dose of myself. They have sent for me, and engaged to pay for me, and I am determined that they shall have me, though I bore them beyond all precedent.

So now I would say something similar to you, my readers. Since *you* are my readers, and I have not been much of a traveller,[7] I will not talk about people a thousand miles off, but come as near home as I can. As the time is short, I will leave out all the flattery, and retain all the criticism.

Let us consider the way in which we spend our lives.

This world is a place of business. What an infinite bustle! I am awaked almost every night by the panting of the locomotive.[8] It interrupts my dreams. There is no sabbath. It would be glorious to see mankind at leisure for once. It is nothing but work, work, work.[9] I cannot easily buy a blank-book to write thoughts in;[10] they are commonly ruled for dollars and cents. An Irishman,[11] seeing me making a minute[12] in the fields, took it for granted that I was calculating my wages. If a man was tossed out of a window when an infant, and so made a cripple for life, or scared out of his wits by the Indians, it is regretted chiefly because he was thus incapacitated for—business! I think that there is nothing, not even crime, more opposed to poetry, to philosophy, ay, to life itself, than this incessant business.

There is a coarse and boisterous money-making fellow in the outskirts of our town,[13] who is going to build a bank-wall[14] under the hill along the edge meadow. The powers have put this into his head to keep him out of mischief, and he wishes me to spend three weeks digging there with him. The result will be that he will perhaps get some more money to hoard, and leave for his heirs to spend foolishly. If I do this, most will commend me as an industrious and hard-working man; but if I choose to devote myself to certain labors which yield more real profit, though but little money, they may be inclined to look on me as an idler. Nevertheless, as I do not need the police of meaningless labor to regulate me, and do not see anything absolutely praiseworthy in this fellow's

7 As Thoreau wrote in *Walden:* "I have travelled a good deal in Concord" [Wa 2]. Thoreau wrote in his journal of 6 August 1851: "It takes a man of genius to travel in his own country, in his native village" [J 2:376]. For Thoreau, "To travel and 'descry new lands' is to think new thoughts, and have new imaginings. . . . The deepest and most original thinker is the farthest travelled" [PJ 1:171]. "When you are starting away, leaving your more familiar fields, for a little adventure like a walk . . . begin to observe and moralize like a traveller," Thoreau urged in his journal of 4 September 1851: "It is worth the while to see your native village thus sometimes, as if you were a traveller passing through it, commenting on your neighbors as strangers" [J 2:452].

8 At the time Thoreau wrote this comment about the railroad, 4 March 1854, he was living at 73 Main Street in Concord, approximately one third of a mile from the depot.

9 In a 19 December 1853 letter to Harrison Gray Otis Blake (1816–1898), Thoreau cited the source of this phrase as Thomas Hood's (1799–1845) 1843 poem, "The Song of the Shirt."

10 Thoreau complained of this in his journal of 21 August and 7 September 1851.

11 This incident is recorded in Thoreau's journal of 3 April 1859.

12 Thoreau's practice was to make a field note, or minute, which was later transcribed into his journal.

13 Unidentified, although in his journal of 24 July 1852 Thoreau more specifically wrote that this fellow lived "in the north part of the town" [J 4:252].

14 Retaining wall to control erosion.

15 Thoreau wrote: "I have told many that I walk every day about half the daylight, but I think they do not believe it" [ITM 302].

16 This passage appeared in Thoreau's journal of 17 June 1853, but he had been working it over the previous year, as indicated by the following journal entries. On 28 December 1852: "One moment of life costs many hours, hours not of business but of preparation and invitation. Yet the man who does not betake himself at once and desperately to sawing is called a loafer, though he may be knocking at the doors of heaven all the while, which shall surely be opened to him" [J 4:433]. And on 24 July 1852: "As I choose to devote myself to labors which yield more real profit, though but little money, they regard me as a loafer" [J 4:252]. Cf. Thoreau's journal of 30 August 1856 passage on berrying: "If anybody . . . should spend an hour thus wading about here in this secluded swamp, barelegged, intent on the sphagnum, filling his pocket only, with no rake in his hand and no bag or bushel on the bank, he would be pronounced insane and have a guardian put over him; but if he'll spend his time skimming and watering his milk and selling his small potatoes for large ones, or generally in skinning flints, he will probably be made guardian of somebody else" [J 9:41].

17 Thoreau names this neighbor as Haden (or Hayden) in his journal of 24 July 1852, without further identification, although possibly the "Hayden senior" of whom in his 1857 journal Thoreau says "he has been at work regularly with his team almost every day" [J 9:247].

18 Colloquial phrase of unknown origin used by several writers before Thoreau, including William Makepeace Thackeray and Charles Lamb (1775–1834).

19 With the preceding emphasis on honesty, an allusion to Proverbs 20:17: "Bread of deceit is sweet to a man."

20 Allusion to the Sacred Band of Thebes, a fourth-century C.E. elite corps of 150 male couples.

21 Samuel Green Wheeler (1792–1865) described

undertaking, any more than in many an enterprise of our own or foreign governments, however amusing it may be to him or them, I prefer to finish my education at a different school.

If a man walk in the woods for love of them half of each day,[15] he is in danger of being regarded as a loafer; but if he spends his whole day as a speculator, shearing off those woods and making earth bald before her time, he is esteemed an industrious and enterprising citizen.[16] As if a town had no interest in its forests but to cut them down!

Most men would feel insulted, if it were proposed to employ them in throwing stones over a wall, and then in throwing them back, merely that they might earn their wages. But many are no more worthily employed now. For instance: just after sunrise, one summer morning, I noticed one of my neighbors[17] walking beside his team, which was slowly drawing a heavy hewn stone swung under the axle, surrounded by an atmosphere of industry,—his day's work begun,—his brow commenced to sweat,—a reproach to all sluggards and idlers,—pausing a breast the shoulders of his oxen, and half turning round with a flourish of his merciful whip, while they gained their length on him. And I thought, Such is the labor which the American Congress exists to protect,—honest, manly toil,—honest as the day is long,[18]—that makes his bread taste sweet,[19] and keeps society sweet,—which all men respect and have consecrated: one of the sacred band,[20] doing the needful, but irksome drudgery. Indeed, I felt a slight reproach, because I observed this from the window, and was not abroad and stirring about a similar business. The day went by, and at evening I passed the yard of another neighbor,[21] who keeps many servants, and spends much money foolishly, while he adds nothing to the common stock, and there I saw the stone of the morning lying beside a whimsical structure intended to adorn this Lord Timothy Dexter's[22] premises, and the dignity forthwith departed from the teamster's labor, in my eyes. In my opinion, the sun was made to light worthier toil than this. I may add, that his employer has since run off, in debt to a good part of the town, and, after passing through Chancery,[23] has settled somewhere else,[24] there to become once more a patron of the arts.

The ways by which you may get money almost without exception lead downward. To have done anything by which you earned money *merely* is to have been truly idle or worse. If the laborer gets no more than the wages which his employer pays him, he is cheated, he cheats himself. If you would get money as a writer or lecturer, you must be popular, which is to go down perpendicularly.[25] Those services which the community will most readily pay for it is most disagreeable to render. You are paid for being something less than a man. The State does not commonly reward a genius any more wisely. Even the poet-laureate would rather not have to celebrate the accidents of royalty. He must be bribed with a pipe of wine;[26] and perhaps another poet is called away from his muse to gauge that very pipe. As for my own business, even that kind of surveying which I could do with most satisfaction my employers do not want. They would prefer that I should do my work coarsely and not too well, ay, not well enough. When I observe that there are different ways of surveying, my employer commonly asks which will give him the most land, not which is most correct. I once invented a rule for measuring cordwood, and tried to introduce it in Boston;[27] but the measurer there told me that the sellers did not wish to have their wood measured correctly, — that he was already too accurate for them, and therefore they commonly got their wood measured in Charlestown before crossing the bridge.[28]

in *Memoirs of Members of the Social Circle in Concord: third Series* as one who "had the externals of wealth, dressed well, lived expensively." After he purchased the "largest and most valuable farm in Concord" in 1850, "the work of improvement began. . . . Money was freely spent, perhaps lavishly." In 1856 "his speculations failed, his notes were protested, his bills unpaid, his farm mortgaged and his establishment broken up, his family scattered."

22 Timothy Dexter (1747–1806), eccentric merchant from Newburyport, Massachusetts, who prefaced his memoir, *A Pickle for the Knowing Ones*, by writing: "Lord Dexter relates how he was created Lord by the People, announces his intention of forming a Museum of great men, that shall be the wonder of the world, and shall confound his enemies."

23 Court of Chancery, at which matters of debt and equity were settled.

24 Chelsea, Massachusetts.

25 As Thoreau wrote in his journal of 6 December 1854: "After lecturing twice this winter I feel that I am in danger of cheapening myself by trying to become a successful lecturer, *i.e.*, to interest my audiences. I am disappointed to find that most that I am and value myself for is lost, or worse than lost, on my audience" [J 7:79].

26 The poet laureate, during the seventeenth and eighteenth centuries in England, was given a cask or pipe (approximately 126 gallons) of wine annually.

27 There is no extant record of this rule for measuring cordwood: wood stacked 4 × 4 × 8 feet.

28 There are several bridges which have connected the peninsula of Charlestown to Boston and other neighboring towns: the Charles River Bridge, which opened in 1786; the Malden Bridge, which opened in 1787; and the Chelsea Bridge, which opened in 1802. The first toll-free bridge connecting Charlestown and Boston was built ca. 1825.

29 Thoreau wrote in his journal of 24 April 1852: "Society, man, has no prize to offer that can tempt me; not one" [J 3:461].
30 Allusion to the nearly five-mile-long railroad tunnel begun in 1848 through the Hoosick range in western Massachusetts.

The aim of the laborer should be, not to get his living, to get "a good job," but to perform well a certain work; and, even in a pecuniary sense, it would be economy for a town to pay its laborers so well that they would not feel that they were working for low ends, as for a livelihood merely, but for scientific, or even moral ends. Do not hire a man who does your work for money, but him who does it for love of it.

It is remarkable that there are few men so well employed, so much to their minds, but that a little money or fame would commonly buy them off from their present pursuit. I see advertisements for *active* young men, as if activity were the whole of a young man's capital. Yet I have been surprised when one has with confidence proposed to me, a grown man, to embark in some enterprise of his, as if I had absolutely nothing to do, my life having been a complete failure hitherto. What a doubtful compliment this is to pay me! As if he had met me half-way across the ocean beating up against the wind, but bound nowhere, and proposed to me to go along with him! If I did, what do you think the underwriters would say? No, no! I am not without employment at this stage of the voyage. To tell the truth, I saw an advertisement for able-bodied seamen, when I was a boy, sauntering in my native port, and as soon as I came of age I embarked.

The community has no bribe that will tempt a wise man.[29] You may raise money enough to tunnel a mountain,[30] but you cannot raise money enough to hire a man who is minding *his own* business. An efficient and valuable man does what he can, whether the community pay him for it or not. The inefficient offer their inefficiency to the highest bidder, and are forever expecting to be put into office. One would suppose that they were rarely disappointed.

Perhaps I am more than usually jealous with respect to my freedom. I feel that my connection with and obligation to society are still very slight and transient. Those slight labors which afford me a livelihood, and by which it is allowed that I am to some extent serviceable to my contemporaries, are as yet commonly a pleasure to me, and I am not often reminded that they are a necessity. So far I am successful. But I foresee, that, if my wants should be much increased, the labor required to supply them would become a drudgery. If I should sell both my forenoons and afternoons to society, as most appear to do, I am sure, that, for me, there would be nothing left worth living for. I trust that I shall never thus sell my birthright for a mess of pottage.[31] I wish to suggest that a man may be very industrious, and yet not spend his time well. There is no more fatal blunderer than he who consumes the greater part of his life getting his living. All great enterprises are self-supporting. The poet, for instance, must sustain his body by his poetry, as a steam planing-mill[32] feeds its boilers with the shavings it makes. You must get your living by loving. But as it is said of the merchants that ninety-seven in a hundred fail,[33] so the life of men generally, tried by this standard, is a failure, and bankruptcy may be surely prophesied.

Merely to come into the world the heir of a fortune is not to be born, but to be still-born, rather. To be supported by the charity of friends, or a government-pension,—provided you continue to breathe,—by whatever fine synonymes you describe these relations, is to go into the almshouse. On Sundays the poor debtor goes to church to take an account of stock, and finds, of course, that his outgoes have been greater than his income. In the Catholic Church, especially, they go into Chancery, make a clean confession, give up all, and think to start again. Thus men will lie on their backs, talking about the fall of man,[34] and never make an effort to get up.

As for the comparative demand which men make on life, it is an important difference between two, that the

31 Allusion to Genesis 25:32–34, in which Esau, son of Isaac, sold his birthright to his brother Jacob for "bread and pottage."
32 This term may refer to either a shop or mill where planing is done, or to the planing machine itself.
33 The same statistic is used in the "Economy" chapter in *Walden* and, similarly, in a 16 November 1857 letter to H. G. O. Blake: "The statement that ninety-six in a hundred doing such business surely break down is perhaps the sweetest fact that statistics have revealed,—exhilarating as the fragrant of sallows in spring. . . . If thousands are thrown out of employment, it suggests that they were not well employed. Why don't they take the hint?" [C 496].
34 Allusion to the Biblical fall as depicted in Genesis 3:1–24.

35 In archery or artillery, a shot from near enough the target to proceed on a level line, with no need for elevation to compensate for the pull of gravity.
36 Quoted from the fable of the lion and the bull in Charles Wilkins's translation *The Hĕĕtōpădēs of Vĕĕshnŏŏ-Sărmā, in a Series of Connected Fables, Interspersed with Moral, Prudential, And Political Maxims,* a selection from which was published in the *Dial,* July 1842, although this quotation was not in that selection.
37 In his journal Thoreau followed this sentence with "Neither the New Testament nor Poor Richard speaks to our condition" [J 2:164]. The *Dial* contained a few pieces on this topic, such as Bronson Alcott's sections on "Vocation" and "Labor" from his "Orphic Sayings," Frederick Henry Hedge's (1805–1890) "The Art of Life, — The Scholar's Calling," and Theodore Parker's (1810–1860) "Thoughts on Labor."
38 Epithet for God found in many works, such as John Milton's *Paradise Lost* VIII:359–360: "how may I / Adore thee, Author of this Universe."

one is satisfied with a level success, that his marks can all be hit by point-blank shots,[35] but the other, however low and unsuccessful his life may be, constantly elevates his aim, though at a very slight angle to the horizon. I should much rather be the last man, — though, as the Orientals say, "Greatness doth not approach him who is forever looking down; and all those who are looking high are growing poor."[36]

It is remarkable that there is little or nothing to be remembered written on the subject of getting a living:[37] how to make getting a living not merely honest and honorable, but altogether inviting and glorious; for if *getting* a living is not so, then living is not. One would think, from looking at literature, that this question had never disturbed a solitary individual's musings. Is it that men are too much disgusted with their experience to speak of it? The lesson of value which money teaches, which the Author of the Universe[38] has taken so much pains to teach us, we are inclined to skip altogether. As for the means of living, it is wonderful how indifferent men of all classes are about it, even reformers, so called, — whether they inherit, or earn, or steal it. I think that society has done nothing for us in this respect, or at least has undone what she has done. Cold and hunger seem more friendly to my nature than those methods which men have adopted and advise to ward them off.

The title *wise* is, for the most part, falsely applied. How can one be a wise man, if he does not know any better how to live than other men? — if he is only more cunning and intellectually subtle? Does Wisdom work in a tread-mill? or does she teach how to succeed *by her example?* Is there any such thing as wisdom not applied to life? Is she merely the miller who grinds the finest logic? It is pertinent to ask if Plato got his *living* in a better way or more successfully than his contemporaries, — or did he succumb to the difficulties of life like other men?

Did he seem to prevail over some of them merely by indifference, or by assuming grand airs? or find it easier to live, because his aunt remembered him in her will? The ways in which most men get their living, that is, live, are mere make-shifts, and a shirking of the real business of life, — chiefly because they do not know, but partly because they do not mean, any better.

The rush to California,[39] for instance, and the attitude, not merely of merchants, but of philosophers and prophets, so called, in relation to it, reflect the greatest disgrace on mankind. That so many are ready to live by luck, and so get the means of commanding the labor of others less lucky, without contributing any value to society! And that is called enterprise! I know of no more startling development of the immorality of trade, and all the common modes of getting a living. The philosophy and poetry and religion of such a mankind are not worth the dust of a puff-ball.[40] The hog that gets his living by rooting, stirring up the soil so, would be ashamed of such company. If I could command the wealth of all the worlds by lifting my finger, I would not pay *such* a price for it. Even Mahomet knew that God did not make this world in jest.[41] It makes God to be a moneyed gentleman who scatters a handful of pennies in order to see mankind scramble for them. The world's raffle! A subsistence in the domains of Nature a thing to be raffled for! What a comment, what a satire on our institutions! The conclusion will be, that mankind will hang itself upon a tree.[42] And have all the precepts in all the Bibles taught men only this? and is the last and most admirable invention of the human race only an improved muck-rake?[43] Is this the ground on which Orientals and Occidentals meet? Did God direct us so to get our living, digging where we never planted, — and He would, perchance, reward us with lumps of gold?[44]

God gave the righteous man a certificate entitling him

39 Gold was discovered at Sutter's Mill in California in January 1848, precipitating the gold rush.
40 Spore-bearing structure of fungi (order: *Lycoperdales*) from which clouds of spores are emitted, with a hollow pop or report, when the ripe puffball is struck.
41 Allusion to the Koran 38:27, which Thoreau wrote in his journal as "God did not make this world in jest; no, nor in indifference" [J 3:368], possibly after hearing it at Thomas Wentworth Higginson's lecture "Muhomed" given at the Concord Lyceum on 21 January 1852.
42 Allusion to Matthew 27:5, in which Judas, after betraying Jesus, "cast down the pieces of silver in the temple, and departed, and went and hanged himself."
43 Possible allusion to Bunyan's *The Pilgrim's Progress*, in which a man who "could look no way but downward, with a muck-rake in his hand" would fail to trade his muck rake for a celestial crown.
44 See "Autumnal Tints," note 46.

45 Allusion to Matthew 6:24–32: "Ye cannot serve God and mammon. Therefore I say unto you, Take no thought for your life, what ye shall eat, or what ye shall drink; nor yet for your body, what ye shall put on. Is not the life more than meat, and the body than raiment? . . . Consider the lilies of the field, how they grow; they toil not, neither do they spin. . . . Therefore take no thought, saying, What shall we eat? or, What shall we drink? or, Wherewithal shall we be clothed? (For after all these things do the Gentiles seek:) for your heavenly Father knoweth that ye have need of all these things."

46 Allusion to Proverbs 13:15: "Good understanding giveth favor: but the way of transgressors is hard."

47 Thoreau was reading William Howitt's (1792–1879) *Land, Labor and Gold; or, Two Years in Victoria: with Visits to Sydney and Van Dieman's Land* on 17 October 1855. The Australian gold-diggings began in 1851 in New South Wales.

to food and raiment, but the unrighteous man found a *facsimile* of the same in God's coffers, and appropriated it, and obtained food and raiment like the former.[45] It is one of the most extensive systems of counterfeiting that the world has seen. I did not know that mankind were suffering for want of gold. I have seen a little of it. I know that it is very malleable, but not so malleable as wit. A grain of gold will gild a great surface, but not so much as a grain of wisdom.

The gold-digger in the ravines of the mountains is as much a gambler as his fellow in the saloons of San Francisco. What difference does it make, whether you shake dirt or shake dice? If you win, society is the loser. The gold-digger is the enemy of the honest laborer, whatever checks and compensations there may be. It is not enough to tell me that you worked hard to get your gold. So does the Devil work hard. The way of transgressors may be hard[46] in many respects. The humblest observer who goes to the mines sees and says that gold-digging is of the character of a lottery; the gold thus obtained is not the same thing with the wages of honest toil. But, practically, he forgets what he has seen, for he has seen only the fact, not the principle, and goes into trade there, that is, buys a ticket in what commonly proves another lottery, where the fact is not so obvious.

After reading Howitt's account of the Australian gold-diggings one evening,[47] I had in my mind's eye, all night, the numerous valleys, with their streams, all cut up with foul pits, from ten to one hundred feet deep, and half a dozen feet across, as close as they can be dug, and partly filled with water,—the locality to which men furiously rush to probe for their fortunes,—uncertain where they shall break ground,—not knowing but the gold is under their camp itself,—sometimes digging one hundred and sixty feet before they strike the vein, or then missing it by a foot,—turned into demons, and regardless of each other's rights, in their thirst for riches—whole valleys, for thirty miles, suddenly honey-combed by the pits of the miners, so that even hundreds are drowned in them,—standing in water, and covered with mud and clay, they work night and day, dying of exposure and disease. Having read this, and partly for-gotten it, I was thinking, accidentally, of my own unsat-isfactory life, doing as others do; and with that vision of the diggings still before me, I asked myself, why *I* might not be washing sonic gold daily, though it were only the finest particles,—why *I* might not sink a shaft down to the gold within me, and work that mine. *There* is a Bal-larat, a Bendigo[48] for you,—what though it were a Sulky Gully?[49] At any rate, I might pursue some path, how-ever solitary and narrow and crooked,[50] in which I could walk with love and reverence. Wherever a man separates from the multitude, and goes his own way in this mood, there indeed is a fork in the road, though ordinary trav-ellers may see only a gap in the paling. His solitary path across-lots will turn out the *higher way* of the two.

Men rush to California and Australia as if the true gold were to be found in that direction; but that is to go to the very opposite extreme to where it lies. They go prospecting farther and farther away from the true lead,[51] and are most unfortunate when they think themselves most successful. Is not our *native* soil auriferous?[52] Does not a stream from the golden mountains flow through our native valley? and has not this for more than geo-logic ages been bringing down the shining particles and forming the nuggets for us? Yet, strange to tell, if a digger steal away, prospecting for this true gold, into the unex-plored solitudes around us, there is no danger that any will dog his steps, and endeavor to supplant him. He may claim and undermine the whole valley even, both the cultivated and the uncultivated portions, his whole life long in peace, for no one will ever dispute his claim.

48 Australian cities founded during the gold rush.
49 Howitt referred to "a small digging, called Sulky Gully, from the looks of the diggers who did not find it very productive."
50 Allusion to Matthew 7:13: "But strait is the gate, and narrow is the way, which leadeth unto life, and few there be that find it."
51 Lead or lode: a deposit of ore.
52 Gold-bearing.

They will not mind his cradles or his toms.[53] He is not confined to a claim twelve feet square, as at Ballarat,[54] but may mine anywhere, and wash the whole wide world in his tom.

Howitt says of the man who found the great nugget which weighed twenty-eight pounds, at the Bendigo diggings in Australia:—"He soon began to drink; got a horse, and rode all about, generally at full gallop, and, when he met people, called out to inquire if they knew who he was, and then kindly informed them that he was 'the bloody wretch that had found the nugget.' At last he rode full speed against a tree, and I think however nearly knocked his brains out." I think, however, there was no danger of that, for he had already knocked his brains out against the nugget. Howitt adds, "He is a hopelessly ruined man."[55] But he is a type of the class. They are all fast men. Hear some of the names of the places where they dig:—"Jackass Flat,"—"Sheep's-Head Gully,"—"Murderer's Bar,"[56] etc. Is there no satire in these names? Let them carry their ill-gotten wealth where they will, I am thinking it will still be "Jackass Flat," if not "Murderer's Bar," where they live.

The last resource of our energy has been the robbing of graveyards on the Isthmus of Darien,[57] an enterprise which appears to be but in its infancy; for, according to late accounts, an act has passed its second reading in the legislature of New Granada,[58] regulating this kind of mining; and a correspondent of the "Tribune" writes:— "In the dry season, when the weather will permit of the country being properly prospected, no doubt other rich 'guacas'[59] [that is, graveyards] will be found." To emigrants he says:—"Do not come before December; take the Isthmus route in preference to the Boca del Toro[60] one; bring no useless baggage, and do not cumber yourself with a tent; but a good pair of blankets will be necessary; a pick, shovel, and axe of good material will be

53 A cradle is a trough on rockers used to separate gold from earth or sand. A tom is a stationary trough used to wash gold from gravel.
54 Howitt wrote that the "holes are put down as close to each other as possible. Twelve feet square are the usual allowance."
55 Thoreau quoted and adapted from Howitt: "He soon began to drink; got a horse, and rode all about, generally at full gallop, and when he met people, called out to inquire if they knew who he was, and then kindly informed them that he was 'the bloody wretch'—that was his phrase—'that had found the nugget.' At last he rode full speed against a tree, and nearly knocked his brains out. He is a hopelessly ruined man; and I fear that will be the fate of hundreds, if not of thousands, who will stumble precipitately on more gold than they have sense and prudence to deal with."
56 Howitt wrote: "In our walk through the diggings we could not help noting the names of places and signs as indications of the character of mind of the people who give such names— Jackass Flat, Donkey Gully, Dead-horse Gully, Sheepshead Gully, Tinpot Gully, Job's Gully, Poverty Gully, and Piccaninny Gullies without end. These, however, are not quite so bad as Murderer's Flat, and Chokem Gully." Thoreau correctly transcribed "Murderer's Flat" in his journal of 19 October 1855 but may have intentionally written "Murderer's Bar" here and in the next line.
57 Now the Isthmus of Panama.
58 Now Colombia. The legislature was passed in October 1859.
59 Specifically, tombs or funeral mounds.
60 Inlet on the east coast of Panama.

almost all that is required": advice which might have been taken from the "Burker's Guide."[61] And he concludes with this line in Italics and small capitals: *"If you are doing well at home,* STAY THERE,"[62] which may fairly be interpreted to mean, "If you are getting a good living by robbing graveyards at home, stay there."

But why go to California for a text?[63] She is the child of New England, bred at her own school and church.

It is remarkable that among all the preachers there are so few moral teachers. The prophets are employed in excusing the ways of men.[64] Most reverend seniors,[65] the *illuminati*[66] of the age, tell me, with a gracious, reminiscent smile, betwixt an aspiration and a shudder, not to be too tender about these things, — to lump all that, that is, make a lump of gold of it. The highest advice I have heard on these subjects was grovelling. The burden of it was, — It is not worth your while to undertake to reform the world in this particular. Do not ask how your bread is buttered;[67] it will make you sick, if you do, — and the like. A man had better starve at once than lose his innocence in the process of getting his bread. If within the sophisticated man there is not an unsophisticated one, then he is but one of the Devil's angels.[68] As we grow old, we live more coarsely, we relax a little in our disciplines, and, to some extent, cease to obey our finest instincts. But we should be fastidious to the extreme of sanity, disregarding the gibes of those who are more unfortunate than ourselves.

In our science and philosophy, even, there is commonly no true and absolute account[69] of things. The spirit of sect and bigotry has planted its hoof amid the stars. You have only to discuss the problem, whether the stars are inhabited or not, in order to discover it.[70] Why must we daub the heavens as well as the earth? It was an unfortunate discovery that Dr. Kane was a Mason, and that Sir John Franklin was another.[71] But it was a

61 Thoreau's facetious title for a guidebook for murderers. A burker specifically is one who murders by suffocation in order to sell the body for dissection, so named after William Burke (1792–1829), who, with his associates, committed seventeen murders and sold the corpses to the Royal College of Surgeons of the City of Edinburgh.
62 Quoted from the *New-York Daily Tribune,* 29 September 1859.
63 In particular, a scriptural passage quoted in proof of a dogmatic position or taken as the subject of a discourse.
64 Possible allusion to Milton's *Paradise Lost* I:26: "And justify the ways of God to man."
65 Allusion to Shakespeare's *Othello* I.iii.78: "Most potent, grave and reverend seniors."
66 Latin: enlightened ones.
67 Allusion to the saying "Know which side your bread is buttered on," which dates back at least to the sixteenth century.
68 Allusion to Matthew 25:41: "the devil and his angels."
69 Thoreau also used this phrase in his journal of 10 November 1851: "No true and absolute account of things, — of the evening and the morning and all the phenomena between them, — but ever a petty reference to man, to society, aye, often to Christianity. What these things are when men are asleep. I come from the funeral of mankind to attend to a natural phenomenon. The so much grander significance of any fact — of sun and moon and stars — when not referred to man and his needs but viewed absolutely! Sounds that are wafted from over the confines of time" [J 3:103–104].
70 Allusion to the controversy regarding the inhabitability of other worlds, in particular debates sparked by William Whewell (1794–1866), who had been a major proponent of the idea, when he changed his mind in 1853. An editorial in the August 1854 issue of *Putnam's Monthly Magazine of American Literature, Science and Art* stated that Whewell "takes the ground that there is little reason to believe the planets and other stars in-

habited. It has received a reply from Sir David Brewster, who, in a work entitled, 'More Worlds than One, the Creed of the Philosopher, and the Hope of the Christian,' has controverted the point with much plausibility and earnestness. A rejoinder has also appeared, under the name of 'A Dialogue on the Plurality of Worlds,' by the writer of the original essay. We are thus presented with the spectacle of a most elaborate and spirited controversy between two of the most eminent men of science in Great Britain, in respect to a subject on which there are no facts to argue."

71 Sir John Franklin (b. 1786), English explorer who was last seen in Baffin Bay, disappeared in 1847 in the Arctic attempting to find the Northwest Passage. His remains were discovered in 1859. Elisha Kent Kane, American explorer and physician who joined the United States Grinnell Expedition in search of Franklin in 1850. The Masons, or Freemasons, are an international fraternal and charitable order of which both men were members.

72 In 1858 Thoreau submitted his "Chesuncook" to the Atlantic Monthly, established the previous year. The editor, James Russell Lowell (1819–1891), expurgated a sentence about the pine tree: "It is as immortal as I am, and perchance will go to as high a heaven, there to tower above me still." Thoreau was outraged at the liberties taken by the editor, writing him a letter on 22 June 1858, in which he stated: "The editor has, in this case, no more right to omit a sentiment than to insert one, or put words into my mouth. . . . I am not willing to be associated in any way, unnecessarily, with parties who will confess themselves so bigoted & timid as this implies. I could excuse a man who was afraid of an uplifted fist, but if one manifests fear at the utterance of a sincere thought, I must think that his life is a kind of nightmare continued into broad daylight" [C 515–516].

73 Doctors of divinity.

74 Allusion to Nathaniel Peabody Rogers (1794–1846), editor of the antislavery newspaper Herald of Freedom, who wrote in "The American Board"

more cruel suggestion that possibly that was the reason why the former went in search of the latter. There is not a popular magazine in this country that would dare to print a child's thought on important subjects without comment.[72] It must be submitted to the D.D.s.[73] I would it were the chickadee-dees.[74]

You come from attending the funeral of mankind to attend to a natural phenomenon. A little thought is sexton[75] to all the world.

I hardly know an *intellectual* man, even, who is so broad and truly liberal that you can think aloud in his society. Most with whom you endeavor to talk soon come to a stand against some institution in which they appear to hold stock,—that is, some particular, not universal, way of viewing things. They will continually thrust their own low roof, with its narrow skylight, between you and the sky, when it is the unobstructed heavens you would view.[76] Get out of the way with your cobwebs, wash your windows, I say! In some lyceums they tell me that they have voted to exclude the subject of religion. But how do I know what their religion is, and when I am near to or far from it? I have walked into such an arena and done my best to make a clean breast of what religion I have experienced, and the audience never suspected what I was about. The lecture was as harmless as moonshine to them. Whereas, if I had read to them the biography of the greatest scamps in history, they might have thought that I had written the lives of the deacons of their church. Ordinarily, the inquiry is, Where did you come from? or, Where are you going? That was a more pertinent question which I overheard one of my auditors put to another once,—"What does he lecture for?"[77] It made me quake in my shoes.

To speak impartially, the best men that I know are not serene, a world in themselves. For the most part, they dwell in forms, and flatter and study effect only more finely than the rest. We select granite for the under-pinning of our houses and barns; we build fences of stone; but we do not ourselves rest on an underpinning of granitic truth, the lowest primitive rock.[78] Our sills are rotten. What stuff is the man made of[79] who is not coexistent in our thought with the purest and subtilest truth? I often accuse my finest acquaintances of an immense frivolity; for, while there are manners and compliments we do not meet, we do not teach one another the lessons of honesty and sincerity that the brutes do, or of steadiness and solidity that the rocks do. The fault is commonly mutual, however; for we do not habitually demand any more of each other.

That excitement about Kossuth,[80] consider how characteristic, but superficial, it was!—only another kind of politics or dancing. Men were making speeches to him all over the country, but each expressed only the thought, or the want of thought, of the multitude. No man stood on truth. They were merely banded together, as usual, one leaning on another, and all together on nothing; as the Hindoos made the world rest on an elephant, the elephant on a tortoise, and the tortoise on a serpent, and had nothing to put under the serpent.[81] For all fruit of that stir we have the Kossuth hat.[82]

Just so hollow and ineffectual, for the most part, is our ordinary conversation. Surface meets surface. When our life ceases to be inward and private, conversation degenerates into mere gossip. We rarely meet a man who can tell us any news which he has not read in a newspaper, or been told by his neighbor; and, for the most part, the only difference between us and our fellow is, that he has seen the newspaper, or been out to tea, and we have not. In proportion as our inward life fails, we go more constantly and desperately to the post-office. You may depend on it, that the poor fellow who walks away with the greatest number of letters, proud of his ex-

(*Herald of Freedom*, 19 September 1845): "The D.D.'s (chick-*adee-dees*) were as thick as hops."

75 Church official one of whose duties was the digging of graves.

76 From his journal of 9 May 1853, in contrast to Bronson Alcott, in whose society Thoreau "can express at my leisure, with more or less success, my vaguest but most cherished fancy or thought. There are never any obstacles in the way of our meeting. He has no creed. He is not pledged to any institution. The sanest man I ever knew; the fewest crotchets, after all, has he" [J 5:130].

77 Written in his journal of 24 April 1852 and probably in reference to his most recent lecture in Boston on the 6th of April. Thomas Wentworth Higginson, who had arranged the lecture, later recalled "the disastrous entertainment" in which he and Thoreau "found a few young mechanics reading newspapers. . . . Some laid down their newspapers, more retained them; the lecture proved to be one of the most introspective chapters from 'Walden.' A few went to sleep, the rest rustled their papers."

78 Possible allusion to Luke 6:47–48: "Whosoever cometh to me, and heareth my sayings, and doeth them, I will shew you to whom he is like: He is like a man which built an house, and digged deep, and laid the foundation on a rock: and when the flood arose, the stream beat vehemently upon that house, and could not shake it: for it was founded upon a rock."

79 Possible allusion to Shakespeare's *The Tempest* IV.i.156–157: "We are such stuff / As dreams are made on."

80 Lajos Kossuth (1802–1894), Hungarian patriot who worked, unsuccessfully, to establish Hungarian independence from Austria in the 1840s. Kossuth spoke in Concord on 7 May 1852 and in Lexington on 11 May during his 1851–1852 lecture tour in the United States, where he was collecting funds for the independence movement.

81 Cf. "Walking," note 116.

82 *Scientific American* reported on 27 December 1851: "Since Kossuth came to New York, the Kos-

suth hat has become quite fashionable. This is a
low crowned hat with a small black ostrich feather
stuck at one side. . . . These are made of felted
wool, and allow gas to pass from the head to escape freely. . . . Oldish people of a sedate turn,
although they would prefer the 'Kossuth hat,' do
not like to adopt it just yet, from a prudential fear
of being conspicuous." The hat was promoted
by the New York merchant John Nicholas Genin
(1819–1878), who distributed several of these hats
to Kossuth's followers and Hungarian refugees
prior to their disembarcation from the ship at
Sandy Hook, creating the new fashion fad.

83 Cf. "Slavery in Massachusetts," note 39.

84 Cf. "Slavery in Massachusetts," note 46.

85 In the journal version of this passage Thoreau
wrote: "In relation to politics, to society, aye, to
the whole outward world, I am tempted to ask,
Why do *they* lay such stress on a particular experience which you have had?—that, after twenty-five
years, you should meet Cyrus Warren again on
the sidewalk!" [J 3:102], referring either to Cyrus
Warren (1789–1866) or his son Cyrus (1824–1901),
a student of the Thoreau brothers in 1839.

86 Small spores.

87 Young shoot not yet differentiated into stem,
root, or leaf.

88 Although he may not have run, Thoreau could
appreciate the entertainment value of such an
event and would have walked around the corner.
Going to Cape Cod on 9 October 1849, Thoreau
decided to travel by way of Cohasset to view a
shipwreck after reading handbills in Boston advertising, "Death! 145 lives lost at Cohasset!"
Similarly, despite the destructive power of a fire,
Thoreau was aware of its power to attract. On
5 June 1850 Thoreau wrote in his journal: "Men go
to a fire for entertainment. When I see how eagerly
men will run to a fire, whether in warm or in cold
weather, by day or by night, dragging an engine at
their heels, I am astonished to perceive how good
a purpose the love of excitement is made to serve.
What other force, pray, what offered pay, what
disinterested neighborliness could ever effect so

tensive correspondence, has not heard from himself this
long while.

I do not know but it is too much to read one newspaper a week. I have tried it recently, and for so long it
seems to me that I have not dwelt in my native region.[83]
The sun, the clouds, the snow, the trees say not so much
to me. You cannot serve two masters.[84] It requires more
than a day's devotion to know and to possess the wealth
of a day.

We may well be ashamed to tell what things we have
read or heard in our day. I do not know why my news
should be so trivial,—considering what one's dreams
and expectations are, why the developments should be
so paltry. The news we hear, for the most part, is not
news to our genius. It is the stalest repetition. You are
often tempted to ask, why such stress is laid on a particular experience which you have had,—that, after
twenty-five years, you should meet Hobbins, Registrar
of Deeds, again on the sidewalk.[85] Have you not budged
an inch, then? Such is the daily news. Its facts appear to
float in the atmosphere, insignificant as the sporules[86] of
fungi, and impinge on some neglected *thallus*,[87] or surface of our minds, which affords a basis for them, and
hence a parasitic growth. We should wash ourselves clean
of such news. Of what consequence, though our planet
explode, if there is no character involved in the explosion? In health we have not the least curiosity about such
events. We do not live for idle amusement. I would not
run round a corner to see the world blow up.[88]

All summer, and far into the autumn, perchance, you
unconsciously went by the newspapers and the news,
and now you find it was because the morning and the
evening were full of news to you. Your walks were full of
incidents. You attended, not to the affairs of Europe, but
to your own affairs in Massachusetts fields. If you chance
to live and move and have your being[89] in that thin

stratum in which the events that make the news transpire, — thinner than the paper on which it is printed, — then these things will fill the world for you; but if you soar above or dive below that plane, you cannot remember nor be reminded of them. Really to see the sun rise or go down every day, so to relate ourselves to a universal fact, would preserve us sane forever. Nations! What are nations? Tartars, and Huns, and Chinamen![90] Like insects, they swarm. The historian strives in vain to make them memorable. It is for want of a man that there are so many men. It is individuals that populate the world. Any man thinking may say with the Spirit of Lodin, —

"I look down from my height on nations,
And they become ashes before me; —
Calm is dwelling in the clouds;
Pleasant are the great fields of my rest."[91]

Pray, let us live without being drawn by dogs, Esquimaux-fashion, tearing over hill and dale, and biting each other's ears.

Not without a slight shudder at the danger, I often perceive how near I had come to admitting into my mind the details of some trivial affair, — the news of the street; and I am astonished to observe how willing men are to lumber their minds with such rubbish, — to permit idle rumors and incidents of the most insignificant kind to intrude on ground which should be sacred to thought. Shall the mind be a public arena, where the affairs of the street and the gossip of the tea-table chiefly are discussed? Or shall it be a quarter of heaven itself, — an Hypaethral temple,[92] consecrated to the service of the gods? I find it so difficult to dispose of the few facts which to me are significant, that I hesitate to burden my attention with those which are insignificant, which only a divine

much? No, these are boys who are to be dealt with, and these are the motives that prevail. There is no old man or woman dropping into the grave but covets excitement" [J 2:30].

89 Allusion to Acts 17:18: "For in him we live, and move, and have our being."

90 Nations which led invasions.

91 Quoted from "Carric. A Poem," in James Macpherson's *The Genuine Remains of Ossian, Literally Translated* (cf. "Walking," note 141). The dash after the second line indicates four lines dropped. Thoreau had copied these lines into his journal of 1 May 1851.

92 A temple open to the sky, a probable allusion to David Roberts's (1796–1864) "The Hypaethral Temple at Philae, Called the Bed of Pharaoh," in his *Egypt and Nubia from Drawings Made on the Spot.*

93 Cf. "Walking," note 100.

94 Thoreau appeared twice in court in 1859. On 11 January he testified to the genuineness of the Reverend Barzillai Frost's will, the signing of which he had witnessed on 4 February 1856. On 6 October, Thoreau appeared in Boston Superior Court in relation to the case that his aunts, Maria and Jane, brought against their neighbor, Eliza Pallies, who had torn down their fence and then erected a spite fence less than two feet from their door. Pallies lost the case.

95 Allusion to phrenology, a popular pseudo-science in Thoreau's day, first proposed by a Viennese doctor, Franz Josef Gall (1758–1828), in which relationships were believed to exist between the shape of the head and character. The degree of mental development was supposed to be indicated by the shape of the skull, reflecting the development of the underlying parts of the brain in which the various mental processes were assumed to take place. A head high but narrow between the ears was an indication of moral and benevolent character, but a low and narrow head indicated a deficiency of human and religious susceptibilities.

96 Like a machine with cogs, with a possible allusion to the Scottish word *coggie*, meaning a small wooden bowl for porridge.

97 Allusion to the principle of presumed innocence as expressed in the phrase "innocent until proven guilty" attributed to the English lawyer Sir William Garrow (1760–1840).

98 Self-referencing pun, as when he wrote in "Paradise (To Be) Regained" about a "thoroughbred business man."

99 Related to Mount Parnassus; cf. "Natural History of Massachusetts," note 42.

mind could illustrate. Such is, for the most part, the news in newspapers and conversation. It is important to preserve the mind's chastity in this respect. Think of admitting the details of a single case of the criminal court into our thoughts, to stalk profanely through their very *sanctum sanctorum*[93] for an hour, ay, for many hours! to make a very bar-room of the mind's inmost apartment, as if for so long the dust of the street had occupied us,— the very street itself, with all its travel, its bustle, and filth had passed through our thoughts' shrine! Would it not be an intellectual and moral suicide? When I have been compelled to sit spectator and auditor in a court-room for some hours,[94] and have seen my neighbors, who were not compelled, stealing in from time to time, and tiptoeing about with washed hands and faces, it has appeared to my mind's eye, that, when they took off their hats, their ears suddenly expanded into vast hoppers for sound, between which even their narrow heads[95] were crowded. Like the vanes of windmills, they caught the broad, but shallow stream of sound, which, after a few titillating gyrations in their coggy[96] brains, passed out the other side. I wondered if, when they got home, they were as careful to wash their ears as before their hands and faces. It has seemed to me, at such a time, that the auditors and the witnesses, the jury and the counsel, the judge and the criminal at the bar,—if I may presume him guilty before he is convicted,[97]—were all equally criminal, and a thunderbolt might be expected to descend and consume them all together.

By all kinds of traps and sign-boards, threatening the extreme penalty of the divine law, exclude such trespassers from the only ground which can be sacred to you. It is so hard to forget what it is worse than useless to remember! If I am to be a thoroughfare,[98] I prefer that it be of the mountain-brooks, the Parnassian streams,[99] and not the town-sewers. There is inspiration, that gossip which comes to the ear of the attentive mind from the courts of heaven. There is the profane and stale revelation of the bar-room and the police court. The same ear is fitted to receive both communications. Only the character of the hearer determines to which it shall be open, and to which closed. I believe that the mind can be permanently profaned by the habit of attending to trivial things, so that all our thoughts shall be tinged with triviality. Our very intellect shall be macadamized,[100] as it were,—its foundation broken into fragments for the wheels of travel to roll over; and if you would know what will make the most durable pavement, surpassing rolled stones, spruce blocks, and asphaltum,[101] you have only to look into some of our minds which have been subjected to this treatment so long.

If we have thus desecrated ourselves,—as who has not?—the remedy will be by wariness and devotion to reconsecrate ourselves, and make once more a fane[102] of the mind. We should treat our minds, that is, ourselves, as innocent and ingenuous children, whose guardians we are, and be careful what objects and what subjects we thrust on their attention. Read not the Times.[103] Read the Eternities. Conventionalities are at length as bad as impurities. Even the facts of science may dust the mind by their dryness, unless they are in a sense effaced each morning, or rather rendered fertile by the dews of fresh and living truth. Knowledge does not come to us by details, but in flashes of light from heaven. Yes, every thought that passes through the mind helps to wear and tear it, and to deepen the ruts, which, as in the streets of Pompeii,[104] evince how much it has been used. How many things there are concerning which we might well deliberate, whether we had better know them,—had better let their peddling-carts be driven, even at the slowest trot or walk, over that bridge of glorious span by which we trust to pass at last from the farthest brink of

100 Paved over, from John McAdam (1756–1836), who engineered the method of road construction involving the compacting of small fragments of stone into a solid layer.
101 Asphalt.
102 Cf. "Thomas Carlyle and His Works," note 76.
103 Many major cities published newspapers entitled the *Times.*
104 Italian city destroyed by an eruption of Mount Vesuvius in 79 C.E., the ruins of which were discovered in 1748. Thoreau read in Sir William Gell's (1777–1836) *Edifices and Ornaments of Pompeii, the Results of Excavations since 1819:* "The streets are paved with large irregular pieces of lava joined neatly together, in which the chariot wheels have worn ruts, still discernible; in some places they are an inch and a half deep, and in the narrow streets follow one track; where the streets are wider, the ruts are more numerous and irregular."

105 George III of England (1738–1820, r. 1801–1820).

106 Latin: public thing.

107 Quoted from Cicero's *Orations* ("Oratio pro Milone" 26–70). Thoreau altered *respublica* to *res-PRIVITA*.

108 Allusion to Francis Scott Key's (1779–1843) "The Star Spangled Banner," each stanza of which ends with "O'er the land of the free, and the home of the brave."

109 Allusion to "Taxation without representation is tyranny," attributed to James Otis (1725–1783).

110 Allusion to the Declaration of Independence, in which it is stated against King George that he is "quartering large Bodies of Armed Troops among us."

111 Common nineteenth-century name for an American, similar to the use of John Bull for the English, but Thoreau also used the name to mean a "raw country bumpkin" [MW 12].

time to the nearest shore of eternity! Have we no culture, no refinement,—but skill only to live coarsely and serve the Devil?—to acquire a little worldly wealth, or fame, or liberty, and make a false show with it, as if we were all husk and shell, with no tender and living kernel to us? Shall our institutions be like those chestnut-burs which contain abortive nuts, perfect only to prick the fingers?

America is said to be the arena on which the battle of freedom is to be fought; but surely it cannot be freedom in a merely political sense that is meant. Even if we grant that the American has freed himself from a political tyrant,[105] he is still the slave of an economical and moral tyrant. Now that the republic—the *res-publica*[106]—has been settled, it is time to look after the res-*privata*,—the private state,—to see, as the Roman senate charged its consuls, "*ne quid res-PRIVATA detrimenti caperet,*"[107] that the *private* state receive no detriment.

Do we call this the land of the free?[108] What is it to be free from King George and continue the slaves of King Prejudice? What is it to be born free and not to live free? What is the value of any political freedom, but as a means to moral freedom? Is it a freedom to be slaves, or a freedom to be free, of which we boast? We are a nation of politicians, concerned about the outmost defences only of freedom. It is our children's children who may perchance be really free. We tax ourselves unjustly. There is a part of us which is not represented. It is taxation without representation.[109] We quarter troops,[110] we quarter fools and cattle of all sorts upon ourselves. We quarter our gross bodies on our poor souls, till the former eat up all the latter's substance.

With respect to a true culture and manhood, we are essentially provincial still, not metropolitan,—mere Jonathans.[111] We are provincial, because we do not find at home our standards,—because we do not worship truth, but the reflection of truth,—because we are warped and narrowed by an exclusive devotion to trade and commerce and manufactures and agriculture and the like, which are but means, and not the end.

So is the English Parliament provincial. Mere country-bumpkins, they betray themselves, when any more important question arises for them to settle, the Irish question,[112] for instance,—the English question why did I not say? Their natures are subdued to what they work in.[113] Their "good breeding" respects only secondary objects. The finest manners in the world are awkwardness and fatuity, when contrasted with a finer intelligence. They appear but as the fashions of past days,—mere courtliness, knee-buckles and small clothes,[114] out of date. It is the vice, but not the excellence of manners, that they are continually being deserted by the character; they are cast-off clothes or shells, claiming the respect which belonged to the living creature. You are presented with the shells instead of the meat, and it is no excuse generally, that, in the case of some fishes, the shells are of more worth than the meat. The man who thrusts his manners upon me does as if he were to insist on introducing me to his cabinet of curiosities, when I wished to see himself. It was not in this sense that the poet Decker called Christ "the first true gentleman that ever breathed."[115] I repeat that in this sense the most splendid court in Christendom is provincial, having authority to consult about Transalpine interests only, and not the affairs of Rome.[116] A praetor or proconsul[117] would suffice to settle the questions which absorb the attention of the English Parliament and the American Congress.

Government and legislation! these I thought were respectable professions. We have heard of heaven-born Numas, Lycurguses, and Solons,[118] in the history of the world, whose *names* at least may stand for ideal legislators; but think of legislating to *regulate* the breeding of slaves,[119] or the exportation of tobacco! What have divine

112 The question of Irish independence from Great Britain.

113 Allusion to Shakespeare's Sonnet 111:6–7: "My nature is subdu'd / To what it works in, like the dyer's hand."

114 Late-eighteenth-century fashions: knee buckles were breeches fastened at the knee with small buckles; small clothes were close-fitting breeches fastened at the knee with buttons.

115 Quoted from Thomas Decker (ca. 1572–1632) and Thomas Middleton's *The Honest Whore* I.13.777.

116 At this time the temporal authority of the papacy in Rome had been minimalized following the 1848 revolution.

117 In the Roman Empire, an annually elected magistrate and a provincial governor of consular rank, respectively.

118 Ancient or legendary lawgivers: Numa Pompilius, legendary king of Rome, successor to Romulus, and supposed originator of ceremonial law and religious rites; Lycurgus, reputed founder of the Spartan constitution; and Solon (ca. 638–558 B.C.E.), Athenian statesman and poet who laid the foundations of Athenian democracy.

119 Although there was no actual legislature regarding slave breeding, Thoreau may have had in mind the Congressional Act to Prohibit the Importation of Slaves implemented on 1 January 1808, the ultimate result of which was to increase slave breeding in Maryland, Virginia, North Carolina, Kentucky, Tennessee, and Delaware; or Harriet Beecher Stowe's (1811–1896) *The Key to Uncle Tom's Cabin; Presenting the Original Facts and Documents Upon Which the Story Is Founded*, which reported debates in the Virginia legislature and elsewhere regarding this practice.

120 Although "Son of God" was used specifically in the New Testament as an epithet for Jesus Christ, in the Old Testament and in several places in the New Testament the word *son* was used to signify not only filiation but also any close connection or intimate relationship, and the term *son(s) of God* was used for persons having any special relationship with God: "Behold, what manner of love the Father hath bestowed upon us, that we should be called the sons of God" (John 3:10), and "For as many as are led by the Spirit of God, they are the sons of God" (Romans 8:14).

121 A common phrase, as Hayward noted in *The New England Gazetteer*: "In regard to commerce, it has often been said of New England, that 'her canvas whitens every sea;' and Massachusetts is the most commercial of this family of states."

122 Allusion to the capture of free black sailors in Charleston, South Carolina. Charles Lyell (1797–1875) in his *A Second Visit to the United States of North America* recounted: "A few years ago a ship from Massachusetts touched at Charleston, having some free blacks on board, the steward and cook being of the number. On their landing, they were immediately put into jail by virtue of a law of South Carolina, not of very old standing. The government of Massachusetts, in a state of great indignation, sent a lawyer to investigate the case and remonstrate. This agent took up his abode at the Charleston Hotel. . . . A few days after his arrival, the hotel was surrounded, to the terror of all the inmates, by a mob of 'gentlemen,' who were resolved to seize the New England envoy. There is no saying to what extremities they would have proceeded, had not the lawyer's daughter, a spirited girl, refused to leave the hotel. The excitement lasted five days, and almost every northern man in Charleston was made to feel himself in personal danger. At length, by the courage and energy of some of the leading citizens, Mr. H——was enabled to escape. . . . The same law has given rise to some very awkward disputes with the captains of English vessels, whose colored sailors have, in like manner, been im-

legislators to do with the exportation or the importation of tobacco? what humane ones with the breeding of slaves? Suppose you were to submit the question to any son of God,[120]—and has He no children in the nineteenth century? is it a family which is extinct?—in what condition would you get it again? What shall a State like Virginia say for itself at the last day, in which these have been the principal, the staple productions? What ground is there for patriotism in such a State? I derive my facts from statistical tables which the States themselves have published.

A commerce that whitens every sea[121] in quest of nuts and raisins, and makes slaves of its sailors for this purpose![122] I saw, the other day, a vessel which had been wrecked, and many lives lost,[123] and her cargo of rags, juniper-berries, and bitter almonds were strewn along the shore. It seemed hardly worth the while to tempt the dangers of the sea between Leghorn and New York for the sake of a cargo of juniper-berries and bitter almonds. America sending to the Old World for her bitters![124] Is not the sea-brine, is not shipwreck, bitter enough to make the cup of life go down here? Yet such, to a great extent, is our boasted commerce; and there are those who style themselves statesmen and philosophers who are so blind as to think that progress and civilization depend on precisely this kind of interchange and activity,—the activity of flies about a molasses-hogshead.[125] Very well, observes one, if men were oysters.[126] And very well, answer I, if men were mosquitoes.

Lieutenant Herndon, whom our Government sent to explore the Amazon, and, it is said, to extend the area of Slavery, observed that there was wanting there "an industrious and active population, who know what the comforts of life are, and who have artificial wants to draw out the great resources of the country."[127] But what are the "artificial wants" to be encouraged? Not the love of luxuries, like the tobacco and slaves of, I believe, his native Virginia, nor the ice and granite and other material wealth of our native New England; nor are "the great resources of a country" that fertility or barrenness of soil which produces these. The chief want, in every State that I have been into,[128] was a high and earnest purpose in its inhabitants. This alone draws out "the great resources" of Nature, and at last taxes her beyond her resources; for man naturally dies out of her. When we want culture more than potatoes, and illumination more than sugar-plums,[129] then the great resources of a world are taxed and drawn out, and the result, or staple production, is, not slaves, nor operatives,[130] but men,—those rare fruits called heroes, saints, poets, philosophers, and redeemers.

In short, as a snow-drift is formed where there is a lull in the wind, so, one would say, where there is a lull of truth, an institution springs up. But the truth blows right on over it, nevertheless, and at length blows it down.

What is called politics is comparatively something so superficial and inhuman, that, practically, I have never fairly recognized that it concerns me at all. The newspapers, I perceive, devote some of their columns specially to politics or government without charge; and this, one would say, is all that saves it; but, as I love literature, and, to some extent, the truth also, I never read those columns at any rate. I do not wish to blunt my sense of right so much. I have not got to answer for having read a single President's Message.[131] A strange age of the world this, when empires, kingdoms, and republics come a-begging to a private man's door, and utter their complaints at his elbow! I cannot take up a newspaper but I find that some wretched government or other, hard pushed, and on its last legs, is interceding with me, the reader, to vote for it,—more importunate than an Italian beggar;[132] and if I have a mind to look at its certificate, made, perchance, by some benevolent merchant's clerk, or the skipper that

prisoned. To obtain redress for the injury, in such cases, is impossible." The lawyer and his daughter were Thoreau's fellow Concordians Samuel Hoar and Elizabeth Hoar (1814–1878).

123 On 19 July 1850 Sarah Margaret Fuller (1810–1850)—author, Transcendentalist, friend of Emerson, editor of the *Dial,* author of *Summer on the Lakes in 1843* and *Women in the Nineteenth Century,* and foreign correspondent for the *New-York Tribune*—together with her husband, Giovanni Angelo, Marchese d'Ossoli (ca. 1820–1850), and their son, Angelo Eugenio Filippo Ossoli (1848–1850), drowned off Fire Island, New York, when the ship *Elizabeth,* on which they were returning to America, wrecked. Emerson sent Thoreau to recover what he could locate of their remains and personal belongings.

124 Liquor infused with bitter herbs and roots.

125 A large butt or cask containing from 100 to 140 gallons.

126 Oysters, as explained by the Wellfleet Oysterman in *Cape Cod,* "merely settled down as they grew; if put down in a square they would be found so."

127 Quoted from William Lewis Herndon (1813–1857) and Lardner Gibbon's (1820–1910) *Exploration of the Valley of the Amazon.*

128 At the time Thoreau was preparing this for publication in February 1862, he had been in eleven states: Connecticut, Illinois, Maine, Massachusetts, Minnesota, New Hampshire, New Jersey, New York, Pennsylvania, Rhode Island, and Vermont, excluding states passed through but not visited by Thoreau on his Minnesota excursion.

129 A small round sweet of flavored boiled sugar. In his journal of 16 November 1858 Thoreau wrote: "The audiences do not want to hear any prophets; they do not wish to be stimulated and instructed, but entertained. They, their wives and daughters, go to the Lyceum to suck a sugar-plum" [J 11:327].

130 Workmen.

131 Official communication from a chief executive to a legislative body.

132 Hawthorne called Italy "beggar-haunted" in *The Marble Faun* and referred to the "multitude of beggars in Italy" in his *French and Italian Note-Books*.

133 The eruption of Mount Vesuvius in Italy in June 1787 was witnessed by Goethe (1749–1832), whose *Die Italiänische Reise* Thoreau read in 1837.

134 The Po, in northern Italy, overflowed its banks annually.

135 Millard Fillmore (1800–1874) when this sentence was originally written in Thoreau's journal, 17 November 1850; Franklin Pierce (1804–1869) when Thoreau began giving this as a lecture, 1854; and James Buchanan when he prepared this lecture for publication. They were the thirteenth (1850–1853), fourteenth (1853–1857), and fifteenth (1857–1861) presidents, respectively.

136 Army garrison on Castle Island in Boston Harbor, at which, according to Thoreau's journal, his father, John, was stationed as commissary during the War of 1812 [J 2:81].

137 Beneath the human.

138 Indigestion.

139 The two major political parties by 1856 were the Republicans (replacing the Whigs) and the Democrats, with smaller parties, such as the Free-Soil and Know-Nothing parties, springing up for short periods.

140 Flatulence, one of the conditions of dyspepsia.

141 Allusion to Wordsworth's "Ode: Intimations of Immortality" 59: "Our birth is but a sleep and a forgetting."

142 Another condition caused by dyspepsia.

143 Those with good digestion.

brought it over, for it cannot speak a word of English itself, I shall probably read of the eruption of some Vesuvius,[133] or the overflowing of some Po,[134] true or forged, which brought it into this condition. I do not hesitate, in such a case, to suggest work, or the almshouse; or why not keep its castle in silence, as I do commonly? The poor President,[135] what with preserving his popularity and doing his duty, is completely bewildered. The newspapers are the ruling power. Any other government is reduced to a few marines at Fort Independence.[136] If a man neglects to read the Daily Times, Government will go down on its knees to him, for this is the only treason in these days.

Those things which now most engage the attention of men, as politics and the daily routine, are, it is true, vital functions of human society, but should be unconsciously performed, like the corresponding functions of the physical body. They are *infra*-human,[137] a kind of vegetation. I sometimes awake to a half-consciousness of them going on about me, as a man may become conscious of some of the processes of digestion in a morbid state, and so have the dyspepsia, as it is called.[138] It is as if a thinker submitted himself to be rasped by the great gizzard of creation. Politics is, as it were, the gizzard of society, full of grit and gravel, and the two political parties are its two opposite halves,—sometimes split into quarters,[139] it may be, which grind on each other. Not only individuals, but States, have thus a confirmed dyspepsia, which expresses itself, you can imagine by what sort of eloquence.[140] Thus our life is not altogether a forgetting,[141] but also, alas! to a great extent, a remembering of that which we should never have been conscious of, certainly not in our waking hours. Why should we not meet, not always as dyspeptics, to tell our bad dreams,[142] but sometimes as *eu*peptics,[143] to congratulate each other on the ever glorious morning? I do not make an exorbitant demand, surely.

Appendix
Excerpts from John Adolphus Etzler

In "Paradise (To Be) Regained" Thoreau silently and sometimes substantially amended quotations from John Adolphus Etzler's *The Paradise within the Reach of all Men, Without Labor, by Powers of Nature and Machinery. An Address to All Intelligent Men,* 2nd English ed. (London: James H. Young, 1842). The following, for the purpose of comparison, are the non-edited texts from Thoreau's source with the page number(s) for the corresponding passage in "Paradise (To Be) Regained" in this edition. They contain portions that Thoreau did not quote in order to provide the context from which he drew his excerpts, and all excerpts have been restored to the original order of Etzler's book. All of Thoreau's excerpts are from Part One.

FELLOW-MEN!

I promise to show the means for creating a paradise within ten years, where every thing desirable for human life may be had for every man in superabundance, without labor, without pay; where the whole face of nature is changed into the most beautiful form of which it be capable; where man may live in the most magnificent palaces, in all imaginable refinements of luxury, in the most delightful gardens; where he may accomplish, without his labor, in one year, more than hitherto could be done in thousands of years; he may level mountains, sink valleys, create lakes, drain lakes and swamps, intersect every-where the land with beautiful canals, with roads for transporting heavy loads of many thousand tons and for

travelling 1000 miles in 24 hours; he may cover the ocean with floating islands moveable in any desired direction with immense power and celerity, in perfect security and in all comforts and luxury, bearing gardens, palaces, with thousands of families, provided with rivulets of sweet water; he may explore the interior of the globe, travel from pole to pole in a fortnight; he may provide himself with means, unheard of yet, for increasing his knowledge of the world; and so his intelligence; he may lead a life of continual happiness, of enjoyments unknown yet, he may free himself from almost all the evils that afflict mankind, except death, and even put death far beyond the common period of human life, and finally render it less afflicting: mankind may thus live in and enjoy a new world, far superior to our present, and raise themselves to a far higher scale of beings.

The Paradise within the Reach of all Men, 5; "Paradise (To Be) Regained," 64–65

We know by experiences, that ships of the first rank carry sails 200 feet high. In order to form an idea near the reality of nature, how much power of wind there may be at our disposal, we have to ascertain, by a deduction from experiences and observations, how large we may construct and expose surfaces to the effects of wind, and how close they may be brought together without intercepting the wind and diminishing its power materially. We know by experiences, that ships of the first rank carry sails 200 feet high. We may, therefore, equally, on land, oppose to the wind surfaces 200 feet high. Imagine a line of such surfaces 200 feet high, and a mile (or about 5000 feet) long; the same would then contain 1,000,000 square feet. Suppose these surfaces intersect the direction of the wind in a right angle, by some contrivances, and receives consequently the full power of the wind at all times. The average power of wind being equal to 1 horse's upon every 100 square feet, the total power these surfaces would receive would then be equal to 1,000,000 divided by 100, or 10,000 horses' power. Allowing the power of 1 horse to be equal to that of 10 men, the power of 10,000 horses is equal to 100,000 men's. But as men cannot uninterruptedly work, and want about half of the time for sleep and repose, the same power would equal to 200,000 men's. Imagine such another line of surfaces just behind or before the former at 1 mile's distance, parallel to the first and in the same circumstances. This second line would then receive the same power of wind again as the first; for the distance being 25 times greater than their height, the one line could not intercept the wind from the other in any considerable degree, both lines would receive the full power of wind, as soon as the direction of it would deviate from the horizontal more than about 2 degrees. It may be easily observed, that the wind will generally strike the ground in a steeper direction, and therefore admit a closer approach of such parallel surfaces. That the wind strikes the ground obliquely is evident on the high sea. Else whence the disturbance and rise of the waves on it? — If the wind moved parallel to the ground, the surface of the sea could not be affected by it, and would remain smooth for ever. But such is never the case. The least breeze ruffles the surface of the water. And it is too well known, to what

size and powerful effects the waves may be raised by wind. Moreover, experiences in navigation teach, that vessels of the first rank sailing along a shore of about 200 feet high, trees etc. included, at their wind-side, at a distance of 1 mile, will not suffer any considerable diminution of wind. If the supposed two lines of surfaces will receive such a power of wind as stated, that is, each equal to 200,000 men's power, a third line of the same height, at the same distance and parallel to the former, under equal circumstances, will receive the same quantity of power, so a fourth, fifth, and so on, as far as may be chosen. The length of each such one may, under the supposed circumstances, be prolonged as far as we please, the power of wind will be every-where the same. Now, if we find the power of wind to be at the end of every mile equal to 200,000 men's power, and so for every mile in breadth, it follows, that every 1 square mile affords such a power. — What an immense power! — The most populous countries in the world contain in an average from 100 to 200 individuals on every square mile, of which hardly one half is able to work, or to be counted for full hands to work. But suppose even 100 full hands to work on 1 square mile, the power of wind within their places of habitation will be 2000 times greater. Yet this will not be the whole power of wind at their disposal. We are not limited to the height of 200 feet. We might extend, if required, the application of this power to the height of the clouds, by means of kites. If we extend it, for instance, to but 2000 feet high, we might increase the power 10 times as much, that is, 20,000 times greater than the inhabitants of the most populous countries could effect with their nerves and sinews. Yet we will get a more proper conception of this power, in extending this comparison over the whole globe. The surface of the globe is about 200,000,000 square miles. According to the foregoing statement of 200,000 men's power for every 1 square mile, the whole extent of the wind's power over the globe amounts to about 200,000,000 times 200,000, i.e., to 40,000,000,000,000,000 men's power. The number of all human individuals on earth will not exceed 1,000,000,000, of which hardly the half may be counted for full hands to work, that is, 500,000,000; consequently, the stated power of wind is 80,000 times greater than all men on earth could effect with their nerves, when the wind is used but to the height of 200 feet.

It may now be objected, that this computation includes the surface of the ocean and uninhabitable regions of the earth, where this power could not be applied for our purposes. But you will recollect, that I have promised to show the means for rendering the ocean as inhabitable as the most fruitful dry land; and I do not even exclude the polar regions.

The Paradise within the Reach of all Men, 9–10;
"Paradise (To Be) Regained," 70–71

Hitherto the power of wind has been applied immediately upon the machinery for use, and they had to wait the chances of the wind's blowing; where the operation is stopped as soon as the wind ceases to blow. But the manner, which I shall state hereafter, to apply this power, is to make it operate only for collecting or storing up power in a manner, and then to take out of this store of power, at any time, as much power for final operation upon the machineries as may be wanted for the intended purposes. The power stored up is to react, just as it may suit the purposes, and may do so long after the original power

of wind has ceased. And, though the wind should cease at intervals of many months, we may have by the same power a uniform perpetual motion in a very simple way.

The Paradise within the Reach of all Men, 11;
"Paradise (To Be) Regained," 77

To form a conception of the power which the tide affords, let us imagine a surface of 100 miles square, or 10,000 square miles, somewhere in the ocean, where the tide rises and sinks, in an average, 10 feet. — How many men would it require for emptying a basin of 10,000 square miles area, and 10 feet deep, filled with sea-water, in 6¼ hours, and filling the same again in 6¼ hours? — Whether this is caused by the gravity of the moon or by labor of men, the effect and requisite power is the same.

Experience teaches, that a common laboring man may raise 20 pounds 2 feet at every second by continual labor. To empty a basin 10 feet deep, the laborer would in the beginning have but little to raise, but he would have to raise the water higher and higher in proportion he would get nearer to the bottom of the vessel, till at the end 10 feet high. His labor would, therefore, be equal, by the best contrivance, to the raising of the basin 5 feet high. If a man raises 20 pounds 2 feet at every second, he can raise the same 5 feet at every 2½ seconds, and 1 cubic foot sea-water, in about 8 or 9 seconds, 5 feet; but for the same of round numbers, say at every 7½ seconds, or 8 cubic feet, at every minute, which would amount to 3000 at every 6½ hours. Suppose a geographical mile to be about 6000 feet long, 1 square mile consequently equal to 36 millions of square feet, and this area would, by a depth of 10 feet, contain a mass of water 360,000,000 cubic feet. Allowing 3000 cubic feet for every man, the raising of such a mass would require 120,000 men.

The Paradise within the Reach of all Men, 13;
"Paradise (To Be) Regained," 73

As we do not know yet the greatest depth of the ocean, it is not for me, now, to tell how far the application of this power may be extended, though it may possibly be co-extensive with the whole ocean, by means which the immense powers of nature afford. However, the application of the tide being by establishments fixed on the ground, it is natural to begin with them near the shores in shallow water, and upon sands, which may be extended gradually farther into the sea. The shores of the continent, and of islands and the sands, being generally surrounded by shallow water, not exceeding from 50 to 100 fathoms in depth, for 20 to 50 till 100 miles and upwards, the coasts of North America with their extensive sand-banks, islands, and rocks, may easily afford, for this purpose, a ground of about 3000 miles long, and in an average 100 miles broad, or 300,000 square miles, with a power of 240,000 men per 1 square mile, as stated, at 10 feet's tide, of 72,000 millions of men, or for every mile of length of the coast a power of 24 millions of men. What an enormous power! And this power may be rendered highly beneficial for men, without occupying even any room on dry land. In what manner? it will be asked. To answer this question now, it will have the appearance of fairy tales; and, reserving the answer, the statement of this gigantic power will appear useless. I will, therefore, give here some slight notice of its applications; though perhaps not one-thousandth part of it may be wanted at our time, yet it will serve to remove the narrow conceptions, prejudices, and all apprehension of having not enough means for any purpose that will come into question hereafter. We have to accustom ourselves to conceive a state of things that must and will be the consequence of the application of these means, quite different from what we are wont to see.

Rafts of any extent, fastened on the ground of the sea along the shore, stretching far into the sea, may be covered with fertile soil, bearing vegetables and trees, of any description, the finest gardens equal to those the dry land may admit of, covered with buildings and machineries, which may operate not only on the sea, where they are, but which also, by means of mechanical connections, extend their operations for many miles into the continent. (Etzler's Mechanical System, page 24.) Thus this power may cultivate the artificial soil for many miles upon the surface of the sea near the shores, and for several miles on the dry land along the shore, in the most superior manner imaginable; it may build cities along the shore, consisting of the most magnificent palaces, every one being surrounded by gardens and the most delightful sceneries; it may level the hills or unevennesses, or raise eminences along the shore; for enjoying open prospects into the country and upon the sea; it may cover the barren shore with fertile soil, and beautify the same in various manners; it may clear the sea of shallows, and make easy the approach, not merely of vessels, but of large floating islands, which may come from, and go to distant parts of the world, islands that have every commodity and security for their inhabitants as may afford the dry land. All such things and many others, which may seem now to be but extravagant fancies, require nothing but the raw materials for their construction, and these are to be found in plenty.

Thus may a power, derived from the gravity of the moon and the ocean, hitherto but the objects of idle curiosity to the studious man, be made eminently subservient for creating the most delightful abodes along the coasts, where men may enjoy in the same time all advantages of sea and dry land. The coasts may be hereafter continual paradisiacal skirts between land and sea, every-where crowded with the densest population. The shores and the sea along them will be no more as raw nature presents them now, but they will be every-where of easy and charming access, not even molested by the roars of waves, shaped as it may suit the purposes of their inhabitants; the sea will be cleared of every obstruction to free passage every-where: its productions in fishes, etc., will be gathered in large, appropriated receptacles, to present them to the inhabitants of the shores and of the sea.

The Paradise within the Reach of all Men, 15–16;
"Paradise (To Be) Regained," 73–75

May this idea be considered as a mere fancy, or as something that only a remote posterity may live to see? — No, it is within our reach within less than 10 years, commencing from the first year of an association for the purpose of constructing and applying the machinery. The accomplishment of such purposes requires nothing but the raw materials for them, that is to say, iron, copper, wood, earth chiefly, and a union of men, whose eyes and understanding are not shut up by preconceptions.

The Paradise within the Reach of all Men, 19;
"Paradise (To Be) Regained," 89

But it will now be objected, that there is not always sun-shine, that the nights and cloudy or foggy weather interrupt the effect.

To obviate such interruptions there are two ways: —

1. By enveloping the boilers with stuffs that keep the heat the longest in themselves; for instance, a thick coat of red-hot iron or other hot metal, enveloped in a thick coat of clay, loam, sand, or other earthen material.

We might thus continue a heat sufficient to boil water for many hours after the sun has ceased to shine, without consuming any material.

2. By contriving a reacting power, caused by the power of the steam, of which hereafter will be given the description, and by which many days, and even many months, the power of steam, caused by sun-shine, may react at will, and thus be rendered perpetual, no matter how often or how long the sun-shine may be interrupted. (Etzler's Mechanical System).

The Paradise within the Reach of all Men, 20;
"Paradise (To Be) Regained," 78–79

How to create rivulets of sweet and wholesome water on floating islands in the midst of the ocean will be no riddle now. Sea-water changed into steam will distil into sweet water, leaving the salt on the bottom. Thus the steam-engines on floating islands for their propulsion and other mechanical purposes, will serve in the same time for the distillery of sweet water, which, collected in basins, may be led through channels over the island, while, where required, it may be refrigerated by artificial means into cool water, surpassing in salubrity the best spring water, because nature hardly ever distils water so purely of itself without some admixture of stuffs of less wholesome influence on the human body, as it may be done here artificially.

The Paradise within the Reach of all Men, 24;
"Paradise (To Be) Regained," 76

Nature plays with these mighty powers before our eyes in the most irregular way. To apply them immediately upon machineries, for certain final purposes, would subject the latter to great irregularities and interruptions. It is probably owing to this circumstance, that men have made so little application of them as yet. These inconveniences will be remedied in putting a medium between the powers and their final application, in order to convert them into uniform operations, or, in other words, into perpetual motions with uniform powers. As we have superabundant powers, irregular as they be, we may then create perpetual motions any power that may be wanted, and any-where.

To effect this purpose, we have to cause a reaction of the power of wind, steam, etc. The weight of a clock being wound up gives us an image of reaction. The sinking of this weight is the reaction of winding it up. It is not just necessary to wait with winding up the weight till it is entirely sunk down; but it may be wound up at any time partly or totally; and if done always before the weight reaches the bottom, the clock will be going perpetually. In a similar, though not in the same way, we may cause a reaction on a larger scale. We may raise, for instance, water by the immediate application of wind or steam, upon some eminence, into a pond, out of which the water may, through an outlet, fall upon some wheel or other contrivance for setting some machinery a-going. Thus we may store up water in some eminent pond, and take out of this store, at any time, as much water through the outlet as we want to employ, by which means the original power may react for many days after it has ceased.

The Paradise within the Reach of all Men, 25–26;
"Paradise (To Be) Regained," 77–78

Such reservoirs of moderate elevation or size need not just be made artificially, but will be found made by nature very frequently, requiring but little aid for their completion. They require no regularity of form. Any valley surrounded by elevations, with some lower grounds in its vicinity, would answer the purpose. Small crevices may be filled up. Such places may be eligible for the beginning of enterprises of this kind; but thereafter, when the powers are rendered operative for the purposes in view, larger and more perfect contrivances may be made without expenses. Hills and mountains afford natural advantages for this purpose. The higher the reservoir the less room is required; for the more power with the same quantity of water will then be effected, by the greater fall. But suppose even an entirely flat country. By the application of any of the stated powers, we may, for instance, excavate a large hole of from 200 to 250 feet deep, and raise, with the stuff that is taken out of it, an elevation of 300 feet at its edge, so as to have then a height of from 500 to 550 feet. Suppose this elevation to be 2000 feet square, its water 100 feet deep, its fall in an average 400 feet; then its reacting power may be brought to 80 times as great as that of the reservoir before stated; for its area will be 4 times, its depth 5 times, its fall 4 times, and consequently its reacting power 4 times 5 times 4 times as great as the calculation in the first case shows. If then the former reservoir afforded a power of 10,000 men for 10 days, this will be capable of 80 times 10,000, or 800,000 men's power for 10 days. Water enough may be found at such a depth any-where. But say it were not; then we may use, instead of water, sand, stones, earth, etc., which will have the advantage of not evaporating, and of being heavier, and therefore requiring less room for equal quantity of power, while these dry materials will cause somewhat more friction than water, which, however, will not counterbalance the advantages. The room which this hole and the adjacent elevation occupies is not lost for cultivation of soil. Both surfaces may be covered with rafts decked with fertile earth and all kinds of vegetables, which may grow there as well as any-where else.

The Paradise within the Reach of all Men, pp. 26–27 — "Paradise (To Be) Regained" p. 78

The science of mechanics is but in a state of infancy. It is true, improvements are made upon improvements, instigated by patents of government; but they are made accidentally or at hap-hazard. There is no general system of this science, mathematical as it is, which developes its principles in their full extent, and the outlines of the application to which they lead. There is no idea of comparison between what is explored and what is yet to be explored in this science; no investigation of powers and their applications for the benefit of man, in all their ramifications and extents; we are in a manner groping along in the dark, and wonder at every new invention and improvement in mechanics. People doubt, reject, and reason at random, with positiveness, on every thing that is new to them, without understanding, without even troubling themselves with examining the matter. It is thus a hard task to inform and convince them of any-thing that may not suit their superficial or erroneous notions. The ancient Greeks placed mathematics at the head of their education and deemed it indispensable to a liberal education, more for teaching and accustoming the mind to good, sound, close reasoning, than even for the matter itself. But we are glad to have filled our memory with notions, without troubling ourselves much with reasoning about them; if

we do it at all, we may do it in secret. Hence this contrariety of opinions, which prove but the state of errors we live in.

The Paradise within the Reach of all Men, 30; "Paradise (To Be) Regained," 91

There was never any system in the productions of human labor; but they came into existence and fashion as chance directed men. Still less was there ever a thought exhibited to make a general science or system of providing for all artificial human wants. My object is to furnish, by an extremely-simple system, all what may be desirable for human life, without taking for pattern any of the existing things of industry. By abstracting from all what is in existence and fashion, I am enabled to devise: means, without any artificial machinery, for producing every thing that man may want for his nourishment, dwelling, garments, furnitures, and articles of fancy and amusements.

But we have to relinquish entirely all our customary notions of human wants, and substitute them by others of a superior and more systematic order.

I shall begin with agriculture.

The first object is here, to clear the ground from all spontaneous growth and stones.

1. A machine of large size is to move along, and, while moving, to take the trees of all sizes with their roots out of the ground, to cut them in convenient pieces, to pile them up, and to take all stones out of the ground to any required depth.

2. A second machine is to follow, for taking up the piles of wood and stones and transporting the some to the places of their destination; this machine may carry thousands of tons at once.

3. The wood removed to its places for final use is then to be formed into planks, boards, beams, rails,

pieces for fuel, and for any other purpose, by a simple contrivance, from whence it is to be removed to the places where it be wanted; this is done by one machine, which may also cut stones of any size.

4. The first-mentioned machine, with a little alteration, is then to level the ground perfectly, in planing it, filling the excavations or taking off the elevations of ground until all is level. If the hills or valleys are considerable, the same machine cuts terraces, winding around them up to the top in elegant shapes.

The same machine may make any excavation or elevation, cut canals, ditches, ponds of any size and shape, raise dams, artificial level roads, walls, and ramparts, with ditches around fields as enclosures, with walks on their top, from walks and paths with elevated borders.

5. The same machine, with some other little alteration, is to give to the ground its final preparation for receiving the seed; it tills the ground, in tearing the soil up to any required depth, refining or mouldering the same, sifting all small roots and stones from it, and putting the seed into the ground in any way required.

6. The same machine may take good fertile ground from one place to some other, for covering, at any required depth, poor soil with fertile soil of the best mixture.

7. The same machine, with a little addition, may reap any kind of grain or vegetable, thrash the seed out in the same time, grind it to meal, or press it to oil; it may also cut or prepare any other vegetable for final use in the kitchen or bakery.

8. Another small machine may sink wells and mines to any required depth and in any direction, and take the contents of the same up to light: it may be in earth, rocks, swamps, or water. (For the description of these machines, see Etzler's Mechanical System, page 11 to 27.)

Architecture

Earth may be baked into bricks, or even vitrified stone, by heat. Stones may be cemented together, so as to break to pieces before their cement yields—a proof, that cement is then harder and more cohesive than the stones themselves. Sand and stone ground to dust may be turned into glass or vitrified substance of the greatest duration, even for thousands of years, out of clayey earth or of stones ground to dust, by the application of burning mirrors. This is to be done in the open air, without other preparation than gathering the substance, grinding, and mixing it with water and cement, moulding or casting it into adapted moulds, and bringing the focus of the burning mirrors of proper size upon the same.

The Paradise within the Reach of all Men, 31–32; "Paradise (To Be) Regained," 79–82, 91

Foundries of any description are to be heated by burning mirrors, and require no labor, except the making of the first moulds and the superintendence for gathering the metal and taking the finished articles away.

The Paradise within the Reach of all Men, 33; "Paradise (To Be) Regained," 82

The walks and roads are to be paved with hard vitrified, large plates, so as to be always clean from all dirt in any weather or season. They may be bordered with the most beautiful beds of flowers, fruitful vegetables, bushes, shrubs, and trees, all rising gradually in rows behind one another, arranged so as to afford almost continually delight to the organs of sight, taste, and smell. Canals and aqueducts with vitrified channels, and if required, covered, filled with the clearest water out of fountains, from the deep subterraneous recesses of water, which may spout and be led anywhere. Some canals may serve for fish-ponds and for irrigating the gardens, others for draining swampy ground. Some aqueducts may be used to lead water into all parts of the garden, for irrigating the ground whenever it be required; this may be done by sprinkling the water in copious showers through moveable tubes with adapted large mouths. This water may be mixed with liquid manure, derived from all the decayed vegetables and other materials fit for manure, prepared and liquified in proper buildings to that effect. Thus the fertility of the garden will not depend from weather. When it rains too much, it may be led off from the ground in proper channels. The canals may be bordered with beautiful growth, in similar manner as the walks. The channels being of vitrified substance, the water being perfectly clear, and filtrated or distilled if required, they may afford the most beautiful sceneries imaginable, while a variety of fishes is seen clear down to the bottom playing about, and while these canals afford in the same time the chance for gliding smoothly along and between these various sceneries of art and nature, upon beautiful gondolas, and while their surface and borders may be covered with fine land and aquatic birds. The canals may end or concentrate in large beautiful ponds, where the bottom is also of vitrified substance. Thus water clear as crystal, in beds or channels like crystal, surrounded and covered by enchanting sceneries, fertilizes and beautifies the gardens, and gives them the relief of a paradise. The aqueducts may be supported by the most splendid colonnades. The walks may be covered with

porticos adorned with magnificent columns, statues, and sculptural works; all of vitrified substance, and lasting for ever, while the beauties of nature around heighten the magnificence and deliciousness.

The Paradise within the Reach of all Men, 34–35;
"Paradise (To Be) Regained," 85

The dwellings ought to be also very different from what is known in that kind, if the full benefit of our means is to be enjoyed. They are to be of a structure for which we have no name yet. They are to be neither palaces, nor temples, nor cities, but a combination of all, superior to whatever is known.

The Paradise within the Reach of all Men, 35;
"Paradise (To Be) Regained," 81

One or two persons are sufficient to direct the kitchen-business. They have nothing else to do but to superintend the cookery and to watch the time of the victuals being done, and then to remove them with the table and vessels into the dining-hall, or to the respective private apartments, by a slight motion of the hand at some crank. From thence are thereafter the remaining victuals to be moved into the store of prepared victuals.

The cleaning of the vessels and all washing of utensils, floors, etc., is to be done by streaming water, the washing of other stuffs by steam. All this requires no work, but is done by slightly moving some crank. Any extraordinary desire of any person may be satisfied by going to the place where the thing is to be had; and any thing that requires a particular preparation in cooking or baking may be done by the person who desires it.

The Paradise within the Reach of all Men, 37;
"Paradise (To Be) Regained," 84

Each adult member has, out of his apartment, a free view into the environs around the habitation, and an immediate communication with the halls in the inside of the square. He may walk, inside or outside of the square, upon the galleries that surround every story. He may ascend to any story above his, or to the flat roof of the whole square, or descend to any gallery below his story, or to the ground, in a box, without trouble, easy and quick, both inside and outside of the square. He may thus move without exertion in a few seconds to any part of the square inside and outside, every individual having a box inside and another one outside for his own use, fixed in a proper manner at the galleries by his apartment. He may procure to himself all common articles of his daily wants, by a short turn of some crank, without leaving his apartment. He may at any time bathe himself in cold or warm water, or in steam, or in some artificially prepared liquor for invigorating health. He may at any time give to the air in his apartment that temperature that suits his feeling best. He may cause at any time an agreeable scent of various kinds. He may at any time meliorate his breathing air—this main vehicle of vital power. The science of chemistry in our days teaches this to be done in a high degree. Man is depending, physically and morally, from the things that surround him, and chiefly from the temperature and the qualities of the air he breathes and absorbs through his pores. Impure and inferior air is more hurtful to health and temper than bad water; the difference is only, that the bad qualities and impurities of water are partly seen and tasted, while those of the air are invisible. Nobody would like to drink out of a stinking pool; still the invisible air, which is continually in hated and immediately transformed into component parts of our own body and life, is of far greater importance for life, so much, at least, that the same human individual, with the same food and habits, may in one kind of air live with a decaying health, pale, and sallow face, general debility, digestion, and all other vital functions enfeebled, susceptible of various diseases, till finally premature death or accelerated decrepitude concludes his existence; while in another kind of air he may enjoy a vigorous health, a cheerful temper, possess a blooming countenance, and the best energies of all vital functions, and thus reach an age far beyond the common period of human life; yet the difference of air would be neither seen nor smelt. Therefore, by a proper application of the physical knowledge of our days, man may be kept in a perpetual serenity of mind, and, if there is no incurable disease or defect in his organism, in constant vigor of health, and his life be prolonged beyond any known period of human life of our present time.

The Paradise within the Reach of all Men, 37–38;
"Paradise (To Be) Regained," 81, 84

The character of the architecture is to be quite different from what it ever has been hitherto. There are vehicles to be used for moving several thousand tons at once and putting them into their destined place. Hence large solid masses are to be baked or cast in one piece, ready shaped in any form that may be desired. The building may therefore consist in columns 200 feet high and upwards, of proportionate thickness, and of one entire piece of vitrified substance. These columns may form colonnades both for surrounding the whole square and dividing and subdividing it into all the required larger and smaller squares, for the private apartments, the halls, and their subdivisions. The floors and ceilings of each such square may be of one entire piece of the same or similar vitrified substance. The intervals of the columns along them are to form the doors, windows, mirrors, pictures, etc., for the partitions and outside walls. All these huge pieces are to be moulded, so as to join and hook into each other firmly by proper joints and folds, and not to yield in any way without breaking.

The Paradise within the Reach of all Men, 38;
"Paradise (To Be) Regained," 82

The 25 halls in the inside of the square, each 200 feet square and high; the 40 corridors, each 1100 feet long and 20 feet wide; the 80 galleries, each from 1000 to 1250 feet long; about 7000 private rooms; the whole surrounded and intersected by the grandest and most splendid colonnades imaginable; floors, ceilings, columns with their various beautiful and fanciful intervals, all shining, and reflecting to infinity all objects and persons, with splendid lustre of all beautiful colors and fanciful shapes and pictures; every-where the most elegant couches, seats, tables, etc.; all galleries, outside and within the halls, are to be provided with many thousand commodious and most elegant vehicles, in which persons may move up and down, like birds, in perfect security and without exertion; the elegant galleries with beautiful balustrades and various ornaments; the flat roof of the whole square, 1250 feet square, with its 25 cupolas, each upwards of 100 feet in diameter, with mazes of pleasant galleries, turrets, places for various purposes, vaulted alleys, pavilions, and many various ornaments and commodities: at night the roof, and the inside and outside of the whole square, are illuminated by gas-light, which, in the mazes of many colored crystal-like colonnades and vaultings and reflectors, is reverberated with a brilliancy that gives to the whole a lustre of precious stones, as far as the eye can see—such are the future abodes of men!

The environs of this residence are no less beautiful. The building is to be erected on an elevated spot, artificially made, if not formed by nature already, with a commanding view upon an extensive landscape of the most fanciful and varied beauties of nature and art, with all the luxuriancy and variety of growth that such a superior culture of soil and a fine climate afford.—And why pass a dreary winter every year, while there is yet room enough on the globe where nature is blessed with a perpetual summer, and with a far greater variety and luxuriance of vegetation?—More than one half of the surface of the globe has no winter. Men will have it in their power to remove and prevent all bad influences of climate, and to enjoy perpetually only that temperature which suits their constitution and feeling best.—There will be afforded the most enrapturing views to be fancied, out of the private apartments, from the galleries, from the roof, from its turrets and cupolas—gardens as far as the eye can see, full of fruits and flowers, arranged in the most beautiful order, with walks, colonnades, aqueducts, canals, ponds, plains, amphitheatres, terraces, fountains, sculptural works, pavilions, gondolas, places for public amusement, etc., to delight the eye and fancy, the taste and smell.

The night affords no less delight to fancy and feelings. An infinite variety of grand, beautiful, and fanciful objects and sceneries, radiating with crystalline brilliancy of all colors every-where, inside and outside of the square, by the illumination of gas-light; the human figures themselves, arrayed in the most beautiful pomp fancy may suggest, and the eye may delight, shining even with brilliancy of stuff and diamond, like stones of various colors, elegantly shaped and arranged around the body; all reflected a thousand-fold in huge mirrors and reflectors of various forms; theatrical scenes of a grandeur and magnificence and enrapturing illusions unknown yet, in which any person may be either a spectator or actor: the speech and the songs reverberating with increased sound, rendered more sonorous and harmonious than by nature, by vaultings that are moveable into any shape at any time; the sweetest and most impressive harmony of music, produced by song and instruments partly not known yet, may thrill through the nerves and vary with other amusements and delights.

Such is the life reserved to true intelligence, but withheld from ignorance, prejudice, and stupid adherence to custom.

And what is all the material for so enchanting and unheard-of abodes, sceneries, ornaments, dress, comforts, luxuries, delights?—Nothing but the most common, the most neglected stuff in nature—earth, sand, clay, stones, the substances of vegetables, that hitherto had no value and no use but for dung. And what is the expense for producing such great things?—None, except for the first machineries, of very simple construction, and for the first moulds of all things to be artificially made; for the machineries themselves, as well as the moulds for casting the materials for use, are to be made by the same machineries, and may then be multiplied to any number required, without any labor or expense.

Such is the domestic life to be enjoyed by every human individual that will partake of it. How different from that of even the mightiest monarch, or the richest man of our times?—No fear of being robbed or cheated, no cares of managing the household, none even for the education of children; for this will be provided for, by a wise people, in a general way, for generating and cultivating good feelings and instructing the mind of all what is to be known; no anxiety for preserving or increasing property; no disgusting objects and occupations vexes there the mind; no low vices and crimes resulting from want, or fear of want, and poverty surround man; there is but one desire predominant in all, this is to live as happy as they can, and in order to live so to please and to be pleased. Love and affection may there be fostered and enjoyed without any of the obstructions that oppose, diminish, and destroy them in the present state of men.

The Paradise within the Reach of all Men, 39–40; "Paradise (To Be) Regained," 83, 85–86

Is perhaps our present generation free from irrationality and error?—Have we perhaps reached now the summit of human wisdom, and need no more to look out for mental or physical improvement?—This is exactly the way of thinking that ever barred the road to intelligence.

The Paradise within the Reach of all Men, 44; "Paradise (To Be) Regained," 90

Not one ten-thousandth part of men in the most civilized countries are actually engaged in any study or investigation of nature.—Still, is there any other source of true and useful knowledges?—Only a few professional men of learning occupy themselves with teaching natural philosophy, chemistry, and the other branches of the sciences of nature, to a very limited extent, for very limited purposes, with very limited means. The rest of men have to pass their lives in drudgery and trivial occupations, and in ignorance. In many erroneous notions of nature, for want of means, time, and chance for information.

The Paradise within the Reach of all Men, 45;
"Paradise (To Be) Regained," 91

I have drawn but the sketch of domestic life within our immediate reach. But man is not to be confined to domestic life; he may roam over the whole world, not in hardships, perils, and deprivations, but with his family and friends in all security, refinements of social life, comforts, and luxury, as well as he may enjoy at home. Large commodious vehicles, for carrying many thousand tons, running over peculiarly adapted level roads, at the rate of 40 miles per hour, or 1000 miles per day, may transport men and things, small houses, and whatever may serve for his comfort and ease, by land. Floating islands, constructed of logs, or of wooden stuffs prepared in a similar manner as it is to be done with stone, and of live trees, which may be reared so as to interweave each other and strengthen the whole, may be covered with gardens and palaces, propelled by powerful engines, and run at equal rate through seas and oceans. Thus man may move, with the celerity of birds' flight, in terrestrial paradises, from one climate to another, and see the world in all its variety, exchanging with distant nations the surplus of productions. The journey from one pole to another may be performed in a fortnight, the visit to a transmarine country in a week or two, a journey around the world in one or two months, by land and water.

The Paradise within the Reach of all Men, 46;
"Paradise (To Be) Regained," 80

All men may plentifully partake of the benefits nature affords to human enjoyment, by a wise application of her powers and means. It would be as ridiculous, then, to dispute and quarrel about the means for our life, as it would be now about water to drink along mighty rivers, or about the permission of breathing air in the atmosphere, or about sticks in our extensive woods.

The Paradise within the Reach of all Men, 47;
"Paradise (To Be) Regained," 80

It may therefore be considered as a moderate sum, brought together in a similar way, when rated at 200,000 to 300,000 dollars for the beginning—(the estimate in Etzler's Mechanical System, page 36 to 46, show that a considerable smaller sum in sufficient);—which may be sufficient to create the first establishment for a whole community of from 3,000 to 4,000 individuals in the described manner.

The Paradise within the Reach of all Men, 48;
"Paradise (To Be) Regained," 89

The whole world might therefore be really changed into a paradise of the described kind, within the first 10 years, beginning with but 200,000 to 300,000 dollars.

The Paradise within the Reach of all Men, 49;
"Paradise (To Be) Regained," 89

It will now be plainly seen, that the execution of the proposals is not proper for individuals. Whether it be qualified for the government at this time, before the subject has become popular, is a question to be decided: it would certainly be a great fortune and glory for the nation, if no prejudice would prevent the majority of the government from bestowing attention upon the subject, and promoting to application for the public benefit whatever be found useful of it by careful examination of some committee.

The Paradise within the Reach of all Men, 49;
"Paradise (To Be) Regained," 88

Man, as an individual, is weak; and whatever his means or abilities be, they are always very limited in comparison to those of many men joined in one body. His contrivances and pursuits can be but for his separate private interest, and must therefore be very limited and transient, like himself. He sees every-where his interest opposed by all, with whom he has to deal, and must therefore oppose his endeavours to all of those who deal with him. Therefore, nothing great for the improvement of his own condition, or that of his fellow-men, can ever be effected by individual enterprise. Man is powerful but in union with many.

The Paradise within the Reach of all Men, 50;
"Paradise (To Be) Regained," 89

The way for putting the matter to the test is pointed out; it is plain and without expenses: the execution of the proposals itself requires no fortune; small shares of 20 dollars will be sufficient; and even these may be accepted partly in work, after a small part is paid to the treasury of the society.

The Paradise within the Reach of all Men, 53;
"Paradise (To Be) Regained," 89

All what is to be done, is, to step forth, after mature reflection, to confess loudly one's conviction, and to constitute societies, which are to increase by offering reception to whomsoever will join, till the subscribed shares afford sufficient means for making the first experiment.

The Paradise within the Reach of all Men, 53;
"Paradise (To Be) Regained," 88

I consider this Address as a touch-stone to try whether our nation is in any way accessible to these great truths, for raising the human creature to a superior state of existence, in accordance with the knowledges and the spirit of the most cultivated minds of the present time—or whether I have to look out for a more congenial spirit somewhere else. For it cannot reasonably be expected, that I should doom such glorious discoveries to the grave, merely out of regard to dullness and unjustifiable prejudice of any nation in the world.

The Paradise within the Reach of all Men, 55;
"Paradise (To Be) Regained," 89–90

Choice of Copy Text

The text for this Yale University Press edition of *Essays: A Fully Annotated Edition* has been newly established upon the following editorial principles established by this editor.

In order to trace Thoreau's projectile as a writer for the outlets of his day—the periodical press, newspapers, and compendiums—and to remain as close as possible to an authoritative text representing the Thoreau presented to and read by his contemporaries, the copy texts for the essays included in *Essays: A Fully Annotated Edition* are the first publication of each essay. Although Thoreau would often make corrections and emendations to his published texts following publication, such postpublication changes are outside the scope of this volume. Except in cases where Thoreau was making a correction to an obvious copy text error caused by a typesetter's misreading of his handwriting, the copy text has not been emended. Substantive emendations worth noting are presented as annotations.

When a line was omitted from his essay "Chesuncook" during periodical publication, Thoreau wrote, "I hardly need to say that this is a liberty which I will not permit to be taken with my MS. The editor has, in this case, no more right to omit a sentiment than to insert one, or put words into my mouth." This is too often taken as Thoreau's final word on editors and the editorial process. As he wrote: "I do not ask anybody to adopt my opinions, but I do expect that when they ask for them to print, they will print them, or obtain my consent to their alteration or omission. I should not read many books if I thought that they had been thus *expurgated*." Thoreau is clear that his thought and opinion must not be altered. He has considerably less concern for other corrections, what he called "other cases of comparatively little importance to me."

As copy texts were prepared under several variant editorial policies, no attempt has been made to impose any consistency in regard to spelling and punctuation, nor has there been any attempt to modernize the spelling. All bracketed interpolations in the text are Thoreau's. Variants of punctuation or capitalization, common practice in Thoreau's day, between texts quoted by Thoreau and his sources have been neither emended nor noted. Stylistic policies of the various publishing houses, such as ligatures, the off-setting of quotations, periods following essay titles, *do n't* for *don't,* or large initial capitals, have not been followed as a matter of course.

Textual Notes and Emendations

Natural History of Massachusetts

Copy text: *The Dial: A Magazine for Literature, Philosophy, and Religion*, July 1842

20:3	*lizzard* emended to *lizard* as in Excursions (1863)
21:5	*wreathes* emended to *wreaths* as in Excursions (1863)

A Winter Walk

Copy text: *The Dial: A Magazine for Literature, Philosophy, and Religion*, October 1843

28:27	*For* emended to *Far* as indicated by Thoreau's corrected copy of the *Dial*
31:35	*lanes* emended to *lawns* as in Thoreau's corrected copy of the *Dial* and as emended in *Excursions* (1863)
32:25	*traveler* emended to *traveller* following usage elsewhere in essay and as emended in *Excursions* (1863)
34:31–32	*expands* emended to *exhales* as in Thoreau's corrected copy of the *Dial* and as emended in *Excursions* (1863)
35:7	*foaming* emended to *fuming* as in Thoreau's corrected copy of the *Dial* and as emended in *Excursions* (1863)
35:12	*phæbes* emended to *phoebes*

37:6	*on* emended to *in* as emended in *Excursions* (1863)
40:22	*plain* emended to *plane* as in Thoreau's corrected copy of the *Dial* and as emended in *Excursions* (1863)
40:26	*dominion* emended to *domain* as emended in *Excursions* (1863)
41:6	*on* emended to *in* as emended in *Excursions* (1863)
41:17	*bird's* emended to *birds'* as emended in *Excursions* (1863)
43:21	*on* emended to *in* as emended in *Excursions* (1863)
44:5	*merry* emended to *cheery* as emended in *Excursions* (1863)
44:21	*cured* emended to *cruel* as emended in *Excursions* (1863)
44:31	*of* emended to *to* as emended in *Excursions* (1863)

A Walk to Wachusett

Copy text: *The Boston Miscellany of Literature and Fashion*, January 1843

46:11	*July,* emended to *July* as in *Excursions* (1863)
48:22	*knowst* emended to *know'st* as in *Excursions* (1863)
49:20	*dark* emended to *dank* as in Thoreau's Journal of 8 August 1842 and *Excursions* (1863)

51:7	*coming* emended to *lowering* as in *Excursions* (1863)
52:21	*far,* emended to *far* as in *Excursions* (1863)
52:24	*there*—a probable typesetting error—emended to *these*
52:33	*Haman* emended to *Hassan* as in *Excursions* (1863) and Thoreau's source: William Collins's *Persian Eclogues*
52:36	*Schina's* emended to *Schiraz'* as emended in *Excursions* (1863) and as found in Thoreau's source: William Collins's *Persian Eclogues*
54:29	*breaking* emended to *brawling* as in *Excursions* (1863)
55:32	*blueberries* emended to *blue berries* as in in *The Writings of Henry David Thoreau* (1906)
57:16	*attis* emended to *altis* as emended in *Excursions* (1863) and as found in Thoreau's source: Virgil's *Eclogue I*
58:30	*nesthatch* emended to *nuthatch* as emended in *Excursions* (1863)
59:30	*or* emended to *on* as in *The Writings of Henry David Thoreau* (1906)
60:14	*bearings,* emended to *bearings* as emended in *Excursions* (1863)
61:5	*use?* emended to *use.* as emended in *Excursions* (1863)
62:10	*Swearers* emended to *Sweavens* as in Thoreau's Journal of 8 April 1847 and Thoreau's source: *Robin Hood: A Collection of All the Ancient Poems, Songs, and Ballads,* compiled by Joseph Ritson
63:23	*desert* emended to *desultory* as emended in *Excursions* (1863)
63:24	*impart* emended to *import* as emended in *Excursions* (1863)

Paradise (To Be) Regained

Copy text: *The United States Magazine and Democratic Review,* November 1843

65:32	*the* emended to *this* as in *A Yankee in Canada, with Anti-Slavery and Reform Papers*
65:36	*and* added as in *A Yankee in Canada, with Anti-Slavery and Reform Papers*
66:5	*paradise* emended to *a paradise* as in *A Yankee in Canada, with Anti-Slavery and Reform Papers*
66:9	*Hygeian* emended to *Hygeia* as in *A Yankee in Canada, with Anti-Slavery and Reform Papers*
68:5	*Arabia* emended to *Achaia* as in Thoreau's source: "The Honey-bee, and Bee-books"
68:18	*Here* emended to *True* as in *A Yankee in Canada, with Anti-Slavery and Reform Papers*
68:33	*a-head* emended to *ahead* as in *A Yankee in Canada, with Anti-Slavery and Reform Papers*
70:20	*he* (dropped t) emended to *the*
73:13	The end-of-line *3,000-000,000,000* emended to *3,000,000,000,000*
78:9	*a going* emended to *a-going* as in Thoreau's source: Etzler's *The Paradise within the Reach of all Men*

79:24   *page* emended to *pages* as in
*A Yankee in Canada, with Anti-
Slavery and Reform Papers*

81:4   *constitntion* emended to *constitution*

81:29–30   *is to* emended to *is to be* as in
Thoreau's source: Etzler's *The Paradise within the Reach of all Men;* and
as emended in *A Yankee in Canada,
with Anti-Slavery and Reform Papers*

82:18   Closing quotation added

84:15   Closing quotation added

85:1   *a* inserted as in *A Yankee in Canada,
with Anti-Slavery and Reform Ppaers*

86:17   Closing quotation added

88:17   *income but our* emended to *income,
but* as in *A Yankee in Canada, with
Anti-Slavery and Reform Papers*

93:19   *Sunma* emended to *Sarma* as in *A
Yankee in Canada, with Anti-Slavery
and Reform Papers*

94:1   *elasity* emended to *clarity* as in
Thoreau's source: Raleigh's *The
History of the World;* and as correctly quoted in Thoreau's "Sir
Walter Raleigh" [EE&M 204] and
as emended in *A Yankee in Canada,
with Anti-Slavery and Reform Papers*

94:4   *"the* emended to *the* as in Thoreau's
source: Raleigh's *The History of the
World;* and as correctly quoted
in Thoreau's "Sir Walter Raleigh"
[EE&M 204] and as emended in A
*Yankee in Canada, with Anti-Slavery
and Reform Papers*

94:23   *almshouses* emended to *almshouse* as

emended in *A Yankee in Canada,
with Anti-Slavery and Reform Papers*

94:27   *gearter* emended to *greater* as
emended in *A Yankee in Canada,
with Anti-Slavery and Reform Papers*

Wendell Phillips Before Concord Lyceum

Copy text: *The Liberator,* 28 March 1845

95:19   *conserver* emended to *conservers* as
demanded by the subject, *descen-
dants,* and as emended in *A Yankee
in Canada, with Anti-Slavery and
Reform Papers*

Thomas Carlyle and His Works

Copy text: *Graham's Magazine,* March 1847, April
1847

100:18   *Stirling* emended to *Sterling* following the correct spelling of the
poet's surname and as in *A Yankee
in Canada, with Anti-Slavery and
Reform Papers*

100:35   *workship* emended to *workshop*
following Thoreau's source: Turnbull's *The Genius of Scotland;* and as
emended in *A Yankee in Canada,
with Anti-Slavery and Reform Papers*

102:25   *mouth to mouth* emended to *month
to month* as in *A Yankee in Canada,
with Anti-Slavery and Reform Papers*

103:1   *Landon* emended to *Landor* following the correct spelling of the
author's surname and as in *A Yankee*

138:21   *Maidstone* emended to *Maidston* following the common spelling of the steward's surname and as the preferred spelling in Thoreau's source: Oliver Cromwell's *Letters and Speeches: With Elucidations.* In the instance from which Thoreau quoted, Carlyle mistakenly used the form *Maidstone.*

144:10   End-of-line *discrimi nating* emended to *discriminating*

Resistance to Civil Government

Copy text: *Aesthetic Papers,* May 1849

A note on the title: "Resistance to Civil Government" was the title of this essay in the copy text. It was revised from the lecture title, "On the Relation of the Individual to the State." When posthumously collected in *A Yankee in Canada, with Anti-Slavery and Reform Papers* (Boston: Ticknor and Fields, 1866) it was given the more common title "Civil Disobedience." Although it is doubtful that Thoreau's sister Sophia, who acted as his literary executor, would have allowed any change which she did not know that her brother had provided and otherwise authorized, and although the new title could have been a response to William Paley's chapter "The Duty of Civil Obedience" in his *The Principles of Moral and Political Philosophy,* there is no extant evidence showing that this change was authorial, and therefore the copy text title has been retained.

146:24   *goverment* emended to *government* as in "Civil Disobedience" in *A Yankee in Canada, with Anti-Slavery and Reform Papers*

151:11   nonhyphenated form of *well-disposed* emended to hyphenated form following usage elsewhere in this essay (147:14 and 156:28) and in "Civil Disobedience" in *A Yankee in Canada, with Anti-Slavery and Reform Papers*

155:28   *be* emended to *he* as in "Civil Disobedience" in *A Yankee in Canada, with Anti-Slavery and Reform Papers*

169:22   *government* emended to *governments* as in Thoreau's source, O. C. Gardiner's *The Great Issue; or, The Three Presidential Candidates,* and as emended in "Civil Disobedience" in *A Yankee in Canada, with Anti-Slavery and Reform Papers*

Slavery in Massachusetts

Copy text: *The Liberator,* 21 July 1854

172:1   Subtitle—"An Address, Delivered at the Anti-Slavery Celebration at Framingham, July 4th, 1854, by Henry D. Thoreau, of Concord, (Mass.)."—deleted as in *A Yankee in Canada, with Anti-Slavery and Reform Papers.* In *A Yankee in Canada, with Anti-Slavery and Reform Papers* the subtitle was placed as a footnote

177:28   *reasonable* emended to *sensible* as in *A Yankee in Canada, with Anti-Slavery and Reform Papers* and as found in his journal after 19 April 1851 [J 2:176]

179:23   *Roxboro*—a likely compositor's

error—emended to *Boxboro* as being a town of which Thoreau had written in his journal

187:32   *store-house* emended to *stone house* as in *A Yankee in Canada, with Anti-Slavery and Reform Papers* and as found in his journal of 17 June 1854

188:11   *secured* emended to *scented* as in *A Yankee in Canada, with Anti-Slavery and Reform Papers* and as found in his journal of 16 June 1854

A Plea for Captain John Brown

Copy text: *Echoes of Harper's Ferry,* edited by James Redpath (Boston: Thayer and Eldridge, 1860)

190:1   Title and subtitle: supplied from *A Yankee in Canada, with Anti-Slavery and Reform Papers*

195:28   *Vallandingham* emended to *Vallandigham* as in Thoreau's corrected copy of Redpath's *Echoes of Harper's Ferry* (Morgan Library) and following the correct spelling of the surname

200:2   *were* emended to *are* as in Thoreau's journal of 19 October 1859

205:25   *Sharpe's*—a common contemporary misspelling—emended to *Sharps'* to reflect the correct name of the inventor, Christian Sharps

205:26   *Sharpe's*—a common contemporary misspelling—emended to *Sharps'* to reflect the correct name of the inventor, Christian Sharps

206:27–28   *Stephens, and Coppic* emended to *Stevens, and Coppoc* following the correct spelling of the names and as emended in *The Writings of Henry David Thoreau* (1906)

206:31   *Vallandingham* emended to *Vallandigham* as in Thoreau's corrected copy of Redpath's *Echoes of Harper's Ferry* (Morgan Library) and following the correct spelling of the surname

209:2   Noncapitalized form of *Vigilant Committee* emended to capitalized form following Thoreau's usage in the preceding and succeeding sentences

211:11   *Sharpe's*—a common contemporary misspelling—emended to *Sharps'* to reflect the correct name of the inventor, Christian Sharps

211:15   *Sharpe's*—a common contemporary misspelling—emended to *Sharps'* to reflect the correct name of the inventor, Christian Sharps

213:5–6   "Unless above himself he doth erect himself,
How poor a thing is man!"
emended to
"Unless above himself he can
Erect himself, how poor a thing is man!"
following Thoreau's corrected copy of Redpath's *Echoes of Harper's Ferry* (Morgan Library) and as in *A Yankee in Canada, with Anti-Slavery and Reform Papers.* Thoreau had

correctly transcribed these lines in
his 1840–1848 literary notebooks

215:24   *friends* emended to *friend* as in
Thoreau's source and as in his
journal of 21 October 1859

The Last Days of John Brown

Copy text: *The Liberator,* 27 July 1860

217:1   Title: supplied from *A Yankee in
Canada, with Anti-Slavery and Reform Papers*

220:4–5   The end-of-line *Demo-rat* emended
to *Democrat* following *A Yankee in
Canada, with Anti-Slavery and Reform Papers*

220:29   *ever* emended to *even* following *A
Yankee in Canada, with Anti-Slavery
and Reform Papers*

223:27   *Sharpe's*—a common contemporary
misspelling—emended to *Sharps'* to
reflect the correct name of the inventor, Christian Sharps

223:36   Mark of elision added as indicated
in Thoreau's journal of 6 December
1859

An Address on the Succession of Forest Trees

Copy text: *New-York Weekly Tribune,* 6 October 1860

228:32   *the of* emended to *the centre of* as in
*Transactions of the Middlesex Agri-
cultural Society for the Year 1860*

228:32   *earthly* emended to *earthy* as in
*Transactions of the Middlesex Agri-
cultural Society for the Year 1860*

229:18   *then the* emended to *then an* as in
*Transactions of the Middlesex Agri-
cultural Society for the Year 1860*

229:28   *abort* emended to *about* as in *Transactions of the Middlesex Agricultural
Society for the Year 1860*

231:30   end-of-line *an other* emended to
another as in *Transactions of the
Middlesex Agricultural Society for the
Year 1860*

232:1   *on* emended to *in* as in *Transactions
of the Middlesex Agricultural Society
for the Year 1860*

232:3   *their ferns* emended to *thin ferns* as
in *Transactions of the Middlesex Agricultural Society for the Year 1860*

232:10   *his* emended to *this* as in *Transactions of the Middlesex Agricultural
Society for the Year 1860*

233:7   *soil* emended to *soil might* as in
*Transactions of the Middlesex Agri-
cultural Society for the Year 1860*

233:7   *bound* emended to *found* as in
*Transactions of the Middlesex Agri-
cultural Society for the Year 1860,* and
as in Thoreau's source: Alexander
Loudon's *Arboretum et Fruticetum
Britannicum*

233:9   *inclosures* emended to *enclosures* following Thoreau's source: Loudon's
Arboretum et Fruticetum Britannicum

233:11   *hight* corrected to *height* following
Thoreau's source: Loudon's *Arbo-
retum et Fruticetum Britannicum,*
and as corrected in *Excursions* (1863)

233:23   *pine* emended to *pines* following

Thoreau's source: Loudon's *Arboretum et Fruticetum Britannicum*

234:26   *chestnuting* corrected to *chestnutting* as corrected in *Excursions* (1863)

235:20   *those* emended to *these* as in *Transactions of the Middlesex Agricultural Society for the Year 1860*

235:22–23   *and these* emended to *for these* as in *Transactions of the Middlesex Agricultural Society for the Year 1860*

236:10   *pick* emended to *pack* as in *Transactions of the Middlesex Agricultural Society for the Year 1860*

237:7   *most* emended to *almost* as in *Transactions of the Middlesex Agricultural Society for the Year 1860*

238:19   *years* emended to *years'* following Thoreau's source: Wilson's *American Ornithology*

238:34   *beach* emended to *beech* following the spelling found in Thoreau's source: Loudon's *Arboretum et Fruticetum Britannicum*

239:2   *sprouted* emended to *sprouted or decayed* as in *Transactions of the Middlesex Agricultural Society for the Year 1860*

240:12   *consider* emended to *I consider* as in *Transactions of the Middlesex Agricultural Society for the Year 1860*

240:13   *seed* emended to *seeds* as in *Transactions of the Middlesex Agricultural Society for the Year 1860*

240:23   *Solanium* emended to *Solanum* as in *Transactions of the Middlesex Agricultural Society for the Year 1860*

241:19   *squash, two* emended to *squash. Two* as in *Transactions of the Middlesex Agricultural Society for the Year 1860*

241:31   *talismen*—an incorrect plural of *talisman*—corrected to *talismans* as corrected in *The Writings of Henry David Thoreau* (1906)

242:13   *farmers* emended to *farmers'* as in *Transactions of the Middlesex Agricultural Society for the Year 1860*

Walking

Copy text: *The Atlantic Monthly,* June 1862

257:36   *longer* corrected to *larger* following Thoreau's source: Head's *The Emigrant*

259:35   *river* emended to *stream* following Thoreau's setting-copy manuscript of "Walking" in the Concord Free Public Library Special Collections (Henry David Thoreau Papers, 1836–[1862], Vault A35, Unit 1)

260:10   *river* emended to *stream* following Thoreau's setting-copy manuscript of "Walking" in the Concord Free Public Library Special Collections (Henry David Thoreau Papers, 1836–[1862], Vault A35, Unit 1)

261:12   *Cummings* corrected to *Cumming* following the correct spelling of the author's surname

263:27   *desert,* emended to *desert* following Thoreau's setting-copy manuscript of "Walking" in the Concord Free Public Library Special Collections

(Henry David Thoreau Papers, 1836–[1862], Vault A35, Unit 1) and his source: Burton's *Personal Narrative to Al-Madinah and Meccah*

267:11 *Nature* emended to *nature* following Thoreau's setting-copy manuscript of "Walking" in the Concord Free Public Library Special Collections (Henry David Thoreau Papers, 1836–[1862], Vault A35, Unit 1)

269:7 the copy text's correct word form *unwieldy* has been retained over *unwieldly,* which is found in Thoreau's setting-copy manuscript of "Walking" in the Concord Free Public Library Special Collections (Henry David Thoreau Papers, 1836–[1862], Vault A35, Unit 1) and as emended in *Excursions* (1863). *The Writings of Henry David Thoreau* (1906) reinstated the copy text form

269:11 *Whoa!* emended to *who!* following Thoreau's setting-copy manuscript of "Walking" in the Concord Free Public Library Special Collections (Henry David Thoreau Papers, 1836–[1862], Vault A35, Unit 1)

269:14 *Whoa!* emended to *Who!* following Thoreau's setting-copy manuscript of "Walking" in the Concord Free Public Library Special Collections (Henry David Thoreau Papers, 1836–[1862], Vault A35, Unit 1). The quotation marks, absent in the

setting-copy manuscript, have been retained from the copy text.

269:27 *this is* emended to *is* following Thoreau's setting-copy manuscript of "Walking" in the Concord Free Public Library Special Collections (Henry David Thoreau Papers, 1836–[1862], Vault A35, Unit 1)

271:14 *mother* emended to *Mother* following Thoreau's setting-copy manuscript of "Walking" in the Concord Free Public Library Special Collections (Henry David Thoreau Papers, 1836–[1862], Vault A35, Unit 1)

271:28 *only!* emended to *only.* following Thoreau's setting-copy manuscript of "Walking" in the Concord Free Public Library Special Collections (Henry David Thoreau Papers, 1836–[1862], Vault A35, Unit 1)

272:4 *Nature* emended to *nature* following Thoreau's setting-copy manuscript of "Walking" in the Concord Free Public Library Special Collections (Henry David Thoreau Papers, 1836–[1862], Vault A35, Unit 1); and as in Thoreau's source, Robert Hunt's *Poetry of Science*

273:18 *besides* emended to *beside* following Thoreau's setting-copy manuscript of "Walking" in the Concord Free Public Library Special Collections (Henry David Thoreau Papers, 1836–[1862], Vault A35, Unit 1)

273:34   italicized *know* emended to roman type following Thoreau's setting-copy manuscript of "Walking" in the Concord Free Public Library Special Collections (Henry David Thoreau Papers, 1836–[1862], Vault A35, Unit 1)

274:8   *child of the mist* emended to *Child of the Mist* following Thoreau's setting-copy manuscript of "Walking" in the Concord Free Public Library Special Collections (Henry David Thoreau Papers, 1836–[1862], Vault A35, Unit 1)

274:11   *laws,* emended to *laws both of heaven and earth,* following Thoreau's setting-copy manuscript of "Walking" in the Concord Free Public Library Special Collections (Henry David Thoreau Papers, 1836–[1862], Vault A35, Unit 1)

274:14   *liberation:* emended to *liberation;* following Thoreau's setting-copy manuscript of "Walking" in the Concord Free Public Library Special Collections (Henry David Thoreau Papers, 1836–[1862], Vault A35, Unit 1)

274:24   *well,* emended to *well* following Thoreau's setting-copy manuscript of "Walking" in the Concord Free Public Library Special Collections (Henry David Thoreau Papers, 1836–[1862], Vault A35, Unit 1)

274:26   *Christ,* inserted as following

Thoreau's setting-copy manuscript of "Walking" in the Concord Free Public Library Special Collections (Henry David Thoreau Papers, 1836–[1862], Vault A35, Unit 1)

274:30   *many* emended to *Christians* following Thoreau's setting-copy manuscript of "Walking" in the Concord Free Public Library Special Collections (Henry David Thoreau Papers, 1836–[1862], Vault A35, Unit 1)

275:1   *breeze,* emended to *breeze* following Thoreau's setting-copy manuscript of "Walking" in the Concord Free Public Library Special Collections (Henry David Thoreau Papers, 1836–[1862], Vault A35, Unit 1); and as in Thoreau's source: James MacPherson's *The Genuine Remains of Ossian, Literally Translated*

276:6   *pine wood* emended to *pine-wood* following Thoreau's setting-copy manuscript of "Walking" in the Concord Free Public Library Special Collections (Henry David Thoreau Papers, 1836–[1862], Vault A35, Unit 1)

277:17   italicized *wings* emended to roman type following Thoreau's setting-copy manuscript of "Walking" in the Concord Free Public Library Special Collections (Henry David Thoreau Papers, 1836–[1862], Vault A35, Unit 1)

277:23–24   gra-a-ate *thoughts, those* gra-a-ate *men you* emended to gra-a-ate *thoughts—those* gra-a-ate *men—you* following Thoreau's setting-copy manuscript of "Walking" in the Concord Free Public Library Special Collections (Henry David Thoreau Papers, 1836–[1862], Vault A35, Unit 1)

278:8   *down.* emended to *down!* following Thoreau's setting-copy manuscript of "Walking" in the Concord Free Public Library Special Collections (Henry David Thoreau Papers, 1836–[1862], Vault A35, Unit 1)

278:28   *by it that is* emended to *by it not in Plato nor the New Testament. It is* following Thoreau's setting-copy manuscript of "Walking" in the Concord Free Public Library Special Collections (Henry David Thoreau Papers, 1836–[1862], Vault A35, Unit 1)

Autumnal Tints

Copy text: *The Atlantic Monthly,* October 1862

281:17–18   *green to sooty* emended to
green
To sooty
as in Thoreau's source, *The Works of the English Poets from Chaucer to Cowper,* and as emended in *The Writings of Henry David Thoreau* (1906)

314:23   *Immanuel* emended to *Emanuel*

following the correct form of the name and as emended in *The Writings of Henry David Thoreau* (1906)

Wild Apples

Copy text: *The Atlantic Monthly,* November 1862

317:27   *way* emended to *ways* as in Thoreau's source: Berthold Georg Niebuhr's *The History of Rome*

324:3   *Hurra!* emended to *Huzza!* following Thoreau's source: Robert Southey's *Southey's Commonplace Book. Fourth Series*

324:24   *so* emended to *do* as in Thoreau's source: Robert Herrick's *Hesperides*

327:9–11   quotation mark moved from its placement here *"if, . . . celebrated for the* to *if, . . . celebrated for "the* to mark the beginning of the quotation from Michaux as indicated in Thoreau's journal of 23 May 1851

332:20   *Palladius* emended to *Columella* to indicate Thoreau's correct source

334:18   *Seek-no-farthers* emended to *Seek-no-furthers* following the spelling of the singular form in Thoreau's source: Downing's *The Fruits and Fruit-Trees of America*

337:23   *Deuxan* emended to *Deuzan* following Thoreau's source: Francis Quarles's *Emblemes*

337:24   *Greening* emended to *Queening* following Thoreau's source: Francis Quarles's *Emblemes*

Life Without Principle

Copy text: *The Atlantic Monthly*, October 1863

335:13–14   *sulky-gully* emended to *Sulky Gully* as in Thoreau's source and in his journal of 18 October 1855.

End-of-Line Hyphenation

The two lists below record end-of-line hyphenations. The following list shows the form adopted in the current text for compound or possible compound words that were hyphenated at the end of a line in the respective copy texts.

NATURAL HISTORY OF MASSACHUSETTS

7:2–3	nuthatch
14:1	muskrat
16:19	north-east
18:31	moth-like
18:34–35	light-bringer
20:28	day-light
24:20–21	flower-stalks

A WINTER WALK

28:4	landscape
33:22	wood-chopper
34:2	henceforth
36:28	housewife
41:10–11	wood-duck
42:5	snow-water

A WALK TO WACHUSETT

50:26	road-side
54:12	Trolhate
54:28	Stillwater
55:26	gooseberries
59:22	north-west
60:9	afterward
61:20	hop-fields

PARADISE (TO BE) REGAINED

66:2	counteracted
69:27	water-power
69:33	sailing-vessel
73:10–11	sea-water
73:13	3,000,000,000,000 (misprinted in copy text as end-of-line *3,000-000, 000, 000*)
75:13	every-where
79:4–5	millwrights
85:36–86:1	gas-light
91:15	haphazard

WENDELL PHILLIPS BEFORE CONCORD LYCEUM

98:14	Red-cross

THOMAS CARLYLE AND HIS WORKS

101:25	chest-shaking
103:34	booksellers
107:24–25	shop-windows
109:34	blueberry-swamps
109:35	shad-blossoms
110:2	mail-coach

111:24–25	peacock's
114:15	super-abundance
115:3–4	ball-room
115:11	side-light
118:4	summer-heat
119:31	stereotyped
125:6	pre-occupied
126:17	background

RESISTANCE TO CIVIL GOVERNMENT

151:8	to-day
151:14	Godspeed
151:18–19	backgammon
152:2	elsewhere
157:5	newspapers
159:28	tax-bill
160:23	schoolmaster
161:32	half-witted
164:33	Chinamen
167:21	tax-gatherer
168:5	imagination-free
168:11	Statesmen
169:12	Notwithstanding

SLAVERY IN MASSACHUSETTS

173:23–24	Commander-in-Chief
175:30	seventy-nine
184:15	backsliders

A PLEA FOR CAPTAIN JOHN BROWN

195:34	daylight
201:1	Office-seekers
211:4	so-called

THE LAST DAYS OF JOHN BROWN

| 220:4–5 | Democrat (misprinted in copy text as end-of-line *Demo-rat*) |
| 221:21 | statesman |

AN ADDRESS ON THE SUCCESSION OF FOREST TREES

225:20	weak-minded
226:3	Moreover
228:21	bird-cherries
234:34	pine-cone
235:6	evergreens
235:13–14	white-pine
235:20	moreover

WALKING

243:24–25	Holy-Lander
246:13	afternoon
246:26	afternoon
247:8–9	dumb-bells
247:11	dumb-bells
249:6–7	landscape
250:3	beanfield
250:7	cigar-smoke
253:5	pleasure-grounds
254:9	Eastward
254:26	southeastward
261:4	stall-fed
263:13	Front-yards
263:27	single-minded
265:24	heirlooms
265:26	bog-hoe
265:31–32	clam-shell

267:32	Englishmen
271:12	jaw-breaking
275:29	far-away
278:4	topmost
279:35	black-veined

AUTUMNAL TINTS

281:31	fortnight
283:15	Woodbine
283:33	Skunk-Cabbage
284:1	hill-side
285:19	purple-veined
287:27	fine-eared
288:31	wine-colored
289:33	hill-sides
294:4	barn-yard
295:6	crimson-spotted
297:5	spruce-knee
298:9	homestead
298:32–33	resting-place
299:20	Loosestrife
299:20	Huckleberry-bird
299:21	woodman
299:30	Sugar-Maples
300:22	to-day
301:30	dye-house
302:8	neighborhood
302:16	maids-of-honor
302:31	rum-sellers
304:10	gun-house
305:6–7	outward
308:12–13	half-dozen
309:3	headlands
310:9	Oak-wine
310:20	evergreens

312:22–23	near-sighted
315:14	head-wind

WILD APPLES

317:30	apple-tree
318:28	apple-spray
320:7	woodpecker
320:15	half-rolled
321:14	handkerchief
321:30	god-like
322:22	three-quarters
324:33	apple-trees
327:8	sweet-meats
327:16	half-fabulous
327:32	Crab-Apple
328:14	Easterbrooks
334:26	high-colored
334:35	hogshead
336:26	plum-tree
336:34	wood-chopper
339:11	cider-mill
339:17	rainbow
340:10	Hedge-Apple
341:17	lurking-places
342:1	hedge-hog

LIFE WITHOUT PRINCIPLE

346:28	anywhere
347:23	money-making
347:31	hard-working
347:36	praiseworthy
351:16	self-supporting
351:25–26	government-pension
352:2	point-blank

353:5	make-shifts
356:6	twenty-eight
359:29–30	newspaper
360:18	twenty-five
360:19	sidewalk
362:19	windmills
365:27	Transalpine
366:21	sea-brine
366:27	molasses-hogshead
368:18	half-consciousness

The following list shows words hyphenated at the end of a line in this edition that should be considered intentionally hyphenated compounds. Any other word that is hyphenated at the end of a line in this edition but does not appear on this list should be considered as a single word.

1:13–14	sharp-shinned
18:34–35	light-bringer
22:6–7	out-door
23:23–24	needle-shaped
24:20–21	flower-stalks
24:22–23	ice-crystals
27:7–8	watch-dog
33:21–22	ice-cutter
41:10–11	wood-duck
42:24–25	North-west
43:36–44:1	wood-chopper
57:3–4	wood-thrush
58:29–30	cherry-birds
69:6–7	ever-varying
73:10–11	sea-water
84:20–21	dining-hall
85:36–86:1	gas-light
100:29–30	ivy-clad

107:14–15	letter-writer
107:24–25	shop-windows
110:1–2	old-line
115:3–4	ball-room
121:34–35	working-man
122:17–18	toil-worn
126:8–9	Revolution-work
127:6–7	ten-pound-ten
133:15–16	fire-baptized
133:29–30	so-called
139:21–22	top-of-the-morning
140:21–22	life-long
151:5–6	prices-current
162:29–30	room-mate
168:4–5	fancy-free
171:8–9	fellow-men
173:24–25	Commander-in-Chief
176:1–2	rub-a-dub
176:16–17	whipping-post
177:14–15	laughing-stock
178:32–33	pick-lock
184:11–12	down-hill
188:33–34	time-serving
199:8–8	figure-heads
208:26–27	fellow-citizens
210:7–8	son-in-law
226:8–9	out-of-the-way
230:21–22	shrub-oak
234:9–10	acorn-cups
235:13–14	white-pine
243:24–25	Holy-Lander
247:8–9	dumb-bells
265:27–28	hard-fought
265:31–32	clam-shell
275:22–23	will-o'-the-wisp
285:34–35	twenty-third

287:14–15	high-colored		325:21–22	apple-trees
287:25–26	horse-raking		326:12–13	apple-tree
287:35–36	Wood-Grass		327:25–26	Crab-Apple
288:33–34	Wood-Grass		338:27–28	straw-colored
296:26–27	mid-channel		338:36–339:1	sea-shore
296:36–297:1	fellow-voyagers		339:32–33	Cellar-Hole
297:3–4	river-bay		339:33–34	Partridge-Apple
298:13–14	Poison-Sumach		341:2–3	Blue-Pearmain
298:32–33	resting-place		344:19–20	wall-side
303:3–4	Cattle-Show		345:14–15	apple-tree
304:35–36	wash-tub		346:26–27	one-eighth
308:12–13	half-dozen		349:30–31	cord-wood
310:14–15	Pine-boughs		351:25–26	government-pension
315:31–32	sink-spout		355:2–3	honey-combed
318:35–36	apple-tree		365:4–5	country-bumpkins
320:15–16	half-carried		367:10–11	sugar-plums
320:36–321:1	still-born			

Bibliography

Books are the treasured wealth of the world and the fit inheritance of generations and nations. —Walden

Abbreviations used in notes for works by Henry D. Thoreau:

C   *The Correspondence of Henry David Thoreau.* Edited by Walter Harding and Carl Bode. New York: New York University Press, 1958.

ITM   *I to Myself: An Annotated Selection from the Journal of Henry D. Thoreau.* Edited by Jeffrey S. Cramer. New Haven: Yale University Press, 2007.

J   *The Journal of Henry D. Thoreau.* Edited by Bradford Torrey and Francis H. Allen. Boston: Houghton Mifflin, 1906.

PJ   *Journal.* Edited by John C. Broderick et al. Princeton: Princeton University Press, 1981–.

MW   *The Maine Woods: A Fully Annotated Edition.* Edited by Jeffrey S. Cramer. New Haven: Yale University Press, 2009.

W   *The Writings of Henry David Thoreau.* Walden ed. Boston: Houghton Mifflin, 1906.

Wa   *Walden: A Fully Annotated Edition.* Edited by Jeffrey S. Cramer. New Haven: Yale University Press, 2004.

All biblical quotations in the notes are from the King James Version.

Aeschylus. *Prometheus Bound.* Trans. Thomas Medwin. London, 1832.

Audubon, John James. *Ornithological Biography; or, An Account of the Habits of the Birds of the United States of America.* 5 vols. London: A. Black, 1831–1849.

Berry, Wendell. *What Are People For?* San Francisco: North Point, 1990.

Bodaeus, Johannes. *Theophrasti Eresii De historia plantarum libri decem, graece et latine . . .* Amsterdam: apud H. Laurentium, 1644.

Brand, John. *Observations on Popular Antiquities: Chiefly Illustrating the Origin of Our Vulgar Customs, Ceremonies, and Superstitions.* Arr. and rev., with additions by Henry Ellis. 2 vols. London: F. C. and J. Rivington, 1813.

Bremer, Frederika. *The Homes of the New World; Impressions of America.* New York: Harpers, 1853.

Browne, Sir Thomas. *Miscellaneous Works.* Ed. Alexander Young. Cambridge, Mass.: Hilliard and Brown, 1831.

———. *Works, Including His Life and Correspondence.* 4 vols. Ed. Simon Wilkins. London: W. Pickering, 1835–1836.

Buber, Martin. "Man's Duty as Man." In *Thoreau in Our Season,* ed. John Hicks. Amherst: University of Massachusetts Press, 1962.

Buffon, Georges Louis Leclerc, comte de. *Natural History, General and Particular.* Trans. and ed. William Smellie. London: W. Strahan and T. Cadell, 1785.

Burton, Richard Francis. *Personal Narrative to Al-Madinah and Meccah.* New York: G. P. Putnam, 1856.

Candolle, Augustin Pyramus de, and Kurt Polycarp Joachim Sprengel. *Elements of the Philosophy of Plants.* Edinburgh: William Blackwood, 1821.

Carlyle, Thomas. *Critical and Miscellaneous Essays.* 4 vols. Boston: J. Munroe, 1838–1839.

———. *The French Revolution: A History.* 2 vols. Boston: C. C. Little and J. Brown, 1838.

———. *The Life of Friedrich Schiller. Comprehending an Examination of His Works . . .* New York: G. Dearborn, 1837.

———. *Oliver Cromwell's Letters and Speeches. With Elucidations.* 2 vols. New York: Wiley and Putnam, 1845.

———. *On Heroes, Hero-Worship, and the Heroic in History. Six Lectures.* London: J. Fraser, 1841.

———. *Past and Present.* Boston: C. C. Little and J. Brown, 1843.

———. *Sartor Resartus.* 3 vols. London: J. Fraser, 1834.

Carpenter, William Benjamin. *Vegetable Physiology and Systematic Botany.* London: H. G. Bohn, 1858.

Chalmers, Alexander, ed. *The Works of the English Poets, from Chaucer to Cowper.* 21 vols. London: J. Johnson, 1810.

Chapin, Loring Dudley. *The Vegetable Kingdom; or, Handbook of Plants and Fruits.* New York: Jerome Loft, 1843.

Chatto, William Andrew (P. Fischer, esq., pseud.). *The Angler's Souvenir.* London: C. Tilt, 1835.

Chaucer, Geoffrey. General Prologue to *The Canterbury Tales.* In Chalmers, *Works of the English Poets.*

Cheever, George Barrell. *Wanderings of a Pilgrim in the Shadow of Mount Blanc.* New York: Wiley and Putnam, 1846.

Collins, William. *Persian Eclogues.* In Chalmers, *Works of the English Poets.*

Concord, Massachusetts: Births, Marriages, and Deaths, 1635–1850. Concord: Printed by the Town, 1895.

Concord Free Public Library. First Parish in Concord Records.

Conway, Moncure Daniel. *Life of Nathaniel Hawthorne.* London: W. Scott, 1890.

Cory, Isaac Preston. *Ancient Fragments of the Phoenician, Chaldaean, Egyptian, Tyrian, Carthaginian, Indian, Persian, and Other Writers: With an Introductory Dissertation and an Inquiry into the Philosophy and Trinity of the Ancients.* London: W. Pickering, 1832

Curzon, Robert. *Visits to Monasteries in the Levant.* New York: George P. Putnam, 1849.

Dante, Alighieri. *Divine Comedy: The Inferno.* Prose trans. John A. Carlyle. New York: Harper and Brothers, 1849.

Darwin, Charles. *Journal of Researches into the Natural History and Geology of the Countries Visited During the Voyage of H.M.S. Beagle Round the World, Under the Command of Capt. Fitz Roy, R.N.* New York: Harper and Brothers, 1846.

Dean, Bradley P. "The Sound of a Flail: Reconstructions of Thoreau's Early 'Life Without Principle' Lectures." 2 vols. M.A. thesis, Eastern Washington University, 1984.

Dean, Bradley P., and Ronald Wesley Hoag. "Thoreau's Lectures After Walden: An Annotated Calendar." In *Studies in the American Renaissance, 1996.*

———. "Thoreau's Lectures Before Walden: An Annotated Calendar" in *Studies in the American Renaissance, 1995.*

Dewey, Chester, and Ebenezer Emmons. *Report on the Herbaceous Flowering Plants of Massachusetts, and on the Quadrupeds of Massachusetts. Massachusetts Zoological and Botanical Survey.* Cambridge, Mass.: Folsom, Wells and Thurston, 1840.

The Dial: A Magazine for Literature, Philosophy and Religion. 4 vols. Boston: Weeks, Jordan, 1840–1844; rpt. New York: Russell and Russell, 1961.

———. Thoreau's copy, with penciled corrections and revisions, Morris Library, Southern Illinois University, Carbondale, Special Collections.

Downing, Andrew Jackson. *The Architecture of Country Houses; Including Designs for Cottages, Farm Houses, and Villas, with Remarks on Interiors, Furniture, and the Best Modes of Warming and Ventilating.* New York: D. Appleton, 1850.

———. *The Fruits and Fruit-Trees of America; or, The Culture, Propagations, and Management in the Garden and Orchard, of Fruit Trees.* New York: Wiley and Putnam, 1845.

Duncumb, John. *General View of the Agriculture of the County of Hereford.* London, 1805.

Ellis, William. *Polynesian Researches, During a Residence of Nearly Six Years in the South Sea Islands.* London: Fischer, Son, and Jackson, 1829.

Emerson, George B. *A Report on the Trees and Shrubs*

Growing Naturally in the Forests of Massachusetts. Boston: Dutton and Wentworth, 1846.

Emerson, Ralph Waldo. *The Collected Works of Ralph Waldo Emerson.* Cambridge: Harvard University Press, 1971–.

———. *The Complete Works of Ralph Waldo Emerson.* Centenary ed. Boston: Houghton Mifflin, 1903.

———. *The Correspondence of Emerson and Carlyle.* Ed. Joseph Slater. New York: Columbia University Press, 1964.

———. *The Journals and Miscellaneous Notebooks of Ralph Waldo Emerson.* Ed. William H. Gilman et al. Cambridge: Harvard University Press, 1960–1982.

———. *The Letters of Ralph Waldo Emerson.* Ed. Ralph L. Rusk and Eleanor Tilton. New York: Columbia University Press, 1939–1995.

———. *Nature, Addresses, and Lectures.* Boston: James Munroe, 1849.

Etzler, John Adolphus. *The New World; or, Mechanical System, to Perform the Labours of Man and Beast by Inanimate Powers, That Cost Nothing, for Producing and Preparing the Substances of Life.* Philadelphia: C. F. Stollmeyer, 1841.

———. *The Paradise within the Reach of all Men, Without Labor, by Powers of Nature and Machinery. An Address to all intelligent Men.* In Two Parts. Pittsburgh: Etzler and Reinhold, 1833.

———. *The Paradise within the Reach of all Men, Without Labor, by Powers of Nature and Machinery. An Address to all intelligent Men.* In Two Parts. London: J. Cleave, 1842.

Evelyn, John. *Sylva; or, A Discourse of Forest-Trees and the Propagation of Timber in His Majesties Dominions . . . Terra, a Philosophical Essay of Earth . . . Also, Kalendarium Hortense; or, The Gard'ners Almanac.* London: Royal Society, 1679.

Fénelon, François de Salignac de La Mothe. *The Lives and Most Remarkable Maxims of the Antient Philosophers.* London: B. Barker and R. Francklin, 1726.

Fischer, P. (pseudonym). *See* Chatto, William Andrew.

Foster, David R. *Thoreau's Country: Journey Through a Transformed Landscape.* Cambridge: Harvard University Press, 1999.

Franklin, John. *Narrative of a Journey to the Shores of the Polar Seas in the Years 1819, 20, 21 & 22.* Philadelphia: H. C. Carey and I. Lea, 1824.

Gell, William. *Edifices and Ornaments of Pompeii, the Results of Excavations since 1819.* London: Maurice, Clark, 1835.

Giesecke, Charles. "Greenland." In the *Edinburgh Encyclopedia* as found in *Library of Useful Knowledge. Natural Philosophy.* London, 1829.

Gilfillan, George. *Sketches of Modern Literature, and Eminent Literary Men.* New York: Appleton, 1846.

Gilpin, William. *Remarks on Forest Scenery and Other Woodland Views, Relative Chiefly to Picturesque Beauty.* London: T. Cadell and W. Davies, 1808.

Goldsmith, Oliver. *A History of the Earth and Animated Nature.* Philadelphia: Grigg and Elliot, 1835.

Gordon-Cumming, Roualeyn George. *Five Years of a Hunter's Life in the Far Interior of South Africa.* 2 vols. New York: Harper and Brothers, 1850.

Gould, Augustus A. *Report on the Invertebrata of Massachusetts, Comprising the Mollusca, Crustacea, Annelida, and Radiata.* Cambridge, Mass.: Folsom, Wells and Thurston, 1841.

Gray, Asa. *Manual of Botany of the Northern United States.* Boston: Monroe, 1848.

Grose, Francis. *A Provincial Glossary; With a Collection of Local Proverbs and Popular Superstitions.* London: Edward Jeffery, 1811.

Guyot, Arnold Henry. *The Earth and Man: Lectures on Comparative Physical Geography, in Its Relation to the History of Mankind.* 3rd rev. ed. Trans. C. C. Felton. Boston: Gould and Lincoln, 1851.

Harding, Walter. *The Days of Henry Thoreau.* Enlarged and corrected ed. New York: Dover, 1982.

Harris, Thaddeus William. *A Report on the Insects of Massachusetts, Injurious to Vegetation.* Cambridge, Mass.: Folsom, Wells and Thurston, 1841.

Hayward, John. *The New England Gazetteer: Containing descriptions of all the states, counties and towns in New England . . .* Concord, N.H.: L. S. Boyd and W. White, 1839.

Head, Sir Francis B. *The Emigrant.* 5th ed. London: J. Murray, 1847.

The Hĕĕtōpădēs of Vĕĕshnŏŏ-Sărmă, in a Series of Connected Fables, Interspersed with Moral, Prudential, and Political Maxims. Trans Charles Wilkins. Bath: R. Cruttwell, 1787.

Herndon, William L., and Lardner Gibbon. *Exploration of the Valley of the Amazon.* 2 vols. Washington, D.C.: R. Armstrong, 1853–1854.

Higginson, Thomas Wentworth. "Glimpses of Authors." *Brains,* 1 December 1891.

Hitchcock, Edward Hitchcock. *Report on the Geology, Mineralogy, Botany, and Zoology of Massachusetts: Made and Published by Order of the Government of that State.* Amherst: Press of J. S. and C. Adams, 1833.

Holland, Henry Richard Vassall. *Foreign Reminiscences.* New York: Harper and Brothers, 1851.

Hosmer, Horace. *Remembrances of Concord and the Thoreaus: Letters of Horace Hosmer to Dr. S. A. Jones.* Ed. George Hendrick. Urbana: University of Illinois Press, 1977.

Howarth, William L. *The Literary Manuscripts of Henry David Thoreau.* Columbus: Ohio State University Press, 1974.

Howitt, William. *Land, Labor and Gold; or, Two Years in Victoria: with Visits to Sydney and Van Dieman's Land.* 2 vols. Boston: Ticknor and Fields, 1855.

Huc, Évariste Régis. *Recollections of a Journey Through Tartary, Thibet, and China, During the Years 1844, 1845, and 1846 . . . a Reprint of the Translation by Mrs. Percy Sinnett.* New York: Appleton, 1852.

Humboldt, Alexander, Freiherr von. *Views of Nature; or, Contemplations on the Sublime Phenomena of Creation.* Trans. C. W. Otte and Henry G. Bohn. London: H. G. Bohn, 1849

Hunt, Robert. *The Poetry of Science; or, Studies of the Physical Phenomena of Nature.* Boston: Gould, Kendall, and Lincoln, 1850.

Jarvis, Edward. *Traditions and Reminiscences of Concord, Massachusetts, 1779–1878.* Ed. Sarah Chapin. Amherst: University of Massachusetts Press, 1993.

The John Brown invasion; an authentic history of the Harper's Ferry tragedy, with full details of the capture, trial, and execution of the invaders, and of all the incidents connected therewith. Compiled by Thomas Drew. Boston: J. Campbell, 1860.

Johnson, Samuel, and John Walker. *A Dictionary of the English Language.* 2nd ed., rev. and corrected. London: J. O. Robinson, 1828.

Jonson, Ben. *The Works of Ben Jonson.* 6 vols. London: J. Walthoe, M. Wotton, J. Nicholson, 1716.

Kane, Elisha Kent. *The U.S. Grinnell Expedition in Search of Sir John Franklin: A Personal Narrative.* New York: Harper and Brothers, 1853.

Kirby, William, and William Spence. *An Introduction to Entomology; or, Elements of the Natural History of Insects.* 4 vols. London: Longman, Hurst, Rees, Orme and Brown, 1814–1826.

Las Cases, Emmanuel Augustin Dieudeonné, comte de. *Journal of the Private Life and Conversation of the Emperor Napoleon at St. Helena.* 3 vols. Boston: Wells and Lilly, 1823.

Lindley, John. *An Introduction to Botany.* London: Longman, Rees, Orme, Brown, Green, and Longman, 1832.

Linnaeus (Carl von Linné). *Lachesis Lapponica; or, A tour of Lapland.* London: White and Cochrane, 1811.

———. *Philosophia botanica, in qua explicantur fundamenta botanica cum definitionibus partium, exemplis terminorum, observationibus, rariorum, adjectis figuris aeniis.* Vienna: J. T. Trotmer, 1763.

———. *Select Dissertations from the Amoenitates Academicae: A Supplement to Mr. Stillingfleet's Tracts Relating to Natural History.* Trans. F. J. Brand. 2 vols. London: G. Robinson, 1781.

Loudon, John Claudius. *Arboretum et Fruticetum Britannicum; or, The trees and shrubs of Britain, native and foreign, hardy and half hardy, pictorially and botanically delineated, and scientifically and popularly described.* 8 vols. London: the author, 1844.

———. *Encyclopedia of Gardening comprising the theory and practice of horticulture, floriculture.* London: Longmann, 1824.

Lyell, Charles. *A Second Visit to the United States of North America.* New York: Harper and Brothers, 1849.

MacPherson, James. *The Genuine Remains of Ossian, Literally Translated.* London: Smith, Elder, 1841.

Mahābhārata. Bhăgvăt-gēētā; or, Dialogues of Krĕĕshnă and Ărjŏŏn. Trans. Charles Wilkin. London, 1785.

Mallet, Paul Henri. *Northern Antiquities; or, An Historical Account of the Manners, Customs, Religion, and Laws, Maritime Expeditions and Discoveries, Language and Literature of the Ancient Scandinavians.* London: Henry G. Bohn, 1847.

Michaux, François André. *The North American Sylva; or, A Description of the Forest Trees of the United States, Canada and Nova Scotia.* Trans. Augustus L. Hillhouse. Paris, 1817–1819.

———. *Voyage à l'Ouest des Monts Alléghanys.* Paris: Dentu, 1808.

Miller, Hugh. *The Testimony of the Rocks; or, Geology in Its Bearing on Two Theologies, Natural and Revealed.* Boston: Gould and Lincoln, 1857.

Mott, Wes, ed. *Biographical Dictionary of Transcendentalism.* Westport: Greenwood, 1996.

———. *Encyclopedia of Transcendentalism.* Westport: Greenwood, 1996.

New Hampshire State Agricultural Society. *Transactions of the New Hampshire Agricultural Society, For the Year 1856.* Concord: Amos Hadley, 1857.

Niebuhr, Barthold Georg. *The History of Rome.* Philadelphia: Thomas Wardel, 1835.

Nuttall, Thomas. *A Manual of the Ornithology of the United States and Canada.* 4 vols. Cambridge: Hilliard and Brown; Boston: Hilliard, Gray, 1832–1834.

Ockley, Simon. *History of the Saracens.* London: R. Knaplock, 1708.

Ogilby, John. *America: Being an Accurate Description of the New World.* London: by the author, 1670.

Palladius, Rutilius Tauru Aemilianus. The Fourteen Books of Palladius Rutilius Taurus AEmilianus, On Agriculture. Trans. T. Owen. London: J. White, 1807.

Parry, William Edward. *Three Voyages for the Discovery of the Northwest Passage from the Atlantic to the Pacific.* New York: Harper's Family Library, 1841.

Pauthier, Jean-Pierre-Guillaume. *Confucius et Mencius: Les Quatre Livres de Philosophie Moral et Politique de la Chine.* Paris: Bibliothèque-Charpentier, 1841.

Phillips, Henry. *History of Cultivated Vegetables.* London: H. Colburn, 1822.

Pliny. *The Natural History of Pliny.* 6 vols. Trans. John Bostock and H. T. Riley. London: H. Bohn, 1855–1857.

Quarles, Francis. *Emblemes, Divine and Moral.* Chiswick: C. and C. Whittington, 1825.

Raleigh, Walter. *The works of Sir Walter Ralegh, Kt. now first collected: to which are prefixed the lives of the author by Oldys and Birch.* 8 vols. Oxford: University Press, 1829.

Redpath, James. *Echoes of Harper's Ferry.* Boston: Thayer and Eldridge, 1860.

Richardson, John. *Fauna Boreali-Americana; or, The Zoology of the Northern Parts of British America . . .* 4 vols. London: J. Murray, 1829–1837.

Roberts, David. *Egypt and Nubia from Drawings Made on the Spot.* London: Moon, 1846–1849.

Robin Hood: A Collection of All the Ancient Poems, Songs, and Ballads. 2 vols. Compiled by Joseph Ritson. London: T. Egerton and J. Johnson, 1795.

Rogers, Nathaniel Peabody. "The American Board." *Herald of Freedom,* 19 September 1845.

Sanborn, Franklin Benjamin. *The life and letters of John Brown: liberator of Kansas, and martyr of Virginia.* Boston: Roberts Brothers, 1885.

Sattelmeyer, Robert. *Thoreau's Reading: A Study in Intellectual History with Bibliographical Catalogue.* Princeton: Princeton University Press, 1988.

Scott, Walter Scott. *The Waverley Novels.* 5 vols. Philadelphia: Carey and Hart, 1845–1948.

Shakespeare, William. *The Dramatic Works of William Shakespeare, Accurately Printed from the Text of the Corrected Copy Left by the Late George Steevens, Esq.* Hartford: Andrus and Judd, 1833.

———. *The Norton Shakespeare Based Upon the Oxford Edition.* Stephen Greenblatt, gen. ed. New York: W. W. Norton, 1997.

Sharp, Richard. *Letters and Essays in Prose and Verse.* Philadelphia: Carey and Hart, 1835.

Shattuck, Lemuel. *A History of the Town of Concord, Middlesex County, Massachusetts: from its Earliest Settlement to 1832; and of the Adjoining Towns, Bedford, Acton, Lincoln, and Carlisle; Containing Various Notices of County and State History Not Before Published.* Boston: Goodspeed's Book Shop, 1973.

Southey, Robert. *Southey's Commonplace Book. Fourth Series.* London: Longman, Brown, Green and Longmans, 1851.

Specimens of English Dramatic Poets, Who Lived About the Time of Shakespeare. Ed. Charles Lamb. New York: Wiley and Putnam, 1845.

Springer, John S. *Forest Life and Forest Trees.* New York: Harper and Brothers, 1851.

Storer, David Humphreys. *Report on the Fishes, Reptiles, and Birds of Massachusetts.* Boston: Dutton and Wentworth, 1839.

Stowell, Robert F. *A Thoreau Gazetteer.* Ed. William L. Howarth. Princeton: Princeton University Press, 1970.

Studies in the American Renaissance. Ed. Joel Myerson. Charlottesville: University Press of Virginia, 1977–1996.

Sturluson, Snorri. *The Heimskringla; or, Chronicle of the Kings of Norway.* Trans. Samuel Laing. London: Longmans, Brown, Green and Longmans, 1844.

Tacitus, Cornelius. *Cornelii Taciti opera ex recensione io.* Boston: Wells and Lily, 1817.

Theophrastus. *The Characters of Theophrastus.* Boston, 1831.

Thomson, James. *The Seasons.* In Chalmers, *Works of the English Poets.*

Thoreau, Henry D. *Collected Poems of Henry Thoreau.* Enlarged ed. Ed. Carl Bode. Baltimore: Johns Hopkins Press, 1965.

———. *The Correspondence of Henry David Thoreau.* Ed. Walter Harding and Carl Bode. New York: New York University Press, 1958.

———. *Early Essays and Miscellanies.* Ed. Joseph J. Moldenhauer and Edwin Moser, with Alexander Kern. Princeton: Princeton University Press, 1975.

———. *Excursions.* Boston: Ticknor and Fields, 1863.

———. *Faith in a Seed: The Dispersion of Seeds and Other Late Natural History Writings.* Ed. Bradley P. Dean. Washington, D.C.: Island Press/Shearwater Books, 1993.

———. *I to Myself: An Annotated Selection from the Journal of Henry D. Thoreau.* Ed. Jeffrey S. Cramer. New Haven: Yale University Press, 2007.

———. *Journal.* Ed. John C. Broderick et al. Princeton: Princeton University Press, 1981–.

———. *The Journal of Henry Thoreau.* Ed. Bradford Torrey and Francis H. Allen. Boston: Houghton Mifflin, 1906.

———. *The Maine Woods: A Fully Annotated Edition.* Ed. Jeffrey S. Cramer. New Haven: Yale University Press, 2009.

———. *Thoreau's Fact Book in the Harry Elkins Widener Collection.* Hartford: Transcendental, 1966.

———. *Thoreau's Literary Notebook in the Library of Congress.* Ed. K. W. Cameron. Hartford: Transcendental, 1964.

———. *Walden: A Fully Annotated Edition.* Ed. Jeffrey S. Cramer. New Haven: Yale University Press, 2004.

———. *Wild Fruits: Thoreau's Rediscovered Last Manuscript.* Ed. Bradley P. Dean. New York: W. W. Norton, 2000.

———. *The Writings of Henry David Thoreau.* Walden ed. Boston: Houghton Mifflin, 1906.

———. *A Yankee in Canada, with Anti-Slavery and Reform Papers* Boston: Ticknor and Fields, 1866.

Topsell, Edward. *The Historie of Foure-Footed Beasts and Serpents*. London: W. Iagard, 1607.

Trench, Richard Chenevix. *The Study of Words*. New York: Redfield, 1852.

Turnbull, Robert. *The Genius of Scotland, or Sketches of Scottish scenery, literature and religion*. New York: R. Carter, 1847.

Tyler, Royall. *The Contrast: A Comedy in Five Acts*. Philadelphia: Prichard and Hall, 1790.

Vishnupurāna. The Vishnu Puráńa: A System of Hindu Mythology and Tradition. London: J. Murray, 1840.

Webb, Richard Davis Webb. *The Life and Letters of Captain John Brown: who was executed at Charlestown, Virginia, Dec. 2, 1859, for an armed attack upon American slavery; with notices of some of his confederates*. Ed. Richard D. Webb. London: Smith and Elder, 1861.

Whitney, Peter. *The History of the County of Worcester, . . . Massachusetts*. In *Memoirs of the American Academy of Arts and Sciences* (1785).

Wilson, Alexander. *American Ornithology*. Philadelphia: Bradford and Inskeep, 1808.

Wood, Alphonso. *A Class-book of Botany, Designed for Colleges, Academies, and Other Seminaries*. 23rd ed., rev. and enl. Boston, 1851.

Wood, William. *Zoography; or, The beauties of nature displayed: In select descriptions from the animal, and vegetable, with additions from the mineral kingdom*. 3 vols. London: Cadell and Davies, 1807.

Wordsworth, William. *Complete Poetical Works*. Philadelphia: Kay, 1837.

Wright, Thomas. *Dictionary of Obsolete and Provincial English*. London: H. G. Bohn, 1857.

Yates, William Holt. *The modern history and condition of Egypt: its climate, diseases, and capabilities; exhibited in a personal narrative of travels in that country: with an account of the proceedings of Mohammed Ali Pascha, from 1801–1843*. 2 vols. London: Smith, Elder, 1843.

Young, Robert M. *Walking to Wachusett: A Re-enactment of Henry David Thoreau's "A Walk to Wachusett."* Leominster: Robert M. Young, 2008.

Index

buckeye, 3

buffalo, 268

Buffon, Comte de, Georges-Louis Leclerc, *Natural History,* 258

Buford, Jefferson, 193

Buford Ruffians, 193

Bull, John. *See* John Bull

Buncombe, 194

Bunyan, John, *The Pilgrim's Progress,* 274, 353

Burke, William, 357

Burker's Guide, 357

Burns, Anthony, xxx, xxxvi, 172–176, 186–188

Burns, Robert, III, 121, 123–124, 134, 140

Burton, Richard Francis, *Personal Narrative to Al-Madinah and Meccah,* 263

business and businessmen, 66, 214, 248, 250, 254, 347, 349–350, 353

Butler, Samuel, "Hudibras," 106

butterfly, 4, 339

caddis fly. *See* Plicipennes

Caesar, Julius, 159

California, 353, 355, 357

Canada, 3–4, 9, 72, 257

Candolle, Augustin Pyramus de, and Kurt Polycarp Joachim Sprengel, *Elements of the Philosophy of Plants,* 25

canker-worm, 320, 344

Cape Cod, 24–25

Carlyle, Jane, 99

Carlyle, Thomas, xiv, xxiii–xxv, 99–144

Carminum Poetarum Nouem, 6

Carpenter, William Benjamin, *Vegetable Physiology and Systematic Botany,* 239, 282

Cass, Lewis, 152

Cassiopeia, 35

Cato, Marcus Porcius (Cato the Younger), 217

cats, 269

cedar waxwing, 58, 320

Celebes, 309

cemeteries, 299

Ceres (Roman mythology),21, 24

Cervantes, Miguel de, 119

Chaldean Oracles, 274

Champney, Benjamin, 259

Channing, William Ellery (The Elder), 213

Channing, William Ellery (The Younger), xvii, 270

Chapin, Loring Dudley, *The Vegetable Kingdom,* 239

Charleston (South Carolina), xxxvi, 3, 157, 366

Charon (Greek mythology), 18, 297

Chatto, William Andrew, 15

Chaucer, Geoffrey, 109, 250, 266; *Canterbury Tales,* 255

Cheever, George Barrell, *Wanderings of a Pilgrim in the Shadow of Mount Blanc,* 144

cherry-bird. *See* cedar waxwing

chestnut, 162, 234–235, 297, 335, 364

"Chesuncook" (Thoreau), xxxii, 358, 383

chickadee, 32, 39, 326, 340, 358

chickaree. *See* squirrels

children, 49, 52, 66, 104, 106, 113, 116, 121, 127, 129, 151, 159, 182, 198, 223, 228, 243–244, 260, 271–272, 279, 299, 300–301, 331, 333, 358, 363–364

Children of the Mist, 274

China and Chinese, 164, 200, 277, 318, 361

China-aster (Callistephus chinensis), 311

chivalry, 98, 244, 259

Christians and Christianity, 92, 98, 121, 129, 138, 142, 199, 207, 220, 251, 274, 357. *See also* Church, the; Jesus Christ